Harcourt

OHIO SCIENCE FUSION

fusion [FYOO • zhuhn] a combination of two or more things that releases energy

This **Write-In Student Edition** belongs to

____

Teacher/Room

____

Consulting Authors

Michael A. DiSpezio

Global Educator
North Falmouth, Massachusetts

Michael DiSpezio is a renaissance educator who segued from the research laboratory of a Nobel Prize winner to the K–12 science classroom. He has authored or coauthored numerous textbooks and trade books. For nearly a decade he worked with the JASON Project, under the auspices of the National Geographic Society, where he designed curriculum, wrote lessons, and hosted dozens of studio and location broadcasts. Over the past two decades, DiSpezio has developed supplementary material for organizations and programs that include PBS *Scientific American Frontiers*, *Discover* magazine, and the Discovery Channel. To all his projects, he brings his extensive background in science and his expertise in classroom teaching at the elementary, middle, and high school levels.

Marjorie Frank

Science Writer and
Content-Area Reading Specialist
Brooklyn, New York

An educator and linguist by training, a writer and poet by nature, Marjorie Frank has authored and designed a generation of instructional materials in all subject areas, including past HMH Science programs. Her other credits include authoring science issues of an award-winning children's magazine, writing game-based digital assessments, developing blended learning materials for young children, and serving as instructional designer and coauthor of pioneering school-to-work software for a nonprofit organization dedicated to improving reading and math skills for middle and high school learners. In addition, she has served on the adjunct faculty of Hunter, Manhattan, and Brooklyn Colleges, teaching courses in science methods, literacy, and writing.

Acknowledgments for Covers

Front cover: *fiber optics* ©Dennis O'Clair/Stone/Getty Images; *gecko* ©Pete Orelup/Getty Images; *mountain biker* ©Jerome Prevost/TempSport/Corbis; *computer monitor* ©Michael Melford/Getty Images; *Giant's Causeway* ©Rod McLean/Alamy.

Back cover: *anenometer* ©Ryan McGinnis/Flickr/Getty Images; *rock formation* ©John Elk III/Alamy; *racecar* ©David Madison/Corbis; *lava* ©Bruce Omori/epa/Corbis.

Printed in the U.S.A.

ISBN 978-0-544-31942-4

18 0928 22

4500848161 ABCDEFG

Michael R. Heithaus

Executive Director, School of Environment, Arts, and Society
Associate Professor, Department of Biological Sciences
Florida International University
North Miami, Florida

Mike Heithaus joined the Florida International University Biology Department in 2003. He has served as Director of the Marine Sciences Program and is now the Executive Director of the School of Environment, Arts, and Society, which brings together the natural and social sciences and humanities to develop solutions to today's environmental challenges. His research focuses on predator-prey interactions and the ecological roles of large marine species including sharks, sea turtles, and marine mammals. His long-term studies include the Shark Bay Ecosystem Project in Western Australia. He also served as a Research Fellow with National Geographic, using remote imaging in his research and hosting a *Crittercam* television series on the National Geographic Channel.

Donna M. Ogle

Professor of Reading and Language
National-Louis University
Chicago, Illinois

Creator of the well-known KWL strategy, Donna Ogle has directed many staff development projects translating theory and research into school practice in schools throughout the United States. She is a past president of the International Reading Association and has served as a consultant on literacy projects worldwide. Her extensive international experience includes coordinating the Reading and Writing for Critical Thinking Project in Eastern Europe and speaking and consulting on projects in several Latin American countries and in Asia. Her books include *Reading Comprehension: Strategies for Independent Learners*; *All Children Read*; and *Literacy for a Democratic Society*.

Ohio Reviewers

Shila Garg
William F. Harn Professor of Physics
Senior Director of India Initiatives
The College of Wooster
Wooster, OH

Brian Geniusz, M.Ed.
Science Curriculum Leader
Worthington Schools
Worthington, OH

Richard J. Johnson Jr., M.Ed.
Science Department Chair
Eastlake Middle School
Eastlake, OH

Robert Mendenhall
Curriculum Director
Toledo Public Schools
Toledo, OH

Donald J. Stierman, Ph.D.
Associate Professor
Department of Environmental Sciences
The University of Toledo
Toledo, OH

Jessica N. Stried
Science Department Chair
Hyatts Middle School
Powell, OH

Jaimie Thomas, M.Ed.
Olentangy Shanahan Middle School
Lewis Center, OH

Content Reviewers

Arkhat Abzhanov, Ph.D.
Associate Professor
Department of Organismic and Evolutionary Biology
Harvard University
Cambridge, MA

Paul D. Asimow, Ph.D.
Professor of Geology and Geochemistry
Division of Geological and Planetary Sciences
California Institute of Technology
Pasadena, CA

Laura K. Baumgartner, Ph.D.
Biology Instructor
Science Department
Front Range Community College
Longmont, CO

Eileen M. Cashman, Ph.D.
Professor and Department Chair, Environmental Resources Engineering
Research Associate, Schatz Energy Research Center
Humboldt State University
Arcata, CA

Wesley N. Colley, Ph.D.
Senior Research Analyst
Center for Modeling, Simulation, and Analysis
The University of Alabama in Huntsville
Huntsville, AL

Joe W. Crim, Ph.D.
Professor Emeritus
Department of Cellular Biology
The University of Georgia
Athens, GA

Elizabeth A. De Stasio, Ph.D.
Raymond H. Herzog Professor of Science
Professor of Biology
Department of Biology
Lawrence University
Appleton, WI

Julia R. Greer, Ph.D.
Professor of Materials Science and Mechanics
Division of Engineering and Applied Sciences
California Institute of Technology
Pasadena, CA

John E. Hoover, Ph.D.
Professor, Department Chair
Department of Biology
Millersville University
Millersville, PA

William H. Ingham, Ph.D.
Professor Emeritus
Department of Physics and Astronomy
James Madison University
Harrisonburg, VA

Charles W. Johnson, Ph.D.
Associate Professor of Physics, Division Chair
Division of Natural Sciences, Mathematics, and Physical Education
South Georgia State College
Douglas, GA

Tatiana A. Krivosheev, Ph.D.
Professor of Physics
Department of Natural Sciences
Clayton State University
Morrow, GA

Joel Leventhal, Ph.D.
Emeritus Scientist
(formerly *Research Geochemist)*
U.S. Geological Survey
Denver, CO

Joseph A. McClure, Ph.D.
Associate Professor Emeritus
Department of Physics
Georgetown University
Washington, DC

Mark B. Moldwin, Ph.D.
Professor of Space Sciences
Department of Atmospheric, Oceanic and Space Sciences
University of Michigan
Ann Arbor, MI

Sten Odenwald, Ph.D.
Astrophysicist
Director of SpaceMath@NASA
National Institute of Aerospace
Hampton, VA

Patricia M. Pauley, Ph.D.
Meteorologist, Data Assimilation Group
Naval Research Laboratory
Monterey, CA

Stephen F. Pavkovic, Ph.D.
Professor Emeritus
Department of Chemistry
Loyola University of Chicago
Chicago, IL

James L. Pazun, Ph.D.
Professor and Chair
Chemistry and Physics
Pfeiffer University
Misenheimer, NC

L. Jeanne Perry, Ph.D.
Director (Retired)
Protein Expression Technology Center
Institute for Genomics and Proteomics
University of California, Los Angeles
Los Angeles, CA

Kenneth H. Rubin, Ph.D.
Professor
Department of Geology and Geophysics
University of Hawaii
Honolulu, HI

Brandon E. Schwab, Ph.D.
Professor and Chair
Department of Geology
Humboldt State University
Arcata, CA

Adam D. Woods, Ph.D.
Associate Professor
Department of Geological Sciences
California State University, Fullerton
Fullerton, CA

Natalie Zayas, M.S., Ed.D.
Lecturer
Division of Science and Environmental Policy
California State University, Monterey Bay
Seaside, CA

Teacher Reviewers

Karen Cavalluzzi, M.Ed., NBCT
Sunny Vale Middle School
Blue Springs, MO

Katie Demorest, M.A. Ed. Tech.
Marshall Middle School
Marshall, MI

Dave Grabski, M.S. Ed.
P. J. Jacobs Junior High School
Stevens Point, WI

Ben Hondorp
Creekside Middle School
Zeeland, MI

Mary Larsen
Science Instructional Coach
Helena Public Schools
Helena, MT

Angie Larson
Bernard Campbell Middle School
Lee's Summit, MO

Christy Leier
Horizon Middle School
Moorhead, MN

Michele K. Lombard, Ed.D.
Swanson Middle School
Arlington, VA

Helen Mihm, NBCT
Crofton Middle School
Crofton, MD

Jeff Moravec, Sr., M.S. Ed.
Teaching Specialist
Milwaukee Public Schools
Milwaukee, WI

Nancy Kawecki Nega, M.S.T., NBCT, PAESMT
Churchville Middle School
Elmhurst, IL

Mark E. Poggensee, M.S. Ed.
Elkhorn Middle School
Elkhorn, WI

Sherry Rich
Bernard Campbell Middle School
Lee's Summit, MO

Heather Wares, M.Ed.
Traverse City West Middle School
Traverse City, MI

Alexandra Workman, M.Ed., NBCT
Thomas Jefferson Middle School
Arlington, VA

Contents in Brief

Power up with Ohio Science Fusion!

Your program fuses . . .

e-Learning and Virtual Labs

Labs and Activities

Write-In Student Edition

. . . to generate energy for today's science learner — you.

S.T.E.M. Engineering & Technology

S.T.E.M. activities throughout the program!

Write-In Student Edition

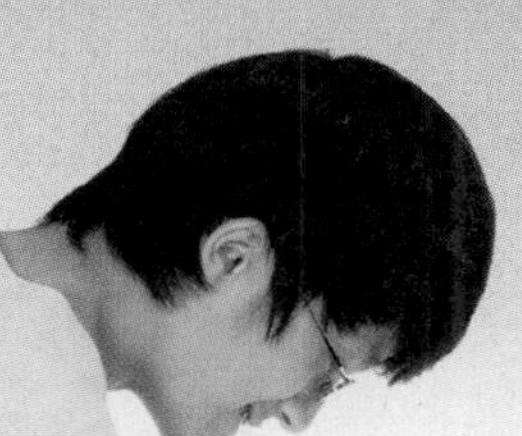

Be an active reader and make this book your own!

You can answer questions, ask questions, create graphs, make notes, write your own ideas, and highlight information right in your book.

Learn science concepts and skills by interacting with every page.

e-Learning and Virtual Labs

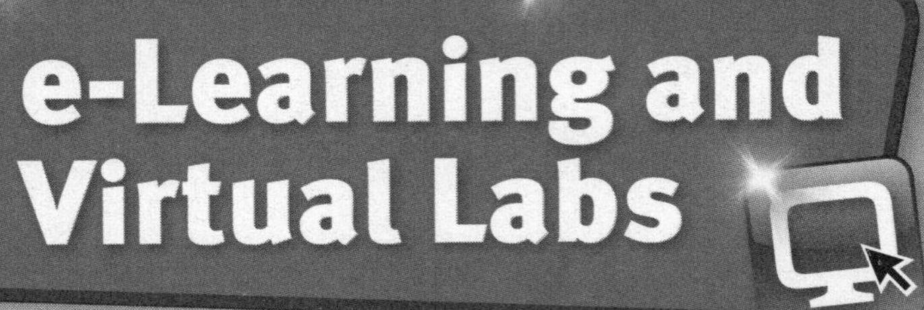

Digital lessons and virtual labs provide e-learning options for every lesson of ScienceFusion.

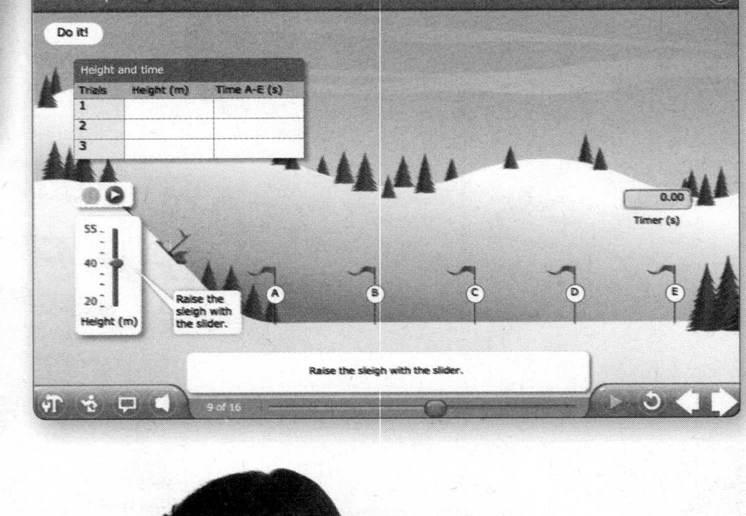

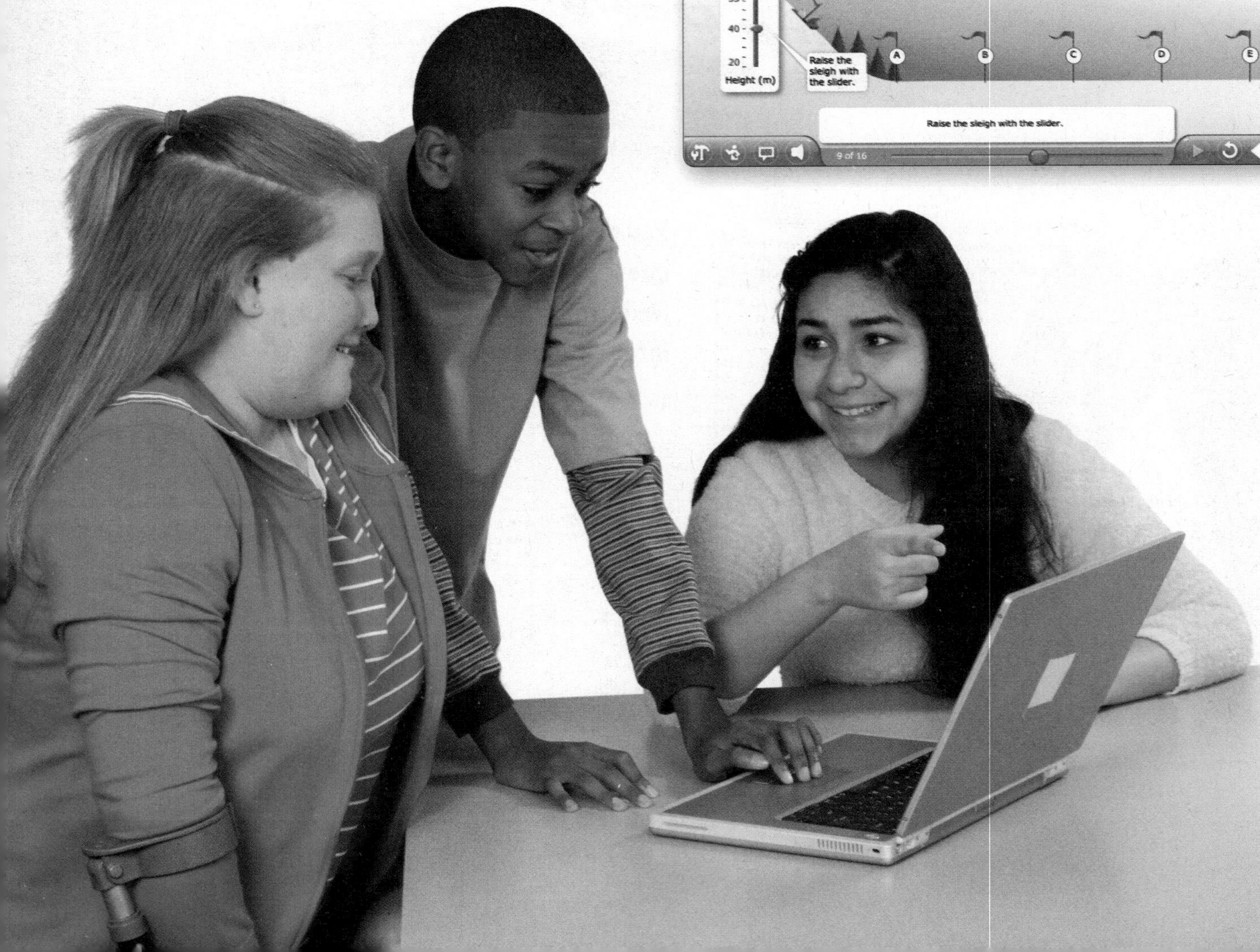

Investigate key science concepts with multiple virtual labs in each unit.

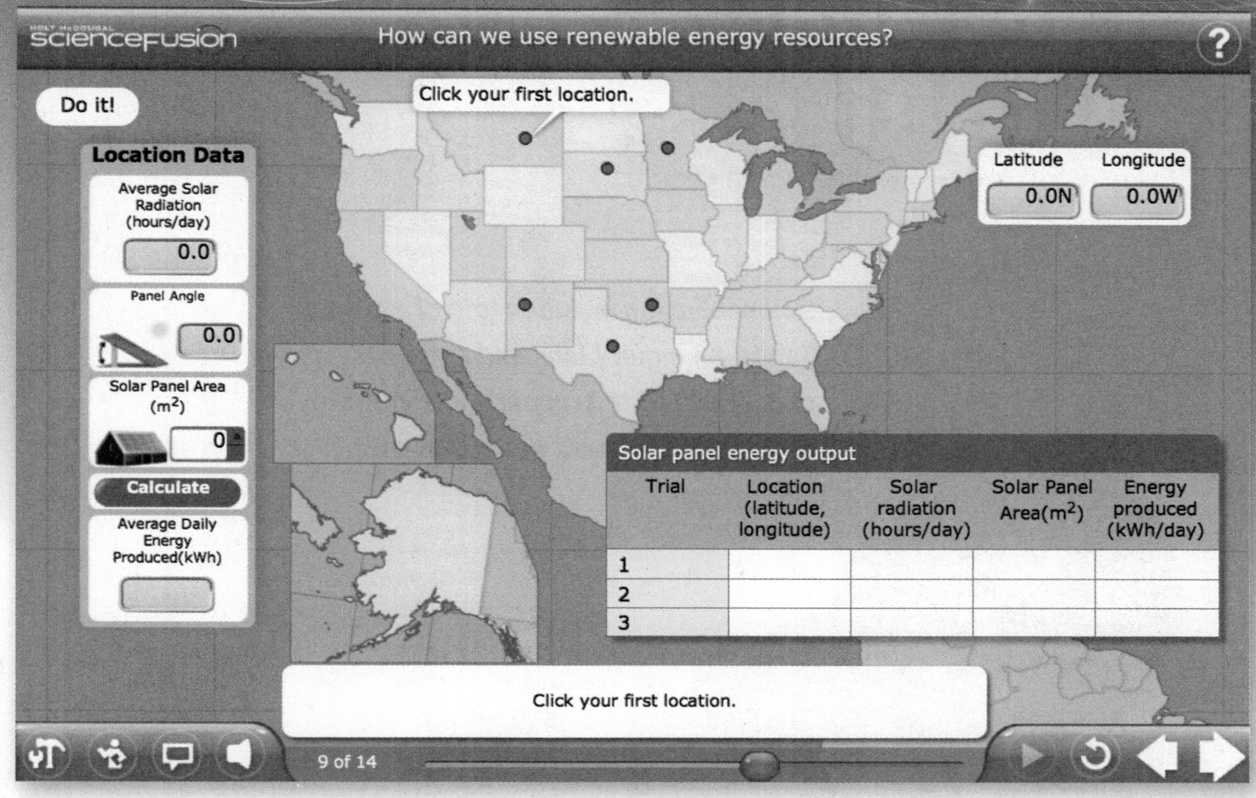

On your own or with a group, explore science concepts in a digital world.

Continue your science explorations with these online tools:

- ScienceSaurus
- NSTA SciLinks
- Video-Based Projects
- People in Science
- Media Gallery
- Digital Glossary

Labs and Activities

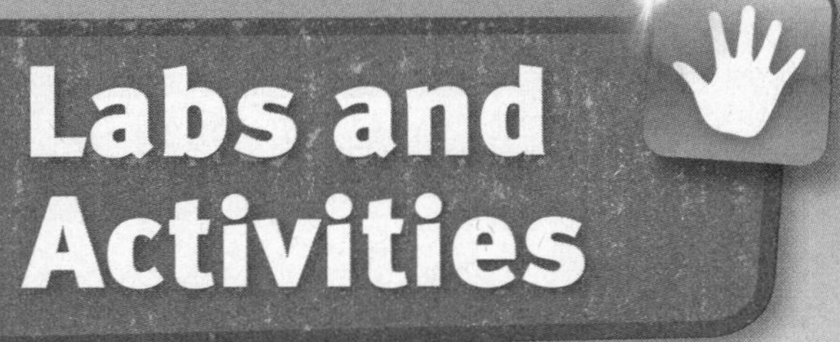

ScienceFusion **includes lots of exciting hands-on inquiry labs and activities, each one designed to bring science skills and concepts to life and get you involved.**

Name ______ Class ______ Date ______

QUICK LAB DIRECTED Inquiry

Extracting DNA

In this lab, you will use common household items to release, unravel, and collect strands of DNA. You will be extracting DNA from raw wheat germ, which is part of the seed of a wheat plant.

OBJECTIVES
- Extract and observe strands of DNA.
- Describe the function and location of DNA in living organisms.

image from http://publications.nigms.nih.gov/thenewgenetics/chapter1.html]

PROCEDURE

1. Use the **balance** to measure 1 g of **raw wheat germ**. Place the raw whe... in the **beaker**.
2. Use the **graduated cylinder** to measure about 50 mL of **warm tap wat**... the water to the beaker containing the wheat germ.

ScienceFusion
Grade 7 Lab Manual 453

Name ______ Class ______ Date ______

FIELD LAB DIRECTED Inquiry

Investigating Parallax

In this lab, you will practice measuring the distances of faraway objects on Earth.

PROCEDURE

ASK A QUESTION

1. In this lab, you will answer the following question: How can you measure the distance to a star?

FORM A HYPOTHESIS

2. Write a hypothesis that might answer this question. Explain your reasoning.

TEST THE HYPOTHESIS

3. Draw a line 4 cm away from the edge of one side of the piece of poster board. Fold the poster board along this line.
4. Tape the protractor to the poster board, with its flat edge against the fold.
5. Use a pencil to carefully punch a hole through the poster board along its folded edge at the center of the protractor.
6. Thread the string through the hole, and tape one end to the underside of the poster board. The other end should be long enough to hang off the far end of the...

MATERIALS
For each pair
- calculator, scientific
- meterstick
- pencil, sharp
- poster board, 16 × 16 cm
- protractor
- ruler, metric
- scissors
- string, 30 cm
- tape measure, metric
- tape, transparent

For each student
- safety goggles

Benchmarks
SC.8.E.5.5 Describe and classify specific physical properties of stars: apparent magnitude (brightness), temperature (color), size, and luminosity (absolute brightness).
SC.8.N.1.5 Analyze the methods used to develop a scientific explanation as seen in different fields of science.

Unit 2, Lesson 1
Photosynthesis & Cell Respiration

Name ______ Class ______ Date ______

EXPLORATION LAB DIRECTED Inquiry

Beach Erosion

In this lab, you will demonstrate the effects of wave action and longshore currents on a beach, and describe ways to decrease the effects of wave action on beach sand.

PROCEDURE

ASK A QUESTION

1. This lab will help you answer the following question: How does wave action affect the amount of sand on a beach, and how can these effects be reduced?

FORM A HYPOTHESIS

2. Form a hypothesis that answers your question. Explain your reasoning.

TEST THE HYPOTHESIS

3. Make a model beach in a large, shallow **plastic container** by placing a mixture of **sand** and small **pebbles** at one end of the container. The beach should occupy about one-fourth of the length of the container.
4. In front of the sand, add **water** to a depth of 2–3 cm. Record what happens.

OBJECTIVES
- Create a model beach to explore the effects of wave action and longshore currents on shorelines.
- Design a breakwater to prevent beach erosion.

MATERIALS
For each group
- blocks, plaster (2)
- block, wooden, large
- container, plastic, large
- paper, blank
- pebbles
- ruler, metric
- sand (5–10 lb)
- water

For each student
- lab apron
- safety goggles

Benchmarks
SC.6.E.6.1
SC.6.E.6.2

ScienceFusion
Grade 6 Labs 4
Unit 2, Unit 2 Lab
Weathering, Erosion, Deposition & Landforms

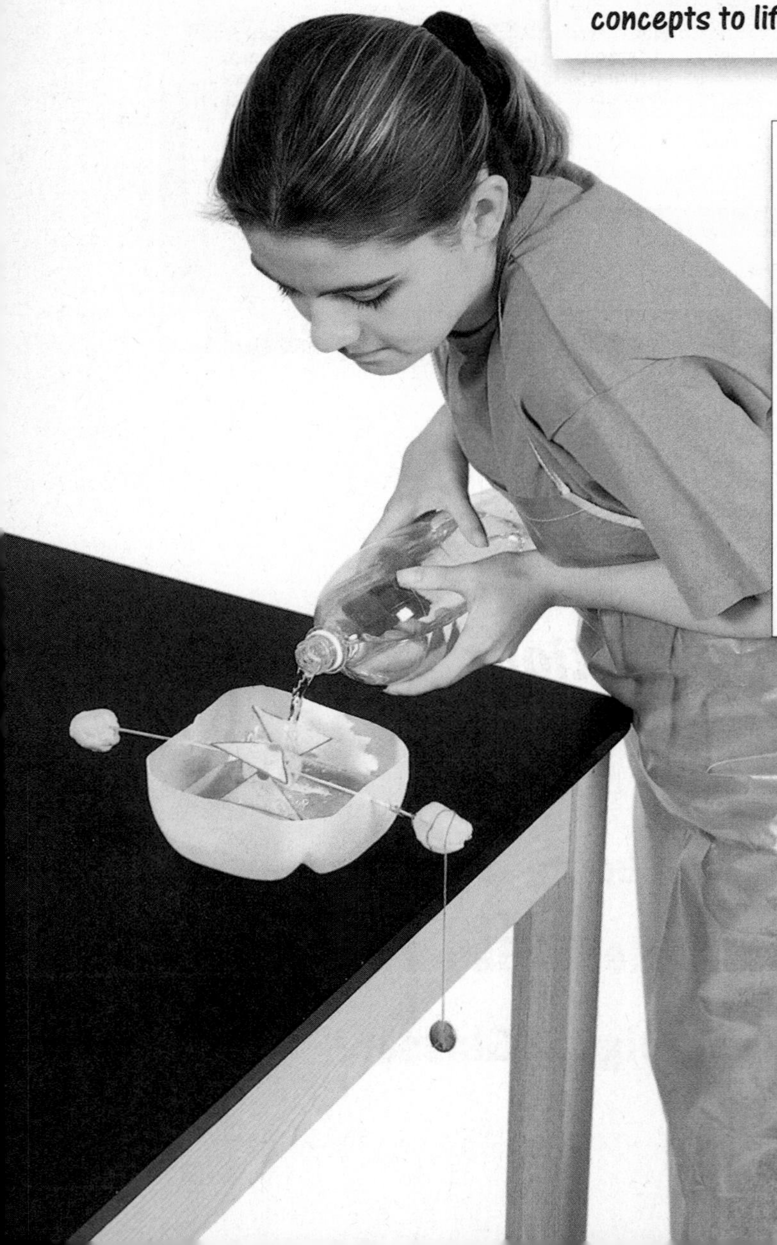

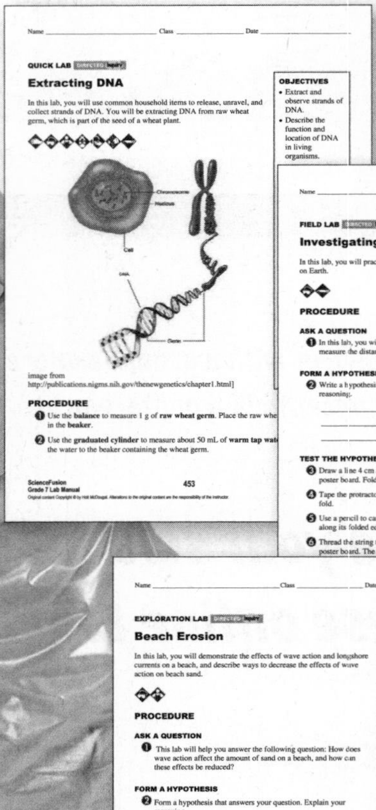

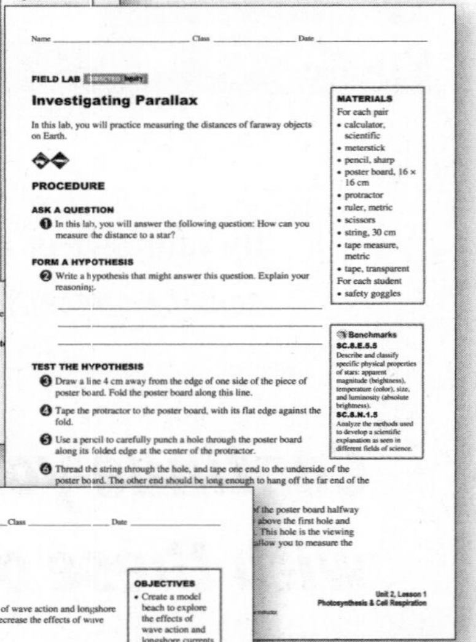

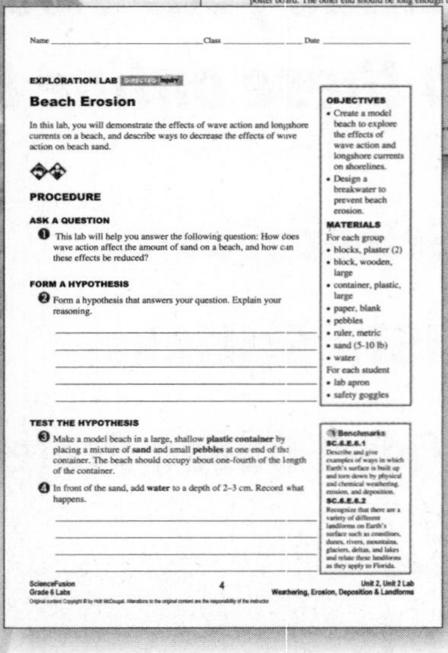

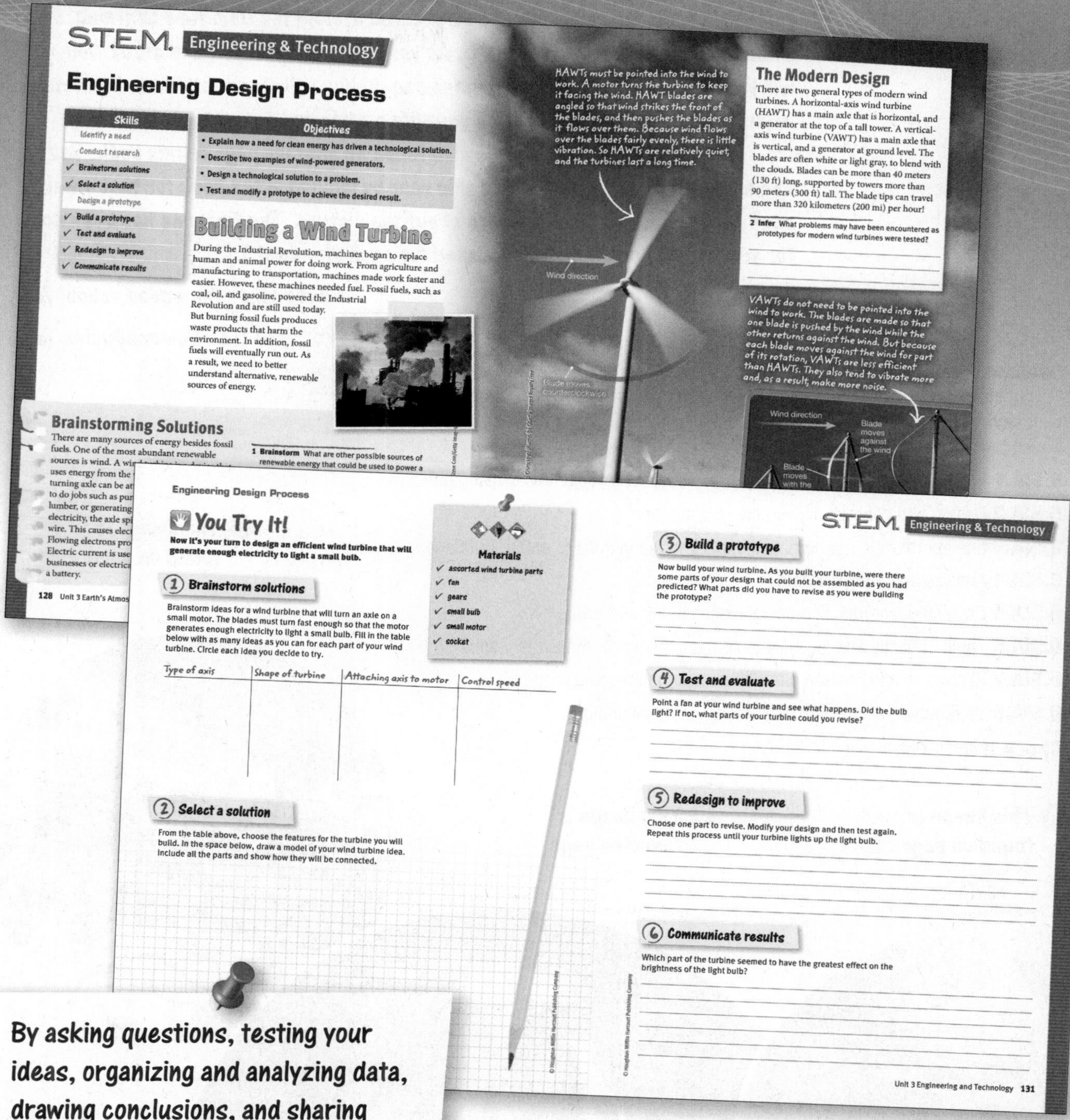

S.T.E.M. Engineering & Technology

Engineering Design Process

Skills
Identify a need
Conduct research
✓ Brainstorm solutions
✓ Select a solution
Design a prototype
✓ Build a prototype
✓ Test and evaluate
✓ Redesign to improve
✓ Communicate results

Objectives

- Explain how a need for clean energy has driven a technological solution.
- Describe two examples of wind-powered generators.
- Design a technological solution to a problem.
- Test and modify a prototype to achieve the desired result.

Building a Wind Turbine

During the Industrial Revolution, machines began to replace human and animal power for doing work. From agriculture and manufacturing to transportation, machines made work faster and easier. However, these machines needed fuel. Fossil fuels, such as coal, oil, and gasoline, powered the Industrial Revolution and are still used today. But burning fossil fuels produces waste products that harm the environment. In addition, fossil fuels will eventually run out. As a result, we need to better understand alternative, renewable sources of energy.

Brainstorming Solutions

There are many sources of energy besides fossil fuels. One of the most abundant renewable sources is wind. A wi... uses energy from the ... turning axle can be at... to do jobs such as pur... lumber, or generating... electricity, the axle spi... wire. This causes elec... Flowing electrons pro... Electric current is use... businesses or electrica... a battery.

1 Brainstorm What are other possible sources of renewable energy that could be used to power a ...

HAWTs must be pointed into the wind to work. A motor turns the turbine to keep it facing the wind. HAWT blades are angled so that wind strikes the front of the blades, and then pushes the blades as it flows over them. Because wind flows over the blades fairly evenly, there is little vibration. So HAWTs are relatively quiet, and the turbines last a long time.

Wind direction

Blade moves counterclockwise

The Modern Design

There are two general types of modern wind turbines. A horizontal-axis wind turbine (HAWT) has a main axle that is horizontal, and a generator at the top of a tall tower. A vertical-axis wind turbine (VAWT) has a main axle that is vertical, and a generator at ground level. The blades are often white or light gray, to blend with the clouds. Blades can be more than 40 meters (130 ft) long, supported by towers more than 90 meters (300 ft) tall. The blade tips can travel more than 320 kilometers (200 mi) per hour!

2 Infer What problems may have been encountered as prototypes for modern wind turbines were tested?

VAWTs do not need to be pointed into the wind to work. The blades are made so that one blade is pushed by the wind while the other returns against the wind. But because each blade moves against the wind for part of its rotation, VAWTs are less efficient than HAWTs. They also tend to vibrate more and, as a result, make more noise.

Wind direction

Blade moves against the wind

Blade moves with the ...

128 Unit 3 Earth's Atmos...

Engineering Design Process

You Try It!

Now it's your turn to design an efficient wind turbine that will generate enough electricity to light a small bulb.

Materials

- ✓ assorted wind turbine parts
- ✓ fan
- ✓ gears
- ✓ small bulb
- ✓ small motor
- ✓ socket

(1) Brainstorm solutions

Brainstorm ideas for a wind turbine that will turn an axle on a small motor. The blades must turn fast enough so that the motor generates enough electricity to light a small bulb. Fill in the table below with as many ideas as you can for each part of your wind turbine. Circle each idea you decide to try.

Type of axis	Shape of turbine	Attaching axis to motor	Control speed

(2) Select a solution

From the table above, choose the features for the turbine you will build. In the space below, draw a model of your wind turbine idea. Include all the parts and show how they will be connected.

S.T.E.M. Engineering & Technology

(3) Build a prototype

Now build your wind turbine. As you built your turbine, were there some parts of your design that could not be assembled as you had predicted? What parts did you have to revise as you were building the prototype?

(4) Test and evaluate

Point a fan at your wind turbine and see what happens. Did the bulb light? If not, what parts of your turbine could you revise?

(5) Redesign to improve

Choose one part to revise. Modify your design and then test again. Repeat this process until your turbine lights up the light bulb.

(6) Communicate results

Which part of the turbine seemed to have the greatest effect on the brightness of the light bulb?

© Houghton Mifflin Harcourt Publishing Company

Unit 3 Engineering and Technology 131

By asking questions, testing your ideas, organizing and analyzing data, drawing conclusions, and sharing what you learn . . .

You are the scientist!

Ohio New Learning Standards for Science

Dear Students and Families,

This book and this class are structured around the Ohio New Learning Standards for Science for Grade 6. As you read, experiment, and study, you will learn the concepts listed on these pages. You will also continue to build your science literacy, which will enrich your life both in and out of school.

Each picture shown below is also found on another page of this book. You can begin your exploration of science this year by looking in the book for that other page, where you can find out more about the picture. The first one has been done for you. (Hint: Look in the units listed for each standard.)

Best wishes for a good school year,

The ScienceFusion Team

OHIO

Science Inquiry and Application

During the years of grades 5–8, all students must use the following scientific processes, with appropriate laboratory safety techniques, to construct their knowledge and understanding in all science content areas:

6.SIA.1 Identify questions that can be answered through scientific investigations.

6.SIA.2 Design and conduct a scientific investigation.

6.SIA.3 Use appropriate mathematics, tools and techniques to gather data and information.

6.SIA.4 Analyze and interpret data.

6.SIA.5 Develop descriptions, models, explanations and predictions.

6.SIA.6 Think critically and logically to connect evidence and explanations.

6.SIA.7 Recognize and analyze alternative explanations and predictions.

6.SIA.8 Communicate scientific procedures and explanations.

Check it out: Unit 1; pages R28–R53

A This image is found on page 44

B This image is found on page ______

C This image is found on page ______

Answers: A. 44; B. 37; C. 79

OHIO

Earth and Space Science

6.ESS.1 Minerals have specific, quantifiable properties.

6.ESS.2 Igneous, metamorphic and sedimentary rocks have unique characteristics that can be used for identification and/or classification.

6.ESS.3 Igneous, metamorphic and sedimentary rocks form in different ways.

6.ESS.4 Soil is unconsolidated material that contains nutrient matter and weathered rock.

6.ESS.5 Rocks, minerals and soils have common and practical uses.

Check it out: Unit 2

G *This image is found on page* ______

D *This image is found on page* ______

E *This image is found on page* ______

F *This image is found on page* ______

Answers: D. 113; E. 128; F. 156; G. 121

OHIO

Life Science

6.LS.1 Cells are the fundamental unit of life.

6.LS.2 All cells come from pre-existing cells.

6.LS.3 Cells carry on specific functions that sustain life.

6.LS.4 Living systems at all levels of organization demonstrate the complementary nature of structure and function.

Check it out: Units 3–4

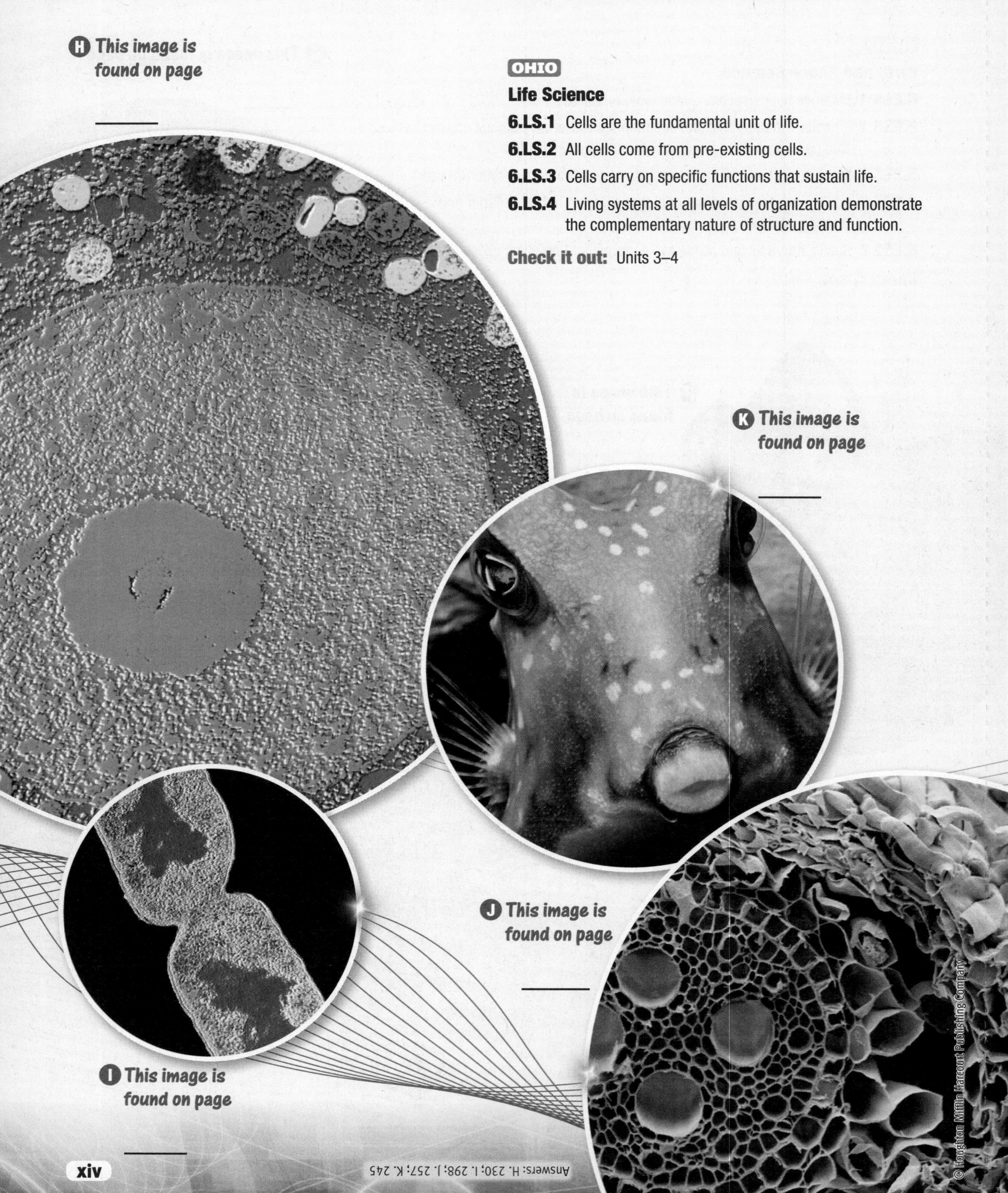
H This image is found on page ______
K This image is found on page ______
J This image is found on page ______
I This image is found on page ______

Answers: H. 230; I. 298; J. 257; K. 245

OHIO

Physical Science

6.PS.1 All matter is made up of small particles called atoms.

6.PS.2 Changes of state are explained by a model of matter composed of atoms and/or molecules that are in motion.

6.PS.3 There are two categories of energy: kinetic and potential.

6.PS.4 An object's motion can be described by its speed and the direction in which it is moving.

Check it out: Units 5–6

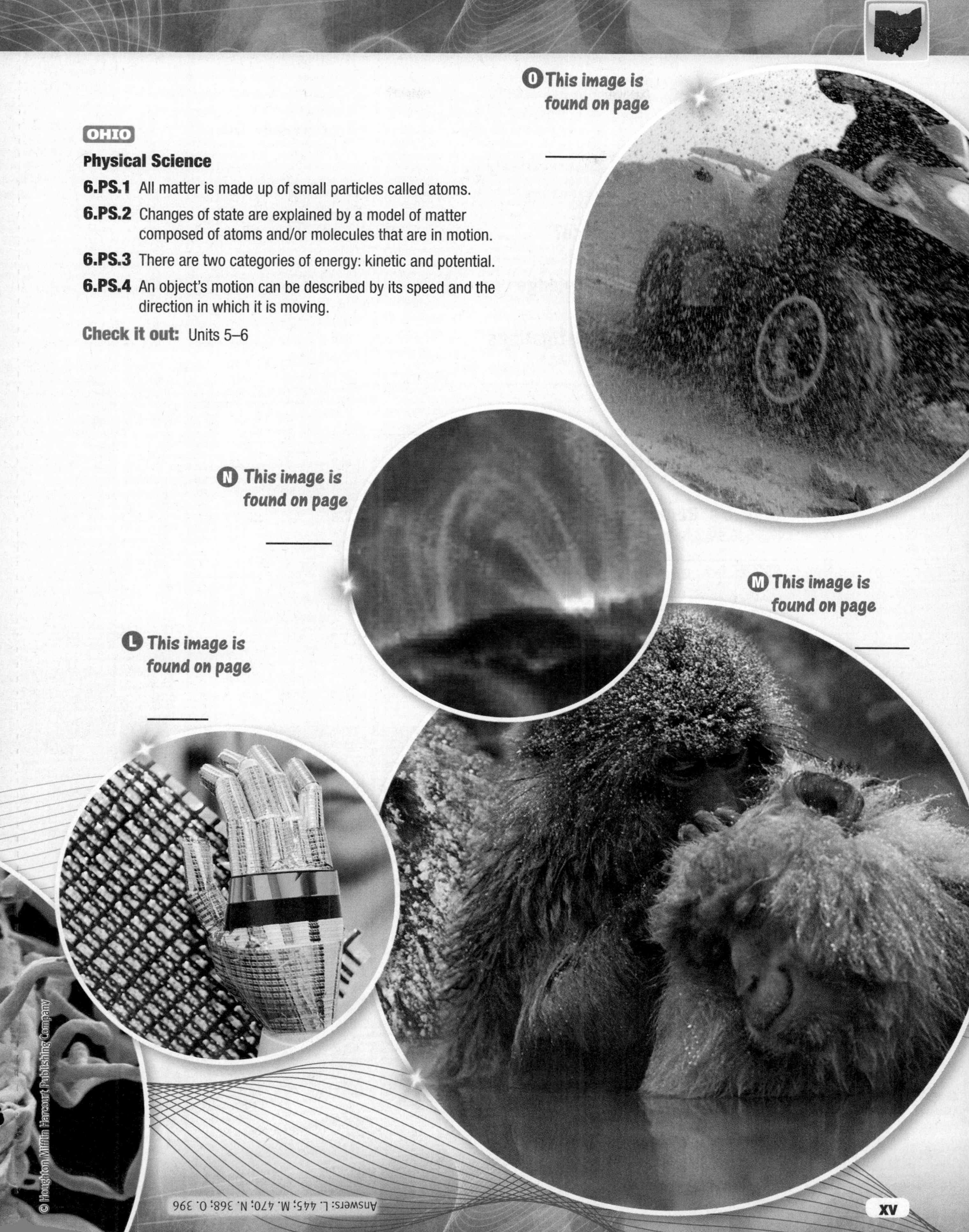

O This image is found on page ____

N This image is found on page ____

M This image is found on page ____

L This image is found on page ____

Answers: L. 445; M. 470; N. 368; O. 396

Contents

Specialized tools are required to collect some types of scientific data. These scientists are using a thermal camera to see how temperatures vary on a volcano.

The huge White Cliffs of Dover were formed from the skeletons of organisms, such as the microscopic marine algae shown here.

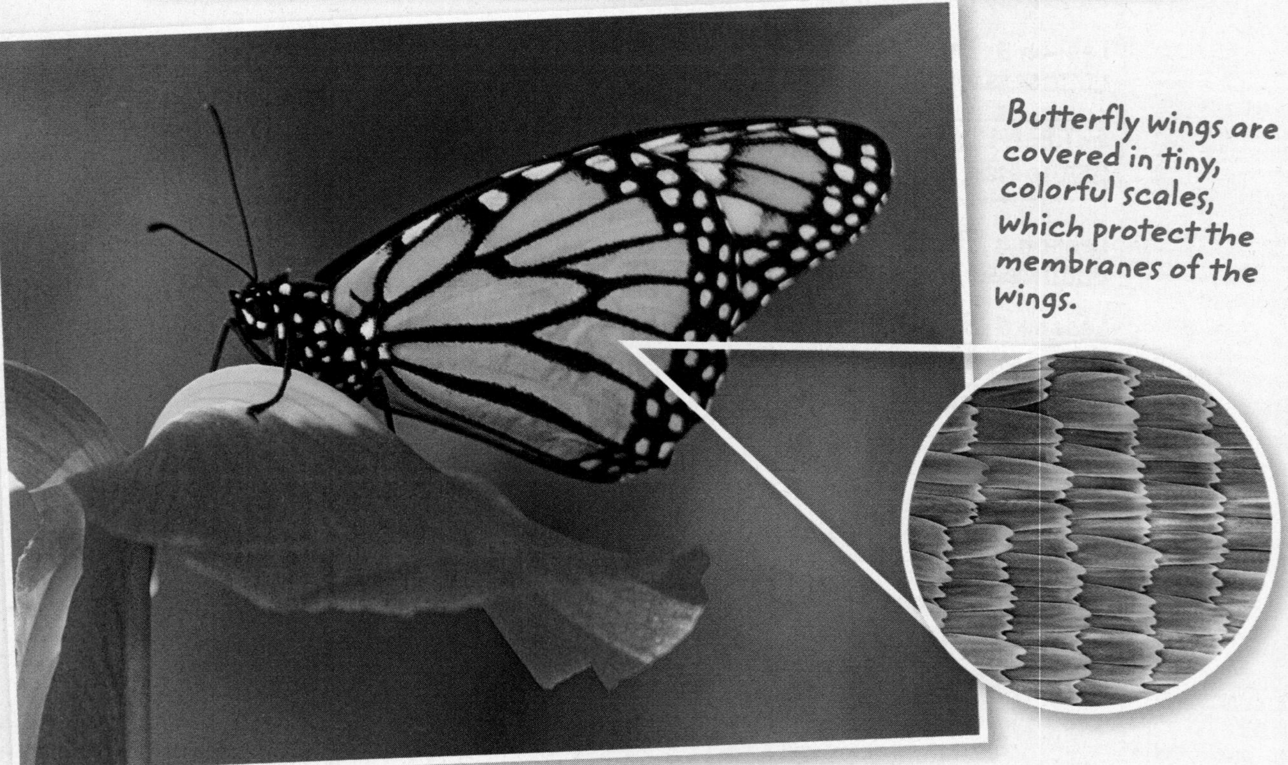

Butterfly wings are covered in tiny, colorful scales, which protect the membranes of the wings.

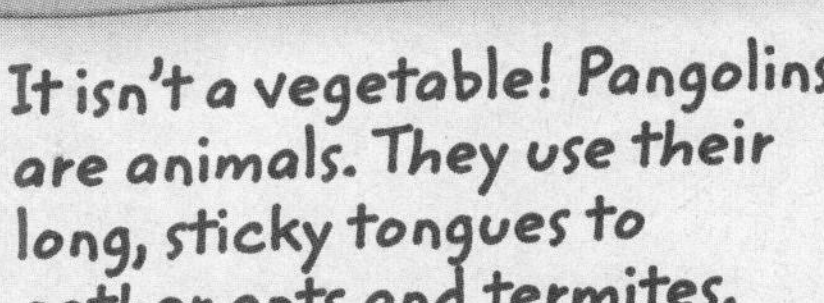
It isn't a vegetable! Pangolins are animals. They use their long, sticky tongues to gather ants and termites.

Don't be fooled by the beautiful red caps of these mushrooms. Unlike their tasty relatives, these mushrooms are highly toxic.

Contents (continued)

Fireworks displays are full of energy! Chemical energy is transformed into sound, light, and energy as heat during each explosion.

The same particles of matter in our bodies today may once have been part of a dinosaur or a star!

Assignments:

UNIT 1

Science, Technology, and Engineering

Big Idea

Scientists and engineers use careful observations and clear reasoning to understand the world around us and to design technology to meet a variety of needs.

People used to think that because Earth was flat, you would fall off the edge if you got too close.

What do you think?

Careful observations and experiments provide us with new information that may change or confirm what we know about the world we live in. What is one way in which science has changed your view of the world?

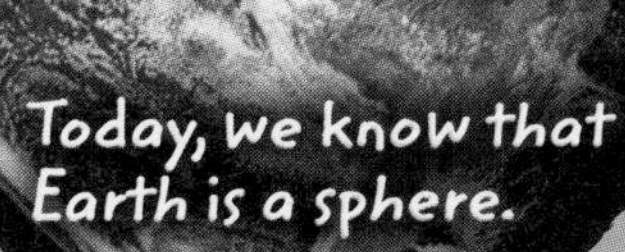

Today, we know that Earth is a sphere.

Unit 1

Science, Technology, and Engineering

CITIZEN SCIENCE

Things Change

People used to have strange ideas about the world in which they lived. How science has changed some of those ideas is shown here.

1687
People used to think that the sun and planets revolved around Earth. In 1687, Newton described gravity and how it affects objects. His work explained why all of the planets, including Earth, must revolve around the much larger sun. Newton's work finally convinced people that the sun and not Earth was at the center of the solar system.

Sir Isaac Newton

1950s

In 1915, people didn't believe Alfred Wegener when he proposed that the continents were moving slowly. It wasn't until the 1950s that advances in technology provided four different lines of evidence, which proved that continents do move. Wegener was right.

1861

People used to think that living things could come from nonliving things such as flies and beetles from rotting meat. This idea was called *spontaneous generation*. It was Pasteur's experiments that finally disproved this idea.

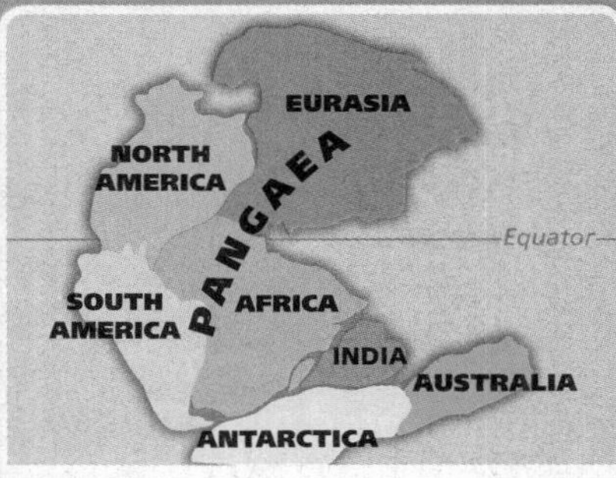

Modern continents used to be a part of Pangaea.

2008

People used to think that there were Martians on Mars. However, probes and landers have replaced ideas of little green men with real information about the planet. In 2008, we discovered water ice there.

Create Your Own Timeline

1 Think About It

Choose a favorite science topic and write it below.

____

2 Conduct Research

Here are some questions to ask as you research your topic:

A What famous people contributed to the development of your topic and when?

____

____

____

B What images can you use to illustrate the changes that occurred to your topic over time?

____

____

____

3 Make A Plan

Sketch out how you would like to organize your information in the space below, including date, people involved, pictures, and brief passages showing the changes in your topic.

Take It Home

Describe what you have learned to adults at home. Then, have them help you create a poster or banner to show how your topic has changed over time.

What Is Science?

Any chef will tell you, cooking is a lot like science. Today, there are a growing number of chefs using scientific knowledge to take traditional foods and recipes in new directions. Here, the chef is using super-cold liquid nitrogen to give a new meaning to the term "Hard-boiled egg."

ESSENTIAL QUESTION

What are the characteristics of science?

By the end of this lesson, you should be able to distinguish what characterizes science and scientific explanations, and differentiate between science and pseudoscience.

OHIO 6.SIA.1 Identify questions that can be answered through scientific investigations.

OHIO 6.SIA.6 Think critically and logically to connect evidence and explanations.

OHIO 6.SIA.7 Recognize and analyze alternative explanations and predictions.

Lesson Labs

Quick Labs
- What's In the Box?
- Investigating the Unseen

Engage Your Brain

1 Predict Check T or F to show whether you think each statement is true or false.

T	F	
☐	☐	Science is the study of the natural world.
☐	☐	Scientific explanations should be logical and testable.
☐	☐	The methods of science can be used in other fields.
☐	☐	Scientific explanations do not change.
☐	☐	Creativity does not play a role in science.

2 Compose In this lamp, heating of the liquid at the bottom causes the wax globs in it to rise and fall in interesting patterns. What is a scientific question you could ask about this lamp? What is a non-scientific question you could ask about this lamp?

____

____

____

____

____

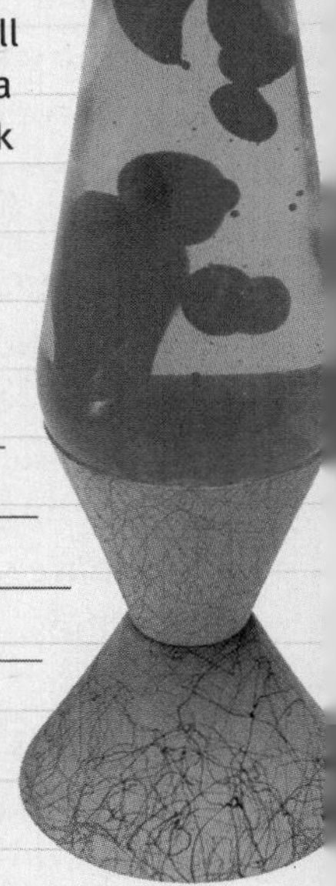

Active Reading

3 Synthesize You can often define an unknown word if you know the meaning of its word parts. Use the word parts and sentence below to make an educated guess about the meaning of the word *pseudoscience*.

Word part	Meaning
pseudo-	false; pretending to be
science	the systematic study of the natural world

Example Sentence
Their belief that space aliens visited the Earth in ancient times is based on pseudoscience and faulty logic.

pseudoscience:

____

____

Vocabulary Terms

- **science**
- **empirical evidence**
- **pseudoscience**

4 Apply As you learn the definition of each vocabulary term in this lesson, create your own definition or sketch to help you remember the meaning of the term.

Character Witness

What characterizes science?

Many people think of science as simply a collection of facts. **Science** is the systematic study of natural events and conditions. Scientific subjects can be anything in the living or nonliving world. In general, all scientific subjects can be broken down into three areas—life science, Earth science, and physical science.

Life science, or biology, is the study of living things. Life scientists may study anything from how plants produce food to how animals interact in the wild. Earth science, or geology, is the study of the surface and interior of Earth. An Earth scientist may study how rocks form or what past events produced the volcano you see in the photo. Physical science includes the subjects of physics and chemistry. Physicists and chemists study nonliving matter and energy. They may study the forces that hold matter together or the ways electromagnetic waves travel through space.

Of course, the three areas contain much more than this. Indeed, the subjects of science can seem practically limitless. As you will see, however, they all share some common characteristics and methods.

5 Identify As you read, underline three areas of science.

Community Consensus

One aspect that really sets the study of science apart from other pursuits is its need for openness and review. Whatever information one scientist collects, others must be able to see and comment upon.

The need for openness is important, because scientific ideas must be testable and reproducible. This means that if one scientist arrives at an explanation based on something he or she observed, that scientist must make the data available to other scientists. This allows others the chance to comment upon the results. For example, a scientist may claim that her evidence shows the volcano will erupt in five days. If the scientist declines to describe what that evidence is or how she collected it, why should anyone else think the claim is accurate?

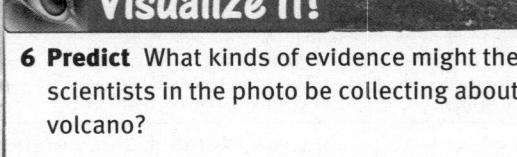

6 Predict What kinds of evidence might the scientists in the photo be collecting about the volcano?

____

____

7 Explain How might the study of volcanoes affect the people who live near them?

____

____

____

Use of Empirical Evidence

If scientific evidence must be open to all, it needs to be the kind of evidence all can observe. It must be something measurable and not just one person's opinion or guess. Evidence in science must be evidence that can be gained by the senses or empirical evidence. **Empirical evidence** includes observations and measurements. It includes all the data that people gather and test to support and evaluate scientific explanations.

For example, a scientist studying a volcano would visit the volcano to get empirical evidence. The scientist might use specialized tools to make observations and take measurements. Many tools help scientists collect more accurate evidence. Tools often make collecting data safer. For example, few scientists would want to go to the top of the volcano and look down into it. Mounting a thermal camera on an airplane allows scientists to get an aerial shot of the volcano's mouth. Not only does the shot show the detail they want, but also it's a lot safer.

Mount St. Helens volcano as seen with thermal photography.

Scientists use special thermal cameras to take photographs that show the temperature regions of volcanoes.

"Give me an explanation..."

What is a scientific explanation?

Active Reading

8 Apply As you read, underline the characteristics of a scientific explanation.

Empirical evidence is the basis for scientific explanations. A scientific explanation provides a description of how a process in nature occurs. Scientific explanations are based on observations and data. Beliefs or opinions that are not based on explanations that can be tested are not scientific.

Scientists may begin developing an explanation by gathering all the empirical evidence they have. This could be the observations and measurements they have made or those from other scientists. Then they think logically about how all of this evidence fits together. The explanation they propose must fit all the available evidence.

Often, other scientists will then further evaluate the explanation by testing it for themselves. The additional observations and tests may provide data that further support the explanation. If the results do not support the explanation, the explanation is rejected or modified and retested.

Consider a scientific explanation for how metal rusts. Rust is a compound of oxygen and a metal, usually iron. Oxygen makes up one-fifth of the air we breathe. Therefore, rust may form when oxygen in the air combines with metal. We observe that most rusted metals have also been exposed to large amounts of water. We also observe that the rate of rusting increases if the water contains salt, as it does near oceans. A scientist would propose that water causes metal to rust and that salt increases the rate of rusting. How might you test this statement?

How is a scientific explanation evaluated?

So, how would you evaluate the explanation of why some metals rust? Look at the explanation below and start to consider what you know.

First, look at your empirical evidence. Think of all the evidence you could gather to support the statement. A few examples are there for you. Think carefully about what you notice when you look at rusty metal.

Second, consider if the explanation is logical. Does it contradict anything you know or other evidence you have seen?

Third, think of other tests you could do to support your ideas. Could you think of a test that might contradict the explanation?

Last, evaluate the explanation. Do you think it has stood up to the tests? Do you think the tests have addressed what they were supposed to?

The Scientific Explanation:
Many metals that rust contain iron that reacts with water and oxygen.

The Evidence

9 Identify What evidence do you have about when some metal objects rust?

- I've seen rust on bridges, cars, and other metal objects exposed to the outdoors
- I left several garden tools outside that rusted

The Logic

Second, consider if the explanation is consistent with other evidence you have seen. Think about whether all metals rust in the same way.

10 Infer Describe how well your explanation fits all of the evidence you have, with all that you know.

- Some metals, like aluminum, don't rust
- Older metals rust more than newer ones

The Tests

Next, think of other tests you could do that would support the explanation.

11 Predict How might you test the conditions under which different metals rust?

- Expose different metals to the same conditions and see if they rust
- Could put metals in regular water and saltwater and note the rate of rusting

The Conclusion

Only after gathering evidence, thinking logically, and doing additional testing do you evaluate the scientific explanation.

12 Evaluate Does this empirical evidence support your explanation? Explain your answer.

Common Habits

What is involved in scientific work?

Even though science and the people who study it are very diverse, scientists have several characteristics in common. Scientists are curious, creative, and careful observers. They are also logical, skeptical, and objective.

You do not have to be a scientist to have these characteristics. When you use these habits of mind, you are thinking like a scientist!

Active Reading

13 Apply Which of the characteristics above do you use most often?

____

____

____

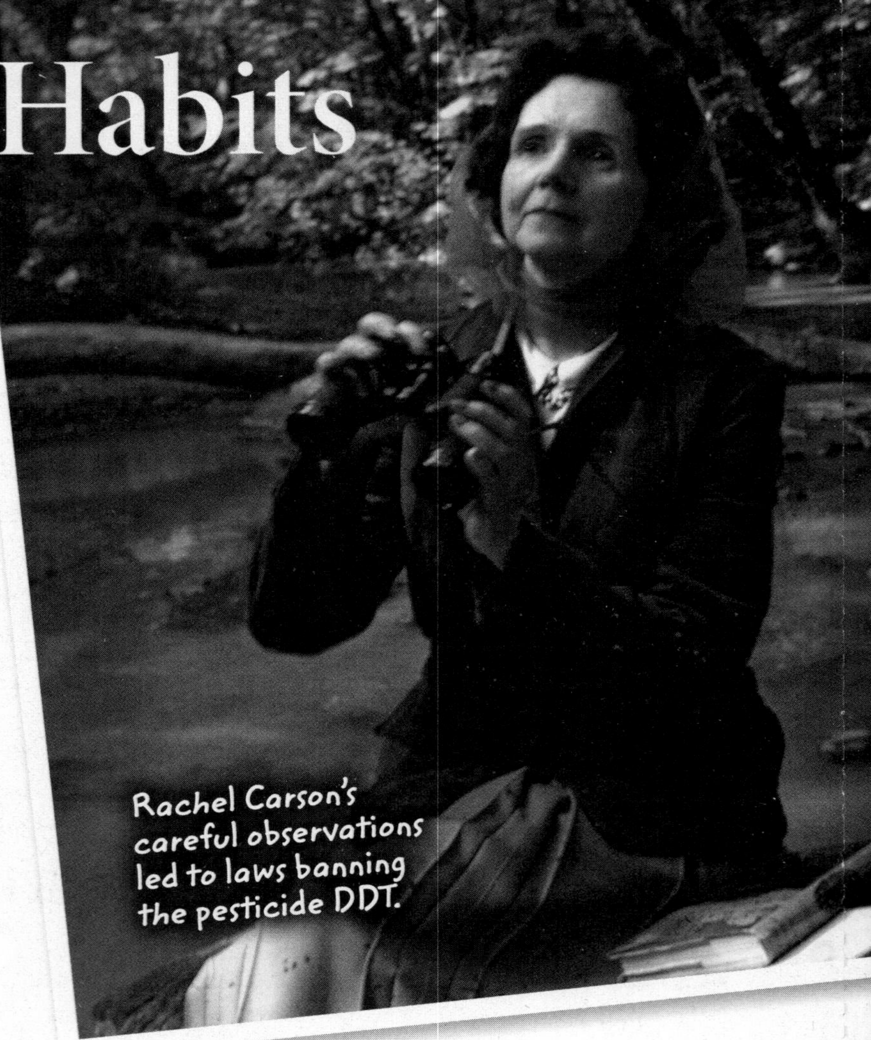

Rachel Carson's careful observations led to laws banning the pesticide DDT.

Careful Observation

Scientists observe with their senses as well as with scientific tools. All observations contribute to the understanding of a subject.

For example, ecologist Rachel Carson spent her entire life observing the natural world around her. She studied the oceans and wrote books and articles about them. She spent years researching and documenting the effects of pesticides, like DDT, on the environment. Her book, *Silent Spring,* drew the world's attention to the problem.

Curiosity

Scientists are curious about the world around them and about the things they observe. Most scientific discoveries are the result of someone asking why or how something happens.

For example, Rachel Carson was curious about all of nature. This curiosity drove her to identify the connections in it. It allowed her to understand how one part affects another.

14 List Name two things you are curious about.

____

____

Creativity

Being creative means to be original. Creative people think for themselves and always try to see other ways things might be.

In science, creativity is used when scientists apply their imaginations to come up with new solutions. For example, prairie fires can start suddenly and cause destruction. Instead of trying to prevent them, some scientists often start them under controlled conditions to minimize the damage.

15 Identify Name an activity you do in which you are creative.

____

19 Apply Research shows that interaction with animals can benefit humans. In the discussion of dolphin therapy to the right, fill in the blanks with the appropriate characteristics scientists are showing.

Scientists saw how well people responded to animals and imagined ______________________ that these interactions might be helpful in some types of therapy.

Scientists were ______________________ about whether dolphins could be used as therapy animals.

Early studies showed that dolphin therapy has helped to improve certain conditions in humans. But scientists must be ______________________. They must not draw conclusions too quickly.

They need to conduct more tests and make ______________________ to determine the effects of dolphin therapy.

When they have more data, they will assess it ______________________ before drawing a conclusion.

They will consider all the evidence ______________________ before making decisions about the advantages and disadvantages of dolphin therapy.

Logic

Thinking logically involves reasoning through information and making conclusions supported by the evidence. Logical thinking is an important tool for the scientist.

For example, toothpaste helps to prevent tooth decay. Some mouthwash also helps to prevent tooth decay. It is logical to think that if the two products are used together they might work even better. This logical conclusion should then be tested.

16 Infer What is another career that relies on logic?

____

Skepticism

Being skeptical means that you don't accept everything you hear or read immediately. You ask questions before deciding whether you will accept information as factual. Scientists are skeptical of drawing conclusions too quickly. Instead, they repeat observations and experiments, and they review and try to replicate the work of others.

17 Conclude Why should you be skeptical of some advertisements?

____

____

Objectivity

Being objective requires that you set aside your personal feelings, moods, and beliefs while you evaluate something. Science requires unbiased observations, experiments, and evaluations. Scientists want their tests to support their ideas. Scientists must be careful not to let this hope influence what they see.

18 Explain Describe a time when it was difficult to be objective.

____

____

____

“Space Aliens built the Pyramids”

How is pseudoscience similar to and different from science?

People have marveled at the pyramids for thousands of years. Even today, scientists still question how ancient people could have built such awesome structures. Some have given a possible explanation for this—the pyramids were built by an advanced race of beings from outer space. Because it is unclear how ancient people could have built the pyramids, supporters of this idea think it provides one possible answer.

Some people will claim to have scientific evidence to support an explanation when in fact they do not. **Pseudoscience** is a belief or practice that is based on incorrectly applied scientific methods. Pseudoscience can seem like real science, but pseudoscientific ideas are based on faulty logic and are supported by claims that can't be tested.

Similarities

Pseudoscience is like science in that it often involves topics related to the natural world. People who believe in pseudoscience have explanations that can sound logical. Like science, pseudoscience uses technical language or scientific-sounding terms. Both science and pseudoscience claim to be based on empirical evidence.

Differences

The biggest difference between science and pseudoscience is that pseudoscience does not use accepted scientific methods. The evidence that supports pseudoscience may be very vague or lack any measurements. Some pseudoscientific claims lack the ability to be tested at all. Other pseudoscientific beliefs are supported only by personal experiences. Unlike scientists, pseudoscientists might claim that results not proven false must be true. This is faulty logic. Scientists must offer evidence for their conclusions. Pseudoscience asks skeptics to prove it false. In the case of the pyramids, pseudoscientists claim the pyramids' complexity is proof of their alien origin. To disprove the claim, you must prove aliens did not visit Earth 5,000 years ago. This is almost impossible to do.

Active Reading **20 Identify** Name two traits of pseudoscience.

Science vs. Pseudoscience

Science	Pseudoscience
Based on logic	Not based on logic or logic is exaggerated
Has testable explanations	Explanations generally not testable
Relies on empirical evidence	Empirical evidence is not available; personal opinions often are used as empirical evidence
Results can be reproduced by others	Results cannot be reproduced by others
Explanations that are not proven false continue to be tested	Explanations that are not proven false are assumed to be true
Explanations are modified by new evidence	Explanations do not change with new evidence

22 Analyze Someone tells you they've heard of a powder that, if worn in a pouch around the neck, will cure a cold. This person claims that the powder has cured everyone with a cold who has worn it. How do you explain to this person that, despite the positive results, this is a pseudoscientific claim?

21 Explain Would it be possible for something to initially be regarded as pseudoscience and then later be supported by science? Explain your answer.

Even today, researchers don't know how ancient people hauled the large stones needed to build the pyramids. Does this prove that aliens did it?

Think Outside the Book

23 Evaluate A popular hoax on the Internet warned of the dangers of the chemical dihydrogen monoxide. The supposed opponents claimed the chemical could cause death if inhaled and severe burns if touched. Do some research to find out what this chemical is. How are the claims made about it like the claims made by pseudoscientists?

Visual Summary

To complete this summary, fill in the blanks with the correct word or phrase. Then use the key below to check your answers. You can use this page to review the main concepts of the lesson.

What Is Science?

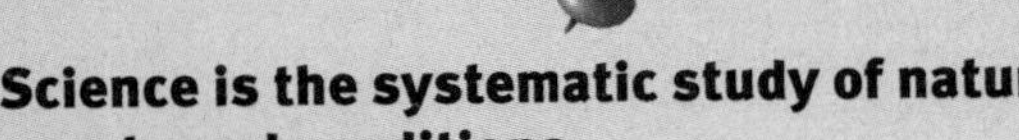

Science is the systematic study of natural events and conditions.

24 Explanations in science must be testable and have ____________________ of other scientists.

25 The ____________________ collected in scientific investigations is often in the form of measurements.

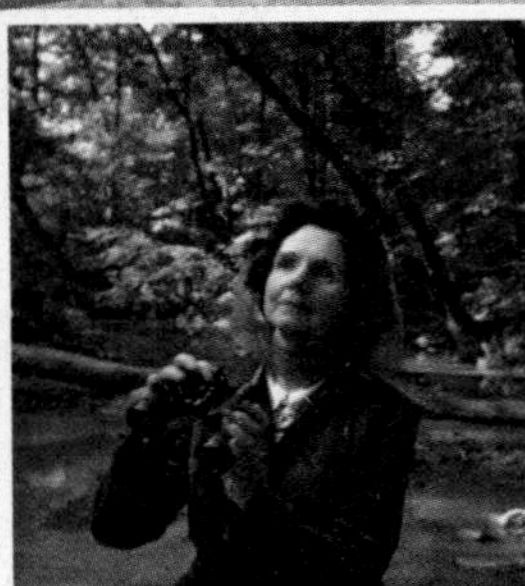

Scientists may study very different things, but they share many common traits.

26 Scientists use empirical evidence, logical thinking, and tests to ____________________ a scientific explanation.

27 Scientists are ____________________ about the subjects they study.

Science and pseudoscience both deal with the natural world, but pseudoscience only deceptively appears to be science.

28 Many claims of pseudoscience are not refutable because they can't be ____________________

Answers: 24 consensus; 25 empirical evidence; 26 evaluate; 27 curious; 28 tested

29 Hypothesize How might the characteristics of a scientist be displayed in a person of your age?

Lesson Review

Vocabulary

Fill in the blank with the term that best completes the following sentences.

1 _______________ is the systematic study of the natural world.

2 ________________________ is often mistakenly regarded as being based on science.

3 _________________ __________________ is the name for the observations and data on which a scientific explanation can be based.

Key Concepts

4 Describe What are two things that characterize the practice of science?

5 Sequence What are the three steps scientists take to evaluate a scientific explanation?

6 Describe What are six traits of a good scientific observer?

7 Justify Why is it good for scientists to be skeptical?

Critical Thinking

Use the table below to answer the following questions.

Characteristic	Science	Pseudoscience
Concerns the natural world		
Explanations can sound logical		
Results can always be tested by others		
Explanations can be proven false		
Allows personal opinions to be used as evidence		

8 Assess Place an "x" in the appropriate box if the characteristic could describe science, pseudoscience, or both. What might this tell you about the relationship between science and pseudoscience?

9 Judge Good scientists use their imagination. What do you think is the difference between being imaginative in doing science and doing pseudoscience?

My Notes

Lesson 2

Scientific Knowledge

ESSENTIAL QUESTION

How do scientists develop explanations?

By the end of this lesson, you should be able to analyze how scientists choose their methods, develop explanations, and identify support for a theory.

Tiny radio transmitters allow scientists to track animals such as this tortoise in the wild. The information about the animal's behavior helps scientists better understand and possibly even protect it.

OHIO 6.SIA.6 Think critically and logically to connect evidence and explanations.

OHIO 6.SIA.7 Recognize and analyze alternative explanations and predictions.

Lesson Labs

Quick Labs

- Does the Evidence Support the Explanation?
- Create a Time Line of a Theory

Engage Your Brain

1 Describe Fill in the blank with the word or phrase that you think correctly completes the following sentences.

Scientists can study in the field or in the ______________________.

A good scientific theory is often ____________ when new evidence is found but is rarely completely rejected.

The results of a scientific investigation either support or do not support a claim; they do not offer conclusive ______________

2 Hypothesize Describe how you might study the butterfly coming out of the cocoon. What actions would you take? What tools would you use? What might you want to avoid doing?

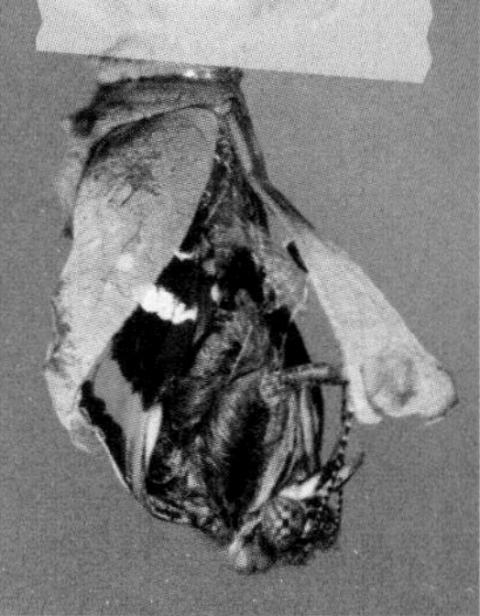

Active Reading

3 Apply Many scientific words such as *method* have everyday meanings. Use context clues to write your own definition for the meaning of the word *method*.

Example Sentence
Gloria felt there was only one method for cooking spaghetti.

Vocabulary

4 Identify As you read, place a question mark next to any words that you don't understand. When you finish reading the lesson, go back and review the words that you marked. If the information is still confusing, consult a classmate or a teacher.

Method Acting

How do scientists choose their methods?

Active Reading

5 Identify As you read, underline examples of tools used in scientific investigations.

Scientists plan investigations to address a specific problem or question. The goal is to come up with a scientific explanation. Each problem or question is unique and so requires a unique method and the proper tools.

You wouldn't lock yourself in a closet to study the birds in your neighborhood. You wouldn't use a microscope to measure the force propelling a model rocket. Science also has methods and tools to study different kinds of problems. Learning to be a scientist is learning how to use these methods and tools properly.

Visualize It!

6 Infer Scientists have all kinds of tools available to them. They select them based on what they study. Can you tell where or how scientist might use the tools in each of the two photos?

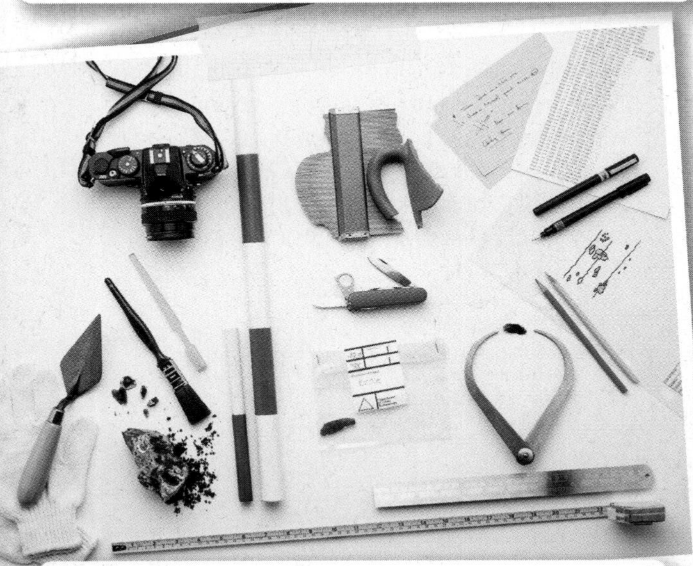

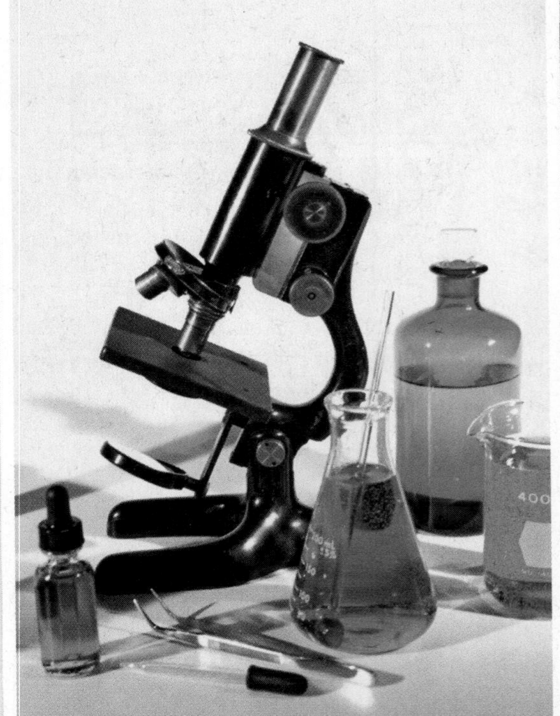

A

____

____

____

B

____

____

____

By the Tools Available

Scientists did not know about cells before there was a microscope. No one had seen the moons of the planet Jupiter before there was the telescope. Severe weather tracking and prediction reached a new level of sophistication with the invention of doppler radar. Scientists need their tools.

Scientists, however, know that they can't always have the tools they may need. Some might be too expensive. Others simply may not exist. So, scientists also need to be creative in the ways they use their tools. For example, astronomers study the light from a star to get an idea of its chemical makeup. Similarly, geologists study what Earth's interior is like by looking at seismograph readings during an earthquake. Tools are only useful if the scientist using them can interpret the data they provide. This skill is a large part of the education of a scientist.

By the Subject Under Study

Generally, scientific investigations fall into two types: experiments and fieldwork. Experiments involve scientists controlling different variables during an investigation. Experiments usually are done under very precise and controlled conditions in a laboratory. Physicists and chemists generally do a lot of experiments.

In contrast, scientists doing fieldwork make observations of what is around them. They watch and observe and try to make sense of what they see. Instead of controlling variables, they try to determine what variables are at work and how they relate to each other. A large part of doing fieldwork is often coming to understand the variables that exist. Biologists and geologists generally do a lot of fieldwork. Sometimes, a scientist will do fieldwork and then take a specimen back to a laboratory to do more testing.

Visualize It!

7 Identify For each photo, identify some tools a scientist might use to study the subject of the photo. Use examples from the photos on the other page for suggestions.

Ⓐ

____

____

____

Ⓑ

____

____

____

Well, Prove It!

How do scientific theories become accepted?

Active Reading **8 Identify** As you read, underline an example of new evidence supporting a theory.

In science, a theory is not the same as an educated guess. A theory is not an explanation for a single fact. A scientific *theory* is a system of ideas that explains many related observations and is supported by a large body of evidence acquired through scientific investigation. Scientific theories may be modified but are rarely rejected.

Being Supported by Evidence

About 65 million years ago, dinosaurs and many other organisms suddenly became extinct. Scientists have offered many explanations for why this happened, from widespread disease to sudden climate change.

In the 1970s, Walter and Luis Alvarez found a thin layer of iridium-rich clay at various places on Earth. These layers dated to 65 million years ago, the same time as the mass extinction. Iridium is a rare element on Earth but is found in large amounts in meteorites. The Alvarezes proposed that perhaps Earth had been struck by a large meteorite at that time. They proposed that this massive impact was what caused the dinosaurs' extinction.

In the 1990s, evidence of a crater of the right size, type, and age was found near the city of Chicxulub (CHIK-shuh-loob) in Mexico. With this evidence, most scientists agreed that a meteorite impact did play a role in the extinction of the dinosaurs.

This rock specimen was collected from the Chicxulub crater. Scientists used samples like this to determine when the meteorite struck Earth. The map shows the location of the crater.

Incorporating New Evidence

Many scientists were skeptical that a single meteorite impact could result in a mass extinction. Further research was needed.

Evidence was found of major volcanic eruptions in India occurring at the end of the dinosaur age. Volcanic ash in the atmosphere can block sunlight and contribute to global cooling. Thus, many scientists thought that volcanoes were the main cause of the mass extinction, and a volcanic-eruption explanation was put forth. But further research showed that these volcanoes had been erupting for about 500,000 years before the Chicxulub impact without having a massive effect on the global environment.

For years scientists studied the evidence using tools and technology from many different fields. Recently, scientists around the world have come to agree that the Chicxulub impact was most likely the trigger that caused tidal waves, earthquakes, landslides, and blasts of dust that, together with the volcanic ash that was already present, darkened the skies. This led to global cooling and reduced plant life, which killed the dinosaurs. With the evidence unified into a well-supported explanation, the meteorite impact explanation for dinosaur extinction could now be called a theory.

Think Outside the Book Inquiry

9 Infer The mass extinction of 65 million years ago is one of the most significant events in Earth's history. Write an essay about why this event was so significant.

The Chicxulub meteorite was about 6 mi (10 km) in diameter. It formed a crater about 3300 ft (1000 m) deep and 110 mi (180 km) wide. The meteorite's impact triggered waves thousands of feet high and darkened the skies with dust.

The modern site for the Chicxulub crater is found buried under limestone in the Yucatan peninsula of Mexico. Finding the crater was evidence in support of the meteorite impact theory.

Chicxulub Crater

Visualize It!

10 Infer Why would the Chicxulub crater be covered up now?

____

____

How can you know who's right?

Active Reading

11 Identify As you read, underline an example of what you need to be aware of when reading a scientific explanation.

The most reliable scientific information is found in professional science journals. These contain articles written and reviewed by other scientists. The reason the information is reliable is simple. It has been checked and rechecked by experts in the same area of science as the journal articles. The downside to reading scientific journals is that they are not easy to understand. They contain many words that nonscientists may not recognize.

You should be very cautious of accepting scientific explanations from advertisers or anyone trying to sell you something. They can be more concerned with getting you to buy their products than with teaching you science.

When you read anything, or assess any scientific claim, you need to ask yourself if it makes sense logically. You should always think critically. When presented with a claim, ask yourself whether the results support it. Do the results agree with what you know about the world? Remember, scientists do not claim to prove anything. Scientists attempt to provide an explanation that agrees with the results of observation and testing.

12 Appraise Conduct library or Internet research to investigate the scientific claims below. Check the appropriate box according to whether you find the theory is supported or not supported by scientific evidence.

The impact of a large meteorite caused the extinction of the dinosaurs.	☐ Results support ☐ Results fail to support Why?
Tests have shown that water exists on Mars and the moon.	☐ Results support ☐ Results fail to support Why?
The moon is made of blue cheese.	☐ Results support ☐ Results fail to support Why?

Why It Matters

FORENSIC SCIENCE

A Theory for the Birds

Dinosaurs Take Flight

The fossil *archaeopteryx*, shown to the right, gave the first solid evidence linking dinosaurs to modern birds. Although it had wings and feathers and may even have been able to fly, it seems to be more dinosaur than bird. It had jaws with teeth, three-fingered claws, and a tail.

Gone But Not Forgotten

Not all dinosaurs of the past were large, like the ones we see reconstructed in museums. Some were small. *Archaeopteryx* was about as big as a medium-sized dog.

Family Resemblance?

Pigeons are thought to be one modern bird that closely resembles its ancient counterpart. Few scientists today debate the dinosaur origins of birds. They do, however, debate how it may have occurred.

Extend

Inquiry

13 Determine Do the fossil remains appear to support or fail to support the idea that today's birds are the descendants of dinosaurs?

14 Relate How might the theory of dinosaurs' relation to birds be modified?

15 Infer Recent DNA evidence shows that dinosaurs and birds are genetically closer than either are to alligators. What does this say about the strength of the theory that birds and dinosaurs are related?

Visual Summary

To complete this summary, fill in the blanks with the correct word or phrase. Then use the key below to check your answers. You can use this page to review the main concepts of the lesson.

Scientific Knowledge

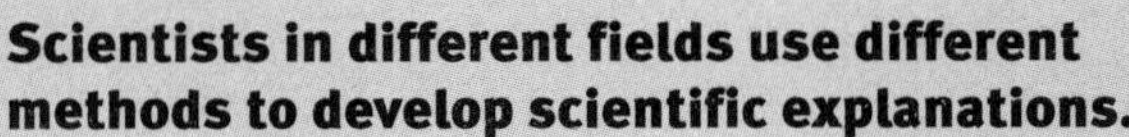

Scientists in different fields use different methods to develop scientific explanations.

16 What might a scientist be doing with the tools shown below?

____

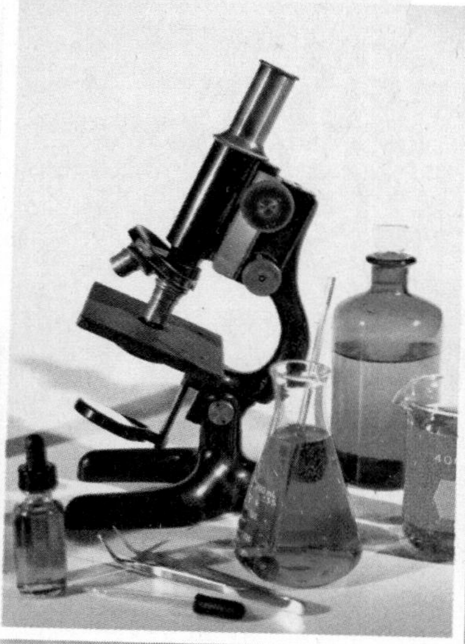

Good scientific theories are supported by a lot of evidence.

17 A good scientific theory is often _______________________ with new evidence but is rarely discarded.

18 Scientists don't claim to _______________ the theory. They just claim that the results _______________ it.

Answers: 16 lab work/experimenting; 17 modified; 18 prove, support

19 Integrate Why do you think scientists claim to offer only supporting evidence for a theory and not proof?

Lesson Review

Vocabulary

Fill in the blank with the term that best completes the following sentence.

1 An explantion in science that has a lot of evidence to back it up is a scientific

____

2 Scientists never say a theory is proven or not. They only say if the evidence ____________ or ________________ it.

Key Concepts

3 List What are two types of scientific investigations?

____

____

4 Infer You've been assigned to observe the habits of the birds living in your neighborhood. What tools might you take along?

____

____

____

5 Describe What kinds of tools might you use in a laboratory?

____

____

6 Judge Any time a scientific theory is challenged, it means it's not a good theory. Do you agree with this statement? Explain.

____

____

____

____

7 Discriminate Why would you be cautious of scientific information you hear from advertisers?

____

____

Critical Thinking

Use the photo below to answer the following questions.

8 Relate What type of investigation would a scientist studying this sinkhole use? What tools might be used to study it?

____

____

____

9 Apply What are some questions a scientist might want to find out about this sinkhole?

____

____

____

10 Assess Do you think it's wise for scientists not to accept a theory immediately, even if the theory has a lot of evidence to support it?

____

____

____

____

My Notes

Lesson 3

Scientific Investigations

ESSENTIAL QUESTION

How are scientific investigations conducted?

By the end of this lesson, you should be able to summarize the processes and characteristics of different kinds of scientific investigations.

Superconducting magnet assemblies such as the one shown here help to guide charged particles moving at almost the speed of light. Scientists study the colliding particles to investigate the nature of matter and energy.

OHIO **6.SIA.1** Identify questions that can be answered through scientific investigations.

OHIO **6.SIA.2** Design and conduct a scientific investigation.

OHIO **6.SIA.3** Use appropriate mathematics, tools and techniques to gather data and information.

OHIO **6.SIA.8** Communicate scientific procedures and explanations.

Lesson Labs

Quick Labs
- The Importance of Replication
- Improving an Electromagnet

Exploration Lab
- Road Safety

Engage Your Brain

1 Evaluate Check T or F to show whether you think each statement is true or false.

T	F	
☐	☐	Every scientific investigation is an experiment.
☐	☐	You could do an experiment to see if eating breakfast helps students raise their grades.
☐	☐	Scientists need fancy instruments to do experiments.
☐	☐	Scientists must repeat an experiment for it to be useful.

2 Infer What do you think the scientists who gathered the data for this graph were studying?

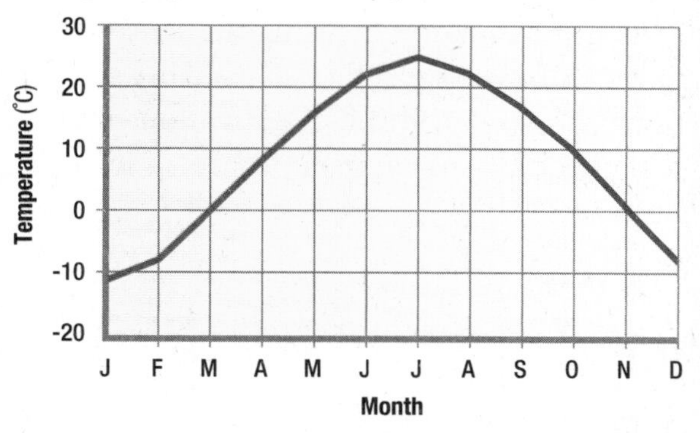

Active Reading

3 Synthesize The word *experiment* comes from the Latin word *experiri*, meaning "to try." What do you think the meaning of the word *experiment* is?

Vocabulary Terms

- experiment
- observation
- hypothesis
- variable
- independent variable
- dependent variable
- data
- control

4 Apply As you learn the meaning of each vocabulary term in this lesson, write a sentence of your own using the term.

Testing, Testing, 1, 2, 3

What are some parts that make up scientific investigations?

An **experiment** is an organized procedure to study something under controlled conditions. Scientists often investigate the natural world through experiments. Scientists also learn about the natural world through observations. **Observation** is the process of getting information by using the senses. The term can also refer to the information collected by using special equipment such as microscopes. Scientific investigations must be planned carefully so that observations can be interpreted in a meaningful way.

Elements of Investigations

Hypothesis

A **hypothesis** (hy•PAHTH•ih•sys) is an idea or explanation that can be tested and that leads to scientific investigation. A scientist may think of a hypothesis after making observations or after reading about other scientists' investigations.

Hypotheses must be carefully constructed so they can be tested in a practical and scientifically sound way. For example, suppose you find a bone fossil. Your hypothesis might be that analyses will date the bone at 200 million years old. You might test your hypothesis by comparing the fossil to other fossils that have been found in the same area or in the same layer of rock. You might also chemically analyze the fossil to determine its age.

If your fossil turned out not to be as old as you hypothesized, that result is still useful. The information from the investigation can help scientists form a better hypothesis for another investigation. Scientists may go through many cycles of testing and analysis before they arrive at a hypothesis that is supported.

Active Reading **5 Explain** Why should hypotheses be testable?

____

____

____

This young plant is growing in a harsh environment.

Visualize It!

6 Infer Write a hypothesis offering a possible explanation of what will happen to the plant above.

____

____

____

Independent and Dependent Variables

Scientists can control conditions in experiments. A **variable** is any factor that can change in a scientific investigation. An **independent variable** is the factor that is deliberately changed in an investigation. The **dependent variable** changes as a result of changes to the independent variable.

Imagine that you want to test the hypothesis that the intensity of heat under a pot of water determines how fast the water boils. You fill three pots with the same amount of water and then heat them until the water boils. The independent variable is the amount of heat. The dependent variable is the time it takes for the water to boil. You measure this variable for all three pots to see whether your hypothesis is supported.

If possible, an experiment should have just one independent variable. Scientists try to keep other variables constant, or unchanged, so they do not affect the results. For example, in the experiment described above, the pots are the constants. Each pot should be made of the same material because some materials change temperature more readily than others do.

Observations and Data

Data are information and measurements gathered by experimentation that can be used in calculating or reasoning. This information may be anything that a scientist senses through his or her own senses or detects with instruments.

In an investigation, everything a scientist observes must be recorded. The setup and procedures need to be recorded. By carefully recording this information, scientists make sure they will not forget anything.

Scientists analyze data to determine the relationship between the independent and dependent variables in an investigation. Then they draw conclusions about whether the data support the investigation's hypothesis.

7 Apply Suppose you want to test the hypothesis that plants grow taller when they receive more sunlight. Identify an independent variable and a dependent variable for this investigation.

____

____

____

____

____

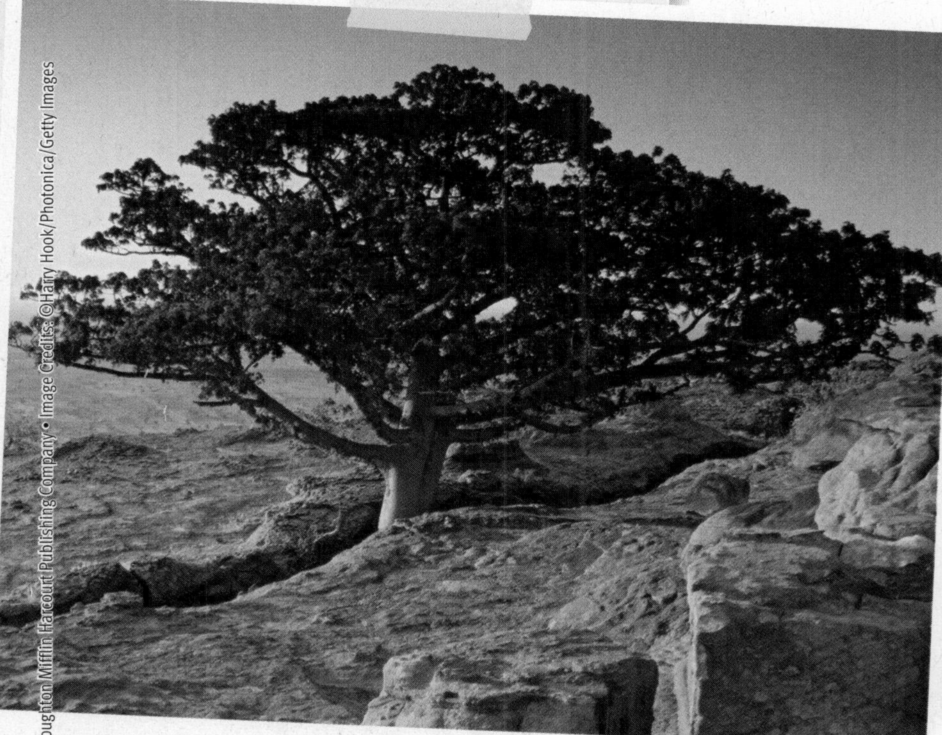

You may have thought that the plant at the left will die. But as this photograph shows, plants can get enough nutrients to thrive under similar conditions.

Many Methods

What are some scientific methods?

Conducting experiments and other scientific investigations is not like following a cookbook recipe. Scientists do not always use the same steps in every investigation or use steps in the same order. They may even repeat some of the steps. The following graphic shows one path that a scientist might follow while conducting an experiment.

8 Diagram Trace the path a scientist might follow if the data from an experiment did not support the hypothesis.

Defining a Problem

After making observations or reading scientific reports, a scientist might be curious about some unexplained aspect of a topic. A scientific problem is a specific question that a scientist wants to answer. The problem must be well-defined, or precisely stated, so that it can be investigated.

Forming a Hypothesis and Making Predictions

When scientists form a hypothesis, they are stating a possible explanation to a question. A hypothesis must be tested to see if it is supported. Before testing a hypothesis, scientists usually make predictions about what will happen in an investigation.

Planning an Investigation

A scientific investigation must be carefully planned so that it tests a hypothesis in a meaningful way. Scientists need to decide whether an investigation should be done in the field or in a laboratory. They must also determine what equipment and technology are needed and how materials for the investigation will be obtained.

Identifying Variables

The dependent and independent variables of an experiment are identified in the hypothesis. Scientists need to decide how the independent variable will change. They must identify other variables that will be controlled. Also, scientists must determine how they will measure the results of the experiment. The dependent variable often can be measured in more than one way. For example, if the dependent variable is fish health, scientists could measure size, weight, or number of offspring.

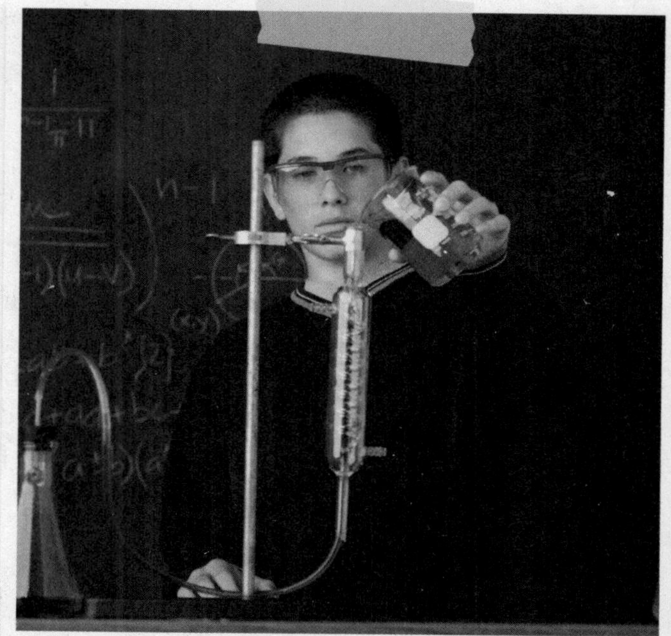

Collecting and Organizing Data

The data collected in an investigation must be recorded and properly organized so that they can be analyzed. Data such as measurements and numbers are often organized into tables, spreadsheets, or graphs.

Interpreting Data and Analyzing Information

After they finish collecting data, scientists must analyze this information. Their analysis will help them draw conclusions about the results. Scientists may have different interpretations of the same data because they analyze it using different methods.

Drawing and Defending Conclusions

Scientists conclude whether the results of their investigation support the hypothesis. If the hypothesis is not supported, scientists may think about the problem some more and try to come up with a new hypothesis to test. Or they may repeat an experiment to see if any mistakes were made. When they publish the results of their investigation, scientists must be prepared to defend their conclusions if they are challenged by other scientists.

Use It or Lose It

How are scientific methods used?

Scientific methods are used to study any aspect of the natural world. They can also be used in the social sciences, which focus on human society. It is often harder to control variables in the social sciences. Nevertheless, the research methods used in these fields are made stronger by the methods developed for physical, life, and earth sciences.

Think Outside the Book Inquiry

9 Plan Suppose that you want to investigate something using scientific methods. First, define a problem. Then, plan a scientific investigation using the methods discussed in the previous pages.

Use of Scientific Methods

Different Situations Require Different Methods

After forming a hypothesis, scientists decide how they will test it. Some hypotheses can be tested only through observation. Others must be tested in laboratory experiments. However, observation and experiments are often used together to build scientific knowledge. For example, if you want to test the strength of a metal used in airplane construction, you may study it in a laboratory experiment. But after conducting the experiment, you may want to inspect airplanes that have flown for a period of time to see how the metal holds up under actual flight conditions.

The results of a well-constructed investigation are useful whether or not the hypothesis is supported. In fact, it can be very interesting to find that a hypothesis is not supported. When a hypothesis is not supported, scientists must reconsider their question, think again about the variables involved, and develop a new hypothesis.

10 Apply Give another example of a scientific investigation that would require both observation and experiments.

____

____

____

____

Scientific Methods Are Used in Physical Science

Physical science includes the study of physics and chemistry. Scientists have used physics to figure out how gecko lizards stick to walls and ceilings.

Various explanations of the gecko's unique ability have been developed. Some scientists thought that static electricity helps geckos stick to walls. Others thought that the gecko produces a kind of glue from its feet. But experiments and observations did not support these hypotheses.

When a team of researchers studied the gecko's feet with a microscope, they found that each foot was covered with hundreds of thousands of tiny hairs. After measuring the force exerted by each hair against a surface, they came up with two possible hypotheses. One hypothesis was that geckos stick to walls because the hairs interact with a thin film of water. The other hypothesis was that the weak forces between the hairs and a surface combine to produce a force great enough to hold the gecko to the surface.

The team designed an experiment to test both hypotheses. The experiment showed that the force of a gecko's hair against a surface was the same whether or not the surface had any water on it. The scientists concluded that geckos stick to walls because of the combined attractive forces of the tiny hairs on their feet.

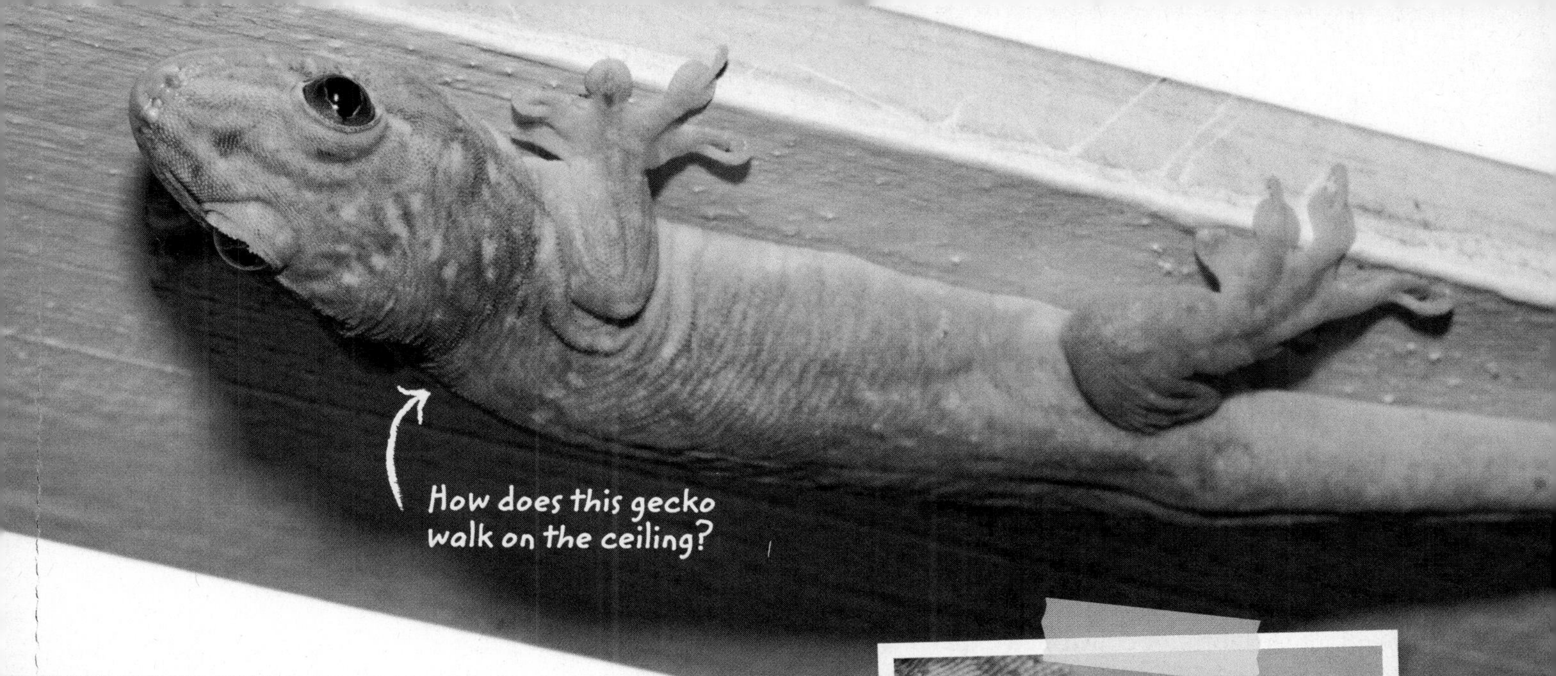

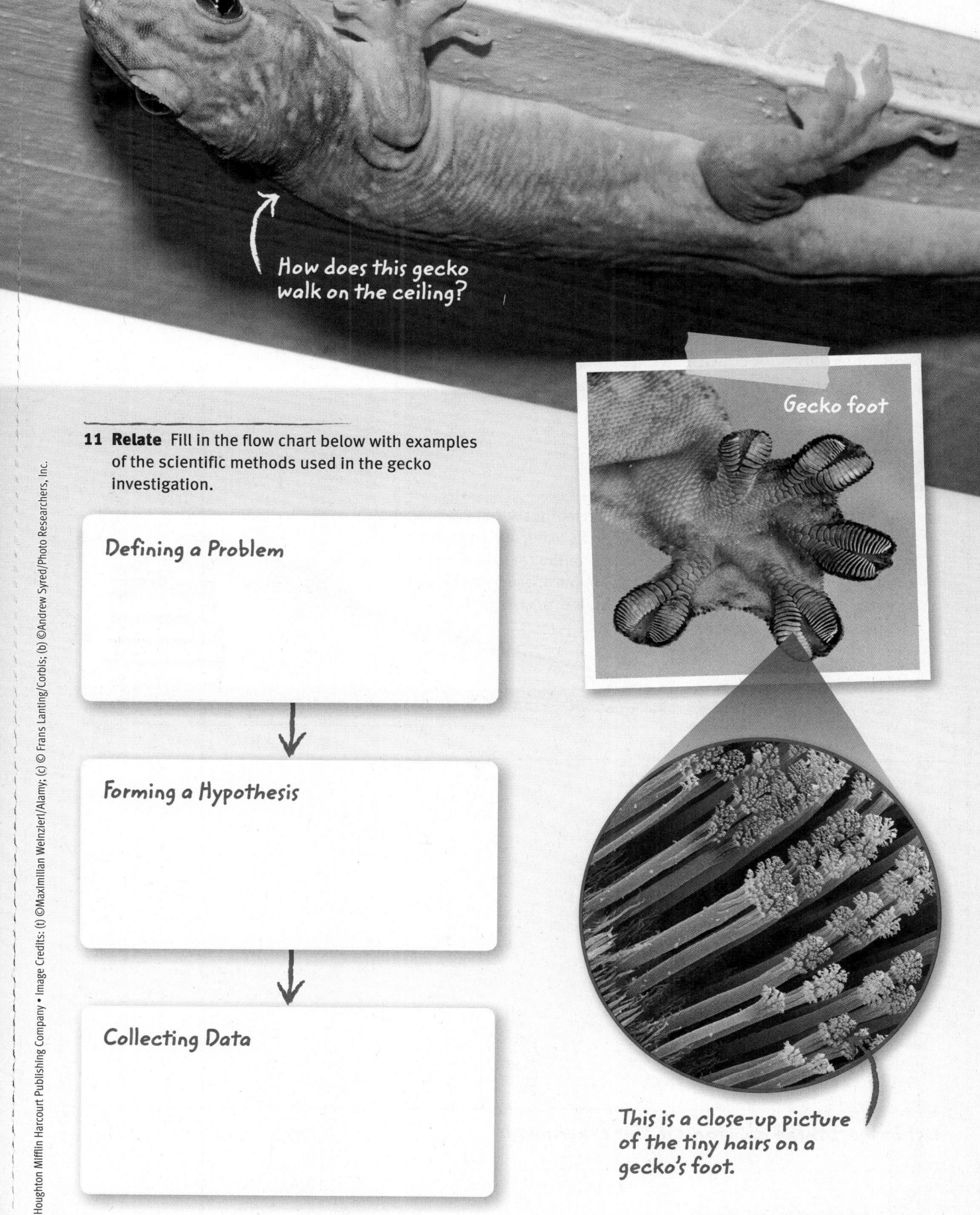

How does this gecko walk on the ceiling?

Gecko foot

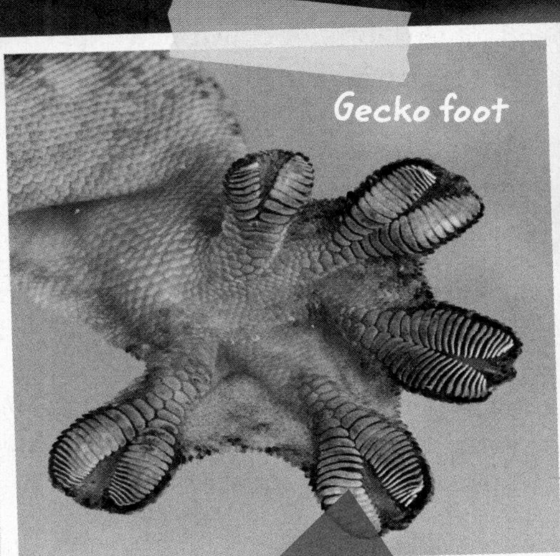

11 Relate Fill in the flow chart below with examples of the scientific methods used in the gecko investigation.

Defining a Problem

↓

Forming a Hypothesis

↓

Collecting Data

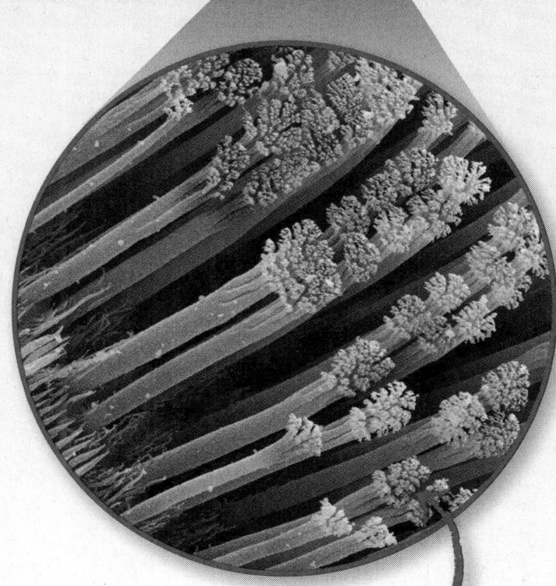

This is a close-up picture of the tiny hairs on a gecko's foot.

Under Control

What are the key components of a controlled investigation?

Components of experiments include independent and dependent variables, constants—also called controlled variables—and controls. A **control** is part of an experiment that is identical to the experimental group except that the independent variable is not manipulated. Scientists compare the results of the investigation with the control. The control should not show any changes in dependent variables. A controlled experiment should have just one independent variable. Other variables remain unchanged.

Visualize It!

12 Infer A class is using this setup to test the hypothesis that lowering the starting position of the car on the ramp results in decreased speed of the toy car. Students time how long it takes for the car to reach a certain point beyond the ramp after it is released. In the space below, make a sketch that shows how you would manipulate, or change, the independent variable to test the hypothesis.

List at least three constants in this experiment. ______________________________

____

Why should investigations be carried out more than once?

Active Reading **13 Identify** As you read, underline two different ways to carry out an investigation more than once.

Scientists verify their results through repetition of their experiments. Repeated trials, or repetition, allow investigators to obtain more accurate and reliable results. Repetition helps identify whether or not results occurred because of chance or error. An experiment that gives the same results when repeated supports the accuracy of the original findings.

Replication occurs when other scientists repeat a particular experiment. When a scientist carries out another scientist's experiment, the results should be the same as they were in the original experiment. Replication of the findings by other scientists provides support for the original results and conclusions of the study. Investigation findings that cannot be replicated are not accepted by the scientific community.

	Trial 1	Trial 2	Trial 3	Mean
Starting position	Speed (cm/s)	Speed (cm/s)	Speed (cm/s)	Speed (cm/s)
1	0.98	0.99	0.97	0.98
2	0.61	0.62	0.61	0.613
3	0. 40	0.41	0.44	0.417

14 Analyze Look at the data in the table collected from the toy car experiment. What conclusion can you draw from the data? Are your conclusions supported by the data? Explain why.

High Quality

What are some characteristics of good scientific investigations?

Scientists may use different ways to test the same hypothesis. But good scientific investigations share some important characteristics. Scientific observations should be well-documented and have supporting evidence. In an experiment, the variables should be controlled as much as possible. However, not all experiments require controls.

Experiments should be repeated multiple times by the original investigator. Scientific investigations should also be able to be replicated by scientists not involved with the original work. If the investigation is valid, the same results will be found.

Before publication, the experiment undergoes peer review by scientists not involved in the original investigation. Scientists must provide answers to the questions raised by their peers.

Scientists take great care with their experiments. Sometimes, however, scientists may not plan properly or collect data properly. These are honest mistakes. Processes of peer review and replication help to ensure that mistakes are identified and corrected. On rare occasions, irresponsible scientists produce false results on purpose. This type of behavior often ends a person's career in the sciences.

According to legend, Galileo dropped two balls from the Leaning Tower of Pisa to demonstrate that objects of different masses fall at the same rate.

Visualize It!

15 Infer When scientists replicate experiments, they will often do so under different conditions than the original investigations. Why might this be helpful? Why do you think the astronaut replicated Galileo's investigation on the moon?

____

____

____

____

____

____

____

How can you evaluate the quality of scientific information?

Scientific information is available on the Internet, on television, and in magazines. Some sources are more trustworthy than others. The most reliable scientific information is published in scientific journals. However, these articles are often difficult to understand. Sometimes, summaries of these articles are written in a way that is easier for non-scientists to understand.

Many scientists and non-scientists write books for the general public. These publications are trustworthy if the person is knowledgeable about the field of study. Usually, the most reliable Internet sources are government or academic webpages. Commercial webpages are often unreliable because they are usually trying to sell something. Commercial webpages are often biased. Bias is a slant that changes how information is presented.

16 Apply Find two sources of information about the same scientific investigation. Then fill out the chart below to explain why you think each source is trustworthy or untrustworthy.

What is this investigation about? ______________________

Source	Trustworthy? Why or why not?

Over 300 years later, scientists were still replicating Galileo's investigation. In 1971, astronaut David Scott traveled to the moon, which has no air. When he dropped a hammer and a feather, they hit the ground at the same time.

Think Outside the Book

17 Design Suppose that you are conducting a field experiment with plants. You are testing the hypothesis that plants grow faster when mulch covers the soil. Plan how you would conduct the experiment. Then plan how you would repeat it.

Visual Summary

Scientific Investigations

To complete this summary, fill in the blanks with the correct word or phrase. Then use the key below to check your answers. You can use this page to review the main concepts of the lesson.

Scientific investigations include experiments, observations, fieldwork, and models.

18 Scientific experiments test relationships between ______________ and ______________ variables.

19 A scientific hypothesis must be ______________

Scientific methods include making and testing hypotheses, collecting data, analyzing data, and drawing conclusions.

20 A(n) ______________ is either supported or unsupported by the results of an investigation.

21 The results of an investigation are the ______________

Reliable scientific information comes from investigations with reproducible results.

22 An investigation that has been done by more than one scientist with similar findings has been ______________

23 The most reliable scientific information is published in ______________

Answers: 18 independent, dependent; 19 testable 20 hypothesis; 21 data; 22 replicated; 23 scientific journals

24 **Apply** Choose an organism that you can observe in its environment. Write a hypothesis that you could test about this organism.

Lesson Review

Vocabulary

Fill in the blank with the term that best completes the following sentences.

1 A scientific ______________________________ is a proposed explanation that can be tested.

2 A(n) ______________________________ is the factor that is deliberately changed in an experiment.

3 The information gathered in an investigation is called ______________________________

4 A(n) ______________________________ should have only one independent variable.

5 ______________________________ can be made in the field or in the laboratory.

Key Concepts

6 Infer What kinds of scientific investigations do not involve experiments?

____

____

7 Explain What is the purpose of a control?

____

____

8 Connect How are independent and dependent variables related?

____

____

____

____

9 Compare How are repetition and replication alike and different?

____

____

____

____

____

____

Critical Thinking

Use the table below to answer the following questions.

Plant	Amount of Water Given	Amount of Fertilizer Given	Height
1	10 mL	none	6 cm
2	20 mL	5 g	8 cm
3	30 mL	10 g	7 cm
4	40 mL	15 g	12 cm

10 Evaluate The table above shows the data collected during an experiment about plant height. Based on the information given, is this a controlled experiment? Why or why not?

____

____

____

____

____

____

11 Describe How would you experiment to find out how much water this plant type needs for optimal growth?

____

____

____

____

12 Recommend Write a checklist that has at least three points to help you evaluate whether scientific information is reliable.

____

____

____

____

____

My Notes

Think Science

OHIO **6.SIA.4** Analyze and interpret data.

OHIO **6.SIA.6** Think critically and logically to connect evidence and explanations.

Supporting Hypotheses

Scientists repeat investigations whenever possible to test the validity of hypotheses. A hypothesis is more strongly supported when more than one investigation gives similar results. But sometimes investigations with similar hypotheses give different results. When this happens, it is important that scientists ask questions to help them judge whether the differences in the results are insignificant or meaningful.

Tutorial

Two groups of students worked together to test a hypothesis. Each group collected four samples of seawater and four samples of drinking water to test. Their hypothesis and the measurements that the students made are shown below. The two groups shared their data and asked the following questions as they evaluated their results.

Conductivity Report

Background: Seawater contains dissolved salts in the form of positive and negative ions. These ions may allow seawater to conduct electric current. Conductivity is a measure of how well a material conducts an electric current.

Hypothesis: The conductivity of seawater is higher than the conductivity of drinking water.

Average Conductivity in Siemens per Meter

	Group 1 Values (S/m)	Group 2 Values (S/m)
Seawater	3.97	4.82
Drinking water	0.005	0.0045

Are the results of the two investigations similar or different? The average conductivity of seawater measured by each group was different.

Do the different results still support the original hypothesis? Even though the groups had different results for seawater conductivity, both groups' results supported the hypothesis that the conductivity of seawater is higher than that of drinking water.

What additional investigations would help to explain the groups' results? The students designed a second investigation in which they would bring all of their samples to the same temperature and then repeat their measurements.

What could account for differences in the results? Students examined the following factors:

- type of equipment
- conditions
- procedure
- materials used

One student did more research and learned that temperature affects conductivity. The students realized that the two groups had made conductivity measurements of seawater samples at different temperatures.

You Try It!

A class was divided into two groups and instructed to investigate the conductivity of rock salt (NaCl) and of quartz (SiO_2). The hypothesis and supporting data collected by the groups are shown below.

Hypothesis: The conductivity of a solid substance increases when the substance is placed in water.

Results of Conductivity Tests

	Group A			Group B		
	NaCl	SiO_2	H_2O	NaCl	SiO_2	H_2O
Conductivity (solid)	No	No	—	No	No	—
Conductivity (in water)	Yes	Yes	No	Yes	No	No

1 Evaluating Data Compare the results of the two groups.

2 Judging Results Based on the results, what would each group conclude about whether their original hypothesis is supported? Explain your reasoning.

3 Evaluating Methods When the students examined their procedures, they found that Group A used a single beaker for both solids, and Group B used a different beaker of water for each solid and for the H_2O. How might this difference in methods explain the difference in their results?

Take It Home

With an adult, find a book or article about experiments in cold fusion. Were the results reproduced? Did they support the original hypothesis? Write a paragraph about your findings.

Scientific Tools and Measurement

ESSENTIAL QUESTION

How do scientists use tools and make measurements?

By the end of this lesson, you should be able to explain how tools and measurements are used in scientific investigations.

This researcher is using sensitive audio equipment to record bird calls in Papua, New Guinea.

OHIO 6.SIA.3 Use appropriate mathematics, tools and techniques to gather data and information.

Lesson Labs

Quick Labs
- Using Tools for Measurement
- Measuring Before and After

Exploration Lab
- Qualitative and Quantitative Observations

Engage Your Brain

1 Describe Write a word or phrase beginning with each letter of the word TOOLS that describes scientific tools.

T ____________________

O ____________________

O ____________________

L ____________________

S ____________________

2 Describe Write your own caption for this image. What tools may have been used to produce it?

____

Active Reading

3 Apply Use context clues to write your own definitions for the words *technology* and *estimate*.

Example sentence
Engineers develop technology that is used to explore space.

technology:

____

Example sentence
After counting the number of leaves on a portion of one tree branch, they estimated that there were about 1000 leaves on the entire tree.

estimate:

____

Vocabulary Terms

- **measurement**
- **quantitative**
- **qualitative**
- **scientific notation**
- **accuracy**
- **precision**

4 Identify This list contains the vocabulary terms you'll learn in this lesson. As you read, circle the definition of each term.

Observe and Report

How are observations and measurements related?

Imagine you are splashing into a swimming pool at the bottom of a water slide. What do you see and hear? Smell? Taste? Feel? When you use your senses in this way, you are observing. To make *observations* is to obtain information using the senses. In other words, observations are descriptions of the natural world. Some observations involve measurements. A **measurement** is a description that includes a number and a unit, such as 5 seconds.

Measurements Can Quantify Observations

Measurements are a type of quantitative observation. **Quantitative** relates to descriptive information that is expressed as a quantity or a number. Imagine an aquarium: the number of fish in the aquarium—say, 11 fish—is an example of a quantitative observation. Observations can be qualitative, too. **Qualitative** relates to descriptive information that is not expressed as a number. For example, the fish in the aquarium may be orange and black.

Some qualitative observations can become quantitative by measuring. You might describe a street as "really wide." A measurement of the actual width could make this observation quantitative. You could then say the street is "11.5 meters wide."

Think Outside the Book Inquiry

5 Apply Choose an event or activity and record qualitative and quantitative observations before, during, and after the event. Write a plan to record and organize this information. Have a teacher approve your plan before beginning your investigation.

6 Analyze Fill in the missing information about the organism in photo A and the event in photo B.

A Quantitative observation:

____

____

____

Qualitative observation:

____

____

____

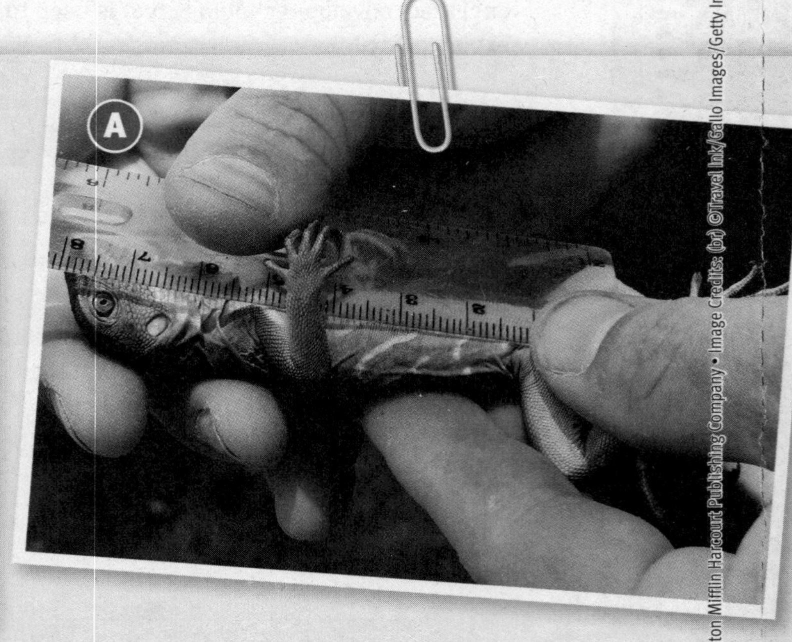

How are measurements expressed?

Scientists use numbers and units to express measurements. A unit is a standard of measurement. For example, the second is a unit of time. A day is also a unit of time. Units vary depending on which measurement system is being used. Many systems exist, but scientists most often use the International System of Units.

By Using the International System of Units

Active Reading **7 Identify** As you read, underline advantages of using the SI.

The International System of Units (SI) is a modern version of the metric system. The SI was developed as an international measurement system for better scientific and technical communication. One advantage of the SI is that it allows scientists to easily share data. It is also a complete system, or one that can measure any quantity. Another advantage is that there is only one unit for each quantity in the SI.

The SI has seven base units and many derived units (combinations of one or more base units). Look at the tables to the right. Weight is measured in newtons (N). $1 \text{ N} = 1 \text{ kg} \times (\text{m/s}^2)$. The kelvin is used for temperature and the cubic meter is used for volume. Scientists also use the degree Celsius (°C) for temperature and the liter (L) for volume. These are not SI units, but are acceptable to use with the SI.

Common SI Base Units

Quantity	Unit and Symbol
time	second (s)
temperature	kelvin (K)
mass	kilogram (kg)
length	meter (m)
amount of substance	mole (mol)
luminous intensity	candela (cd)
electric current	ampere (A)

Common SI Derived Units

Quantity	Unit and Symbol
area	square meter (m^2)
volume	cubic meter (m^3)
weight	newton (N)

B Quantitative observation:

______

______

______

Qualitative observation:

______

______

______

By Using Prefixes and Scientific Notation

With large or small measurements, word parts called prefixes are added to unit names. *Milli-* is a prefix meaning "thousandth." A milligram is one thousandth of a gram. Saying a grain of sand is 11 milligrams is easier than saying it is 0.011 grams. Look at the table to the right. *Kilo-* means 1000 times. One kilogram equals 1000 grams.

Scientific notation is also used to express large or small measurements. **Scientific notation** is a method of writing a quantity as a number multiplied by ten to a power, or $a \times 10^b$. The letter a is found by moving the decimal to get a number between 1 and 10, and b is equal to how many places the decimal was moved. If moved left, b is positive. If moved right, b is negative. For example, the speed of light is 300,000,000 m/s. To find a, move the decimal to make a number between 1 and 10. The decimal would move left 8 places to make $a = 3.0$ and $b = 8$. In scientific notation, the speed of light is 3.0×10^8 m/s.

SI Prefixes and Notation

Prefix	Scientific Notation	Standard Notation	Name
kilo-	1×10^3	1000	thousand
hecto-	1×10^2	100	hundred
deca-	1×10^1	10	ten
(none)	1×10^0	1	one
deci-	1×10^{-1}	0.1	tenth
centi-	1×10^{-2}	0.01	hundredth
milli-	1×10^{-3}	0.001	thousandth

Do the Math

The average mass of an adult male African elephant is about 4,800,000 grams (g). Write this mass in kilograms (kg). Then, write your answer using scientific notation.

Sample Problem

A. Write how many grams equal one kilogram:

$1000\ g = 1\ kg$

B. Write a fraction and multiply it by the elephant's mass:

$$\frac{1\ kg \times 4{,}800{,}000\ g}{1000\ g} = 4800\ kg$$

C. Write 4800 kg in scientific notation: $a \times 10^b$

To find a, move the decimal to make a number between 1 and 10:

$a = 4.8$

D. To find b, count how many places and which direction the decimal moved: I moved the decimal 3 places to the left, so $b = 3$. The answer is 4.8×10^3 kg

You Try It

8 Calculate An ecologist finds that some cliff swallows can migrate about 11,000,000 meters. Write this in kilometers, then write it using scientific notation.

A. Write how many meters equal one kilometer:

B. Write a fraction and multiply it by the distance:

C. Next, write this answer in scientific notation: $a \times 10^b$

First, find a by moving the decimal to make a number between 1 and 10. Write this number below:

D. To find b, count how many places and which direction you moved the decimal. Write your answer below:

What common measurements are made with scientific tools?

Scientists use many different tools to measure objects, organisms, and events. A metric ruler and a GPS (Global Positioning System) device, for example, can both measure length. Different situations call for different tools. A very exact measurement, for example, may require a high-tech tool. If a scientist is measuring something just to get a rough idea, a simple tool might be the best option.

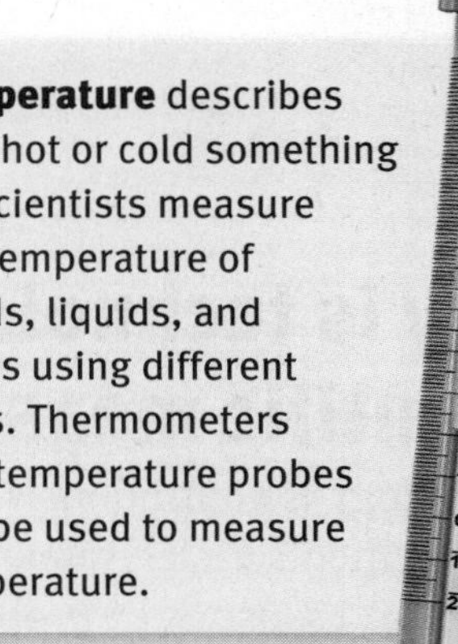

Temperature describes how hot or cold something is. Scientists measure the temperature of solids, liquids, and gases using different tools. Thermometers and temperature probes can be used to measure temperature.

Mass describes how much matter an object contains. Mass can be measured using a triple beam balance or an electronic balance.

Time describes how long something takes to occur. Time is often measured while scientists are measuring other properties, such as temperature change over time. Time can be measured with a clock or stopwatch.

Position describes the location of an object in space. A compass and map, a motion detector, and a GPS device can all be used to measure position.

Volume describes how much space something takes up. The volume of objects with definite shapes can be measured with a metric ruler. The volume of irregularly shaped objects can be measured with a graduated cylinder filled with liquid. The liquid in the cylinder is displaced when the object is set inside.

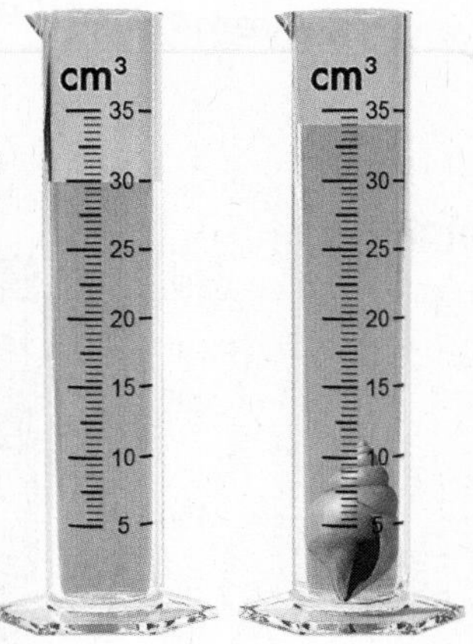

Visualize It!

9 Calculate Find the shell's volume by calculating the difference between the volumes of the liquid above.

____

Weight describes the force of gravity pulling on an object. A spring scale is a common tool used to measure weight. Mass and weight are often confused. An object's mass is the same in all places, but weight depends on gravity, which can be different depending on the location.

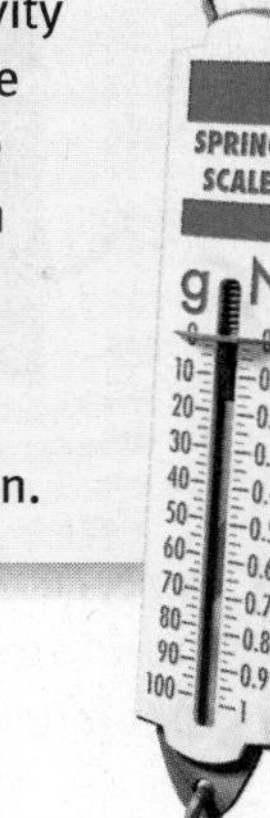

Length describes the distance between two points. A metric ruler and a GPS can be used to measure length.

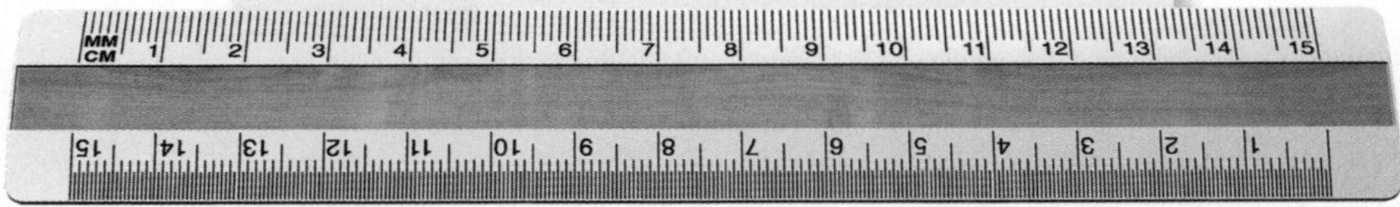

New and Improved

Why is technology important to scientific measurements?

Technology is continuously making scientific measurements easier, safer, and more accurate. Probes and sensors, or probeware, are devices that make measurements and can connect to a computer. Probeware enables scientists to monitor long-term projects; they do not have to always be present while the probeware collects and records measurements. Computers and probeware also allow scientists to collect and organize data more quickly. Computers are used to store, calculate, and analyze data; make graphs to display trends; and to create models and run simulations.

GPS devices are set up and left in selected areas to measure and record the slow movement of Earth's surface over time.

Visualize It!

Rainfall and Streamflow in Wolf Creek, March 7–11

Rainfall (cm): 0, 0.5, 1.0, 1.5, 2.0, 2.5

Streamflow (m³/s): 0, 50, 100, 150, 200, 250

Time (days): 0, 1, 2, 3, 4, 5

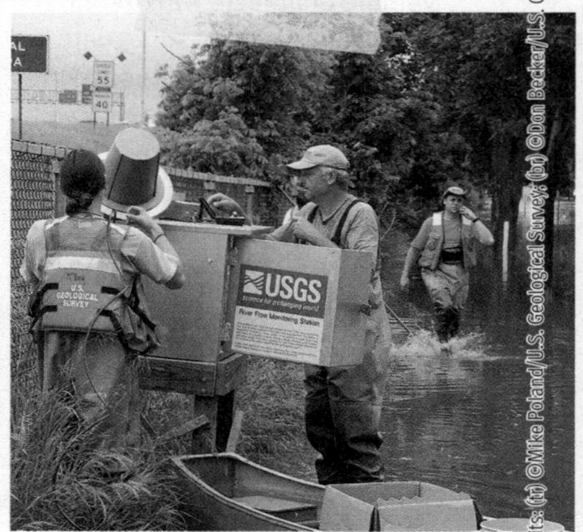

10 Analyze Study the graph. The blue bars show rainfall. The green line shows streamflow, or the volume of water moving over time. Describe streamflow before, during, and after the peak rainfall (tallest blue bar).

Before peak rainfall	During peak rainfall	After peak rainfall

Data from these GPS devices are downloaded to a computer to be stored, shared, analyzed, and to make maps.

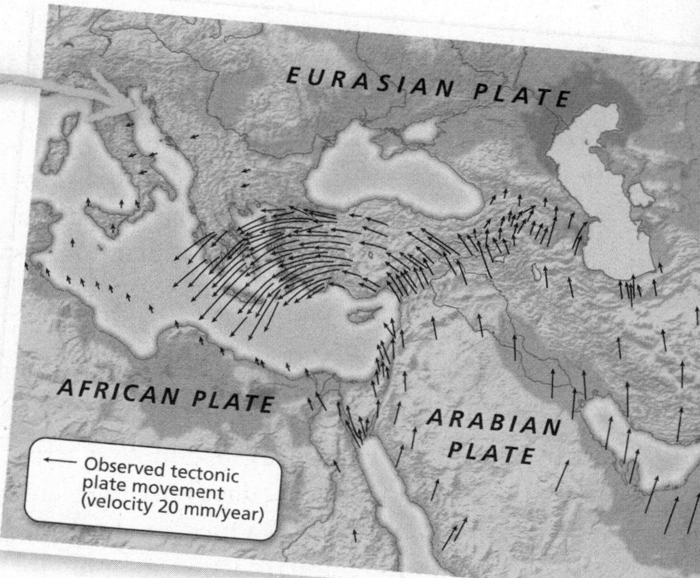

This map was made by using GPS data and a computer. The arrows show the direction and speed of moving pieces of Earth.

Technology Makes Difficult Measurements Possible

Active Reading **11 Identify** As you read, underline examples of measurements that have been made possible by technology.

Technology allows scientists to measure things that would have previously been impossible to measure. Technology has made it possible for scientists to measure the temperature of scorching hot lava and the diameter of a tiny atom. Before GPS devices, scientists could not detect the incredibly slow movement of tectonic plates, nor could they gather and analyze soil samples on distant planets and moons. Technology has enabled scientists to go where no humans have gone before.

Probeware, microscopes, robots, satellites, and other technologies have vastly expanded our knowledge of the universe. We now know that the diameter of an atom can be as small as 0.5 nanometers (5×10^{-10} meters) and there may be as many as 1 septillion, or 10^{24}, stars in the universe. GPS devices are used for various reasons, not just to study the motion of Earth's plates. They have even been attached to sea turtles to collect position and time data that help scientists understand their migration patterns.

Technology Improves Measurements and Saves Time

New scientific technologies are constantly being introduced. These developments improve tools and measurements, make devices more portable, and increase data storage space and calculating speeds. New technology for computers provides ways to display useful information with computer-generated graphs, tables, and models.

Probeware is often used to monitor long-term projects. Temperature probes, for example, are used to gather data in an area over a long period of time. They send the information to a computer. The scientist conducting the study no longer has to be on-site all the time.

12 Justify Give an example of how probeware could increase how much work a scientist can get done.

How do scientists evaluate tools and measurements?

When selecting tools, a scientist must consider how close a measurement needs to be to the true value. An exact measurement or just a rough number may be needed. The tools and methods used also affect the precision and accuracy of the measurements.

By Considering Precision and Accuracy

Computers and other types of technology have made more accurate and precise measurements possible. **Accuracy** compares a measured value of a property with the standard value accepted for that property. The smaller the difference between the measured value and the standard value, the more accurate the measurement.

Precision is the exactness and repeatability of a measurement. Do repeated measurements show very similar results? If so, the measurements are precise.

A measurement can be both accurate and precise. It can also be one or the other, or neither. Scientists strive for both accuracy and precision. The tools used to collect data affect the accuracy and precision of measurements.

With Estimates and Approximations

Active Reading **13 Identify** As you read, underline why scientists use estimates and approximations.

An *approximation* is a number value of limited accuracy. For example, each grain of sand on a beach might have a slightly different volume, but most grains are about 1 mm^3. So, 1 mm^3 is an approximation. An *estimate* is a rough value representing an actual amount. For example, to estimate how many fish are in a small lake, scientists could count fish in a few sample areas of the lake. They could then make calculations to estimate the total number of fish. Scientists may use approximations and estimates to see if data are reasonable or to determine which tool is best suited for making the measurements they need.

14 Infer A student is practicing pitching a baseball using a tire swing. The student has five baseballs and tries to throw each one through the center of the tire. Each snapshot at the right shows one trial. Write your own caption for the fourth trial. Is this trial accurate? Is it precise?

Precise and accurate

Accurate, but not precise

Precise, but not accurate

____

____

Why It Matters

Mixed-up Measurements

When scientists make a mistake in measurement, it usually doesn't cost $125 million. But that's exactly what a metric mess-up cost the National Aeronautics and Space Administration (NASA) in 1999.

Next Stop: Mars

NASA planned a space mission to Mars to study the planet's atmosphere and climate. After a journey of 286 days, the Mars Climate Orbiter finally reached its destination. The engine of the spacecraft fired to send the craft into orbit around Mars. That is when problems arose—the spacecraft came much too close to the planet. It could not maintain an orbit. The mission failed.

Small Details, Big Problems

Scientists soon figured out the problem. The team at NASA had been using **SI** units to calculate the spacecraft's orbit. The team at the private company that built the spacecraft, however, programmed the craft using English units, such as miles.

Extend

15 Infer What can you infer about the relationship between SI units and English units from this article?

16 Research Find out how NASA responded to this problem. What did NASA do to ensure that costly mistakes such as this one do not happen again?

17 Justify People in the United States still use English units such as inches and pounds for many types of measurements, while most other countries use the SI. Do you think the United States should switch exclusively to the SI? Why or why not?

Visual Summary

To complete this summary, circle the correct word or phrase. Then, use the key below to check your answers. You can use this page to review the main concepts of the lesson.

One way to make observations is by taking measurements.

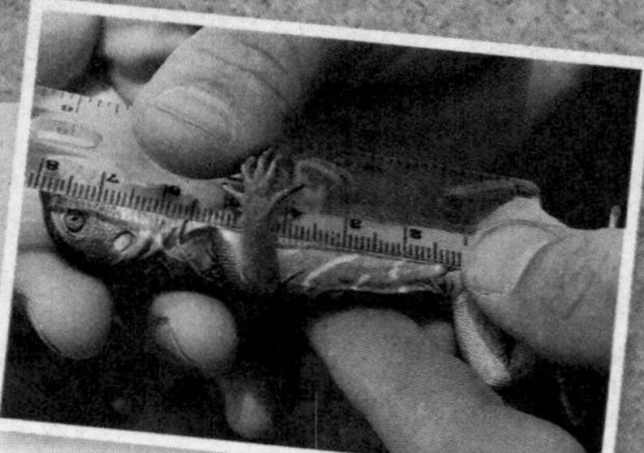

18 One example of a quantitative observation would be saying that this lizard is 8 centimeters long / bright green.

Scientists use SI units, prefixes, and scientific notation to express measurements.

19 The SI unit for measuring mass is the liter / kilogram.

Scientific Tools and Measurement

Scientists use simple tools and advanced technology to take measurements.

20 A GPS measures position / volume.

Scientists consider the accuracy and precision of their measurements.

21 A numerical value of limited accuracy is precise / approximate.

Answers: 18. 8 centimeters long; 19. kilogram; 20. position; 21. approximate

22 Evaluate Make qualitative and quantitative observations about an event. For example, observe an ice cube melting or a seed sprouting. Then categorize your measurements as estimates, approximations, precise, and/or accurate. Explain your reasoning.

Lesson Review

Vocabulary

In your own words, define the following terms.

1 measurement: ______

2 quantitative: ______

3 qualitative: ______

4 scientific notation: ______

5 accuracy: ______

Key Concepts

6 **Solve** The diameter of a human red blood cell is 0.000006 m. Write this number using scientific notation, in the form $a \times 10^b$.

In the table below, write the name of the scientific tool that is being described.

Example	Type of Tool
7 **Identify** This tool is used to measure the volume of a shell.	
8 **Identify** This tool is used to measure the mass of a small sample of soil.	
9 **Identify** This tool is used to measure the speed of a runner.	

Critical Thinking

Use this map to answer the following questions.

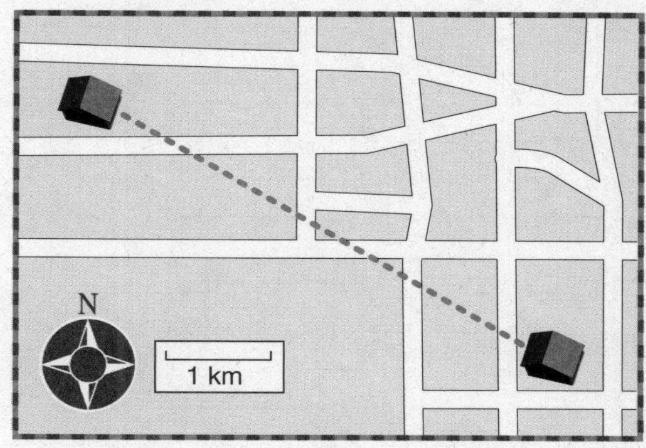

10 **Assess** What tool would you use to measure the distance between the two buildings on this map?

11 **Solve** Use the scale bar to estimate the actual distance in kilometers.

12 **Apply** Draw a new route between the buildings, using the roads. Use the scale bar to estimate the actual distance.

13 **Assess** How do you think current scientific knowledge would be different if we did not have technology?

My Notes

Representing Data

ESSENTIAL QUESTION

How do scientists learn from data?

By the end of this lesson, you should be able to use tables and graphs to organize and analyze scientific data.

This clay tablet, which dates back to 2400 BCE, displays accounting records written in cuneiform script. Cuneiform is a picture-writing system that uses symbols. Today the tablet is located in the Louvre, in Paris, France.

OHIO **6.SIA.4** Analyze and interpret data.

OHIO **6.SIA.5** Develop descriptions, models, explanations and predictions.

Lesson Labs

Quick Labs
- Heart Rate and Exercise
- Modeling Heights of Students

Field Lab
- Investigate Water Usage

Engage Your Brain

1 Evaluate Check T or F to show whether you think each statement is true or false.

T	F	
☐	☐	A graph should always have a title describing what the graph is about.
☐	☐	The factor that is manipulated in an experiment is usually plotted on the vertical axis of a graph.
☐	☐	A table can be used to organize a set of data.

2 Assemble Write a word or phrase beginning with each letter of the word *data* that is a way to represent data. You can think of data as any information collected in an investigation.

D ______________________

A ______________________

T ______________________

A ______________________

Active Reading

3 Apply Use context clues to write your own definition for the words *independent* and *dependent*.

Example sentence
After <u>independent</u> studies, the two scientists reached very different conclusions.

independent:

____

____

Example sentence
The cost of the service is <u>dependent</u> on its availability.

dependent:

____

____

Vocabulary Terms

- **independent variable**
- **dependent variable**

4 Apply As you learn the definition of each vocabulary term in this lesson, create your own definition or sketch to help you remember the meaning of the term.

Modeling Data with Graphs

How do scientists make sense of data?

There are many different kinds of scientific investigations conducted in science, all of which involve the collection of data. *Data* are the facts, figures, and other evidence scientists gather when they conduct an investigation.

Scientists Organize the Data

Scientists use data tables to organize and record the data that they collect. By creating a data table, they can record their observations and measurements in an orderly way.

Data tables often have two columns. One column lists the **independent variable**. This is the variable that is manipulated in an investigation. The other column lists the **dependent variable**. This is the variable that changes as a result of the manipulation of the independent variable. When creating a data table, any units of measurement, such as seconds or degrees, should be included in the table's column headings and not in the individual cells.

The data table below shows the high temperatures for certain days and the number of cold drinks sold at a concession stand on those days.

Drink Sales

High temperature (°F)	Number of cold drinks sold
25	43
40	55
58	60
70	72
81	70

Visualize It!

5 **Apply** Name the independent variable and the dependent variable in the data table. Explain your answer.

Scientists Graph and Analyze the Data

Scientists often analyze data for patterns by constructing graphs of the data. The type of graph they construct depends upon the data they collected and what they want to show.

A *scatter plot* is a graph with points plotted to show a possible relationship between two sets of data. A scatter plot has a horizontal *x*-axis and a vertical *y*-axis. The *x*-axis usually represents the independent variable in the data table. The *y*-axis usually represents the dependent variable.

To show the general relationship between the two variables in the graph, a line of best fit is often used. A *line of best fit* is a line that is drawn to fit, or come close to, most of the data points.

The graphs below show steps used to construct a scatter plot of the drink sales data at the left.

6 Identify Which axis of a graph usually represents the independent variable?

Visualize It!

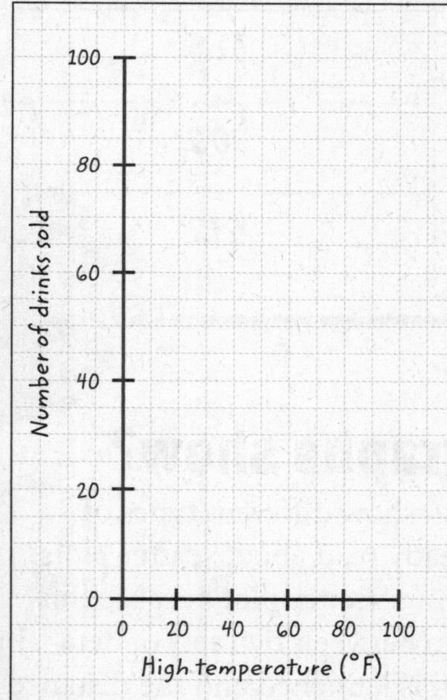

Step 1 Label the Axes Label each axis on a graph with the name of the variable that is represented. Each axis can have its own range and scale so that the data can be seen easily. The range is the difference between the greatest value and the least value of a variable. The scale is the size that is used for each box or grid mark on the graph.

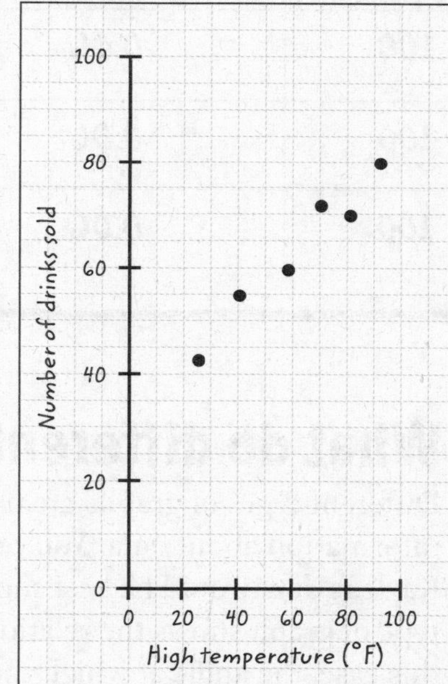

Step 2 Plot the Data Points Plot the data from the table as data points on the graph.

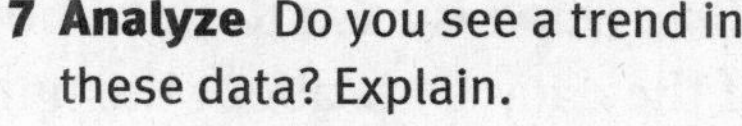

7 Analyze Do you see a trend in these data? Explain.

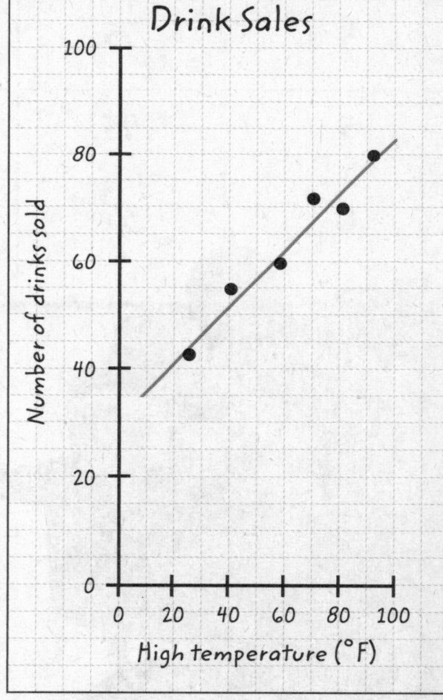

Step 3 Draw a Line of Best Fit Draw a line that comes close to most of the data points. The line shows the pattern described by the data. It also shows how the data differ from the pattern.

Experimental Data

Kaylee has set up an experiment to find out how the angle at which a ball is launched affects the horizontal distance that the ball travels. She launched a ball from several different angles. She stood in the same spot and used the same launcher each time. The table below shows her results.

8 Identify Underline the independent and the dependent variables in the table below.

Trial	Angle	Force(N)	Mass of Ball (kg)	Distance Traveled (m)
1	46	100	0.06	62.6
2	15	100	0.06	31.4
3	30	100	0.06	53.1
4	75	100	0.06	31.5
5	45	100	0.06	70.2
6	35	100	0.06	59.7

What do different graphs show?

Different types of graphs are used to show different types of information about data. You've already read about scatter plots. Kaylee's data would be best shown in a scatter plot because this type of graph shows the relationship between two sets of data—in this case, the angle at which the ball is launched and the distance traveled by the ball. Other graphs include bar graphs and circle graphs. A *bar graph* is used to display and compare data that are in separate, or distinct, categories. Data about the number of inches it rained each month can be displayed in a bar graph. A *circle graph* is used to show how each group of data relates to all of the data. Data about the number of boys and girls in your class could be displayed in a circle graph.

Active Reading **9 List** Name three different types of graphs.

____

____

____

You Try It

Use the steps below to graph and analyze Kaylee's data.

Step 1
Label each axis with the name of the variable that is represented.

Step 2
Find the range for each axis. Remember that the range is the difference between the greatest value and the least value of a variable. The range of the independent variable usually goes on the *x*-axis.

Step 3
Decide the scale for each axis. Recall that the scale is the size that is used for each box or grid mark on the graph. For the distance data, you may want to use a scale of 3 m for each grid mark.

Step 4
Graph the points by putting a dot on the graph for each pair of data in the data table.

Step 5
Title the graph. A good title tells a reader what the graph is all about.

10 Graph Use Kaylee's data to construct a scatter plot. The steps on the left will help you to construct the graph. The horizontal and vertical axes have been drawn for you.

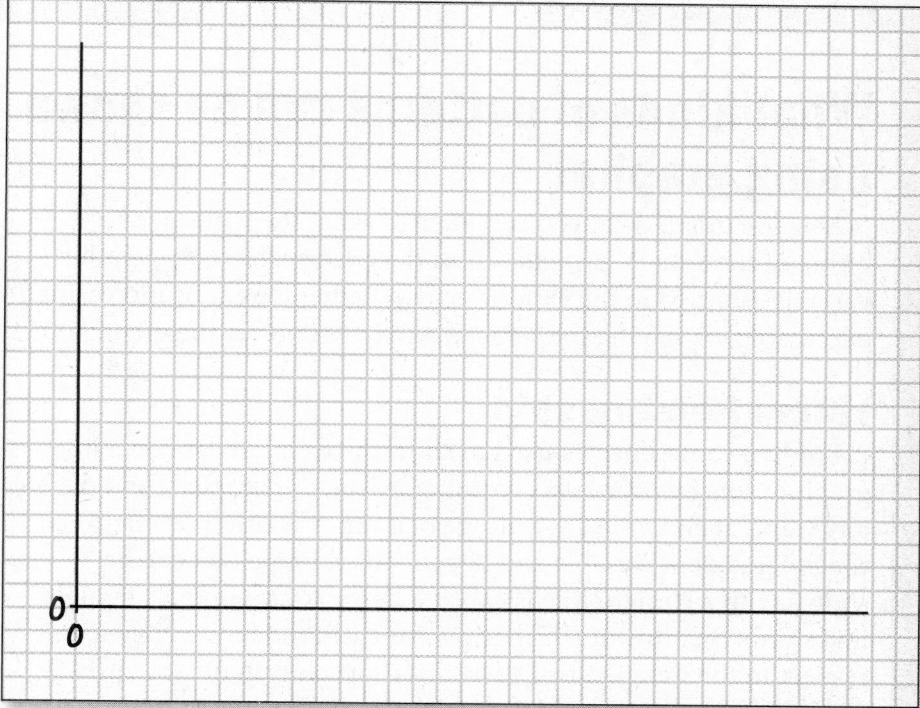

11 Analyze According to the graph, from which angle should Kaylee launch the ball to produce the maximum horizontal distance? How do you know?

The Search for Meaning

What kinds of patterns can be shown using graphs?

When you graph data, you can identify what the pattern, or trend, of the data is. A *trend* shows the relationship between the variables studied in the experiment. Whether a trend is increasing, decreasing, or staying the same, it will be visible on the graph.

Jupiter and one of its moons

Linear Relationships

A line can sometimes be used to show the trend of data on a line graph. A *line graph* shows continuous data, or data that can take on any value, such as the gas mileage of a car. A relationship between the independent variable and dependent variable that can be shown with a straight line is called a *linear relationship*. A straight line shows that the rate of change of the dependent variable with respect to the independent variable is constant. In other words, y always increases or decreases by the same value in relation to x.

This line graph shows an example of a linear relationship.

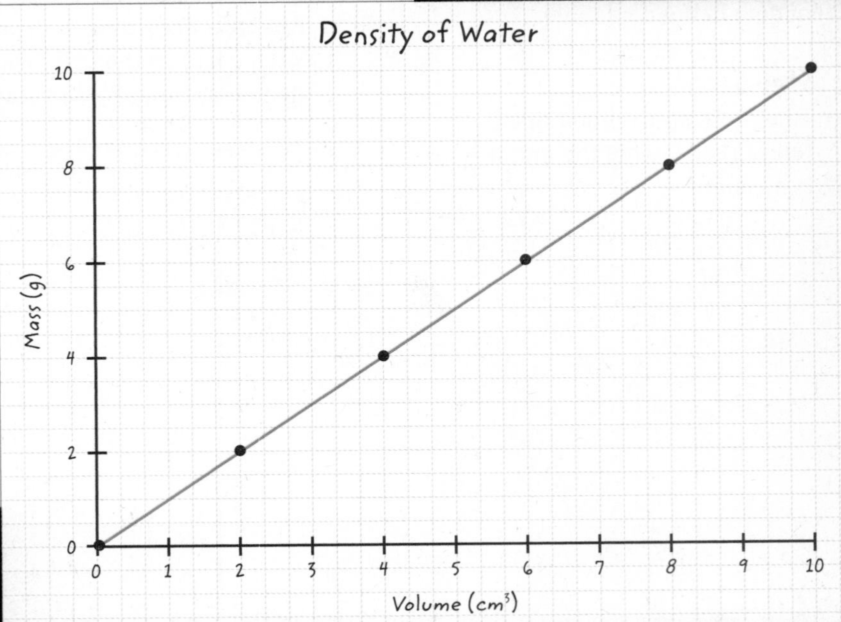

Visualize It!

12 Interpret Use the graph to determine the mass of 7 cm³ of water.

____

____

____

____

____

____

Frequency Distributions

A *line plot* shows the frequency distribution of data, or how often data fall into certain intervals or categories on a horizontal number line. The graph below is a line plot. It is based on data given in the table below about the number of moons associated with different planets. Four planets have 0 to 9 moons. So four *X*s, each one representing a planet, are plotted on the number line above the proper value. You can see from the line plot below that planets tend to have only a few moons or many moons.

A *histogram* is a type of bar graph that also shows the frequency of data within equal intervals. Histograms use bars rather than *X*s to represent data. Each bar on a histogram is an interval. A histogram looks similar to a bar graph. However, there are no spaces between the bars on a histogram.

This line plot shows that four planets have nine moons or fewer.

Number of Moons per Planet	
0–9	4
10–19	1
20–29	1
30–39	0
40–49	0
50–59	0
60–69	2

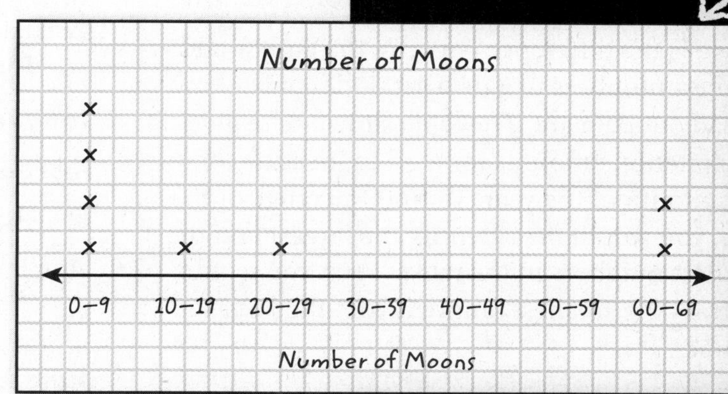

13 Infer Make a histogram based on the data in the table above.

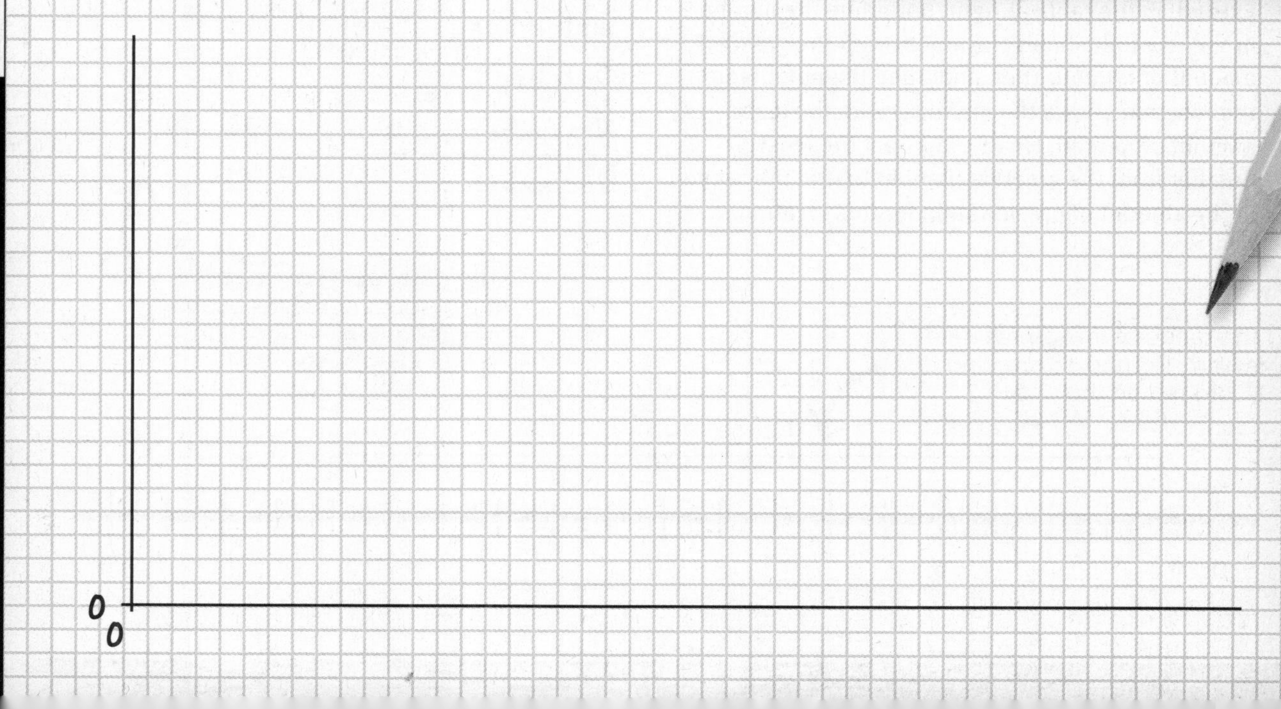

Finding the Center

How are data described?

Statistics is the branch of math that analyzes data. One term used in statistics is central tendency. *Central tendency* describes a data set using only one number. The number is often a middle value. There are several measures of central tendency, including *mean*, *median*, and *mode*. Data also are described by how dispersed, or spread out, they are. This measure is called *range*.

Range

Range is the difference between the largest and smallest numbers in a data set. It describes how spread out data are. The table shown here gives precipitation amounts for a given location for each month of the year. To find the range of the data, you would first identify the largest and the smallest numbers in the table. Then you would subtract the smallest number from the largest number.

Do the Math You Try It

14 Extend In the table at right, underline the number in the row that shows the month with the greatest amount of rainfall. Then underline the number in the row that shows the month(s) with the least amount of rainfall. Finally, subtract the least number from the greatest number to find the range in the amount of precipitation for this location.

Rainfall Data

Month	Rainfall (cm)
January	8
February	10
March	7
April	3
May	5
June	1
July	3
August	4
September	3
October	1
November	16
December	11

The data table above shows the amount of rainfall each month for a given location.

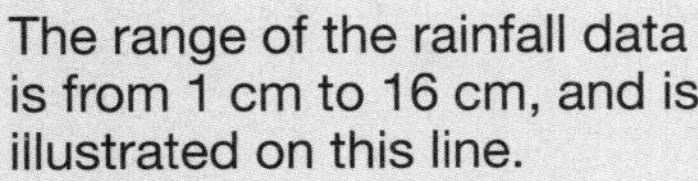

The range of the rainfall data is from 1 cm to 16 cm, and is illustrated on this line.

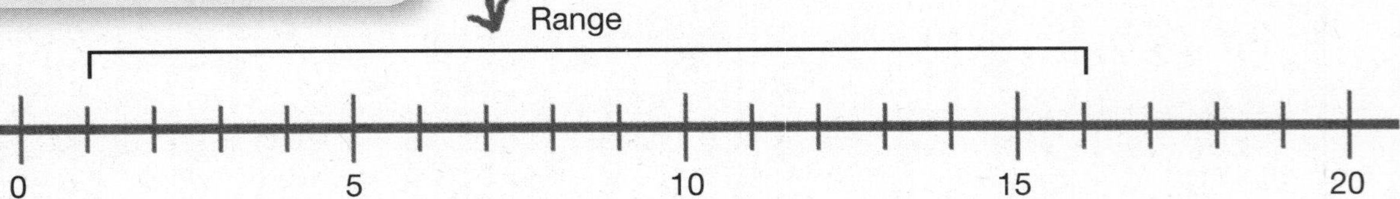

Mean

The mean, or average, is the sum of all the values in a data set divided by the number of items in the data set. So to find the mean of the ages of students in your class, you would add up all the ages and then divide that number by the number of students in your class.

The mean is also commonly known as the average. It is a way of describing a data set using only one number.

15 Extend Find the mean of the rainfall data. Add up all the precipitation amounts in the data table. Then divide that number by the number of months in the data set. Once you have found the mean, label it on the number line on the previous page.

Median

The median is the middle number in an ordered data set with an odd number of data points. An ordered data set simply means that the data are placed in numerical order. If the data set has an even number of data points, then the median is the mean of the two middle numbers.

Like mean, median is a way to describe a data set using a middle number. In a data set, half the data are above the median, and half are below the median.

Do the Math You Try It

16 Extend Find the median of the rainfall data. Arrange the data in numerical order from least to greatest. When there is an even number of data points, identify the two middle numbers, and calculate their mean. Label the median on the number line.

Mode

Mode is the number or numbers that occur most frequently in a data set. For example, suppose the ages of the students in your science lab group are 13, 14, 13, and 12. The number 13 represents the mode of the group because it occurs most often.

When all numbers in a data set occur with the same frequency, there is no mode. Conversely, a data set can have multiple modes. Suppose the ages of students in your science lab group are 14, 13, 13, and 14. The data set would have two modes: 13 and 14.

Do the Math You Try It

17 Extend To find the mode of the rainfall data, arrange identical numbers together. Determine which number occurs most often in the data set. Label the mode on the number line.

You Try It

Kaylee wanted to know how mass might affect the distance traveled by a ball. She formed a hypothesis and wrote a description of her investigation. Shown below are her hypothesis, description, and results.

HYPOTHESIS

If I use the same amount of force and launch a ball from the same angle, then a ball with a lighter mass will travel farther than a ball with a heavier mass.

DESCRIPTION

I will use five balls of different masses. I will launch the balls from the same launcher and measure the distance that they travel. I will graph my results and analyze the graph to form a conclusion about how mass affects the distance traveled by a ball.

18 Infer Why didn't Kaylee vary the angle at which the balls were launched?

Mass of Ball and Distance Traveled

Trial	Angle	Force(N)	Mass of Ball (kg)	Distance Traveled (m)
1	45	100	0.1	62.4
2	45	100	0.3	57.2
3	45	100	0.5	55.1
4	45	100	0.2	60.8
5	45	100	0.4	56.7

RESULTS

19 Calculate Use the data table to find the range of the masses of the balls and the range of the distances traveled by the balls. Use these numbers to help you draw the axes on your graph in the next step.

Mass of Ball (kg)	Distance Traveled (m)
0.1	62.4
0.3	57.2
0.5	55.1
0.2	60.8
0.4	56.7
Range:	Range:

20 Graph Look over the data in the table above. Decide which kind of graph would best display the data. Draw the graph in the space below.

CONCLUSIONS

21 Conclude What conclusions can you draw from Kaylee's data?

Visual Summary

To complete this summary, circle the correct word. Then use the key below to check your answers. You can use this page to review the main concepts of the lesson.

Representing Data

Scientists use data tables to organize and record the data they collect.

Drink Sales

High temperature (°F)	Number of cold drinks sold
25	43
40	55
58	60

22 Units of measurements are written in the cells / column headings of a data table.

Graphs are visual displays of data that show relationships.

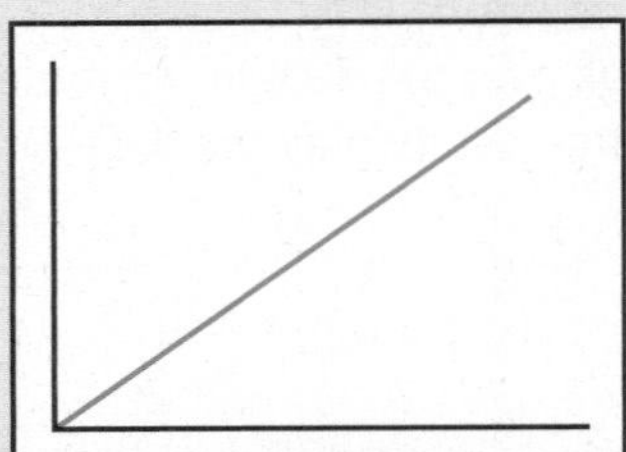

23 The dependent / independent variable is usually found on the x-axis of a graph.

Mean, median, and mode summarize data using a middle value; range shows how dispersed data are.

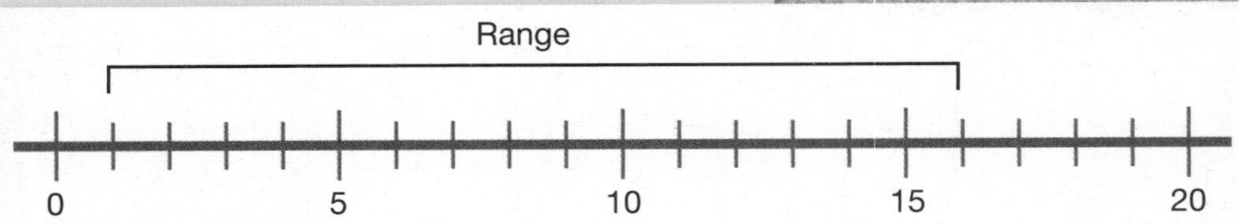

24 Range / Mode is the difference between the largest and smallest numbers in a data set.

Answers: 22 column headings; 23 independent; 24 Range

25 Provide Give examples of the kind of information scientists can obtain from different types of graphs.

Lesson Review

Vocabulary

Fill in the blank with the term that best completes the following sentences.

1 The ______________________________ variable in an investigation is the variable that is deliberately manipulated.

2 The ______________________________ variable in an investigation is the variable that changes in response to changes in the investigation.

3 The ______________________________ is the number or numbers that occur most frequently in a data set.

Key Concepts

4 Plan Alfonso is conducting an experiment to determine whether temperature affects how fast earthworms move. He is making a data table. What column headings would be appropriate?

5 Apply When creating a graph, why is an appropriate title for a graph important?

6 Compare How are mean and median alike? How are they different?

Critical Thinking

Use this graph to answer the following questions.

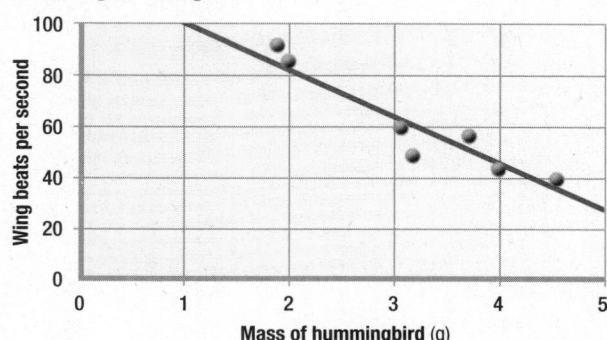

Hummingbird Wing Beats

Wing beats per second: 0, 20, 40, 60, 80, 100

Mass of hummingbird (g): 0, 1, 2, 3, 4, 5

7 Identify In this graph, what are the independent and dependent variables?

8 Describe Explain a trend or pattern you observe in the graph.

9 Apply You want to determine the frequency distribution of data on student height. What kind of graph would you use?

My Notes

S.T.E.M. **Engineering & Technology** OHIO 6.SIA.3, 6.SIA.4, 6.SIA.8

Engineering Design Process

Skills
Identify a need
Conduct research
✓ Brainstorm solutions
✓ Select a solution
Design a prototype
✓ Build a prototype
✓ Test and evaluate
✓ Redesign to improve
✓ Communicate results

Objectives
• Identify different uses of mirrors and lenses.
• Use mirrors and lenses to design and build a periscope.
• Test and evaluate the periscope you built.

Building a Periscope

A *periscope* is a device that uses mirrors and lenses to help people see around obstacles. You might be surprised to learn how many other important technologies benefit from mirrors and lenses.

Early Uses of Mirrors and Lenses

For many centuries, people have used mirrors and lenses to bend light. In ancient times, people used shiny metal to see their reflections and pieces of curved glass to start fires. In the 17th century, scientists began using lenses and mirrors to make telescopes, microscopes, and other devices that helped them make new discoveries.

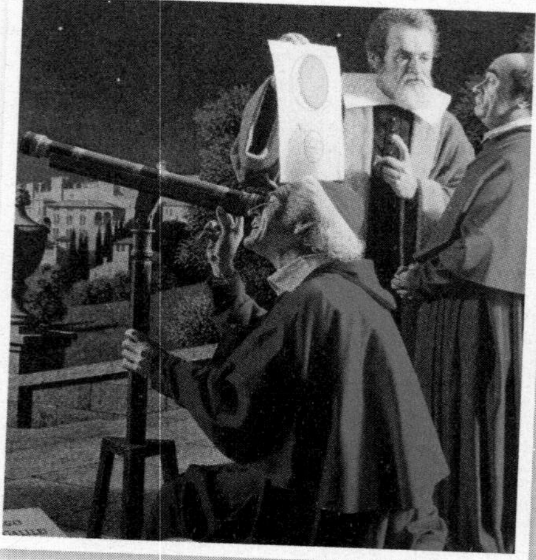

In 1610, Italian astronomer Galileo used a two-lens telescope to discover Jupiter's moons.

1 Identify List devices that use mirrors, lenses, or a combination of both. Then describe the purpose of each device, and identify whether it uses mirrors, lenses, or both.

Device	Purpose	Mirrors, Lenses, or Both
telescope	magnifies far away objects	both

Lasers

Mirrors bend light by reflecting it in a different direction. Lenses bend light by slowing it as it passes through the lens material. Many modern technologies also take advantage of mirrors and lenses. Devices such as DVD players and barcode scanners operate by using laser light. A *laser* is a device that produces a coherent beam of light of a specific wavelength, or color. Laser light is created in a chamber that has mirrors on each end. A single color of light is produced by reflecting light back and forth between the two mirrors. The distance between the mirrors determines the wavelength of light that is amplified. When the light is of the proper wavelength, it can exit the transparent center of one of the mirrors. Lenses are often found in devices that use laser light. Lenses can focus the laser light in devices such as DVD players.

2 Identify Conduct research about the uses of laser light. What are some objects that use lasers?

____

____

____

This device uses mirrors and lasers to measure the wind speed during an aircraft test. Wind speed is measured as the laser interacts with dust in the wind.

Periscopes

A periscope is another type of device that uses mirrors and lenses. The mirrors in a periscope bend light in order to allow a person to see around obstacles or above water. Most people think of periscopes in submarines, but periscopes are also used to see over walls or around corners, to see out of parade floats, and to see inside pipes or machinery.

Submarine periscopes use lenses and mirrored prisms to allow people to see above the water without surfacing.

You Try It!

Now it's your turn to use mirrors and lenses to design and build a periscope.

 You Try It!

Mirrors are used to bend light, and lenses are used to focus light. Now it's your turn to use mirrors and lenses to design and build a periscope that can see at least six inches above eye level.

You Will Need

- ✓ cardboard boxes or poster board
- ✓ cardboard or plastic tubes
- ✓ lenses
- ✓ mirrors
- ✓ scissors
- ✓ tape

1 Brainstorm Solutions

A You will build a periscope to see things at least six inches above eye level. Brainstorm some ideas about how your periscope will work. Check a box in each row below to get started.

Length of periscope:	☐ 6 inches	☐ 12 inches	☐ other ________
Shape of periscope:	☐ tube	☐ box	☐ other ________
User will look with:	☐ one eye	☐ both eyes	
Your periscope:	☐ will	☐ will not	magnify objects

B Once you have decided what your periscope needs to do, look at the materials available to you, and brainstorm how you can build your periscope. Write down the materials you will use and how you will use them.

____

____

____

2 Select a Solution

Choose one of the ideas that you brainstormed. In the space below, draw a sketch of how your prototype periscope will be constructed. Include arrows to show the path of light through your periscope.

3 Build a Prototype

Use your materials to assemble the periscope according to your design. Write down the steps you took to assemble the parts.

____

____

____

____

4 Test, Evaluate, and Redesign to Improve

Test your periscope, and fill in the first row of the table below. Make any improvements, and test your periscope again, filling in an additional row of the table for each revised prototype.

Prototype	What I saw through the periscope	Improvements to be made
1		
2		
3		

5 Communicate Results

Write a paragraph summarizing what you wanted the periscope to do, how you designed and built it, whether the finished periscope worked as planned, and how you made improvements.

____

____

____

____

____

____

____

The Engineering Design Process

ESSENTIAL QUESTION

What is the engineering design process?

By the end of this lesson, you should be able to explain how the engineering design process leads to technical solutions that meet people's needs.

Engineers designed the Millau Viaduct, located in France, to allow vehicles to safely cross a wide valley.

OHIO 6.SIA.3 Use appropriate mathematics, tools and techniques to gather data and information.

OHIO 6.SIA.5 Develop descriptions, models, explanations and predictions.

OHIO 6.SIA.8 Communicate scientific procedures and explanations.

Lesson Labs

Quick Labs
- Defining a Problem
- Simple and Complex Technology

S.T.E.M. Lab
- Design Your Own Car

Engage Your Brain

1 Predict Check T or F to show whether you think each statement is true or false.

T	F	
☐	☐	People have been using technology for only the past few hundred years.
☐	☐	Technology can be a product, a process, or a system.
☐	☐	Technological items must be made up of many engineered parts.
☐	☐	Identifying a problem or need is the first step of the design process.
☐	☐	A prototype is the final model of a product.

2 Explain Draw an item you use at school that was developed through the engineering design process. Write a caption that explains how technology helps you to learn.

Active Reading

3 Apply Use context clues to write your own definitions for the words *communicate* and *evaluate*.

Example sentence:
Engineers communicate with one another as they design a product.

communicate:

____

____

Example sentence:
Engineers test and evaluate how well a model works.

evaluate:

____

____

Vocabulary Terms

- **technology**
- **engineering**
- **prototype**

4 Identify As you read, create a reference card for each vocabulary term. On one side of the card, write the term and its meaning. On the other side, draw an image that illustrates or makes a connection to the term. These cards can be used as bookmarks in the text so that you can refer to them while studying.

We Have the TECHNOLOGY

What is technology?

Since the dawn of human history, people have invented tools to help them work. Ancient hunters developed processes to transform pieces of flint or obsidian into arrow points and blades. Thousands of years later, people manufactured sharper spears from copper and iron. Today, ceramic kitchen knives can cut tomato slices that are as thin as a piece of paper.

Each of these tools was designed to meet a human need. **Technology** is the use of tools, machines, materials, and processes to meet human needs. Technology includes simple everyday products, such as toothbrushes, and complex mechanisms with many parts, such as communication satellites. Technology also refers to processes that meet people's needs. The processing of wheat to make flour is an example of a technological process.

Technology changes and grows over time. The basic function of houses, drinking vessels, and roads remains the same. But the designs and materials used to make these tools become increasingly more efficient or useful.

5 Compare Write a sentence about each of these mathematical tools that uses the word *technology*.

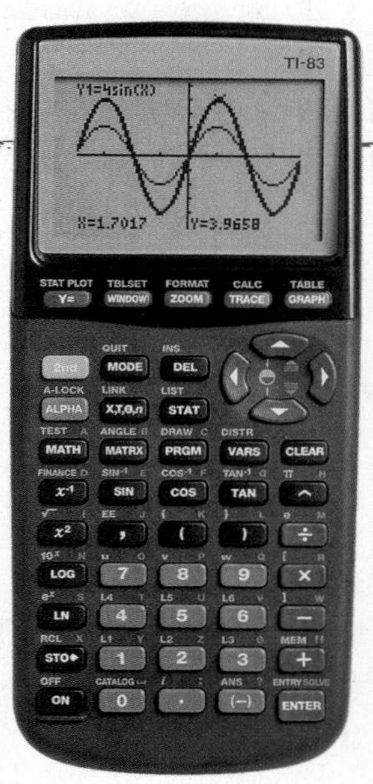

A ______________________________

____

____

____

____

B ______________________________

____

____

____

____

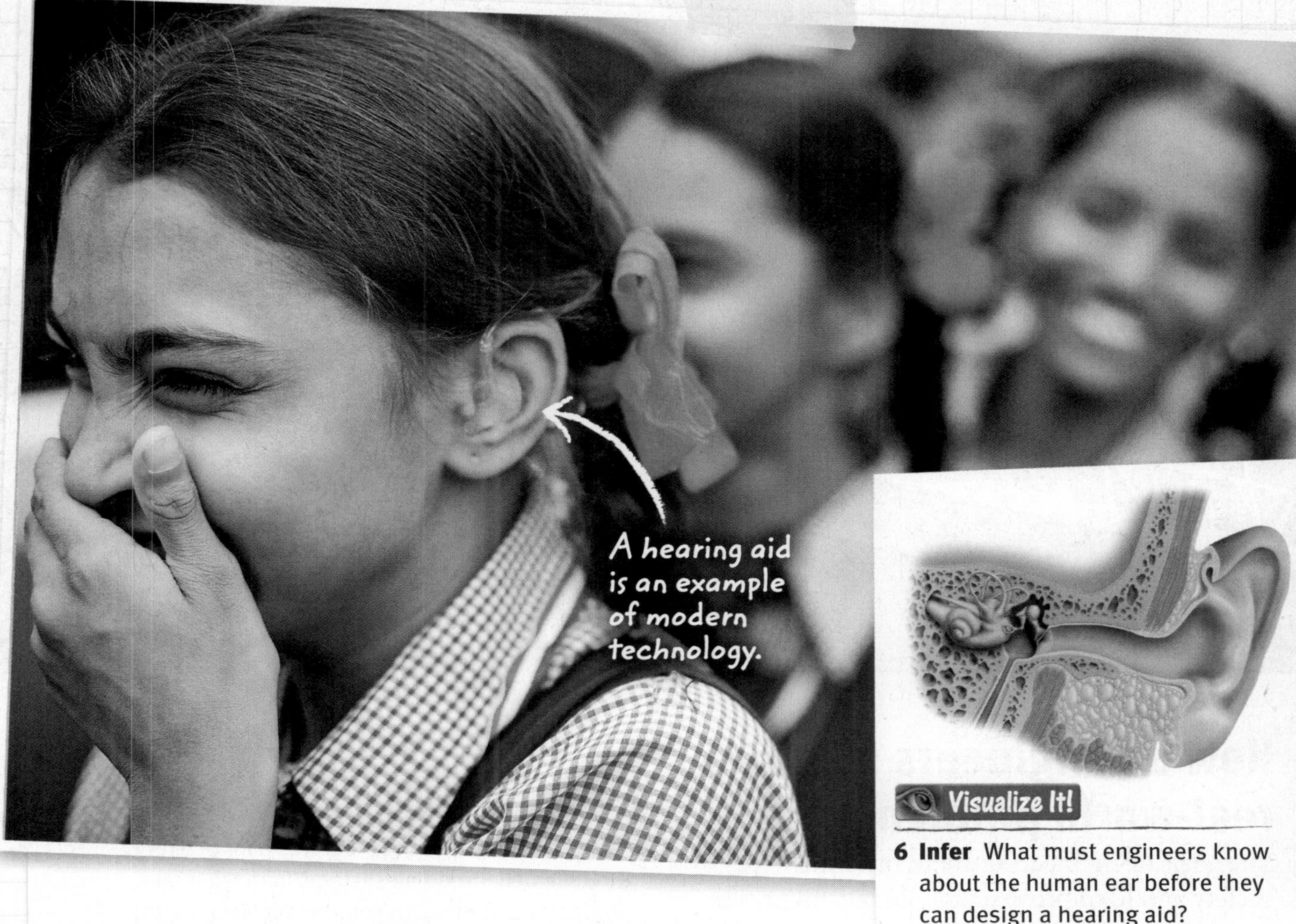

A hearing aid is an example of modern technology.

Visualize It!

6 Infer What must engineers know about the human ear before they can design a hearing aid?

How does technology relate to science?

The words *science* and *technology* are related, but they do not mean the same thing. Science is the study of the natural world. A scientist observes objects and events in the natural world and analyzes data to explain their structure or function. Technology, on the other hand, is the use of designed materials and processes to improve people's lives. Much of the technology we use today is the result of engineering. **Engineering** is the application of science and mathematics to solve real-life problems.

Scientific advances can improve technology, and technological advances can improve scientific research. For example, scientific knowledge about electromagnetic waves is an essential building block in the development of modern communication systems. Scientific knowledge continues to grow as engineers develop new technology to improve observations and analysis. Weather instruments can gather data remotely in the upper atmosphere. Computers can analyze the resulting data, improving the ability to predict weather.

Active Reading

7 Apply Give an example of how technology can be used to gather scientific data.

Going Up?

The windows in the Empire State building are being replaced with modern windows that are more energy efficient.

How do engineers solve real-world problems?

The goals of engineering are to meet the needs of society and to improve quality of life. Engineers provide solutions for civil and economic needs. For example, police and emergency services must be coordinated and efficient to address city emergencies. Radio towers made of inexpensive, durable materials satisfy an economic need and are a means of communication.

By Thinking Creatively and Methodically

Engineers employ creative thinking to solve problems. Creativity leads to new ways of doing things that are more efficient or enjoyable. However, there are still *constraints,* or limitations, that an engineer must consider. For example, imagine that an engineer wants to design a grabbing tool for a person with a physical condition that limits reach. In order to be useful, such a tool must be lightweight, easy to use, and affordable for the person who is to use it. Together, creative and methodical thinking can lead the engineer to develop an appropriate solution.

8 Design A large building requires a lot of energy to run air conditioning systems in the summer. Brainstorm alternative solutions to keeping the building cool while limiting energy costs. Sketch one idea in the space below, and label your drawing.

Making a building as large as the Empire State Building more efficient is a huge engineering challenge.

By Using Science Skills, Math Skills, and Technology

Active Reading **9 Identify** As you read, underline examples of skills that engineers use.

Engineering involves the application of science skills, math skills, and technical skills. Science skills include the ability to conduct valid investigations and thorough research. Engineers follow the scientific method as they test and improve their designs. They research how similar problems have been addressed in the past and explore potential drawbacks to proposed solutions. Math skills allow engineers to draw blueprints in correct scale, calculate safe loads for bridges, or make the parts of a pacemaker work together to improve heart function. Proper scale and sizing of parts is critical to creating a usable product or process. Technical skills include the ability to use computers and other types of technology to collect and analyze data.

10 Plan Imagine that you are part of a team of engineers working to make the Empire State Building more energy efficient. In the first column of the table below, write three questions you need to answer before beginning the project. In the second column, circle *Research* for each question that can be researched. Circle *Investigation* for each question that is testable through investigation.

Question	How to address	
	Research	Investigation
	Research	Investigation
	Research	Investigation

STEP by STEP

What are the steps of the engineering design process?

In some ways, the engineering design process is similar to the scientific method. Because the goals of engineering design are different from those of scientific research, there is some variation in the research approach. However, an engineer, like a scientist, must perform controlled experiments and determine that solutions are reproducible.

Active Reading

11 Identify As you read this page and the next, underline examples of each step in the engineering design process.

1. Identifying a Need

The first step in the engineering design process is identifying a practical need. For example, in some remote locations, cell phone service is not available. There is a need for an economical way to provide communication in these places. As part of defining the need, engineers consider constraints and limitations to the problem. Some solutions may be too expensive to work.

2. Conducting Research

Engineering research includes learning more details about a problem and about previous attempts to address it. To design a phone that works in remote locations, engineers might need to research environmental conditions and existing telephone technology. New ways to send a signal might be possible based on recent scientific research.

3. Brainstorming and Selecting Solutions

Brainstorming is a creative process in which many potential solutions are considered. Often, teams work together to generate and evaluate a number of ideas. Solutions for providing cell phone service could include a different type of tower, increased signal strength, different wavelengths, or satellite relays. The many options generated through brainstorming are then narrowed, leaving only the solutions that show the most promise for success.

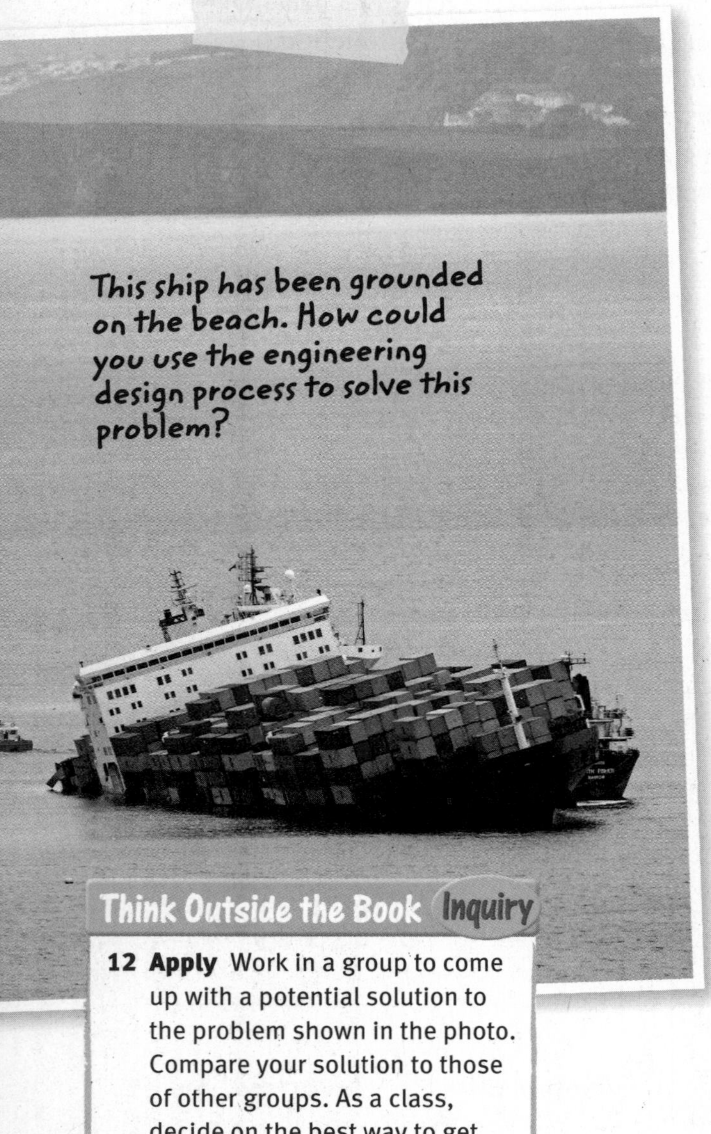

This ship has been grounded on the beach. How could you use the engineering design process to solve this problem?

Think Outside the Book **Inquiry**

12 Apply Work in a group to come up with a potential solution to the problem shown in the photo. Compare your solution to those of other groups. As a class, decide on the best way to get the ship back into the water.

4. Building a Prototype

After the best potential solution is chosen, the next step is building a prototype. A **prototype** is a test model of the product. Prototypes allow engineers to see if their design works the way they expected. Sometimes, several prototypes are built to compare the benefits and drawbacks of each. If the team chose to use satellite relays for phone signals, for example, several prototypes could be used to determine what frequencies establish the most stable link to the satellite.

5. Testing, Evaluating, and Redesigning a Prototype

The next step involves testing, evaluating, and redesigning the prototype. Engineers troubleshoot during this step. What works? What doesn't? They also test and evaluate for efficiency and the overall ability of the prototype to address the problem. If a prototype phone tends to lose contact with the satellite, they determine what interferes with the link. After testing, engineers observe what worked and what requires improvement. The prototype is redesigned. It is tested and evaluated again. Sometimes, the prototype must be abandoned. If so, engineers use what they learned from the first prototype as they begin the design process again.

6. Communicating Results

Like scientists, engineers must communicate with each other before, during, and after the design process. They may publish details of the design process in academic journals so that their peers can build on their work. This allows other researchers to suggest alternative explanations for questions or solutions to problems. They must also be able to communicate with the public. For example, they may explain and promote the communication technology to potential customers and manufacturers. Or they may communicate with the public through news releases or advertisements.

Visualize It!

13 Identify Place a number in each box to identify which step of the engineering design process is shown.

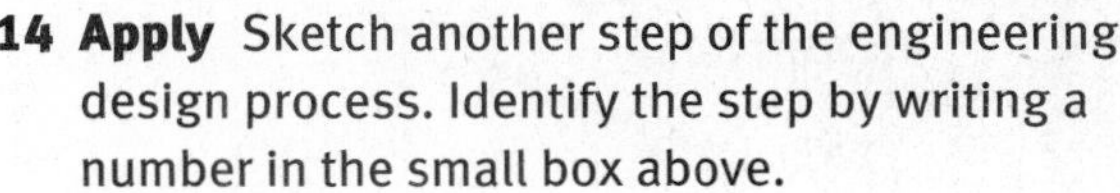

14 Apply Sketch another step of the engineering design process. Identify the step by writing a number in the small box above.

How does the engineering design process work?

Engineers follow different paths through the design process, depending on the need being addressed and the results of research and development. Sometimes, they backtrack because of unexpected constraints or even unexpected benefits. Whether engineers are designing a new automobile or a garden where travelers can take a break, the first step in the process is always the same: identify a need.

The diagram below illustrates the steps of the engineering design process. It shows different paths to follow based on the answers to the questions in the diagram. Notice the diamond-shaped decision points. These indicate a step where the engineer evaluates how well the product solves the problem. Depending on the answer to the question, the process moves to the next step or returns to an earlier step.

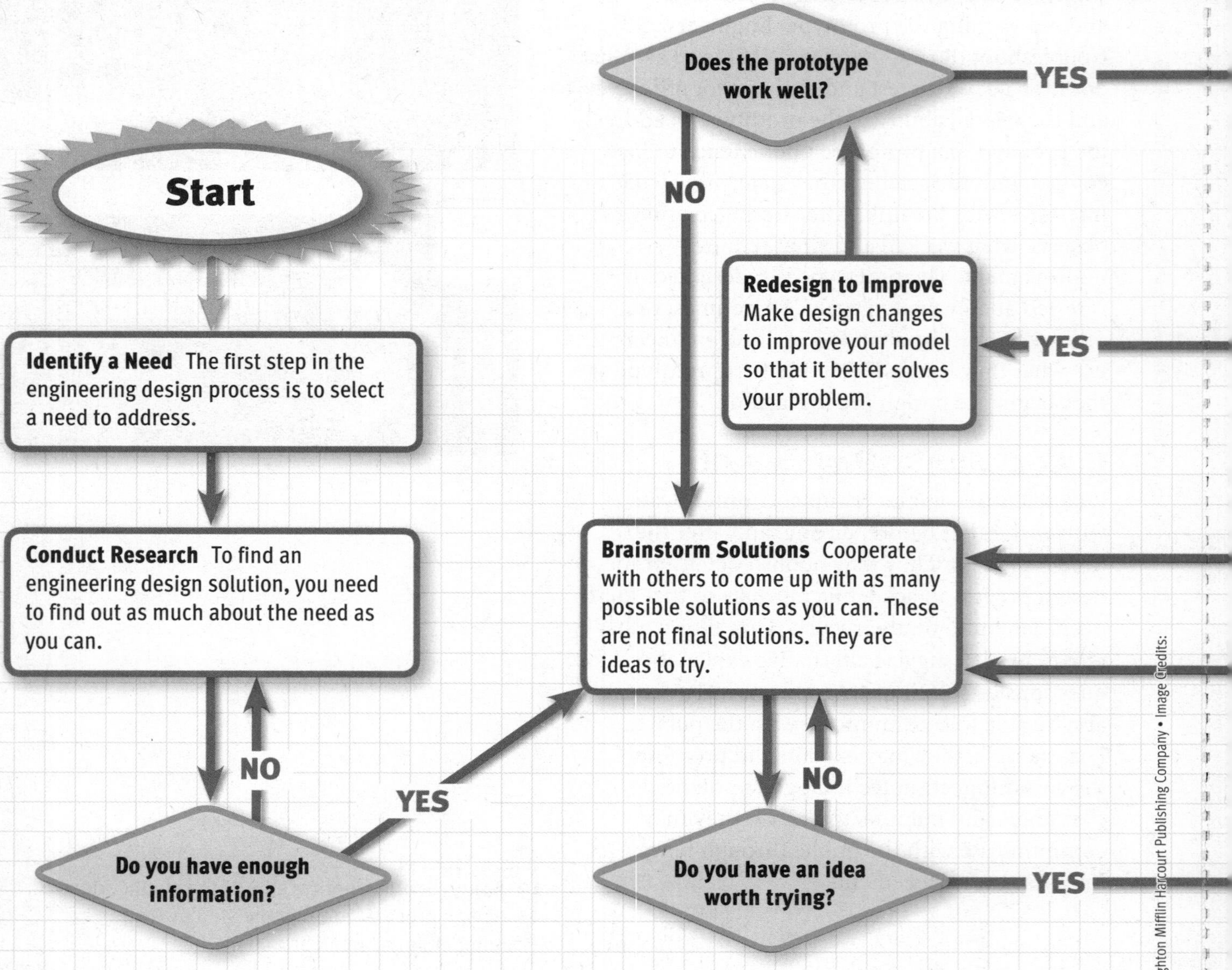

Start

Identify a Need The first step in the engineering design process is to select a need to address.

Conduct Research To find an engineering design solution, you need to find out as much about the need as you can.

Do you have enough information? — NO / YES

Brainstorm Solutions Cooperate with others to come up with as many possible solutions as you can. These are not final solutions. They are ideas to try.

Do you have an idea worth trying? — NO / YES

Redesign to Improve Make design changes to improve your model so that it better solves your problem.

YES

Does the prototype work well? — NO / YES

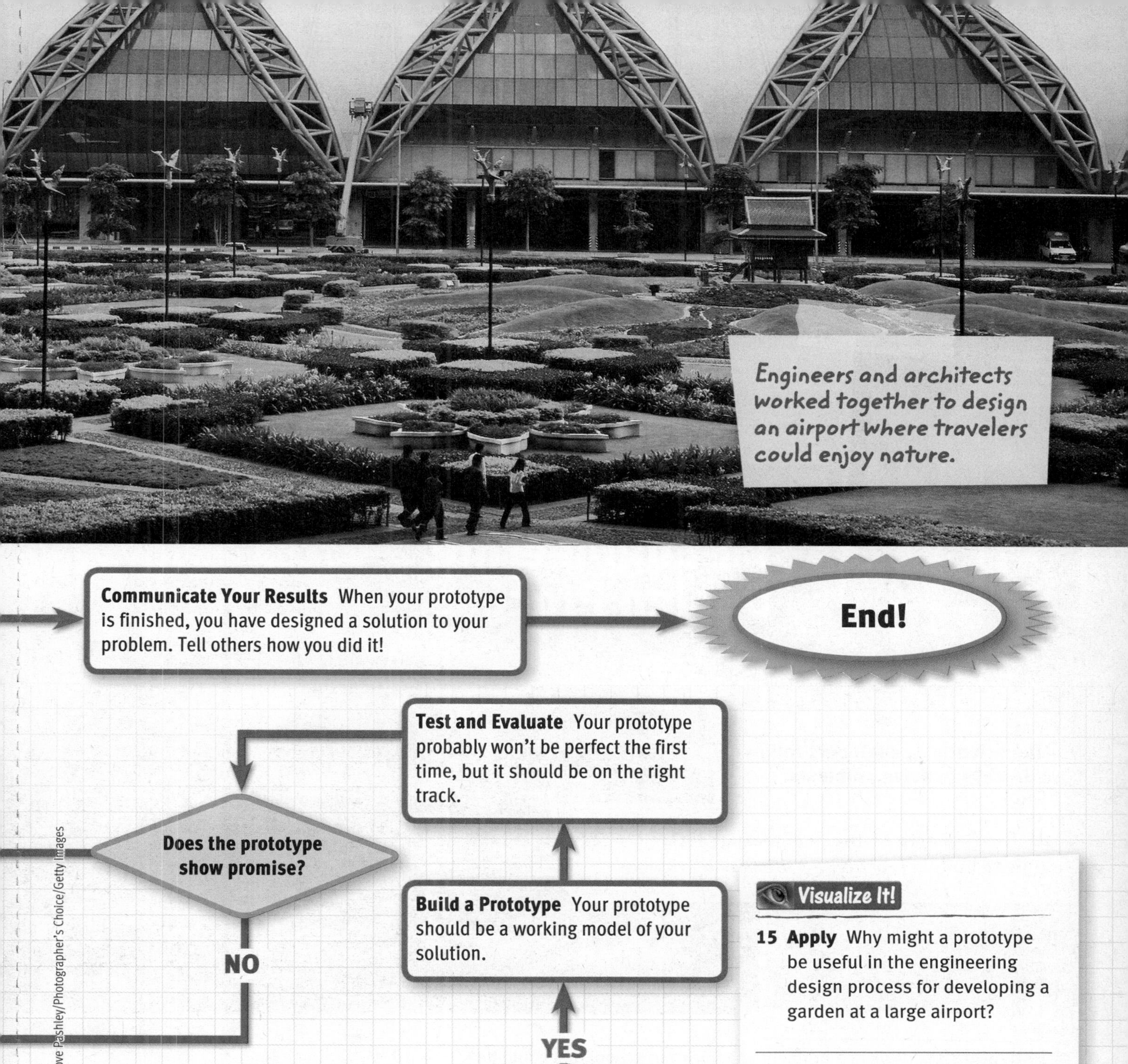

Engineers and architects worked together to design an airport where travelers could enjoy nature.

Communicate Your Results When your prototype is finished, you have designed a solution to your problem. Tell others how you did it!

End!

Test and Evaluate Your prototype probably won't be perfect the first time, but it should be on the right track.

Does the prototype show promise?

NO

Build a Prototype Your prototype should be a working model of your solution.

YES

NO

Can you make a prototype?

Select a Solution Which of your ideas do you want to try? Pick one, and plan how you want to try it.

Visualize It!

15 Apply Why might a prototype be useful in the engineering design process for developing a garden at a large airport?

Visual Summary

To complete this summary, circle the correct word. Then, use the key below to check your answers. You can use this page to review the main concepts of the lesson.

Technology is advanced by science, and science is advanced by technology.

16 A hearing aid is an example of technology / brainstorming.

Engineers use different types of thinking and skills to solve problems.

17 Researching is a math / science skill used by engineers.

Like scientists, engineers follow a process to solve problems.

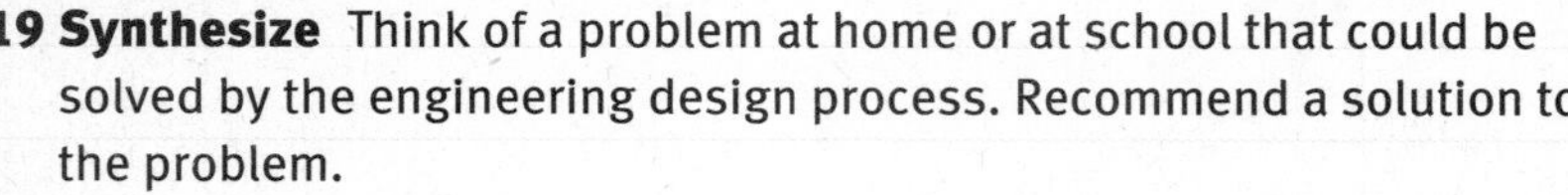

18 The first step of the engineering design process is to build a prototype / identify a problem.

Answers: 16. technology; 17. science; 18. identify a problem

19 Synthesize Think of a problem at home or at school that could be solved by the engineering design process. Recommend a solution to the problem.

Lesson Review

Vocabulary

Fill in the blanks with the terms that best complete the following sentences.

1 A ________________________ is a test model of a product.

2 ________________________ is the application of science and mathematics to solve real-life problems.

3 ________________________ is the use of tools, machines, materials, and processes to meet human needs.

Key Concepts

4 Compare How are simple technology and complex technology similar? How are they different?

5 Apply Give an example of how engineers use math skills in their work. Why are math skills important for engineering?

6 Identify Give an example of a technology that benefitted from scientific discoveries.

Critical Thinking

Use this graph to answer the following questions.

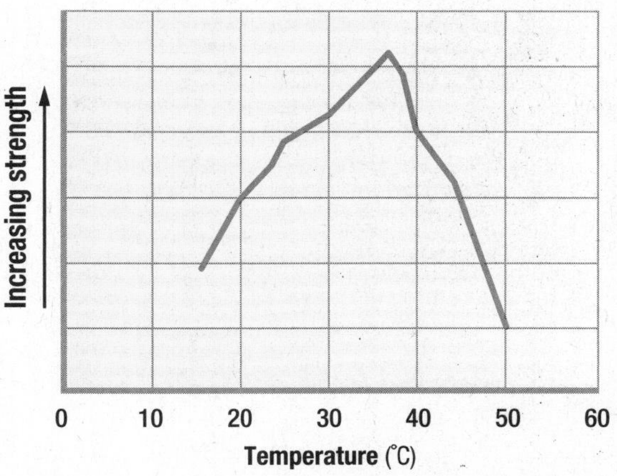

7 Analyze The graph shows data collected by a digital probe. What trend do you see in the graph?

8 Infer How would an engineer use the information on the graph to determine whether this plastic is suitable for a particular application?

9 Explain Why might it be necessary to repeat a step in the engineering design process more than once?

My Notes

Unit 1 Big Idea

Scientists and engineers use careful observations and clear reasoning to understand the world around us and to design technology to meet a variety of needs.

Lesson 1
ESSENTIAL QUESTION
What are the characteristics of science?

Distinguish between science and scientific explanations, and differentiate between science and pseudoscience.

Lesson 2
ESSENTIAL QUESTION
How do scientists develop explanations?

Analyze how scientists choose their methods, develop explanations, and identify support for a theory.

Lesson 3
ESSENTIAL QUESTION
How are scientific investigations conducted?

Summarize the processes and characteristics of different kinds of scientific investigations.

Lesson 4
ESSENTIAL QUESTION
How do scientists use tools and make measurements?

Explain how tools and measurements are used in scientific investigations.

Lesson 5
ESSENTIAL QUESTION
How do scientists learn from data?

Use tables and graphs to organize and analyze scientific data.

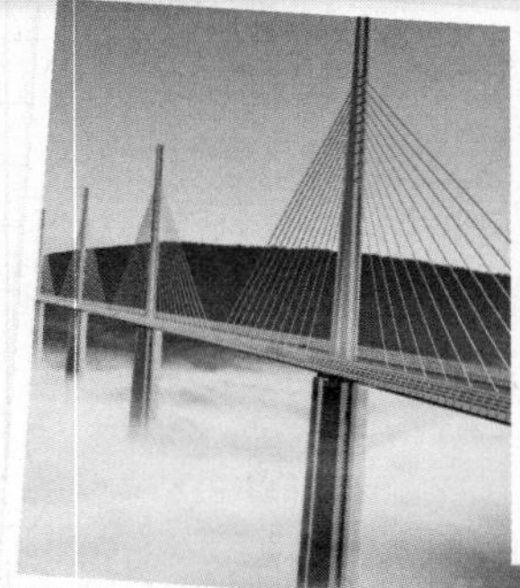

Lesson 6
ESSENTIAL QUESTION
What is the engineering design process?

Explain how the engineering design process develops technical solutions to meet people's needs.

Connect ESSENTIAL QUESTIONS
Lessons 1 and 3

1 **Evaluate** How are repetition and replication important with regard to credibility in scientific investigations?

Think Outside the Book

2 **Synthesize** Choose one of these activities to help synthesize what you have learned in this unit.

- ☐ Using what you learned in Lessons 1, 2, and 3, draw a flow chart to illustrate the process by which a hypothesis can eventually lead to a theory. In the steps, show how a theory results from many investigations. Include loops for revising ideas.
- ☐ Using what you learned in Lessons 3 and 6, differentiate between the process of scientific investigation and the engineering design process by drawing a Venn diagram.

Unit 1 Review

Name ______________________

Vocabulary

Check the box to show whether each statement is true or false.

T	F	
☐	☐	**1** The dependent variable is the factor that is changed in order to test the effect of the change on other variables.
☐	☐	**2** An organized procedure to study something under controlled conditions is called an experiment.
☐	☐	**3** The median is the difference between the largest and the smallest numbers in a data set.
☐	☐	**4** The observations, measurements, and other data gathered to evaluate an explanation is called empirical evidence.
☐	☐	**5** In science, conclusions may be based on faulty logic and lack substantial support from valid scientific data.

Key Concepts

Read each question below, and circle the best answer.

6 What are the limits on the things that scientists can study in their work?

A They can study only phenomena that they can observe or model.

B They can study only the events that take place on Earth.

C They can investigate only questions that they were the first to ask.

D They can investigate only the areas of science in which they are experts.

7 Wen is a bike messenger. He has found that it is difficult to carry large packages on his bike. After conducting some research, Wen has come up with an idea for a new type of backpack that might help him carry packages. What is Wen's next step?

A revise the solution

B conduct research

C create a prototype

D communicate results

8 This line graph shows a company's average annual salary over nine years.

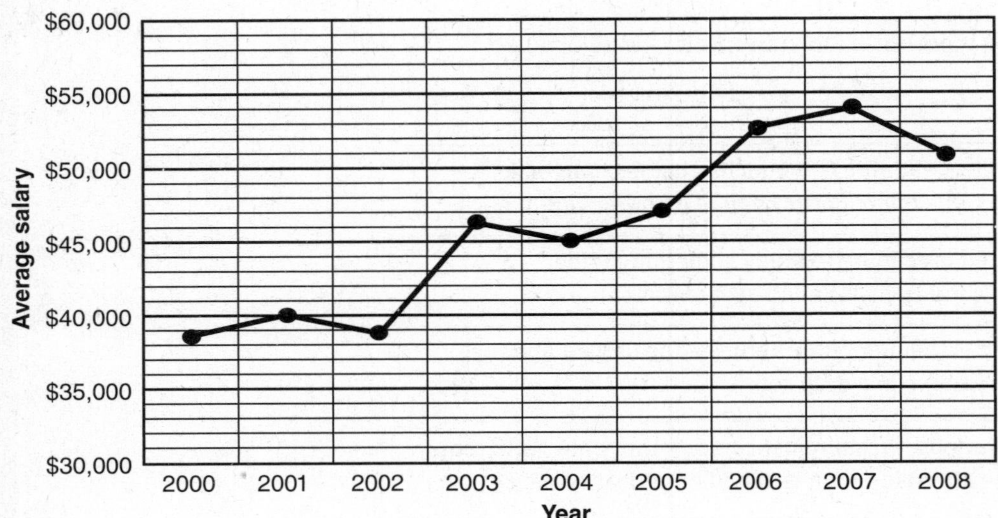

From 2000 to 2008, how many times did the average annual salary decrease?

A once

B twice

C three times

D four times

9 Which action is a characteristic of both science and engineering?

A conducting research

B developing prototypes

C incorporating personal bias

D conducting controlled experiments

10 Imagine that the label on a sunscreen product reads, "Recommended by nine out of ten doctors." No other information regarding this claim is provided. Why would a scientist tell a consumer to be wary of this statistical claim?

A Sunscreen products are ineffective.

B The supporting scientific data are missing.

C The claim is impossible to confirm or refute.

D The claim cannot be reevaluated when new information emerges.

Name ____________________

11 The figure below shows a manatee wearing a radio tracking device that biologists use to track its migration pattern.

Why is this method of evidence collection a good way to study the manatee's migration pattern?

A It restricts the manatees to the biologists' facility.

B It records manatees' breeding habits for biologists to study.

C It allows manatees to travel freely.

D It requires the team of biologists to do in-person checks on the manatees.

12 Astrology is an example of pseudoscience. Astrologers use horoscopes that are based upon the positions of planets and stars to make predictions about a person's life. How is science different from pseudoscience?

A Pseudoscience does not involve making observations.

B Pseudoscience does not examine phenomena in the natural world.

C Pseudoscience does not attempt to provide explanations for phenomena.

D Pseudoscientific conclusions are not supported by data gathered using scientific methods.

13 What is the purpose of repeated trials in an investigation?

A to develop a new theory

B to verify the results of the experiment

C to conduct experiments with more variables

D to revise each step of their research procedure

14 Mrs. Rehak shows her students a model of the three states of matter.

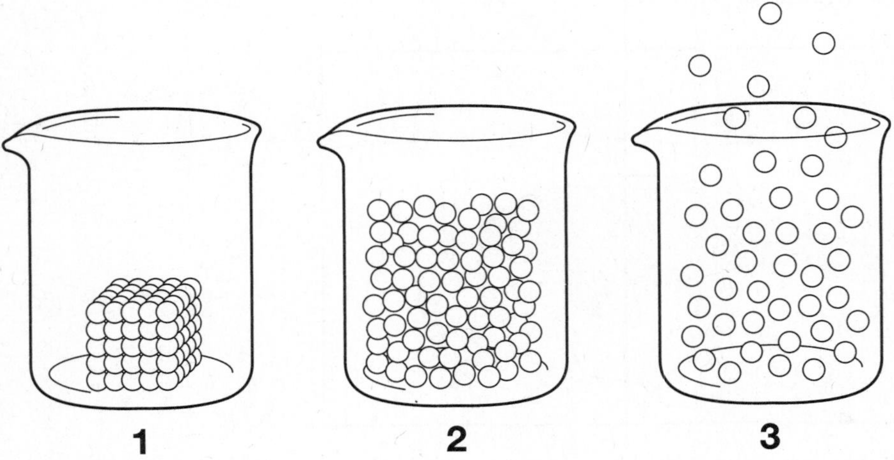

Which part(s) of Mrs. Rehak's model represents a gas?

A 1 and 2

B 3

C 2

D 1

15 Scientific investigations involve many steps and processes. Which characteristics define a laboratory experiment?

A hypotheses, models, and calculations

B test variables, data, and uncontrolled conditions

C data, conclusions, and unregulated environment

D independent and dependent variables, data, and controlled conditions

16 Ella paints two identical pieces of metal different colors. She places them near each other in direct sunlight for 30 minutes and records her data in a table.

Color of metal	Temperature of metal (°C)
white	40
black	70

Which statement best explains why the temperatures are not the same?

A Each color absorbs a different amount of heat energy.

B A different amount of sunlight strikes each piece of metal.

C The mass of each sample varies, which affects heat absorption.

D The samples were different types of metal that absorb sunlight differently.

Name ___________________________

17 A biomedical company uses a certain type of bacteria to manufacture a new medicine. A researcher for the company studies how temperature affects the rate at which the bacteria reproduce. He records his results in a graph.

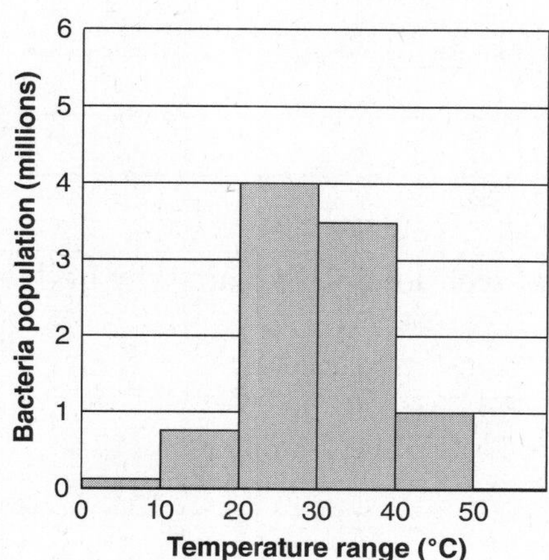

Currently, the company grows the bacteria in a lab maintained at 18 °C. If the company wants to grow the bacteria as quickly as possible, which recommendation should the researcher make?

A The current lab temperature is ideal for growing the bacteria.

B The lab temperature should be increased to between 20 °C and 30 °C.

C The lab temperature should be increased to between 30 °C and 40 °C.

D The lab temperature should be increased to between 40 °C and 50 °C.

18 Kirstin measures the temperature of water before adding ice cubes. What is the SI base unit abbreviation for temperature?

A K

B °C

C C

D °F

Critical Thinking

Answer the following questions in the spaces provided.

19 For each of the following measurements, list one tool that could be used to make the measurement. 2.9 g, 35.20 s, 17 cm, 37 °C

____

____

____

20 You conduct an investigation to determine how long it takes for a rock, dropped from a height of 1 m, to hit the ground. Describe how you would incorporate multiple trials in the experiment, and explain why this practice is a good one.

21 Both a toothbrush and a car are examples of technology. Explain why both are considered technology.

Explain the relationships between engineering, science, and technology..

Connect ESSENTIAL QUESTIONS
Lessons 3, 4, and 6

Answer the following question in the space provided.

22 Explain how the work of scientists benefits engineering, and how the work of engineers benefits science.

UNIT 2

Earth's Resources

The rock in this abandoned Australian copper mine has been colored by different compounds of copper.

Big Idea

Natural resources are classified by their properties, and these properties help explain how the resources formed and help determine how they can be used.

What do you think?

Minerals and rocks have a variety of uses in products that people use every day. What minerals or rocks are mined in your community?

Copper was one of the first metals used by humans, because it can be found in a nearly pure form, like this native copper.

Unit 2

Earth's Resources

CITIZEN SCIENCE

Mineral Resources

Minerals and rocks are mined in large open-pit mines or quarries, or within deep underground tunnels. These natural resources are used to build homes, to pave roads, and to manufacture many everyday consumer items. Some common mineral resources are granite, limestone, and marble; sand and gravel; gypsum; coal; and iron and copper ore.

1 Think About It

A Ask your classmates to identify different types of minerals and rocks that are used in the construction of a house, apartment, or school.

____

____

____

____

____

B How is each of these resources used?

____

____

____

____

____

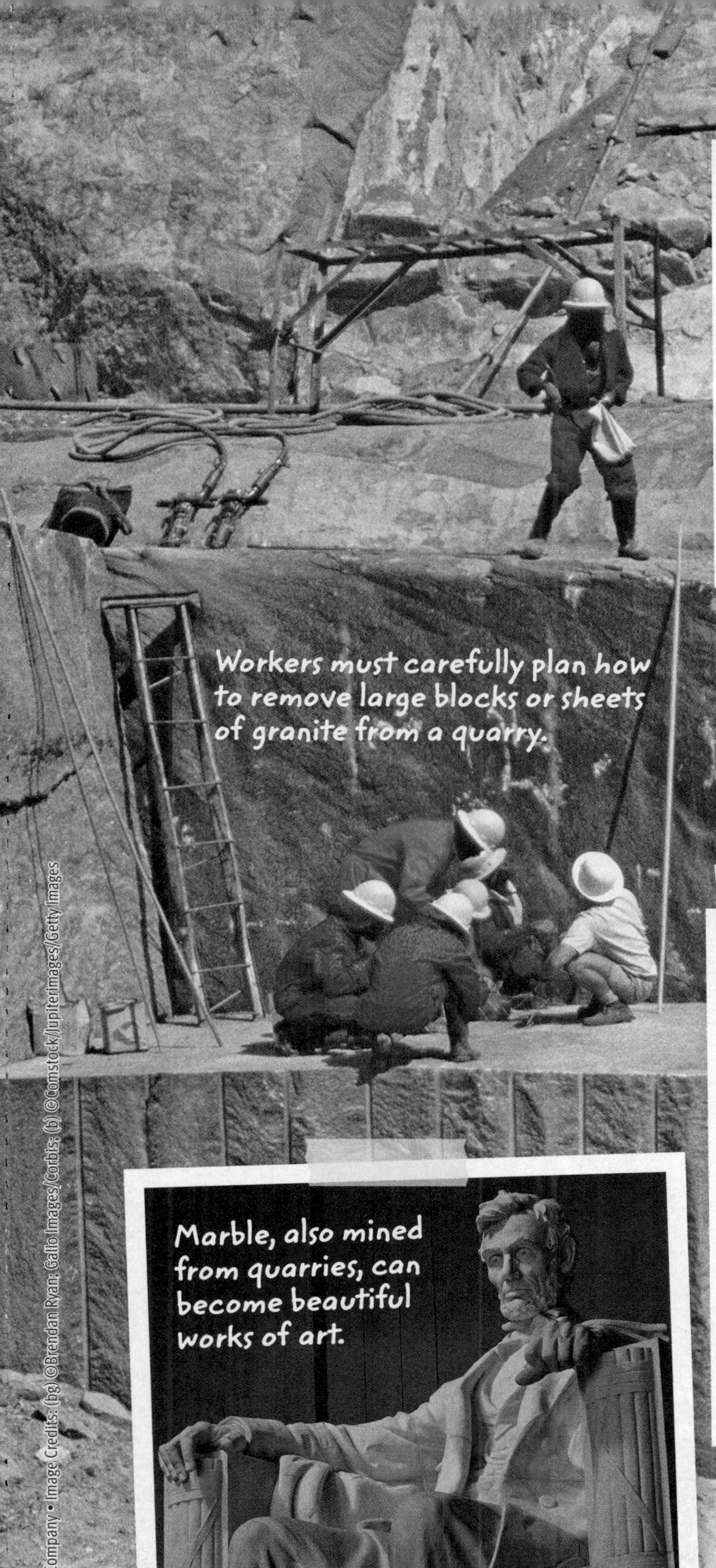

Workers must carefully plan how to remove large blocks or sheets of granite from a quarry.

Marble, also mined from quarries, can become beautiful works of art.

2 Ask a Question

What is the environmental impact of mining minerals and rocks?
Opening a mine requires clearing the land and moving soil and rock. Do some research on how mining affects the environment. What are some ways in which mining can harm the environment?

____

____

____

____

____

3 Make a Plan

Imagine that a mining operation is coming to a place near you. Make a plan for two regulations you would like to see the mining company have to follow in order to protect the environment.

____

____

____

____

____

____

____

____

Take It Home

Search your local newspaper or the Internet for news stories that involve the environmental impact of mining.

Lesson 1

Natural Resources

ESSENTIAL QUESTION

What are Earth's natural resources?

By the end of this lesson, you should be able to describe the types and uses of Earth's natural resources.

Light produced from electrical energy helps people see at night. Natural resources are needed to produce electrical energy.

OHIO 6.ESS.5 Rocks, minerals and soils have common and practical uses.

Lesson Labs

Quick Labs
Renewable or Not?
Production Impacts
Investigating Local Geologic Resources

Field Labs
Natural Resources Used at Lunch

Engage Your Brain

1 Predict Check T or F to show whether you think each statement is true or false.

T	F	
☐	☐	Energy from the sun can be used to make electrical energy.
☐	☐	All of Earth's resources will last forever.
☐	☐	Food, cloth, rope, lumber, paper, and rubber can come from plants.
☐	☐	Humans depend on soil, minerals, and rock.

2 Describe Name one item that you use every day. Describe how you think that item is made.

Active Reading

3 Apply Many scientific words, such as *natural* and *resource,* also have everyday meanings. Use context clues to write your own definition for each underlined word.

Oranges are a natural source of vitamin C.

natural:

His curly hair is natural.

natural:

A dictionary is a useful resource for learning words.

resource:

In the desert, water is a limited resource.

resource:

Vocabulary Terms

- **natural resource**
- **renewable resource**
- **nonrenewable resource**
- **fossil fuel**
- **material resource**
- **energy resource**
- **conservation**
- **stewardship**

4 Identify This list contains the key terms you'll learn in this lesson. As you read, circle the definition of each term.

It's Only Natural

What are natural resources?

What do the water you drink, the paper you write on, the gasoline used in cars, and the air you breathe all have in common? They all come from Earth's natural resources. A **natural resource** is any natural material that is used by humans. Natural resources include air, soil, minerals, water, oil, plants, and animals.

Earth's natural resources provide everything needed for life. The atmosphere contains the air we breathe. Rain forms in the atmosphere. Rainfall renews the water in oceans, rivers, lakes, streams, and underground. In turn, these water sources provide water for drinking, cleaning, and growing crops. Earth's soil gives plants a place to grow and has nutrients they need to live. Plants are food for some animals. Animals can be food as well. Many of Earth's resources, such as oil and wind, are a source of energy for human use. The energy in these resources originally comes from the sun's energy. Earth's resources are also used to make people's lives easier and more comfortable.

Active Reading

5 Identify List four examples of natural resources.

____

____

____

____

Visualize It!

6 Illustrate Draw or label the missing natural resources in the circles labeled "A" and "B."

Bauxite is a rock that is used to make aluminum.

A

How can we categorize natural resources?

There are many different types of natural resources. Some can be replaced more quickly than others. A natural resource may be categorized as a renewable resource or a nonrenewable resource.

Think Outside the Book **Inquiry**

7 Discuss Research why water or soil can become a nonrenewable resource. With a classmate, discuss how you could keep soil or water from becoming a nonrenewable resource.

Renewable Resources

Some natural resources can be replaced in a relatively short time. A natural resource that can be replaced at least as quickly as it is used is a **renewable resource**. Solar energy, water, and air are all renewable resources. Some renewable resources are considered to be *inexhaustible resources* because they cannot be used up by human activities. Solar energy and wind energy, which are both powered by the sun, are examples of inexhaustible resources. Other renewable resources are not inexhaustible. Trees and crops that are used for food must be replanted. Water use must be managed so that water does not become scarce or polluted.

Nonrenewable Resources

A resource that forms much more slowly than it is consumed is a **nonrenewable resource**. Some nonrenewable resources, such as minerals, form very slowly. Quartz, calcite, and copper are examples of minerals. A **fossil fuel** is a nonrenewable resource formed from the buried remains of plants and animals that lived long ago. Coal, oil (petroleum), and natural gas are types of fossil fuels. Fossil fuels can take millions of years to form. If these resources are used up, humans will need to find other resources to use instead. Some renewable resources, such as water, soil, and wood, may become nonrenewable if they are used faster than they can be replenished.

8 Compare List some examples of renewable and nonrenewable resources.

Renewable resources	Nonrenewable resources

Natural fibers from cotton plants are processed to make fabric.

B

Material World

How do we use natural resources?

When you turn on a computer, take a shower, or eat food, you are using natural resources. A variety of natural resources are used to make common objects. The energy needed for many of the activities that we do also comes from natural resources. Earth's natural resources can be divided into material resources and energy resources depending on how the resource is used.

Active Reading

9 Identify As you read this page and the next, underline examples of material resources and energy resources.

As Material Resources

A **material resource** is a natural resource that humans use to make objects or to consume as food or drink. Material resources can come from Earth's atmosphere, crust, fresh waters, and oceans, as well as from plants and animals.

Earth's atmosphere provides the oxygen needed by plants and animals, including humans. Minerals and rock in Earth's crust are used for construction and other industries. Salt, a mineral, comes from ocean water. Fresh water sources and the oceans provide drinking water and food. Some plants, such as cotton, have fibers that are woven into cloth or braided into ropes. Trees are resources for food, lumber, and paper. The sap of some trees is used to make rubber and maple syrup. Animals provide meat, leather, and dairy and egg products. Oil is processed to make plastics, synthetic rubber, nylon, and polyester.

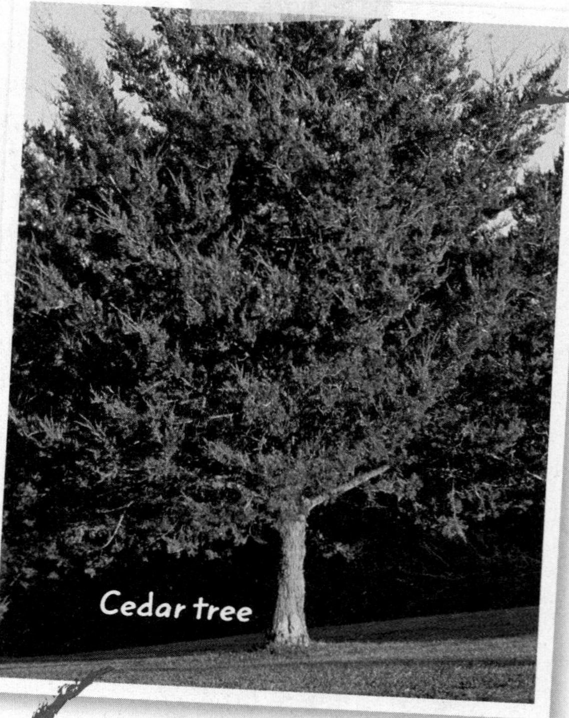

Cedar tree

Trees are a material resource when they are used to make products, such as this guitar.

10 Apply What other items can you think of that are made of wood?

____

____

____

____

As Energy Resources

Energy resources drive the world. An **energy resource** is a natural resource that humans use to generate energy. Most of this energy comes from fossil fuels. For example, oil is processed to make gasoline. When fossil fuels are burned, they release energy in the form of heat. Power plants and machines use that heat to generate mechanical and electrical energy. In turn, electrical energy is used to power lights and many of the appliances we use every day.

Some renewable energy resources are moving water, solar power, and wind power. Trees can be cut to make firewood. Horses, camels, and other animals are used as transportation in some places.

Trees are an energy resource when they are burned in a campfire.

11 Infer What other resources might these campers use?

12 List Think about all the products you use every day. Fill in the chart with three of these products and the resources needed to make them or use them.

Product	Material and Energy Resources Needed
computer	plastic from oil, metal and glass from minerals, electrical energy from fossil fuels

Rockin' Resources

What are some geologic resources?

Active Reading

13 Identify As you read, underline examples of geologic resources.

Did you know that the average American born today will use about 1.36 million kilograms (3 million pounds) of geologic resources in his or her lifetime? Rock, minerals, soil, and fossil fuels are all geologic resources. Most geologic resources are nonrenewable.

Believe it or not, we need rocks and minerals to live healthy, comfortable lives. Cell phones and computers are made from minerals and elements such as silica, aluminum, copper, gold, and tin. Sinks, bathtubs, and sidewalks contain limestone and clay. Soil is another geologic resource. Soil supports plant and animal life.

Rocks and Minerals

The buildings and roads we see today would not exist without rock, sand, and gravel. Crushed rock is a key ingredient in concrete. Concrete is used to build houses, skyscrapers, roads, and sidewalks. Many statues, walls, and floors are made from rocks such as granite, limestone, and marble. However, limestone and marble can be dissolved by acid rain because of their chemical makeup. This can make them less desirable for use in some areas.

Minerals are used differently depending on their properties. You may have heard of rubies or sapphires (SAF•yrz). These gemstones are used in jewelry and come from the mineral corundum (kuh•RUHN•duhm). *Gemstones* are cut and polished minerals with bright lusters that are not easily scratched. Corundum is hard and brittle, so it is also used to make sandpaper.

Minerals are important in technology and electronics. For example, what do you think tennis rackets and spaceships have in common? They are both improved by adding titanium (ty•TAY•nee•uhm) to steel to make a lighter, stronger material. Titanium comes from minerals such as rutile (ROO•teel). Copper is another important mineral. Copper is used in electronics because it conducts electricity well. It is also *ductile*, meaning it can be drawn out into a thin wire.

Soil

Farmers, gardeners, insects, and burrowing animals all benefit from healthy soil. *Soil* is a mixture of rock fragments, organic matter, water, and air. Most plants, and even some animals, need soil for a place to live. Soil holds water for plants and provides them with nutrients. In turn, humans need plants for food, shelter, and oxygen.

Soil can be polluted by activities that have to do with mining and agriculture. Polluted soil can harm plants and animals. Overgrazing can also affect soil. When animals eat too many plants, there are fewer roots to hold the soil in place. That means that soil can be carried away by heavy rains, flooding, and wind.

14 Infer In what ways do animals besides humans depend on soil? Write at least two examples.

Crushed rock, sand, and gravel are used in roads. In the paved road, concrete or asphalt binds rock material. Oil is used to make asphalt. Gypsum, limestone, and clay are used to make concrete.

This native sulfur is a mineral made up entirely of the element sulfur. Sulfur is also found in other minerals. It can be used to control crop pests and disease.

The steel in this tractor is made from iron and carbon, which are found in minerals and rock. Oil is needed to make fuel and tires for the tractor.

Gypsum is a key mineral used to make this wall. It helps make the wall fire-resistant due to its chemical makeup. Gypsum is also a soil fertilizer. It contains calcium and sulfur, which are plant nutrients.

15 Connect How is gypsum related to sulfur, soil, and crops?

___

___

___

___

___

These windows and this computer both contain the mineral silica. Sand is an important source of silica.

Making Materials

What are some ways to extract geologic resources?

Geologic resources are not spread evenly through the ground. Instead, they are concentrated in deposits. An *ore* is a deposit that has a high enough concentration of valuable material to be extracted for a profit. Geologic resources are extracted by mining or drilling.

Think Outside the Book

16 Apply Research what geologic resources are found in your state. Choose one and write a summary about how it is extracted.

Drilling

Oil and natural gas are fossil fuels that give us much of the energy we use today. They can be found together in pockets underground. These fossil fuels are held in spaces between rock grains, like water is held in a sponge. Geologists drill into the ground to reach oil and natural gas. Drilling is done on land and on the ocean floor. The image to the right shows an offshore oil rig. Below the rig, drills go down through the ocean and into the ocean floor. Once the drill reaches the gas and oil, they can be pumped, or they flow up to the surface.

This drilling platform is anchored off the coast of Brazil.

Mining

Ore is taken from the ground by a process called mining. Surface mining is done by removing material to extract ore near the surface. One type of surface mining involves digging large pits in the ground. This is called *open-pit mining*. Another method of surface mining is called *quarrying* (KWOR•ee•ing). Sand, gravel, and crushed rock are collected in quarries.

Tunnels are dug to reach deposits deep underground. This is called subsurface mining. Iron ore, such as the rock magnetite, is often mined in this way. Some underground deposits contain minerals such as halite (HAL•yt). Halite is the same as the salt you can eat. Halite and similar types of minerals can be dissolved by pumping hot water into the ground. The water dissolves the halite, then it is brought to the surface. This is called *solution mining*.

Ore containing silver is being taken from this subsurface mine in Mexico.

What are some ways to process geologic resources?

Active Reading **17 Identify** As you read, number the steps that describe how leaching works.

It may be hard to imagine how rock, minerals, and oil can become a cell phone, a can of paint, or a glass window. Most of the time, geologic resources must be processed to make usable products.

There are different ways to process ore. Ore can be crushed and melted to separate out metals. This is called *smelting*. In another process called *leaching*, a liquid solution is poured on the ore. As the liquid passes through the ore, it dissolves certain materials. Next, the liquid carries the dissolved materials out of the ore and the liquid is collected. Finally, the dissolved materials are taken out of the liquid solution.

Oil pumped from the ground is called *crude oil*. Crude oil has to be processed to make things that we use. *Refining* (rih•FYN•ing) is a process in which fuels and products are made from crude oil. For example, gasoline is a fuel refined from crude oil. The asphalt in parking lots, the polyester in clothing, and the rubber in tires are all products refined from oil. Plastics made from oil are found in computers, medical devices, and food containers.

Metals such as silver, gold, and copper can be separated from ore by smelting.

Silver is malleable, so it can be shaped into this bracelet.

18 Summarize How do you think the metal nickel went from being a part of a rock to these batteries?

____

____

____

____

____

How Resourceful!

How can we conserve resources?

Active Reading

19 Identify As you read, underline ways to conserve natural resources.

You depend on natural resources for the food you eat, the clothes you wear, the paint you use in art class, and the sidewalk you walk on. It is important that natural resources are used wisely, because many are nonrenewable. **Conservation** (kahn•ser•VAY•shuhn) is the protection and wise use of resources. Without conservation, resources may run out.

By Reducing Use of Resources

You can conserve by using less resources. Think of all the lights, televisions, computers, and other devices that you can plug in. They need electrical energy, which often comes from burning coal, a nonrenewable fossil fuel. Natural gas is another nonrenewable fossil fuel used to heat some homes and buildings.

You can conserve resources by turning the heat down when no one is home. You can turn off lights that are not needed or water that is not being used. When you are not on the computer, you can turn the power off. Many vehicles run on gasoline or diesel, both made from crude oil. What if the people on the bus shown above each drove a car instead? The bus likely uses less fossil fuels than all of those cars would. Walking and bicycling are also ways to reduce the use of resources.

By Reusing and Recycling Resources

One way to conserve is to reuse resources. For example, you could drink filtered water from a reusable stainless steel water bottle instead of a new, disposable plastic bottle. Clothes can be donated to a secondhand store or exchanged with a friend or family member. Reusable shopping bags could be used instead of getting new bags from the store.

Some homes, businesses, and schools have recycling programs for paper, metal, glass, and plastic. Buying recycled products helps to conserve resources. For example, recycled notebooks can be bought so fewer trees are cut down. Construction companies can often use materials from old buildings to build new ones. In many cases, electronics and batteries are able to be recycled.

20 Provide In the table below, write two ways to practice conservation that were not mentioned previously. Be sure to fill in each column.

Activity	Resource Use	Way(s) to Practice Conservation
Buying and drinking bottled water	Plastic is made from crude oil, a fossil fuel.	• use filtered water pitcher and reusable bottle • recycle bottles instead of throwing them away
Riding in a gas-powered vehicle	Gasoline is made from crude oil, a fossil fuel.	• carpool, walk, ride a bike, or skateboard • take a train or bus

What is stewardship?

Stewardship is important to practice in places where we extract and process resources. **Stewardship** (STOO•erd•ship) is the careful and responsible management of resources. Wastes from mining and processing can pollute soil and waterways and harm plants and animals. An important part of stewardship is protecting and reviving water, soil, and living things that can be harmed by human activities. Sometimes, chemicals used in processing can be reused or recycled instead of being released into the environment or thrown away. For example, heat generated from making glass or steel can be captured and used to warm buildings. Sulfur can be captured in coal-processing plants and then be used as a fertilizer to grow crops.

This stream was polluted from mining operations upstream.

The pollution was cleaned up, and this is what the stream looked like five years later.

21 Defend Imagine that a company decides to mine an area near a wildlife preserve. Explain what the company can do to practice stewardship.

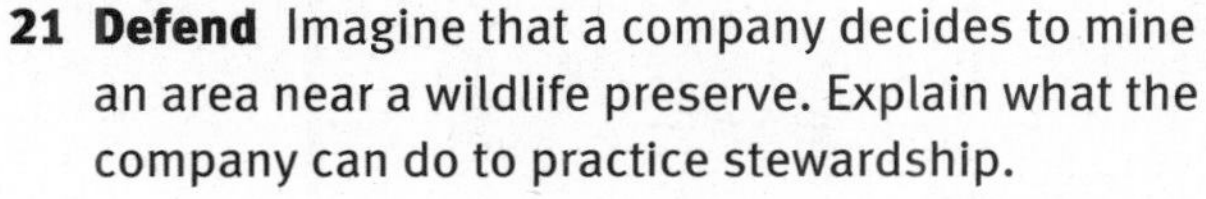

Visual Summary

To complete this summary, circle the correct word. Then use the key below to check your answers. You can use this page to review the main concepts of the lesson.

Natural Resources

Natural resources can be nonrenewable or renewable depending on the rate at which we use them.

22 A resource is renewable/nonrenewable if it is used more quickly than it can be replaced.

Natural resources can be material or energy resources, depending on how they are used.

23 When wood is burned for warmth, it is a(n) material/energy resource.

24 When wood is used to build a house, it is a(n) material/energy resource.

Geologic resources are extracted from Earth's crust and processed to make different products.

25 Rock, minerals, fossil fuels, and plants/soil are geologic resources.

Conservation and stewardship are important because many resources are nonrenewable.

26 Drinking from a reusable bottle is one way to practice recycling/conservation.

Answers: 22 nonrenewable; 23 energy; 24 material; 25 soil; 26 conservation

27 Illustrate Think of a geologic resource that can be used as both a material resource and as an energy resource. Draw pictures to illustrate each use of the resource.

Lesson Review

Vocabulary

Fill in the blank with the term that best completes the following sentences.

1 Nonrenewable and renewable are two categories of ______________________________.

2 A(n) ____________________________ can be used to make objects.

Key Concepts

3 Evaluate Why are natural resources important to humans?

____

____

____

____

4 Identify Give an example of a geologic resource and how it can be extracted.

____

____

5 Compare How do nonrenewable resources and renewable resources differ?

____

____

____

____

____

6 List Choose one mineral, one rock, and one fossil fuel. List an example and a use for each.

Critical Thinking

Use the graph to answer the following questions.

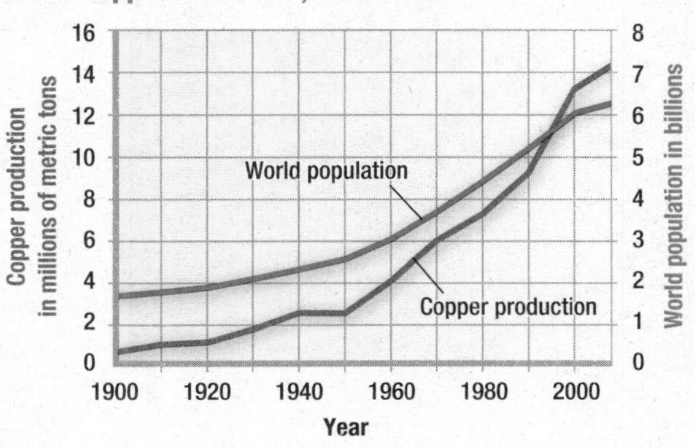

Sources: U.S. Bureau of Mines, U.S. Geological Survey, and U.S. Census Bureau

7 Interpret In what year was the most copper produced?

____

8 Analyze What is the trend in copper production over the past 100 years?

____

____

____

9 Apply Copper is used in making electronic devices. Describe how the use of copper might change as copper becomes more scarce.

____

____

____

____

10 Infer How does human activity affect Earth's natural resources? Explain.

____

____

____

____

____

____

My Notes

Minerals

ESSENTIAL QUESTION

What are minerals, how do they form, and how can they be identified?

By the end of this lesson, you should be able to describe the basic structure of minerals and identify different minerals by using their physical properties.

This cave was once full of water. Over millions of years, dissolved minerals in the water slowly formed these gypsum crystals, which are now considered to be the largest mineral crystals in the world!

OHIO 6.ESS.1 Minerals have specific, quantifiable properties.

OHIO 6.ESS.5 Rocks, minerals and soils have common and practical uses.

OHIO 6.SIA.3 Use appropriate mathematics, tools and techniques to gather data and information.

Lesson Labs

Quick Labs
- Cooling Rate and Crystal Size
- Scratch Test

Exploration Lab
- Intrinsic Identification of Minerals

Engage Your Brain

1 Identify Which of the materials listed below is a mineral?

Yes	No	
☐	☐	ice
☐	☐	gold
☐	☐	wood
☐	☐	diamond
☐	☐	table salt

2 Explain Describe how you think the minerals in the picture below may have formed.

Active Reading

3 Synthesize Many of this lesson's vocabulary terms are related to each other. Locate the terms in the Glossary and see if you can find connections between them. When you find two terms that are related to each other, write a sentence using both terms in a way that shows the relationship. An example is done for you.

Example Sentence
Each element is made of only one kind of atom.

Vocabulary Terms

- **mineral**
- **element**
- **atom**
- **compound**
- **matter**
- **crystal**
- **streak**
- **luster**
- **cleavage**

4 Apply As you learn the definition of each vocabulary term in this lesson, create your own definition or sketch to help you remember the meaning of the term.

Animal, Vegetable,

What do minerals have in common?

When you hear the word *mineral,* you may think of sparkling gems. But, in fact, most minerals are found in groups that make up rocks. So what is a mineral? A **mineral** is a naturally occurring, usually inorganic solid that has a definite crystalline structure and chemical composition.

Definite Chemical Composition

To understand what a definite chemical composition is, you need to know a little about elements. **Elements** are pure substances that cannot be broken down into simpler substances by ordinary chemical means. Each element is made of only one kind of atom. All substances are made up of atoms, so **atoms** can be thought of as the building blocks of matter. Stable particles that are made up of strongly bonded atoms are called *molecules.* And, if a substance is made up of molecules of two or more elements, the substance is called a **compound.**

The chemical composition of a mineral is determined by the element or compound that makes up the mineral. For example, minerals such as gold and silver are composed of only one element. Such a mineral is called a *native element.* The mineral quartz is a compound in which silicon atoms can each bond with up to four oxygen atoms in a repeating pattern.

Inquiry

5 Synthesize What is the relationship between elements, atoms, and compounds?

____

____

____

____

Solid

Matter is anything that has volume and mass. *Volume* refers to the amount of space an object takes up. For example, a golf ball has a smaller volume than a baseball does. Matter is generally found in one of three states: solid, liquid, or gas. A mineral is a solid—that is, it has a definite volume and shape. A substance that is a liquid or a gas is not a mineral. However, in some cases its solid form is a mineral. For instance, liquid water is not a mineral, but ice is because it is solid and has all of the other mineral characteristics also.

Atoms The mineral quartz is made up of atoms of oxygen and silicon.

Compound An atom of silicon can typically bond with up to four oxygen atoms to form a molecule. One or more of these molecules form a compound.

or Mineral?

Usually Inorganic

Most substances made by living things are categorized as organic substances, such as kidney stones and wood. However, a few substances made by animals, such as clam shells, are categorized as inorganic. An inorganic substance is usually one that is not made up of living things or the remains of living things. And, although a few organic substances such as kidney stones are categorized as minerals, most minerals are inorganic. And, unlike clam shells, most of the processes that form minerals usually take place in the non-living environment.

Crystalline Structure

Minerals have a crystalline structure because they are composed of crystals. A **crystal** is a solid, geometric form that results from a repeating pattern of atoms or molecules. A crystal's shape is produced by the arrangement of the atoms or molecules within the crystal. This arrangement is determined by the kinds of atoms or molecules that make up the mineral and the conditions under which it forms. All minerals can be placed into crystal classes according to their specific crystal shape. This diagram shows how silica compounds can be arranged in quartz crystals.

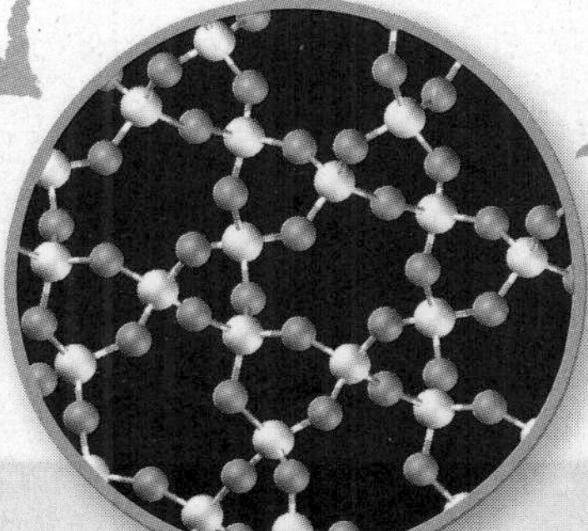

Crystal Structure In crystals, molecules are arranged in a regular pattern.

Mineral Crystal Billions of molecules arranged in a crystalline structure form these quartz crystals.

Naturally Occurring

Minerals are formed by many different natural processes that occur on Earth and throughout the universe. On Earth, the mineral halite, which is used for table salt, forms as water evaporates and leaves behind the salt it contained. Some minerals form as molten rock cools. Talc, a mineral that can be used to make baby powder, forms deep in Earth as high temperature and pressure change the rock. Some of the other ways in which minerals form are on the next page.

6 Classify Circle *Y* for "yes" or *N* for "no" to determine whether the two materials below are minerals.

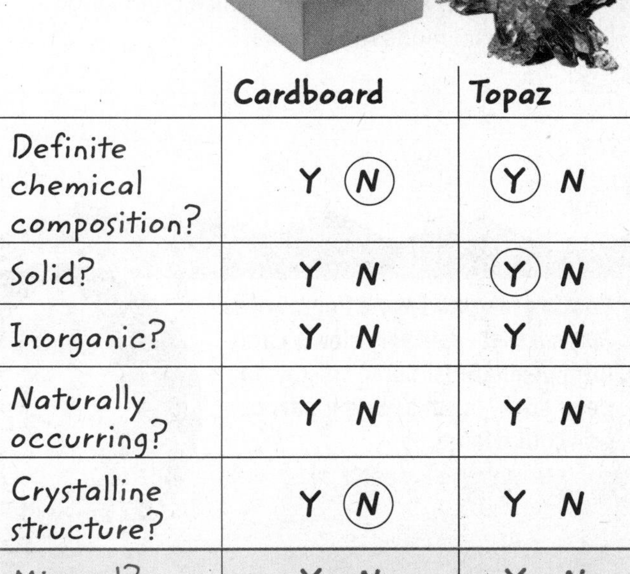

	Cardboard	Topaz
Definite chemical composition?	Y N	Y N
Solid?	Y N	Y N
Inorganic?	Y N	Y N
Naturally occurring?	Y N	Y N
Crystalline structure?	Y N	Y N
Mineral?	Y N	Y N

Crystal Clear!

How are minerals formed?

Minerals form within Earth or on Earth's surface by natural processes. Recall that each type of mineral has its own chemical makeup. Therefore, which types of minerals form in an area depends in part on which elements are present there. Temperature and pressure also affect which minerals form.

As Magma and Lava Cool

Many minerals grow from magma. Magma—molten rock inside Earth—contains most of the types of atoms that are found in minerals. As magma cools, the atoms join together to form different minerals. Minerals also form as lava cools. Lava is molten rock that has reached Earth's surface. Quartz is one of the many minerals that crystallize from magma and lava.

By Metamorphism

Temperature and pressure within Earth cause new minerals to form as bonds between atoms break and reform with different atoms. The mineral garnet can form and replace the minerals chlorite and quartz in this way. At high temperatures and pressures, the element carbon in rocks forms the mineral diamond or the mineral graphite, which is used in pencils.

Visualize It!

7 Compare How are the ways in which pluton and pegmatite minerals form similar?

____

____

Cooling Magma Forms Plutons As magma rises, it can stop moving and cool slowly. This forms rocks like this granite, which contains minerals like quartz, mica, and feldspar.

Cooling Magma Forms Pegmatites Magma that cools very slowly can form pegmatites. Some crystals in pegmatites, such as this topaz, can grow quite large.

Metamorphism Minerals like these garnets form when temperature and pressure causes the chemical and crystalline makeup of minerals to change.

From Solutions

Water usually has many substances dissolved in it. As water evaporates, these substances form into solids and come out of solution, or *precipitate*. For example, the mineral gypsum often forms as water evaporates. Minerals can also form from hot water solutions. Hot water can dissolve more materials than cold water. As a body of hot water cools, dissolved substances can form into minerals such as dolomite, as they precipitate out of solution.

8 Summarize Describe three ways minerals form.

A ______________________________

____

B ______________________________

____

C ______________________________

____

Precipitating from an Evaporating Solution When a body of salt water evaporates, minerals such as this halite precipitate and are left behind on the shoreline.

Precipitating from a Cooling Solution on Earth's Surface Dissolved materials can come out of a solution and accumulate. Dolomite, can form this way.

Precipitating from a Cooling Solution Beneath Earth's Surface Water works its way downward and is heated by magma. It then reacts with minerals to form a solution. Dissolved elements, such as gold, precipitate once the fluid cools to form new mineral deposits.

Think Outside the Book

9 Apply Find out what your state mineral is and how it forms.

Sort It Out

How are minerals classified?

The most common classification of minerals is based on chemical composition. Minerals are divided into two groups based on their composition. These groups are the silicate (SIL'ih•kayt) minerals and the nonsilicate (nawn•SIL'ih•kayt) minerals.

Silicate Minerals

Silicon and oxygen are the two most common elements in Earth's crust. Minerals that contain a combination of these two elements are called *silicate minerals.* Silicate minerals make up most of Earth's crust. The most common silicate minerals in Earth's crust are feldspar and quartz. Most silicate minerals are formed from basic building blocks called *silicate tetrahedrons.* Silicate tetrahedrons are made of one silicon atom bonded to four oxygen atoms. Most silicate minerals, including mica and olivine, are composed of silicate tetrahedrons combined with other elements, such as aluminum or iron.

Active Reading **10 Explain** Why is Earth's crust made up mostly of silicate minerals?

____

____

The mineral zircon is a silicate mineral. It is composed of the element zirconium and silicate tetrahedrons.

Nonsilicate Minerals

Minerals that do not contain the silicate tetrahedron building block form a group called the *nonsilicate minerals.* Some of these minerals are made up of elements such as carbon, oxygen, fluorine, iron, and sulfur. The table on the next page shows the most important classes of nonsilicate minerals. A nonsilicate mineral's chemical composition determines its class.

Do the Math **You Try It**

11 Calculate Calculate the percent of non-silicates in Earth's crust to complete the graph's key.

Minerals in Earth's Crust

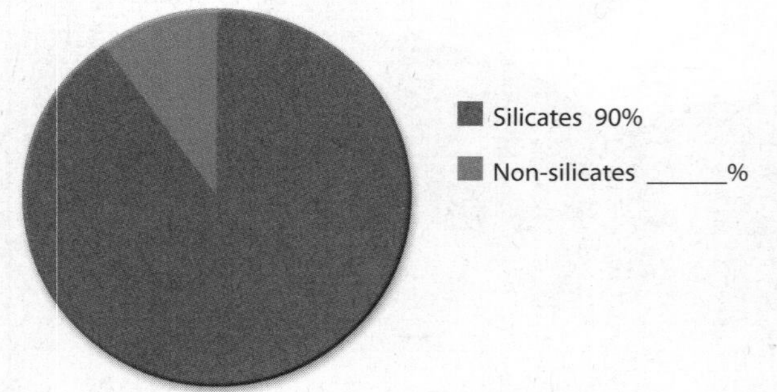

Classes of Nonsilicate Minerals

Native elements are minerals that are composed of only one element. Copper (Cu) and silver (Ag) are two examples. Native elements are often used to make electronics.

Silver, Ag

Carbonates are minerals that contain carbon (C) and oxygen (O) in the form of the carbonate ion CO_3^{2-}. We use carbonate minerals in cement, building stones, and fireworks.

Calcite, $CaCO_3$

Halides are compounds that form when elements such as fluorine (F) and chlorine (Cl), combine with elements such as calcium (Ca). Halides are used in the chemical industry and in detergents.

Fluorite, CaF_2

Oxides are compounds that form when an element, such as aluminum (Al) or iron (Fe), combines with oxygen. Oxide minerals are used to make abrasives, aircraft parts, and paint.

Corundum, Al_2O_3

Sulfates are minerals that contain sulfur (S) and oxygen (O) in the form of the sulfate ion SO_4^{2-}. Sulfates are used in cosmetics, toothpaste, cement, and paint.

Barite, $BaSO_4$

Sulfides are minerals that contain one or more elements, such as lead (Pb), or iron (Fe), combined with sulfur (S). Sulfide minerals are used to make batteries and medicines.

Pyrite, FeS_2

Visualize It!

12 Classify Examine the chemical formulas for the two minerals at right. Classify the minerals as a silicate or nonsilicate. If it is a nonsilicate, also write its class.

Gypsum, $CaSO_4 \cdot 2H_2O$

Kyanite, Al_2SiO_5

_______________________ _______________________

_______________________ _______________________

Name That Mineral!

What properties can be used to identify minerals?

If you closed your eyes and tasted different foods, you could probably determine what the foods are by noting properties such as saltiness or sweetness. You can also determine the identity of a mineral by noting different properties. In this section, you will learn about the properties that will help you identify minerals.

Color

The same mineral can come in different colors. For example, pure quartz is colorless. However, impurities can make quartz pink, orange, or many other colors. Other factors can also change a mineral's color. Pyrite is normally golden, but turns black or brown if exposed to air and water. The same mineral can be different colors, and different minerals can be the same color. So, color is helpful but usually not the best way to identify a mineral.

Active Reading

13 Identify Underline the name of the property on this page that is most reliable for identifying a mineral.

Streak

The color of the powdered form of a mineral is its **streak**. A mineral's streak is found by rubbing the mineral against a white tile called a *streak plate*. The mark left is the streak. A mineral's streak is not always the same as the color of the mineral, but all samples of the same mineral have the same streak color. Unlike the surface of a mineral, the streak is not affected by air or water. For this reason, streak is more reliable than color in identifying a mineral.

Visualize It!

14 Evaluate Look at these two mineral samples. What property indicates that they may be the same mineral?

____

____

____

Mineral Lusters

Metallic **Silky** **Vitreous** **Waxy**

Submetallic **Pearly** **Resinous** **Earthy**

Luster

The way a surface reflects light is called **luster**. When you say an object is shiny or dull, you are describing its luster. The two major types of luster are metallic and nonmetallic. Pyrite has a metallic luster. It looks as if it is made of metal. A mineral with a nonmetallic luster can be shiny, but it does not appear to be made of metal. Different types of lusters are shown above.

Cleavage and Fracture

The tendency of a mineral to split along specific planes of weakness to form smooth, flat surfaces is called **cleavage**. When a mineral has cleavage, it breaks along flat surfaces that generally run parallel to planes of weakness in the crystal structure. For example, mica tends to split into parallel sheets. Many minerals, however, do not break along cleavage planes. Instead, they fracture, or break unevenly, into pieces that have curved or irregular surfaces. Scientists describe a fracture according to the appearance of the broken surface. For example, a rough surface has an irregular fracture, and a curved surfaces has a conchoidal (kahn•KOY•duhl) fracture.

Visualize It!

15 Identify Write the correct description, either *cleavage* or *fracture,* under the two broken mineral crystals shown here.

____

____

Mohs Scale

1	Talc
2	Gypsum
3	Calcite
4	Fluorite
5	Apatite
6	Feldspar
7	Quartz
8	Topaz
9	Corundum
10	Diamond

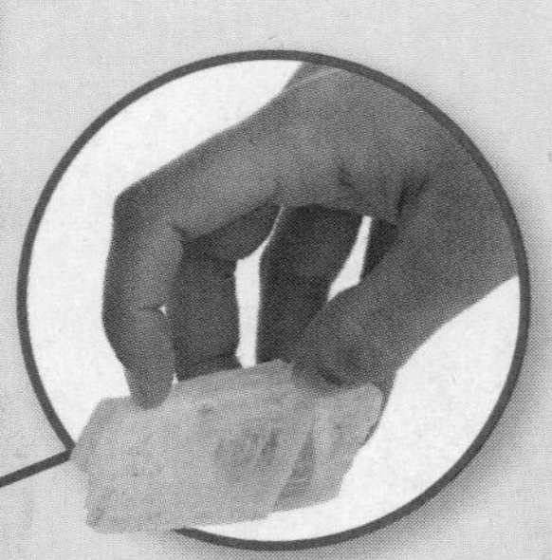

Your fingernail has a hardness of about 2.5, so it can scratch talc and gypsum.

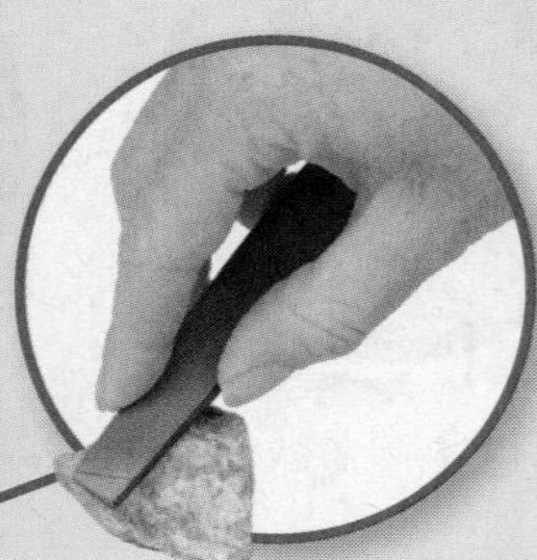

A steel file has a hardness of about 6.5. You can scratch feldspar with it.

Diamond is the hardest mineral. Only a diamond can scratch another diamond.

16 Determine A mineral can be scratched by calcite but not by a fingernail. What is its approximate hardness?

____

Density

If you pick up a golf ball and a table-tennis ball, which will feel heavier? Although the balls are of similar size, the golf ball will feel heavier because it is denser. *Density* is the measure of how much matter is in a given amount of space. Density is usually measured in grams per cubic centimeter. Gold has a density of 19 g/cm^3. The mineral pyrite looks very similar to gold, but its density is only 5 g/cm^3. Because of this, density can be used to tell gold from pyrite. Density can also be used to tell many other similar-looking minerals apart.

Hardness

A mineral's resistance to being scratched is called its *hardness*. To determine the hardness of minerals, scientists use the Mohs hardness scale, shown at left. Notice that talc has a rating of 1 and diamond has a rating of 10. The greater a mineral's resistance to being scratched, the higher its hardness rating. To identify a mineral by using the Mohs scale, try to scratch the surface of a mineral with the edge of one of the 10 reference minerals. If the reference mineral scratches your mineral, the reference mineral is as hard as or harder than your mineral.

Special Properties

All minerals exhibit the properties that were described earlier in this section. However, a few minerals have some additional, special properties that can help identify those minerals. For example, the mineral magnetite is a natural magnet. The mineral calcite is usually white in ordinary light, but in ultraviolet light, it often appears red. Another special property of calcite is shown below.

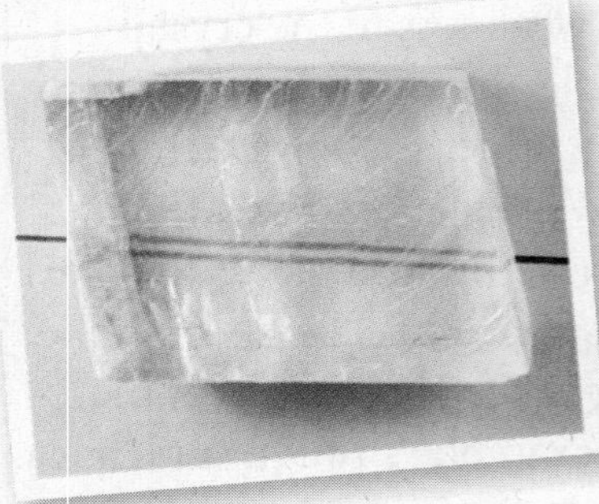

A clear piece of calcite placed over an image will cause a double image.

Why It Matters

SOCIETY AND TECHNOLOGY

Made from Minerals

Many minerals contain useful substances. Rutile and several other minerals contain the metal titanium. Titanium can resist corrosion and is about as strong as steel, but it is 47% lighter than steel. These properties make titanium very valuable.

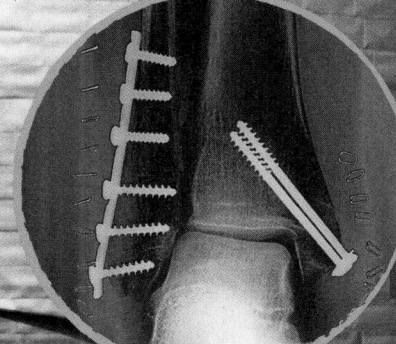

Devices for Doctors

Surgical procedures like joint replacements require metal implantations. Titanium is used because it can resist body fluid corrosion and its low density and elasticity is similar to human bone.

Marvels for Mechanics

Motorcycle exhaust pipes are often made out of titanium, which dissipates heat better than stainless steel.

An Aid to Architects

Titanium doesn't just serve practical purposes. Architect Frank Gehry used titanium panels to cover the outside of the Guggenheim Museum in Bilbao, Spain. He chose titanium because of its luster.

Extend

Inquiry

17 Infer How do you think the density of titanium-containing minerals would compare to the density of minerals used to make steel? Explain.

18 List Research some other products made from minerals. Make a list summarizing your research.

19 Determine Choose one of the products you researched. How do the properties of the minerals used to make the product contribute to the product's characteristics or usefulness?

Visual Summary

To complete this summary, fill in the blanks with the correct words or phrase. Then use the key below to check your answers. You can use this page to review the main concepts of the lesson.

Minerals

Minerals make up Earth's crust.

20 A mineral:

- has a definite chemical composition
- is a solid
- is usually inorganic
- is formed in nature
- ____________________

Minerals are classified by composition.

21 Minerals are classified in two groups as:

Quartz, SiO_2

____

Calcite, $CaCO_3$

____

Minerals form by natural processes.

22 Minerals form by:

- metamorphism
- the cooling of magma and lava
- ____________________

Minerals are identified by their properties.

23 Properties used to identify minerals include:

- color and luster
- ____________________
- cleavage or fracture
- density and hardness
- special properties

Answers: 20 has a crystalline structure; 21 silicates (left), nonsilicates (right); 22 precipitating from solutions; 23 streak

24 Apply Ice (H_2O) is a mineral. Classify it as silicate or nonsilicate. List two of its properties.

Lesson Review

Vocabulary

Fill in the blank with the term that best completes the following sentence.

1 The way light bounces off a mineral's surface is described by the mineral's ________________

2 The color of a mineral in powdered form is the mineral's ________________

3 Each element is made up of only one kind of ________________

Key Concepts

4 Explain How could you determine whether an unknown substance is a mineral?

____

5 Determine If a substance is a mineral, how could you identify what type of mineral it is?

____

6 Organize In the space below, draw a graphic organizer showing how minerals can be classified. Be sure to include the six main classes of nonsilicate minerals.

Critical Thinking

Use the diagram below to answer question 7.

Carbon Bonds in Graphite

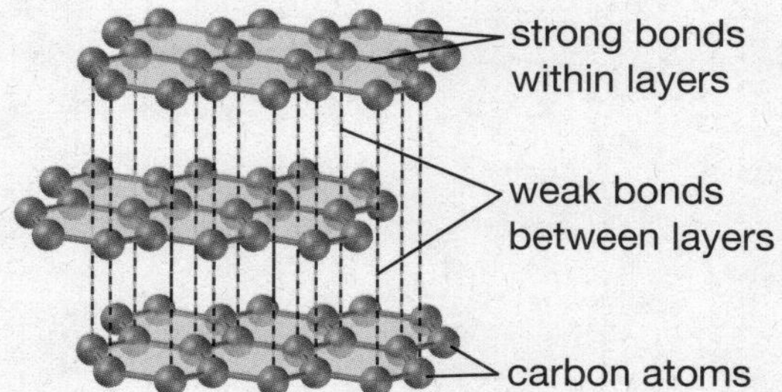

7 Evaluate The diagram above shows the crystal structure of graphite, a mineral made up of carbon atoms that are bonded together in a regular pattern. Do you think graphite would most likely display cleavage or fracture? Explain your answer.

____

8 Infer How do you think the hardness and density of a mineral that formed through metamorphism would compare to a mineral that formed through evaporation? Explain.

____

My Notes

The Rock Cycle

ESSENTIAL QUESTION

What is the rock cycle?

By the end of this lesson, you should be able to describe the series of processes and classes of rocks that make up the rock cycle.

It may be hard to believe, but these mountains actually move. Wyoming's Teton Mountains rise by millimeters each year. An active fault is uplifting the mountains. In this lesson, you will learn about uplift and other processes that change rock.

OHIO 6.ESS.2 Igneous, metamorphic and sedimentary rocks have unique characteristics that can be used for identification and/or classification.

OHIO 6.ESS.3 Igneous, metamorphic and sedimentary rocks form in different ways.

Lesson Labs

Quick Labs
- Crayon Rock Cycle
- Modeling Weathering

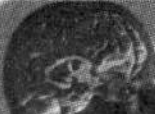

Engage Your Brain

1 Describe Fill in the blank with the word or phrase that you think correctly completes the following sentences.

Most of Earth is made of ____________

Rock is ____________ changing.

The three main classes of rock are igneous, metamorphic, and ________________

2 Describe Write your own caption for this photo.

____

____

____

Active Reading

3 Synthesize Many English words have their roots in other languages. Use the Latin words below to make an educated guess about the meaning of the words *erosion* and *deposition*.

Latin Word	Meaning
erosus	eaten away
depositus	laid down

Erosion:

____

____

Deposition:

____

____

Vocabulary Terms

- **weathering**
- **erosion**
- **deposition**
- **igneous rock**
- **sedimentary rock**
- **metamorphic rock**
- **rock cycle**
- **uplift**
- **subsidence**
- **rift zone**

4 Apply As you learn the definition of each vocabulary term in this lesson, create your own definition or sketch to help you remember the meaning of the term.

Let's Rock!

What is rock?

The solid parts of Earth are made almost entirely of rock. Scientists define rock as a naturally occurring solid mixture of one or more minerals that may also include organic matter. Most rock is made of minerals, but some rock is made of nonmineral material that is not organic, such as glass. Rock has been an important natural resource as long as humans have existed. Early humans used rocks as hammers to make other tools. For centuries, people have used different types of rock, including granite, marble, sandstone, and slate, to make buildings, such as the pyramids shown below.

It may be hard to believe, but rocks are always changing. People study rocks to learn how areas have changed through time.

5 List How is rock used today?

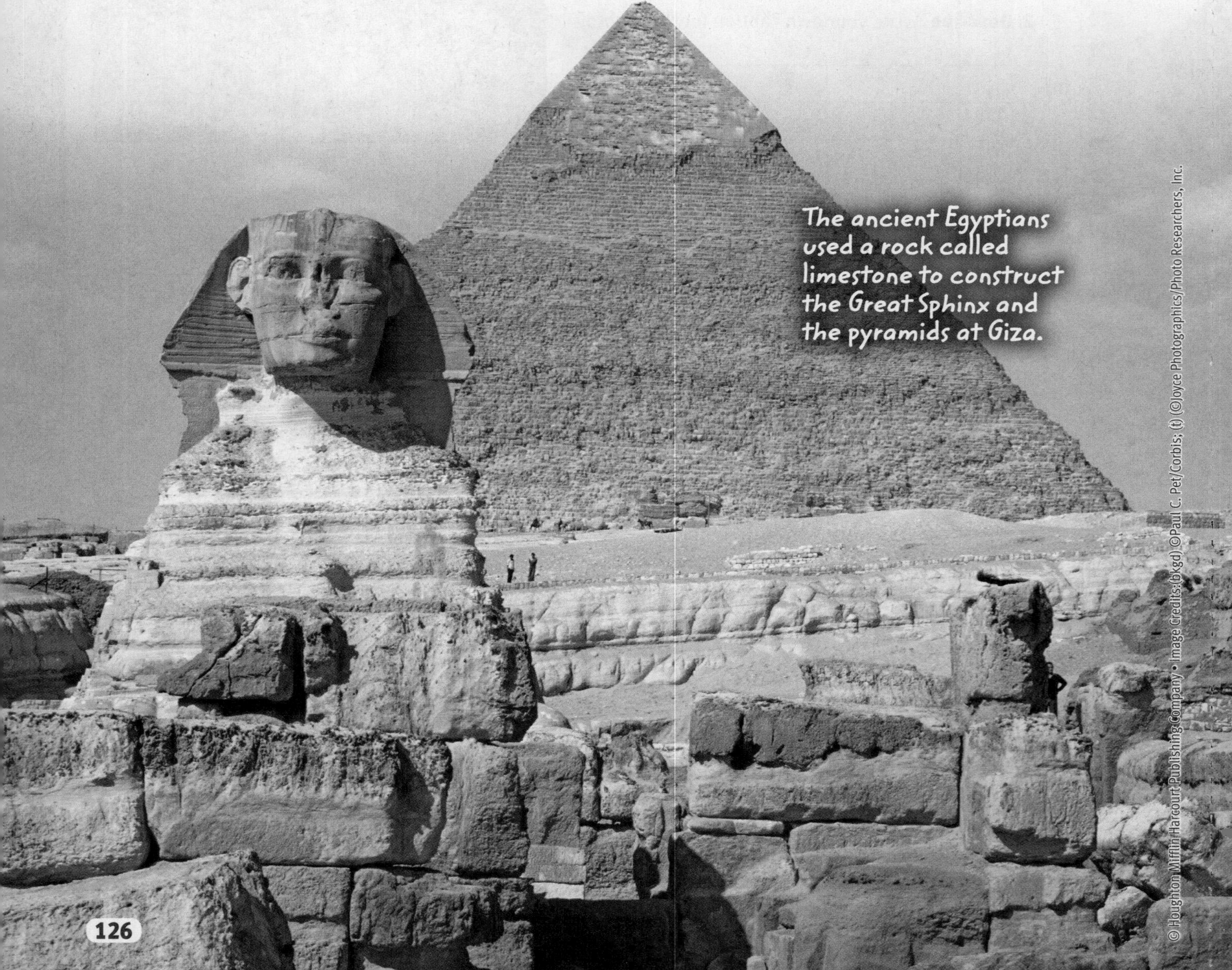

The ancient Egyptians used a rock called limestone to construct the Great Sphinx and the pyramids at Giza.

These rock formations in Goreme, Turkey, are known as fairy chimneys. They were shaped by erosion.

Think Outside the Book

6 Design Create a travel brochure for Goreme, Turkey.

What processes change rock?

Natural processes make and destroy rock. They change each type of rock into other types of rock and shape the features of our planet. These processes also influence the type of rock that is found in each area of Earth's surface.

Active Reading **7 Identify** As you read, underline the processes and factors that can change rock.

Weathering, Erosion, and Deposition

The process by which water, wind, ice, and changes in temperature break down rock is called **weathering**. Weathering breaks down rock into fragments called *sediment*. The process by which sediment is moved from one place to another is called **erosion.** Water, wind, ice, and gravity can erode sediments. These sediments are eventually deposited, or laid down, in bodies of water and other low-lying areas. The process by which sediment comes to rest is called **deposition.**

Temperature and Pressure

Rock that is buried can be squeezed by the weight of the rock or the layers of sediment on top of it. As pressure increases with depth beneath Earth's surface, so does temperature. If the temperature and pressure are high enough, the buried rock can change into metamorphic rock. In some cases, the rock gets hot enough to melt and forms *magma*, or molten rock. If magma reaches Earth's surface, it is called *lava*. The magma or lava eventually cool and solidify to form new rock.

Classified Information!

What are the classes of rocks?

Rocks fall into three major classes based on how they form. **Igneous rock** forms when magma or lava cools and hardens to become solid. It forms beneath or on Earth's surface. **Sedimentary rock** forms when minerals that form from solutions or sediment from older rocks get pressed and cemented together. **Metamorphic rock** forms when pressure, temperature, or chemical processes change existing rock. Each class can be divided further, based on differences in the way rocks form. For example, some igneous rocks form when lava cools on Earth's surface, and others form when magma cools deep beneath the surface. Therefore, igneous rock can be classified based on how and where it forms.

Active Reading

8 Identify As you read the paragraph, underline the three main classes of rocks.

Think Outside the Book Inquiry

9 Apply With a classmate, discuss the processes that might have shaped the rock formations in the Valley of Fire State Park.

These formations in Valley of Fire State Park in Nevada are made of sandstone, a sedimentary rock.

sandstone

Sedimentary

Sedimentary rock is composed of minerals formed from solutions or sediments from older rock. Sedimentary rock forms when the weight from above presses down on the layers of minerals or sediment, or when minerals dissolved in water solidify between sediment pieces and cement them together.

Sedimentary rocks are named according to the size and type of the fragments they contain. For example, the rock shown here is made of sand and is called sandstone. Rock made primarily of the mineral calcite (calcium carbonate) is called limestone.

Enchanted Rock in Texas is a large dome made of granite, an intrusive igneous rock.

Igneous Rock

granite

Igneous rock forms from cooling lava and magma. As molten rock cools and becomes solid, the minerals crystallize and grow. The longer the cooling takes, the more time the crystals have to grow. The granite shown here cooled slowly and is made of large crystals. Rock that forms when magna cools beneath Earth's surface is called intrusive igneous rock. Rock that forms when lava cools on Earth's surface is called extrusive igneous rock.

Metamorphic Rock

Metamorphic rock forms when high temperature and pressure change the texture and mineral content of rock. For example, a rock can be buried in Earth's crust, where the temperature and pressure are high. Over millions of years, the solid rock changes, and new crystals are formed. Metamorphic rocks may be changed in four ways: by temperature, by pressure, by temperature and pressure combined, or by fluids or other chemicals. Gneiss, shown here, is a metamorphic rock. It forms at

gneiss

Gneiss is a metamorphic rock that is made up of bands of light and dark minerals.

10 Compare Fill in the chart to compare and contrast sedimentary, igneous, and metamorphic rock.

Classes of Rocks

Sedimentary rock	Igneous rock	Metamorphic rock

What is the rock cycle?

Active Reading **11 Apply** As you read, underline the rock types that metamorphic rock can change into.

Rocks may seem very permanent, solid, and unchanging. But over millions of years, any of the three rock types can be changed into another of the three types. For example, igneous rock can change into sedimentary or metamorphic rock, or back into another kind of igneous rock. This series of processes in which rock changes from one type to another is called the **rock cycle**. Rocks may follow different pathways in the cycle. Examples of these pathways are shown here. Factors, including temperature, pressure, weathering, and erosion, may change a rock's identity. Where rock is located on a tectonic plate and whether the rock is at Earth's surface also influence how it forms and changes.

When igneous rock is exposed at Earth's surface, it may break down into sediment. Igneous rock may also change directly into metamorphic rock while still beneath Earth's surface. It may also melt to form magma that becomes another type of igneous rock.

When sediment is pressed together and cemented, the sediment becomes sedimentary rock. With temperature and pressure changes, sedimentary rocks may become metamorphic rocks, or they may melt and become igneous rock. Sedimentary rock may also be broken down at Earth's surface and become sediment that forms another sedimentary rock.

Under certain temperature and pressure conditions, metamorphic rock will melt and form magma. Metamorphic rock can also be altered by heat and pressure to form a different type of metamorphic rock. Metamorphic rock can also be broken down by weathering and erosion to form sediment that forms sedimentary rock.

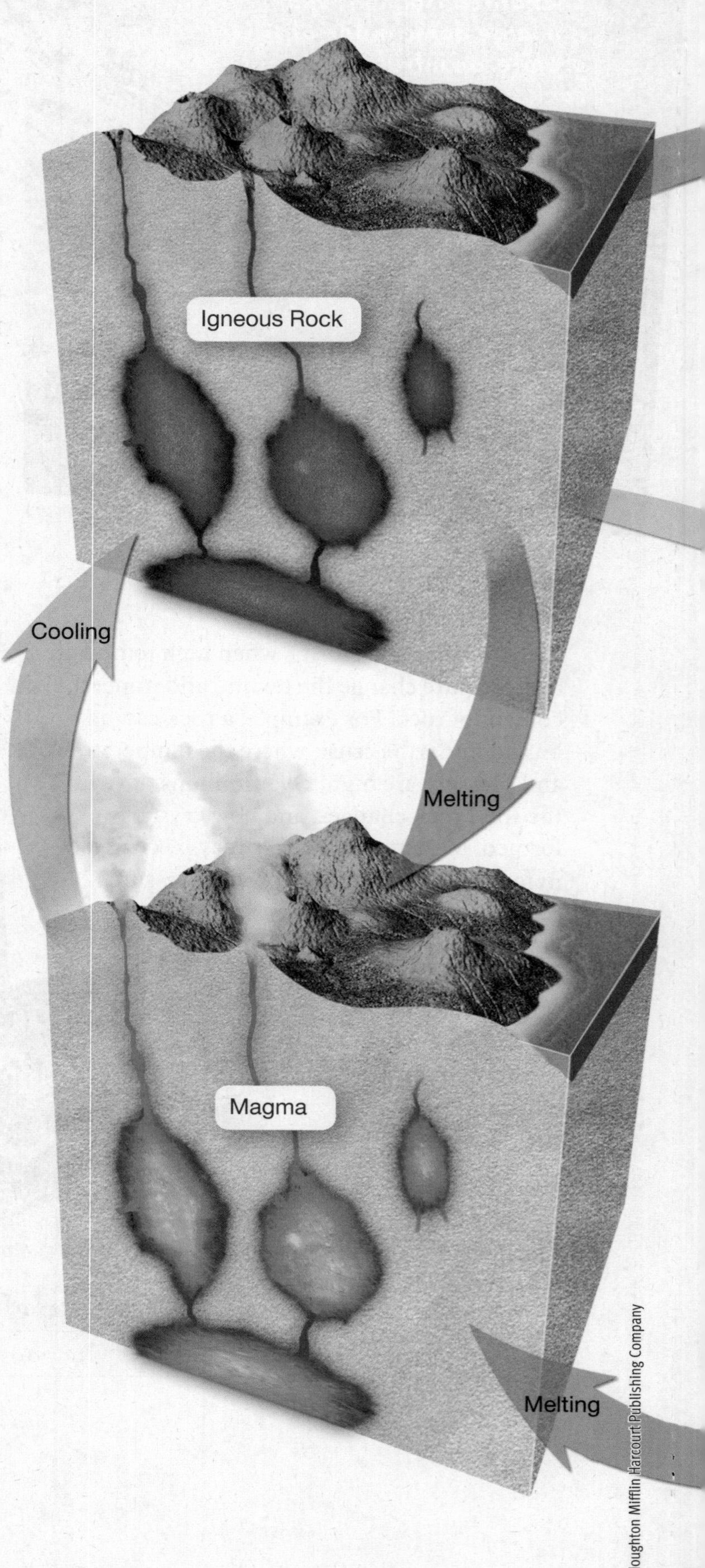

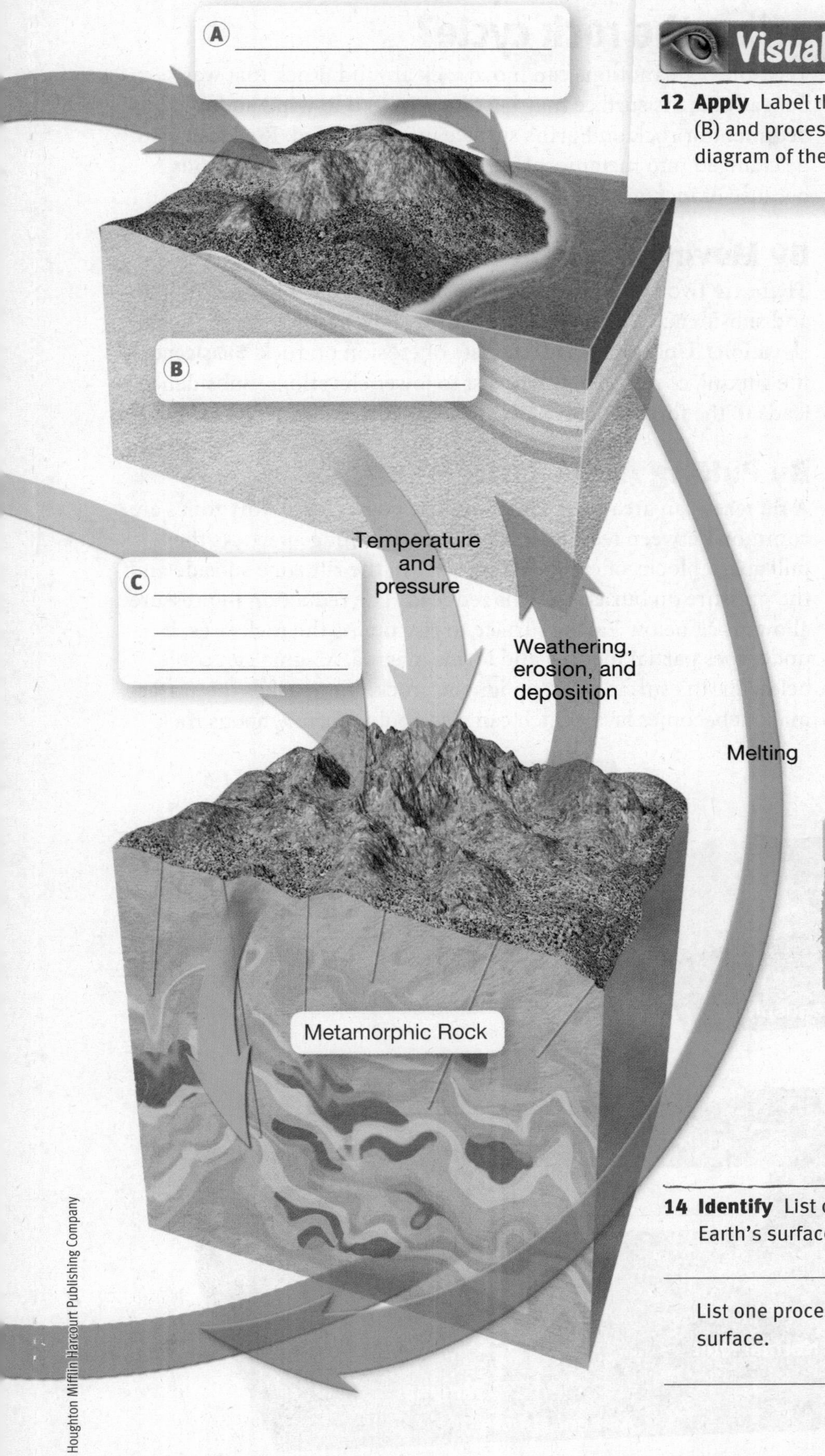

Ⓐ ______________________
____

Ⓑ ______________________

Temperature and pressure

Ⓒ ______________________
____
____

Weathering, erosion, and deposition

Melting

Metamorphic Rock

Visualize It!

12 Apply Label the missing rock type (B) and processes (A and C) on the diagram of the rock cycle.

Think Outside the Book

13 Apply Write a series of blog entries from the viewpoint of igneous rock that is changing into sedimentary rock.

14 Identify List one process that happens above Earth's surface.

____

List one process that happens below Earth's surface.

____

How do tectonic plate motions affect the rock cycle?

Tectonic plate motions can move rock around. Rock that was beneath Earth's surface may become exposed to wind and rain. Sediment or rock on Earth's surface may be buried. Rock can also be changed into metamorphic rock by tectonic plate collisions because of increased temperature and pressure.

By Moving Rock Up or Down

There are two types of vertical movements in Earth's crust: uplift and subsidence. **Uplift** is the rising of regions of the crust to higher elevations. Uplift increases the rate of erosion on rock. **Subsidence** is the sinking of regions of the crust to lower elevations. Subsidence leads to the formation of basins where sediment can be deposited.

15 Compare How does uplift differ from subsidence?

By Pulling Apart Earth's Surface

A **rift zone** is an area where a set of deep cracks form. Rift zones are common between tectonic plates that are pulling apart. As they pull apart, blocks of crust in the center of the rift zone subside and the pressure on buried rocks is reduced. The reduction in pressure allows rock below Earth's surface to rise up. As the rock rises, it undergoes partial melting and forms magma. Magma can cool below Earth's surface to form igneous rock. If it reaches the surface, magma becomes lava, which can also cool to form igneous rock.

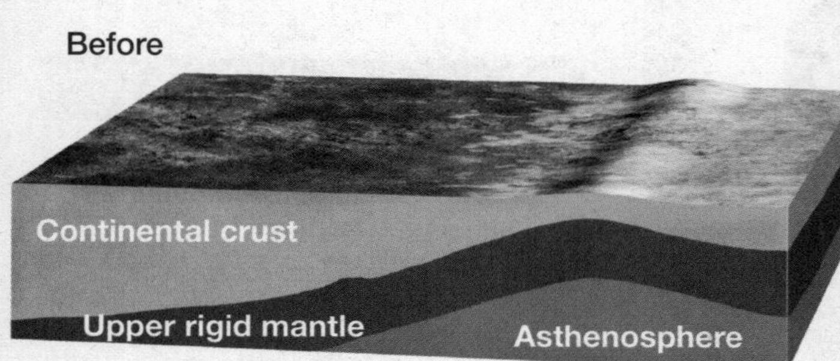

16 Predict Label uplift and subsidence on this diagram. What pathway in the rock cycle might rock take next if it is subjected to uplift? Explain.

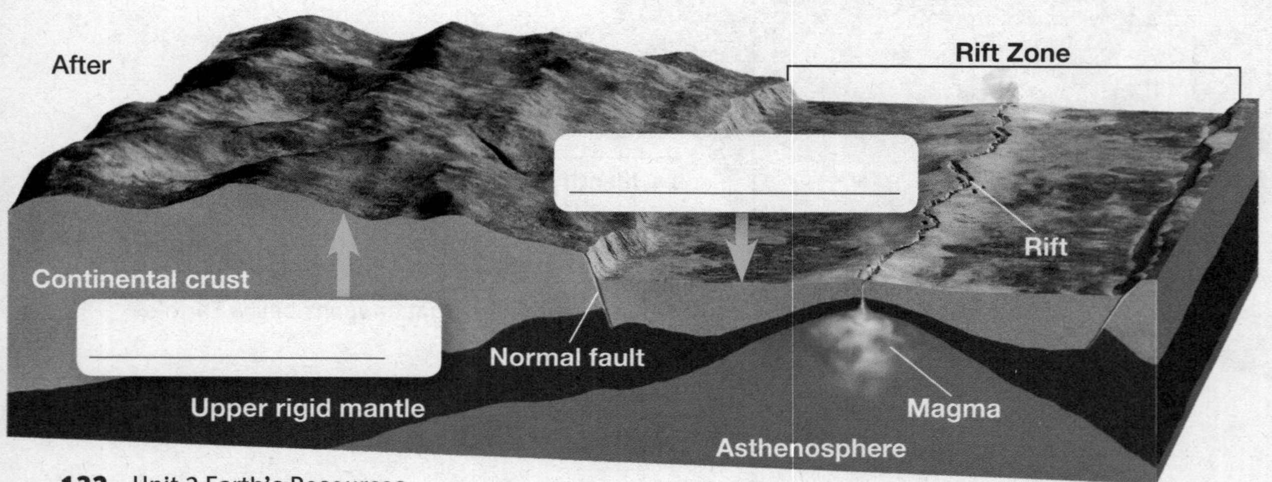

Why It Matters

WEIRD SCIENCE

Cliff Dwellings

Can you imagine living on the side of a cliff? Some ancient peoples could! They created dwellings from cliff rock. They also decorated rock with art, as you can see in the pictographs shown below.

Cliff Palace
This dwelling in Colorado is called the Cliff Palace. It was home to the Ancient Puebloans from about 550 to 1300 CE.

Cliff Art
These pictographs are located at the Gila Cliff Dwellings in New Mexico.

A Palace in Rock
Ancient cliff dwellings are also found outside the United States. These dwellings from about 70 CE are located in Petra, Jordan.

Extend

Inquiry

17 Identify Describe how ancient people used rock to create shelter.

18 Research Find out how people lived in one of the cliff dwelling locations. How did living in a rock environment affect their daily lives?

19 Produce Illustrate how the people lived by doing one of the following: write a play, write a song, or create a graphic novel.

Visual Summary

To complete this summary, use what you know about the rock cycle to fill in the blanks below. Then use the key below to check your answers. You can use this page to review the main concepts of the lesson.

Each rock type can change into another of the three types.

20 When sediment is pressed together and cemented, the sediment becomes

____

21 When lava cools and solidifies, _______________ forms.

22 Metamorphic rock can be altered by temperature and pressure to form a different type of

____

Rock Cycle

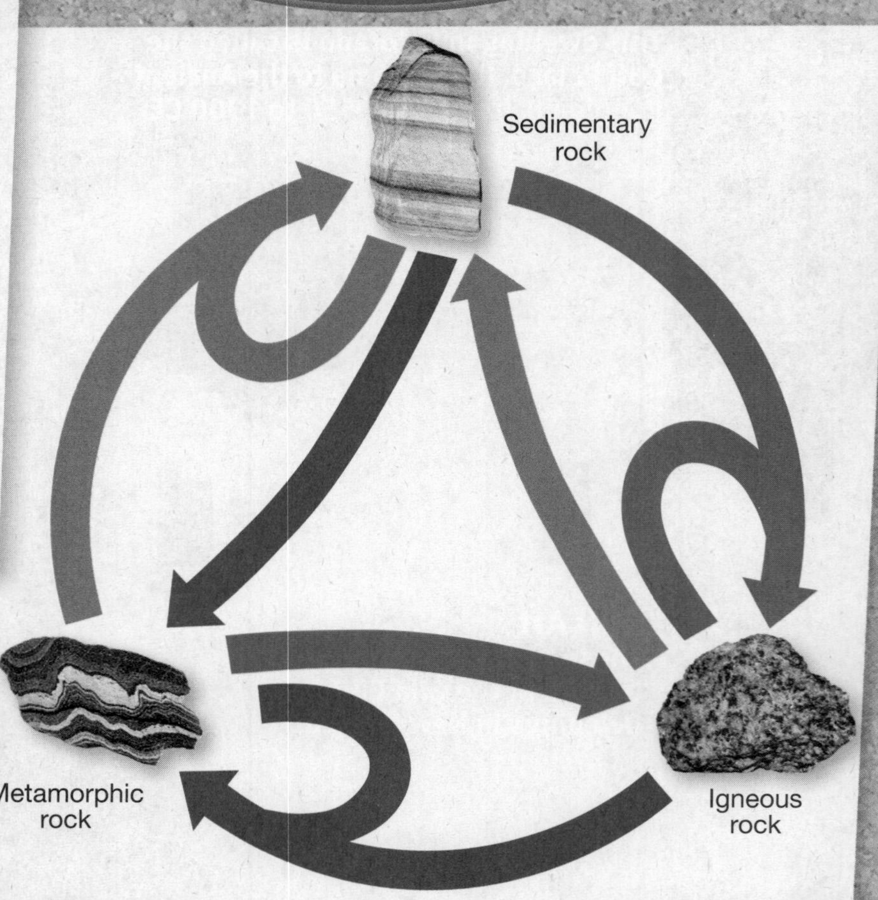

Answers: 20 sedimentary rock; 21 igneous rock; 22 metamorphic rock

23 **Explain** What factors and processes can affect the pathway that igneous rock takes in the rock cycle?

Lesson Review

Vocabulary

In your own words, define the following terms.

1 Rock cycle

2 Weathering

3 Rift zone

Key Concepts

Use these photos to classify the rock as sedimentary, igneous, or metamorphic.

Example	Type of rock
4 Classify This rock is made up of the mineral calcite, and it formed from the remains of organisms that lived in water.	
5 Classify Through high temperature and pressure, this rock formed from a sedimentary rock.	
6 Classify This rock is made of tiny crystals that formed quickly when molten rock cooled at Earth's surface.	

7 Describe How can sedimentary rock become metamorphic rock?

8 Explain How can subsidence lead to the formation of sedimentary rock?

9 Explain Why are rift zones common places for igneous rock to form?

Critical Thinking

10 Hypothesize What would happen to the rock cycle if erosion did not occur?

11 Criticize A classmate states that igneous rock must always become sedimentary rock next, according to the rock cycle. Explain why this statement is not correct.

12 Predict Granite is an igneous rock that forms from magma cooled below Earth's surface. Why would granite have larger crystals than igneous rocks formed from lava cooled above Earth's surface?

My Notes

S.T.E.M. Engineering & Technology

OHIO 6.ESS.5, 6.SIA.7, 6.SIA.8

Analyzing Technology

Skills
Identify risks
Identify benefits
✓ Evaluate cost of technology
✓ Evaluate environmental impact
✓ Propose improvements
Propose risk reduction
✓ Compare technology
✓ Communicate results

Objectives
• Analyze the life cycle of an aluminum can.
• Analyze the life cycle of a glass bottle.
• Evaluate the cost of recycling versus disposal of technology.
• Analyze the environmental impact of technology.

Analyzing the Life Cycles of Aluminum and Glass

A life cycle analysis is a way to evaluate the real cost of a product. The analysis considers how much money an item costs to make. It also examines how making the product affects the economy and the environment through the life of the product. Engineers, scientists, and technologists use this information to improve processes and to compare products.

Costs of Production

Have you ever wondered where an aluminum soda can comes from? Have you wondered where the can goes when you are done with it? If so, you have started a life cycle analysis by asking the right questions. Aluminum is a metal found in a type of rock called *bauxite.* To get aluminum, first bauxite must be mined. The mined ore is then shipped to a processing plant. There, the bauxite is melted to get aluminum in a process called *smelting.* After smelting, the aluminum is processed. It may be shaped into bicycle parts or rolled into sheets to make cans. Every step in the production involves both financial costs and environmental costs that must be considered in a life cycle analysis.

Many bicycles are made of aluminum because it is lightweight and strong.

Costs of Disposal

After an aluminum can is used it can travel either to a landfill or to a recycling plant. The process of recycling an aluminum can does require the use of some energy. However, the financial and environmental costs of disposing of a can and mining ore are much greater than the cost of recycling a can. Additionally, smelting bauxite produces harmful wastes. A life cycle analysis of an aluminum can must include the cost and environmental effects of mining, smelting, and disposing of the aluminum can.

1 **Analyze** After a can is recycled, which steps are no longer part of the life cycle?

Life Cycle of an Aluminum Can

Bauxite mining

Most bauxite mining occurs far away from where aluminum is used. Large ships or trains transport the ore before it is made into aluminum products.

Smelting

Fabrication

Aluminum is one of the easiest materials to recycle. Producing a ton of aluminum by shredding and remelting uses about 5% of the energy needed to process enough bauxite to make a ton of aluminum.

Remelting

Shredding

Recycling

Manufacturing

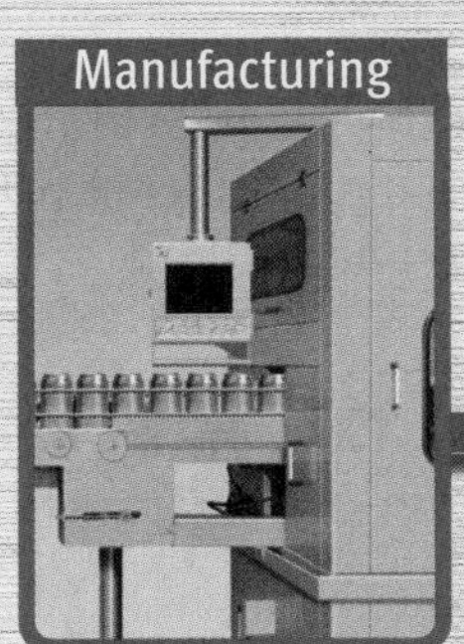

Consumer use

2 **Evaluate** In the life cycle shown here, which two steps could include an arrow to indicate disposal?

You Try It!

Now it's your turn to analyze the life cycle of a product.

Now, apply what you have learned about the life cycle of aluminum to analyze the life cycle of a glass bottle. Glass is made by melting silica from sand or from mineral deposits mined from the Earth. A kiln heats the silica until it melts to form a red-hot glob. Then, the glass is shaped and cooled to form useful items.

1 Evaluate Cost of Technology

As a group, discuss the steps that would be involved in making a glass bottle. List the steps in the space below. Start with mining and end at a landfill. Include as many steps in the process as you can think of. Beside each step, tell whether there would be financial costs, environmental costs, or both.

Life Cycle of a Glass Bottle

2 Evaluate Environmental Impact

Use the table below to indicate which of the steps listed above would have environmental costs, and what type of cost would be involved. A step can appear in more than one column.

Cause pollution	Consume energy	Damage habitat

3 Propose Improvements

In your group, discuss how you might improve the life cycle of a glass bottle and reduce the impact on the environment. Draw a life cycle that includes your suggestions for improvement.

4 Compare Technology

How does your improved process decrease the environmental effects of making and using glass bottles?

5 Communicate Results

Imagine that you are an accountant for a company that produces glass bottles. In the space below, write an argument for using recycled glass that is based on financial savings for your company.

Three Classes of Rock

ESSENTIAL QUESTION

How do rocks form?

By the end of this lesson, you should be able to describe the formation and classification of sedimentary, igneous, and metamorphic rocks.

Wind and water have eroded the softer rock surrounding Ship Rock, an igneous landform in New Mexico.

OHIO **6.ESS.2** Igneous, metamorphic and sedimentary rocks have unique characteristics that can be used for identification and/or classification.

OHIO **6.ESS.3** Igneous, metamorphic and sedimentary rocks form in different ways.

Lesson Labs

Quick Labs
- Stretching Out
- Observing Rocks

S.T.E.M. Lab
- Modeling Rock Formation

Engage Your Brain

1 Predict Check T or F to show whether you think each statement is true or false.

T	F	
☐	☐	All rocks form deep beneath Earth's surface.
☐	☐	Some rocks are made up of materials from living things.
☐	☐	Some rocks take millions of years to form.
☐	☐	All rocks are made up of the same kinds of minerals.
☐	☐	Some rocks form from particles of other rocks.

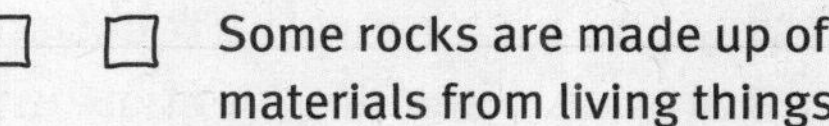

2 Identify How do you think rocks might form as a result of the volcanic activity shown here?

____

____

____

____

Active Reading

3 Apply Use context clues to write your own definition for the words *composition* and *texture*.

Example sentence:
The composition of the trail mix was 50% nuts, 30% dried fruit, and 20% granola.

composition:

____

____

Example sentence:
Because glass is smooth, flat, and shiny, it has a much different texture than wood does.

texture:

____

____

Vocabulary Terms

- rock
- texture
- composition

4 Apply As you learn the definition of each vocabulary term in this lesson, create your own definition or sketch to help you remember the meaning of the term.

A Rocky World

How are rocks classified?

Active Reading

5 Identify As you read, underline two properties that are used to classify rock.

A combination of one or more minerals or organic matter is called **rock**. Scientists divide rock into three classes based on how each class of rock forms. The three classes of rock are igneous, sedimentary, and metamorphic. Each class of rock can be further divided into more specific types of rock. For example, igneous rocks can be divided based on where they form. All igneous rock forms when molten rock cools and solidifies. However, some igneous rocks form on Earth's surface, and others form within Earth's crust. Sedimentary and metamorphic rocks are also divided into more specific types of rock. How do scientists understand how to classify rocks? They observe their composition and texture.

By Mineral Composition

The minerals and organic matter a rock contains determine the **composition**, or makeup, of that rock. Many rocks are made up mostly of the minerals quartz and feldspar, which contain a large amount of the compound silica. Other rocks have different compositions. The limestone rock shown below is made up mostly of the carbonate mineral calcite.

Do the Math

6 Graph Fill in the percentage grid on the right to show the amounts of calcite and aragonite in limestone.

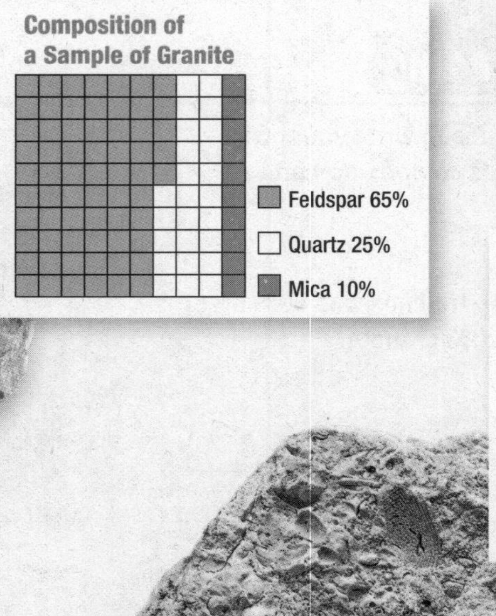

Granite is made of silica minerals.

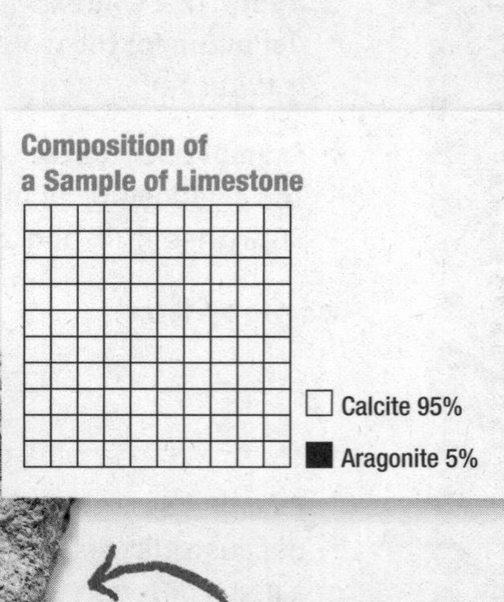

Limestone is made of carbonate minerals.

By Texture

The size, shape, and positions of the grains that make up a rock determine a rock's **texture**. Coarse-grained rock has large grains that are easy to see with your eyes. Fine-grained rock has small grains that can only be seen by using a hand lens or microscope. The texture of a rock may give clues as to how and where it formed. Igneous rock can be fine-grained or coarse-grained depending on the time magma takes to cool. The texture of metamorphic rock depends on the rock's original composition and the temperature and pressure at which the rock formed. The rocks shown below look different because they formed in different ways.

Visualize It!

7 Describe Observe the sedimentary rocks on this page, and describe their texture as coarse-grained, medium-grained, or fine-grained.

This sandstone formed from sand grains that once made up a sand dune.

A ______________________________

____

This mudstone is made up of microscopic particles of clay.

B ______________________________

____

This breccia is composed of broken fragments of rock cemented together.

C ______________________________

____

The Furnace Below

What are two kinds of igneous rock?

Igneous rock forms when hot, liquid magma cools into solid rock. Magma forms when solid rock melts below Earth's surface. Magma flows through passageways up toward Earth's surface. Magma can cool and harden below Earth's surface, or it can make its way above Earth's surface and become lava.

Intrusive Igneous Rock

When magma does not reach Earth's surface, it cools in large chambers, in cracks, or between layers in the surrounding rock. When magma pushes into, or intrudes, surrounding rock below Earth's surface and cools, the rock that forms is called *intrusive igneous rock*. Magma that is well insulated by surrounding rock cools very slowly. The minerals form large, visible crystals. Therefore, intrusive igneous rock generally has a coarse-grained texture. Examples of intrusive igneous rock are granite and diorite. A sample of diorite is shown at the left.

Diorite is an example of intrusive igneous rock.

8 Infer How can you tell that diorite is an intrusive igneous rock?

____

____

Deep Inside Earth The amount of time magma takes to cool determines the texture of an igneous rock.

Crystals Slow-cooling magma has time to form large mineral crystals. The resulting rock is coarse-grained.

Magma chamber Magma chambers deep inside Earth contain pools of molten rock. Magma cools slowly in large chambers such as this.

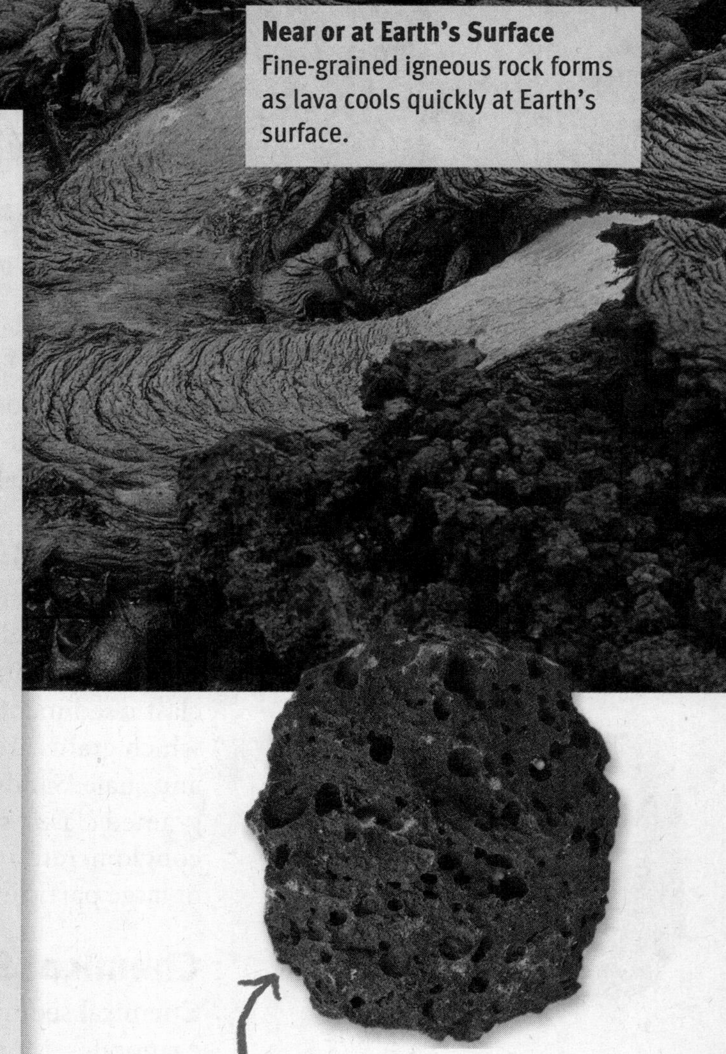

Near or at Earth's Surface
Fine-grained igneous rock forms as lava cools quickly at Earth's surface.

Extrusive Igneous Rock

Igneous rock that forms when lava erupts, or extrudes, onto Earth's surface is called *extrusive igneous rock*. Extrusive igneous rock is common around the sides and bases of volcanoes. Lava cools very quickly at Earth's surface. So there is very little time for crystal formation. Because there is little time for crystals to form, extrusive rocks are made up of very small crystals and have a fine-grained texture. Obsidian (ahb•SID•ee•uhn) is an extrusive rock that cools so rapidly that no crystals form. Obsidian looks glassy, so it is often called *volcanic glass*. Other common extrusive igneous rocks are basalt and andesite.

Lava flows form when lava erupts from a volcano. The photo above shows an active lava flow. Sometimes lava erupts and flows from long cracks in Earth's crust called *fissures*. It also flows on the ocean floor at places where tension is causing Earth's crust to pull apart.

Active Reading **9 Explain** How does the rate at which magma cools affect the texture of igneous rock?

Basalt is an example of extrusive igneous rock.

10 Compare Use the Venn diagram to compare and contrast intrusive igneous rock and extrusive igneous rock.

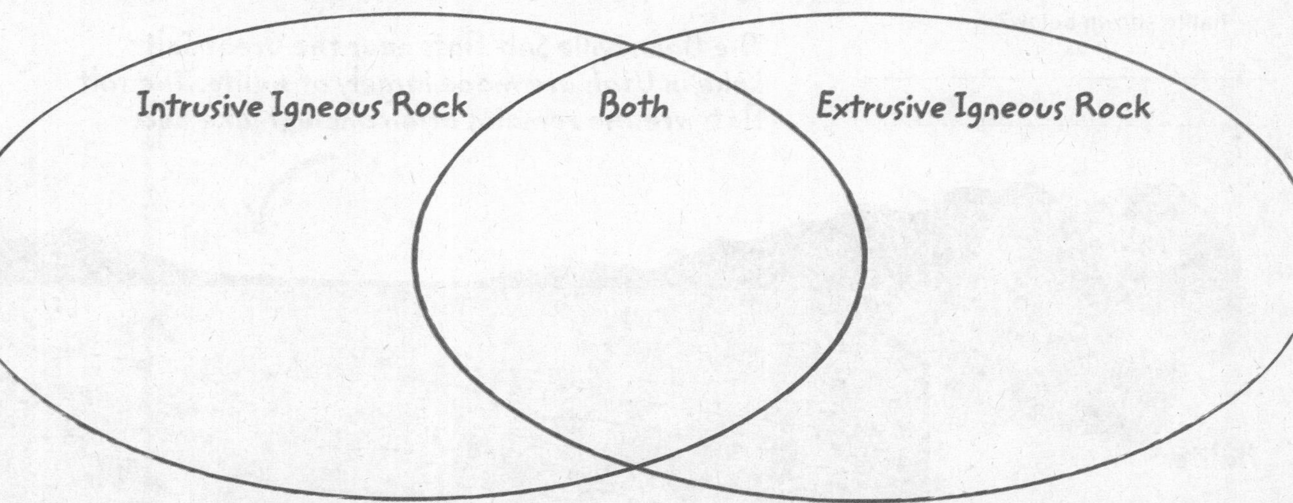

Lay It On!

Horizontal layers of clastic sedimentary rock and volcanic ash are exposed at Badlands National Park in South Dakota.

What are three types of sedimentary rock?

All the processes that form sedimentary rock occur mainly at or near the surface of Earth. Some of these processes include weathering, erosion, deposition, burial, and cementation. Based on the way that they form, scientists classify sedimentary rocks as clastic, chemical, and organic sedimentary rock.

Clastic Sedimentary Rock

Clastic sedimentary rock forms when sediments are buried, compacted, and cemented together by calcite or quartz. The size of the sediment, or clasts, that makes up the rock is used to classify clastic sedimentary rocks. Fine-grained sedimentary rocks, in which grains are too small to be seen, include mudstone, siltstone, and shale. Sandstone, which is shown at the left, is a medium-grained clastic sedimentary rock with visible grains. Breccia and conglomerate are coarse-grained clastic sedimentary rocks made of large particles, such as pebbles, cobbles, and boulders.

Sandstone

Chemical Sedimentary Rock

Chemical sedimentary rock forms when water, usually seawater, evaporates. Most water contains dissolved minerals. As water evaporates, the minerals in water become concentrated to the point that they precipitate out of solution and crystallize. Halite, or rock salt, is an example of chemical sedimentary rock. It is made of sodium chloride, NaCl. Halite forms when sodium ions and chlorine ions in shallow bodies of water become so concentrated that halite crystallizes from solution.

11 Identify How would you describe the texture of the halite shown below?

____

____

The Bonneville Salt Flats near the Great Salt Lake in Utah are made largely of halite. The salt flats are the remains of an ancient lake bed.

Halite

The White Cliffs of Dover on the English sea coast are made up of the skeletons of the marine alga that is shown below.

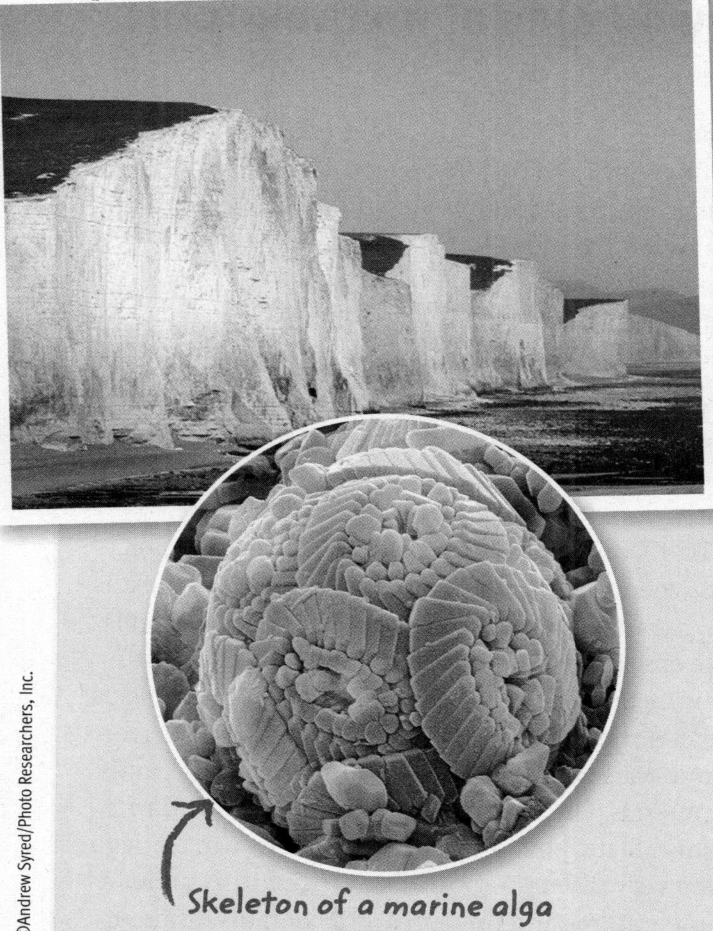

Skeleton of a marine alga

Organic Sedimentary Rock

Organic sedimentary rock forms from the remains, or fossils, of once-living plants and animals. Most limestone forms from the fossils of organisms that once lived in the ocean. Over time, the skeletons of these marine organisms, which are made of calcium carbonate, collect on the ocean floor. These animal remains, together with sediment, are eventually buried, compacted, and cemented together to form *fossiliferous* (fahs•uh•LIF•er•uhs) limestone.

Coquina is a fossiliferous limestone that consists of the shells of marine mollusks that have been cemented together by calcite. Chalk is a soft, white limestone that is made up of the skeletons of microorganisms that collect in huge numbers on the floor of the deep ocean.

Coal is another type of organic sedimentary rock. It forms when plant material is buried and changes into coal as a result of increasing heat and pressure. This process occurs over millions of years.

Active Reading **12 Identify** What are two types of organic sedimentary rock?

____

____

13 Compare Use the table to compare and contrast clastic, chemical, and organic sedimentary rock.

Three Types of Sedimentary Rock

Clastic	Chemical	Organic

The Heat Is On!

Sedimentary shale

Slate

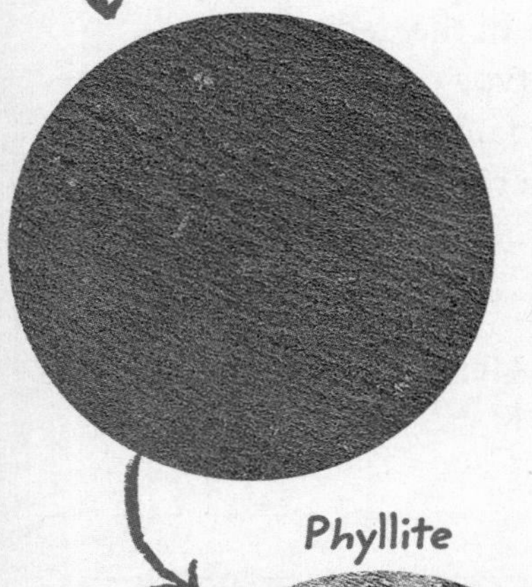

Phyllite

What are two types of metamorphic rock?

As a rock is exposed to high temperature and pressure, the crystal structures of the minerals in the rock change to form new minerals. This process results in the formation of metamorphic rock, which has either a foliated texture or a nonfoliated texture.

Foliated Metamorphic Rock

The metamorphic process in which mineral grains are arranged in planes or bands is called *foliation* (foh•lee•AY•shuhn). Foliation occurs when pressure causes the mineral grains in a rock to realign to form parallel bands.

Metamorphic rocks with a foliated texture include slate, phyllite, schist (SHIST), and gneiss (NYS). Slate and phyllite are commonly formed when shale, a fine-grained sedimentary rock, is exposed to an increase in temperature and pressure. The minerals in slate and phyllite are squeezed into flat, sheet-like layers. With increasing temperature and pressure, phyllite may become schist, a coarse-grained foliated rock. With further increases in temperature and pressure, the minerals in schist separate into alternating bands of light and dark minerals. Gneiss is a coarse-grained, foliated rock that forms from schist. Slate, phyllite, schist, and gneiss can all begin as shale, but they are very different rocks. Each rock forms under a certain range of temperatures and pressures and contains different minerals.

Schist

Gneiss

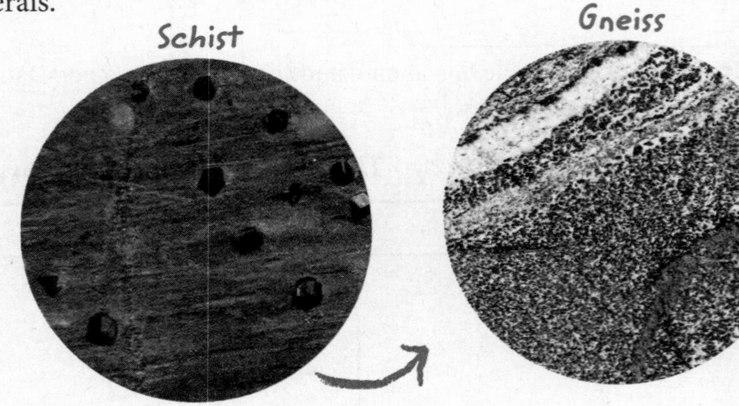

When shale is exposed to increasing temperature and pressure, different foliated metamorphic rocks form.

14 Describe What happens to the minerals as gneiss forms from schist?

____

____

Nonfoliated Metamorphic Rock

Metamorphic rocks that do not have mineral grains that are aligned in planes or bands are called *nonfoliated*. Nonfoliated metamorphic rocks are commonly made of one or only a few minerals. During metamorphism, mineral grains or crystals may change size or shape, and some may change into another mineral.

Two common nonfoliated metamorphic rocks are quartzite and marble. Quartzite forms when quartz sandstone is exposed to high temperature and pressure. This causes the sand grains to grow larger, and the spaces between the sand grains disappear. For that reason, quartzite is very hard and not easily broken down.

When limestone undergoes metamorphism, the limestone becomes marble. During the process of metamorphism, the calcite crystals in the marble grow larger than the calcite grains in the original limestone.

The mineral grains in quartzite (top) and crystals in marble (bottom) do not form bands.

Active Reading **15 Apply** What are two characteristics of nonfoliated metamorphic rocks?

____

____

Marble is a nonfoliated metamorphic rock that forms when limestone is metamorphosed. Marble is used to build monuments and statues.

Think Outside the Book **Inquiry**

16 Apply With a classmate, discuss how different types of rocks can be used as building or construction materials.

Visualize It!

Rock Classification

The table below describes the general composition and some common uses for each rock type shown. Read the descriptions, and study the images. Then answer the questions below.

IGNEOUS ROCKS

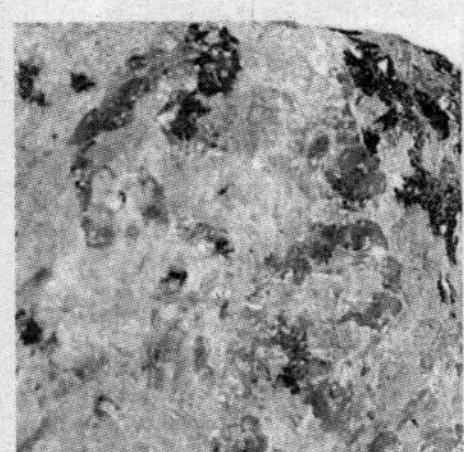

granite
- igneous intrusive rock composed mostly of quartz and feldspar; light in color
- commonly used as a building stone, such as facing stone on buildings, for countertops, and in statues

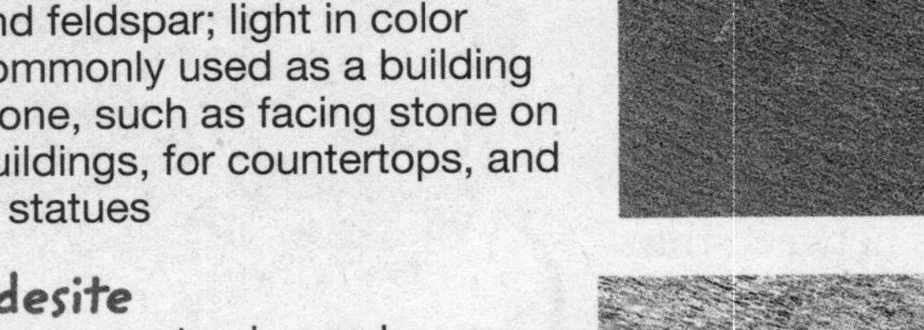

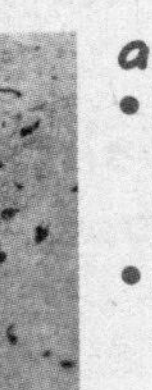

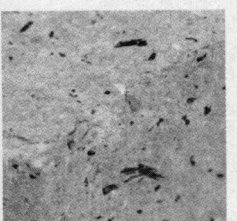

andesite
- igneous extrusive rock composed largely of feldspar; light in color
- commonly used in the construction of roads

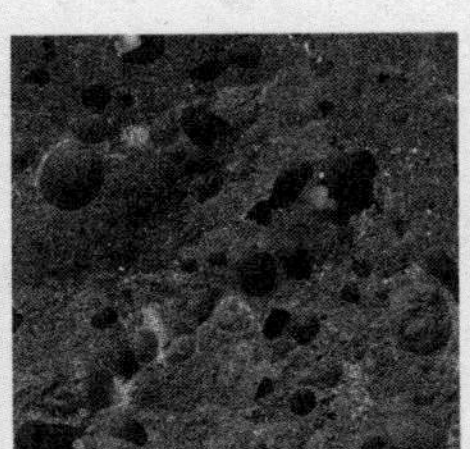

basalt
- igneous extrusive rock composed largely of dark minerals; typically brown to black in color
- commonly used to construct roads and railroads

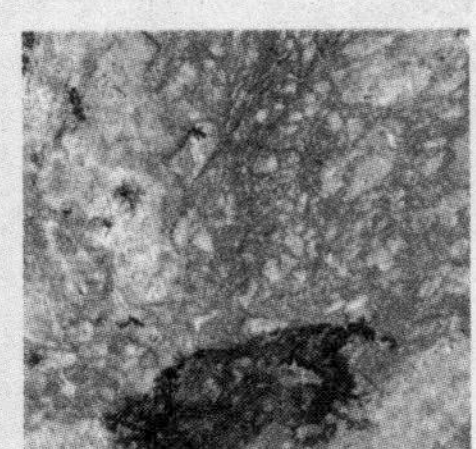

rhyolite
- igneous extrusive rock composed largely of quartz and feldspar; light in color
- commonly used in the construction of roads

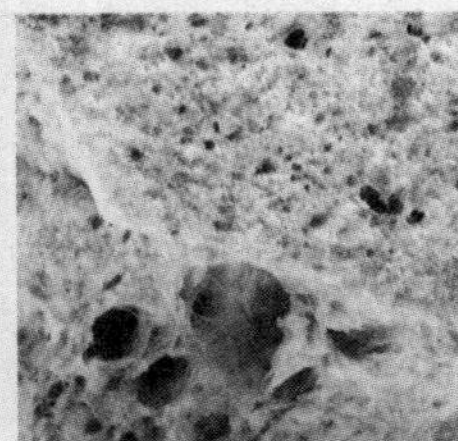

pumice
- igneous extrusive rock composed largely of silica; light in color; light enough to float on water
- commonly used in soaps and cleansers, concrete and plaster

obsidian
- igneous extrusive rock composed largely of silica; dark due todark-colored minerals distributed within
- commonly used to make jewelry and surgical instruments

METAMORPHIC ROCKS

slate
- foliated metamorphic rock commonly composed of clay minerals and micas; ranges from light gray to black in color; breaks into thin sheets
- commonly used as a roofing tile or for flooring

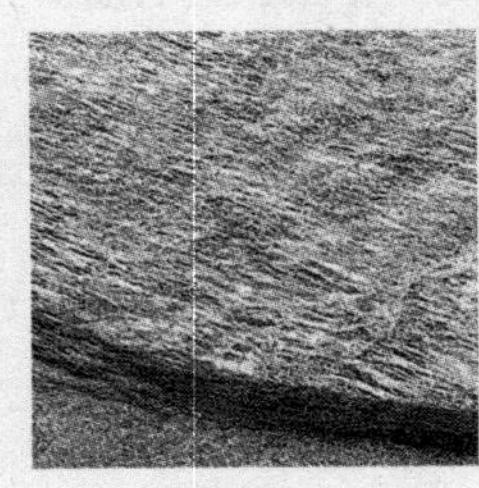

phyllite
- foliated metamorphic rock that breaks into thin sheets; composed mostly of quartz and mica; silvery luster
- commonly used for countertops

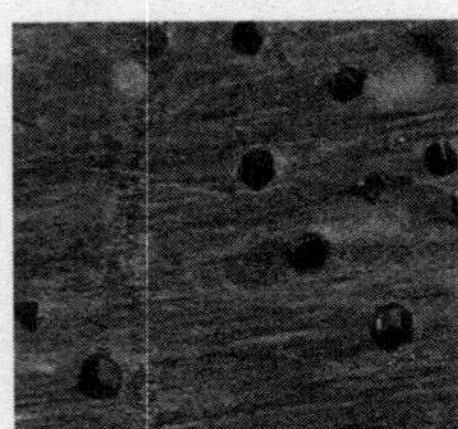

schist
- foliated metamorphic rock that can be split into thin layers due to the parallel arrangement of minerals
- commonly used for decorative stones in gardens

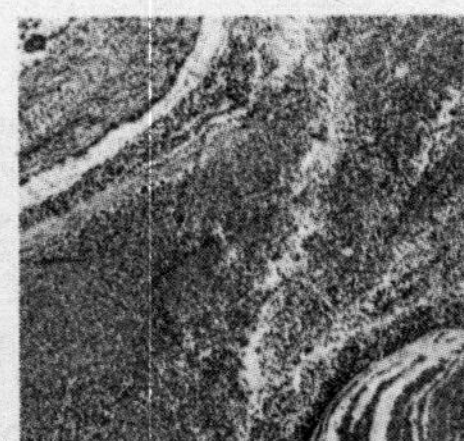

gneiss
- foliated metamorphic rock in which the mineral grains have been arranged into a banded structure
- common uses are in building, such as flooring, roof tiles, and facing stones on buildings

marble
- nonfoliated metamorphic rock composed of calcite or, less commonly, dolomite; light in color
- commonly used for building stone and statues

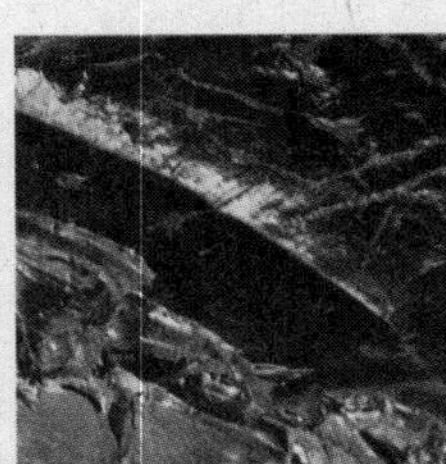

anthracite coal
- the only form of coal that is of metamorphic formation; has the highest carbon content and fewest impurities of any form of coal; metallic luster
- commonly burned to produce electrical energy

SEDIMENTARY ROCKS

shale
- clastic sedimentary rock composed of silt and clay; forms thin layers along which it splits
- dark, organic shale contains oil and natural gas; can be used to produce clay and cement

sandstone
- clastic sedimentary rock that is made of sand grains that have been cemented together; often stained red by iron oxide
- commonly used as a construction material for buildings

conglomerate
- clastic sedimentary rock composed of rounded rocks of different sizes that are cemented together
- commonly used for building construction and monuments

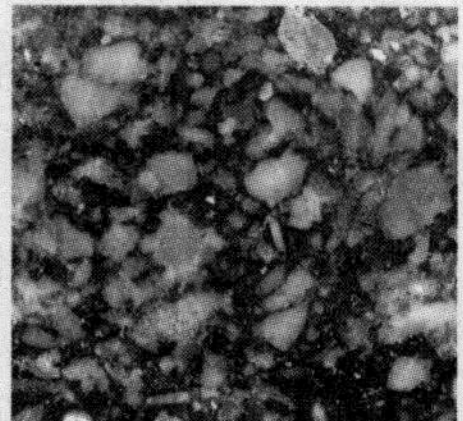

breccia
- clastic sedimentary rock composed of angular rocks of different sizes that are cemented together
- commonly used for building construction and as decorations for use inside of buildings

limestone
- chemical sedimentary rock composed almost entirely of the mineral calcite
- many common uses, such as the construction of buildings, the production of cement, fertilizer, glass, and paint

coquina
- variety of limestone composed of shell fragments cemented together
- commonly used in the production of fertilizer, as paving material, and as a building stone

chert
- variety of hard, siliceous sedimentary rock; composed of silica microcrystals; breaks with a conchoidal fracture; occurs commonly as nodules
- in the past, chert was used for weapons and utensils

bituminous coal
- carbon-rich, banded sedimentary rock that is found in veins in sedimentary layers; the most common form of coal found in the U.S.
- commonly burned to produce electrical energy

17 Compare Pumice and obsidian are both forms of volcanic glass. What are one similarity and one difference in the composition of these two rocks?

18 Contrast Anthracite and bituminous coal are two varieties of coal that have the same use. What are two differences between anthracite and bituminous coal?

19 Infer Of the rock types shown on these two pages, what factor usually determines the color of the rock?

20 Justify Suppose you are designing a new building. Identify three rock types you may incorporate into your design, and describe how you would use them.

Visual Summary

To complete this summary, fill in the blanks. Then, use the key below to check your answers. You can use this page to review the main concepts of the lesson.

Three Classes of Rock

Sedimentary rock may form from layers of sediment that are cemented together.

21 Sedimentary rocks can be classified into three groups:

______________________________,

______________________, and

____

Igneous rock forms from magma or lava that has cooled and hardened.

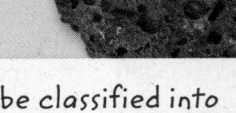

22 Igneous rocks can be classified into two groups:

____

and ______________________________

Metamorphic rock forms under high temperature or pressure deep within Earth's crust.

23 Metamorphic rocks can be classified into two groups:

____

and ______________________________

Answers: 21 clastic, chemical, organic; 22 intrusive, extrusive; 23 foliated, nonfoliated

24 Synthesize While hiking in the mountains, you see a large outcrop of marble. Describe one process by which the metamorphic rock marble forms from the sedimentary rock limestone.

Lesson 3

Lesson Review

Vocabulary

Fill in the blank with the term that best completes the following sentences.

1 Sedimentary rocks that are made up of large pebbles and stones have a coarse-grained

____

2 Most granite has a _______________ of quartz, mica, and feldspar.

3 _______________ can be considered to be mixtures of minerals.

Key Concepts

4 Summarize How does the cooling rate of magma or lava affect the texture of the igneous rock that forms?

5 Describe How does clastic sedimentary rock form?

6 Explain What is the difference between foliated and nonfoliated metamorphic rock?

Critical Thinking

Use this photo to answer the following questions.

7 Identify What type of rock is shown here? How do you know?

8 Describe How did this rock form?

9 Infer Suppose this rock were exposed to high temperature and pressure. What would most likely happen to it?

10 Infer What information can a foliated metamorphic rock provide you about the conditions under which it formed?

My Notes

Lesson 5

Soil Formation

ESSENTIAL QUESTION

How does soil form?

By the end of this lesson, you should be able to describe the physical and chemical characteristics of soil layers and identify the factors that affect soil formation, including the action of living things.

Living things, such as this shelf fungus **(Laetiporus sulphureus)**, help to break down organic matter. The organic matter mixes with minerals, weathered sediment, water, and air to form soil.

OHIO 6.ESS.4 Soil is unconsolidated material that contains nutrient matter and weathered rock.

OHIO 6.ESS.5 Rocks, minerals and soils have common and practical uses.

Lesson Labs

Quick Labs
- Observing Life in Soil
- Modeling a Soil Profile
- Observing the Impact of Earthworms on Soil

Field Lab
- Comparing Soil Characteristics

Engage Your Brain

1 Predict Check T or F to show whether you think each statement is true or false.

T	F	
☐	☐	Soil contains air and water.
☐	☐	Soil does not contain living things.
☐	☐	Soils are the same from place to place.
☐	☐	Climate can affect how fertile soils are.

2 Explain How might the burrows formed by ants affect the soil?

Active Reading

3 Apply Many scientific words, such as *weather*, have more than one meaning. Use context clues to write your own definition for each meaning of the word *weather*.

Example sentence
The weather outside is nice.

weather:

Example sentence
Wind, water, and plant roots weather rock into sediment.

weather:

Vocabulary Terms

- soil
- humus
- soil profile
- soil horizon

4 Apply As you learn the definition of each vocabulary term in this lesson, write your own definition or sketch to help you remember the meaning of the term.

The Dirt on Soil

What causes soil to form?

Active Reading

5 Identify As you read, underline the different substances that make up soil.

Soil is important to your life. You walk on grass that is rooted in soil. You eat foods that need soil in order to grow. But what exactly is soil? Where does it come from? How does it form?

A scientist might define **soil** as a loose mixture of small rock fragments, organic matter, water, and air that can support the growth of vegetation. The very first step in soil formation is the weathering of *parent rock.* Parent rock is the source of inorganic soil particles. Soil forms directly above the parent rock. Soil either develops here, or it is eroded and transported to another location.

Weathering of Parent Rock

Weathering breaks down parent rock into smaller and smaller pieces. These pieces of rock eventually become very small particles that are mixed in with organic matter to form soil. The process of soil formation can take a very long time. The amount of time it takes depends on many factors that you will learn about later in this lesson.

Soil formation begins when parent rock weathers into small fragments.
Plant roots grow and can break down sediment even further.
Burrowing animals increase the rate of weathering. They mix the soil, allowing more air to enter. They bring sediment to the surface where it is weathered more quickly by water, wind, and organisms.

Decomposition and Mixing by Living Things

Some microorganisms, such as bacteria and fungi, are decomposers that live in soil. These tiny decomposers perform the important task of breaking down the remains of plants and animals. These remains are decayed organic matter called **humus**. Humus is found in the top layer of soils. It is important because it contains nutrients that plants need to grow. Plants take up these nutrients through their roots. When plants or animals die, they are broken down by decomposers, and the nutrients are returned to the soil.

Larger animals, such as earthworms and moles, also live in soil. They loosen and mix the soil as they burrow through it. The mixing increases the amount of air in soil and improves the ability of soil to drain water.

6 Apply How might a fallen leaf eventually become part of soil?

7 Summarize How do decomposers and plants cycle nutrients in soil?

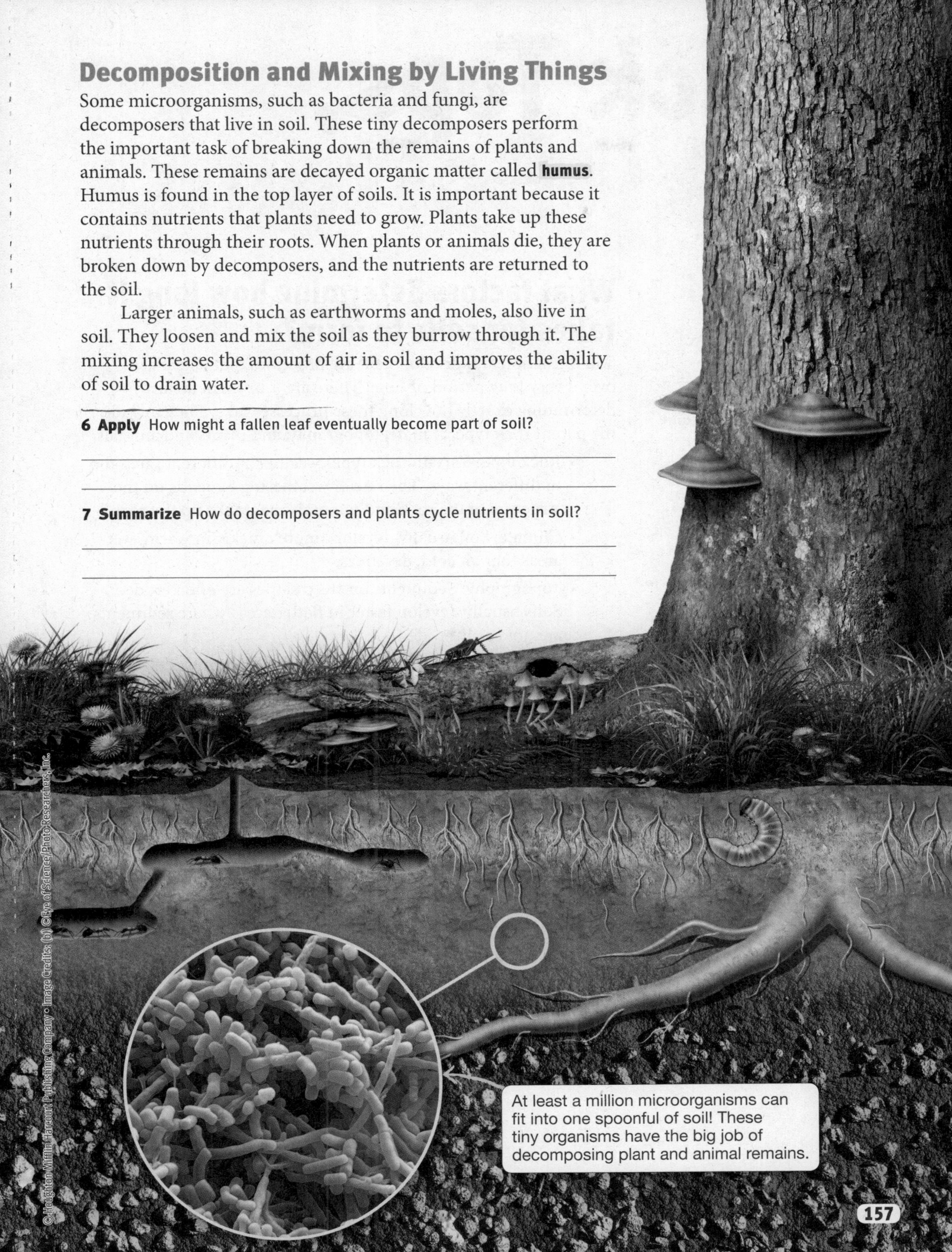

At least a million microorganisms can fit into one spoonful of soil! These tiny organisms have the big job of decomposing plant and animal remains.

Thick Tops, Rocky Bottoms

What factors determine how long it takes for soils to form?

Active Reading

8 Identify As you read, underline the factors that affect how long it takes for soils to form and develop.

Soil formation and development are processes that take place over a very long period of time. There are four main factors in determining exactly how long these processes take. They include the parent rock type, climate, topography, and plants and animals.

- Rock type: Certain rock types weather at different rates and in different ways. The rate of weathering depends on the structure of the rock and minerals that make up the rock.
- Climate: Soil usually develops more quickly in warm, wet areas than in cold, dry areas.
- Topography: Sediments on steep slopes are often eroded. Soils usually develop faster in flatter areas where sediments are not easily eroded.
- Plants and animals: Plant roots hold sediments in place, allowing soil to develop quickly. Areas teeming with life have higher rates of decomposition and mixing. Soils tend to develop more quickly in these areas. Without a lot of plants and animals, soil tends to develop slowly.

9 Compare List some possible characteristics of an area where soils would develop quickly. Then do the same for an area where soils would develop slowly.

Area where Soils Develop Quickly	Area where Soils Develop Slowly

What are the main soil horizons?

Picture the rich, dark soil in a garden. Now imagine what the soil looks like as you dig deeper beneath the surface. Does the soil look and feel the same as you dig deeper? A vertical section of soil that shows all of the different layers is a **soil profile**. Each layer in the soil profile that has different physical properties is called a **soil horizon**. The main horizons include the A horizon, B horizon, and C horizon. There are many other horizons as well.

A Horizon

The A horizon is at the top of the soil profile. It is often referred to as *topsoil*. Decomposers live in this horizon, so it has the most decayed organic matter. This humus gives it a dark color. Plant roots break up fragments and animals burrow and mix the the soil. These processes increase the rate of weathering, so the A horizon is usually the most developed. As you'll learn later in this lesson, rich soils generally have high amounts of humus. Dead leaves, branches, and other organic matter may cover the surface of the A horizon.

B Horizon

The B horizon lies below the A horizon. It is not as developed as the A horizon and has less humus. Following precipitation events, water seeps down through the A horizon. Water carries material, such as iron minerals and clay, from the A horizon down to the B horizon. This is known as *leaching*. The leached materials commonly give the B horizon a reddish or brownish color.

C Horizon

The C horizon lies below the B horizon. It is the least-developed soil horizon. It contains the largest rock fragments and usually has no organic matter. The C horizon lies directly above the parent rock. Recall that this is the weathered rock from which the soil was formed.

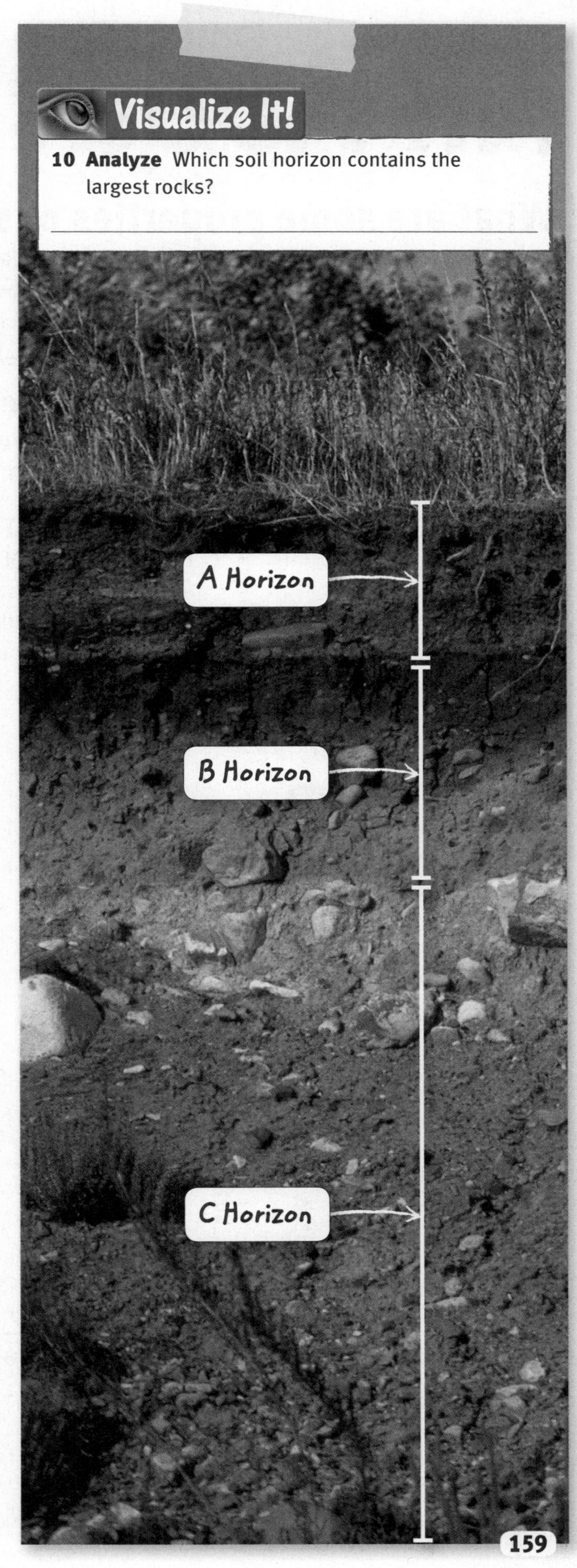

All About Soil

What are some properties of soil?

Plants grow well in some soils and poorly in others. Soils look and feel different. They also contain different minerals and particles. Soil properties are used to classify different soils. These properties include soil texture, color, chemistry, pore space, and fertility.

Active Reading

11 Identify As you read, underline the three kinds of soil particles.

Soil Texture

The term *soil texture* is a property that describes the relative amounts of differently sized soil particles. Soil particles are classified as sand, silt, or clay. Most soils are a mixture of all three. Sand is the largest particle, ranging from 0.05 mm to 2 mm. Soils containing a lot of sand feel coarse. Silt particles are smaller than sand particles. They range from 0.002 mm to 0.05 mm. Silty soils have a smooth, silky feel. At less than 0.002 mm, clay particles are the smallest soil particles. Clayey soils feel very smooth and are usually sticky when they are wet.

Visualize It!

12 Distinguish The last space in each row contains three circles. Fill in the circle that shows the correct relative size of the particle shown in that row.

Particle	Size Range	Relative Size
sand	0.05 mm–2 mm	○ ○ ○
silt	0.002 mm–0.05 mm	○ ○ ○
clay	less than 0.002 mm	○ ○ ○

Soil Color

Soils can be black, brown, red, orange, yellow, gray, and even white. Soil color is a clue to the types and amounts of minerals and organic matter in the soil. Iron minerals make soil orange or reddish. Soils that contain a lot of humus are black or brown. Color can also be a clue about the environmental conditions. Gray soil can indicate that an area is often wet and has poor drainage.

Soils are usually a mixture of colors, such as reddish brown. Scientists use the Munsell System of Color Notation to describe soil colors. The system uses a book of color chips, much like the paint chips found in a paint store. Scientists compare a soil to the color chips in the book to classify soils.

Think Outside the Book

13 Apply Find out about the qualities of your local soil. Describe its texture, color, chemistry, pore space, and fertility. Choose one of these activities to present your description: draw a poster or diagram, create a brochure, or write a poem.

Soil and Climate

Climate can affect how soil forms in different regions on Earth. Warm, rainy regions produce tropical soils and temperate soils. Dry regions produce desert soils and arctic soils.

Tropical Soils form in warm, wet regions. Heavy rains wash away and leach soils, leaving only a thin layer of humus. Soil development is fast in these regions. They are not suitable for growing most crops.

Desert Soils form in dry regions. These soils are shallow and contain little organic matter. Because of the low rainfall, chemical weathering and soil development is slow in desert regions.

Temperate Soils form in regions with moderate rainfall and temperatures. Some temperate soils are dark-colored, rich in organic matter and minerals, and good for growing crops.

Arctic Soils form in cold, dry regions where chemical weathering is slow. They typically do not have well-developed horizons. Arctic soils may contain many rock fragments.

Soil Chemistry

Soil pH is determined by the combination of minerals, sediment, and organic matter found in soil. The pH of soil is a measure of how acidic or basic a soil is. The pH is based on a scale of 0 to 14. If pH is less than 7, the soil is acidic. If pH is above 7, the soil is basic. In the middle of the pH scale is 7, which means the soil is neither acidic nor basic; it is neutral. Scientists measure soil pH to determine whether the soil can support different plants. For example, soybeans grow best in a soil with a pH between 6.0 and 7.0. Peanuts thrive when the pH of soil is between 5.3 and 6.6.

Farmers can adjust the pH of soil to meet the needs of their plants. They can add lime to make acidic soils more basic. They can add acids to make basic soils more acidic.

The pH of a soil can be tested to make sure it will support the plants being grown.

Pore Space

Pore space describes the spaces between soil particles. Water and air are found in the pore spaces of soils. Water and air move easily through soils with many well-connected pore spaces. Soils with this property are well-drained and typically good for plant growth.

Plants need both water and air to grow. About 25 to 60 percent of the volume of most soils is pore space. The best soil for growing most plants has about 50 percent of its volume as pore space, with that volume equally divided between water and air.

Visualize It!

14 Describe Write a caption that describes the pore space for each diagram below.

A ______________________________

B ______________________________

Soil Fertility

Soil fertility describes how well a soil can support plant growth. This quality is affected by factors that include the climate of the area; the amount of humus, minerals, and nutrients in the soil; and the topography of the area.

Fertile soils are often found in areas with moderate rainfall and temperatures. Soils with a lot of humus and the proper proportions of minerals and nutrients have high soil fertility. Soils found in dry areas or on steep hillsides often have low fertility. Farmers can add chemical fertilizers or organic material to soils to improve soil fertility. They also can grow crops, such as legumes, to restore certain nutrients to soil or leave cropland unplanted for a season to replenish its fertility.

Active Reading **15 Apply** What could you do to improve the fertility of the soil in your garden?

____

____

This meadow's bluebonnets thrive in well-drained soil. Bluebonnets also grow best in slightly basic soils.

Inquiry

16 Infer Use what you have learned to infer why Soils A and B have the following soils properties.

Soil Properties	Possible Reasons for Soil Properties
Soil A is black, well-drained, and good for growing plants.	
Soil B feels smooth and sticky and is gray in color.	

Visual Summary

To complete this summary, fill in the blanks with the correct word. Then use the key below to check your answers. You can use this page to review the main concepts of the lesson.

Soil Formation

Soil formation involves weathering of rock, addition of organic material, and actions by plants and animals that live in the soil.

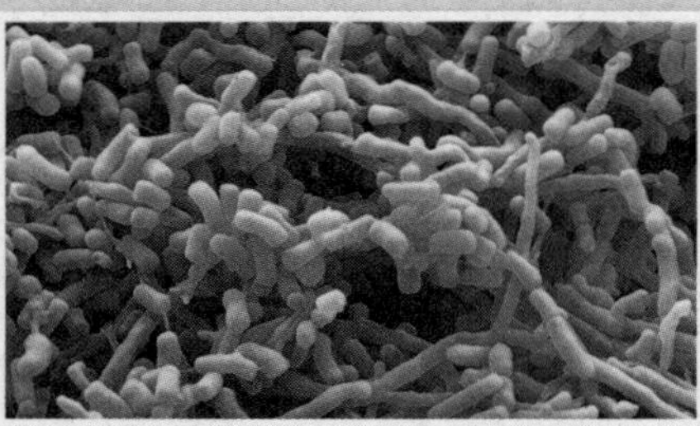

17 In general, soils in cold, dry areas will take ________________ to develop than soils in warm, wet areas.

Characteristics of soil include texture, color, chemistry, pore space, and soil fertility.

19 ________________ describes the spaces between soil particles.

A soil profile commonly has the A horizon, B horizon, and C horizon. They each have distinct physical characteristics.

18 The ________________ contains the most organic matter; leaching carries minerals and humus down to the ________________.

Answers: 17 longer; 18 A horizon, B horizon; 19 Pore space

20 **Summarize** Describe how living things can affect the different characteristics and development of soil.

Lesson Review

Vocabulary

Draw a line to connect the following terms to their definitions.

1 soil

2 humus

3 soil profile

4 soil horizon

A decomposed organic matter

B layer of soil with distinct physical properties in a soil profile

C vertical section showing the soil horizons

D mixture of weathered sediment, organic material, water, and air

Key Concepts

5 Identify What is the first step of soil formation?

6 Explain What are the main factors that determine how long it takes for a soil to form and develop?

7 Describe How would a soil that developed in a warm, wet place be different than one that developed in a hot, dry place?

8 Compare How might a dark colored, coarse soil differ from a reddish, smooth soil?

Critical Thinking

Use this table to answer the following question.

Climate Data for Locations A and B

	Average Yearly Temperature (°C)	Average Yearly Precipitation (cm)
Location A	27	190
Location B	3	26

9 Analyze In which location would soils develop faster? Explain.

10 Infer Which soil would you expect to be better developed: the soil on a hillside or the soil on a valley floor? Why?

11 Synthesize Describe the cycle that involves soil, decomposers, and other living things.

My Notes

Lesson 6

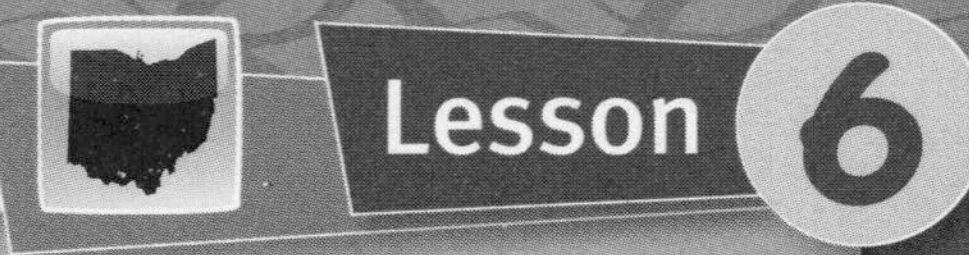

Nonrenewable Energy Resources

ESSENTIAL QUESTION

How do we use nonrenewable energy resources?

By the end of this lesson, you should be able to describe how humans use energy resources and the role of nonrenewable energy resources in society.

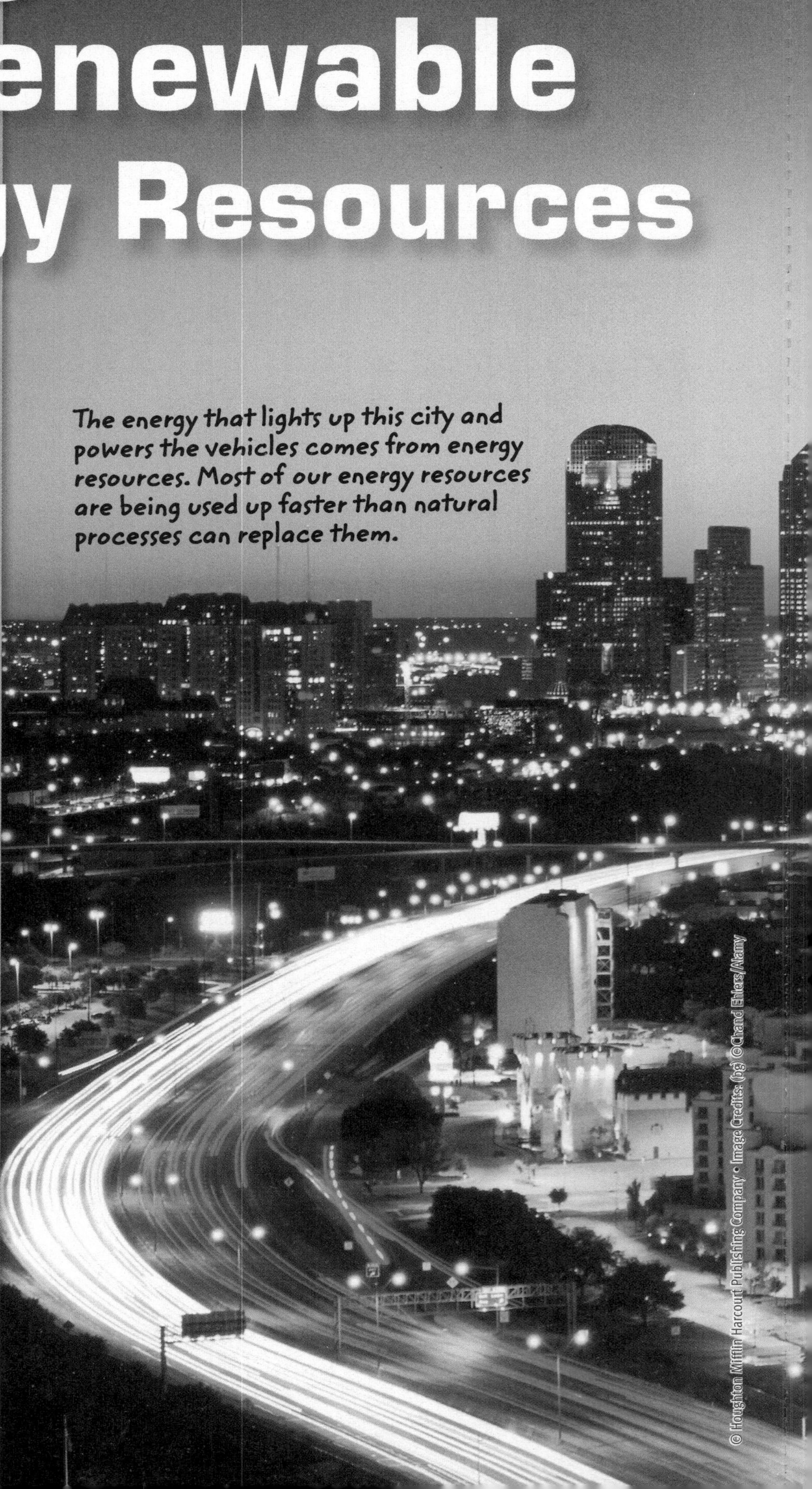

The energy that lights up this city and powers the vehicles comes from energy resources. Most of our energy resources are being used up faster than natural processes can replace them.

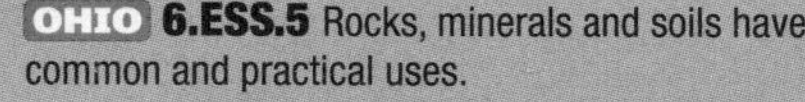

OHIO 6.ESS.5 Rocks, minerals and soils have common and practical uses.

OHIO 6.SIA.6 Think critically and logically to connect evidence and explanations.

OHIO 6.SIA.7 Recognize and analyze alternative explanations and predictions.

Lesson Labs

Quick Labs
- Modeling Nonrenewable Resources
- Modeling Nuclear Fission

Engage Your Brain

1 Identify Unscramble the letters below to find substances that are nonrenewable resources.

ALCO ______________________

AUNTRLA SGA ______________________

NUUIMAR ______________________

MLPEOUTRE ______________________

2 Describe Write your own caption for this photo.

____

____

____

Active Reading

3 Synthesize Many English words have their roots in other languages. Use the Latin word below to make an educated guess about the meaning of the word *fission*.

Latin word	Meaning
fissus	to split

Example sentence
An atomic nucleus can undergo fission.

fission:

____

____

Vocabulary Terms

- **energy resource**
- **fossil fuel**
- **nuclear energy**
- **fission**

4 Identify This list contains the vocabulary terms you'll learn in this lesson. As you read, circle the definition of each term.

Be Resourceful!

What are the two main types of nonrenewable energy resources?

An **energy resource** is a natural resource that humans use to generate energy and can be renewable or nonrenewable. *Renewable resources* are replaced by natural processes at least as quickly as they are used. *Nonrenewable resources* are used up faster than they can be replaced. Most of the energy used in the United States comes from nonrenewable resources.

Fossil Fuels

A **fossil fuel** is a nonrenewable energy resource that forms from the remains of organisms that lived long ago. Fossil fuels release energy when they are burned. This energy can be converted to electricity or used to power engines. Fossil fuels are the most commonly used energy resource because they are relatively inexpensive to locate and process.

Nuclear Fuel

The energy released when the nuclei of atoms are split or combined is called **nuclear energy**. This energy can be obtained by two kinds of nuclear reactions—fusion and fission. Today's nuclear power plants use fission, because the technology for fusion power plants does not currently exist. The most common nuclear fuel is uranium. Uranium is obtained by mining and processing uranium ore, which is a nonrenewable resource.

Do the Math

You Try It

Nonrenewable Energy Resources Consumed in the U.S. in 2009

Fossil Fuels 90.37%
Nuclear Fuel 9.63%

5 Calculate In 2009, 86.8 quadrillion BTUs of the energy used in the United States was produced from nonrenewable energy resources. Using the graph above, calculate how much of this energy was produced from nuclear fuel.

____

6 Compare Fill in the Venn diagram to compare and contrast fossil fuels and nuclear fuel.

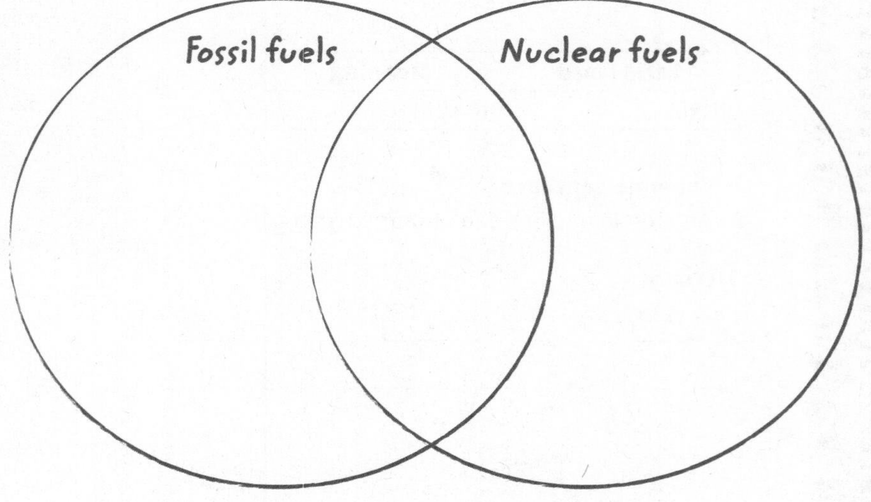

What are the three main types of fossil fuels?

All living things contain the element carbon. Fossil fuels form from the remains of living things, so they also contain carbon. Most of this carbon is in the form of hydrocarbons, which are compounds made of hydrogen and carbon. Fossil fuels can be liquids, gases, or solids. Fossil fuels include petroleum, natural gas, and coal.

Active Reading **7 Identify** As you read, underline the state of matter for each fossil fuel.

Petroleum

Petroleum, or *crude oil,* is a liquid mixture of complex hydrocarbon compounds. Crude oil is extracted from the ground by drilling then processed for use. This process, called *refining,* separates the crude oil into different products such as gasoline, kerosene, and diesel fuel. More than 35 percent of the world's energy comes from crude oil products. Crude oil is also used to make products such as ink, bubble gum, and plastics.

This crude oil will be refined into gasoline, diesel fuel, heating oil, kerosene, and other products.

Natural Gas

Natural gas is a mixture of gaseous hydrocarbons. Most natural gas is used for heating and cooking, but some is used to generate electricity. Also, some vehicles use natural gas as fuel.

Methane is the main component of natural gas. Butane and propane can also be separated from natural gas. Butane and propane are used as fuel for camp stoves and outdoor grills. Some rural homes also use propane as a heating fuel.

Natural gas is a popular fuel for cooking because it is inexpensive.

Coal

The fossil fuel most widely used for generating electrical power is a solid called coal. Coal was once used to heat homes and for transportation. In fact, many trains in the 1800s and early 1900s were pulled by coal-burning steam locomotives. Now, most people use gasoline for transportation fuel. But more than half of our nation's electricity comes from coal-burning power plants.

Coal is a fossil fuel often used to generate electricity.

How do fossil fuels form?

How might a sunny day 200 million years ago relate to your life today? If you traveled to school by bus or car, you likely used energy from sunlight that warmed Earth that long ago.

Fossil fuels form over millions of years from the buried remains of ancient organisms. Fossil fuels differ in the kinds of organisms from which they form and in how they form. This process is continuing, too. The fossil fuels forming today will be available for use in a few million years!

Petroleum and Natural Gas Form from Marine Organisms

Petroleum and natural gas form mainly from the remains of microscopic sea organisms. When these organisms die, their remains sink and settle on the ocean floor. There, the dead organisms are gradually buried by sediment. The sediment is compacted by more layers of dead organisms and sediment. Over time the sediment layers become layers of rock.

Over millions of years, heat and pressure turn the remains of the organisms into petroleum and natural gas. The petroleum and natural gas, along with groundwater, flow into pores in the rock. A rock with pores is a *permeable rock*. Permeable rocks become reservoirs where the petroleum and natural gas are trapped and concentrated over time. Humans can extract the fuels from these reservoirs.

Think Outside the Book *Inquiry*

8 Apply With a classmate, discuss how the process of petroleum formation might affect oil availability in the future.

Petroleum and Natural Gas Formation

1 Microscopic marine organisms die and settle to the bottom of the sea.

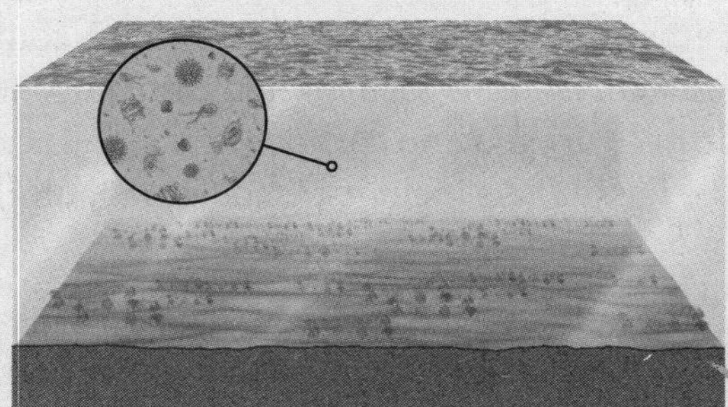

2 Layers of sediment slowly bury the dead marine organisms.

3 Heat and pressure on these layers slowly turn the remains of these organisms into petroleum and natural gas.

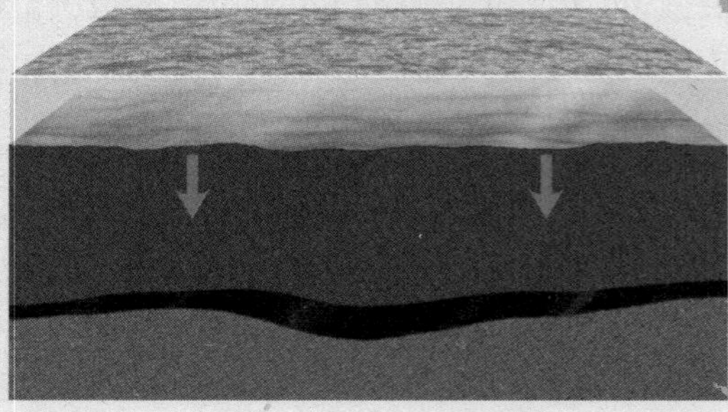

4 Petroleum and natural gas flow through permeable rocks, where they are trapped and become concentrated into reservoirs.

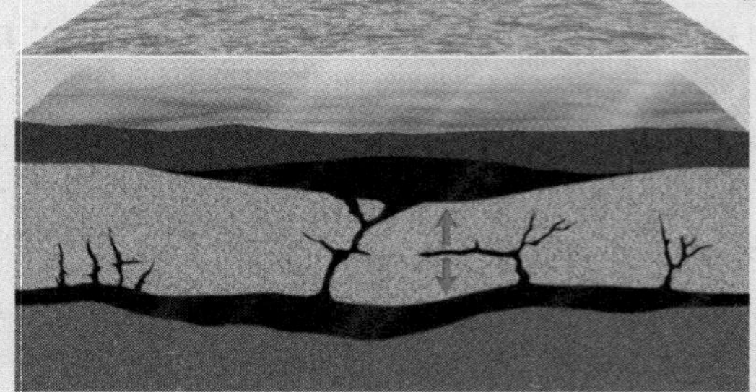

Coal Formation

1 Peat Partially decayed swamp plants sink and change into peat.

2 Lignite As sediment buries the peat, increases in temperature and pressure change peat to lignite.

3 Bituminous Coal As sediment builds, increased temperature and pressure change lignite to bituminous coal.

4 Anthracite As sediments accumulate and temperature and pressure rise, bituminous coal changes to anthracite.

Coal Forms from Plant Remains

Active Reading **9 Identify** As you read, underline the factors that convert the buried plants into coal.

Coal is formed over millions of years from the remains of swamp plants. When the plants die, they sink to the swamp floor. Low oxygen levels in the water keep many plants from decaying and allow the process of coal formation to begin. Today's swamp plants may eventually turn into coal millions of years from now.

The first step of coal formation is plant matter changing into peat. Peat is made mostly of plant material and water. Peat is not coal. In some parts of the world, peat is dried and burned for warmth or used as fuel. Peat that is buried by layers of sediment can turn into coal after millions of years.

Over time, pressure and high temperature force water and gases out of the peat. The peat gradually becomes harder, and its carbon content increases. The amount of heat and pressure determines the type of coal that forms. Lignite forms first, followed by bituminous coal and, finally, anthracite. Anthracite is highly valued because it has the highest carbon content and gives off the most energy as heat when burned.

Today, all three types of coal are mined around the world. When burned, coal releases energy as heat and pollutes the air. The greater the carbon content of the coal, the fewer pollutants are released and the cleaner the coal burns.

Visualize It!

10 Compare What is similar about the way petroleum and coal form? What is different?

Power Trip

How are fossil fuels used as energy sources?

11 Identify As you read, underline the uses of fossil fuels.

In the United States, petroleum fuels are mainly used for transportation and heating. Airplanes, trains, boats, and cars all use petroleum for energy. Some people also use petroleum as a heating fuel. There are some oil-fired power plants in the United States, but most are found in other parts of the world.

Natural gas can be used as transportation fuel but is mainly used for heating and cooking. The use of natural gas as a source of electrical power is increasing. The U.S. Department of Energy projects that most power plants in the near future will use natural gas. Today, coal is mainly used in the U.S. to generate electricity, which we use for lighting and to power appliances and technology.

Burning coal heats water to produce steam. The steam turns the turbines to generate electricity. Scrubbers and filters in the smokestack help reduce air pollution.

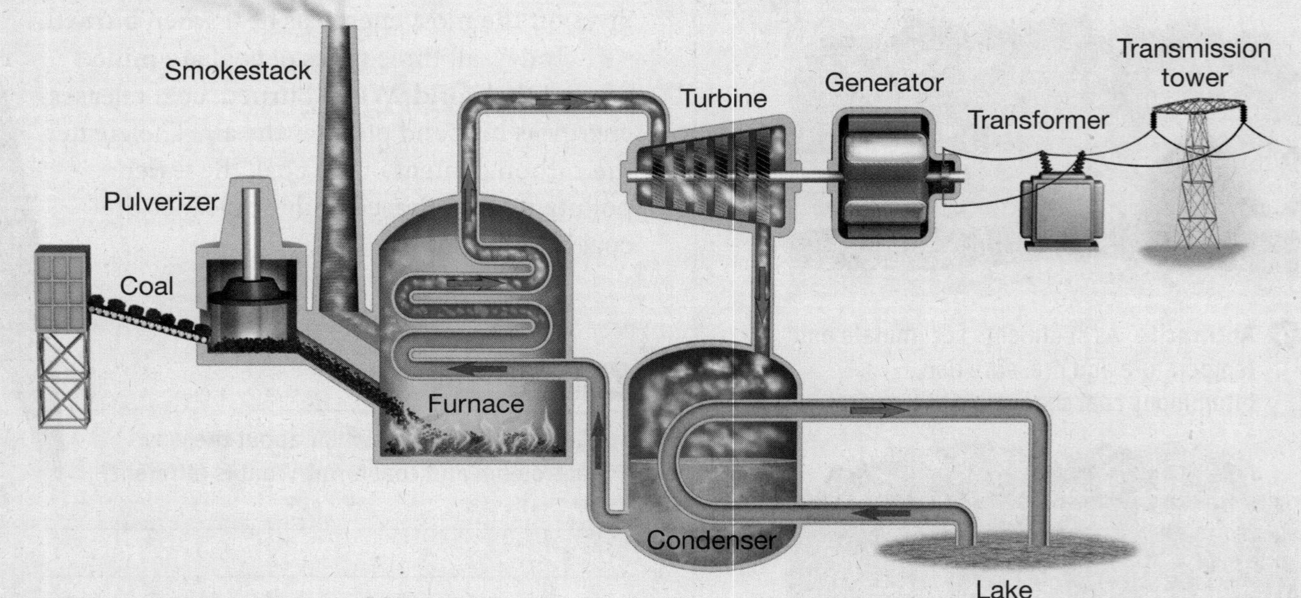

How is energy produced from nuclear fuels?

During **fission**, the nuclei of radioactive atoms are split into two or more fragments. A small particle called a neutron hits and splits an atom. This process releases large amounts of energy as heat and radiation. Fission also releases more neutrons that bombard other atoms. The process repeats as a chain reaction. Fission takes place inside a reactor core. Fuel rods containing uranium, shown in green below, provide the material for the chain reaction. Control rods that absorb neutrons are used to regulate the chain reaction. The energy is released, which is used to generate electrical power. A closed reactor system contains the radioactivity. Nuclear wastes are contained separately for disposal.

During nuclear reactions, energy in the form of heat is released, which turns water into steam. Steam turns the turbines to generate electricity.

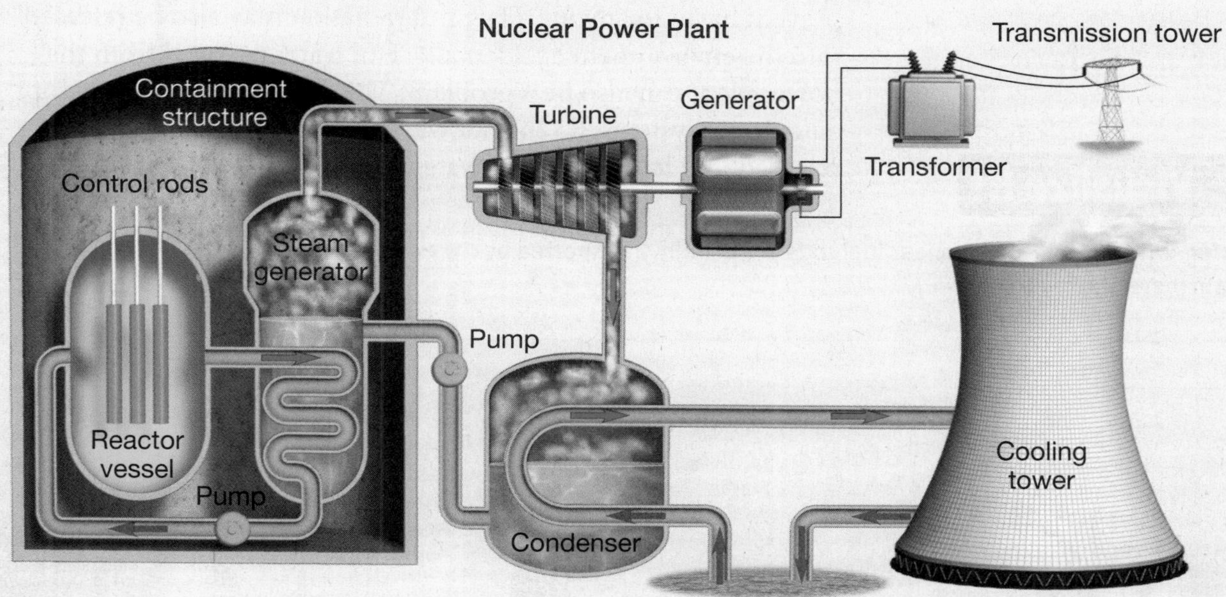

12 Compare How are the two types of power plants similar? How are they different?

Similar

Different

The Pros and Cons

How can we evaluate nonrenewable energy resources?

There are advantages and disadvantages to using nonrenewable energy resources. Nonrenewable resources provide much of the energy that humans need to power transportation, warm homes, and produce electricity relatively cheaply. But the methods of obtaining and using these resources can have negative effects on the environment.

Active Reading

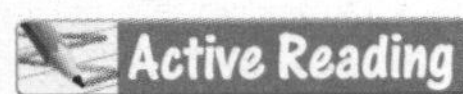

13 Identify As you read, underline the effects that nuclear power plants have on their surroundings.

The Pros and Cons of Nuclear Fuel

Nuclear fission produces a large amount of energy and does not cause air pollution because no fuel is burned. Mining uranium also does not usually result in massive strip mines or large loss of habitats.

However, nuclear power does have drawbacks. Nuclear power plants produce dangerous wastes that remain radioactive for thousands of years. So the waste must be specially stored to prevent harm to anyone. Harmful radiation may also be released into the environment accidentally. Hot water released from the power plant can also be a problem. This heated water can disrupt aquatic ecosystems. So the hot water must be cooled before it is released into local bodies of water.

Visualize It!

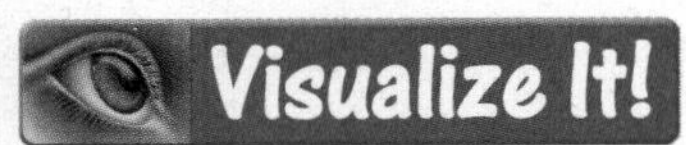

14 Infer Why do you think nuclear fuel rods are usually transported by train instead of by trucks?

____

____

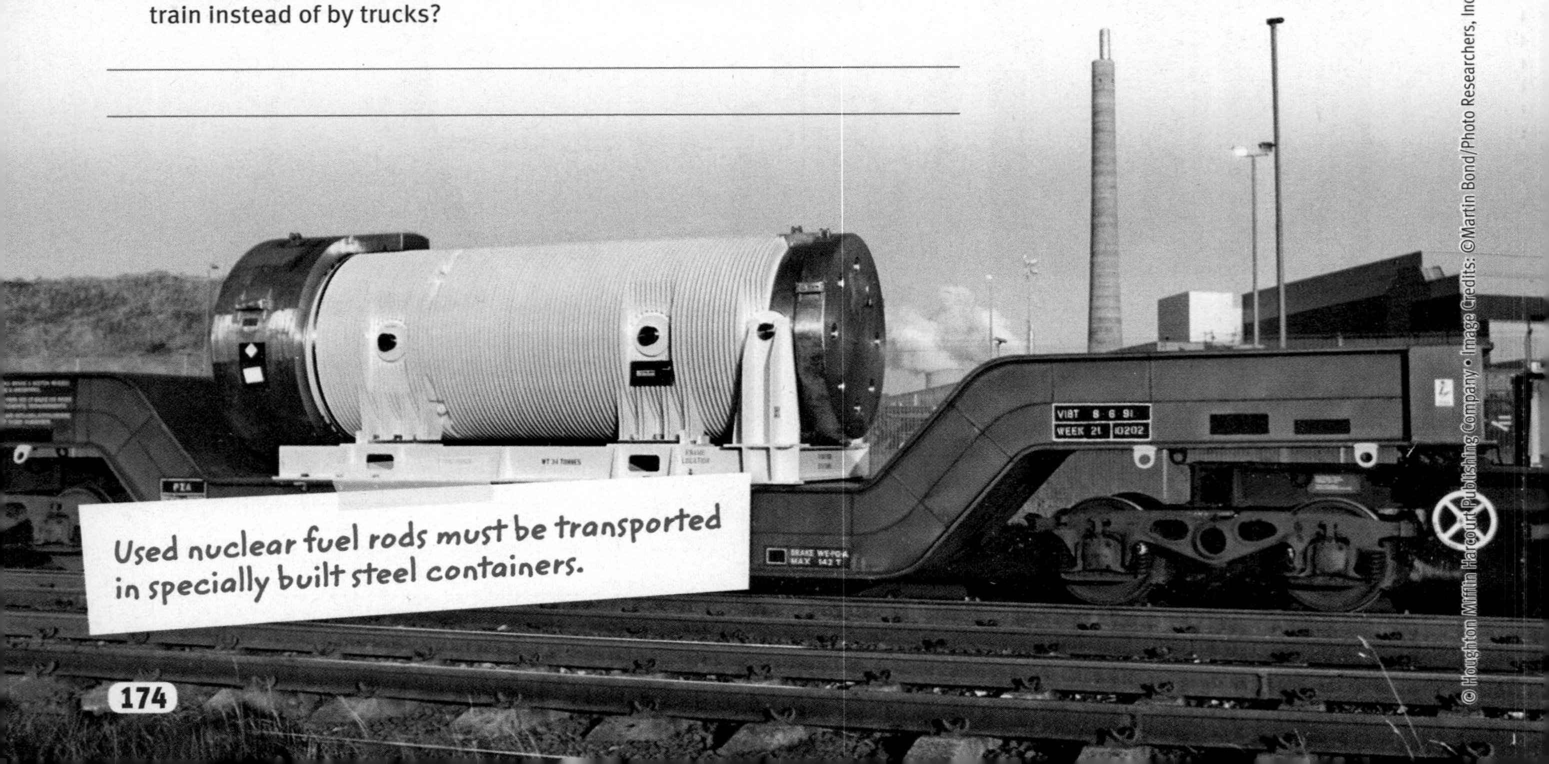

Used nuclear fuel rods must be transported in specially built steel containers.

The Pros and Cons of Fossil Fuels

Fossil fuels are relatively inexpensive to obtain and use. However, there are problems associated with their use. Burning coal can release sulfur dioxide, which combines with moisture in the air to form acid rain. Acid rain causes damage to structures and the environment. Coal mining also disturbs habitats, lowers water tables, and pollutes water.

Environmental problems are also associated with using oil. In 2010, a blown oil well spilled an estimated 200 million gallons of crude oil in the Gulf of Mexico for 86 days. The environmental costs may continue for years.

Burning fossil fuels can cause smog, especially in cities with millions of vehicles. Smog is a brownish haze that can cause respiratory problems and contribute to acid rain. Burning fossil fuels also releases carbon dioxide into the atmosphere. Increases in atmospheric carbon dioxide can lead to global warming.

Some coal is mined by removing the tops of mountains to expose the coal. This damages habitats and can cause water pollution as well.

15 Evaluate In the chart below, list the advantages and disadvantages of using nuclear fuel and fossil fuels.

Type of fuel	Pros	Cons
nuclear fuel		
fossil fuels		

Visual Summary

To complete this summary, check the box that indicates true or false. Then use the key below to check your answers. You can use this page to review the main concepts of the lesson.

Nonrenewable Energy Resources

Nuclear fuel is an energy resource that undergoes the process of fission to release energy for human use.

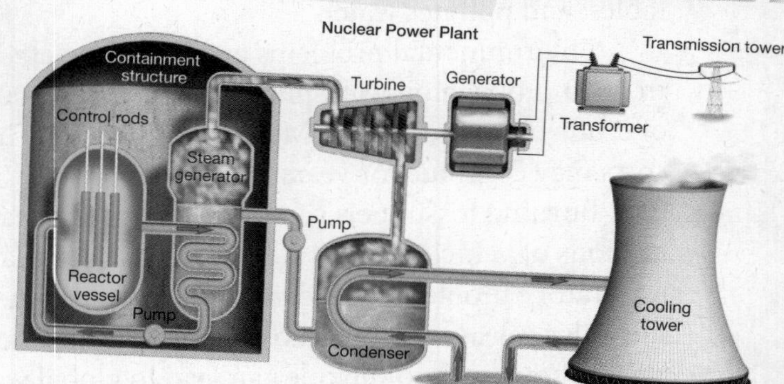

	T	F	
16	☐	☐	Uranium is often used as fuel in nuclear fission.
17	☐	☐	One disadvantage of nuclear fission is that it produces only a small amount of energy.

Most of the energy used today comes from fossil fuels, which include petroleum, natural gas, and coal.

	T	F	
18	☐	☐	Natural gas forms from microscopic marine organisms.
19	☐	☐	Most transportation fuels are products of coal.
20	☐	☐	Burning fossil fuels decreases the amount of carbon dioxide in the atmosphere.

Answers: 16 True; 17 False; 18 True; 19 False; 20 False

21 Summarize Identify the advantages and disadvantages for both fossil fuels and nuclear fuels.

Lesson Review

Vocabulary

Fill in the blank with the term that best completes the following sentences.

1 ____________________ is energy in an atom's nucleus.

2 Crude oil is a liquid kind of ____________

3 ____________________ can be renewable or nonrenewable.

4 During the process of ____________________, the nuclei of radioactive atoms are split into two or more smaller nuclei.

Key Concepts

5 **Describe** Describe how fossil fuels are converted into usable energy?

____

____

____

____

____

6 **Sequence** Which of the following sequences of processes best describes how electricity is generated in a nuclear power plant?

A fission reaction, produce steam, turn turbine, generate electricity, cool water

B produce steam, fission reaction, turn turbine, generate electricity, cool water

C cool water, fission reaction, produce steam, turn turbine, generate electricity

D produce steam, turn turbine, cool water, fission reaction, generate electricity

7 **Identify** Which is an example of how people use nonrenewable energy resources?

A eating a banana

B sailing a boat

C walking to school

D driving a car

Critical Thinking

8 **Hypothesize** Why do some places in the United States have deposits of coal but others have deposits of petroleum and natural gas?

____

____

____

____

____

Use the graph to answer the following questions.

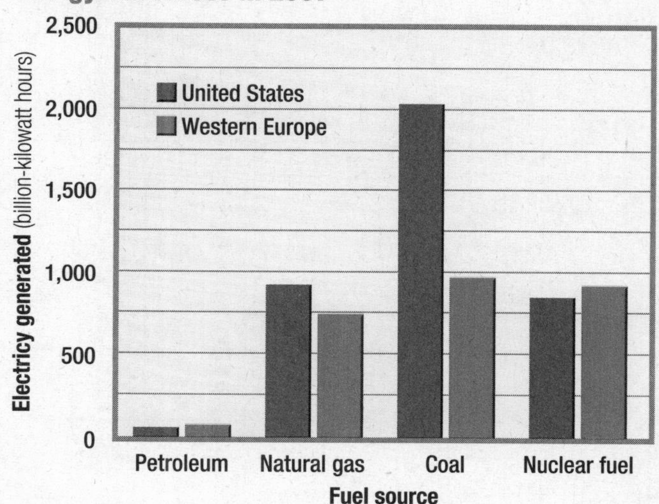

9 **Calculate** About how much more coal than petroleum is used to generate electricity in the United States and Western Europe?

____

____

____

____

10 **Analyze** What patterns of energy resource use do you see in the graph?

____

____

____

____

My Notes

OHIO **6.ESS.5** Rocks, minerals and soils have common and practical uses.

OHIO **6.SIA.6** Think critically and logically to connect evidence and explanations.

OHIO **6.SIA.8** Communicate scientific procedures and explanations.

Scientific Debate

Not all scientific knowledge is gained through experimentation. It is also a result of a great deal of research, debate, and risk analysis.

Tutorial

As you research a topic about which there is much debate, look for the following from your sources.

Reliability Reliable research can strengthen your argument. Scientific studies published in major journals are reviewed by other scientists and are more reliable than non-reviewed studies.

Lack of bias Bias is the tendency to favor a particular point of view or outcome. Determine whether your source favors a particular side of the topic. Science journals and university and government publications are less likely to be affected by bias than articles in magazines, newspapers, blogs, and commercial webpages.

Fact-based conclusions Scientific studies in journals are called primary sources. Secondary sources are reports that explain the findings of scientific studies. A tertiary source is a news item or magazine report about a scientific study. If using a secondary or tertiary source, does it provide references to its source information? Does it contain information for which you cannot find a source? Or does it have phrases such as "Experts say . . ." or "Most people know . . . " without providing reliable references?

Read the passage, and answer the questions.

Extracting natural gas and oil from places that were once too difficult to mine is now possible. One process involves injecting large amounts of fluids under high pressure deep into layers of shale, a type of sedimentary rock. This process is called *hydraulic fracturing,* or *fracking*. The fluid "pushes out" gas or oil trapped in the shale. The extracted gas or oil rises up the well and is collected at the surface. A well may be deeper than 2.5 km (about 1.5 miles) below the surface. Fracking fluid is approximately 90% water, 9% sand, and 1% additives. The additives include chemicals that reduce bacterial growth and reduce friction for the drilling equipment.

There is debate about the safety and environmental impact of fracking. Opponents of fracking are concerned about the potential health effects the additives have on people and animals, the high noise levels and high traffic volumes caused by fracking operations, and where the fracking fluids can leak to once underground. Supporters of fracking say that the drilling methods are safe, the fluids used do not pose a health risk, natural gas is a cleaner fuel than coal or oil, and fracking creates many jobs.

Sources: *American Petroleum Institute; Chesapeake Energy; U.S. Environmental Protection Agency; U.S. Dept. of Energy.*

1 Identify the argument in favor of fracking.

2 What is fracking fluid made of?

You Try It!

Imagine a fracking well is to be built near your community. You want to learn more about the fracking process. Review this diagram and answer the questions that follow to help you develop an understanding of the debate.

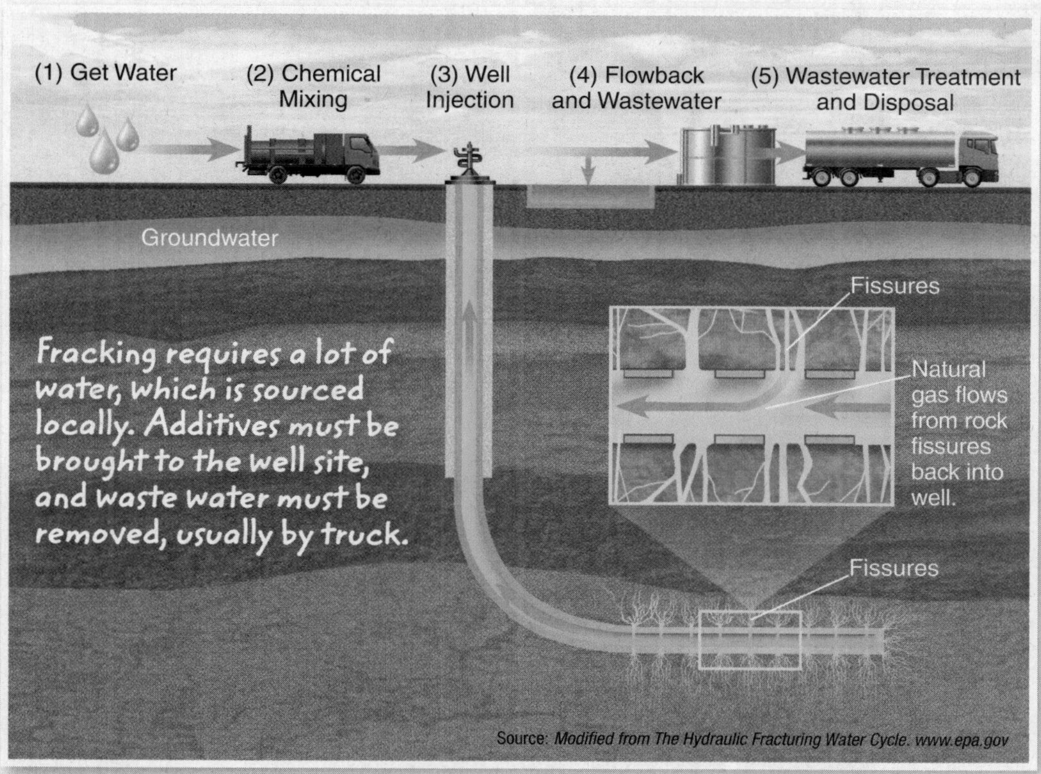

(1) Get Water
(2) Chemical Mixing
(3) Well Injection
(4) Flowback and Wastewater
(5) Wastewater Treatment and Disposal
Groundwater
Fissures
Natural gas flows from rock fissures back into well.
Fissures
Fracking requires a lot of water, which is sourced locally. Additives must be brought to the well site, and waste water must be removed, usually by truck.

Source: *Modified from The Hydraulic Fracturing Water Cycle. www.epa.gov*

1 Interpreting Graphics Using the image above, explain the fracking process in your own words.

2 Investigating Sources What additional information do you want to know about fracking that is not shown in the graphic? Is this information in the reading passage at left?

3 Communicating Ideas Do you think the benefits of fracking outweigh the risks? Discuss and debate your position with a classmate. Complete the table below to show the points on which you agree and disagree.

Agree	Disagree

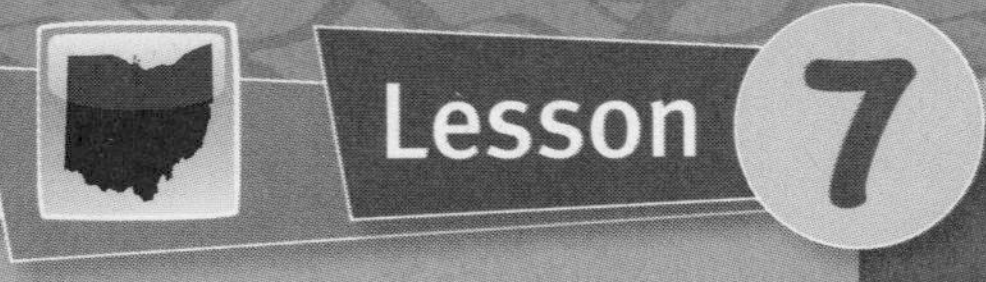

Renewable Energy Resources

ESSENTIAL QUESTION

How do humans use renewable energy resources?

By the end of this lesson, you should be able to describe how humans use energy resources and the role of renewable energy resources in society.

Panels such as these can turn an unused city roof into a miniature solar energy plant.

OHIO 6.ESS.5 Rocks, minerals and soils have common and practical uses.

OHIO 6.SIA.7 Recognize and analyze alternative explanations and predictions.

Lesson Labs

Quick Labs
- Design a Turbine
- Understanding Solar Panels

S.T.E.M. Lab
- Modeling Geothermal Power

Engage Your Brain

1 Predict Check T or F to show whether you think each statement is true or false.

T	F	
☐	☐	Renewable energy resources can never run out.
☐	☐	Renewable energy resources do not cause any type of pollution.
☐	☐	Solar energy is the most widely used renewable energy resource in the United States.
☐	☐	Renewable energy resources include solar energy, wind energy, and geothermal energy.

2 Describe Write a caption to explain how the sun's energy is being used in this photo.

____

____

____

____

____

Active Reading

3 Synthesize You can often define an unknown word if you know the meaning of its word parts. Use the word parts and sentence below to make an educated guess about the meaning of the word *geothermal*.

Word part	Meaning
geo-	Earth
therm-	heat

Example sentence

A geothermal power plant uses steam produced deep in the ground to generate electricity.

geothermal:

____

____

____

Vocabulary Terms

- **energy resource**
- **wind energy**
- **hydroelectric energy**
- **solar energy**
- **biomass**
- **geothermal energy**

4 Apply As you learn the definition of each vocabulary term in this lesson, create your own definition or sketch to help you remember the meaning of the term.

Energy *Déjà Vu*

What are the two main sources of renewable energy?

An **energy resource** is a natural resource used to generate electricity and other forms of energy. Most of the energy used by humans comes from *nonrenewable resources.* These resources are used more quickly than they can be replaced. But *renewable resources* can be replaced almost as quickly as they are used. Most renewable energy resources come from the sun and some from Earth itself.

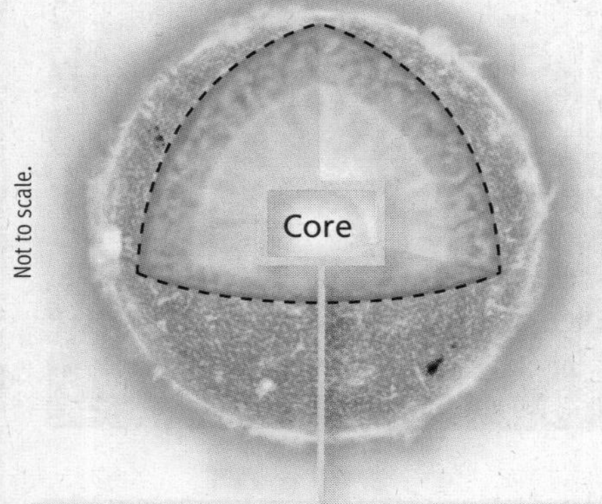

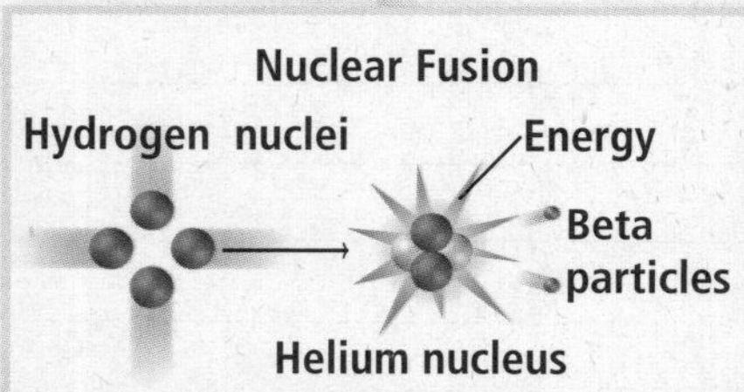

When atomic nuclei fuse, energy is released.

The Sun

The sun's energy is a result of nuclear fusion. Fusion is the process by which two or more nuclei fuse together to form a larger nucleus. Fusion produces a large amount of energy, which is released into space as light and heat.

Solar energy warms Earth, causing the movement of air masses. Moving air masses form winds and some ocean currents. Solar energy also fuels plant growth. Animals get energy by eating plants. Humans can harness energy from wind, moving water, plant and animal materials, and directly from the light and heat that comes from the sun.

Earth

Energy from within Earth comes from two sources. One source is the decay of radioactive elements in Earth's mantle and crust, caused by nuclear fission. Fission is the splitting of the nuclei of radioactive atoms. The second source of energy within Earth is energy stored during Earth's formation. The heat produced from these sources radiates outward toward Earth's surface. Humans can harness this heat to use as an energy source.

5 Contrast Explain how energy production in the sun differs from energy production in Earth's interior.

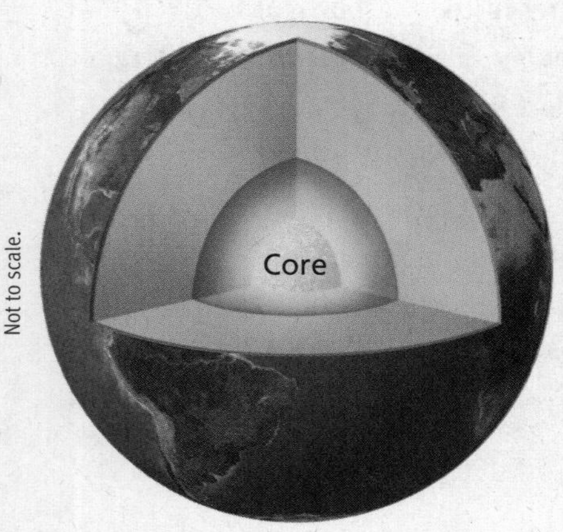

Earth's internal energy comes from the process of nuclear fission and the events that formed Earth.

How might a renewable energy resource become nonrenewable?

All of the energy resources you will learn about in this lesson are renewable. That doesn't mean that they can't become nonrenewable resources. Trees, for example, are a renewable resource. Some people burn wood from trees to heat their homes and cook food. However, some forests are being cut down but are not being replanted in a timely manner. Others are being cut down and replaced with buildings. If this process continues, eventually these forests will no longer be considered renewable resources.

7 Distinguish What is the difference between nonrenewable and renewable energy resources?

6 Apply Read the caption below, then describe what might happen if the community uses too much of the water in the reservoir.

Think Outside the Book

8 Apply Write an interview with a renewable resource that is afraid it might become nonrenewable. Be sure to include questions and answers.

A community uses this reservoir for water. The dam at the end of the reservoir uses moving water to produce electricity for the community.

Turn, Turn, Turn

How do humans use wind energy?

Wind is created by the sun's uneven heating of air masses in Earth's atmosphere. **Wind energy** uses the force of moving air to drive an electric generator or do other work. Wind energy is renewable because the wind will blow as long as the sun warms Earth. Wind energy is harnessed by machines called wind turbines. Electricity is generated when moving air turns turbine blades that drive an electric generator. Clusters of wind turbines, called wind farms, generate large amounts of electricity.

Although wind energy is a renewable energy resource, it has several disadvantages. Wind farms can be placed only in areas that receive large amounts of wind. The equipment required to collect and convert wind energy is also expensive to produce and maintain. And the production and maintenance of this equipment produces a small amount of pollution. The turbine blades can also be hazardous to birds.

Windmills such as these have been used for centuries to grind grain and pump surface water for irrigation.

A wind-powered water pump can pull water from deep underground when electricity is not available.

9 Infer What is the main benefit of placing these turbines in open water?

Wind farms are a form of clean energy, because they do not generate air pollution as they generate electricity.

How do humans get energy from moving water?

Active Reading

10 Identify Underline the kind of energy that is found in moving water.

Like wind, moving water has kinetic energy. People have harnessed the energy of falling or flowing water to power machines since ancient times. Some grain and saw mills still use water to power their equipment. Electrical energy produced by moving water is called **hydroelectric energy**. Hydroelectric energy is renewable because the water cycle is driven by the sun. Water that evaporates from oceans and lakes falls on higher elevations and flows downhill in streams, rivers, and waterfalls. The energy in flowing water is converted to electrical energy when it spins turbines connected to electric generators inside the dam.

Hydroelectric energy is a good source of energy only in locations where there are large, reliable amounts of flowing water. Another disadvantage of hydroelectric energy is that hydroelectric dams and their technology are expensive to build. The dams also can block the movement of fish between the sea and their spawning grounds. Special fish ladders must be built to allow fish to swim around the dam.

11 Explain What is the purpose of the lake that is located behind the dam of a hydroelectric plant?

____

____

____

____

____

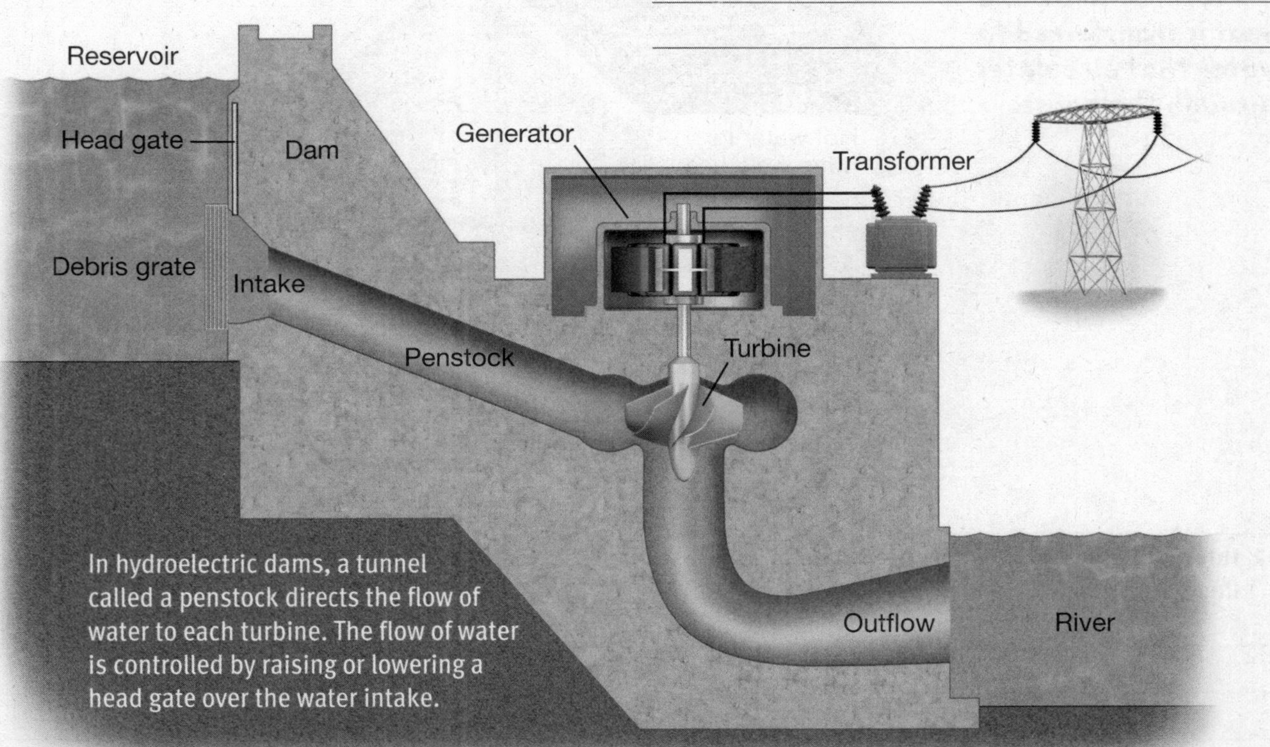

In hydroelectric dams, a tunnel called a penstock directs the flow of water to each turbine. The flow of water is controlled by raising or lowering a head gate over the water intake.

Let the Sunshine In

How do humans use solar energy?

Most forms of energy come from the sun—even fossil fuels begin with the sun as an energy resource. **Solar energy** is the energy received by Earth from the sun in the form of radiation. Solar energy can be used to warm buildings directly. Solar energy can also be converted into electricity by solar cells.

To Provide Energy as Heat

We can use liquids warmed by the sun to warm water and buildings. Some liquids, such as water, have a high capacity for absorbing and holding heat. When the heat is absorbed by the liquid in a solar collector, it can be transferred to water that circulates through a building. The hot water can be used for bathing or other household uses, or to warm the building. The only pollution generated by solar heating systems comes from the manufacture and maintenance of their equipment. Solar heating systems work best in areas with large amounts of sunlight.

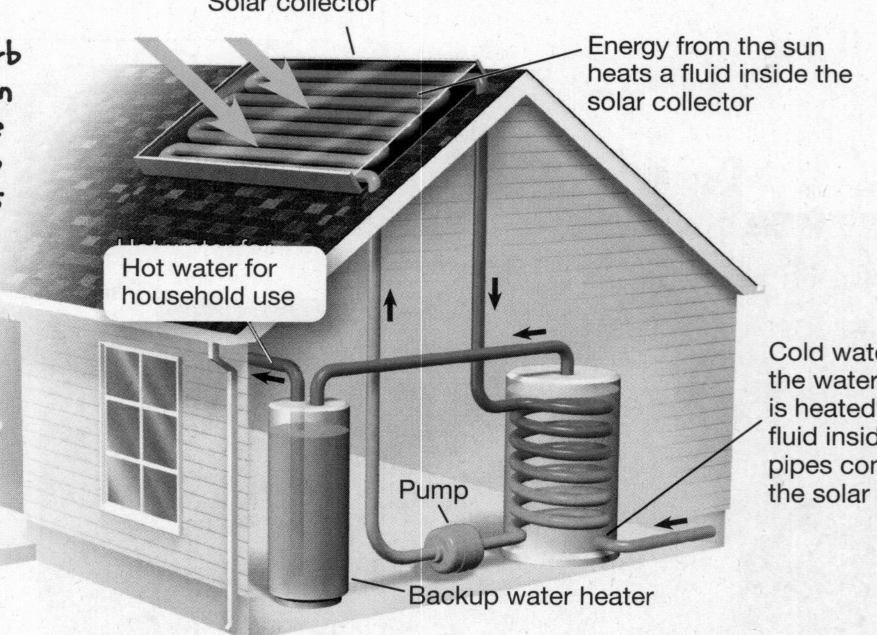
Solar collector
Energy from the sun heats a fluid inside the solar collector
Hot water for household use
Cold water from the water supply is heated by hot fluid inside the pipes coming from the solar collector
Pump
Backup water heater

Solar collectors absorb energy from the sun in the form of heat. The heat is transferred to water that circulates through the house.

12 Infer Not all solar collectors use water to absorb energy from the sun. Why might a solar heating system use a liquid other than water?

Active Reading **13 Identify** As you read, underline the characteristics of a photovoltaic cell.

To Produce Electricity

Solar collectors can also be used to generate electricity. First, heated fluid is used to produce steam. Then, the steam turns a turbine connected to an electric generator.

Electricity can also be generated when sunlight is absorbed by a photovoltaic cell. A single photovoltaic cell produces a small amount of electricity. The electricity from joined photovoltaic cells can power anything from calculators to entire communities. Many cells must be joined together to form each solar panel, as shown in the solar power plant below. Solar power plants must be built in places with adequate space and abundant sunshine year-round. These requirements increase the costs of solar power.

This calculator is powered by solar cells instead of a battery.

Visualize It! Inquiry

14 Infer Based on this image and your reading, what might be a disadvantage to using solar energy to supply electricity to a large community?

____

____

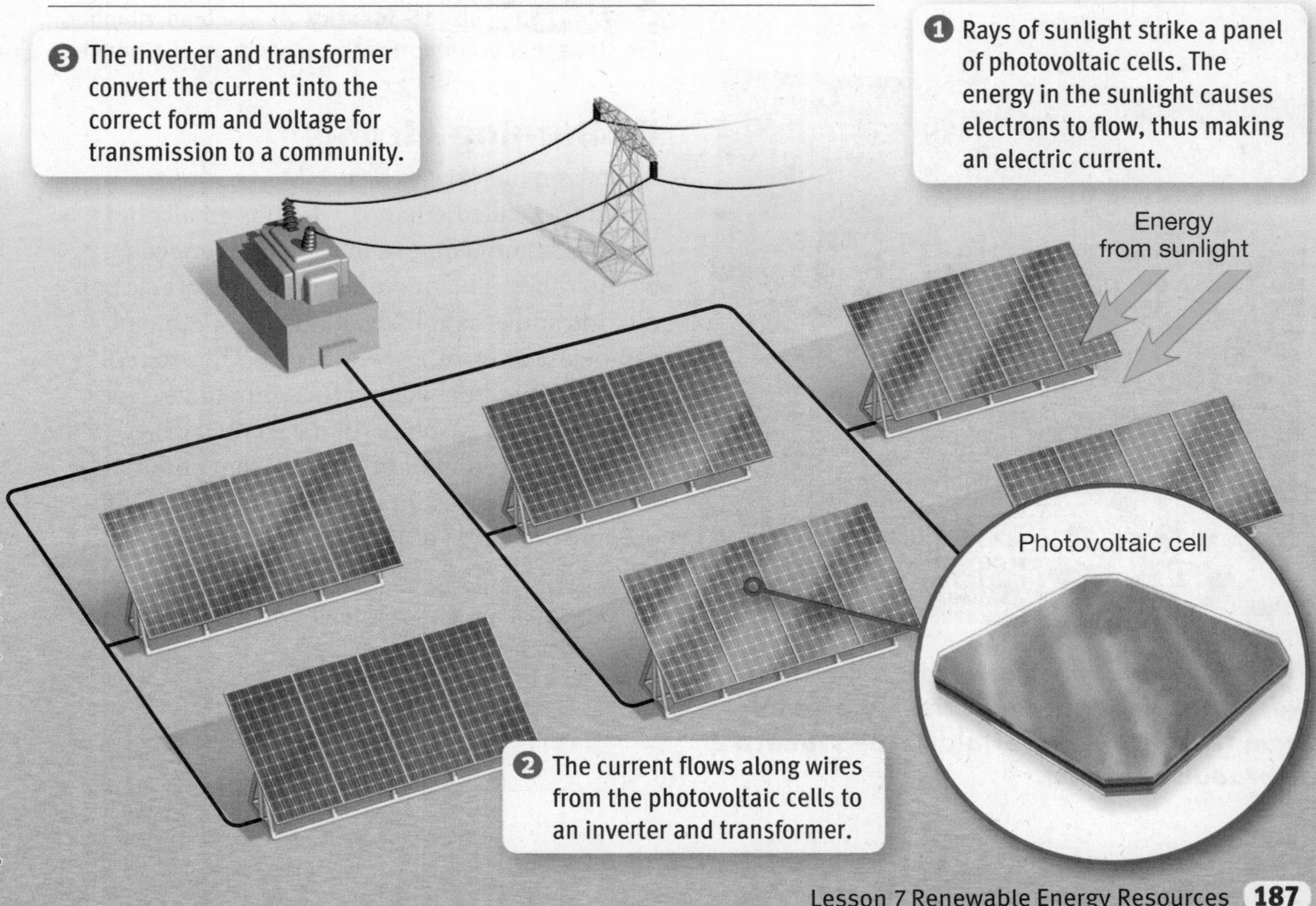

❸ The inverter and transformer convert the current into the correct form and voltage for transmission to a community.

❶ Rays of sunlight strike a panel of photovoltaic cells. The energy in the sunlight causes electrons to flow, thus making an electric current.

Energy from sunlight

Photovoltaic cell

❷ The current flows along wires from the photovoltaic cells to an inverter and transformer.

How do humans get energy from living things?

Plants absorb light energy from the sun and convert it to chemical energy through *photosynthesis.* This energy is stored in leaves, stems, and roots. Chemical energy is also present in the dung of animals. These sources of energy make up biomass.

By Burning Biomass

Biomass is organic matter from plants and from animal waste that contains chemical energy. Biomass can be burned to release energy. This energy can be used to cook food, provide warmth, or power an engine. Biomass sources include trees, crops, animal waste, and peat.

Biomass is inexpensive and can usually be replaced relatively quickly, so it is considered to be a renewable resource. Some types of biomass renew more slowly than others. Peat renews so slowly in areas where it is used heavily that it is treated as a nonrenewable resource. Like fossil fuels, biomass produces pollutants when it burns.

These peat pellets will be used to generate steam in the power plant in the background. The steam will generate electricity by turning turbines.

Active Reading **15 Identify** As you read, number the steps that occur during the production of ethanol.

These wagons are loaded with sugar cane wastes from sugar production. The cellulose from these plant materials will be processed to produce ethanol.

By Burning Alcohol

Biomass material can be used to produce a liquid fuel called ethanol, which is an alcohol. The sugars or cellulose in the plants are eaten by microbes. The microbes then give off carbon dioxide and ethanol. Over 1,000 L of ethanol can be made from 1 acre of corn. The ethanol is collected and burned as a fuel. Ethanol can also be mixed with gasoline to make a fuel called gasohol. The ethanol produced from about 40% of one corn harvest in the United States would provide only 10% of the fuel used in our cars!

16 List What are three examples of how biomass can be used for energy?

How do humans use geothermal energy?

The water in the geyser at right is heated by geothermal energy. **Geothermal energy** is energy produced by heat from Earth's interior. Geothermal energy heats rock formations deep within the ground. Groundwater absorbs this heat and forms hot springs and geysers where the water reaches Earth's surface. Geothermal energy is used to produce energy as heat and electricity.

Because Earth's core will be very hot for billions of years, geothermal energy will be available for a long time.

To Provide Energy as Heat

Geothermal energy can be used to warm and cool buildings. A closed loop system of pipes runs from underground into the heating system of a home or building. Water pumped through these pipes absorbs heat from the ground and is used to warm the building. Hot groundwater can also be pumped in and used in a similar way. In warmer months, the ground is cooler than the air, so this system can also be used for cooling.

To Produce Electricity

Geothermal energy is also used to produce electricity. Wells are drilled into areas of superheated groundwater, allowing steam and hot water to escape. Geothermal power plants pump the steam or hot water from underground to spin turbines that generate electricity, as shown at right. A disadvantage of geothermal energy is pollution that occurs during production of the technology needed to capture it. The technology is also expensive to make and maintain.

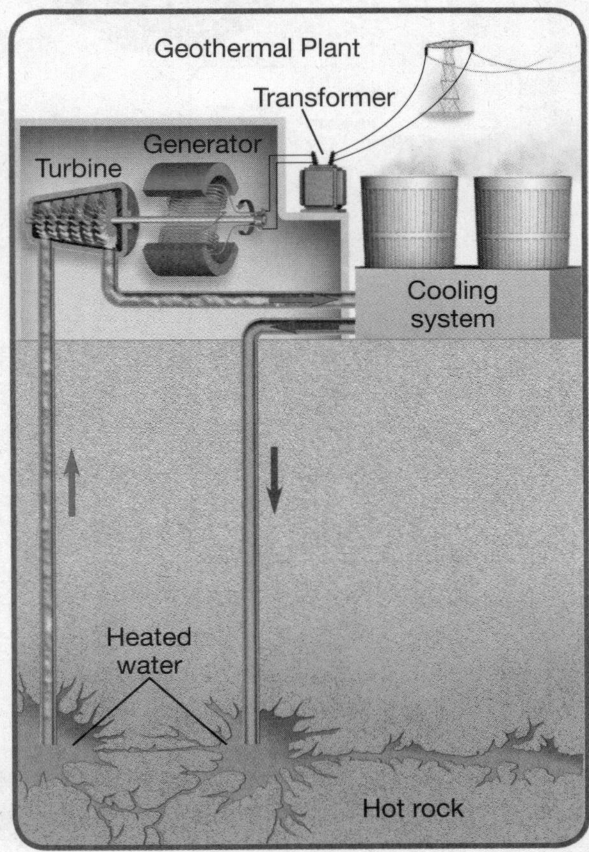

17 List What are some advantages and disadvantages to using geothermal energy?

Advantages	Disadvantages

Visual Summary

To complete this summary, fill in the blanks with the correct word or phrase. Then, use the key below to check your answers. You can use this page to review the main concepts of the lesson.

Renewable Energy Resources

The source of geothermal energy is energy from within Earth.

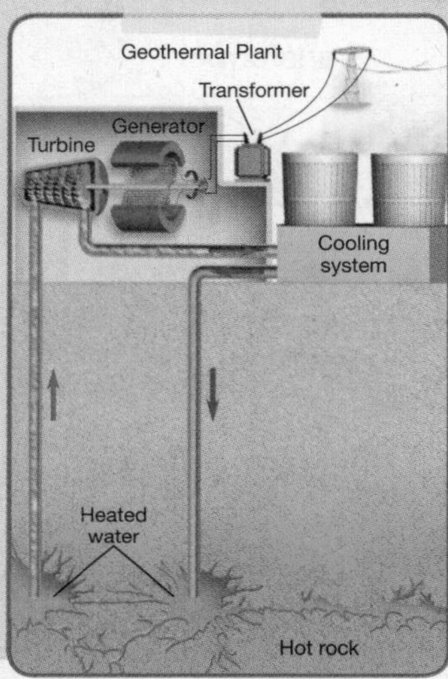

18 In geothermal power plants, hot water or ________________ is pumped from within Earth's crust to produce electricity.

Most of the renewable energy resources that people use come from the sun.

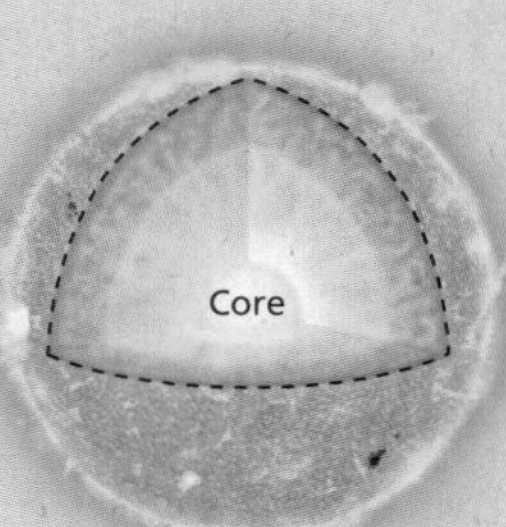

19 Renewable resources that come from the sun include ________________
____
____

Answers: 18 steam; 19 biomass, solar energy, wind energy, and hydroelectric energy

20 Synthesize Which type of renewable energy resource would be best to use to provide electricity for your town? Explain your answer.

Lesson Review

Vocabulary

Fill in the blanks with the term that best completes the following sentences.

1 Organic matter that contains stored energy is called ______________________

2 A resource that humans can use to produce energy is a(n) ______________________

3 ______________________ is an energy resource harnessed from flowing water.

Key Concepts

4 Describe Identify a major advantage and a major disadvantage of using renewable energy resources to produce electricity.

____

5 Explain If renewable energy resources can be replaced, why do we need to conserve them? Use an example to support your answer.

____

6 Describe What is the source of energy that powers wind and flowing water?

____

Critical Thinking

Use this graph to answer the following questions.

Total Renewable Energy Resources Consumed in 2009 in the United States

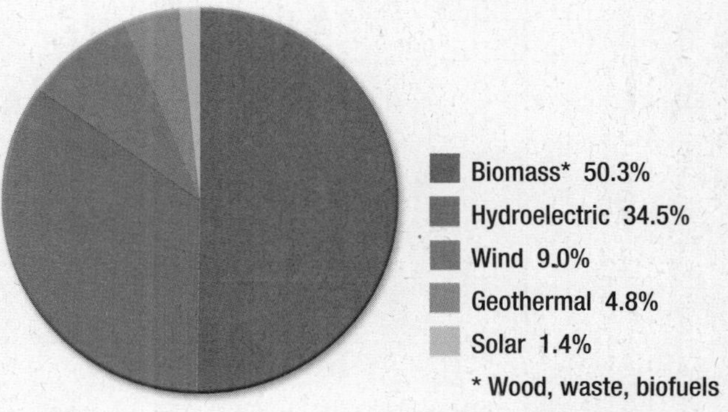

Source: Annual Energy Review 2009, U.S. Energy Information Administration

7 Evaluate Which is the most used renewable energy resource in the United States? Why do you think this is the case?

____

8 Evaluate Which is the least used renewable energy resource in the United States? Why do you think this is the case?

____

9 Relate How are biomass and alcohol production related to energy from the sun?

____

My Notes

Unit 2 Big Idea

Natural resources are classified by their properties, and these properties help explain how the resources formed and help determine how they can be used.

Lesson 1

ESSENTIAL QUESTION

What are Earth's natural resources?

Describe the types and uses of Earth's natural resources.

Lesson 2

ESSENTIAL QUESTION

What are minerals, how do they form, and how can they be identified?

Describe the basic structure of minerals, and identify different minerals by using their physical properties.

Lesson 3

ESSENTIAL QUESTION

What is the rock cycle?

Describe the series of processes and classes of rocks that make up the rock cycle.

Lesson 4

ESSENTIAL QUESTION

How do rocks form?

Describe the formation and classification of sedimentary, igneous, and metamorphic rocks.

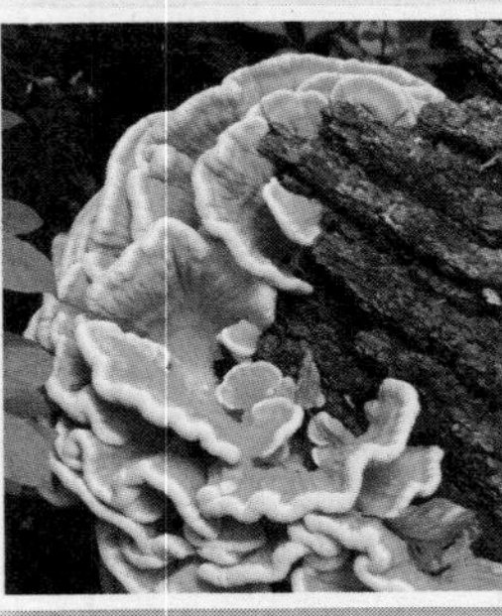

Lesson 5

ESSENTIAL QUESTION

How does soil form?

Describe the physical and chemical characteristics of soil layers, and identify the factors that affect soil formation, including the action of living things.

Lesson 6

ESSENTIAL QUESTION

How do we use nonrenewable energy resources?

Describe how humans use energy resources and the role of nonrenewable energy resources in society.

Lesson 7

ESSENTIAL QUESTION

How do humans use renewable energy resources?

Describe how humans use energy resources and the role of renewable energy resources in society.

Connect ESSENTIAL QUESTIONS

Lessons 2 and 4

1 Synthesize Describe a process by which one mineral can change into another mineral.

____

____

Think Outside the Book

2 Synthesize Choose one of these activities to help synthesize what you have learned in this unit.

☐ Using what you learned in lessons 2, 3, and 4, explain in a short essay how a chemical sedimentary rock formed, beginning with a lake full of dissolved gypsum minerals.

☐ Using what you learned in lessons 1, 6, and 7, create a poster presentation to describe and compare renewable resources and nonrenewable resources.

Unit 2 Review

Name ___________________________

Vocabulary

Check the box to show whether each statement is true or false.

T	F	
☐	☐	1 Petroleum is a fossil fuel that can be used to make plastics.
☐	☐	2 An energy resource is a resource that humans can use to make food or beverages.
☐	☐	3 Biomass energy comes from organic matter such as plant material and manure.
☐	☐	4 A material resource is a renewable resource that is used to make objects.
☐	☐	5 Rocks, water, air, minerals, plants, animals, and soil are all examples of natural resources.

Key Concepts

Choose the letter of the best answer.

6 What is the original source of the energy stored in coal?

A wind

B the sun

C plants

D soil

7 The chemicals released by burning petroleum in car engines contribute to which local and worldwide effects?

A smog and global warming

B fog and radioactivity

C acid rain and UV radiation

D cloudy weather and ozone buildup

Unit 2 Review continued

8 The diagram shows portions of the rock cycle.

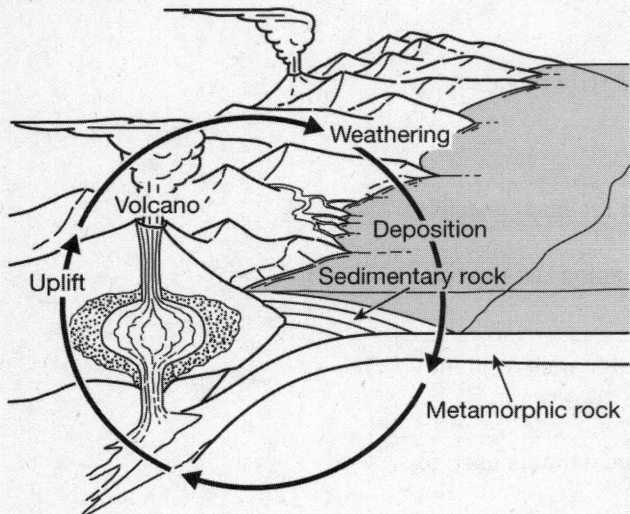

Suppose you were to add an arrow to show subsidence in the diagram. How would you draw the arrow?

A It would extend horizontally across the diagram.

B It would point upward toward the metamorphic rock.

C It would point downward from the metamorphic rock.

D It would point in the same direction as the uplift arrow.

9 Sometimes a renewable resource can be considered nonrenewable because it is used up faster than it can be replenished. Which of the following is an example of this?

A coal supply dwindling because it takes millions of years to form

B forests being cut down at a quicker rate than they can grow

C solar energy being used to provide electricity to a home

D water in streams replaced by rainfall from the atmosphere

10 As part of a natural resources management plan, the owner of an apartment building wants to reduce overall water usage. Which recommendation should she give that would help her renters conserve water?

A Buy drinking water from the store.

B Don't let water run while brushing your teeth.

C Bathe only in the afternoon while others are out.

D Shower before entering the swimming pool.

Name ___________________________

11 The picture shows a scene from a campground.

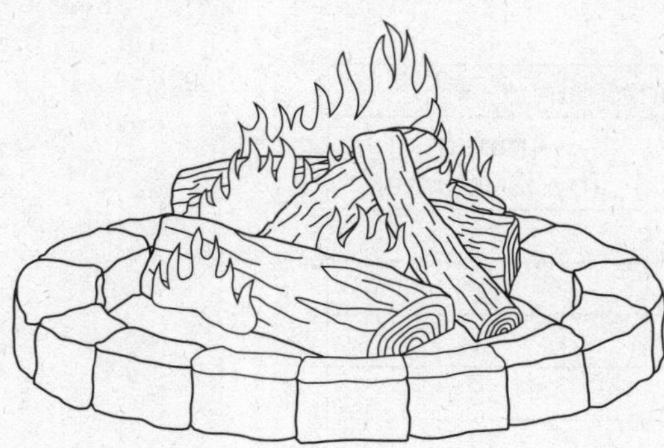

Which energy conversion is taking place in the picture?

A chemical energy to thermal energy

B nuclear energy to chemical energy

C electrical energy to mechanical energy

D electromagnetic energy to chemical energy

12 Which of the following best describes how sedimentary rock forms?

A Molten rock beneath the surface of the Earth cools and becomes solid.

B Layers of material become compressed to form rock .

C Chemical processes or changes in pressure or temperature change the texture and composition of a rock .

D Molten rock reaches Earth's surface and cools to become solid rock.

13 Fossil fuels and soil are categorized as which of the following?

A material resources

B geologic resources

C mineral resources

D energy resources

14 You have just analyzed a 100 g soil sample. You have organized your findings in the following data table.

Soil Analysis	
Soil Material	Amount (by % volume)
Air	25
Silt	18
Clay	9
Sand	18
Water	25
Organic matter	5

Which two materials make up at least 50 percent of the composition of your soil sample?

A air and silt

B silt and sand

C air and water

D clay and organic matter

15 A student is shining a light on several different mineral samples. For which type of mineral should the student expect the greatest luster?

A a dull, chalky mineral

B a rough, gray mineral

C a shiny, metallic mineral

D a clear, translucent mineral

Name ______________________________

Critical Thinking

Answer the following questions in the spaces provided.

16 Below is a graph of the production and use of petroleum in the United States in the past and present and likely usage in the future.

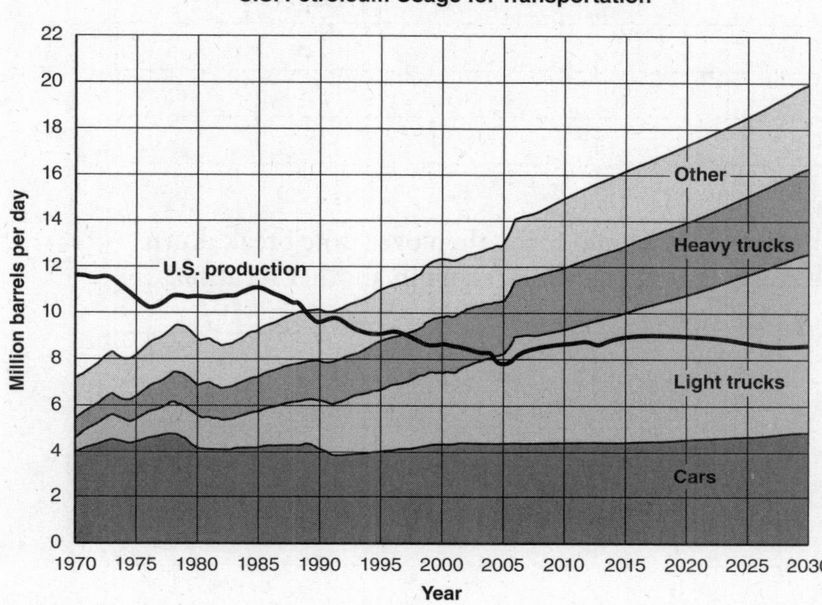

Based on current production and current usage, what could you predict about petroleum resources? Design a logical plan that could help to conserve petroleum resources.

17 Explain how both the texture and the composition of a rock can provide scientists with information on the rock's history. Give an example of each.

18 Explain a way that a sedimentary rock could form, then over time break down into smaller pieces, and become sedimentary rock again in another location.

Connect ESSENTIAL QUESTIONS

Lessons 1 and 7

Answer the following questions in the spaces provided.

19 The picture shows technology used for alternative energy. What type of energy does the equipment in the picture harness?

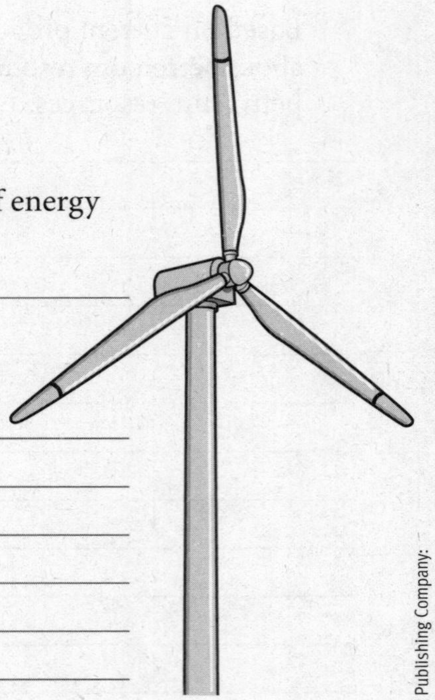

Name one benefit and one disadvantage of using this type of energy.

UNIT 3

Cells

Big Idea

All organisms are made up of one or more cells.

Colorized picture of the organelles of a cell through a modern microscope

What do you think?

As microscopes have become more powerful, our understanding of cells and their functions has also increased. What kinds of questions would you use a microscope to answer?

Cells seen through an early microscope

Unit 3

Cells

CITIZEN SCIENCE

Seeing through Microscopes

Microscopes have come a long way. Today, we can see the details of the surface of metals at the atomic level. Microscopes have allowed us to study our world at some of the smallest levels.

Circa 1000 CE

Although people may have used rock crystals to magnify things thousands of years ago, it wasn't until about 1000 CE that people were able to form and polish clear-glass partial spheres. Placing these reading stones on top of a page made it easier to read the words.

Reading stones magnify the words on a page.

1665
Robert Hooke was interested in many areas of science. In 1665, Hooke invented a light microscope to look at small creatures like fleas. Hooke's microscope was similar to a telescope, but it also had a way to shine light on the object.

1931
Ernst Ruska developed the electron microscope, which shows much greater detail than do light microscopes. The electron microscope uses an electron beam instead of light to show things as small as the structure of viruses. Ruska received the Nobel Prize in Physics in 1986 for his breakthrough.

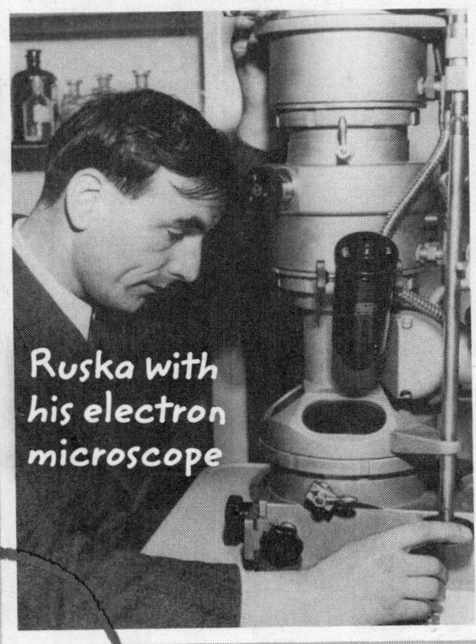
Ruska with his electron microscope

Atoms at platinum's surface

1981
The scanning tunneling microscope changed again the way scientists look at things. Using this microscope, we can look at images of surfaces at the atomic level. The microscope uses a beam of electrons to map a surface. This information is collected and processed so that it can be viewed on a computer screen.

What's in a Microscope?

1 Think About It

A What characteristics do different microscopes have?

B Why are microscopes used?

2 Conduct Research

Choose a specific kind of microscope and research how it is used, whether it is used to view live or dead samples, and its range of magnification.

Take It Home

With an adult, prepare an oral presentation for your class on the microscope that you have researched.

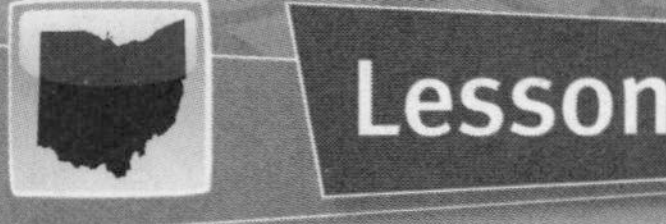

The Characteristics of Cells

ESSENTIAL QUESTION

What are living things made of?

By the end of this lesson, you should be able to explain the components of the scientific theory of cells.

People communicate to others through talking, signing, body language, and other methods. Inside your body, cells communicate too. Brain cells, like the ones shown here, control balance, posture, and muscle coordination.

OHIO 6.LS.1 Cells are the fundamental unit of life.

OHIO 6.LS.2 All cells come from pre-existing cells.

OHIO 6.LS.3 Cells carry on specific functions that sustain life.

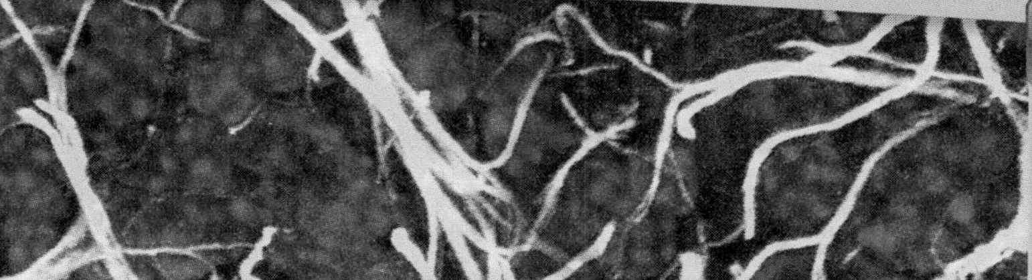

Lesson Labs

Quick Labs
- How Do Tools that Magnify Help Us Study Cells?
- Investigating Cell Size

Exploration Lab
- Using a Microscope to Explore Cells

Engage Your Brain

1 Predict Check T or F to show whether you think each statement is true or false.

T	F	
☐	☐	All living things are made up of one or more cells.
☐	☐	Rocks are made up of cells.
☐	☐	All cells are the same size.
☐	☐	Cells perform life functions for living things.

2 Describe Sketch your idea of what a cell looks like. Label any parts you include in your sketch.

Active Reading

3 Synthesize Many English words have their roots in other languages. Use the Greek words below to make an educated guess about the meanings of the words *prokaryote* and *eukaryote*. Here *kernel* refers to the nucleus where genetic material is contained in some cells.

Word part	Meaning
pro-	before
eu-	true
karyon	kernel

prokaryote:

eukaryote:

Vocabulary Terms

- cell
- organism
- cell membrane
- cytoplasm
- organelle
- nucleus
- prokaryote
- eukaryote

4 Apply As you learn the definition of each vocabulary term in this lesson, create your own sketches of a prokaryotic cell and a eukaryotic cell and label the parts in each cell.

Cell-*ebrate!*

What is a cell?

Like all living things, you are made up of cells. A **cell** is the smallest functional and structural unit of all living organisms. An **organism** is any living thing. All organisms are made up of cells. Some organisms are just one cell. Others, like humans, contain trillions of cells. An organism carries out all of its own life processes.

Robert Hooke was the first person to describe cells. In 1665, he built a microscope to look at tiny objects. One day, he looked at a thin slice of cork from the bark of a cork tree. The cork looked as if it was made of little boxes. Hooke named these boxes *cells*, which means "little rooms" in Latin.

Active Reading

5 Identify As you read, underline the reasons why cells are important.

6 Compare Looking at the photos of the three different cells, what do the cells have in common?

____

____

____

____

____

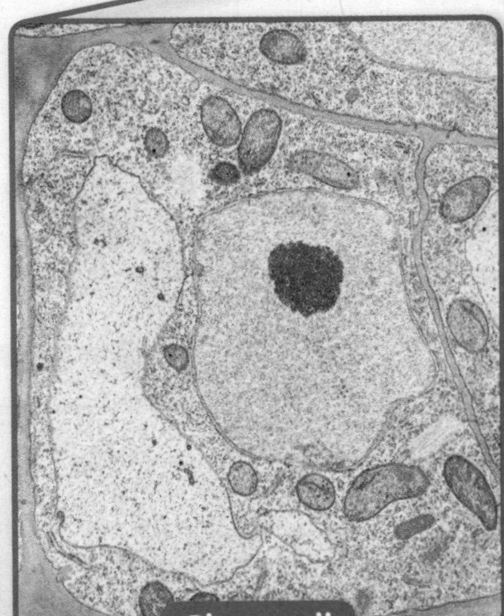

Plant cell

Plant cells range in size from 10 µm to 100 µm. They can be much larger than animal cells.

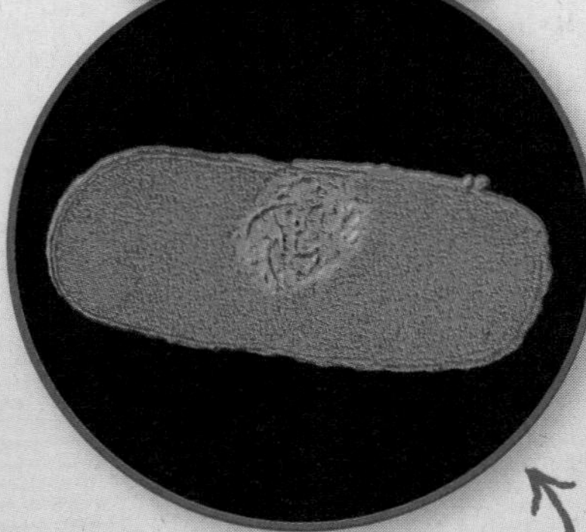

Bacterial cell

Bacterial cells are up to 1000 times smaller than human cells.

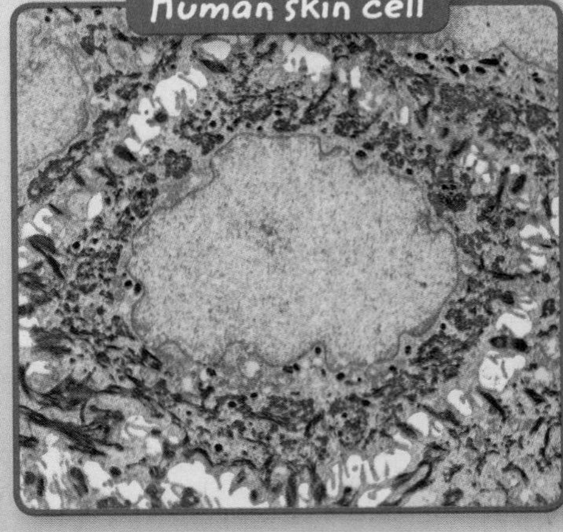

The average size of a human cell is 10 µm. It would take about 50 average human cells to cover the dot on this letter i.

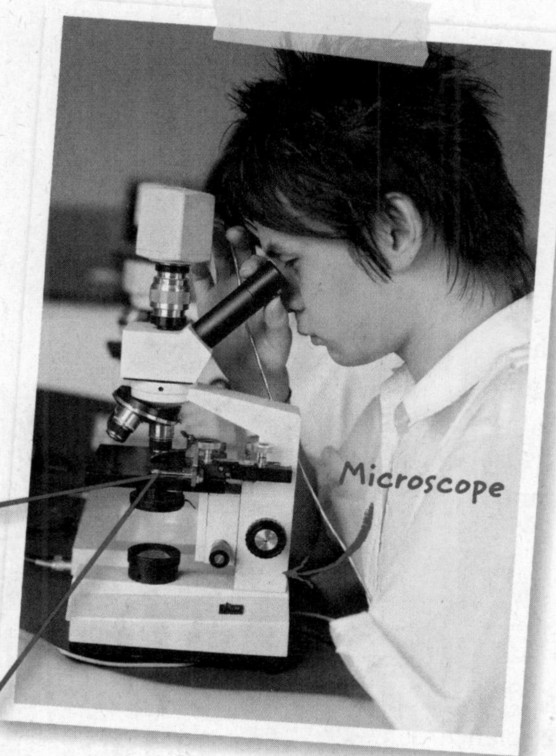

Why are most cells small?

Most cells are too small to be seen without a microscope. Cells are small because their size is limited by their outer surface area. Cells take in food and get rid of wastes through their outer surface. As a cell grows, it needs more food and produces more waste. Therefore, more materials pass through its outer surface. However, as a cell grows, the cell's volume increases faster than the surface area. If a cell gets too large, the cell's surface area will not be large enough to take in enough nutrients or pump out enough wastes. The ratio of the cell's outer surface area to the cell's volume is called the *surface area-to-volume ratio*. Smaller cells have a greater surface area-to-volume ratio than larger cells.

Do the Math

Here's an example of how to calculate the surface area-to-volume ratio of the cube shown at the right.

Sample Problem

A Calculate the surface area.

surface area of cube =

number of faces × area of one face

surface area of cube = $6(2\ cm \times 2\ cm)$

surface area of cube = $24\ cm^2$

B Calculate the volume.

volume of cube = side × side × side

volume of cube = $2\ cm \times 2\ cm \times 2\ cm$

volume of cube = $8\ cm^3$

C Calculate the surface area-to-volume ratio. A ratio is a comparison between numbers. It can be written by placing a colon between the numbers being compared.

surface area : volume = $24\ cm^2 : 8\ cm^3$

surface area : volume = $3\ cm^2 : 1\ cm^3$

You Try It

7 Calculate What is the surface area-to-volume ratio of a cube whose sides are 3 cm long?

A Calculate the surface area.

B Calculate the volume.

C Calculate the surface area-to-volume ratio.

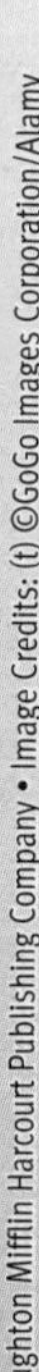

Cell *Hall of Fame*

What is the cell theory?

Scientific knowledge often results from combining the work of several scientists. For example, the discoveries of Matthias Schleiden (muh•THY•uhs SHLY•duhn), Theodor Schwann (THEE•oh•dohr SHVAHN), and Rudolf Virchow (ROO•dawlf VIR•koh) led to one very important theory called the *cell theory*. The cell theory lists three basic characteristics of all cells and organisms:

- All organisms are made up of one or more cells.
- The cell is the basic unit of all organisms.
- All cells come from existing cells.

The cell theory is fundamental to the study of organisms, medicine, heredity, evolution, and all other aspects of life science.

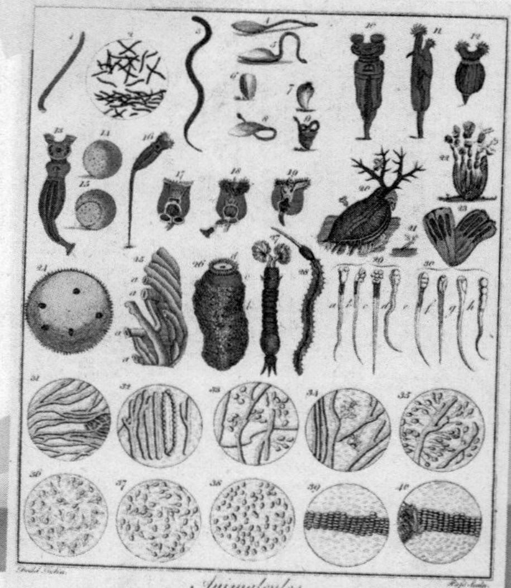

Visualize It!

8 Provide As you read, fill in the missing events on the timeline.

1673
Anton van Leeuwenhoek made careful drawings of the organisms he observed.

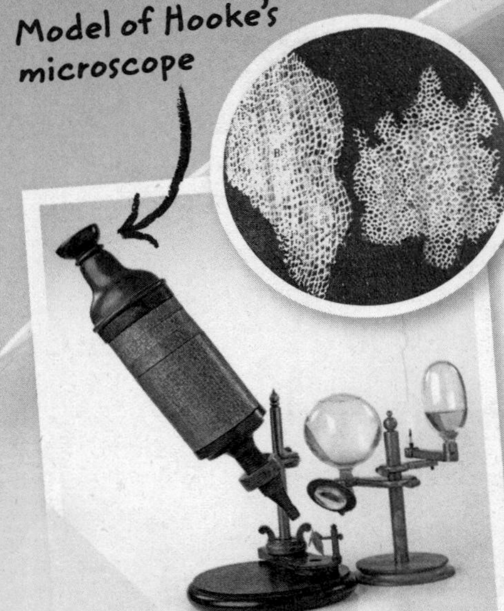

Model of Hooke's microscope

1665
Robert Hooke sees tiny, box-like spaces when using a microscope like this to observe thin slices of cork. He calls these spaces cells.

1858
Rudolf Virchow ______________

____

____

____

Think Outside the Book *Inquiry*

9 Explain How can microscopes help you see cells? First, think of a good place to collect a sample of cells. Then, in a paragraph, describe how to prepare a microscope slide to observe those cells.

Cells of an iris petal

This iris and butterfly are multicellular organisms made up of many cells.

All Organisms Are Made Up of One or More Cells

Anton van Leeuwenhoek (AN•tahn VAN LAY•vuhn•huk) was the first person to describe actual living cells when he looked at a drop of pond water under a microscope. These studies made other scientists wonder if all living things were made up of cells. In 1838, Matthias Schleiden concluded that plants are made of cells. Then in 1839, Theodor Schwann determined that all animal tissues are made of cells. He concluded that all organisms are made up of one or more cells.

Organisms that are made up of just one cell are called *unicellular organisms*. The single cell of a unicellular organism must carry out all of the functions for life. Organisms that are made up of more than one cell are called *multicellular organisms*. The cells of multicellular organism often have specialized functions.

The Cell Is the Basic Unit of All Organisms

Based on his observations about the cellular make up of organisms, Schwann made another conclusion. He determined that the cell is the basic unit of all living things. Thus, Schwann wrote the first two parts of the cell theory.

All Cells Come from Existing Cells

In 1858, Rudolf Virchow, a doctor, proposed that cells could form only from the division of other cells. Virchow then added the third part of the cell theory that all cells come from existing cells.

Active Reading

10 Summarize What is the cell theory?

On the Cellular

What parts do all cells have in common?

Different cells vary in size and shape. However, all cells have some parts in common, including cell membranes, cytoplasm, organelles, and DNA. These different parts help the cell to carry out all the tasks needed for life.

Active Reading

11 Identify As you read, underline the function of cell membranes, organelles, and DNA.

Cell Membrane

A **cell membrane** is a protective layer that covers a cell's surface and acts as a barrier between the inside of a cell and the cell's environment. It also controls materials, such as water and oxygen, that move into and out of a cell.

Cytoplasm

The region enclosed by the cell membrane that includes the fluid and all of the *organelles* of the cell is called the **cytoplasm** (SY•tuh•plaz•uhm).

Organelles

An **organelle** is a small body in a cell's cytoplasm that is specialized to perform a specific function. Cells can have one or more types of organelles. Most, but not all, organelles have a membrane.

DNA

Deoxyribonucleic acid, or DNA, is genetic material that provides instructions for all cell processes. Organisms inherit DNA from their parent or parents. In some cells, the DNA is contained in a membrane-bound organelle called the **nucleus**. In other types of cells, the DNA is not contained in a nucleus.

What are the two types of cells?

Although cells have some basic parts in common, there are some important differences. The way that cells store their DNA is the main difference between the two cell types.

Active Reading

12 Define As you read, underline the differences between prokaryotes and eukaryotes.

Prokaryotic

A **prokaryote** (proh•KAIR•ee•oht) is a single-celled organism that does not have a nucleus or membrane-bound organelles. Its DNA is located in the cytoplasm. Prokaryotic cells contain organelles called *ribosomes* that do not have a membrane. Some prokaryotic cells have hairlike structures called *flagella* that help them move. Prokaryotes, which include all bacteria and archaea, are smaller than eukaryotes.

Eukaryotic

A **eukaryote** (yoo•KAIR•ee•oht) is an organism made up of cells that contain their DNA in a nucleus. Eukaryotic cells contain membrane-bound organelles, as well as ribosomes. Not all eukaryotic cells are the same. Animals, plants, protists, and fungi are eukaryotes. All multicellular organisms are eukaryotes. Most eukaryotes are multicellular. Some eukaryotes, such as amoebas and yeasts, are unicellular.

Visualize It!

13 Identify Use the list of terms below to fill in the blanks with the matching cell parts in each cell. Some terms are used twice.

DNA in cytoplasm
DNA in nucleus
Cytoplasm
Cell membrane
Organelles

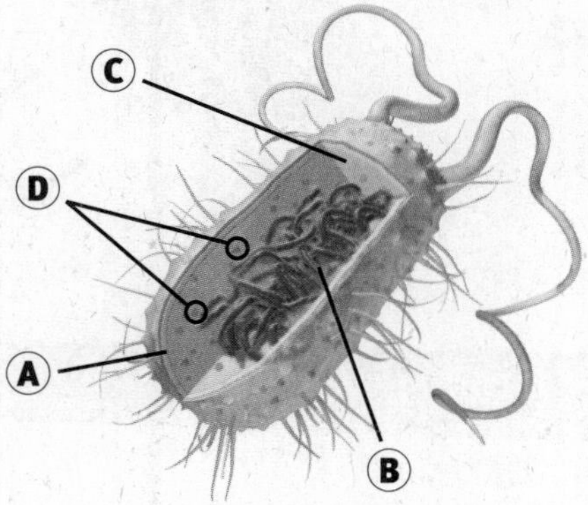

Prokaryotic

Eukaryotic

A ____________________

B ____________________

C ____________________

D ____________________

E ____________________

F DNA in nucleus

G ____________________

H ____________________

Visual Summary

To complete this summary, fill in the blanks with the correct word or phrase. Then use the key below to check your answers. You can use this page to review the main concepts of the lesson.

Cells and Cell Theory

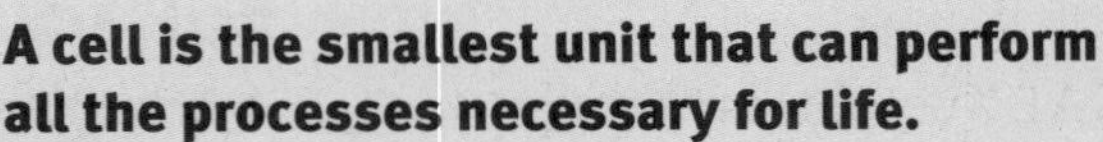

A cell is the smallest unit that can perform all the processes necessary for life.

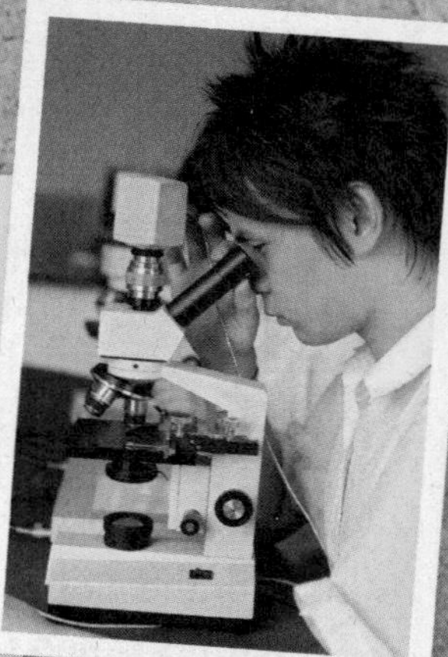

14 The cell of a ______________ organism must carry out all of its life functions; an organism made up of more than one cell is called a ______________ organism.

The cell theory lists three basic principles of all cells and organisms.

15 All cells come from existing ______________

All cells have a cell membrane, cytoplasm, organelles, and DNA.

16 The organelle that contains DNA in eukaryotic cells is called a ______________

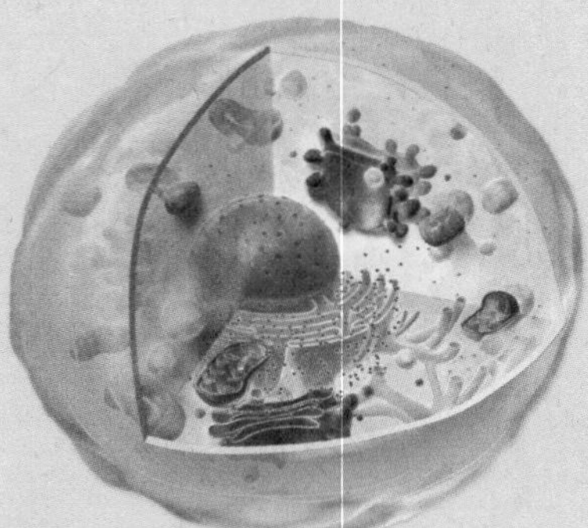

Eukaryotic

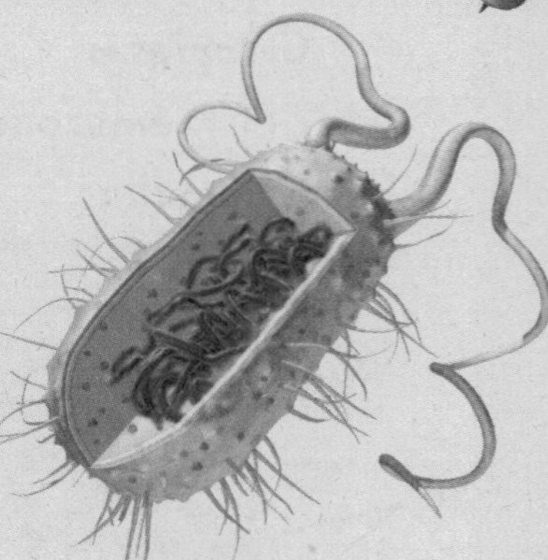

Prokaryotic

Answers: 14 unicellular, multicellular; 15 cells; 16 nucleus

17 Relate Choose an organism that you are familiar with, and explain how the three parts of the cell theory relate to that organism.

Lesson Review

Vocabulary

Fill in the blank with the term that best completes the following sentences.

1 The ________________________ is the smallest functional and structural unit of all living things.

2 All cells are surrounded by a(n) ________________________

3 A living thing is called a(n) ________________________

Key Concepts

4 Describe Discuss two ways that all cells are alike.

5 List What are the main ideas of the cell theory?

6 Compare How do prokaryotes differ from eukaryotes? How are they similar?

Critical Thinking

Use this figure to answer the following questions.

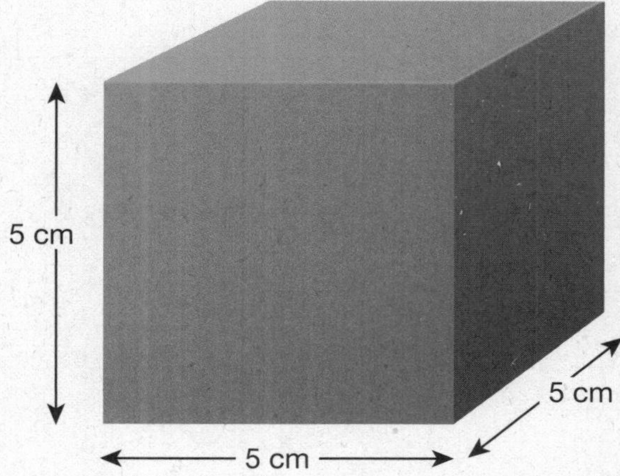

7 Apply What is the surface area-to-volume ratio of this cube?

8 Apply Cells are not as large as this cube. Explain why in terms of a cell's surface area-to-volume ratio.

9 Compare How is the structure of a unicellular organism different than the structure of a multicellular organism? How does this affect function?

My Notes

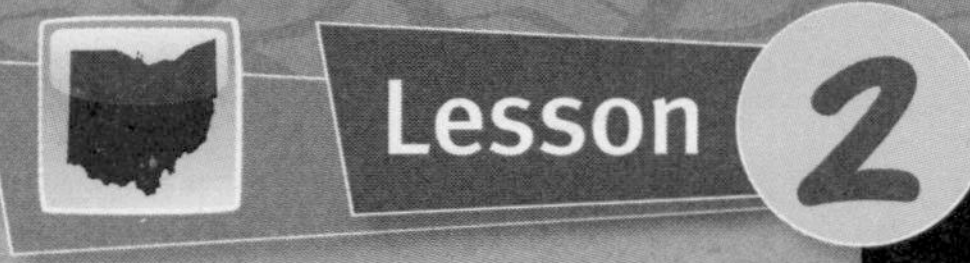

Chemistry of Life

ESSENTIAL QUESTION

What are the building blocks of organisms?

By the end of this lesson, you should be able to discuss the chemical makeup of living things.

These fungi are bioluminescent, which means they produce light from chemical reactions in their bodies. The light attracts insects that disperse the fungi's spores.

OHIO **6.LS.1** Cells are the fundamental unit of life.

OHIO **6.LS.3** Cells carry on specific functions that sustain life.

Lesson Labs

Quick Labs

- Analyzing Cell Components
- Molecules for Life Processes

Engage Your Brain

1 Describe Fill in the blank with the word or phrase that you think correctly completes the following sentences.

The chemical formula for ____________________

is H_2O. The *H* stands for hydrogen and the

____________________ stands for oxygen.

If you don't get enough water, you might

____

____

2 Relate What do you think you are made of?

____

____

____

____

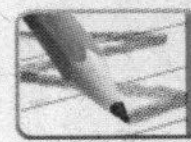

Active Reading

3 Synthesize You can often define an unknown word if you know the meaning of its word parts. Use the word parts and sentence below to make an educated guess about the meaning of the word *atom*.

Word part	Meaning
a–	not
tom	to cut

Example sentence

Air is mostly made up of oxygen and nitrogen atoms.

atom:

____

____

Vocabulary Terms

- **atom**
- **molecule**
- **lipid**
- **protein**
- **carbohydrate**
- **nucleic acid**
- **phospholipid**

4 Identify This list contains the key terms you'll learn in this lesson. As you read, circle the definition of each term.

It's Elementary

What are atoms and molecules?

Think about where you live. The streets are lined with many types of buildings. But these buildings are made from a lot of the same materials, such as bricks, glass, wood, and steel. Similarly, all cells are made from the same materials. The materials in cells are made up of atoms that can join together to form molecules.

Atoms Are the Building Blocks of Matter

The matter that you encounter every day, both living and nonliving, is made up of basic particles called **atoms.** Not all atoms are the same. There are nearly one hundred types of atoms that occur naturally on Earth. These different types of atoms are known as *elements.* Each element has unique properties. For example, oxygen is a colorless gas made up of oxygen atoms. The element gold is a shiny metal made up of gold atoms. Just six elements make up most of the human body. These and other elements are important for cell processes in all living things.

Active Reading

5 Relate How do atoms relate to cells?

____

____

____

____

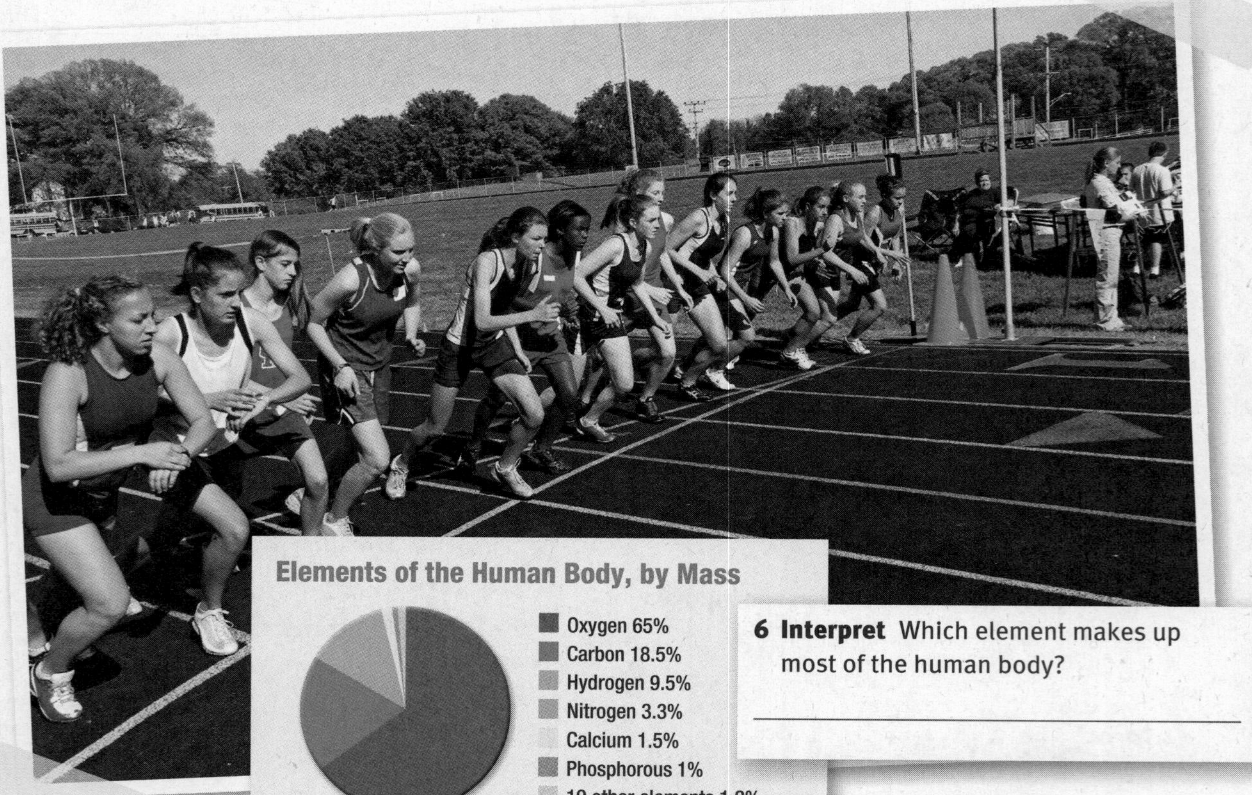

6 Interpret Which element makes up most of the human body?

____

Atoms and Molecules

The human body has trillions of cells made up of many different molecules.

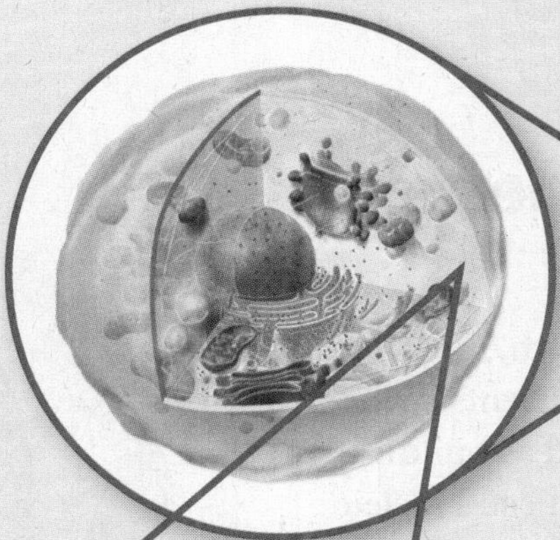

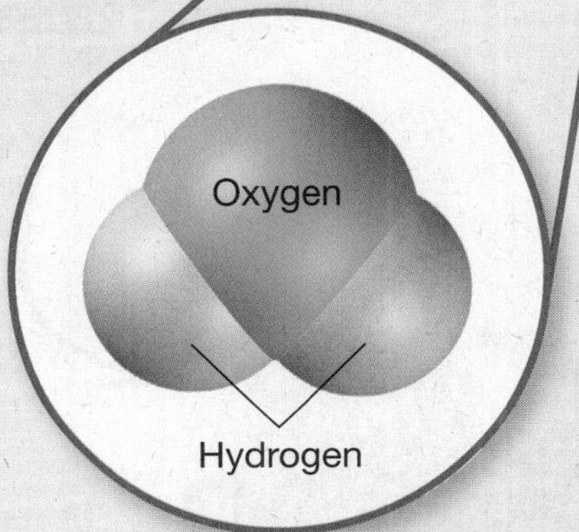

Water molecules are made of one oxygen atom joined to two hydrogen atoms.

If you could see the gold atoms that make up the outer coating of this medal, they would all look the same.

7 Synthesize How are the gold medal and the human cell similar? How do they differ?

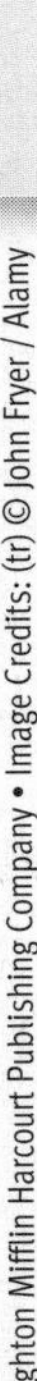

Molecules Are Made of Two or More Atoms

A **molecule** is a group of atoms that are held together by chemical bonds. For example, the molecule of water shown above is made of one oxygen atom bonded to two hydrogen atoms. If you separated the oxygen and hydrogen atoms, then you would no longer have a water molecule.

Some molecules are made up of only one type of atom. For example, a molecule of oxygen gas is made of two oxygen atoms. Other molecules contain different types of atoms. A substance made up of atoms of two or more elements joined by chemical bonds is called a *compound.* Most of the molecules found in cells are also compounds.

Cell Fuel

What are some important types of molecules in cells?

Organisms need certain types of molecules for growth, repair, and other life processes. For example, organisms use nutrients such as lipids, proteins, and carbohydrates for energy and as building materials. You get these nutrients from the food you eat. Nucleic acids are molecules that contain instructions for cell functions. Each of these types of molecules has a role in cell processes.

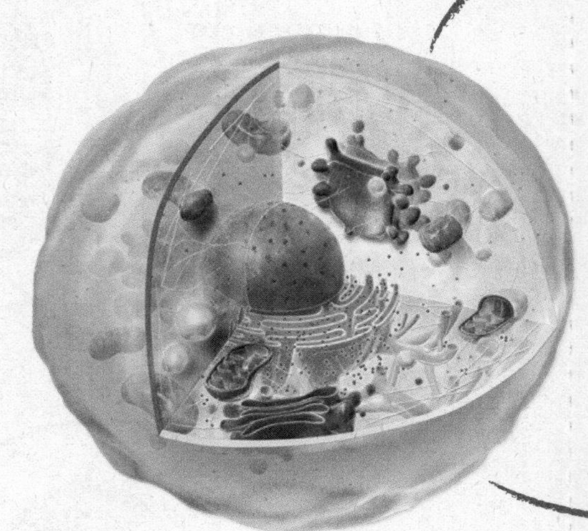

8 Identify What are some examples of nutrients?

____

____

____

Lipids

A **lipid** is a fat molecule or a molecule that has similar properties. Lipids do not mix with water. They have many jobs in cells, such as storing energy. Fats and oils are lipids that store energy that organisms can use when they need it. Your cells get lipids from foods such as olive oil and fish. Waxes and steroids are other types of lipids.

Proteins

A **protein** is a molecule made up of smaller molecules called *amino acids*. When you eat foods high in proteins, such as peanut butter and meat, the proteins are broken down into amino acids. Amino acids are used to make new proteins. Proteins are used to build and repair body structures and to regulate body processes. Proteins called *enzymes* (EHN•zymz) help chemical processes happen in cells.

9 Describe What are the building blocks of proteins?

____

Carbohydrates

Molecules that include sugars, starches, and fiber are called **carbohydrates**. Cells use carbohydrates as a source of energy and for energy storage. Cells break down carbohydrates to release the energy stored in them. Carbohydrates contain carbon, hydrogen, and oxygen atoms. Simple carbohydrates, such as table sugar, are made up of one sugar molecule or a few sugar molecules linked together. Complex carbohydrates, such as starch, are made of many sugar molecules linked together. Pasta, made from grains, is a good source of complex carbohydrates.

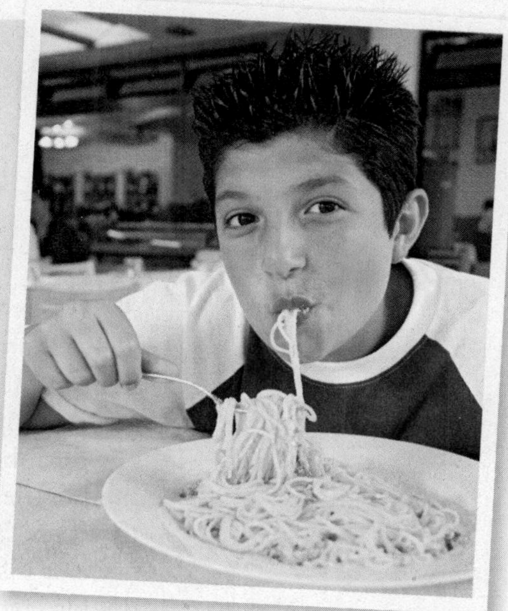

Nucleic Acids

A **nucleic acid** is a molecule that carries information in cells. Nucleic acids are made up of smaller molecules called *nucleotides* (NOO•klee•oh•TYDZ). Deoxyribonucleic acid, or DNA, is one type of nucleic acid that is found in all cells. DNA contains the information that cells need to make molecules, such as proteins. The order of nucleotides in DNA reads like a recipe. Each nucleotide tells the cell the order of amino acids needed to build a certain protein.

DNA

10 Summarize Fill in the table with a function of each nutrient in the cell.

Nutrient	Function in the cell
Lipids	
Proteins	
Carbohydrates	
Nucleic acids	

Waterworks

What are phospholipids?

All cells are surrounded by a cell membrane. The cell membrane helps protect the cell and keep the internal conditions of the cell stable. A lipid that contains phosphorus is called a **phospholipid** (FOSS•foh•LIH•pyd). Phospholipids form much of the cell membrane. The head of a phospholipid molecule is attracted to water. The tail repels water, or pushes it away. Because there is water inside and outside the cell, the phospholipids form a double layer. One layer lines up so that the heads face the outside of the cell. A second layer of phospholipids line up so the heads face the inside of the cell. The tails from both layers face each other, forming the middle of the cell membrane. Molecules, such as water, are regulated into and out of a cell through the cell membrane.

Active Reading **11 Explain** Describe how phospholipids form a barrier between water inside the cell and water outside the cell.

Visualize It!

12 Identify Write *attracts* next to the end of the phospholipid that attracts water. Write *repels* next to the end that repels water.

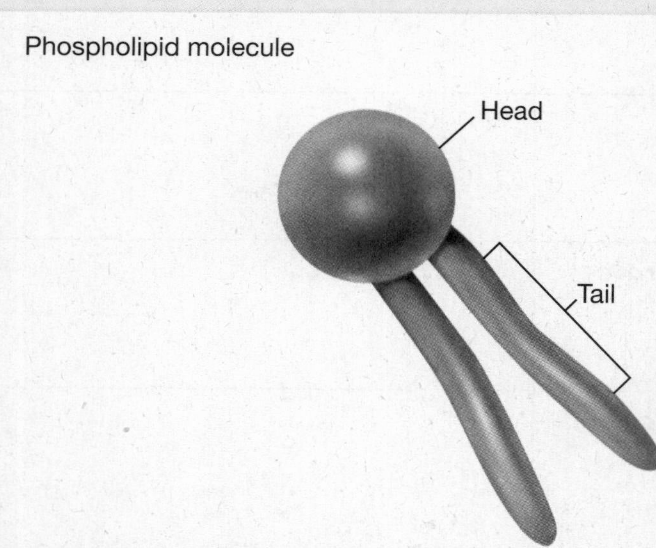

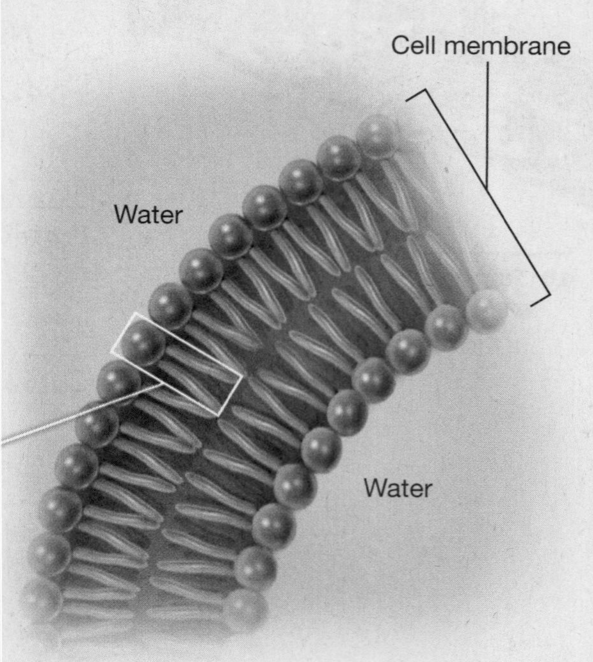

Why is water important?

Many cell processes require water, which makes up nearly two-thirds of the mass of the cell. Thus, water is an important nutrient for life. Water moves through the cell membrane by a process called *osmosis*. Osmosis depends on the concentration of the water inside and outside of the cell. Pure water has the highest concentration of water molecules. If the water concentration inside the cell is lower than the water concentration outside the cell, then water will move into the cell. If the environment outside a cell has a low concentration of water, such as in a salty solution, water will move out of the cell.

Think Outside the Book **Inquiry**

14 Associate Think of an object that could be an analogy to the cell membrane. Draw a picture of the object and explain how it is similar to and different from a cell membrane.

Losing too much water can cause a cell to shrivel and die.

The right balance of water allows a cell to function normally.

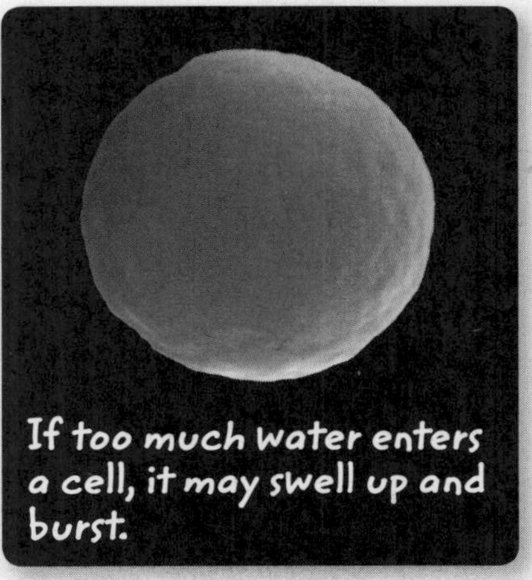

If too much water enters a cell, it may swell up and burst.

These gates control the people who enter and exit a sports stadium.

13 Apply How do these gates function in a similar way to the cell membrane?

____

____

____

____

Visual Summary

To complete this summary, circle the correct word and fill in the blanks with the correct word or phrase. Then, use the key below to check your answers. You can use this page to review the main concepts of the lesson.

Cell Chemistry

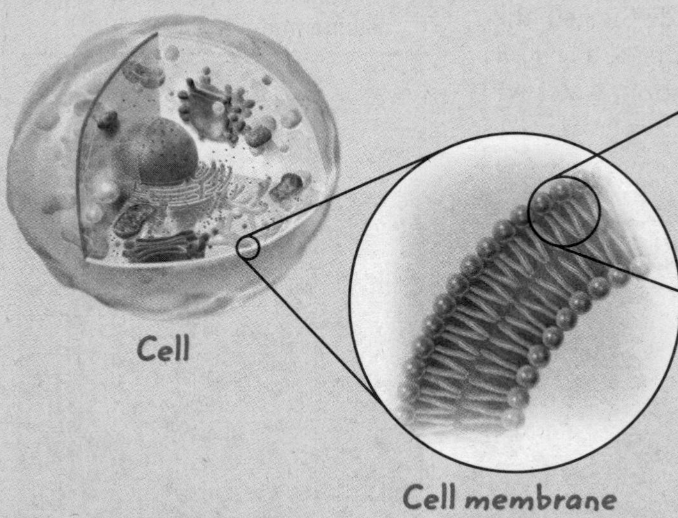

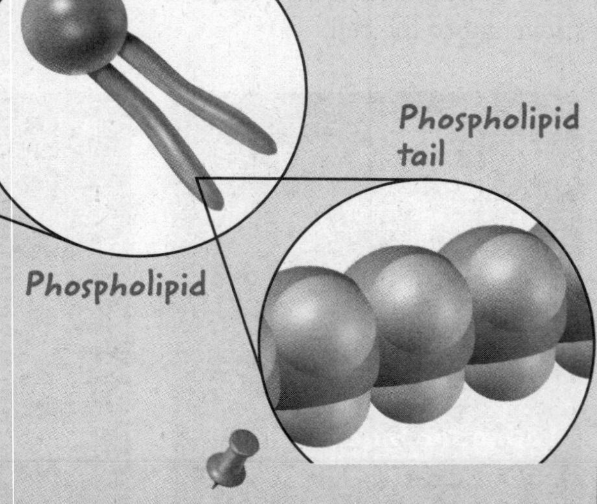

Cells are made up of atoms and molecules.

15 A cell membrane is made of phospholipid atoms / molecules.

16 The tail of the phospholipid is made up of carbon and hydrogen atoms / molecules.

Cells use different molecules for life processes.

17 List four types of molecules important for cell processes.

____

____

____

____

18 Water moves into and out of a cell through the

____

Answers: 15 molecules; 16 atoms; 17 lipids, carbohydrates, proteins, nucleic acids; 18 cell membrane

19 **Relate** Explain how atoms and molecules are important to cell processes.

Lesson Review

Vocabulary

Fill in the blank with the term that best completes the following sentences.

1 The smallest unit of an element is a(n) ______________________

2 A(n) ______________________ is a group of atoms joined by chemical bonds.

Key Concepts

3 Contrast What is the difference between atoms and molecules?

4 Identify What are the functions of proteins in organisms?

5 List Name four important types of molecules found in cells.

6 Describe How does the structure of the cell membrane help the cell regulate water?

Critical Thinking

Use this diagram to answer the following questions.

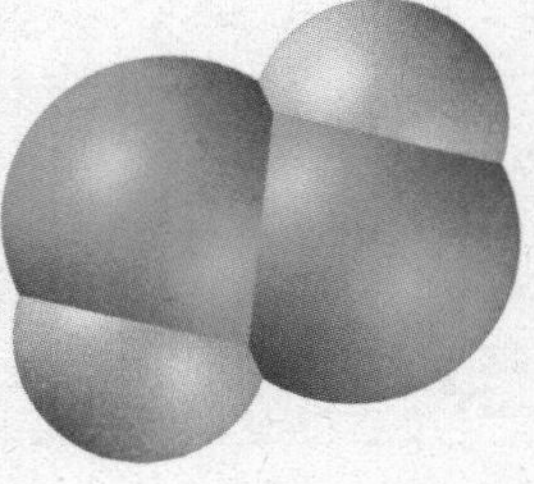

7 Identify Is this an atom or a molecule? Explain.

8 Recognize The red spheres represent oxygen atoms, and the blue spheres represent hydrogen atoms. Is this substance a compound? Explain.

9 Summarize Why is water important in cells?

My Notes

Cell Structure and Function

ESSENTIAL QUESTION

What are the different parts that make up a cell?

By the end of this lesson, you should be able to compare the structure and function of cell parts in plant and animal cells.

Cells have many parts. This part is called a Golgi complex. It functions like a shipping facility, packaging and distributing proteins and other materials for use in the cell.

OHIO 6.LS.1 Cells are the fundamental unit of life.

OHIO 6.LS.3 Cells carry on specific functions that sustain life.

OHIO 6.LS.4 Living systems at all levels of organization demonstrate the complementary nature of structure and function.

Lesson Labs

Quick Labs
- Comparing Cells
- Making a 3-D Cell Model
- Cell Walls and Wilting

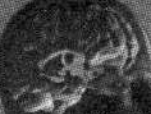

Engage Your Brain

1 Predict Check T or F to show whether you think each statement is true or false.

T	F	
☐	☐	All cells have the same structure and function.
☐	☐	Prokaryotes do not have a nucleus.
☐	☐	Plant cells are the same as animal cells.
☐	☐	All organisms are multicellular.

2 Relate How does the structure of this umbrella relate to its function?

Active Reading

3 Synthesis You can often define an unknown word if you know the meaning of its word parts. Use the word parts and sentence below to make an educated guess about the meaning of the word *chloroplast.*

Word part	Meaning
chloro-	green
plast	structure

Example sentence
Plant cells have chloroplasts, which contain a green pigment used for making their own food.

chloroplast:

Vocabulary Terms

- **cytoskeleton**
- **mitochondrion**
- **ribosome**
- **endoplasmic reticulum**
- **Golgi complex**
- **cell wall**
- **vacuole**
- **chloroplast**
- **lysosome**

4 Apply As you learn the definition of each vocabulary term in this lesson, create your own definition or sketch to help you remember the meaning of the term.

Being Eu-nique

What are the characteristics of eukaryotic cells?

Active Reading

5 Identify As you read, underline the characteristics of eukaryotic cells.

All organisms are made up of one or more cells, but what kinds of cells? There are two types of organisms: prokaryotes and eukaryotes. Prokaryotes are made up of a single prokaryotic cell. Eukaryotes are made up of one or more eukaryotic cells. Prokaryotic cells do not have a nucleus or membrane-bound organelles. Eukaryotic cells have membrane-bound organelles, including a nucleus.

Eukaryotic cells can differ from each other depending on their *structure* and *function*. A cell's structure is the arrangement of its parts. A cell's function is the activity the parts carry out. For example, plant cells and animal cells have different parts that have different functions for the organism. This is what make plants and animals so different from each other. Even cells within the same organism can differ from each other depending on their function. Most of the cells in multicellular organisms are specialized to perform a specific function. However, all eukaryotic cells share some characteristics. They all have a nucleus, membrane-bound organelles, and parts that protect and support the cell.

Visualize It!

6 Apply A euglena is a unicellular organism. Why is it a eukaryote like the plant and animal cells shown here?

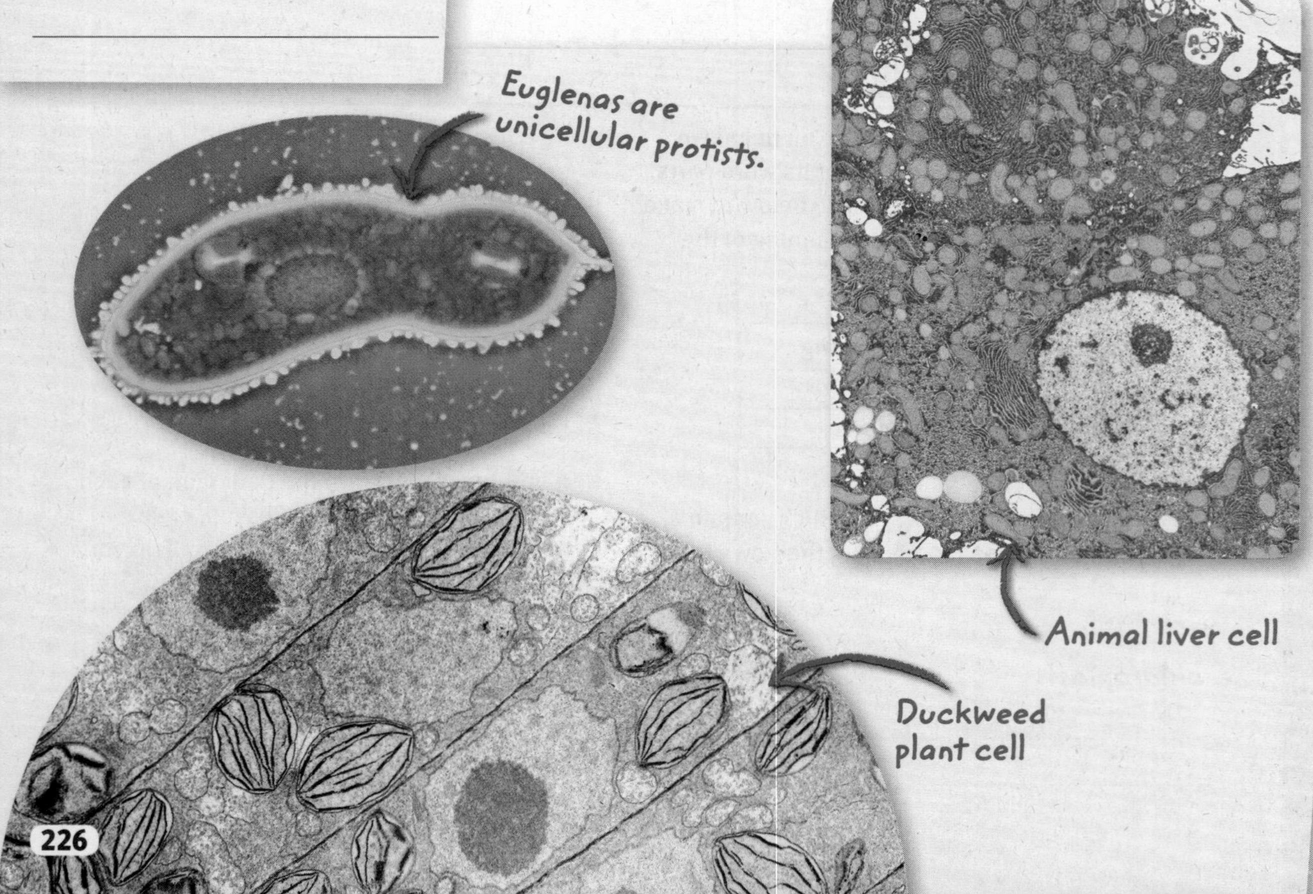

Euglenas are unicellular protists.

Animal liver cell

Duckweed plant cell

Parts that Protect and Support the Cell

Every cell is surrounded by a cell membrane. The cell membrane acts as a barrier between the inside of a cell and the cell's environment. The cell membrane protects the cell and regulates what enters and leaves the cell.

The cytoplasm is the region between the cell membrane and the nucleus that includes fluid and all of the organelles. Throughout the cytoplasm of eukaryotic cells is a **cytoskeleton**. The cytoskeleton is a network of protein filaments that gives shape and support to cells. The cytoskeleton is also involved in cell division and in movement. It may help parts within the cell to move. Or it may form structures that help the whole organism to move.

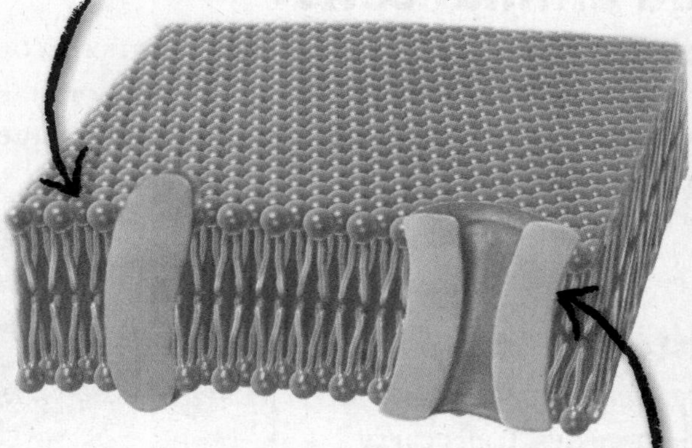

The cell membrane is a double layer of phospholipids. Water molecules and some gas molecules can pass through the cell membrane.
Other larger materials must pass through protein channels in the membrane.

7 Describe What are two functions of the cell membrane?

____

____

____

____

Genetic Material in the Nucleus

The nucleus is an organelle in eukaryotic cells that contains the cell's genetic material. Deoxyribonucleic acid, or DNA, is stored in the nucleus. DNA is genetic material that contains information needed for cell processes, such as making proteins. Proteins perform most actions of a cell. Although DNA is found in the nucleus, proteins are not made there. Instead, instructions for how to make proteins are stored in DNA. These instructions are sent out of the nucleus through pores in the nuclear membrane. The nuclear membrane is a double layer. Each layer is similar in structure to the cell membrane.

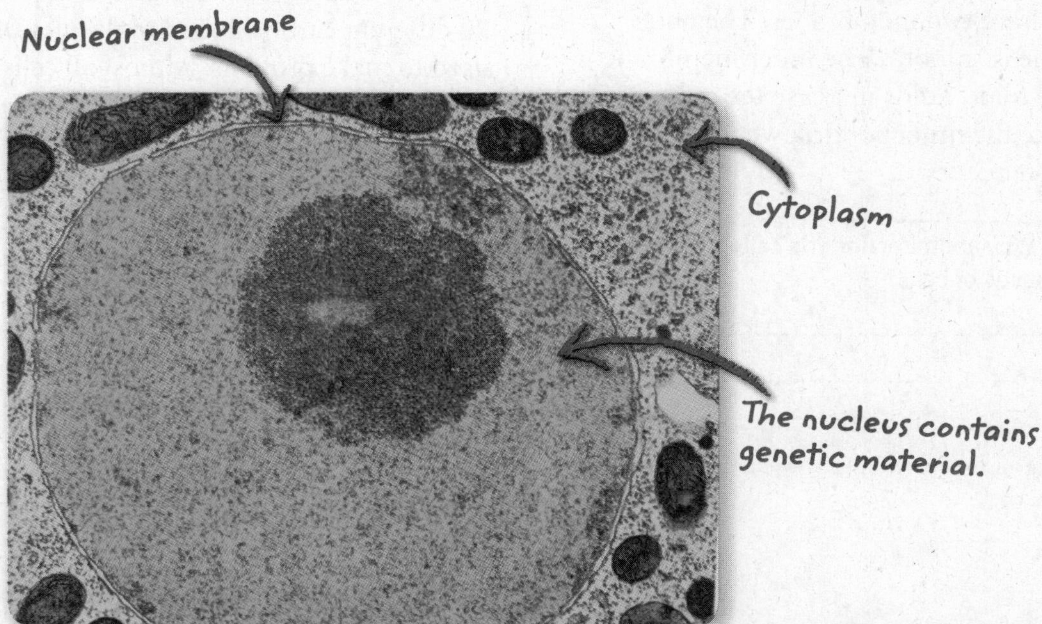

Part-iculars

What organelles are found in plant and animal cells?

Even though plant and animal cells are microscopic, they are very complex. They have many parts that function to keep the cell alive. Many of these parts are membrane-bound organelles that perform a specific function.

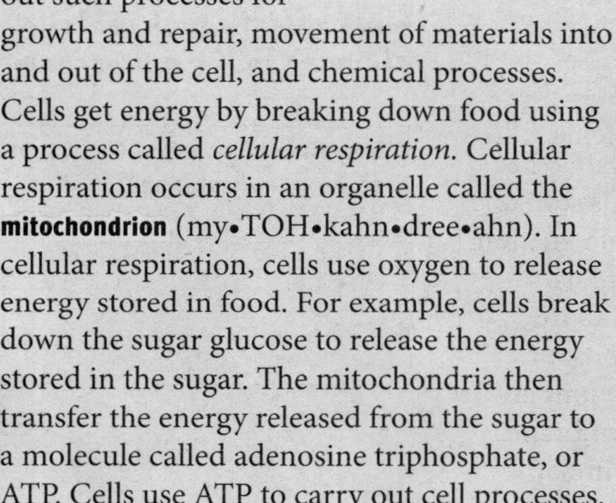

Mitochondria

Organisms need energy for life processes. Cells carry out such processes for growth and repair, movement of materials into and out of the cell, and chemical processes. Cells get energy by breaking down food using a process called *cellular respiration.* Cellular respiration occurs in an organelle called the **mitochondrion** (my•TOH•kahn•dree•ahn). In cellular respiration, cells use oxygen to release energy stored in food. For example, cells break down the sugar glucose to release the energy stored in the sugar. The mitochondria then transfer the energy released from the sugar to a molecule called adenosine triphosphate, or ATP. Cells use ATP to carry out cell processes.

Mitochondria have their own DNA and they have two membranes. The outer membrane is smooth. The inner membrane has many folds. Folds increase the surface area inside the mitochondria where cellular respiration occurs.

8 Explain Why are mitochondria called the powerhouses of cells?

____

____

____

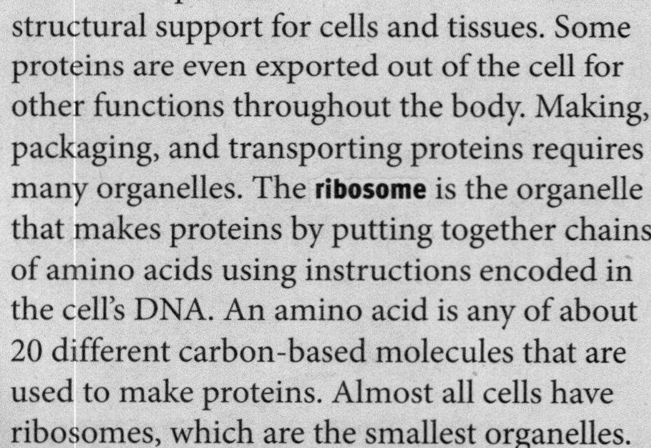

Ribosomes

Proteins control most chemical reactions of cells and provide structural support for cells and tissues. Some proteins are even exported out of the cell for other functions throughout the body. Making, packaging, and transporting proteins requires many organelles. The **ribosome** is the organelle that makes proteins by putting together chains of amino acids using instructions encoded in the cell's DNA. An amino acid is any of about 20 different carbon-based molecules that are used to make proteins. Almost all cells have ribosomes, which are the smallest organelles.

Ribosomes are not enclosed in a membrane. In prokaryotes, the ribosomes are suspended freely in the cytoplasm. In eukaryotes, some ribosomes are free, and others are attached to another organelle called the *endoplasmic reticulum.*

9 Describe How do ribosomes make proteins?

____

____

____

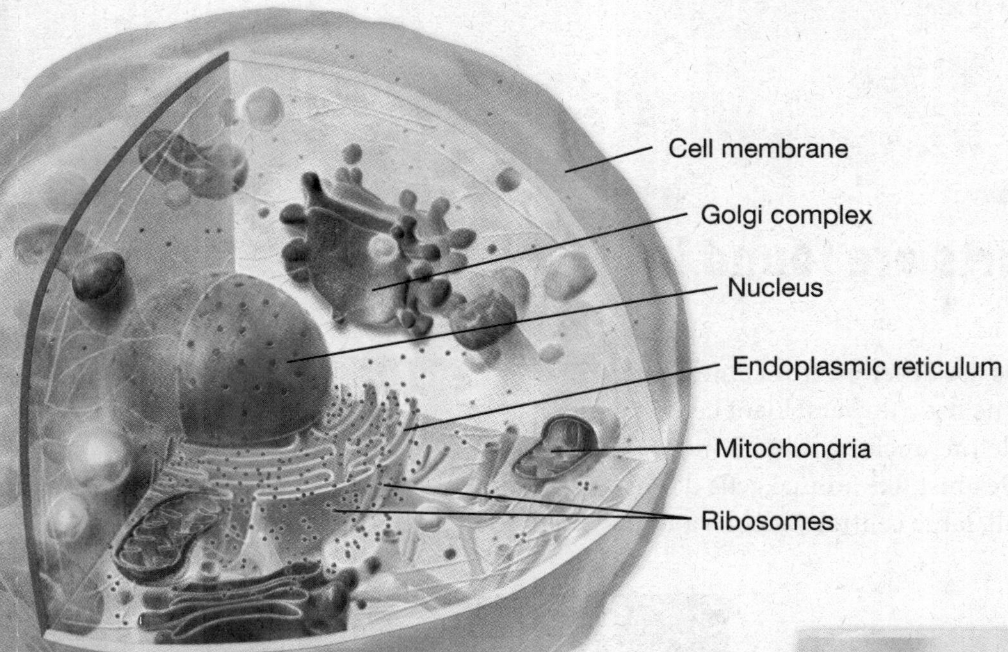

Endoplasmic Reticulum

In the cytoplasm is a system of membranes near the nucleus called the **endoplasmic reticulum** (ehn•doh•PLAHZ•mick rhett•ICK•yoo•luhm), or ER. The ER assists in the production, processing, and transport of proteins and in the production of lipids. The ER is either smooth or rough. Rough ER has ribosomes attached to its membrane, while smooth ER does not. Ribosomes on the rough ER make many of the cell's proteins. Some of these proteins move through the ER to different places in the cell. The smooth ER makes lipids and breaks down toxic materials that could damage the cell.

10 Compare How does rough ER differ from smooth ER in structure and function?

____

____

____

Golgi complex

Golgi Complex

The membrane-bound organelle that packages and distributes materials, such as proteins, is called the **Golgi complex** (GOHL•ghee COHM•plehkz). It is named after Camillo Golgi, the Italian scientist who first identified the organelle.

The Golgi complex is a system of flattened membrane sacs. Lipids and proteins from the ER are delivered to the Golgi complex where they may be modified to do different jobs. The final products are enclosed in a piece of the Golgi complex's membrane. This membrane pinches off to form a small bubble, or vesicle. The vesicle transports its contents to other parts of the cell or out of the cell.

11 Describe What is the function of the Golgi complex?

____

____

____

Now Showing:

The Plant Cell

What additional parts are found in plant cells?

Think about some ways that plants are different from animals. Plants don't move around, and some have flowers. Plant cells do have a cell membrane, cytoskeleton, nucleus, mitochondria, ribosomes, ER, and a Golgi complex just like animal cells do. In addition, plant cells have a cell wall, large central vacuole, and chloroplasts.

12 Identify As you read, underline the functions of the cell wall, large central vacuole, and the chloroplasts.

Cell Wall

In addition to the cell membrane, plant cells have a **cell wall**. The cell wall is a rigid structure that surrounds the cell membrane, identified by the yellow line around the plant cell in this photo. Cell walls provide support and protection to the cell. Plants don't have a skeleton like many animals do, so they get their shape from the cell wall. The cells of fungi, archaea, bacteria, and some protists also have cell walls.

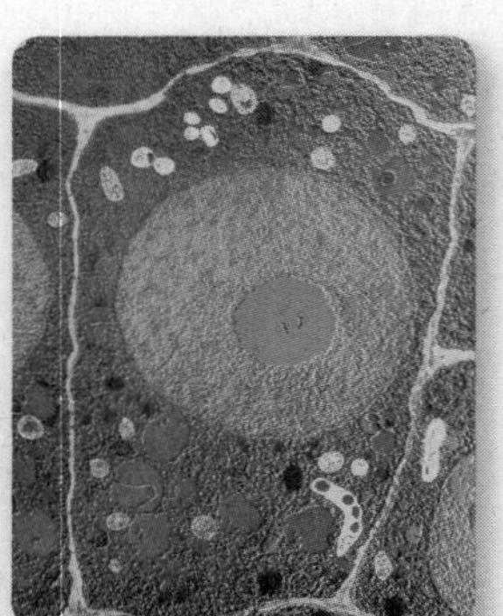

Large Central Vacuole

A **vacuole** (VAK•yoo•ohl) is a fluid-filled vesicle found in the cells of most animals, plants, and fungi. A vacuole may contain enzymes, nutrients, water, or wastes. Plant cells also have a large central vacuole that stores water. Central vacuoles full of water help support the cell. Plants may wilt when the central vacuole loses water.

13 Compare How do large central vacuoles differ from vacuoles?

Visualize It!

14 Identify Label these cell parts on the plant cell shown here:

- Mitochondrion
- Golgi complex
- Nucleus
- Endoplasmic reticulum
- Ribosomes
- Cell wall
- Cell membrane
- Cytoskeleton

Large central vacuole

A ______________________

B ______________________

C ______________________

D ______________________

E ______________________

F ______________________

G ______________________

H ______________________

Chloroplasts

Animals must eat food to provide their cells with energy. However, plants, and some protists, can make their own food using photosynthesis. These organisms have **chloroplasts** (KLOHR•oh•plahstz), organelles where photosynthesis occurs. Photosynthesis is the process by which cells use sunlight, carbon dioxide, and water to make sugar and oxygen. Chloroplasts are green because they contain a green pigment called *chlorophyll* (KLOHR•oh•fill). Chlorophyll absorbs the energy in sunlight. This energy is used to make sugar, which is then used by mitochondria to make ATP. Chloroplasts have two outer membranes.

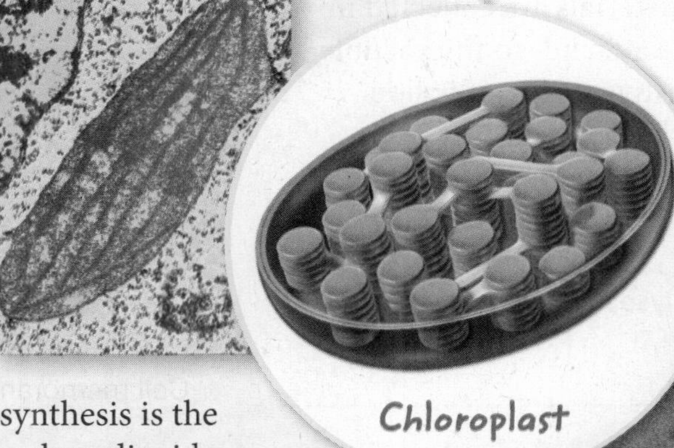
Chloroplast

15 Describe What is the role of chlorophyll inside chloroplasts?

____

____

____

Think Outside the Book Inquiry

16 Describe Cyanobacteria and green algae are similar to plants. Choose one of these organisms and explain why they are similar to plants but are not classified as plants.

Introducing:

The Animal Cell

What additional part is found in animal cells?

Animal cells are eukaryotic cells that contain a nucleus and are surrounded by a cell membrane. They contain many of the same organelles as most plant cells, including mitochondria, ribosomes, ER, and a Golgi complex. Most animal cells also contain a membrane-bound organelle called a *lysosome*.

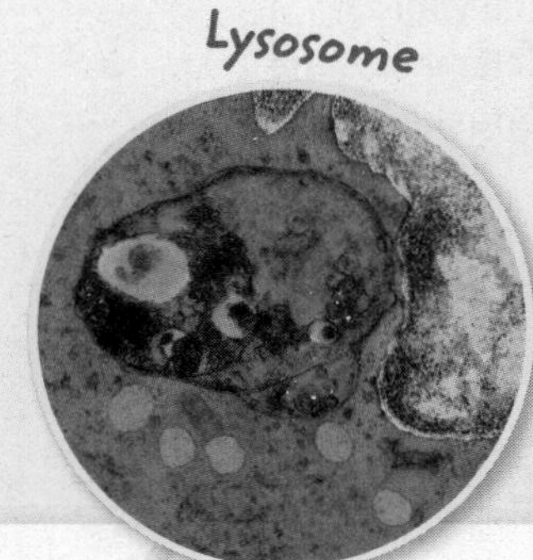

Active Reading **17 Recognize** As you read, underline the function of lysosomes.

Lysosomes

Organelles called **lysosomes** (LY•soh•zohmz) contain digestive enzymes, which break down worn-out or damaged organelles, waste materials, and foreign invaders in the cell. Some of these materials are collected in vacuoles. A lysosome attaches to the vacuole and releases the digestive enzymes inside. Some of these materials are recycled and reused in the cell. For example, a human liver cell recycles half of its materials each week.

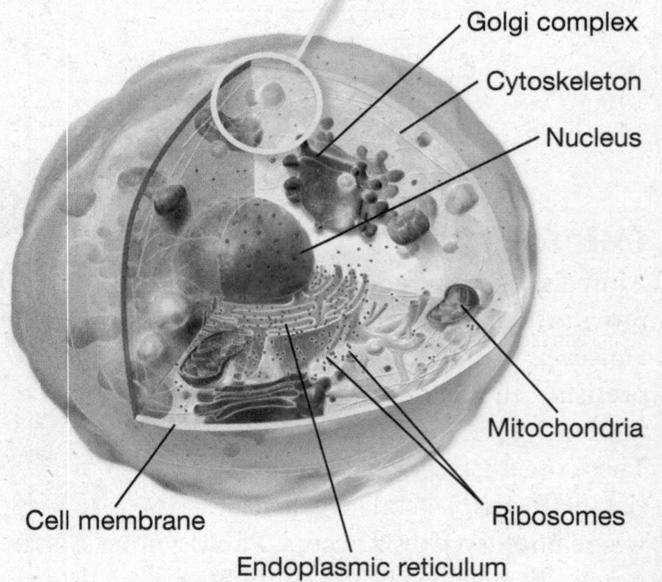

18 Compare How are lysosomes similar to vacuoles?

____

____

____

____

19 Compare Draw a sketch for each organelle identified in the *Structure* column. Put check marks in the last two columns to identify whether the cell structure can usually be found in plant cells, animal cells, or both.

Structure	Function	In plant cell?	In animal cell?
Nucleus	Contains the genetic material		
Endoplasmic reticulum	Processes and transports proteins and makes lipids		
Golgi complex	Packages and distributes materials within or out of the cell		
Ribosome	Makes proteins		
Chloroplast	Uses sunlight, carbon dioxide, and water to make food by photosynthesis		
Mitochondrion	Breaks down food molecules to release energy by cellular respiration		
Large central vacuole	Stores water and helps give shape to the cell		
Lysosome	Produces enzymes that digest wastes, cell parts, and foreign invaders		

Visual Summary

To complete this summary, fill in the blanks to identify the organelles in each cell. Then, use the key below to check your answers. You can use this page to review the main concepts of the lesson.

Compare Plant Cells and Animal Cells

Structures in plant cells

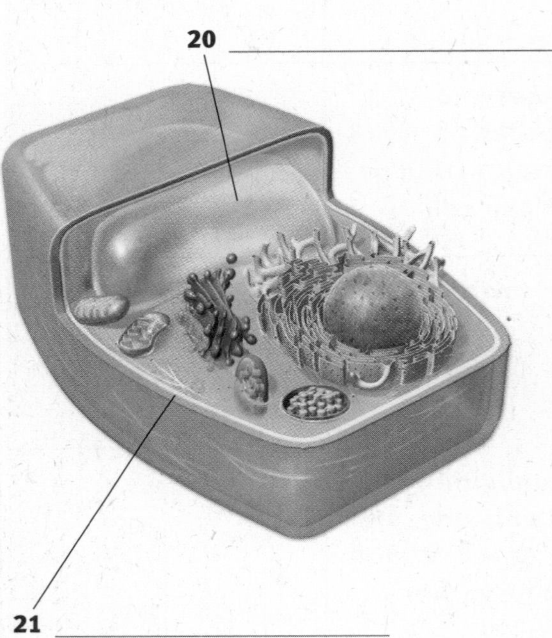

Structures in animal cells

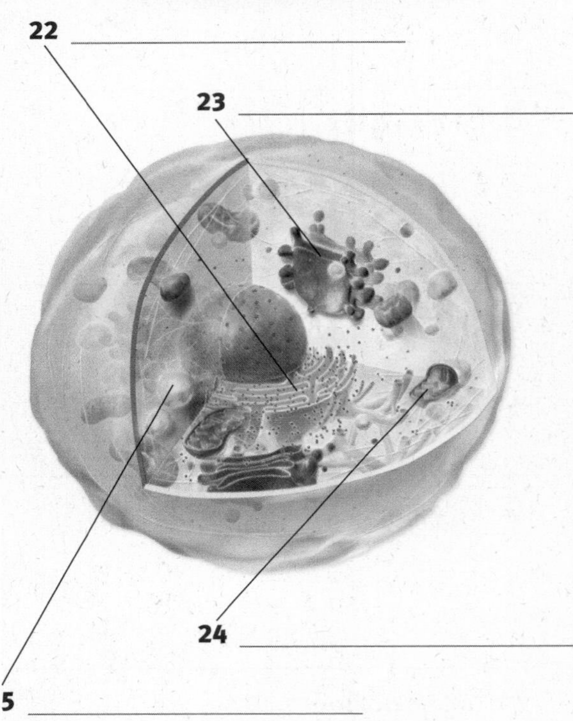

Plants and animals are eukaryotes. The structures inside a eukaryotic cell work together to keep the cell and the entire organism alive.

Answers: 20 large central vacuole; 21 cell wall; 22 endoplasmic reticulum; 23 Golgi complex; 24 mitochondrion; 25 lysosome

26 Summarize How do eukaryotic cells differ from each other?

Lesson Review

Vocabulary

Circle the term that best completes the following sentences.

1 A *Golgi complex / ribosome* makes proteins that are transported through the endoplasmic reticulum.

2 The *nucleus / large central vacuole* contains genetic material of a eukaryotic cell.

3 The *cell membrane / cytoplasm* acts as a barrier between the inside of a cell and the cell's environment.

4 The organelle in which photosynthesis takes place is the *cell wall / chloroplast*.

Key Concepts

5 Recognize What do all eukaryotic cells have in common?

6 Compare How are the functions of the cytoskeleton and the cell wall similar?

7 Contrast What structures are found in plant cells that are not found in animal cells?

Critical Thinking

Use this diagram to answer the following questions.

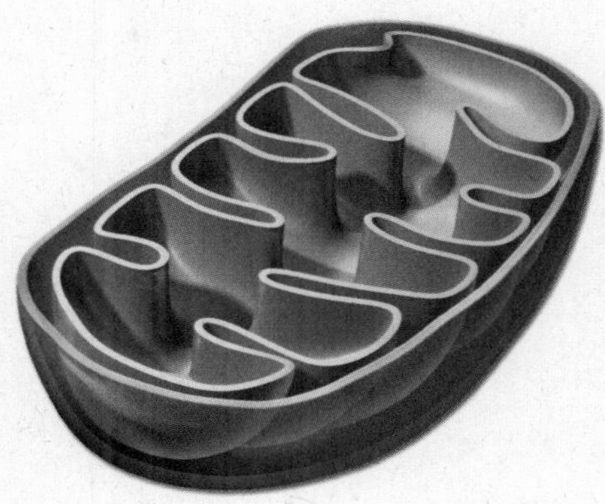

8 Identify What is this organelle?

9 Explain How does its structure affect its function?

10 Compare Which cells contain this organelle: plant cells, animal cells, or both?

11 Apply Explain the function of ribosomes and why cells need them.

My Notes

Think Science

OHIO 6.LS.2 All cells come from pre-existing cells.

OHIO 6.SIA.5 Develop descriptions, models, explanations and predictions.

Making Predictions

Scientists try to answer questions about the world by developing hypotheses, making predictions, and conducting experiments to test those predictions. To make a prediction, a scientist will analyze a general idea and then predict specific results. Predictions often take the form of "if–then" statements. For example, "If living organisms are made of small units called cells, then we predict that we will see cells if we look at organisms up close under a microscope."

A dividing frog cell showing microtubules (green) and DNA (blue)

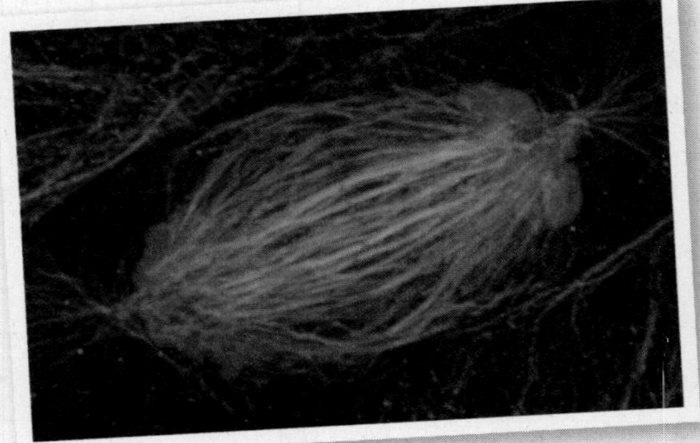

Tutorial

For an organism to grow and reproduce, chromosomes must replicate and cells must divide. The following steps will teach you how to make predictions from hypotheses about the role of protein fibers, called microtubules, in cell division.

Question: How do chromosomes move and separate during cell division?

Hypothesis: Microtubules play an important role in the movement of the chromosomes during cell division.

What is the hypothesis? A hypothesis is a plausible answer to a scientific question. Form a hypothesis based on prior experience, background knowledge, or your own observations.

Prediction: If microtubules were inhibited during cell division, then chromosomes would not be able to move and separate from each other during cell division.

What would we expect or predict to see if the hypothesis were true? When scientists summarize their data, they look for observations and measurements that will support their hypothesis.

Observations: When microtubules are exposed to a drug that blocks microtubule formation, movement of chromosomes is inhibited and cell division stops.

Does the prediction match the observations? If the data matches the predictions generated by the hypothesis, then the hypothesis is supported. Sometimes errors occur during the scientific investigation, which can lead to incorrect results. There is also the possibility that correct data will not match the hypothesis. When this happens, generate a new hypothesis.

You Try It!

Scientists often propose hypotheses about the causes of events they observe. Read the following scenario, and answer the questions that follow.

Scenario: A cell biologist has three cell cultures of human skin cells. The cells in each culture are taken from the same cell line. Each cell culture is placed in a solution for observation. The cells in culture A are growing faster than the cells in cultures B and C.

Question: Why are the cells in culture A growing at a faster rate than the cells in cultures B and C?

Hypothesis 1: The waste level is higher in cultures B and C than in culture A.

Hypothesis 2: The nutrient levels are higher in culture A than in cultures B and C.

1 Making Predictions Read each of the hypotheses above and then make a prediction for each about what might be observed.

Hypothesis 1:

____

____

____

Hypothesis 2:

____

____

____

2 Testing a Hypothesis Identify a possible experiment for each hypothesis that you can perform or observations that you can make to find out whether the hypothesis is supported.

Hypothesis 1:

____

____

____

Hypothesis 2:

____

____

____

____

3 Predicting Outcomes Fill in the two tables below with plausible data that supports each hypothesis.

Culture	Waste level	Rate of growth (cells/hour)
A		
B		
C		

Culture	Nutrient level	Rate of growth (cells/hour)
A		
B		
C		

Take It Home

Find a recent newspaper or magazine article that makes a conclusion based on a scientific study. Carefully evaluate the study and identify the predictions that were tested in the study. Bring the article to class and be prepared to discuss your analysis of the article.

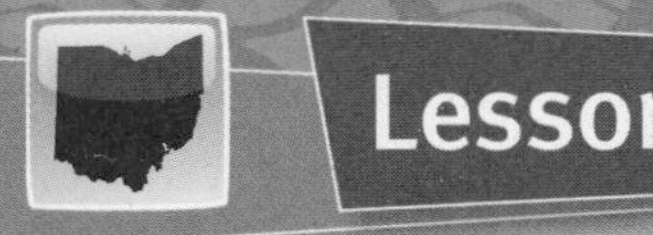
Lesson 4

Levels of Cellular Organization

ESSENTIAL QUESTION

How are living things organized?

By the end of this lesson, you should be able to describe the different levels of organization in living things.

The eye of a green iguana is an organ made of millions of cells and many layers of tissues.

OHIO **6.LS.3** Cells carry on specific functions that sustain life.

OHIO **6.LS.4** Living systems at all levels of organization demonstrate the complementary nature of structure and function.

Lesson Labs

Quick Labs
- Evaluating Specialization
- Observing Plant Organs

Exploration Lab
- The Organization of Organisms

Engage Your Brain

1 Describe Fill in the blank with the word or phrase you think correctly completes the following sentences.

Your body has many organs, such as a heart and ______________________

Plant organs include stems and ______________________

Animal and plant organs are organized into organ systems, much like you organize your homework in ______________________

2 Explain How is the structure of a hammer related to its function?

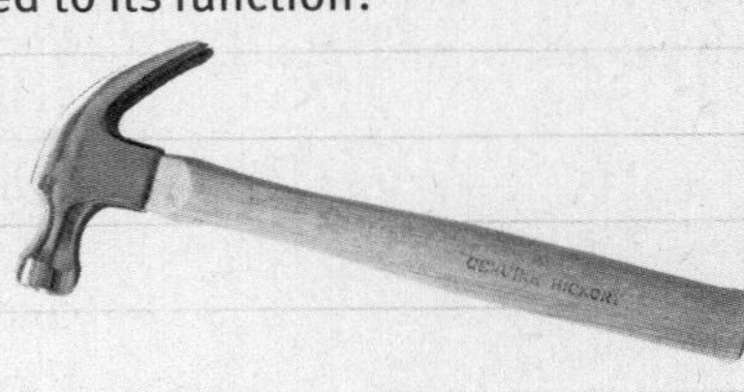

Active Reading

3 Relate Many scientific words, such as *organ* and *tissue,* also have everyday meanings. Use context clues to write your own definition for each underlined word.

It is helpful to use a <u>tissue</u> when sneezing to prevent the spread of droplets carrying bacteria.

tissue:

An <u>organ</u> can be very difficult to play.

organ:

Vocabulary Terms

- **organism**
- **tissue**
- **organ**
- **organ system**
- **structure**
- **function**

4 Apply As you learn the definition of each vocabulary term in this lesson, create your own definition or sketch to help you remember the meaning of the term.

Body Building

How are living things organized?

Active Reading

5 Identify As you read, underline the characteristics of unicellular and multicellular organisms.

An **organism** is a living thing that can carry out life processes by itself. *Unicellular organisms* are made up of just one cell that performs all of the functions necessary for life. Unicellular organisms do not have levels of organization. Having only one cell has advantages and disadvantages. For example, unicellular organisms need fewer resources and some can live in harsh conditions, such as hot springs and very salty water. However, a disadvantage of being unicellular is that the entire organism dies if the single cell dies.

Into Cells

Multicellular organisms are made up of more than one cell. These cells are grouped into different levels of organization, including tissues, organs, and organ systems. The cells that make up a multicellular organism, such as humans and plants, are specialized to perform specific functions. Many multicellular organisms reproduce through sexual reproduction, during which a male sex cell fertilizes a female sex cell. The single cell that results from fertilization divides repeatedly. This cell division forms the basic tissues of an embryo, which further develop into all of the specialized tissues and organs within a multicellular organism. Other characteristics of multicellular organisms include a larger size and a longer lifespan than unicellular organisms.

There are some disadvantages to being multicellular. Multicellular organisms need more resources than do unicellular organisms. Also, the cells of multicellular organisms are specialized for certain jobs, which means that cells must depend on each other to perform all of the functions that an organism needs to live.

Humpback whales are multicellular organisms.

Diatoms are microscopic unicellular organisms that live in water.

Into Tissues

A **tissue** is a group of similar cells that perform a common function. Humans and many other animals are made up of four basic types of tissue: nervous, epithelial, connective, and muscle. Nervous tissue functions as a messaging system within the body. Epithelial tissue is protective and forms boundaries, such as skin. Connective tissue, including bones and blood, holds parts of the body together and provides support and nourishment to organs. Muscle tissue helps produce movement.

Plants have three types of tissue: transport, protective, and ground. Transport tissue moves water and nutrients through the plant. Protective tissue protects the outside of the plant. Ground tissue provides internal support and storage and absorbs light energy to make food in photosynthesis (foh•toh•SIN•thuh•sis).

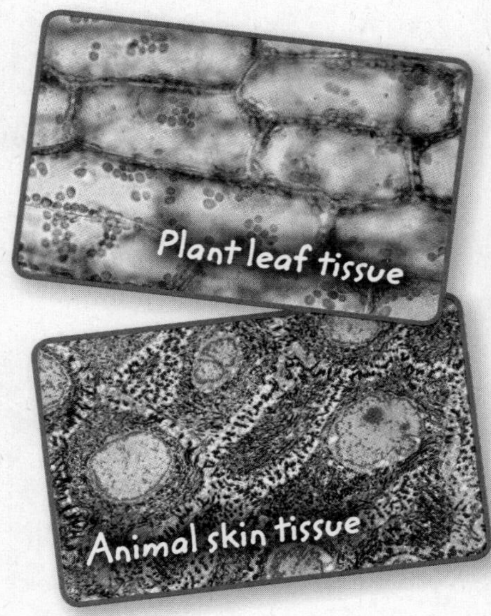
Plant leaf tissue

Animal skin tissue

6 Compare Fill in the Venn diagram to compare the functions of animal tissues and plant tissues. What functions do they share?

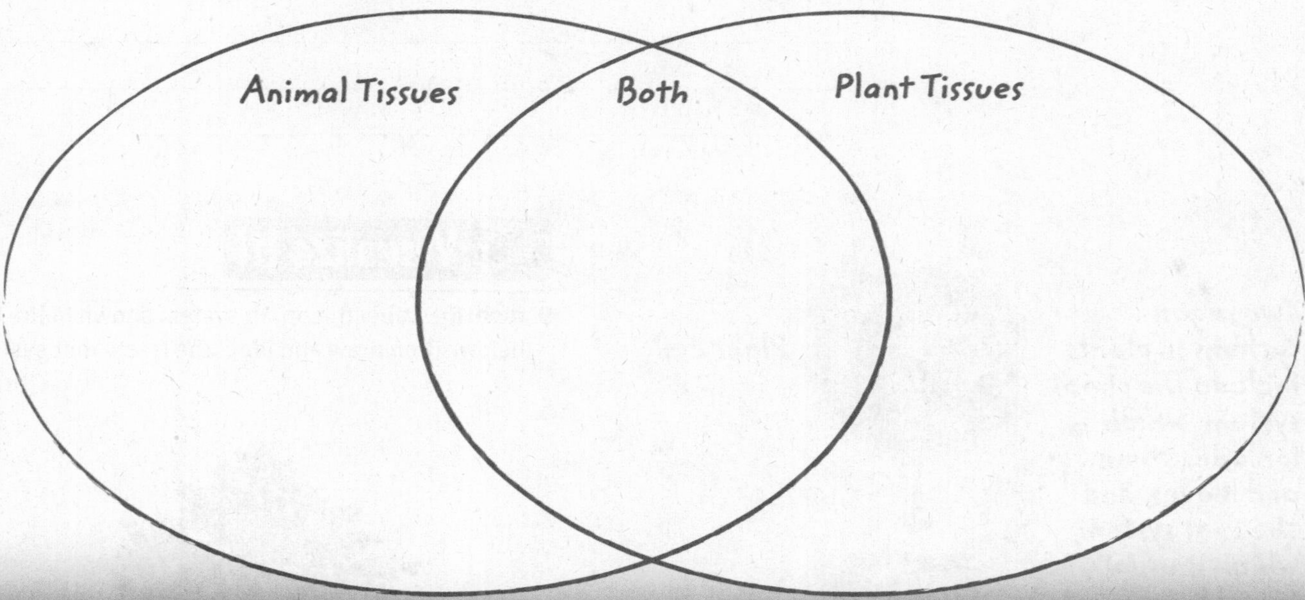

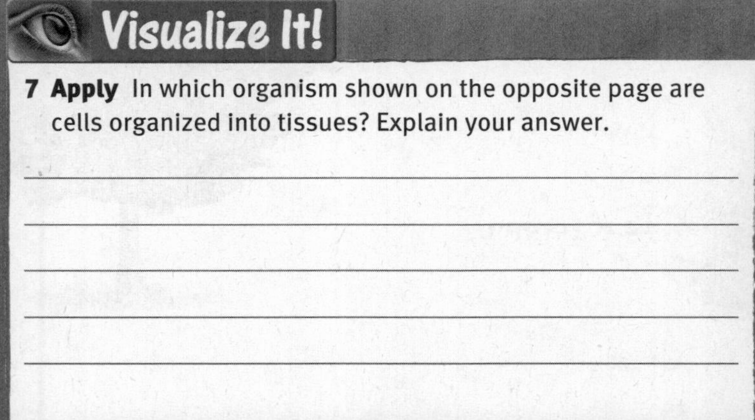

Visualize It!

7 Apply In which organism shown on the opposite page are cells organized into tissues? Explain your answer.

Into Organs

A structure made up of a collection of tissues that carries out a specialized function is called an **organ**. The stomach is an organ that breaks down food for digestion. Different types of tissues work together to accomplish this function. For example, nervous tissue sends messages to the stomach's muscle tissue to tell the muscle tissue to contract. When the muscle tissue contracts, food and stomach acids are mixed, and the food breaks down.

Plants also have organs that are made up of different tissues working together. For example, a leaf is an organ that contains protective tissue to reduce water loss, ground tissue for photosynthesis, and transport tissue to move nutrients from leaves to stems. Stems and roots are organs that function to transport and store water and nutrients in the plant. The trunk of most trees is a stem. Roots are usually below the ground.

8 Apply How do organs relate to cells and tissues?

___

___

___

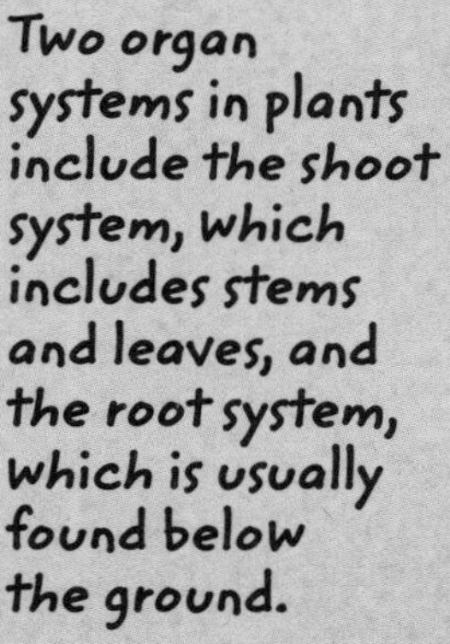

Two organ systems in plants include the shoot system, which includes stems and leaves, and the root system, which is usually found below the ground.

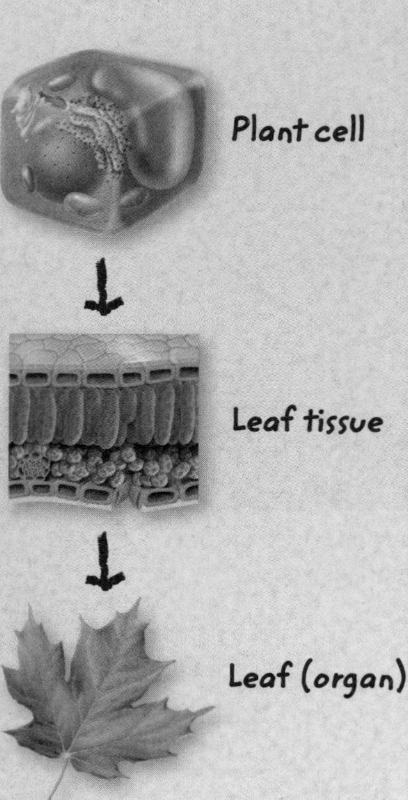

9 Identify Label the organ system shown in the tree below. Then draw and label the tree's root system.

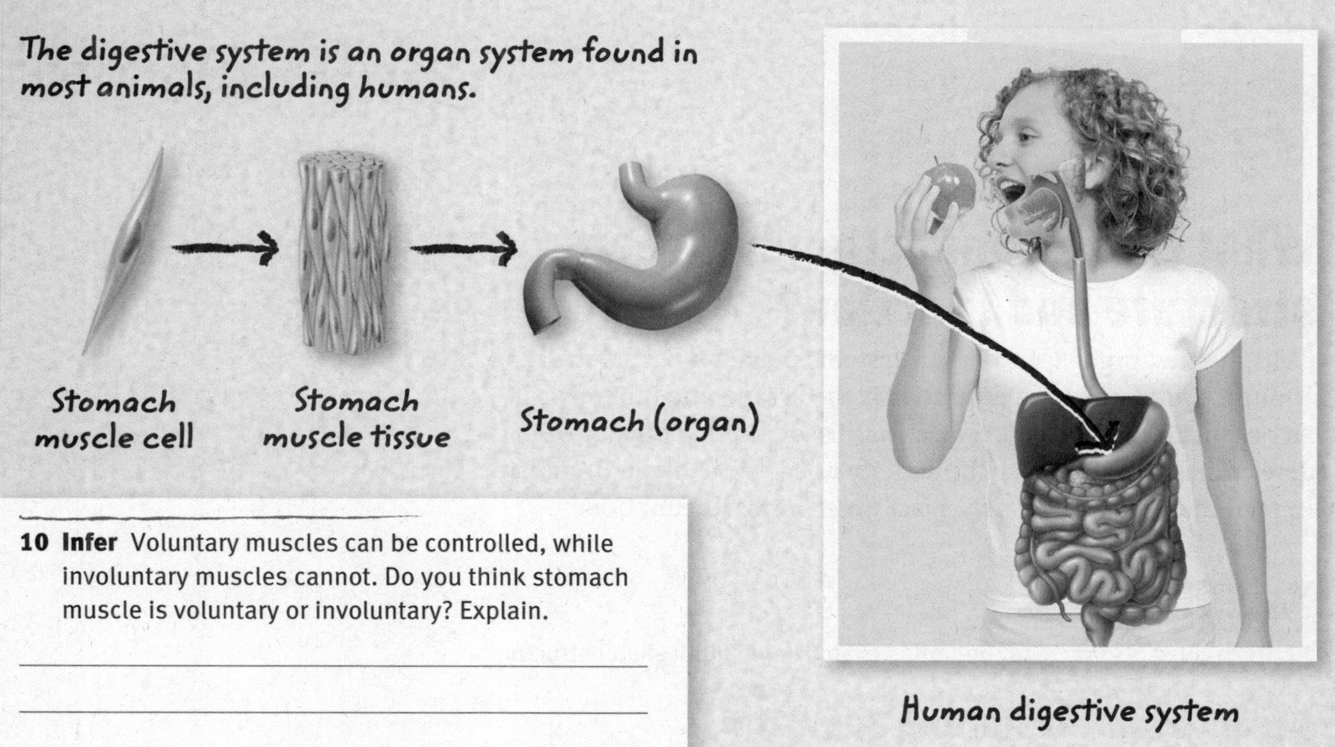

Human digestive system

10 Infer Voluntary muscles can be controlled, while involuntary muscles cannot. Do you think stomach muscle is voluntary or involuntary? Explain.

____

____

____

Into Organ Systems

An **organ system** is a group of organs that work together to perform body functions. Each organ system has a specific job to do for the organism. For example, the stomach works with other organs of the digestive system to digest and absorb nutrients from food. Other organs included in the digestive system are the esophagus and the small and large intestines.

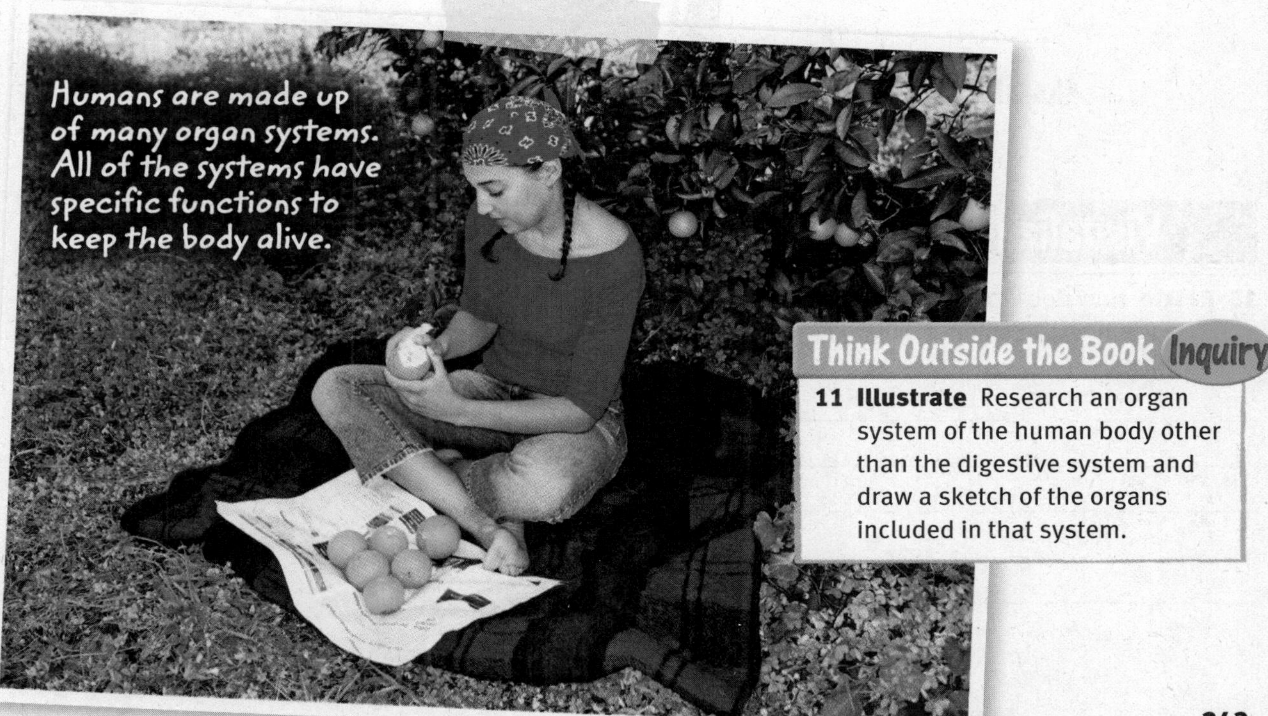

Humans are made up of many organ systems. All of the systems have specific functions to keep the body alive.

Think Outside the Book Inquiry

11 Illustrate Research an organ system of the human body other than the digestive system and draw a sketch of the organs included in that system.

What's Your Function?

What is the connection between structure and function?

Cells, tissues, organs, and organ systems make up the structure of a multicellular organism. **Structure** is the arrangement of parts in an organism or an object. The structure of a cell, tissue, or organ determines its **function**, or the activity of each part in an organism. In fact, the structure of any object determines its function.

Active Reading

12 Recognize As you read, underline examples of multicellular structures.

Structure Determines Function

Cells, tissues, and organs vary in structure. For example, bone cells look different from plant leaf cells. A lung differs from a stomach because they have different functions. Cells, tissues, and organs are specialized to perform specific functions. For example, a lung is an organ made up of cells and tissues that work together to help you breathe. The lungs are made up of millions of tiny air sacs called *alveoli* (singular, *alveolus*). The large number of alveoli increases the surface area of the lungs to let enough oxygen and carbon dioxide move between the lungs and the blood.

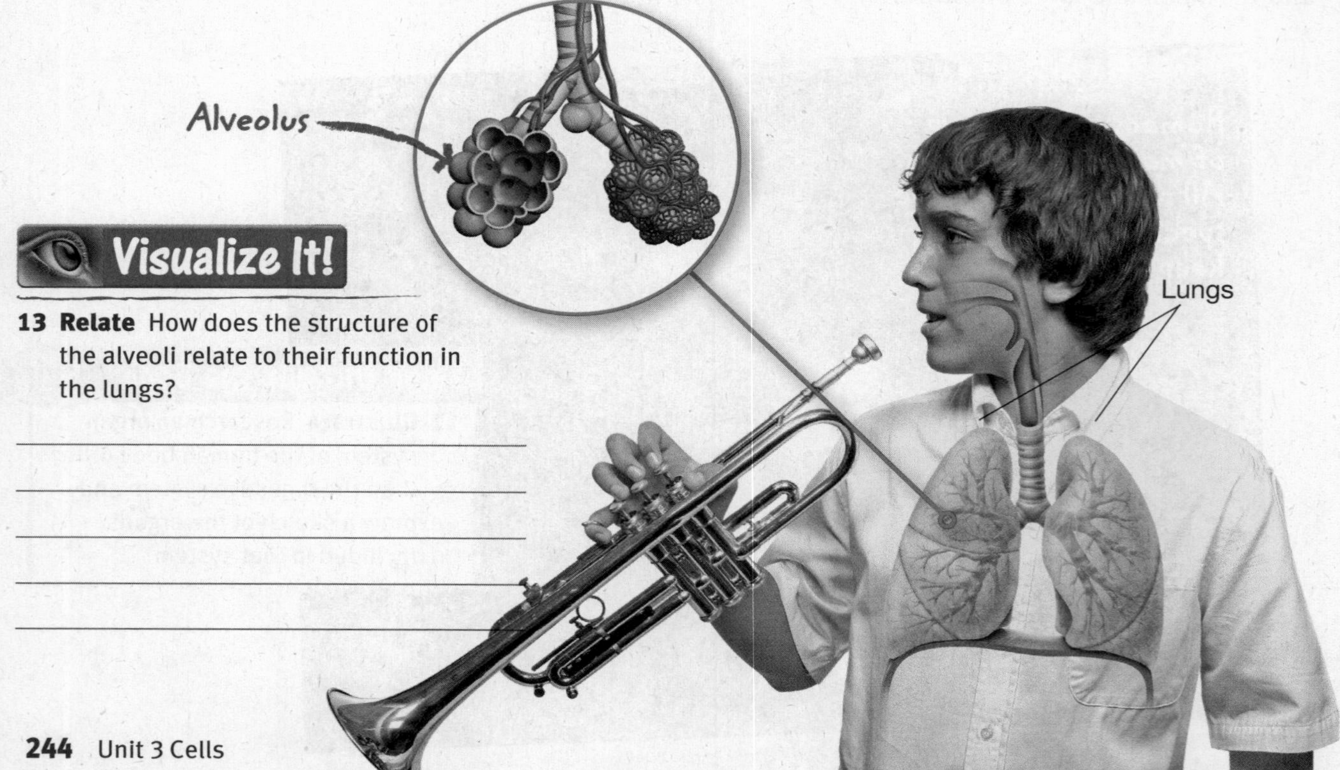

Visualize It!

13 Relate How does the structure of the alveoli relate to their function in the lungs?

____

____

____

____

____

Why It Matters

Odd Bodies

With millions of different organisms that exist on Earth, it's no wonder there are so many different body structures. Some organisms have special structures that can help them eat—or not be eaten!

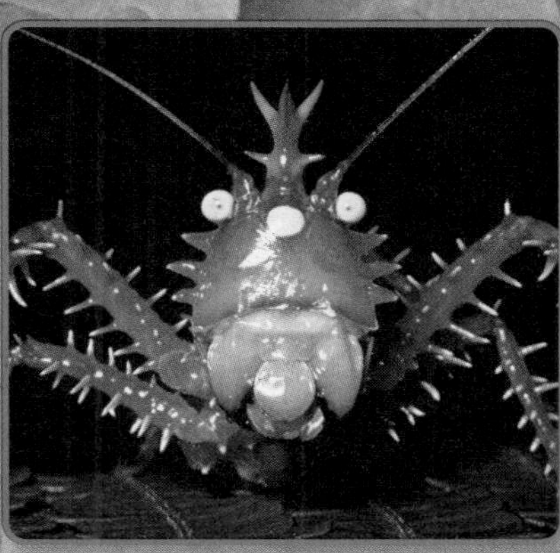

Can't Touch This!

Named for its prickly body, the spiny katydid doesn't make much of a meal for its predator. Male katydids sing loudly at night to attract female katydids. The singing can also attract predators, such as bats, who hunt for food at night. Its spines provide the katydid with some protection from being eaten.

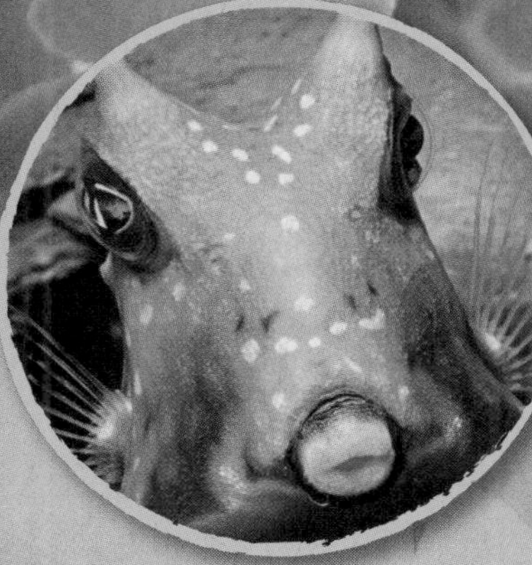

Blow on Your Food

The longhorn cowfish is a marine organism that lives on the sandy ocean bottom at depths up to 50 m. Its permanently puckered mouth helps the cowfish find food. The cowfish blows jets of water into the sand to find and feed on tiny organisms.

Night Vision

The tarsier's huge eyes provide excellent vision for hunting insects at night. Its eyes average 16 mm in diameter, but the tarsier's overall body size ranges from 85 mm to 165 mm. In comparison, your eyes would be the size of apples! When the tarsier spots its prey, it leaps through the air to pounce on it. The tarsier's long fingers help it grasp branches when it's on the move.

Extend

Inquiry

14 Relate How does the body structure of each of these organisms contribute to a particular function?

15 Contrast How do structures in living organisms compare with structures of nonliving things such as construction cranes, buildings, ships, airplanes, or bridges?

16 Imagine Describe an organism that might live in an extreme environment such as inside a volcano, deep in the ocean, or in an icy cave. What type of organism is it? What special structures would it have in order to survive in that environment?

Systems at Work

What tasks do systems perform to meet the needs of cells?

Complex organisms are made up of many systems. These systems work together to perform actions needed by cells to function properly. Whether it is a bone cell or a skin cell, each cell in the organism needs to receive nutrients, exchange carbon dioxide and oxygen, and have waste products taken away.

A unicellular organism must perform all functions necessary for life, such as getting nutrients, exchanging gases, and removing wastes. The functions must be performed by a single cell, because there is no opportunity for cell specialization.

Multicellular organisms face different challenges. Multicellular organisms have different cell types that can work together in groups to perform specific functions. Groups of cells that work together form tissues. Groups of tissues that work together form organs, and groups of organs that work together form systems. Systems work with other systems. In most animals, the digestive, respiratory, and excretory systems interact with the circulatory system to maintain healthy cells. A circulatory system delivers nutrients to body cells and carries away wastes. It carries oxygen to cells and removes carbon dioxide.

Some plants have a vascular system that transports water and nutrients to and from cells throughout the plant. Xylem and phloem are tissues that make up the vascular system. Xylem transports water from roots to cells. Phloem transports nutrients made in leaf cells to all parts of the plant.

Active Reading

17 Compare How do unicellular organisms and multicellular organisms compare in meeting their needs to stay alive?

____

____

____

____

____

Visualize It!

18 Analyze This diagram shows the xylem and phloem that make up the plant's vascular system. How does a vascular system serve the needs of plant cells?

____

____

____

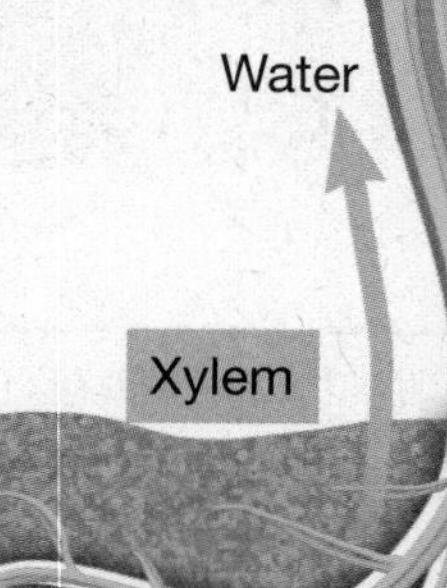
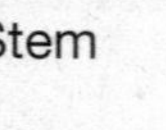

Delivering Nutrients

The digestive system in most animals breaks down food mechanically and chemically. In most animals, the digestive system works with a circulatory system. In the small intestine, nutrients are absorbed through thousands of finger-like projections in the wall of the small intestine and then into the blood vessels of the circulatory system. Once in the blood, the nutrients are delivered to cells throughout the body.

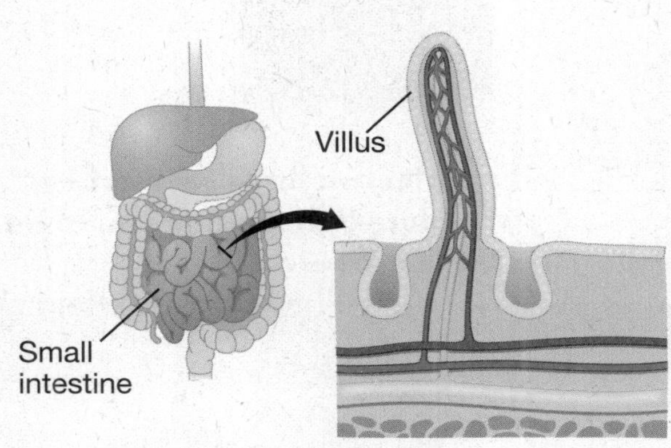

Delivering Oxygen

In animals, taking in oxygen is a function of the respiratory system. Depending on the animal, oxygen enters a body through skin, gills, spiracles, or lungs. There, it comes in contact with the circulatory system. Oxygen enters the bloodstream and is carried to the cells of the body. Once in the cells, oxygen is used to release energy from nutrients from digestion.

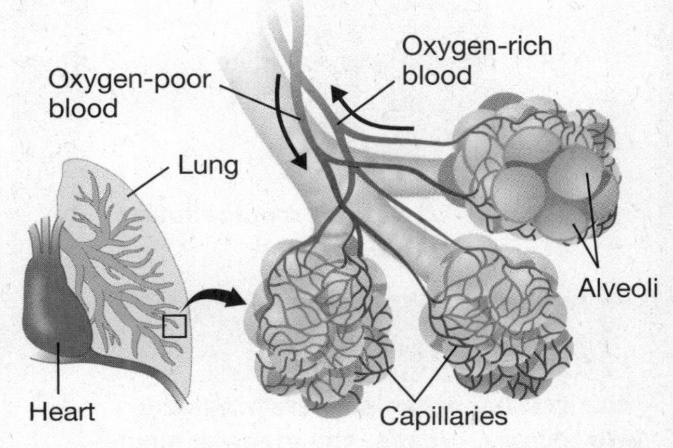

Removing Wastes

Skin, lungs, the digestive system, and the kidneys all have processes for removing waste products from the body. Sweat evaporates from the skin. Solid wastes and some water move out as part of the digestive system. Carbon dioxide and some water are breathed out through the respiratory system. In humans, the largest amount of excess water and waste products from cells is carried by the blood to the kidneys. There, wastes are filtered out of the blood through a complex series of tubules in the kidneys and leave the body as urine.

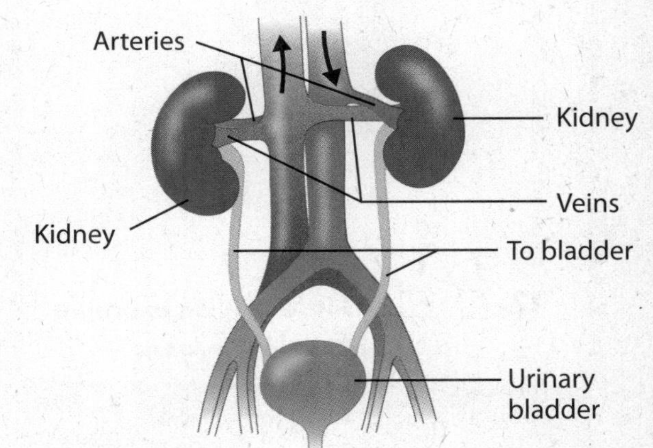

Visualize It!

19 Synthesize Notice that oxygen-poor blood (blue) and oxygen-rich blood (red) are shown in all three diagrams. Describe the role of blood in the transportation of materials throughout the body.

____
____
____
____
____

Visual Summary

To complete this summary, fill in the blanks with the correct word. Then, use the key below to check your answers. You can use this page to review the main concepts of the lesson.

Cellular Organization

All organisms are made up of one or more cells.

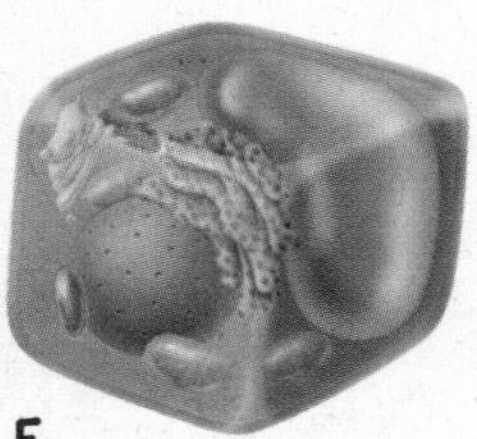

	T	F	
20	☐	☐	A plant is a unicellular organism.

The structures of cells, tissues, and organs determine their functions.

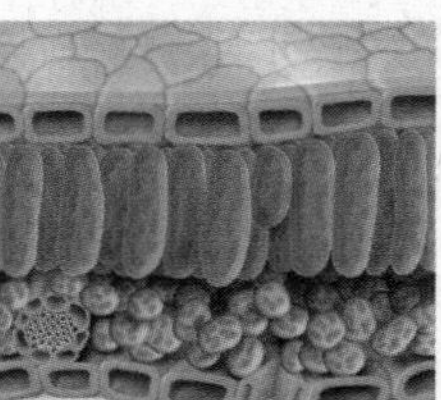

	T	F	
21	☐	☐	The protective tissue on a leaf has a structure that keeps the moisture in the leaf from drying out.

Multicellular organisms are organized into tissues, organs, and organ systems.

	T	F	
22	☐	☐	This leaf is an example of a plant organ.

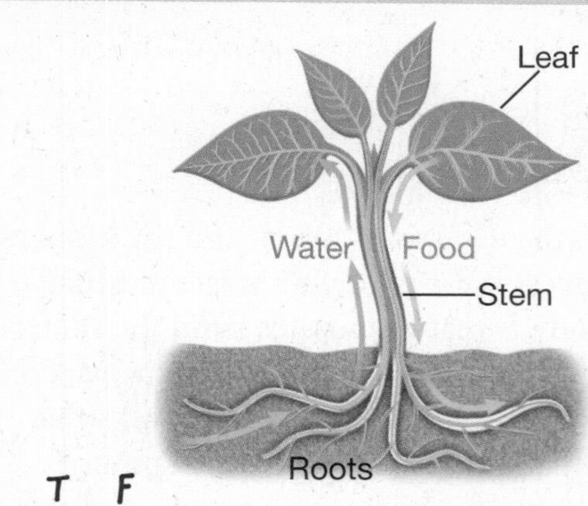

	T	F	
23	☐	☐	A plant obtains water from its environment through the root system.

Answers: 20 False; 21 True; 22 True; 23 True

24 Synthesize How do cells, tissues, organs, and organ systems work together in a multicellular organism?

Lesson Review

Vocabulary

Fill in the blank with the term that best completes the following sentences.

1 Animals have four basic types of ________________: nervous, epithelial, muscle, and connective.

2 Together, the esophagus, stomach, and intestines are part of a(n) ________________

Key Concepts

3 Describe What are the levels of organization in multicellular organisms?

4 Analyze Discuss two benefits of multicellular organisms' having some specialized cells rather than all the cells being the same.

5 Relate How do the structures in an organism relate to their functions?

Critical Thinking

Use the figure to answer the next two questions.

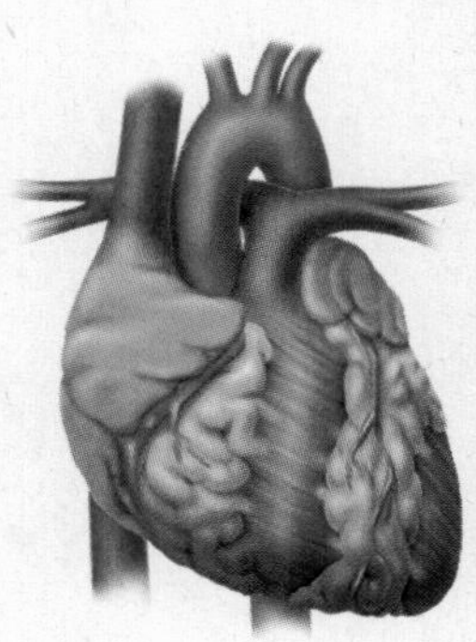

Human heart

6 Apply What level of organization is shown here?

7 Relate How does this level of organization relate to cells? To organ systems?

8 Analyze Explain why a circulatory system is important in meeting the needs of all cells throughout an animal's body.

My Notes

S.T.E.M. Engineering & Technology

OHIO 6.SIA.4, 6.SIA.8

Analyzing Technology

Skills
✓ Identify risks
✓ Identify benefits
Evaluate cost of technology
Evaluate environmental impact
Propose improvements
Propose risk reduction
Plan for technology failures
✓ Compare technology
✓ Communicate results

Objectives
• Identify different resources for nutritional values.
• Compare the nutritional value of common foods.

Analyzing Nutrients

Technology includes products, processes and systems developed to meet people's needs. Therefore, food is a kind of technology. Food supplies materials, called *nutrients*, that the body needs to perform its life functions. Your body gets nutrients from the food that you eat and the beverages that you drink. Each nutrient plays a role in keeping your body healthy. To make good decisions about what to eat, use nutrition guidelines such as the ChooseMyPlate.gov recommendations and the Nutrition Facts panels and ingredient labels on food packages.

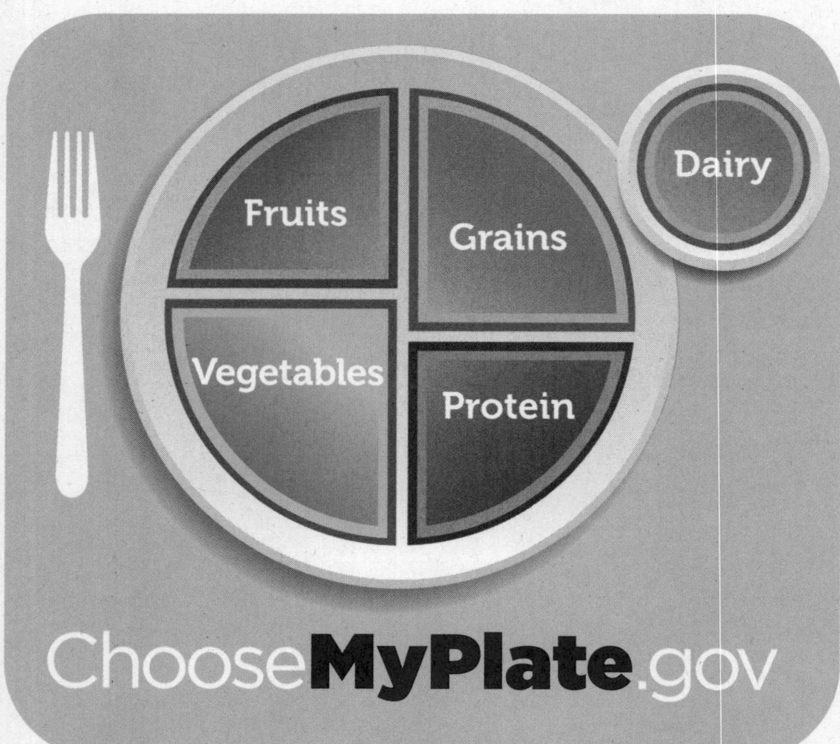

The MyPlate image was designed to help people make healthy food choices. As shown on the MyPlate icon, a healthy meal should be made up primarily of fruits and vegetables. The rest should be made up of lean protein, whole grains, and low-fat dairy products.

1 Infer According to the MyPlate icon, what kinds of food should you eat to maintain a healthy body?

____

____

____

What's in Your Food?

Nutrients are listed on food labels by amounts and as percentages of Daily Values. The Daily Value (DV) of a nutrient is the recommended amount that a person should consume in a day. The percentage of the DV of a nutrient tells you what percentage of the recommended amount is provided by one serving of the food if your diet contains 2,000 Calories. A Calorie is a measurement of the amount of energy your body gets from a food. Your body gets energy from carbohydrates, proteins, and fats. So when is the amount of a nutrient in a food item low, and when is it high? If a food item has less than 5% of the DV of a nutrient, the Food and Drug Administration (FDA) says it's low in that nutrient. If the item has more than 20% of the DV of a nutrient, the FDA says it's high in that nutrient.

2 Calculate If a person consumes an entire can of this product, what percentage of his or her Daily Value of saturated fat would he or she consume?

____

____

____

____

____

Fat Builds cell membranes, excess linked with heart disease
Sodium Needed for nerve function, excess linked with heart and kidney disease
Dietary Fiber Lowers risk of diabetes and heart disease
Protein Important for heart, brain, kidney, muscles
Vitamin A Important for eyes, skin
Calcium Important for bones, teeth, heart
Vitamin C Helps body absorb iron
Iron Vital for red blood cells

Nutrition Facts

Serving Size 8 ounces　Servings in can 2

Amount Per Serving	
Calories 155	Calories from Fat 93
	% Daily Value*
Total Fat 11g	**16%**
Saturated Fat 3g	**15%**
Trans Fat	
Polyunsaturated Fat 5g	
Monounsaturated Fat 3g	
Cholesterol 0mg	**0%**
Sodium 148mg	**6%**
Potassium 45mg	**1%**
Total Carbohydrate 14g	**5%**
Dietary Fiber 1g	**5%**
Sugars 1g	
Protein 2g	
Vitamin A 0% • Vitamin C 9%	
Calcium 1% • Iron 3%	

* Percent Daily Values are based on a 2,000 calorie diet. Your Daily Values may be higher or lower depending on your calorie needs.

You Try It!

Now it's your turn to compare the nutritional value of some food items.

You Try It!

Now it's your turn to use a Pugh chart and to compare the nutritional value of some common food items. You will analyze which foods are most likely to provide better nutrition, which allows you to make objective comparisons.

You Will Need

✓ Make a list of 5 common foods that you like to eat, including some that you think are healthy and some that you think are not very healthy.

____

____

____

____

____

1 Identify Risks

Using Nutrition Facts labels from Internet or supermarket resources, find out what nutrients are in each food on your list. Which foods are high in nutrients that are associated with health risks, such as saturated fat and cholesterol? Are there other health risks in these foods—for example, few healthy nutrients, or too many calories based on your recommended daily allowance? Use the information you find to fill in the table.

Food item	Unhealthy nutrients	Other health risks
1		
2		
3		
4		
5		

2 Identify Benefits

Now use the same resources to identify which foods from your list are high in nutrients associated with health benefits. Are there other benefits you should consider for your foods? Use your information to fill in the table.

Food item	Healthy nutrients	Other health benefits
1		
2		
3		
4		
5		

3 Compare Technologies

Now make a Pugh chart to compare nutritional values numerically. Write the names of the five foods you chose in the top row of the chart below. Fill in the boxes under each food item, ranking the food on a scale of 1–5, based on how it compares to the other foods for each nutrient.

Key for Ranking:
Each food is assigned 1 if it has the least of the listed nutrient and a 5 if it has the most.

1= lowest

5= highest

Fiber					
Protein					
Vitamin A					
Calcium					
Vitamin C					
Iron					
Total					

4 Communicate Results

Summarize your comparison of your food items, and interpret the information. Which of your foods has the highest total? Which has the lowest? What do your results tell you about the nutritional value of these foods?

Lesson 5

Homeostasis and Cell Processes

ESSENTIAL QUESTION

How do organisms maintain homeostasis?

By the end of this lesson, you should be able to explain the important processes that organisms undergo to maintain stable internal conditions.

These American alligators are warming themselves in the sun. Body temperature is one factor that an organism can control to maintain stable internal conditions.

OHIO 6.LS.1 Cells are the fundamental unit of life.

OHIO 6.LS.2 All cells come from pre-existing cells.

OHIO 6.LS.3 Cells carry on specific functions that sustain life.

OHIO 6.LS.4 Living systems at all levels of organization demonstrate the complementary nature of structure and function.

Lesson Labs

Quick Labs
- Investigate Microorganisms
- Homeostasis and Adaptations

Exploration Lab
- Diffusion

Engage Your Brain

1 Explain How is this person able to stay on the skateboard?

____

____

2 Describe Fill in the blanks with the word or phrase that you think correctly completes the following sentences.

Eating ________________ provides your body with nutrients it needs for energy.

Cells can ________________ to make more cells.

Trucks, airplanes, and trains are used to ________________ people and supplies from one place to another.

Active Reading

3 Synthesis You can often define an unknown word if you know the meaning of its word parts. Use the word parts and sentence below to make an educated guess about the meaning of the word *photosynthesis*.

Word part	Meaning
photo-	light
synthesis	to make

Example sentence
Plants use a process called photosynthesis to make their own food.

photosynthesis:

____

____

Vocabulary Terms

- **homeostasis**
- **photosynthesis**
- **cellular respiration**
- **binary fission**
- **mitosis**
- **passive transport**
- **diffusion**
- **osmosis**
- **active transport**
- **endocytosis**
- **exocytosis**

4 Identify As you read, place a question mark next to any words that you don't understand. When you finish reading the lesson, go back and review the text that you marked. If the information is still confusing, consult a classmate or a teacher.

Stayin' Alive

What is homeostasis?

We all feel more comfortable when our surroundings are ideal—not too hot, not too cold, not too wet, and not too dry. Cells are the same way. However, a cell's environment is constantly changing. **Homeostasis** (hoh•mee•oh•STAY•sis) is the maintenance of an internal balance of conditions in a changing external environment. In order to survive, your cells need to be able to obtain and use energy, make new cells, exchange materials, and eliminate wastes. Maintaining an internal balance allows cells to carry out these tasks.

Organisms behave in ways that maintain homeostasis and improve survival. For example, eating is important because it provides nutrients the body needs for growth and repair. An organism will search out food when it is hungry because the need to maintain homeostasis drives food-seeking behavior.

Think Outside the Book Inquiry

5 Select Many mechanisms are used to regulate different things in our lives. Choose one of the following devices, and do some research to describe what it regulates and how it works:

- thermostat
- insulin pump
- dam

Active Reading **6 Summarize** What are four things that cells can do to maintain homeostasis?

____

____

Visualize It!

7 Apply Think about how this girl is feeling after she exercises. What things can you see that are helping to keep her body temperature stable?

____

____

____

____

Balance in Organisms

All cells need energy and materials in order to carry out life processes. A unicellular organism exchanges materials directly with its environment. The cell membrane and other parts of the cell regulate what materials get into and out of the cell. This is one way that unicellular organisms maintain homeostasis.

Cells in multicellular organisms must work together to maintain homeostasis for the entire organism. For example, multicellular organisms have systems that transport materials to cells from other places in the organism. The main transport system in your body is your cardiovascular system. The cardiovascular system includes the heart, blood vessels, and blood. The heart pumps blood through branched blood vessels that come close to every cell in the body. Blood carries materials to the cells and carries wastes away from the cells. Other multicellular organisms have transport systems, too. For example, many plants have two types of vascular tissues that work together as a transport system. *Xylem* is the tissue that transports water and minerals from the roots to the rest of the plant. Another tissue called *phloem* transports food made within plant cells.

Active Reading

8 Compare As you read, underline how unicellular organisms and multicellular organisms exchange materials.

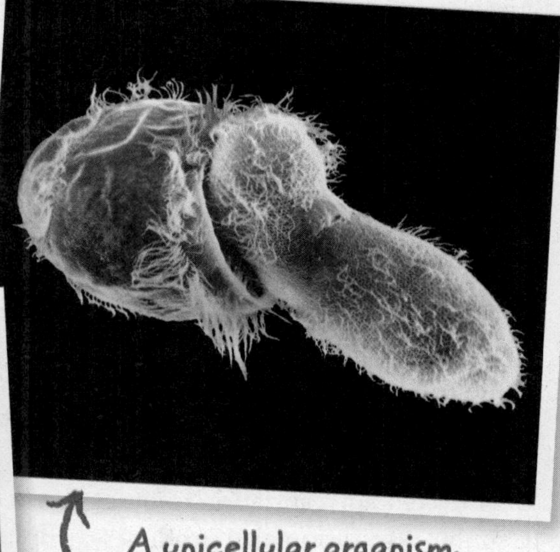

A unicellular organism, ***Didinium***, is eating another unicellular organism, called a ***Paramecium***.

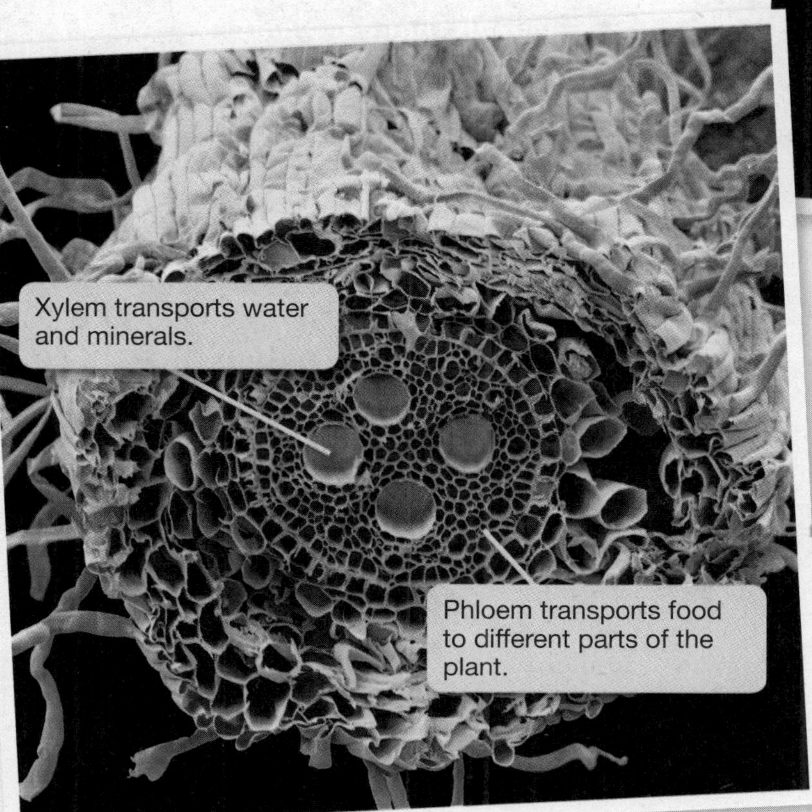
Xylem transports water and minerals.
Phloem transports food to different parts of the plant.

Plants have two types of vascular tissue that they use to transport materials.

Get Growing!

How do cells get energy?

Cells need energy to perform cell functions. Cells get energy by breaking down materials, such as food, in which energy is stored. Breaking down food also provides raw materials the cell needs to make other materials for cell processes.

Photosynthesis

The sun provides the energy for plants to grow and make food. Plants use sunlight to change carbon dioxide and water into sugar and oxygen. This process by which plants, algae, and some bacteria make their own food is called **photosynthesis**. Inside plant and algal cells are special organelles, called chloroplasts, where photosynthesis takes place.

Cellular Respiration

All living things need food to produce energy for cell processes. The process by which cells use oxygen to produce energy from food is called **cellular respiration**. Plants, animals, and most other organisms use cellular respiration to get energy from food.

Nearly all the oxygen around us is made by photosynthesis. Animals and plants use oxygen during cellular respiration to break down food. Cellular respiration also produces carbon dioxide. Plants need carbon dioxide to make sugars. So, photosynthesis and respiration are linked, each one depending on the products of the other.

Plants provide the food for nearly all living thing on land. Some organisms eat plants for food. Other organisms eat animals that eat plants.

9 Synthesize Fill in the blanks with the materials that are involved in photosynthesis and cellular respiration.

Photosynthesis	________ + carbon dioxide —sunlight→ ________ + oxygen
Cellular respiration	sugar + ________ ——→ water + ________ + energy

Why do cells divide?

Active Reading **10 Identify** As you read, underline what happens to a cell's DNA before it can divide.

Cells grow, divide, and die. All new cells are made when existing cells divide. Cell division enables organisms to grow and reproduce. Unicellular organisms reproduce by cell division. Multicellular organisms grow by adding more cells to themselves. For example, cells in the lower layers your skin are constantly dividing to replace those that are dead, damaged, or were removed. Dead or dying cells around your body are constantly being replaced by healthy, new cells and homeostasis is maintained.

Cell division is a complex process. Before a cell can divide, its DNA is copied. Then, the DNA copies are packaged into what will become two new cells. This process happens in unicellular and multicellular organisms, but in slightly different ways.

To Reproduce

One unicellular organism divides into two unicellular organisms. As the organism is made of a single cell, unicellular organisms divide to reproduce. Prokaryotic, unicellular organisms such as bacteria divide by a process called binary fission. **Binary fission** is a type of asexual reproduction in which a prokaryotic cell divides into two cells. The parent cell divides, producing two offspring cells. Eukaryotic unicellular organisms reproduce by cell division too, in a process called mitosis. Before mitosis occurs, the DNA of the parent cell forms structures called chromosomes (croh•moh•SOHMS). The chromosomes are copied within the parent cell's nucleus. During **mitosis** the chromosome copies are separated and the nucleus and cell divide to form two identical cells.

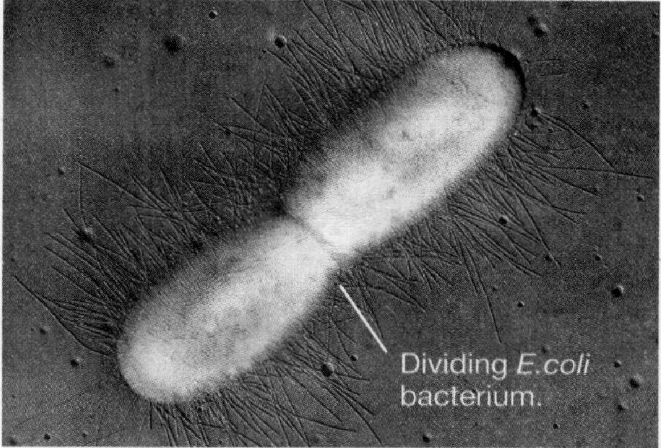
Dividing *E.coli* bacterium.

To Grow and Repair Damage

Multicellular organisms grow by adding more cells to themselves. For example, a young fox, called a *kit*, grows larger by adding cells to its body. Likewise, it heals from injuries such as cuts and bruises by replacing dead or dying cells with new cells. The new cells are made when existing, healthy cells divide by mitosis.

As the two offspring cells resulting from mitosis have identical genetic material to the parent cell, all the cells in a multicellular organism tend to have identical genetic material.

Visualize It!

11 Apply How would mitosis be important in helping the fox recover from a scratch wound?

____

____

____

Move It!

How do cells exchange materials?

What would happen to a factory if its supply of raw materials never arrived or it couldn't get rid of its garbage? Like a factory, an organism must be able to obtain materials for energy, make new materials, and get rid of wastes. The exchange of materials between a cell and its environment takes place at the cell's membrane. Cell membranes are *semi-permeable* because they allow only certain particles to cross into or out of the cell.

Passive Transport

The movement of particles across a cell membrane without the use of energy by the cell is called **passive transport**. For example, when a tea bag is added to a cup of water, the molecules in the tea will eventually spread throughout the water. **Diffusion** is the movement of molecules from high concentrations to low concentrations. Some nutrients move into a cell by diffusion. Some waste products move out of the cell by diffusion. **Osmosis** is the diffusion of water through a semi-permeable membrane. Many molecules are too large to diffuse through the cell membrane. Some of these molecules enter and exit cells through protein channels embedded in the cell membrane. When molecules move through these protein channels from areas of higher concentration to areas of lower concentration, the process usually requires no energy.

Active Reading

12 Relate As you read, underline the similarity between diffusion and osmosis.

The tea has a higher concentration of molecules in the tea bag than in the rest of the mug.

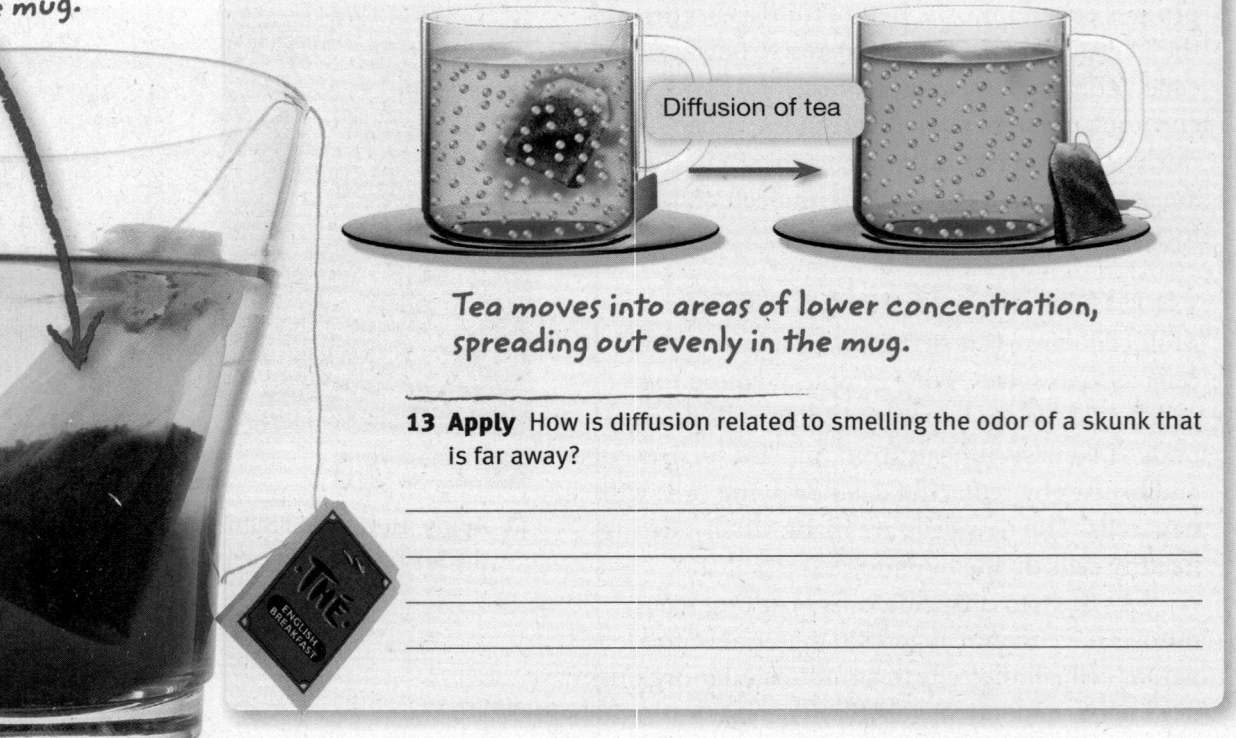

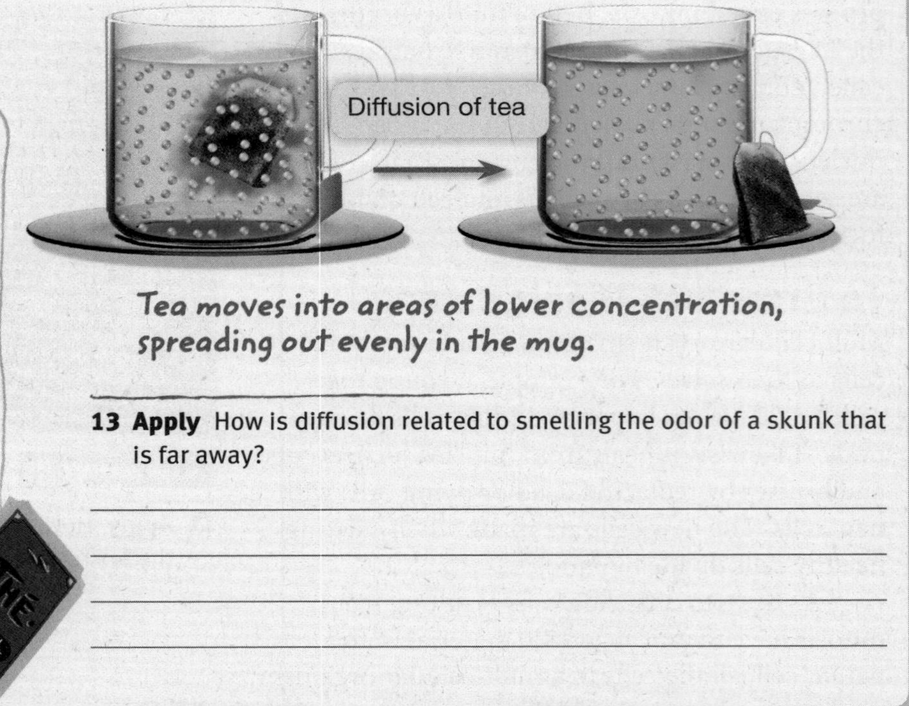

Tea moves into areas of lower concentration, spreading out evenly in the mug.

13 Apply How is diffusion related to smelling the odor of a skunk that is far away?

Active Transport

Cells often need to move materials across the cell membrane from areas of low concentration into areas of higher concentration. This is the opposite direction of passive transport. **Active transport** is the movement of particles against a concentration gradient and requires the cell to use energy. Some large particles that do not fit through the protein channels may require active transport across the cell membrane by processes called *endocytosis* and *exocytosis*.

Visualize It!

14 Identify Place a check mark next to the box that describes diffusion. Explain your answer.

____

____

____

____

Chemical energy
Passive transport moves materials into and out of a cell to areas of lower concentration. ☐
Active transport uses energy to move materials into and out of a cell to areas of higher concentration. ☐

Endocytosis

The process by which a cell uses energy to surround a particle and enclose the particle in a vesicle to bring the particle into the cell is called **endocytosis** (en•doh•sye•TOH•sis). Vesicles are sacs formed from pieces of the cell membrane. Unicellular organisms, such as amoebas, use endocytosis to capture smaller organisms for food.

The cell comes into contact with a particle.

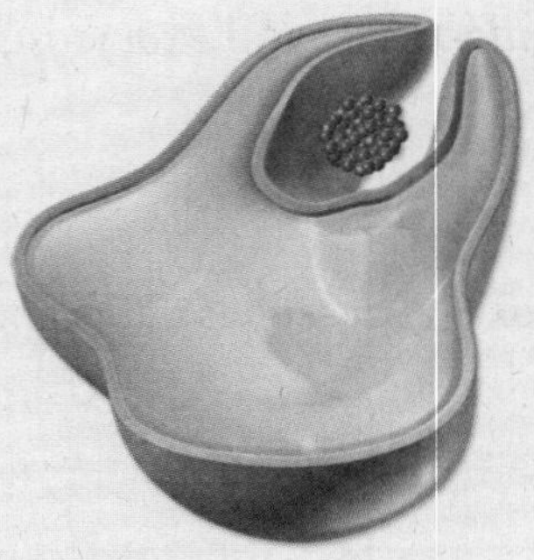

The cell membrane begins to wrap around the particle.

15 Describe What is happening in this step?

____

____

____

____

Exocytosis

When particles are enclosed in a vesicle and released from a cell, the process is called **exocytosis** (ek•soh•sye•TOH•sis). Exocytosis is the reverse process of endocytosis. Exocytosis begins when a vesicle forms around particles within the cell. The vesicle fuses to the cell membrane and the particles are released outside of the cell. Exocytosis is an important process in multicellular organisms.

Large particles that must leave the cell are packaged in vesicles.

16 Describe What is happening in this step?

____

____

____

____

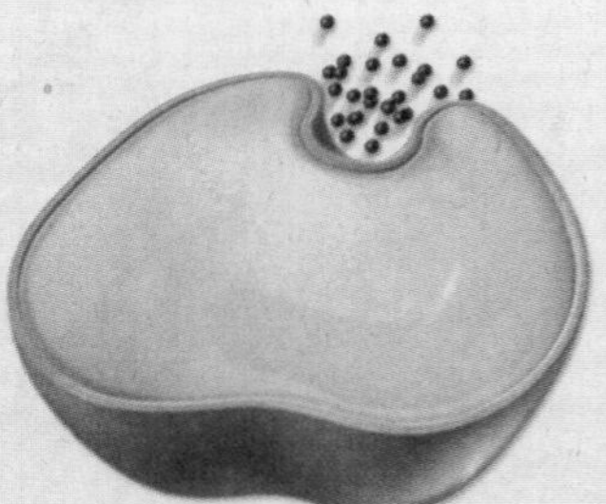

The cell releases the particles to the outside of the cell.

How do organisms maintain homeostasis?

As you have read, cells can obtain energy, divide, and transport materials to maintain stable internal conditions. In multicellular organisms, the cells must work together to maintain homeostasis for the entire organism. For example, when some organisms become cold, the cells respond in order to maintain a normal internal temperature. Muscle cells will contract to generate heat, a process known as shivering.

Some animals adapt their behavior to control body temperature. For example, many reptiles bask in the sun or seek shade to regulate their internal temperatures. When temperatures become extremely cold, some animals hibernate. Animals such as ground squirrels are able to conserve their energy during the winter when food is scarce.

Some trees lose all their leaves around the same time each year. This is a seasonal response. Having bare branches during the winter reduces the amount of water loss. Leaves may also change color before they fall. As autumn approaches, chlorophyll, the green pigment used for photosynthesis, breaks down. As chlorophyll is lost, other yellow and orange pigments can be seen.

Active Reading

17 Identify As you read, underline the different ways that organisms can respond to changes in the environment.

Visualize It!

18 Describe How is this boy's body responding to the cold weather?

____

____

____

The leaves of some trees change colors when the season changes.

Visual Summary

To complete this summary, fill in the blanks with the correct word or phrase. Then use the key below to check your answers. You can use this page to review the main concepts of the lesson.

Cells need to take in energy and matter to perform cell functions.

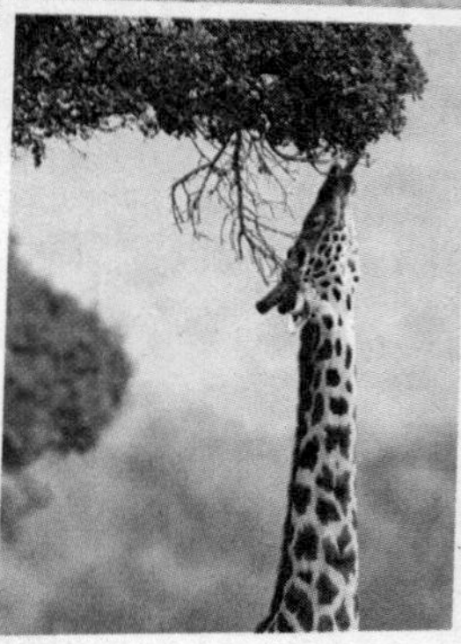

19 Food is made during ________________
Energy is produced from food during ________________

Cell division allows organisms to grow and also to repair damaged cells and tissues.

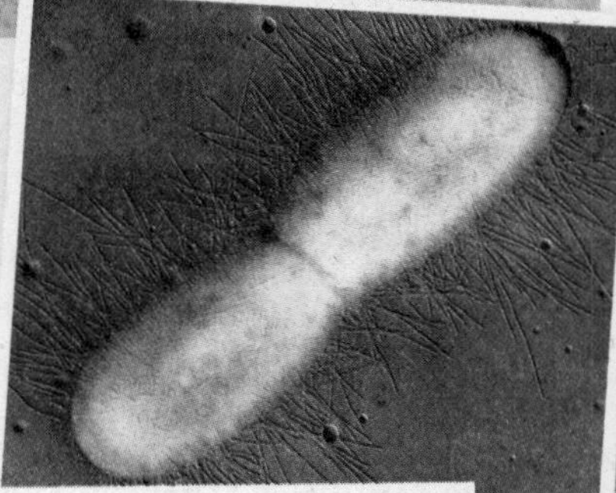

20 ________________ occurs when cells divide to form two new nuclei that are identical to each other.

Maintaining Homeostasis: Balance In Organisms

Materials move into and out of cells through the cell membrane.

21 ________________ uses energy to release particles from a cell.

Organisms respond to changes in the environment.

22 The change in leaf color on these trees is one way the trees maintain ________________

Answers: 19 photosynthesis; cellular respiration; 20 Mitosis; 21 Active transport; 22 homeostasis

23 Summarize Explain why organisms need to maintain homeostasis.

Lesson Review

Vocabulary

In your own words, define the following terms.

1 homeostasis

2 endocytosis

Key Concepts

3 Compare What is the difference between passive and active transport?

4 Identify Why do cells divide?

5 Describe What happens during mitosis?

6 Apply How do the cells in your body get energy?

Critical Thinking

Use the graphs to answer the next two questions.

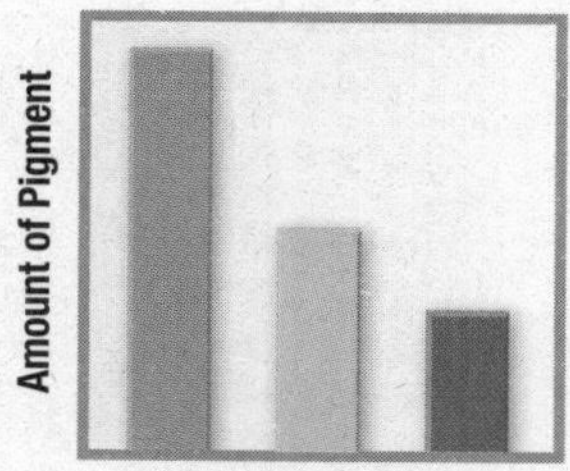

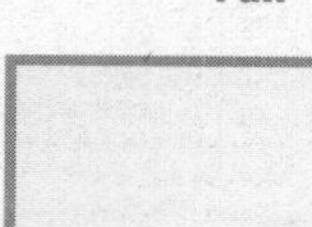

7 Compare How do the amounts of green pigment, chlorophyll, differ from summer to fall?

8 Infer How do you think the change in chlorophyll levels is a response to changes in the length of day from summer to fall?

9 Explain Why is homeostasis important for cells as well as for an entire organism?

My Notes

Unit 3 Big Idea

All organisms are made up of one or more cells.

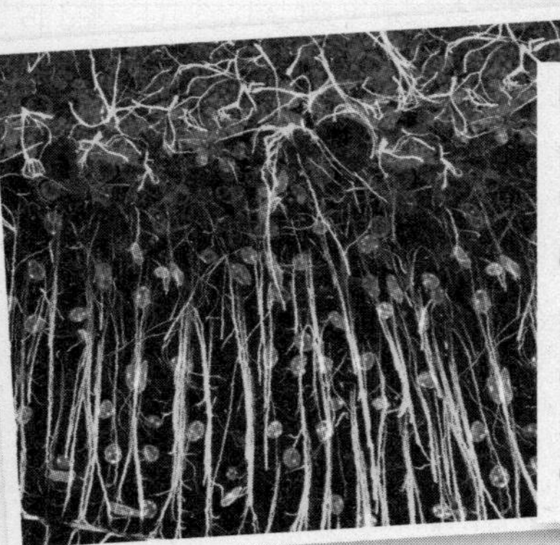

Lesson 1

ESSENTIAL QUESTION

What are living things made of?

Explain the components of the scientific theory of cells.

Lesson 2

ESSENTIAL QUESTION

What are the building blocks of organisms?

Discuss the chemical makeup of living things.

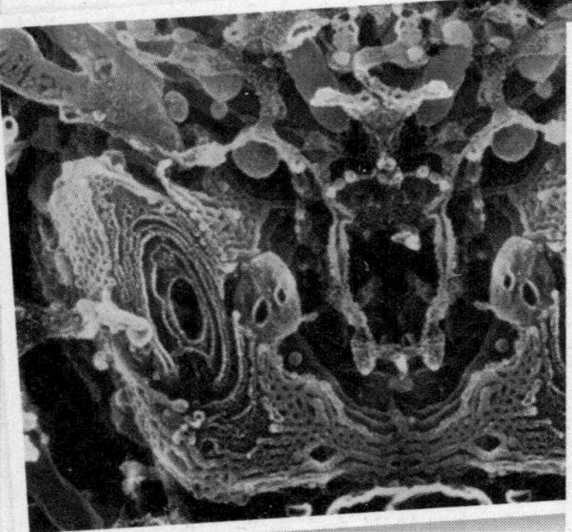

Lesson 3

ESSENTIAL QUESTION

What are the different parts that make up a cell?

Compare the structure and function of cell parts in plant and animal cells.

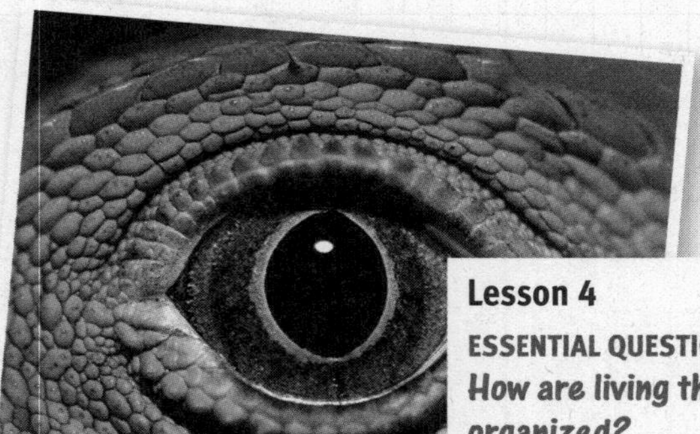

Lesson 4

ESSENTIAL QUESTION

How are living things organized?

Describe the different levels of organization in living things.

Lesson 5

ESSENTIAL QUESTION

How do organisms maintain homeostasis?

Explain the important processes that organisms undergo to maintain stable internal conditions.

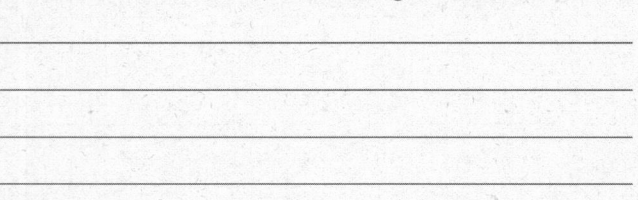

Connect ESSENTIAL QUESTIONS

Lessons 3 and 5

1 Synthesize Explain the role of a cell membrane and how it aids in maintaining homeostasis.

____

____

____

____

Think Outside the Book

2 Synthesize Choose one of the activities to help synthesize what you learned in this unit.

☐ Using what you learned in lessons 1, 3, and 4, choose a plant or an animal and create a poster that shows its levels of organization from a single cell to the whole organism. Include a diagram of a cell and one example of the organism's tissues, organs, and organ systems.

☐ Using what you learned in lessons 4 and 5, draw a diagram of a plant's vascular system. Identify how this system maintains homeostasis in the plant.

Unit 3 Review

Name ______________________

Vocabulary

Check the box to show whether each statement is true or false.

T	F	
☐	☐	**1** A cell organelle that is found in animal cells but usually not in plant cells is a lysosome.
☐	☐	**2** A cell structure that is found in both animal cells and plant cells is a cell wall.
☐	☐	**3** A tissue is a group of similar cells that perform a common function.
☐	☐	**4** A molecule is made up of atoms that are joined together.
☐	☐	**5** A eukaryote has cells that do not contain a nucleus, whereas a prokaryote has cells that have a nucleus.

Key Concepts

Choose the letter of the best answer.

6 Organisms can respond to changes in their environment. What might a plant growing in a dark corner of an otherwise sunny room do in response to its conditions, and what is this response called?

A The plant will die. This is called death.

B The plant will stop all life processes. This is called dormancy.

C The plant will slow down all life processes. This is called hibernation.

D The plant will bend and grow toward the light. This is called phototropism.

7 Juana made the following table.

Structure or organelle	Function
mitochondrion	cellular respiration
ribosome	DNA synthesis
chloroplast	photosynthesis
cell membrane	endocytosis
Golgi complex	packages proteins

Juana's table lists cell structures and organelles and their functions, but she made an error. Which structure or organelle listed in the table shows the wrong function?

A mitochondrion

B ribosome

C cell membrane

D Golgi complex

8 If you were to compare the function of a cell to the function of a city, which of the following organelles would be the city's power plant?

A nucleus

B lysosome

C mitochondrion

D Golgi complex

9 Plants contain xylem and phloem tissue. What organ system in animals performs a similar function as the xylem and phloem of plants?

A digestive system

B excretory system

C respiratory system

D circulatory system

Name ______________________

10 Which statement correctly tells why the cells of unicellular and multicellular organisms divide?

A The cells of unicellular organisms divide to reproduce; those of multicellular organisms divide to replace cells and to grow.

B The cells of unicellular organisms divide to replace cells and to grow; those of multicellular organisms divide to reproduce.

C The cells of both kinds of organisms divide to reproduce.

D The cells of both kinds of organisms divide to replace cells and to grow.

Critical Thinking

Answer the following question in the space provided.

11 The following picture shows the process of photosynthesis.

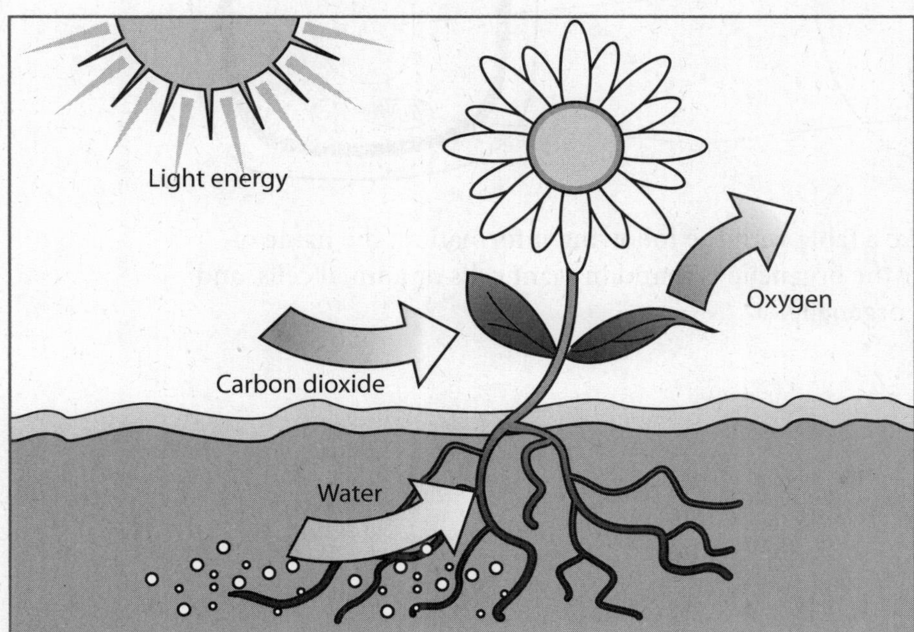

In which plant organ and organelle does photosynthesis take place? One of the products of photosynthesis is not shown in the diagram. What is the missing product? Describe the role of this substance in cells. How do animals get this substance?

____

____

____

____

____

Connect ESSENTIAL QUESTIONS
Lessons 3, 4, and 5

Answer the following question in the space provided.

12 The following picture shows a plant cell and an animal cell.

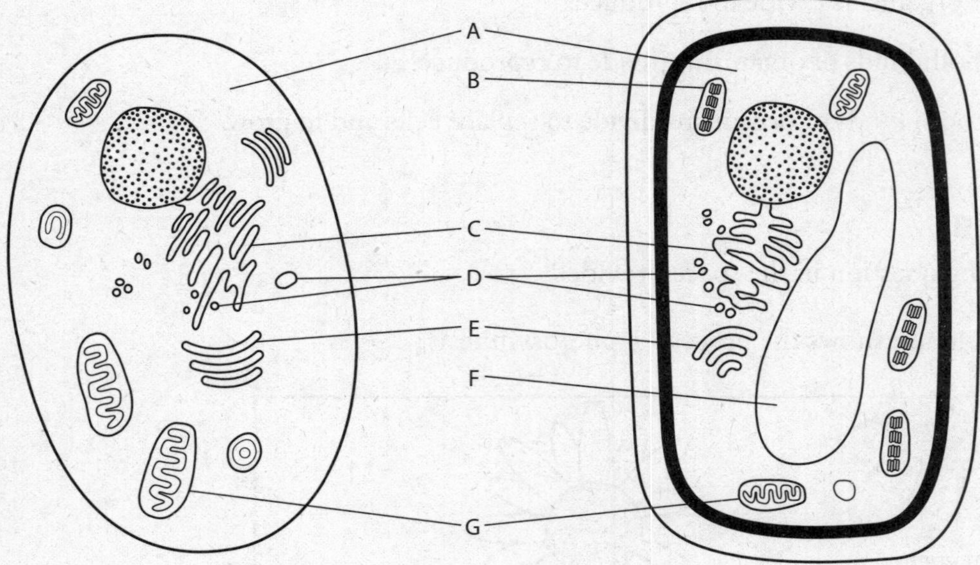

In the space below, make a table with the following information: the name of each organelle, whether the organelle is found in plant cells or animal cells, and the function(s) of each organelle.

UNIT 4

Earth's Organisms

Webbed feet allow flamingos to stand in the soft mud of their shallow water environment.

Big Idea

Living systems at all levels of organization demonstrate the complementary nature of structure and function.

What do you think?

Organisms have many different characteristics that help them survive in their environment. Humans and birds are both animals that use two legs and two feet to move. How else are they alike? Different?

Human feet allow for walking and running easily on solid ground.

Unit 4

Earth's Organisms

CITIZEN SCIENCE

Native and Nonnative Species

Some species have grown and thrived in a given area for hundreds or thousands of years. These organisms are called native species. When nonnative species are introduced, they can outcompete and outproduce the native species. The result might be a decline in or even extinction of the native species.

1 Think About It

The introduction of some nonnative species has been helpful. How can initially useful organisms become harmful to an ecosystem?

Asian carp are considered a serious threat to native fish species. Asian carp eat more of the available food and reproduce faster than the native fish populations.

Perch are native to the Great Lakes region. They are one species threatened by nonnative species.

2 Ask a Question

What species live in your community?

As a class, assess an area in your community to identify the native and nonnative species that live there. Check off the items on the checklist below as you consider them in your discussion.

Things to Consider

- ☐ What area should be assessed?
- ☐ Should garden plants and family pets be included in your assessment, or should you include only wild organisms?
- ☐ How can you determine which organisms in the assessment area are native species?

The Great Lakes are being threatened by nonnative species that could arrive from regional rivers or boat traffic, or through the careless release by humans of certain species directly into the lakes.

3 Make a Plan

A Describe the area that you are assessing.

____

____

B List the native and nonnative organisms in your assessment area.

____

____

____

____

____

C Choose one nonnative species and describe its impact on the assessment area. List ideas for reducing that impact in your community.

____

____

____

____

____

Take It Home

Do you have nonnative plants or animals in your yard or home? Discuss with an adult the pros and cons of keeping nonnative species.

Classification of Living Things

ESSENTIAL QUESTION

How are organisms classified?

By the end of this lesson, you should be able to describe how people sort living things into groups based on shared characteristics.

Scientists use physical and chemical characteristics to classify organisms. Is that a spider? Look again. It's an ant mimicking a jumping spider!

OHIO 6.LS.1 Cells are the fundamental unit of life.

OHIO 6.LS.4 Living systems at all levels of organization demonstrate the complementary nature of structure and function.

OHIO 6.SIA.5 Develop descriptions, models, explanations and predictions.

Lesson Labs

Quick Labs
- Using a Dichotomous Key
- Identifying Leaves

Exploration Lab
- Developing Scientific Names

Engage Your Brain

1 Predict Check T or F to show whether you think each statement is true or false.

T	F	
☐	☐	The classification system used today has changed very little since it was introduced.
☐	☐	To be classified as an animal, an organism must have a backbone.
☐	☐	Organisms can be classified according to whether they have nuclei in their cells.
☐	☐	Scientists can study genetic material to classify organisms.
☐	☐	Organisms that have many physical similarities are always related.

2 Analyze The flowering plant shown above is called an Indian pipe. It could be mistaken for a fungus. Write down how the plant is similar to and different from other plants you know.

Active Reading

3 Word Parts Many English words have their roots in other languages. Use the Latin suffix below to make an educated guess about the meaning of the word *Plantae*.

Latin suffix	Meaning
-ae	a group of

Example sentence
Maples are part of the kingdom Plantae.

Plantae:

Vocabulary Terms

- **species**
- **genus**
- **domain**
- **Bacteria**
- **Archaea**
- **Eukarya**
- **Protista**
- **Fungi**
- **Plantae**
- **Animalia**

4 Apply As you learn the definition of each vocabulary term in this lesson, write your own definition or make a sketch to help you remember the meaning of each term.

Sorting Things Out!

Why do we classify living things?

There are millions of living things on Earth. How do scientists keep all of these living things organized? Scientists *classify* living things based on characteristics that living things share. Classification helps scientists answer questions such as:

- How many kinds of living things are there?
- What characteristics define each kind of living thing?
- What are the relationships among living things?

Sharks have fins and gills.
Dolphins also have fins, but not gills.

Visualize It!

5 Analyze The photos show two organisms. In the table, place a check mark in the box for each characteristic that the organisms have.

Yellow pansy butterfly

American goldfinch

	Wings	Antennae	Beak	Feathers
Yellow pansy butterfly				
American goldfinch				

6 Summarize What characteristics do yellow pansy butterflies have in common with American goldfinches? How do they differ?

____

____

____

How do scientists know living things are related?

If two organisms look similar, are they related? To classify organisms, scientists compare physical characteristics. For example, they may look at size or bone structure. Scientists also compare the chemical characteristics of living things.

The two pandas below share habitats and diets. They look alike, but they have different DNA.

Physical Characteristics

How are chickens similar to dinosaurs? If you compare dinosaur fossils and chicken skeletons, you will see that chickens and dinosaurs share many physical characteristics. Scientists look at physical characteristics, such as skeletal structure. They also study how organisms develop from an egg to an adult. For example, animals with similar skeletons and development may be related.

Chemical Characteristics

Scientists can identify the relationships among organisms by studying genetic material such as DNA and RNA. They study mutations and genetic similarities to find relationships among organisms. Organisms that have very similar gene sequences or have the same mutations are likely related. Other chemicals, such as proteins and hormones, can also be studied to learn how organisms are related.

The red panda is a closer relative to a raccoon than it is to a giant panda.

The giant panda is a closer relative to a spectacled bear than it is to a red panda.

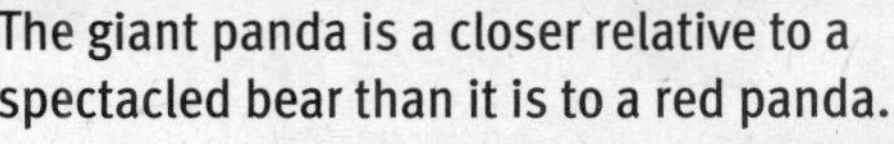

7 List How does DNA lead scientists to better classify organisms?

What's in a Name?

How are living things named?

Early scientists used names as long as 12 words to identify living things, and they also used common names. So, classification was confusing. In the 1700s, a scientist named Carolus Linnaeus (KAR•uh•luhs lih•NEE•uhs) simplified the naming of living things. He gave each kind of living thing a two-part *scientific name.*

HELLO
my name is
Carolus Linnaeus

Scientific Names

Each species has its own scientific name. A **species** (SPEE•sheez) is a group of organisms that are very closely related. They can mate and produce fertile offspring. Consider the scientific name for a mountain lion: *Puma concolor*. The first part, *Puma,* is the genus name. A **genus** (JEE•nuhs; plural, *genera*) includes similar species. The second part, *concolor,* is the specific, or species, name. No other species is named *Puma concolor.*

A scientific name always includes the genus name followed by the specific name. The first letter of the genus name is capitalized, and the first letter of the specific name is lowercase. The entire scientific name is written either in italics or underlined.

The A.K.A. Files

Some living things have many common names. Scientific names prevent confusion when people discuss organisms.

Scientific name:
Puma concolor

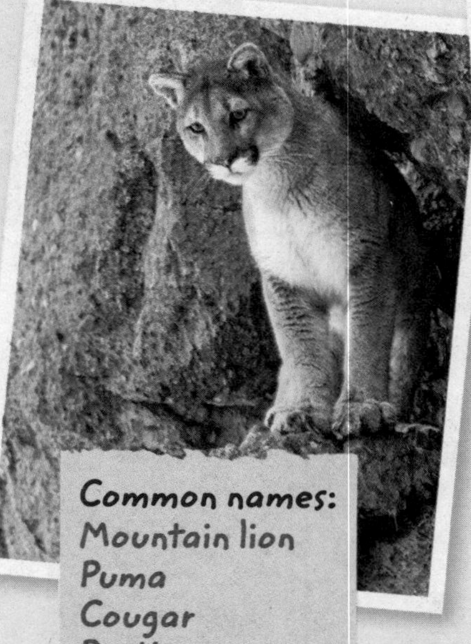

Common names:
Mountain lion
Puma
Cougar
Panther

Scientific name:
Acer rubrum

Common names:
Red maple
Swamp maple
Soft maple

8 Apply In the scientific names above, circle the genus name and underline the specific name.

What are the levels of classification?

9 Identify As you read, underline the levels of classification.

Linnaeus's ideas became the basis for modern taxonomy (tak•SAHN•uh•mee). *Taxonomy* is the science of describing, classifying, and naming living things. At first, many scientists sorted organisms into two groups: plants and animals. But numerous organisms did not fit into either group.

Today, scientists use an eight-level system to classify living things. Each level gets more specific. Therefore, it contains fewer kinds of living things than the level above it. Living things in the lower levels are more closely related to each other than they are to organisms in the higher levels. From most general to more specific, the levels of classification are domain, kingdom, phylum (plural, *phyla*), class, order, family, genus, and species.

Classifying Organisms

Domain **Domain Eukarya** includes all protists, fungi, plants, and animals.

Kingdom **Kingdom Animalia** includes all animals.

Phylum Animals in **Phylum Chordata** have a hollow nerve cord in their backs. Some have a backbone.

Class Animals in **Class Mammalia**, or mammals, have a backbone and nurse their young.

Order Animals in **Order Carnivora** are mammals that have special teeth for tearing meat.

Family Animals in **Family Felidae** are cats. They are carnivores that have retractable claws.

Genus Animals in **Genus *Felis*** are cats that cannot roar. They can only purr.

Species The **species *Felis domesticus***, or the house cat, has unique traits that other members of genus *Felis* do not have.

From domain to species, each level of classification contains a smaller group of organisms.

10 Apply What is true about the number of organisms as they are classified closer to the species level?

Triple Play

What are the three domains?

Active Reading

11 Identify As you read, underline the shared characteristics of Bacteria and Archaea.

Once, kingdoms were the highest level of classification. Scientists used a six-kingdom system. But scientists noticed that organisms in two of the kingdoms differed greatly from organisms in the other four kingdoms. So scientists added a new classification level: domains. A **domain** represents the largest differences among organisms. The three domains are Bacteria (bak•TIR•ee•uh), Archaea (ar•KEE•uh), and Eukarya (yoo•KAIR•ee•uh).

Bacteria

Domain **Bacteria** contains all organisms within Kingdom Bacteria. This domain is made up of prokaryotes that usually have a cell wall and reproduce by cell division. Prokaryotes are single-cell organisms that lack a cell nucleus. Bacteria live in almost any environment—soil, water, and even inside the human body!

Archaea

Domain **Archaea** includes all organisms in Kingdom Archaea. This group is also made up of prokaryotes that reproduce by cell division. They differ from bacteria in their genetics and in the makeup of their cell walls. Many Archaea live in harsh environments in which other organisms could not survive. Some Archaea live in the open ocean or soil.

Bacteria from the genus *Streptomyces* are commonly found in soil.

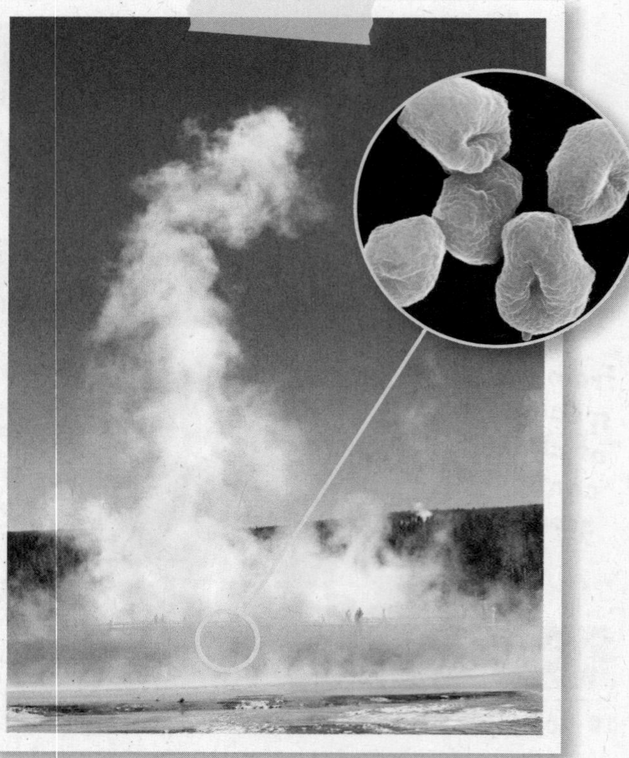

Archaea from the genus *Sulfolobus* are found in hot springs.

Eukarya

What do algae, mushrooms, trees, and humans have in common? All of these organisms are *eukaryotes.* Eukaryotes are made up of cells that have a nucleus and membrane-bound organelles. The cells of eukaryotes are more complex than the cells of prokaryotes. For this reason, the cells of eukaryotes are usually larger than the cells of prokaryotes. Some eukaryotes, such as many protists and some fungi, are single-celled. Many eukaryotes are multicellular organisms. Some protists and many fungi, plants, and animals are multicellular eukaryotes. Domain **Eukarya** is made up of all eukaryotes.

It may look like a pinecone, but the pangolin is actually an animal from Africa. It is in Domain Eukarya.

Visualize It!

12 Identify Fill in the blanks with the missing labels.

Bacteria

A ______________

Archaea

Protist

B ______________

C ______________

D ______________

13 Compare What are the differences between Bacteria and Eukarya?

____

____

____

My Kingdom for a

What are the four kingdoms in Eukarya?

Scientists have classified four types of Eukarya. They ask questions to decide in which kingdom to classify an organism.

- Is the organism single-celled or multicellular?
- Does it make its food or get it from the environment?
- How does it reproduce?

Kingdom Protista

Members of the kingdom **Protista**, called *protists,* are single-celled or multicellular organisms such as algae and slime molds. Protists are very diverse. Members may have plant-like, animal-like, or fungus-like characteristics. Some protists reproduce sexually, while others reproduce asexually. Algae are *autotrophs,* which means that they make their own food. Some protists are *heterotrophs.* They eat other organisms for food.

Kingdom Plantae

Kingdom **Plantae** consists of multicellular organisms that have cell walls, mostly made of cellulose. Most plants are autotrophs; they make their own food through the process of photosynthesis. Plants are found on land and in water that light can pass through. Some plants reproduce sexually, such as when pollen from one plant fertilizes another plant. Other plants reproduce asexually, such as when potato buds grow into new potato plants. While plants can grow, they cannot move by themselves.

14 Categorize Name one example organism from each kingdom.

____

____

Eukaryote!

Kingdom Fungi

The members of the kingdom **Fungi** are heterotrophs,and their cell walls contain chitin. Fungal cells do not have chloroplasts. Fungi are single-celled or multicellular and include yeasts, molds, and mushrooms. Fungi use digestive juices to break down materials around them for food. Fungi reproduce sexually, asexually, or in both ways, depending on their type.

Active Reading **15 Identify** As you read, underline the characteristics of the kingdom Animalia.

Kingdom Animalia

Kingdom **Animalia** contains multicellular organisms that lack cell walls. They do not have chloroplasts like plants and algae, so they must get nutrients by consuming other organisms. Therefore, they are heterotrophic. Animals have specialized sense organs, and most animals are able to move around. Birds, fish, reptiles, amphibians, insects, and mammals are just a few examples of animals. Most animals reproduce sexually, but a few types of animals reproduce asexually, such as by budding.

16 Classify Place a check mark in the box for the characteristic that each kingdom displays.

	Cells		Nutrients		Reproduction	
Kingdom	Unicellular	Multicellular	Autotrophic	Heterotrophic	Sexual	Asexual
Protista						
Plantae						
Fungi						
Animalia						

How do classification systems change over time?

Millions of organisms have been identified and classified, but millions have yet to be discovered and named. Not only are scientists still identifying new species, but sometimes these new species do not fit into existing genera or phyla. For example, many scientists argue that protists are so different from one another that they should be classified into several kingdoms instead of one. The number of kingdoms may change as new data are collected. Our classification system changes as we learn more about living things.

Active Reading

17 Predict How might the classification of protists change in the future?

How do branching diagrams show classification relationships?

How do you organize your closet? What about your books? People organize things in many different ways. Linnaeus' two-name system worked for scientists long ago, but the system does not represent what we know about living things today. Scientists use different tools to organize information about classification.

Scientists often use a type of branching diagram called a *cladogram* (KLAD•uh•gram). A cladogram shows relationships among species. Organisms are grouped according to common characteristics. Usually these characteristics are listed along a line. Branches of organisms extend from this line. Organisms on branches above each characteristic have the characteristic. Organisms on branches below lack the characteristic.

Visualize It!

18 Apply How can you use the branching diagram to tell which plants produce seeds?

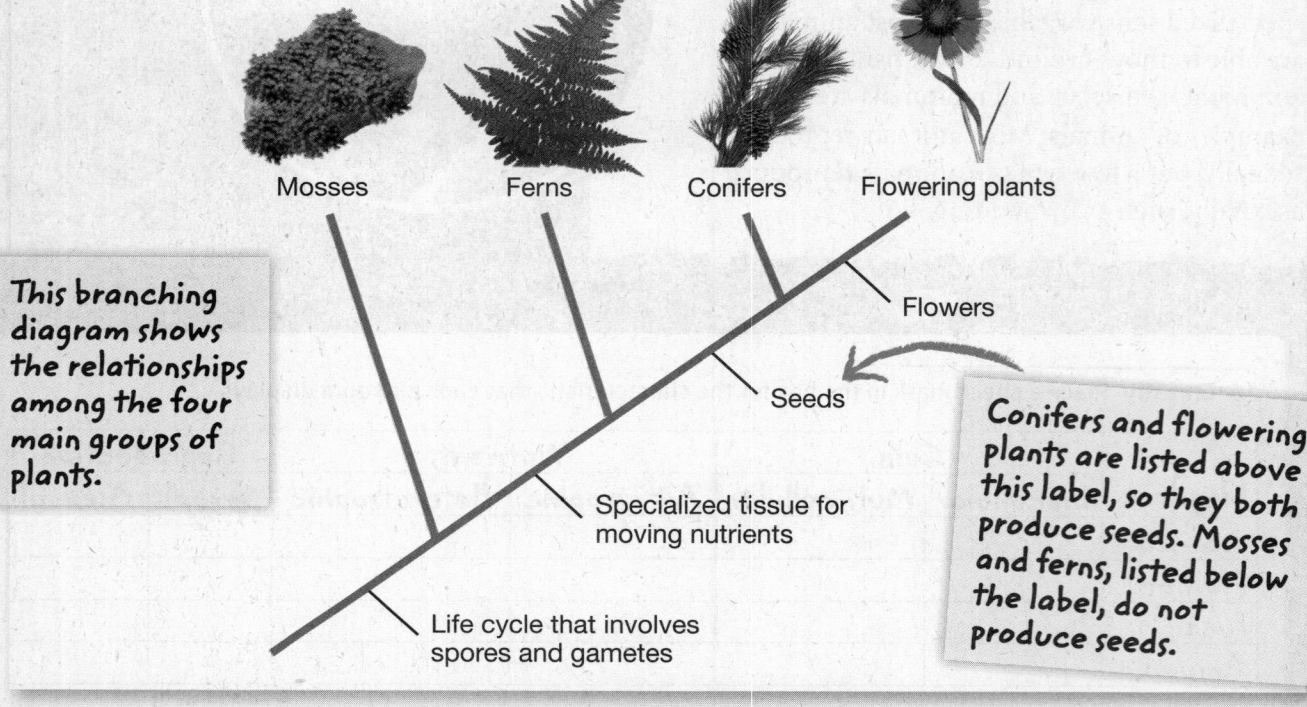

This branching diagram shows the relationships among the four main groups of plants.

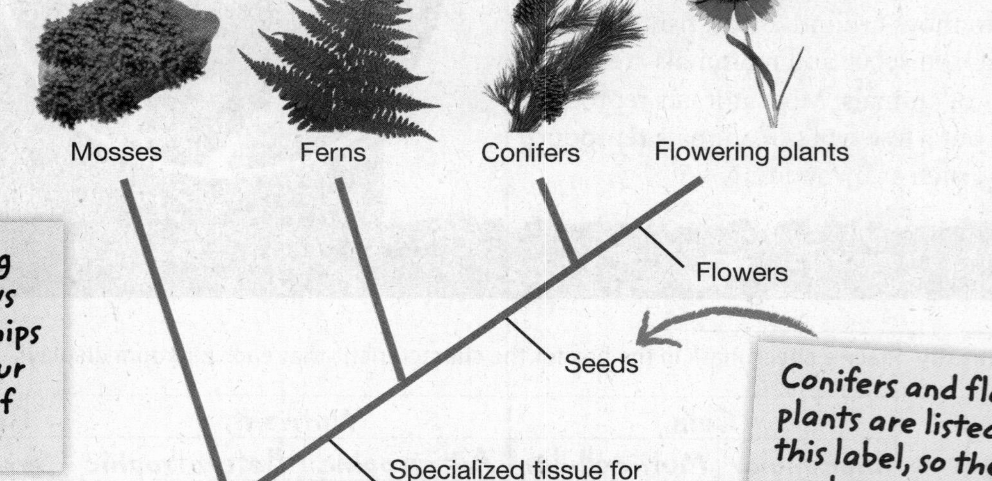

Conifers and flowering plants are listed above this label, so they both produce seeds. Mosses and ferns, listed below the label, do not produce seeds.

Why It Matters

A Class by Themselves

As scientists find more living things to study, they find that they may not have made enough classifications, or that their classifications may not describe organisms well enough. Some living things have traits that fall under more than one classification. These organisms are very difficult to classify.

Sea spider

Euglena

Euglena

Another strange group of creatures is Euglena. Euglena make their own food as plants do. But, like animals, they have no cell walls. They also have a flagellum, a tail-like structure that allows them to move. With this unusual combination of characteristics, Euglena are classified as protists.

Sea Spider

The sea spider is a difficult-to-classify animal. It is an arthropod because it has body segments and an exoskeleton. The problem is in the sea spider's body structure, which is unlike any known arthropod's. Sea spiders have a straw-like mouth, a tiny abdomen, and portions of their intestines are in their legs! Scientists must decide if they need to make a new classification or change an existing one to account for such unusual body structures.

Extend

Inquiry

19 Explain In which domain would the sea spider be classified? Explain your answer.

20 Research Investigate how scientists use DNA to help classify organisms such as the sea spider.

21 Debate Find more information on Euglena and sea spiders. Hold a class debate on how scientists should classify the organisms.

Keys to Success

How can organisms be identified?

Imagine walking through the woods. You see an animal sitting on a rock. It has fur, whiskers, and a large, flat tail. How can you find out what kind of animal it is? You can use a dichotomous key.

Dichotomous Keys

A *dichotomous key* (dy•KAHT•uh•muhs KEE) uses a series of paired statements to identify organisms. Each pair of statements is numbered. When identifying an organism, read each pair of statements. Then choose the statement that best describes the organism. Either the chosen statement identifies the organism, or you will be directed to another pair of statements. By working through the key, you can eventually identify the organism.

22 Apply Use the dichotomous key below to identify the animals shown in the photographs.

Dichotomous Key to Six Mammals in the Eastern United States

1	**A** The mammal has no hair on its tail.	**Go to step 2**
	B The mammal has hair on its tail.	**Go to step 3**
2	**A** The mammal has a very short naked tail.	**Eastern mole**
	B The mammal has a long naked tail.	**Go to step 4**
3	**A** The mammal has a black mask.	**Raccoon**
	B The mammal does not have a black mask.	**Go to step 5**
4	**A** The mammal has a flat, paddle-shaped tail.	**Beaver**
	B The mammal has a round, skinny tail.	**Possum**
5	**A** The mammal has a long furry tail that is black on the tip.	**Long-tailed weasel**
	B The mammal has a long tail that has little fur.	**White-footed mouse**

Visualize It!

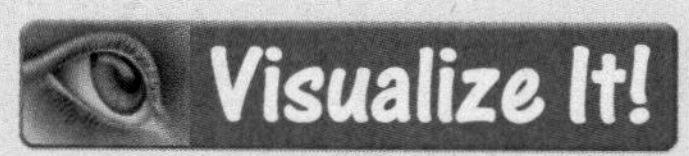

23 Apply Some dichotomous keys are set up as diagrams instead of tables. Work through the key below to identify the unknown plant.

Think Outside the Book Inquiry

24 Summarize With a partner, choose six plants or animals in a local ecosystem. Then design a dichotomous key that can be used to identify the organisms. When you have finished, trade keys with your classmates and work through their keys with your partner.

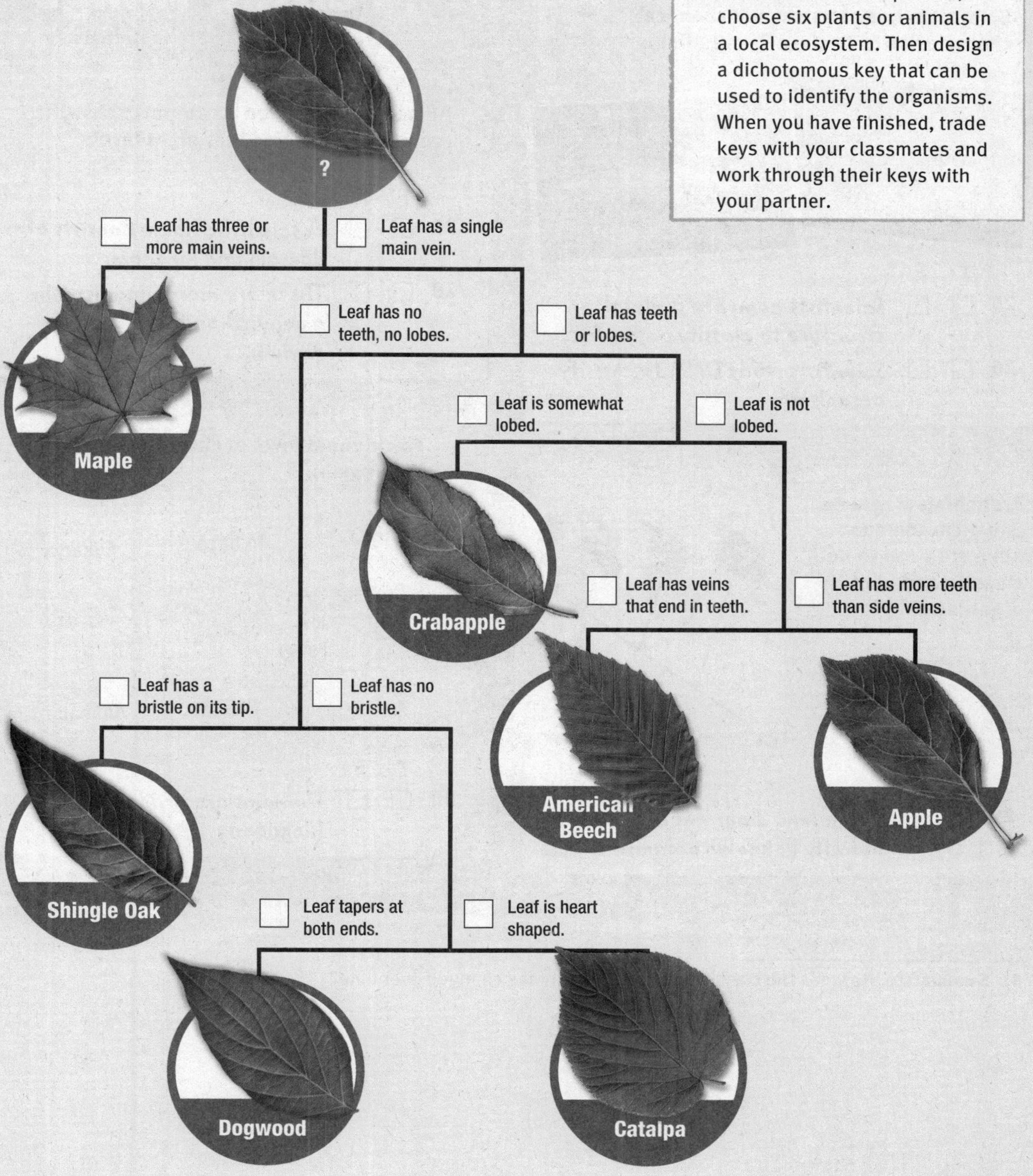

?
Leaf has three or more main veins.
Leaf has a single main vein.
Maple
Leaf has no teeth, no lobes.
Leaf has teeth or lobes.
Leaf is somewhat lobed.
Leaf is not lobed.
Crabapple
Leaf has veins that end in teeth.
Leaf has more teeth than side veins.
American Beech
Apple
Leaf has a bristle on its tip.
Leaf has no bristle.
Shingle Oak
Leaf tapers at both ends.
Leaf is heart shaped.
Dogwood
Catalpa

Visual Summary

To complete this summary, check the box that indicates true or false. Then, use the key below to check your answers. You can use this page to review the main concepts of the lesson.

Classification of Living Things

Scientists use physical and chemical characteristics to classify organisms.

T F

25 ☐ ☐ Scientists compare skeletal structure to classify organisms.

26 ☐ ☐ Scientists study DNA to classify organisms.

Branching diagrams and dichotomous keys are used to help classify and identify organisms.

T F

29 ☐ ☐ Branching diagrams are used to identify unknown organisms.

All species are given a two-part scientific name and classified into eight levels.

T F

27 ☐ ☐ A scientific name consists of domain and kingdom.

28 ☐ ☐ There are more organisms in a genus than there are in a phylum.

The highest level of classification is the domain.

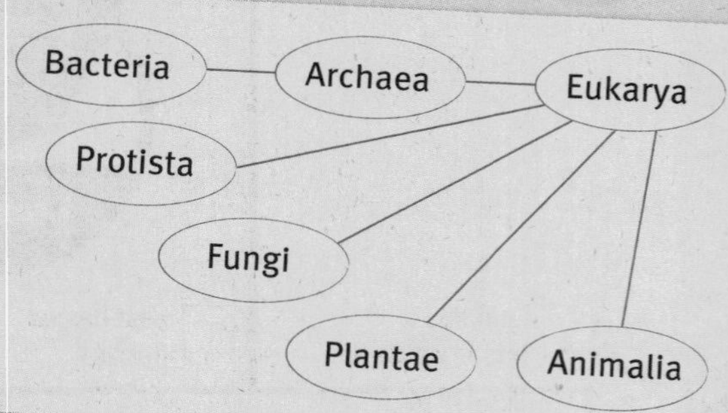

T F

30 ☐ ☐ Domains are divided into kingdoms.

Answers: 25 T; 26 T; 27 F; 28 F; 29 F; 30 T

31 Summarize How has the classification of living things changed over time?

Lesson Review

Vocabulary

Fill in the blanks with the term that best completes the following sentences.

1 A ______________________________ contains paired statements that can be used to identify organisms.

2 The kingdoms of eukaryotes are ____________________, Fungi, Plantae, and Animalia.

3 Domains ____________________ and ____________________ are made up of prokaryotes.

Key Concepts

4 **List** Name the eight levels of classification from most general to most specific.

5 **Explain** Describe how scientists choose the kingdom in which a eukaryote belongs.

6 **Identify** What two types of evidence are used to classify organisms?

7 **Compare** Dichotomous keys and branching diagrams organize different types of information about classification. How are these tools used differently?

Critical Thinking

Use the figure to answer the following questions.

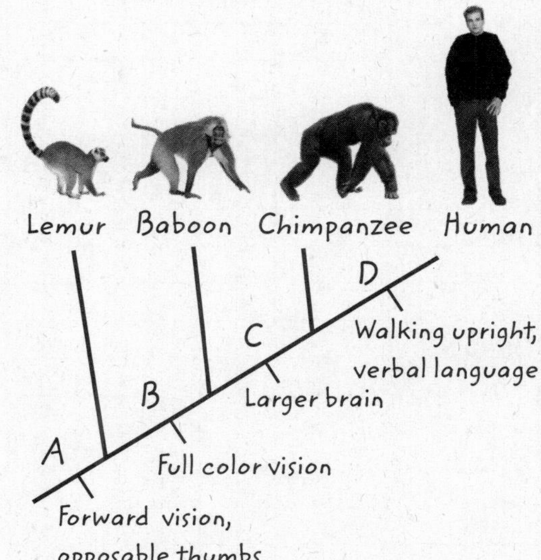

8 **Identify** Which traits do baboons have?

9 **Analyze** Which animal shares the most traits with humans?

10 **Synthesize** Do both lemurs and humans have the trait listed at point D? Explain.

11 **Classify** A scientist finds an organism that cannot move. It has many cells, produces spores, and gets food from its environment. In which kingdom does it belong? Explain.

My Notes

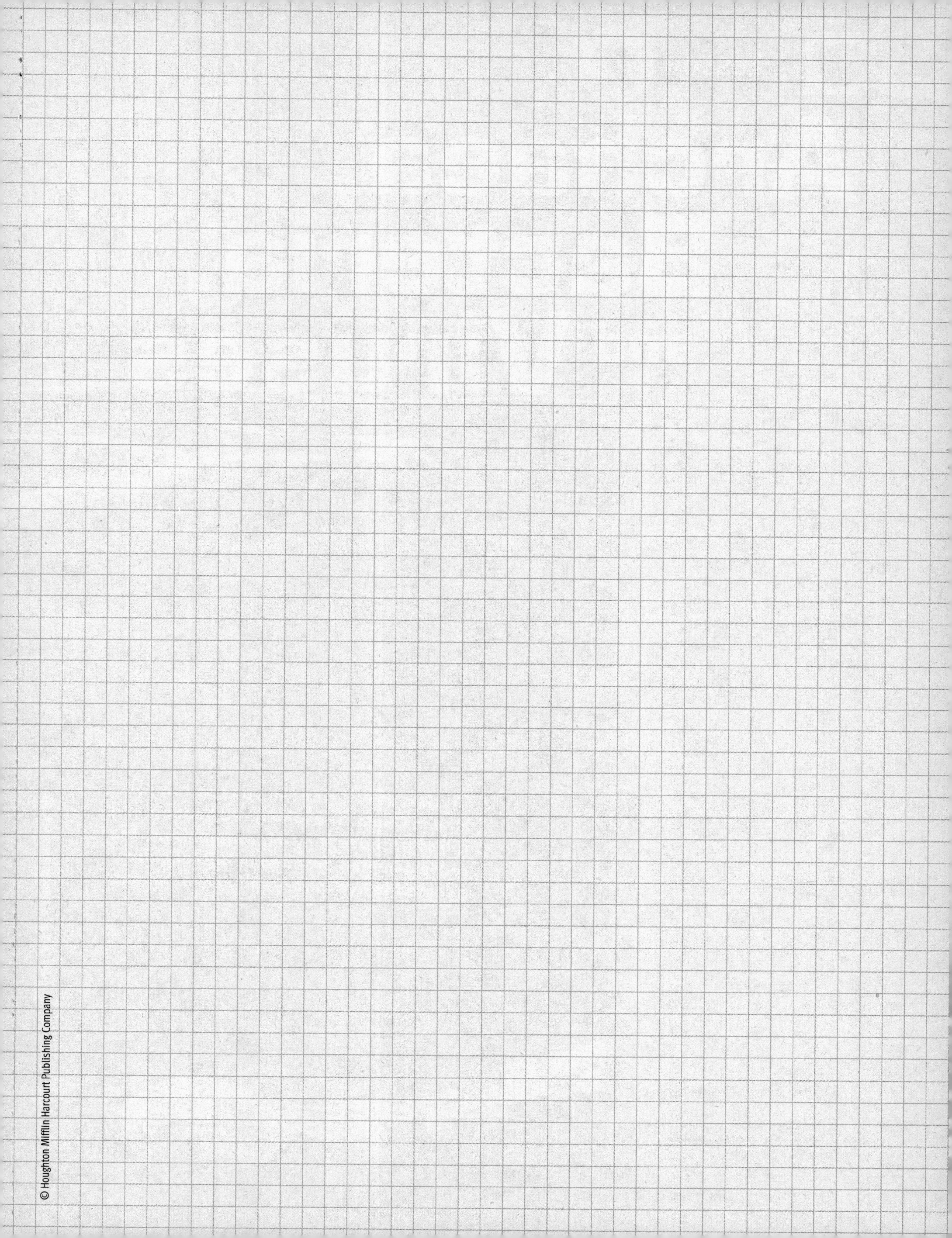

Archaea, Bacteria, and Viruses

ESSENTIAL QUESTION

What are microorganisms?

By the end of this lesson, you should be able to describe the characteristics of archaea, bacteria, and viruses, and explain how they reproduce or replicate.

Crystals of salt ring the edge of this salt lake in China. The lake is red because it is full of archaea, tiny microorganisms. The red-pigmented archaea in this lake are adapted to live in very salty environments.

OHIO **6.LS.1** Cells are the fundamental unit of life.

OHIO **6.LS.4** Living systems at all levels of organization demonstrate the complementary nature of structure and function.

Lesson Labs

Quick Labs
- Observing Bacteria
- Modeling Viral Replication

Field Lab
- Culturing Bacteria from the Environment

Engage Your Brain

1 Predict Check T or F to show whether you think each statement is true or false.

T	F	
☐	☐	Some bacteria are helpful.
☐	☐	Viruses are living things.
☐	☐	A single bacterium can produce many offspring at one time.

2 Predict Using the photo on the right and what you know of bacteria, how do you think bacteria and archaea are similar?

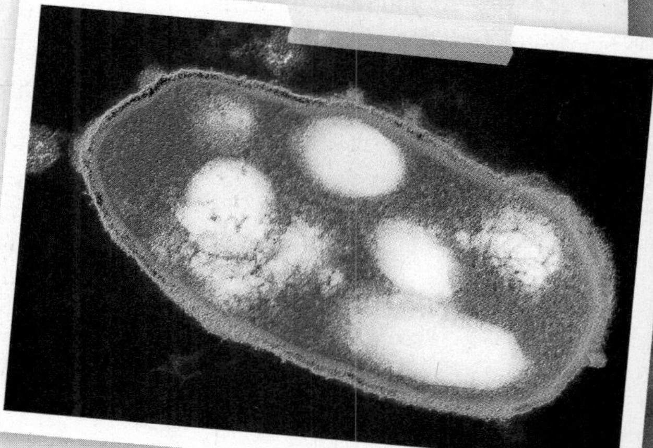

This organism is a member of the domain Archaea. It is a halophile, which means "salt lover." It lives in extremely salty environments like the one shown to the left.

Active Reading

3 Apply Many scientific words, such as *host*, also have everyday meanings. Use context clues to write your own definition for each meaning of the word *host*.

Example sentence
The host greeted the guests as they arrived at her house for the party.

host:

Example sentence
A virus takes over a host cell and causes it to make new viruses.

host:

Vocabulary Terms

- **Bacteria**
- **Archaea**
- **binary fission**
- **virus**
- **host**

4 Identify This list contains the vocabulary terms you'll learn in this lesson. As you read, circle the definition of each term.

SIZED Extra-Small

What is a prokaryote?

Active Reading

5 Identify As you read, underline characteristics of prokaryotes.

All living things fit into one of two major groups: prokaryote or eukaryote (yoo•KAIR•ee•oht). Eukaryotes are made up of one or many cells that each have a nucleus enclosed by a membrane. Prokaryotes do not have a nucleus or membrane-bound organelles and almost all are single-celled. Prokaryotes are so small we can only see them with a microscope, so they are called *microorganisms*. Prokaryotes are divided into two domains. **Bacteria** is a domain of prokaryotes that usually have a cell wall and that usually reproduce by cell division. **Archaea** (ar•KEE•uh) is a domain of prokaryotes that are genetically very different from bacteria and that have unique chemicals in their cell walls. Although they are very small, prokaryotes can get energy and reproduce, and many can move. A handful of soil may contain trillions of prokaryotes!

Visualize It!

6 On the lines below, describe the characteristics of prokaryotic cells and eukaryotic cells.

Prokaryotic Cell

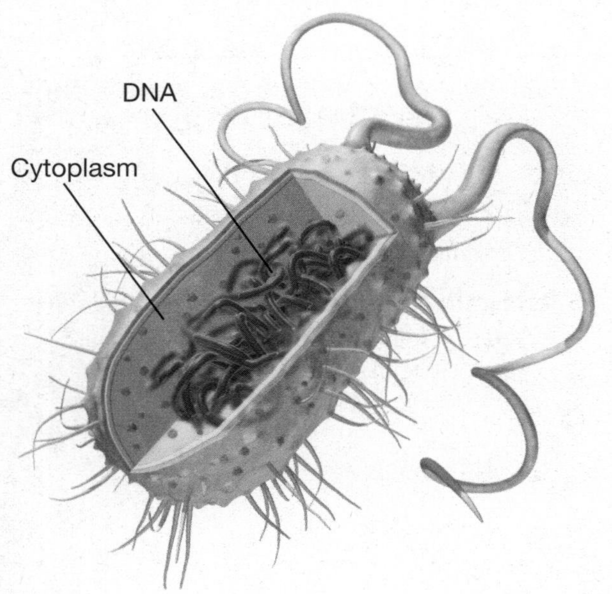

____

____

____

Eukaryotic Cell

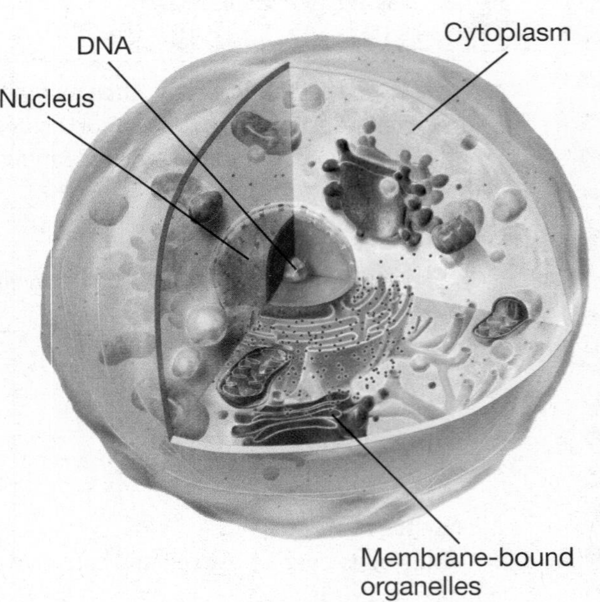

____

____

____

What are some characteristics of archaea?

Active Reading **7 Identify** As you read, underline unusual places where archaea can live.

Archaea are organisms that have many unique molecular traits. Like bacteria, archaea are prokaryotes. But the cell walls of archaea are chemically different from those of bacteria. Some of the molecules in archaea are similar to the molecules in eukaryotes. Some of the molecules in archaea are not found in any other living things.

Archaea often live where nothing else can. Scientists have found them in the hot springs at Yellowstone National Park. They can live in extremely acidic and extremely salty habitats. They flourish near deep-sea vents where no light reaches, and they can use sulfur to convert energy. Archaea have even been found living 8 km below the Earth's surface! It was once thought that archaea only lived in extreme environments. But recent research has shown that archaea are everywhere!

8 Explain What evidence suggests that archaea are more closely related to eukaryotes than bacteria are?

____

____

____

Some archaea can live in hot springs that reach near boiling temperatures.

Some archaea can live in deep-sea vents where there is no oxygen.

Beautiful Bacteria

What are some characteristics of bacteria?

Most known prokaryotes are bacteria. The domain Bacteria has more individuals than all other domains combined do. Many bacteria are *consumers* that get their nutrients by feeding on other organisms. Some bacterial consumers are *decomposers*, which feed on dead organisms. Other bacterial consumers live in or on the body of another organism. Bacteria that make their own food are called *producers*. These bacteria use energy from sunlight to make food, and are often green.

Most bacteria are round, spiral, or rod shaped.

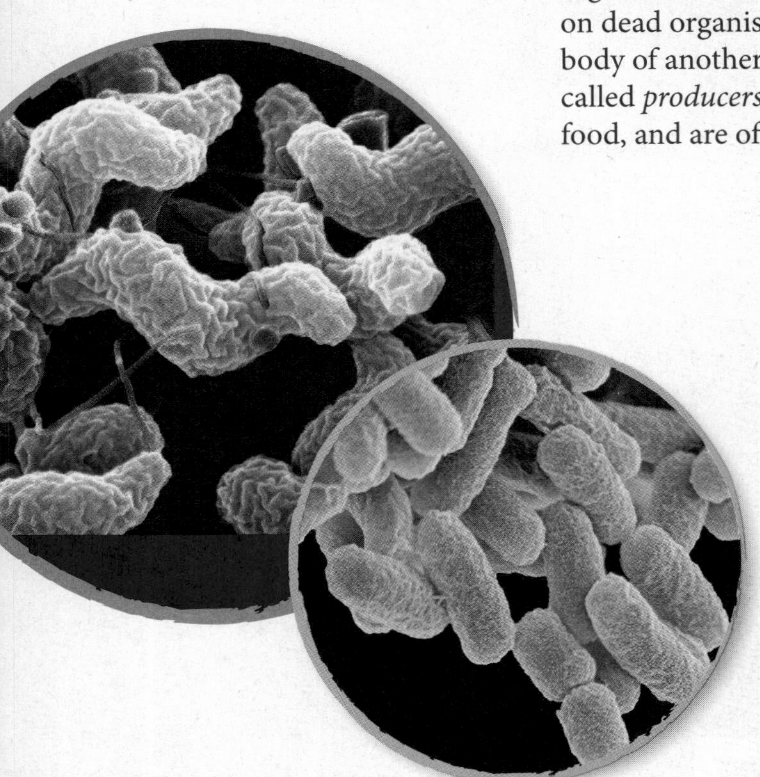

They Are Single-Celled

Bacteria are small, single-celled organisms. Some bacteria stick together to form strands or films, but usually each bacterium still functions as an independent organism. Each bacterium must take in nutrients, release energy from food, get rid of wastes, and grow on its own.

They Are Round, Spiral, or Rod Shaped

Most bacteria have a rigid cell wall that gives them their shape. Each shape helps bacteria in a different way. Bacteria that are shaped like spirals can move like corkscrews. Bacteria shaped like rods quickly absorb nutrients. Round bacteria do not dry out quickly.

Visualize It!

9 Illustrate Draw an example of each of the three bacteria shapes described above.

They Live Everywhere

Bacteria can be found almost everywhere on Earth. They can be found breaking down dead material in soil, making nitrogen available inside plant roots, and breaking down nutrients in animal intestines. They can be found at the tops of mountains and even in Antarctic ice. Some bacteria can survive during periods when environmental conditions become harsh by forming *endospores*. An endospore is made up of a thick, protective coating, the bacteria's genetic material, and cytoplasm. Many endospores can survive in hot, cold, and very dry places. When conditions improve, the endospores break open, and the bacteria become active again.

Active Reading

10 Relate What is the advantage for bacteria that form endospores?

____

____

____

____

A close-up look at leaves from this pond reveals that bacteria live here.

Visualize It!

11 Predict This pond is full of decaying leaves and wood as well as living aquatic plants and animals. In what parts of the pond do you think bacteria might live?

____

____

____

____

____

____

SPLIT Personality

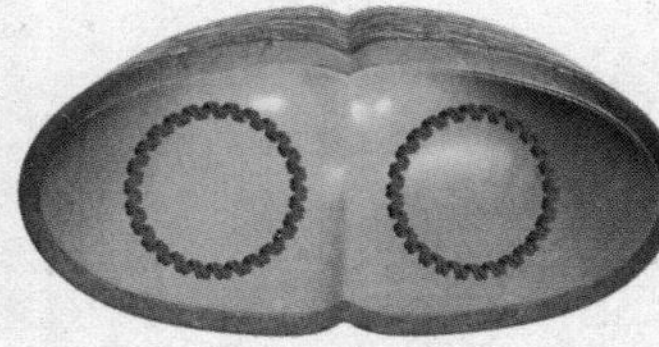

In binary fission, a bacterial cell copies its DNA. The DNA separates, and the cell divides into two new cells.

How do bacteria reproduce?

Bacteria grow if they have the space and food they need. When a bacterial cell has reached its full size, it will generally begin to reproduce. Bacteria reproduce by dividing in two. Some bacteria can divide every 20 minutes!

By Binary Fission

Active Reading **12 Identify** As you read, underline the steps that occur when a bacterium reproduces using binary fission.

Both archaea and bacteria reproduce by binary fission. **Binary fission** is reproduction in which one single-celled organism splits into two single-celled organisms. The first step in bacterial reproduction is copying the cell's genetic information. Bacteria have their genetic information in the form of a long, circular strand of DNA. This loop, called a *chromosome,* is copied. Then the two chromosomes separate, with one on each side of the cell. Next, the cell's membrane starts to grow inward, separating the two halves of the cell. Finally, a new cell wall forms and separates the two new cells. At the end of binary fission, there are two identical bacterial cells, each with identical DNA. This type of reproduction, in which one parent produces offspring that are genetically identical to the parent, is called *asexual reproduction.* The cells will grow until they reach full size, and the process will begin again.

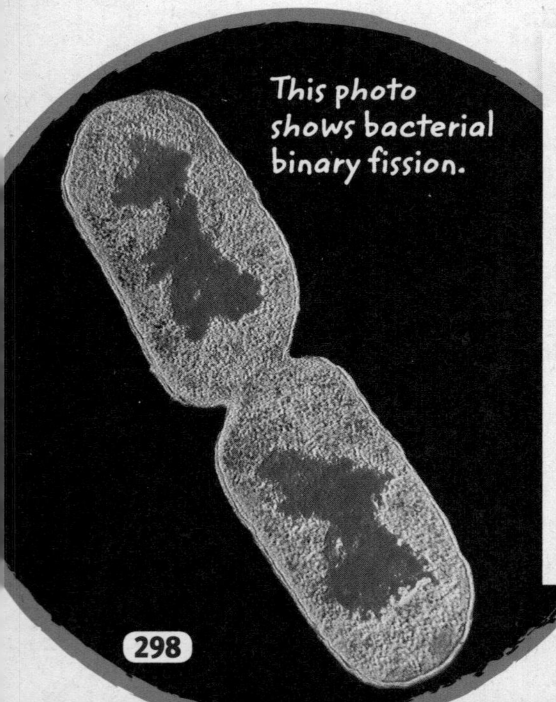

This photo shows bacterial binary fission.

Do the Math You Try It

13 A bacterium undergoes binary fission. After thirty minutes, both new cells are ready to divide again. If this generation divides, and so does the following generation, how many total bacteria will there be? You may want to draw a diagram to check your answer.

How do bacteria exchange DNA?

How do bacteria get new genes? There are three ways that bacteria can acquire new genetic information. One way, called *transformation,* occurs when bacteria take up DNA from the environment. Another way, *transduction,* happens when a virus injects DNA into a bacterium. Sometimes the DNA is incorporated into the cell and may be useful. The third way is called *conjugation*. Some bacteria have a second loop of DNA, smaller than the main chromosome, called a plasmid. During conjugation, a plasmid is transferred from one bacterium to another when the two bacteria temporarily join together. The bacterium that gets the plasmid now has new genes that it can use. An example of a trait found on plasmid DNA is antibiotic resistance.

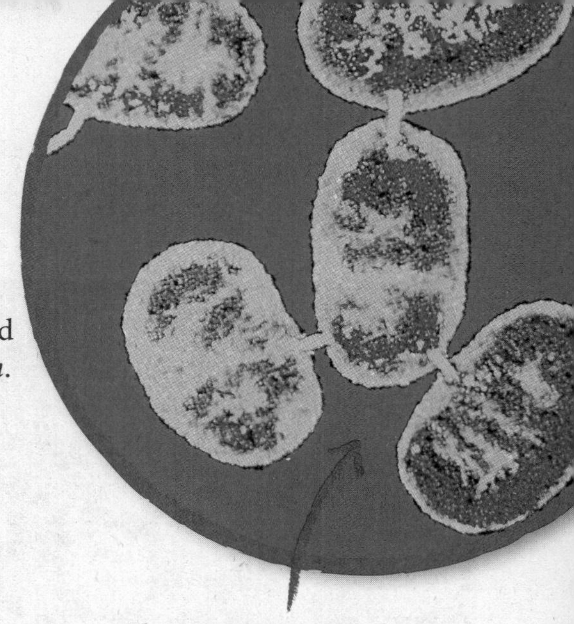

This photo shows bacterial conjugation.

14 Diagram Fill in the missing labels in this flow chart to complete the description of conjugation.

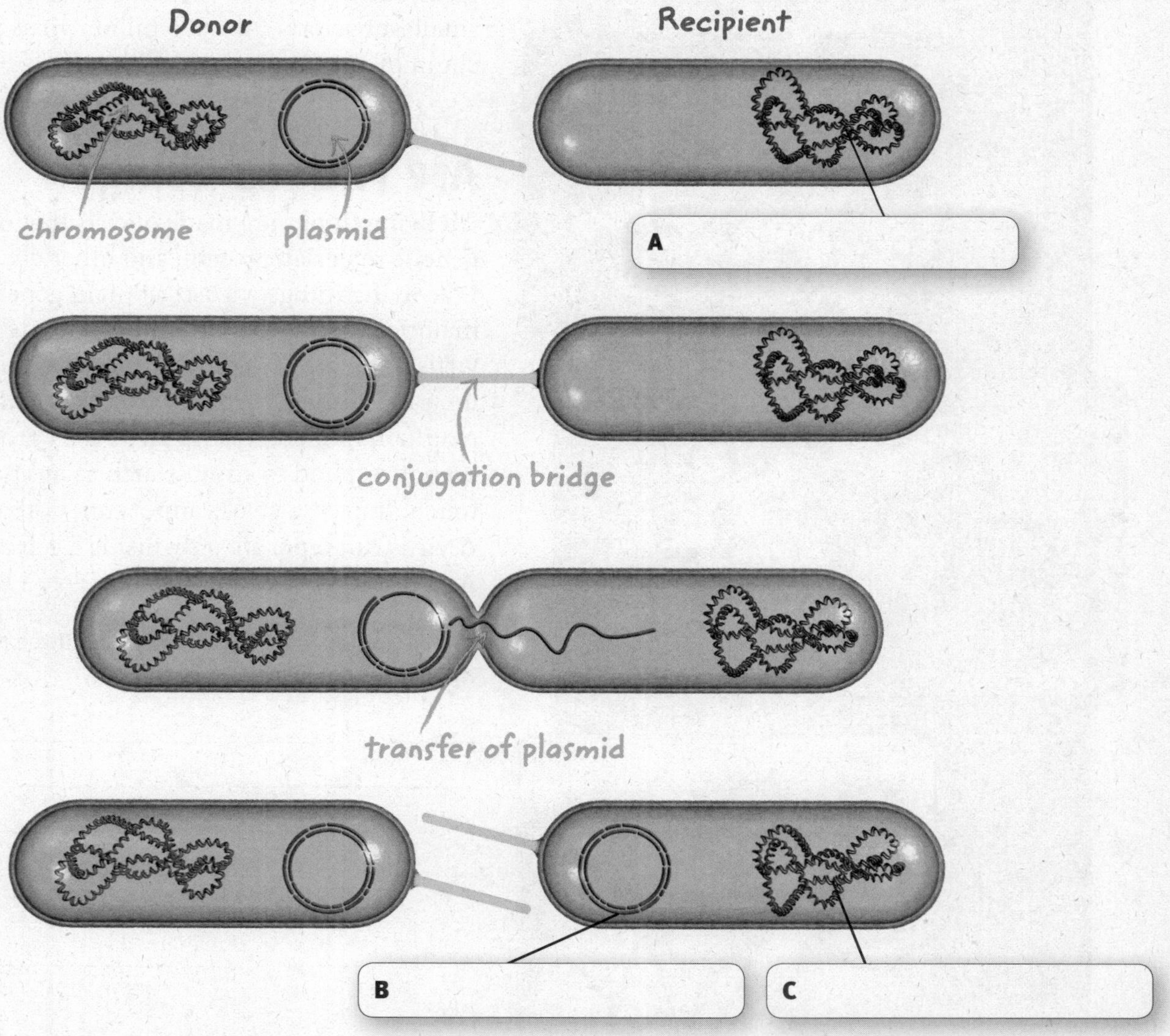

Donor

Recipient

chromosome

plasmid

A

conjugation bridge

transfer of plasmid

B

C

Alive *or* NOT Alive?

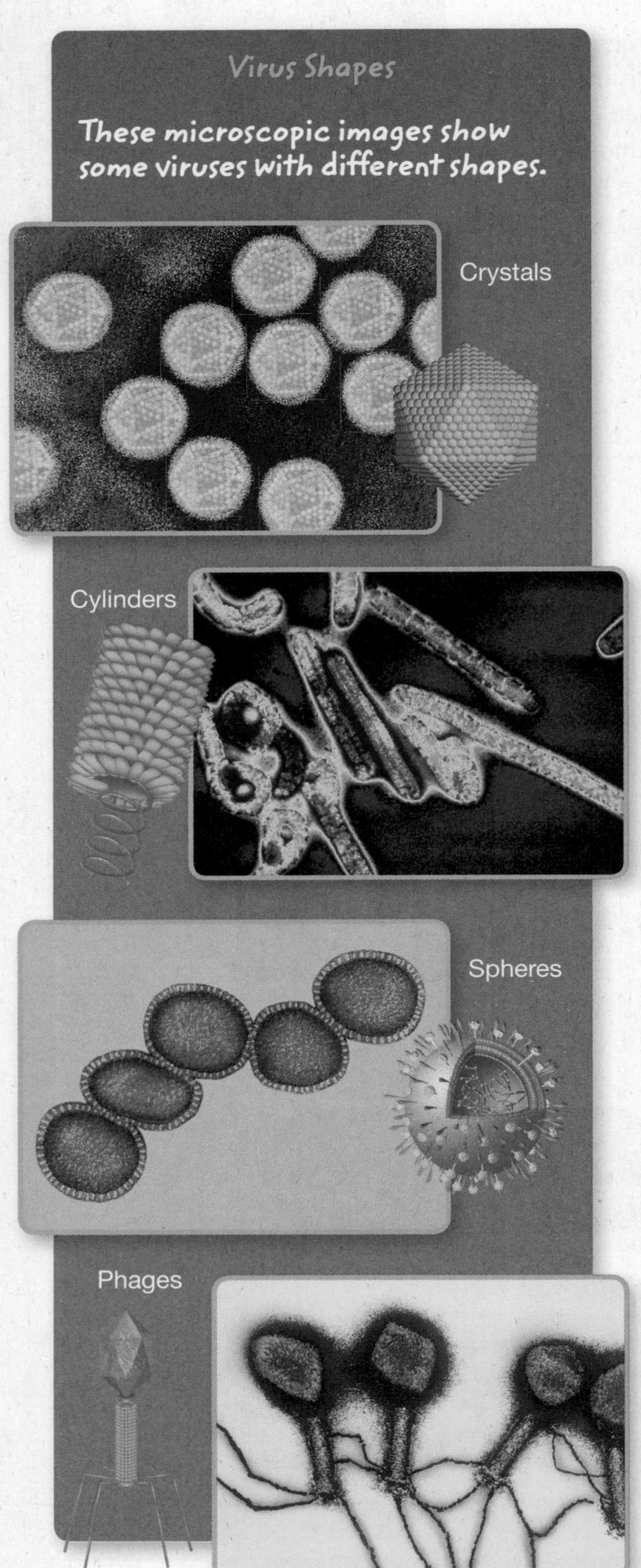

Virus Shapes
These microscopic images show some viruses with different shapes.
Crystals
Cylinders
Spheres
Phages

What are some characteristics of viruses?

A **virus** is a microscopic particle that cannot replicate on its own. It either gets inside a cell or injects a cell with its DNA, often destroying the cell. Many viruses cause diseases, such as the common cold, flu, and acquired immune deficiency syndrome (AIDS). People, plants, animals, and prokaryotes can all be infected by viruses. Viruses are made of a protein coat and genetic material. The genetic material can be either DNA or RNA. The protein coat gives the virus its shape. Most viruses are smaller than the smallest bacteria. About 5 billion virus particles could fit in a single drop of blood.

Are viruses living?

All living things are made of cells that contain genetic material, protein, and other chemicals. Like living things, viruses contain genetic material and protein. But, unlike living things, viruses do not perform any life functions. Viruses do not use energy from nutrients. Viruses do not maintain homeostasis. A virus can't grow. Viruses do not respond to stimuli such as light, sound, or touch. In fact, a virus cannot function on its own. A virus can replicate only inside a cell it infects. As a result, viruses are not considered living.

Active Reading **15 Identify** List three reasons viruses are not living things.

Why It Matters

The Flu

You probably know someone who has had the flu. But did you know that many different influenza viruses cause the flu? Most of these viruses are not very harmful, and healthy people usually recover quickly from the flu. Sometimes, however, a new influenza virus develops that causes serious illness. A flu pandemic occurs when a new flu virus spreads to many people around the world.

The Great Pandemic

Starting in June of 1917, a particularly deadly strain of flu virus began spreading around the world. By the end of 1919, the flu had killed more than 50 million people worldwide! More than 500 million had been infected. Called the 1918 Flu, it was one of the worst epidemics in human history. Scientists are still working to understand what made this strain of flu so deadly.

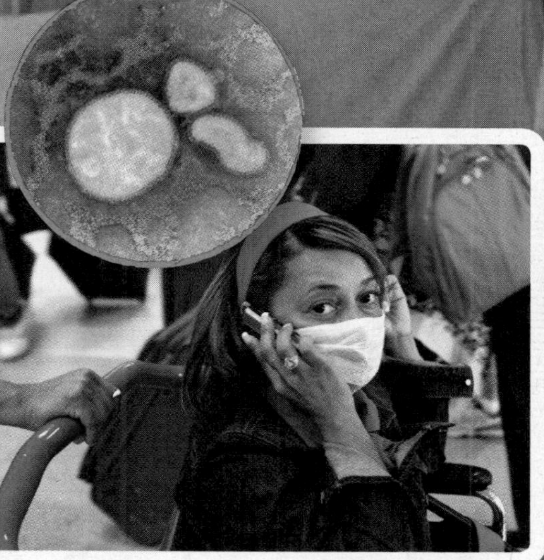

Modern Threats

New strains of flu virus are constantly developing. Scientists monitor outbreaks of new strains closely. The virus that causes the outbreak is studied so that vaccines can be made.

Extend

Inquiry

16 Describe How did the 1918–1919 flu differ from other strains of the flu?

17 Research In 2009, H1N1 flu caused many cases of the flu around the world. Research how H1N1 flu differs from the 1918–1919 flu.

18 Predict How would a flu pandemic be different today than in 1918? In what ways would it be easier or harder to fight a new flu virus now?

A Gift for the Host...

How do viruses replicate?

Why do people stay home when they have a cold? They may not feel well enough to work or to learn. But people also want to prevent other people from getting sick. Some viruses, like the virus that causes the cold, are easily spread from person to person. How do viruses replicate and spread?

By Entering Host Cells

Because viruses are not alive, they can replicate only inside a living cell that serves as a host. A **host** is a living thing that a virus or parasite uses for resources or shelter. Viruses attack specific types of host cells. Proteins on the surface of the virus match proteins on the surface of the host cell. This allows the virus to attach to the host cell and invade it. Many viruses cannot be spread from one type of organism to another, and most can only attack certain types of cells in their host. Some viruses only attack certain types of bacteria. The tobacco mosaic virus can only attack certain types of plants, like the tomato plant shown here.

19 Explain Why can't plants catch a cold?

Both the person and the plant in these pictures are infected with viruses.

By Multiplying their DNA

The first step in viral replication occurs when a virus enters a cell or when the virus's genetic material is injected into a cell. Once the virus's genes are inside, they take over the host cell. The host cell begins following the instructions coded in the viral DNA. The host cell replicates the viral DNA. The host cell makes new protein parts for the virus. Then the parts of the new viruses assemble in the host cell. When the cell is full of new viruses, the viruses burst out of the host cell. This step, called *lysis* (LY•sis), kills the host cell. The new viruses find new host cells, and the *lytic cycle* begins again.

Some viruses insert their genes into the host cell, but new viruses are not made right away. The genes can stay inactive for a long time. When the genes do become active, they begin the lytic cycle and make copies of the virus.

Think Outside the Book Inquiry

21 Apply With a classmate, discuss why some scientists say that viruses replicate instead of reproduce.

Visualize It!

20 Identify Fill in the blank labels with the terms *virus*, *host cell*, and *new viruses* as you study the image to understand the lytic cycle.

A virus infects a host cell and injects genetic material.
A
B
Virus genetic material

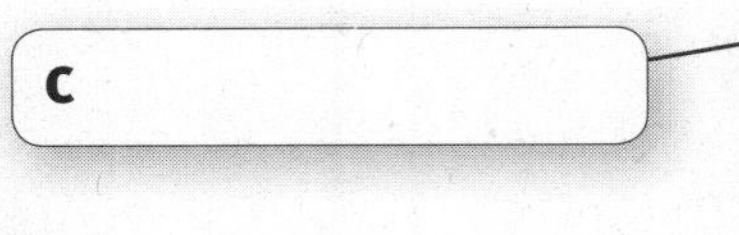
C

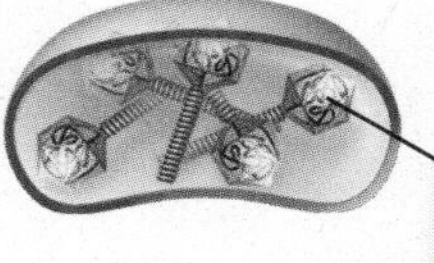
The virus's genetic material takes over the host cell to make more viruses.
new viruses
The host cell bursts, releasing new viruses.

Visual Summary

To complete this summary, circle the correct word or words. Then use the key below to check your answers. You can use this page to review the main concepts of the lesson.

Archaea, Bacteria, and Viruses

Archaea are prokaryotes with variable cell walls made up of unique molecules.

22 Archaea are more/less similar to eukaryotes than bacteria are.

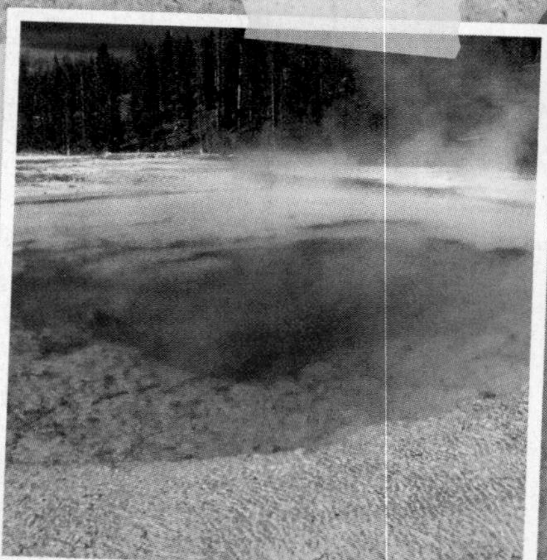

Bacteria are prokaryotes that can have a round, rod, or spiral shape.

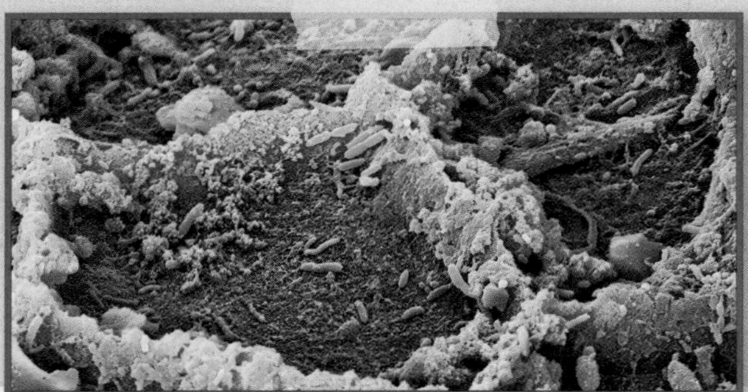

23 Binary fission is asexual reproduction because the offspring are copies of/different from the original cell.

Viruses are nonliving particles made of a protein coat and genetic material.

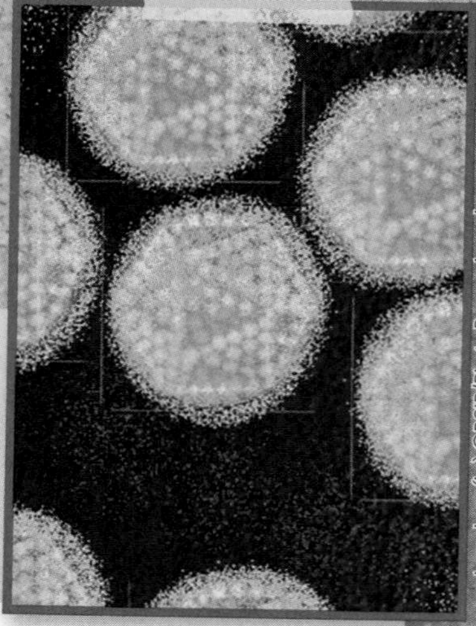

24 Viruses are not alive because they do not release energy/have DNA or RNA.

Answers: 22 more; 23 copies of; 24 release energy.

25 **Compare** What is the difference between bacterial reproduction and viral replication?

Lesson Review

Vocabulary

Fill in the blanks with the terms that best complete the following sentences.

1 A(n) ______________________ is made of genetic material and a protein coat.

2 ______________________ is when one cell reproduces by dividing in half to become two cells.

3 A virus needs a(n) ______________________ to reproduce.

Key Concepts

4 Compare How do prokaryotes and eukaryotes differ?

5 Describe What are the characteristics of archaea?

6 Identify In the lytic cycle, the host cell

A destroys the virus

B becomes a virus

C is destroyed

D undergoes cell division

7 Explain How do the cell walls of archaea and bacteria differ?

Critical Thinking

Use the image below to answer the question that follows.

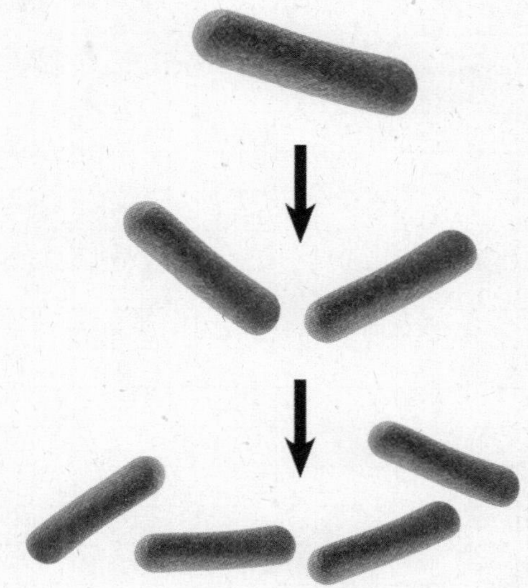

8 Explain Describe the process illustrated in the diagram above. How many individuals would exist if the process continued for one more generation?

9 Apply Unlike some archaea, most bacteria die when their environment reaches extremely high temperature. How can people kill harmful bacteria that might live in some human foods?

My Notes

Think Science

OHIO 6.SIA.3 Use appropriate mathematics, tools and techniques to gather data and information.

OHIO 6.SIA.4 Analyze and interpret data.

Mean, Median, Mode, and Range

You will often find that the samples you study in science vary in size. How do you estimate the size of such varying data sets? You can analyze both the measures of central tendency and the variability of data using mean, median, mode, and range.

Tutorial

Imagine that a public health research group is comparing the number of cases of flu in a specific country. Data has been collected for the last five years.

When working with numerical data, it is helpful to find a value that describes the data set. These representative values can describe a typical data value, or describe how spread out the data values are.

Number of Cases of Flu

Year	Number of Cases
2004	800
2005	300
2006	150
2007	300
2008	200

Mean The mean is the sum of all of the values in a data set divided by the total number of values in the data set. The mean is also called the *average*.	$\frac{800 + 300 + 150 + 300 + 200}{5}$ **mean** = 350 cases/year
Median The median is the value of the middle item when data are arranged in numerical order. If there is an odd number of values, the median is the middle value. If there is an even number of values, the median is the mean of the two middle values.	If necessary, reorder the values from least to greatest: 150, 200, 300, 300, 800 → ← 300 is the middle value **median** = 300 cases/year
Mode The mode is the value or values that occur most frequently in a data set. If all values occur with the same frequency, the data set is said to have no mode. Values should be put in order to find the mode.	If necessary, reorder the values from least to greatest: 150, 200, 300, 300, 800 The value 300 occurs most frequently. **mode** = 300 cases/year
Range Range is another way to measure data. It measures how variable, or spread out, the data are. The range is the difference between the greatest value and the least value of a data set.	800 − 150 = 650 **range** = 650

You Try It!

The data table below shows the reported number of flu cases in four different countries.

Reported Number of Cases of Flu				
Year	**Country 1**	**Country 2**	**Country 3**	**Country 4**
2004	800	none	650	750
2005	300	350	450	450
2006	150	450	500	400
2007	300	200	550	350
2008	200	350	600	600

1

Using Formulas Find the mean, median, and mode of the data for Country 2.

2

Using Formulas Find the mean, median, and mode of the data for Country 3.

3

Analyzing Data Find the mean number of reported flu cases for only years in which cases were reported in Country 2. Compare this with the mean value for all years in Country 2. What conclusion can you draw about the effect of zeros on the mean of a data set?

Mean number of cases for years in which cases were reported: ___________

Mean number of cases for all years: _________

Effect of zeros on the mean:

____

____

4

Evaluating Data Would the country with the greatest total number of flu cases from 2004 to 2008 have the greatest mean? Explain your reasoning.

____

____

____

5

Analyzing Methods Calculate the range for Country 3.

When do you think you might need to use range instead of mean, median or mode?

____

____

____

Lesson 3

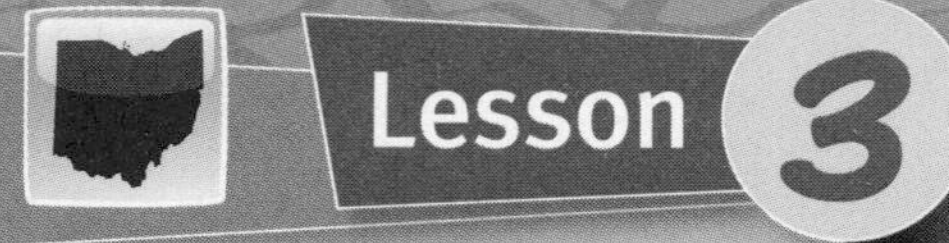

Protists and Fungi

ESSENTIAL QUESTION

What are protists and fungi?

By the end of this lesson, you should be able to describe the characteristics of protists and fungi, and explain how they grow and reproduce.

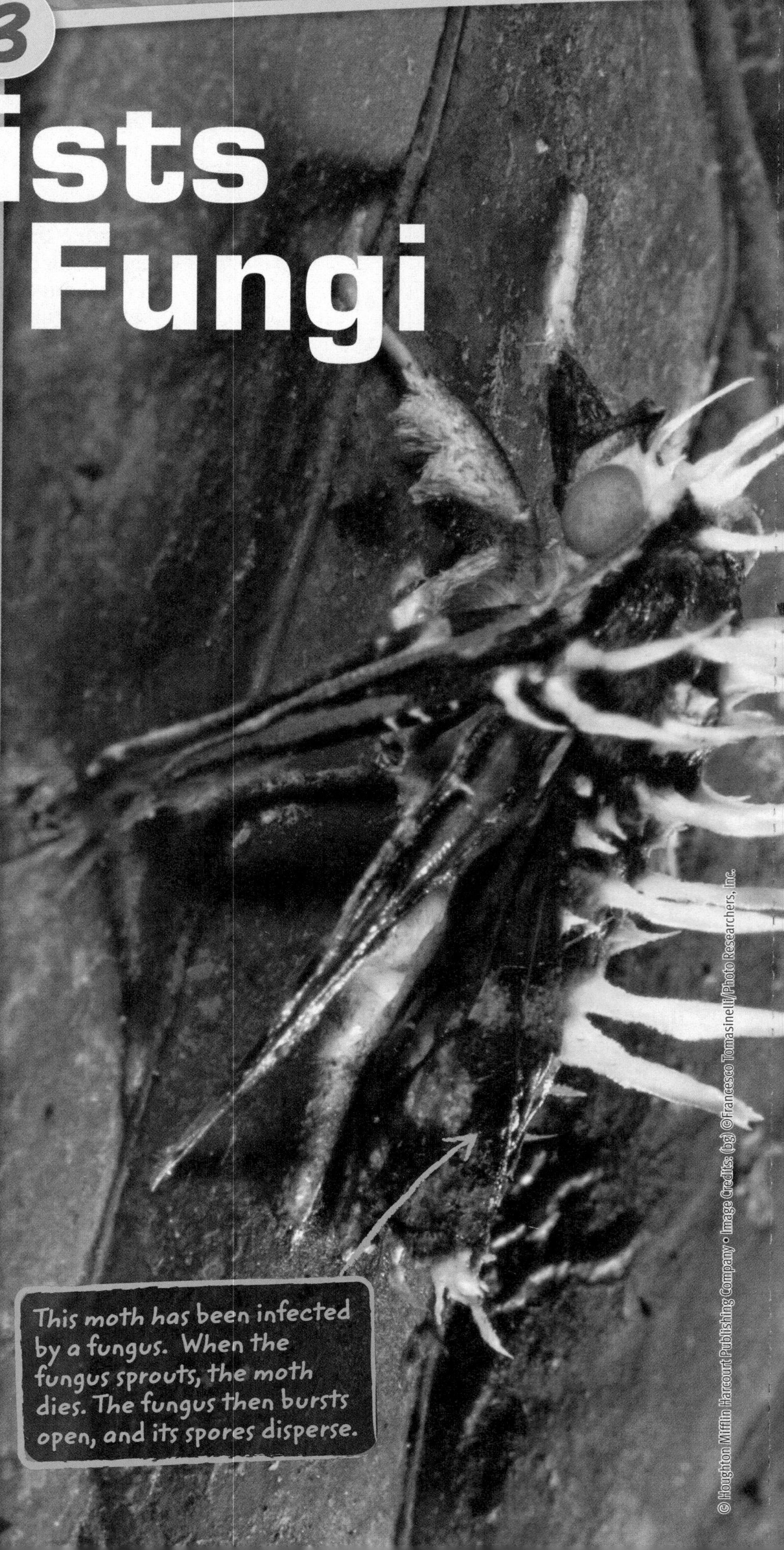

This moth has been infected by a fungus. When the fungus sprouts, the moth dies. The fungus then bursts open, and its spores disperse.

OHIO 6.LS.1 Cells are the fundamental unit of life.

OHIO 6.LS.4 Living systems at all levels of organization demonstrate the complementary nature of structure and function.

Lesson Labs

Quick Labs
- What Do Protists Look Like?
- Observing a Mushroom's Spores and Hyphae

Exploration Lab
- Survey of Reproduction in Protists and Fungi

Engage Your Brain

1 Predict Check T or F to show whether you think each statement is true or false.

T	F	
☐	☐	Mushrooms belong to the kingdom Plantae.
☐	☐	Algae use sunlight to make food through photosynthesis.
☐	☐	Spores are important in fixing atmospheric nitrogen.
☐	☐	Protists can reproduce both asexually and sexually.

2 Describe The photo below shows a protist you might be familiar with—seaweed. Write a caption for the photo that describes this protist.

Active Reading

3 Synthesize Many English words have their roots in other languages. Use the Greek words below to make an educated guess about the meaning of the words spores and hyphae.

Latin word	Meaning
spora	seed, sowing
huphe	web

Example sentence
Fungi reproduce asexually by means of spores.

spores:

Example sentence
Mushrooms are made up of tangled hyphae.

hyphae:

Vocabulary Terms

- **Protista**
- **gamete**
- **spore**
- **algae**
- **Fungi**
- **hyphae**
- **mycorrhiza**
- **lichen**

4 Identify This list contains the vocabulary terms you'll learn in this lesson. As you read, circle the definition of each term.

On the Move!

What are some characteristics of protists?

The kingdom **Protista** is a group of eukaryotic organisms that cannot be classified as fungi, plants, or animals. Members of the kingdom Protista are called protists. Protists are a very diverse group of organisms. Many members of this kingdom are not closely related to each other and some are more closely related to members of other kingdoms. As a result, classification of protists is likely to change. So are there traits that are shared by all protists? As eukaryotes, they all have a nucleus and membrane-bound organelles.

5 Compare The two organisms shown below look very different. Why do scientists classify both as protists?

___

___

___

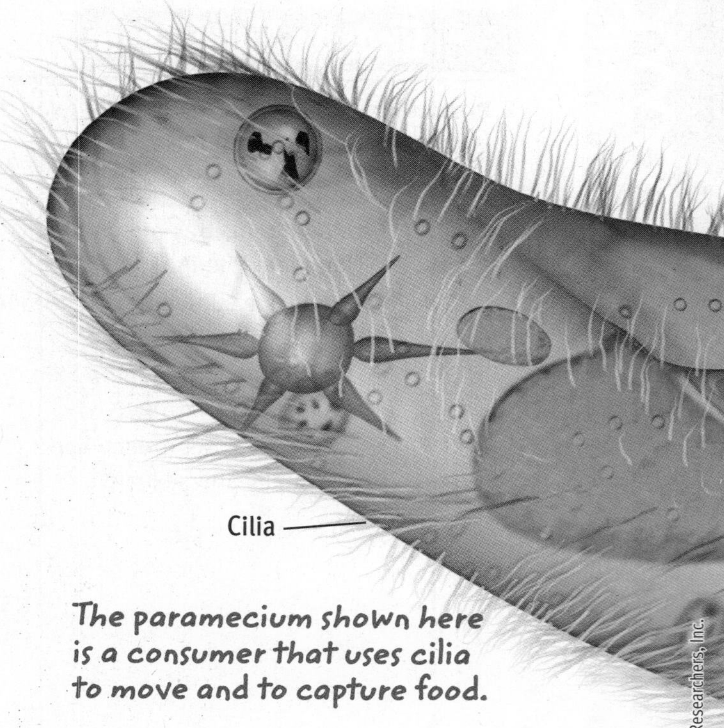

The paramecium shown here is a consumer that uses cilia to move and to capture food.

They Have One or Many Cells

Most protists are single-celled organisms. These protists cannot be seen without a microscope. Diatoms are single-celled protists that have cell walls with unusual shapes. Some protists have many cells. Brown algae are multicellular protists that grow many meters long. Other protists live in colonies. Volvox, a kind of green algae, has cells that form spherical colonies. These colonies can have thousands of cells that all work together.

The brown algae shown here is a multicellular protist.

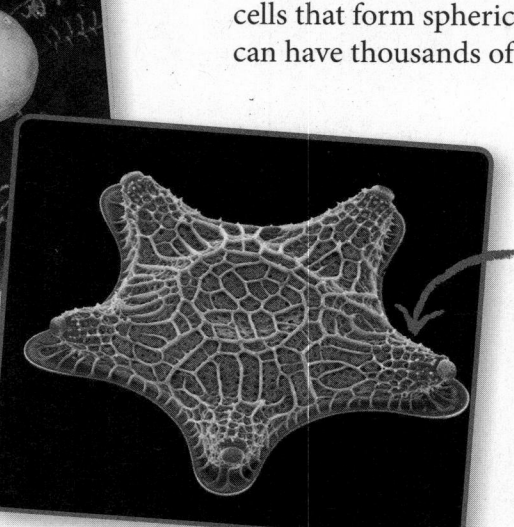

The diatom shown here is a microscopic single-celled protist.

They Have Membrane-Bound Organelles

Like all eukaryotes, protists have membrane-bound organelles. Organelles are structures that carry out jobs inside a cell. For example, some protists have chloroplasts that make food from the sun's energy. Many protists have contractile vacuoles that remove excess water from the cell. Some protists have organelles that sense light.

They Have Complex Structures for Movement

Some protists have structures for movement. Most protists that move do so in order to find food. Some protists use cilia to move. Cilia are hairlike structures that beat rapidly back and forth. Other protists use a flagellum or many flagella to move. A flagellum is a whiplike structure that propels the cell forward. Amoebas are protists that move by stretching their bodies. This forms a *pseudopod* (SOO•duh•pahd) or "false foot." When cytoplasm flows into the pseudopod, the rest of the cell follows.

Contractile vacuole

Visualize It!

6 Draw Each protist shown below is missing the structures it uses for movement. Draw the missing parts for each individual.

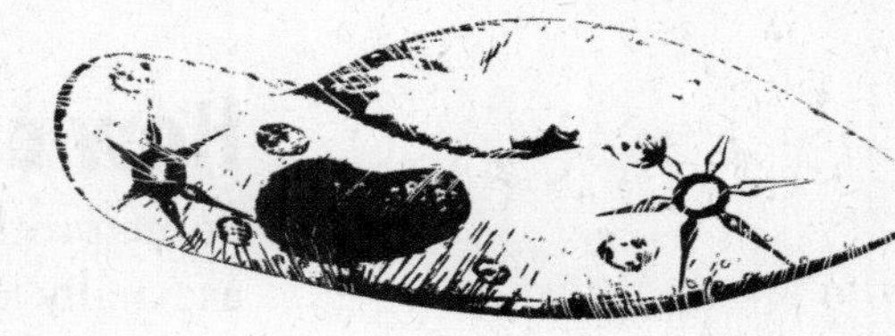

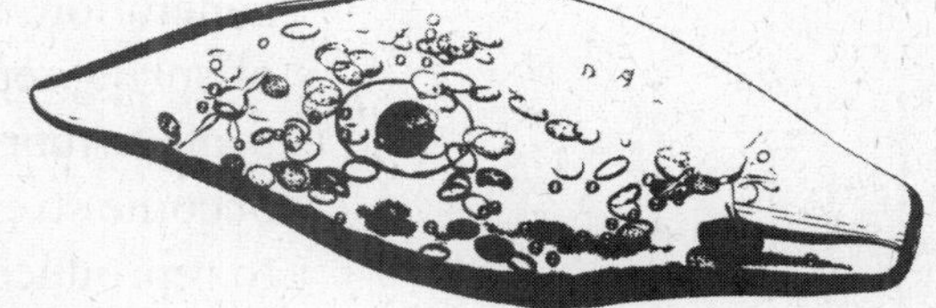

Chloroplast

Flagellum

The euglena is a producer that uses light to make food. It uses its flagellum to move toward light and to escape from predators.

7 Identify How can structures for movement help protists to survive?

____

____

____

____

____

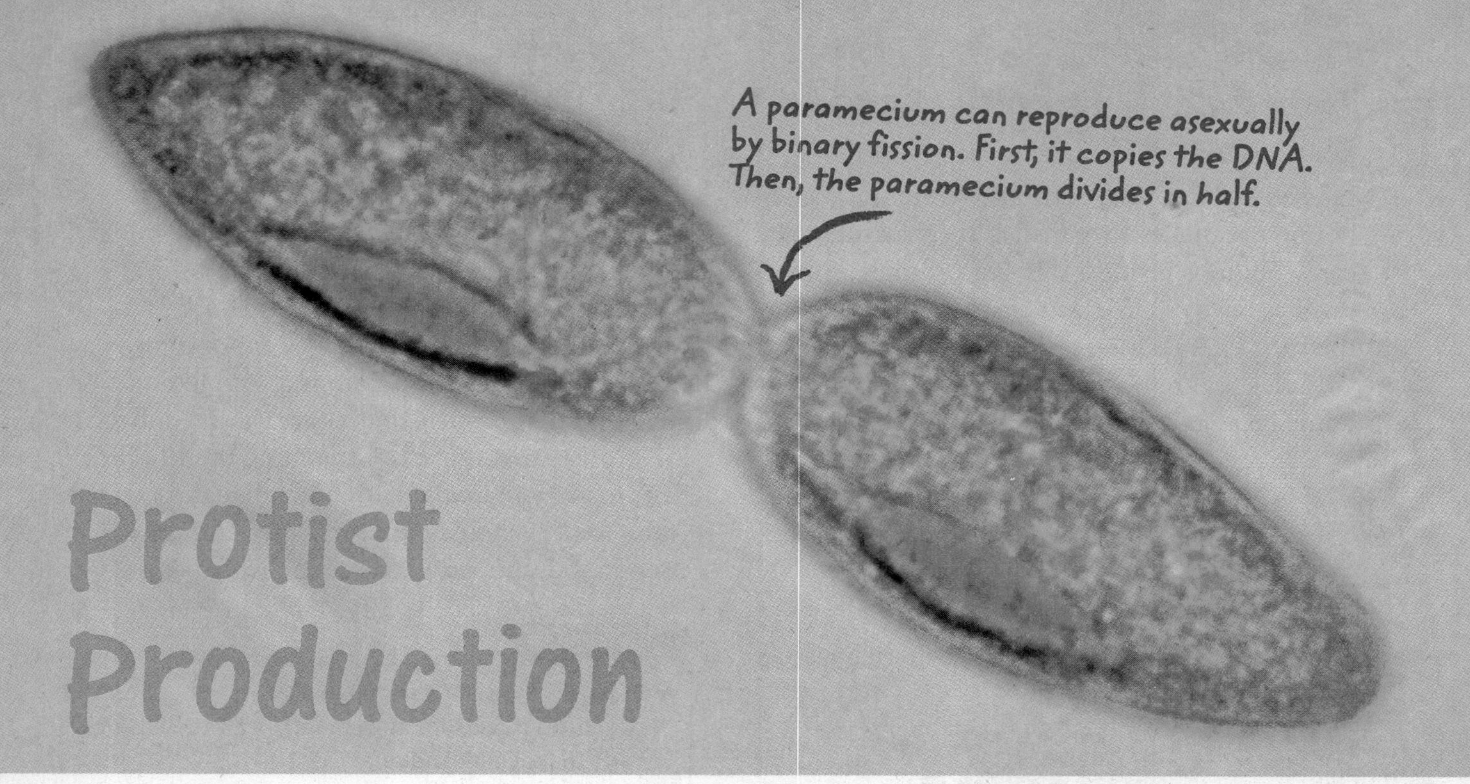

A paramecium can reproduce asexually by binary fission. First, it copies the DNA. Then, the paramecium divides in half.
Protist Production

Protist Production

How can protists reproduce?

Some protists reproduce only asexually. Others reproduce asexually at one stage in their life cycle and sexually at another stage. For some protists, the type of reproduction alternates by generation. For example, a parent reproduces asexually, and its offspring reproduce sexually. Then the cycle starts again. Other protists reproduce asexually until environmental conditions become stressful. A lack of food or water can trigger these protists to reproduce sexually until conditions improve.

By Asexual Reproduction

Most protists can reproduce asexually. In asexual reproduction, the offspring come from just one parent. So every organism can produce offspring on its own. These offspring are genetically identical to the parent. When environmental conditions are favorable and there is plenty of food and water, asexual reproduction produces many offspring very quickly.

Protists can reproduce asexually in different ways. These include binary fission and fragmentation. During binary fission, a single-celled protist copies its DNA. The protist then divides into two cells. Each new cell has a copy of the DNA. The paramecium shown above is splitting through binary fission. Fragmentation is a process in which a piece breaks off of an organism and develops into a new individual. Many multicellular protists can reproduce by fragmentation.

Active Reading

8 Identify On this page and the next, underline the benefits of asexual reproduction and the benefits of sexual reproduction.

Think Outside the Book

9 Compare Both protists and bacteria can reproduce asexually using binary fission. Research to find out how protist fission differs from bacterial fission.

By Sexual Reproduction

Some protists reproduce sexually. In sexual reproduction, two cells, called **gametes**, join together. Each gamete contains a single copy of the genes for the organism. A cell with only one copy of genetic material is described as being *haploid.* A cell with two copies is *diploid.* Each gamete comes from a different parent. When the haploid gametes join, the diploid offspring have a unique combination of genetic material. Genetic diversity increases a species' chance of survival when the environment changes.

In some protists, generations alternate between using sexual or asexual reproduction. The haploid generation adults are called *gametophytes* (guh•MEET•uh•fyts). The diploid generation adults are called *sporophytes* (SPOHR•uh•fyts). Diploid adults undergo meiosis to make haploid spores. **Spores** are reproductive cells that are resistant to stressful environmental conditions. These spores develop into haploid adults. The haploid adults undergo mitosis to form haploid gametes. Two gametes join to form a diploid zygote. The zygote then grows into a diploid adult. This continuing cycle is called *alternation of generations.*

Ulva, or sea lettuce, is an algae that reproduces by alternation of generations.

Visualize It!

10 Draw Use the terms *diploid*, *haploid*, and *adult* to fill in the blanks describing how *Ulva* reproduces with alternating generations of diploid and haploid cells.

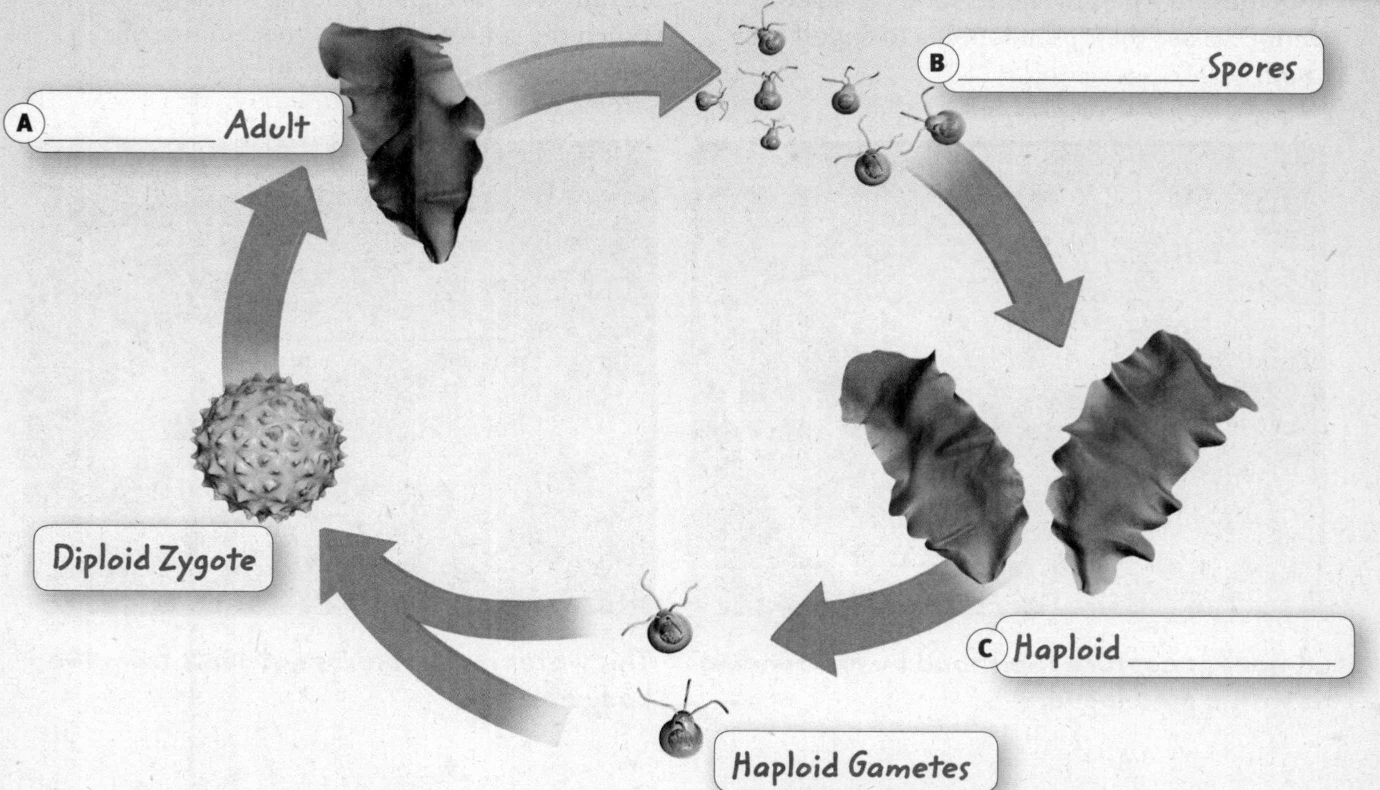

A Diverse Group

What are different kinds of protists?

Because protists are so diverse, grouping them can be difficult. One useful way to group protists is by how they get food. Some capture food, like animals do. Some absorb nutrients, like fungi do. Some make food, like plants do.

Active Reading **11 Identify** On this page and the next, underline how each kind of protist gets its food.

Animal-like Protists

Animal-like protists cannot make their own food. Instead, they get nutrients by ingesting other organisms. Many animal-like protists eat small organisms such as bacteria, yeast, or other protists.

Most animal-like protists can move around their environment. This allows them to search for food in the environment. Sometimes, the same structures that aid movement can also help protists get food. For example, cilia sweep food toward a paramecium's food passageway. Amoebas use their pseudopodia to engulf their food.

Fungus-like Protists

Usually, fungus-like protists cannot move on their own. So capturing live organisms would be hard for these protists. Since they cannot make their own food, how do they get nutrients? Fungus-like protists absorb nutrients from the environment. Many fungus-like protists absorb nutrients from living or dead organisms.

Fungus-like protists produce spores that are used in reproduction. The protists release the spores into the environment, and the spores can survive through periods of harsh conditions. When the spores land on a good source of nutrients, they develop into an adult.

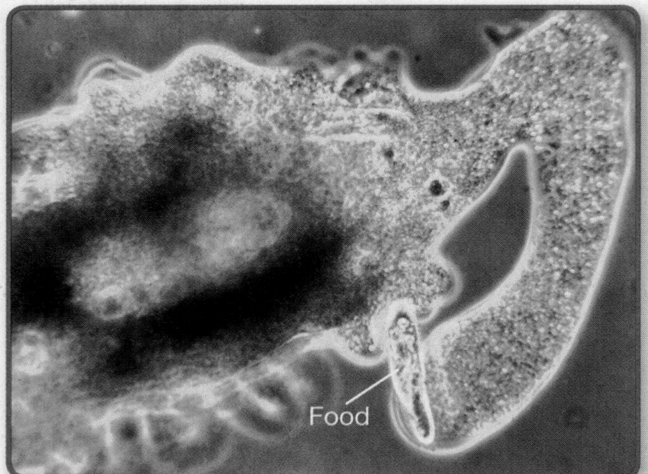

Amoebas capture their food by surrounding it with a pseudopod.

This water mold absorbs nutrients from the body of a fish.

Plant-like Protists

Plant-like protists are producers. This means they use the sun's energy to make food through photosynthesis. Single-celled, free-floating, plant-like protists are a main part of the ocean's phytoplankton. Phytoplankton are tiny, floating organisms that provide food for many larger organisms. They also produce much of the world's oxygen.

Multicellular plant-like protists are called **algae**. All algae have the green pigment chlorophyll in their cells. Many also have other pigments. Algae are grouped by color. The three main groups of algae are brown algae, red algae, and green algae. The pigment color determines what wavelengths of light the algae can absorb.

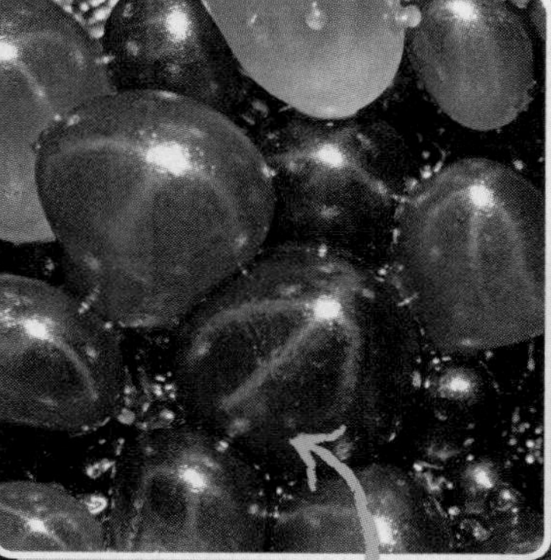

This green algae lives in shallow tide pools.

Some brown algae can grow to be many meters long.

Red algae live in tropical water.

12 Infer Because plant-like protists make their own food from sunlight, in what kind of environment would they not be able to survive? Why?

______

13 Summarize For each kind of protist on the chart below, list three characteristics.

Animal-like Protists	Fungus-like Protists	Plant-like Protists

Lots of Fun(gi)!

What are some characteristics of fungi?

Fungi (FUHN•jy; singular, fungus) are spore-producing organisms that absorb nutrients from the environment. Fungi are so different from other organisms that they are placed in their own kingdom.

Fungi are *consumers*, which means they cannot make their own food. Also, fungi cannot move. This means they cannot catch organisms to ingest as food. Fungi get nutrients by secreting digestive juices onto a food source. Then, they absorb nutrients from the dissolved food. Many fungi are *decomposers*. Decomposers get nutrients from dead matter.

All fungi are made of eukaryotic cells that have nuclei. Fungi are unique because their cell walls contain *chitin*. Chitin is a hard substance that strengthens the cell walls. Some fungi are single-celled. Most are made up of many cells that form chains. These chains are threadlike fungal filaments called **hyphae** (HY•fee; singular, hypha).

We can only see a small part of many fungi. That's because most of the organism is underground or woven into its food source. Most hyphae in a fungus form a twisted mass called a *mycelium* (mie•SEE•lee•uhm). The hidden mycelium makes up the major part of the body of a fungus. Just a small part of a fungus is visible. The visible part of a mushroom includes a stalk, a cap, and gills that release spores.

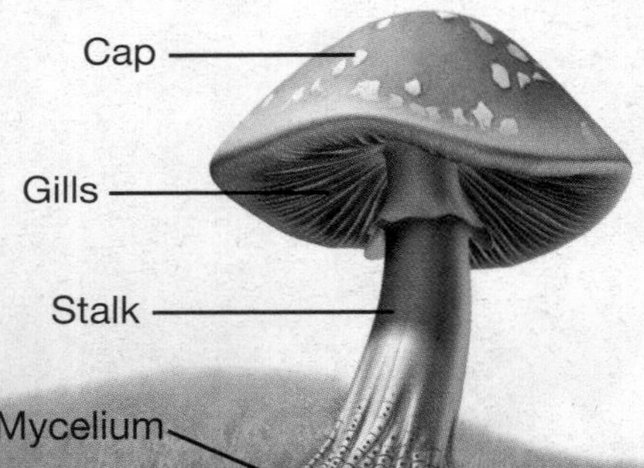

Thread-like strands called hyphae make up the body of this mushroom. Most of the hyphae are underground.

Visualize It!

14 Apply Fungi come in all shapes and sizes. Draw an organism that is a mushroom with all the parts shown in the image at left but that is shaped according to your imagination. Label each part of the mushroom.

How can fungi reproduce?

Fungi reproduce both asexually and sexually. In asexual reproduction, offspring are genetically identical to the parent. In sexual reproduction, offspring are genetically unique.

By Asexual Reproduction

Asexual reproduction in fungi occurs in three ways. In fragmentation, hyphae break apart, and each piece becomes a new fungus. In budding, a small portion of a parent cell pinches off to become a new individual. In asexual reproduction by spores, hyphae produce a long stalk called a *sporangium* (spuh•RAN•jee•uhm). Here, spores develop through mitosis. Spores are light and easily spread by wind. So spores can travel long distances even though fungi cannot move on their own. When conditions are favorable, a spore develops into a new fungus.

By Sexual Reproduction

In most fungi, sexual reproduction occurs when hyphae from two individuals join together. The fused hyphae produce a special reproductive structure, such as a mushroom. Genetic material from both individuals fuse to form diploid cells. Then the cells undergo meiosis to become haploid again. The spores are then released. These spores are much like asexual spores. Both can spread easily through the environment and survive until favorable conditions arise.

Active Reading **15 Identify** Describe the role of spores in both asexual and sexual fungus reproduction.

____

____

This bread mold sporangium will release spores to spread through the environment.

This collared earthstar fungus releases its spores by shooting them into the air.

Inquiry

16 Infer Why is it important for spores to spread easily to other locations?

____

____

What are some kinds of fungi?

Fungi are classified based on their shape and the way they reproduce. Many species of fungi fit into three main groups. These groups are zygote fungi, sac fungi, and club fungi.

17 Identify On this page and the next, underline the characteristics that define each kind of fungus.

Zygote Fungi

Zygote fungi are named for sexual reproductive structures that produce zygotes inside a tough capsule. Most of the fungi in this group live in the soil and are decomposers. Some zygote fungi are used to process foods like soybeans. Other types of zygote fungi are used to fight bacterial infections. However, some zygote fungi can cause problems for people. Have you ever seen moldy bread? A mold is a fast-growing, fuzzy fungus that reproduces asexually. Bread mold and molds that rot fruits and vegetables are examples of this asexual stage of a zygote fungus life cycle. Some molds also have a stage during which they reproduce sexually.

This bread mold is a fuzzy example of a zygote fungus.

Morels are an edible type of sac fungus that grow at the base of trees.

Sac Fungi

Sac fungi are the largest group of fungi. Sac fungi include yeasts, powdery mildews, morels, and bird's-nest fungi. Sac fungi reproduce asexually and sexually. Sexually produced spores develop within a microscopic sac that then opens to release the spores. This structure gives sac fungi their name. Most sac fungi are multicellular. Yeasts are typically single-celled sac fungi that usually reproduce asexually by budding. Budding occurs when a new cell pinches off from an existing cell. Under certain conditions a yeast will reproduce sexually and form spores in sacs. Yeasts are used to make bread and alcohol. Other sac fungi make antibiotics and vitamins.

These mushrooms are club fungi.

Club Fungi

Mushrooms, bracket fungi, puffballs, smuts, and rusts are club fungi. Club fungi are named for the microscopic structures in which the spores develop. Only the spore-producing part of a club fungus is visible. These structures usually grow at the edges of the mycelium. A fungal mycelium can be incredibly large. One of the world's largest living organisms is a honey mushroom in Oregon whose mycelium spans almost 9 km^2.

Club fungi are very important decomposers of wood. Without fungi, the nutrients in wood could not be recycled. Smuts and rusts are plant parasites. They often attack crops such as corn and wheat.

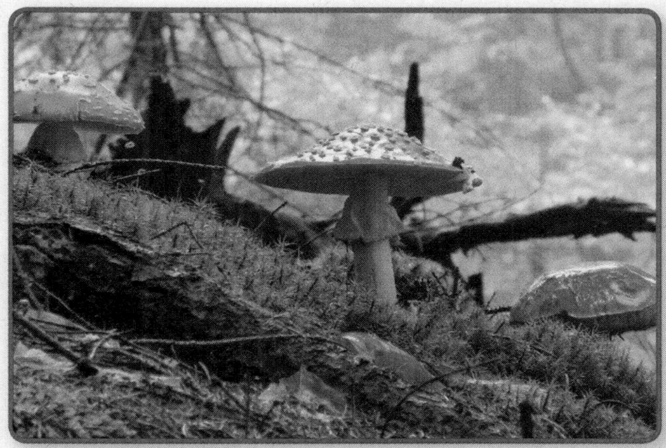
These red ***Amanita*** are highly toxic, yet beautiful, club fungi.

How do fungi form partnerships?

Fungi form two very important partnerships. Some fungi grow on or in the roots of plants. These plants provide nutrients to the fungus. In return, the fungus usually helps the roots absorb minerals. This partnership is called a **mycorrhiza** (my•kuh•RY•zuh).

A **lichen** is a partnership between a fungus and a green alga or cyanobacterium. They are so inseparable that scientists give lichens their own scientific names. The alga or cyanobacterium uses photosynthesis to make food. The fungus gives protection, water, and minerals. Lichens provide food for animals in polar climates. Also, because lichens are very sensitive to pollution, the presence of lichens indicates that an environment has clean air.

18 Infer Suppose that the number of kinds of lichens at a city park is decreasing each year. What might explain this disappearance?

___

___

___

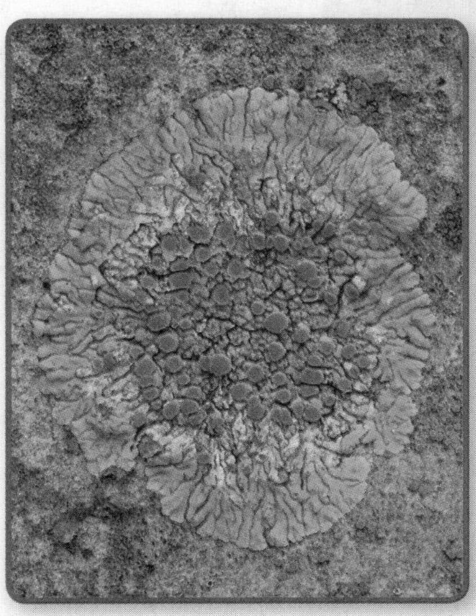
Lichens can grow on rocks. They release acids that break down rock over time to make soil.

Visual Summary

To complete this summary, fill in the blank with the correct word or phrase. Then use the key below to check your answers. You can use this page to review the main concepts of the lesson.

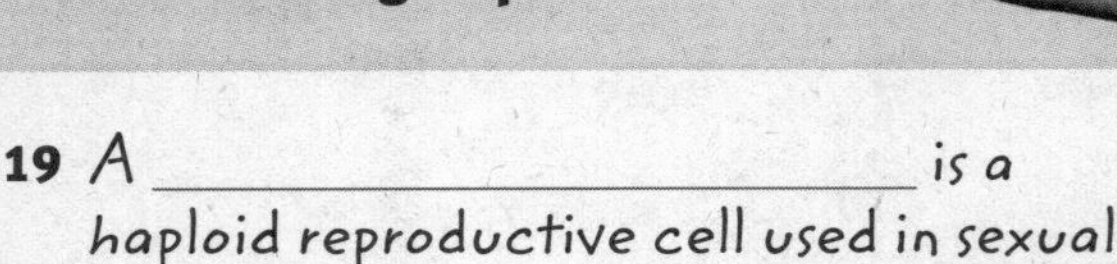

Protists are eukaryotes that don't fit in other classification groups.

19 A _______________ is a haploid reproductive cell used in sexual reproduction.

Protists can be grouped as fungus-like, plant-like, and animal-like protists.

20 _______________-like protists can produce their own food from the sun's energy.

Protists and Fungi

Fungi absorb nutrients and have chitinous cell walls.

21 Fungi are _______________ because they have a nucleus and other membrane-bound organelles.

Fungi can partner with other organisms.

22 _______________ can indicate levels of air pollution.

Answers: 19 gamete; 20 plant; 21 eukaryotes; 22 lichens

23 Describe This lesson groups protists informally by the way they get food. Think of another way to categorize the different kinds of protists and describe your system below.

Lesson Review

Vocabulary

Draw a line to connect the following terms to their definitions.

1	fungi	**A**	reproductive cell that resists harsh environmental conditions
2	protists	**B**	extremely diverse group of eukaryotic organisms; some have cilia
3	spore	**C**	reproductive cell that unites with another reproductive cell
4	gamete	**D**	spore-producing organisms that absorb nutrients

Key Concepts

5 Compare Why are protists discussed in groups such as animal-like, plant-like, and fungus-like protists?

____

____

____

____

____

6 List Write the three major types of fungi and an example of each.

____

____

____

____

7 Identify What are two ways that protists can reproduce asexually?

____

____

8 Describe What are two ways in which fungi reproduce?

____

____

____

____

Critical Thinking

Use this image to answer the following question.

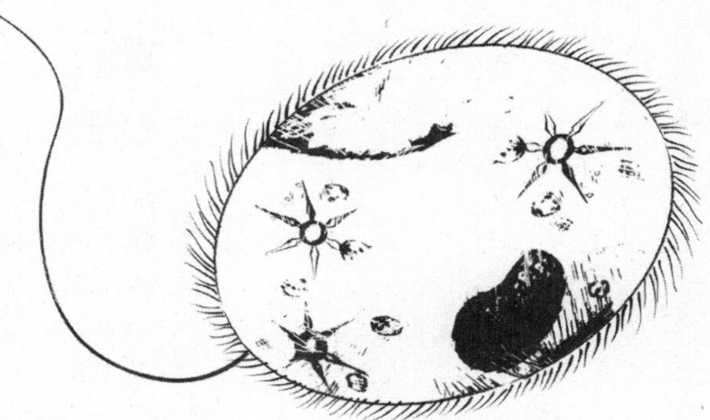

9 Hypothesize Do you think this protist can make its own food? Explain.

____

____

____

____

____

10 Synthesize In humans, infections by fungi and protists are usually more difficult to treat than bacterial infections. Suggest an explanation that is based on cell structure.

____

____

____

____

____

11 Apply Suppose that when crops developed a fungal infection, a farmer decided to spray the soil with a fungicide. Just after spraying, the plants looked healthier, but soon they showed signs of mineral deficiency. What might explain this response?

____

____

____

____

____

My Notes

Lesson 4

Introduction to Plants

ESSENTIAL QUESTION

What are plants?

By the end of this lesson, you should be able to list the characteristics that all plants share, and explain how plants are classified into major plant divisions.

OHIO 6.LS.1 Cells are the fundamental unit of life.

OHIO 6.LS.4 Living systems at all levels of organization demonstrate the complementary nature of structure and function.

Is this an alien spacecraft? No, it's a passion flower plant! Plants come in many different shapes and sizes.

Lesson Labs

Quick Labs
- Investigating Flower Parts
- Observing Transport

Engage Your Brain

1 Predict Check T or F to show whether you think each statement is true or false.

T	F	
☐	☐	All plants have a special transport system that delivers water and nutrients.
☐	☐	The majority of plants have roots, stems, and leaves.
☐	☐	Conifer trees, such as pine trees, produce flowers.
☐	☐	Plants are multicellular eukaryotes.

2 Categorize Write a caption for this magnified cross section of a buttercup plant stem.

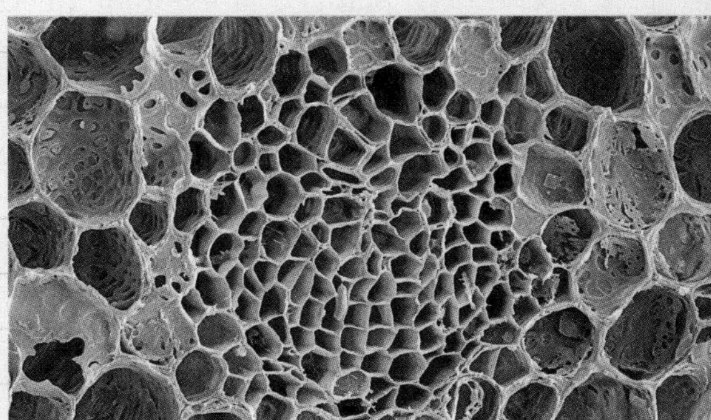

___

___

___

___

Active Reading

3 Synthesize You can often define an unknown word if you know the meaning of its word parts. Use the word parts and sentences below to make an educated guess about the meaning of the words *gymnosperm* and *angiosperm*.

Word part	Meaning
gymno-	naked, bare
angio-	vessel, container
sperm	seed

Example sentence
Gymnosperms are seed plants that do not produce fruit.

gymnosperm:

___

Example sentence
Angiosperms are seed plants that do produce fruit.

angiosperm:

___

Vocabulary Terms

- producers
- photosynthesis
- chlorophyll
- vascular system
- seed
- pollen
- gymnosperm
- angiosperm

4 Identify As you learn the definition of each vocabulary term in this lesson, create your own definition or sketch to help you remember the meaning of the term.

Plants Alive

What are the characteristics of plants?

The kingdom Plantae includes a wide variety of organisms known as plants. Plants range in size from the tallest giant sequoia trees, reaching more than 80 meters (270 ft) to the smallest flowering plant, which can fit on the tip of your finger. So what do these plants have in common with one another?

They Are Multicellular Eukaryotes

All plants are multicellular. Their bodies are made up of more than one cell. They are also eukaryotes. This means that their cells contain membrane-bound organelles, including a nucleus which contains the cell's DNA.

They Have a Two-Stage Life Cycle

All plants have a life cycle that is made up of two stages: a *sporophyte* stage and a *gametophyte* stage. These are the two stages in which plants reproduce and disperse to new areas. In the sporophyte stage, plants make spores that are genetically identical to the parent plant. In a suitable environment, such as in damp soil, spores can grow into new plants that are the gametophytes.

In the gametophyte stage, plants produces gametes. Female gametophytes produce eggs. Male gametophytes produce sperm. Eggs and sperm are sex cells. By themselves, the sex cells cannot grow directly into new plants. For a new plant to be produced, a sperm cell must fuse with, or *fertilize,* an egg. This type of reproduction is called sexual reproduction. The fertilized egg can grow into a sporophyte, and the cycle can begin again.

Think Outside the Book

5 Apply Imagine a plant is running for president of the garden club. Write a campaign speech stating its unique characteristics.

Chlorophyll gives plants their green color.

They Have Walls and Vacuoles

Plant cells are surrounded by a rigid cell wall that lies outside the cell membrane. The cell wall supports and protects the plant cell. The cell wall also determines the size and shape of a plant cell. A chemical called *cellulose* is the main component of plant cell walls. The strength of the cell wall helps plants stand upright. Some plant cells also have a *secondary cell wall.* This wall forms after the cell is mature, and gives woody plants their strength. Once the secondary cell wall forms, the plant cell cannot grow larger.

Inside a plant cell is a large central vacuole. The vacuole is a membrane-bound organelle that stores water and also helps to keep the plant upright. When the vacuole is full, water presses on the inside of the cell wall. This keeps the cell firm, like an inflated balloon. If the vacuole loses water, the pressure inside the cell decreases, and the plant begins to wilt.

They Make Their Own Food

Almost all plants are producers. **Producers** make their own food by using energy from their surroundings. The process by which plants and other organisms convert solar energy to chemical energy is called **photosynthesis** (foh•toh•SIN•thih•sis).

In plants, photosynthesis occurs in an organelle called a chloroplast. Chloroplasts contain special pigments called chlorophyll. **Chlorophyll** (KLOHR•uh•fil) is a green pigment that captures energy from sunlight. Chloroplasts use this energy, along with carbon dioxide and water, to make food in the form of a sugar called *glucose.* It is chlorophyll that gives plants their green color.

Active Reading **6 Identify** Name the function of chlorophyll in plants.

____

Visualize It!

7 Identify In which part of the cell is chlorophyll found?

____

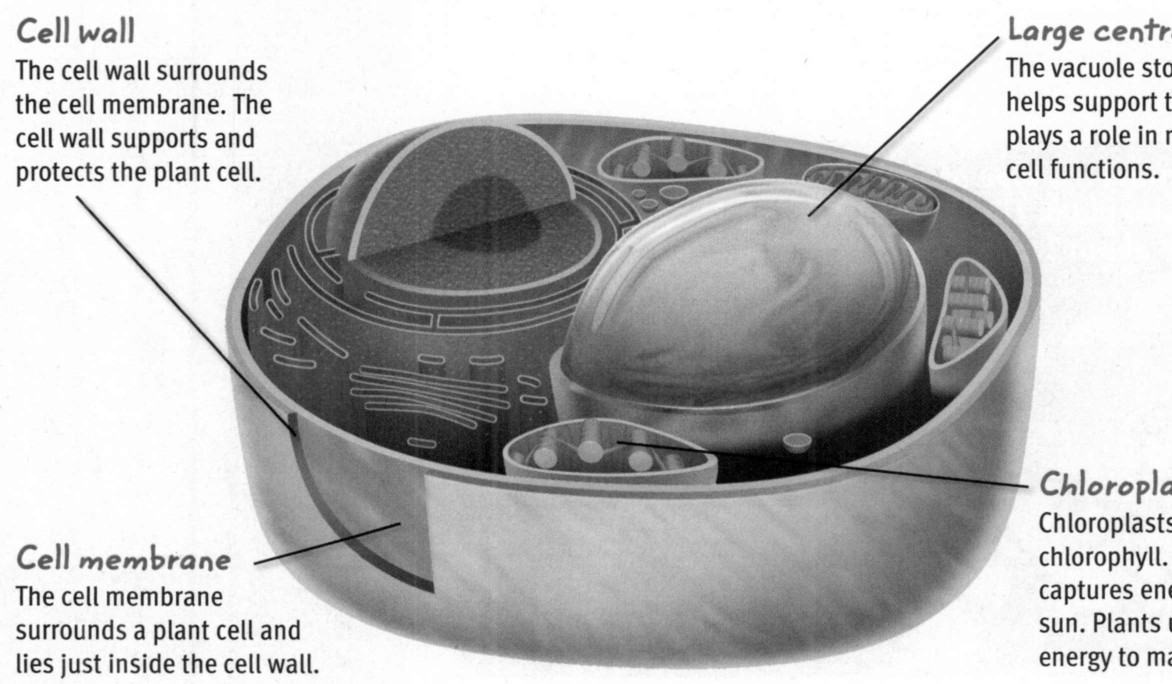

Cell wall
The cell wall surrounds the cell membrane. The cell wall supports and protects the plant cell.

Large central vacuole
The vacuole stores water, helps support the cell, and plays a role in many other cell functions.

Cell membrane
The cell membrane surrounds a plant cell and lies just inside the cell wall.

Chloroplast
Chloroplasts contain chlorophyll. Chlorophyll captures energy from the sun. Plants use this energy to make food.

A Wide World of Plants

What are the two main groups of plants?

Plants can be grouped into two broad categories: nonvascular plants and vascular plants. A plant that has a vascular system is called a vascular plant. A **vascular system** is a system of tube-like tissues that transports water, nutrients, and other materials from one part of an organism to another part. Nonvascular plants do not have a vascular system.

Nonvascular Plants

Have you ever walked through a cool forest with a moist green carpet on the ground? Chances are, the green "carpet" was made up of tiny plants called moss. Mosses, and their relatives such as liverworts and hornworts, are nonvascular plants. Nonvascular plants do not have vascular systems to transport water and nutrients throughout their bodies. Instead, water must move from the environment and throughout the plant by a process called *diffusion*. If nonvascular plants were large, the cells of the plants that are far from the ground would not get enough water. Likewise, cells that are far from the leaves would not get enough nutrients. For this reason, nonvascular plants are all fairly small.

Active Reading **8 Explain** Why are nonvascular plants so small?

____

____

This liverwort is a type of nonvascular plant. The liverwort stalks are about 1 cm tall.

This giant sequoia transports water and nutrients through a vascular system. The materials move between the roots and the leaves, nearly 72 m (200 ft) above ground.

Vascular Plants

Active Reading

9 List As you read, underline the importance of a plant's vascular system.

Vascular plants have a vascular system that transports water and nutrients throughout the plant's body. The vascular system allows these plants to grow large and still move water and materials effectively. As a result, many vascular plants are very tall. Some, such as the giant redwoods of California, reach heights of over 91 meters (300 ft)!

The body of a vascular plant is divided into two systems: the root system and the shoot system. The root system is made up of roots and other underground structures. The above ground structures, such as stems, leaves and flowers, make up the shoot system. Roots, stems, and leaves are the three major kinds of organs in vascular plants. Water and materials are transported between the roots and the shoots through vascular tissue.

Leaves
Most leaves grow above ground. They make food for the plant by photosynthesis. The outer surfaces of a leaf are covered by a waxy cuticle that prevents water loss. Tiny openings in leaves, called *stomata,* allow for gas exchange.

Stem
Stems are usually above ground. They provide support, and they transport water and minerals from the roots up to the leaves. Stems also transport the glucose that is made in the leaves to other parts of the plant. Some stems store materials, such as water.

Roots
Most roots are underground. They supply plants with water and minerals from the soil. Roots also anchor plants in the soil and can store extra food made through photosynthesis.

10 Compare In the table below, compare the functions of the three parts of the plant.

Roots	Stems	Leaves

Spore Power to Ya!

How are seedless nonvascular plants classified?

When you think of growing a plant, you probably imagine planting a seed. But not all plants make seeds. In fact, all nonvascular plants and some vascular plants are seedless. These plants, like all plants, spread by producing spores.

Mosses

Mosses grow on moist soil or on rocks, forming a fuzzy mat of tiny green plants. Mosses have leafy stalks and rhizoids (RY•zoydz). A *rhizoid* is a nonvascular rootlike structure that helps mosses attach to surfaces such as rocks and trees. Rhizoids help the plants get water and nutrients. Mosses can grow even in harsh environments. They have been found above the tree line on mountains and can survive even the freezing temperatures of Antarctica!

Active Reading

11 Identify As you read, underline the structure in nonvascular plants that is like a root.

Liverworts and Hornworts

Like mosses, liverworts and hornworts are small nonvascular plants that usually live in damp environments. Liverworts can be leafy and mosslike or broad and flattened. Hornworts also have broad, flattened leaflike structures. Both liverworts and hornworts have rhizoids to hold them in place.

Mosses and other nonvascular seedless plants dominated the land for many millions of years.

Visualize It!

12 Inquiry Study the photo of the moss. What evidence suggests that mosses produce their own food?

How are seedless vascular plants classified?

Seedless vascular plants include ferns, horsetails, and club mosses. These plants all have vascular tissue, and generally have roots, stems, and leaves. Like seedless nonvascular plants, seedless vascular plants reproduce using spores.

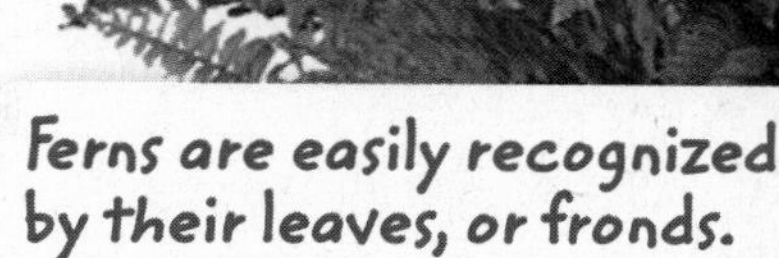

Ferns are easily recognized by their leaves, or fronds.

Ferns and Whisk Ferns

Ferns are seedless vascular plants often grown as house plants. Ferns have roots, and most ferns also have rhizomes that help them spread. A *rhizome* (RY•zohm) is an underground stem from which new leaves and roots grow. Ferns have leaves, called *fronds,* that uncurl as they grow. Whisk ferns are related to ferns, but look very different. They have rhizoids instead of roots, and small growths that look like buttons instead of leaves.

Horsetails

Horsetails have cane-like stems with leaves that grow in a unique whorl pattern around the stems. Horsetails can be up to eight meters tall, but many are smaller. They usually grow in wet, marshy places. Their stems are hollow and contain silica. The silica gives horsetails a gritty, rough texture. In fact, early American pioneers used horsetails to scrub pots and pans.

Club Mosses

Club mosses look similar to true mosses. But unlike true mosses, club mosses have vascular tissue, roots, stems, and tiny leaves. Prehistoric club mosses were tall trees. Some even grew up to 40 m tall! Today's club mosses are small. An example of a modern club moss is the ground pine. Like the name suggests, the ground pine looks like a miniature pine tree. Club mosses grow in woodlands and near streams and marshes.

On the underside of a fern frond are clusters of spore-producing containers called sori.

13 Compare In the graphic organizer below, compare seedless nonvascular plants to seedless vascular plants. How are they similar and different?

Seedless nonvascular plants

Both

Seedless vascular plants

Seeds of Success

How are seed plants classified?

Seed plants are vascular plants that reproduce by making seeds. A **seed** is a plant embryo enclosed in a protective coating. Seed plants also produce **pollen**, a tiny structure in which sperm forms. A sperm cell from pollen fertilizes an egg cell, which develops into an embryo inside a seed. Seed plants are classified based on whether or not their seeds are enclosed in a fruit.

Gymnosperms

Active Reading

14 Identify As you read, underline the characteristics of gymnosperms.

Gymnosperms (JIM•nuh•spermz) are plants that produce seeds that are not enclosed in a fruit. This group includes cycads (SY•kadz), ginkgoes (GING•kohz), and conifers. Cycads produce seeds in large, woody structures called *cones* that grow at the center of a thick trunk. Ginkgoes produce round, grape-like seeds that are not covered by a cone. Ginkgo seeds smell like rotting butter. The word *conifer* comes from two words that mean "cone-bearing." Conifers, such as pine trees, also produce cones. The wood of conifer trees is used for building and for paper products. Pine trees also produce a sticky fluid called resin used to make soap, paint, and ink.

Cycads are gymnosperms found in the tropics that have short stems and palm-like leaves. Cycads produce seeds on large, protective cones. Only about 140 species of cycads still exist.

Ginkgoes are gymnosperms that are pollution tolerant and are used in traditional medicine. Only the *Ginkgo biloba* is still alive today. Its leaves are fan-shaped, and its seeds are round and not covered by a cone.

Conifers are the most common type of gymnosperm. This group includes pine trees, cedars, redwoods, and junipers. They produce seeds in cones and have needle-like leaves. Many are green all year.

15 Identify Which type of gymnosperm does not reproduce with cones?

____

Angiosperms

Angiosperms (AN•jee•uh•spermz) are vascular plants that produce flowers, and fruits which surround and protect seeds. Angiosperms are the most abundant type of plant alive today. At least 260,000 living species of angiosperms are known, and new species are still being discovered. They can be found in almost every ecosystem.

Flowers are the reproductive structures of angiosperms. Flowers are typically made up of sepals, petals, stamens, and a pistil. Sepals are modified leaves that cover and protect the flower while it is budding. Flower petals are often colorful and fragrant. A stamen is the male reproductive structure in a flower. It is made up of an anther, which is attached to a filament. Pollen is made in the anther. A pistil is the female reproductive structure in a flower. The seed develops within the ovary at the base of the pistil. As the seed develops, the ovary matures into a fruit which covers the seed.

16 Label Fill in the structure of each of the flower parts described below.

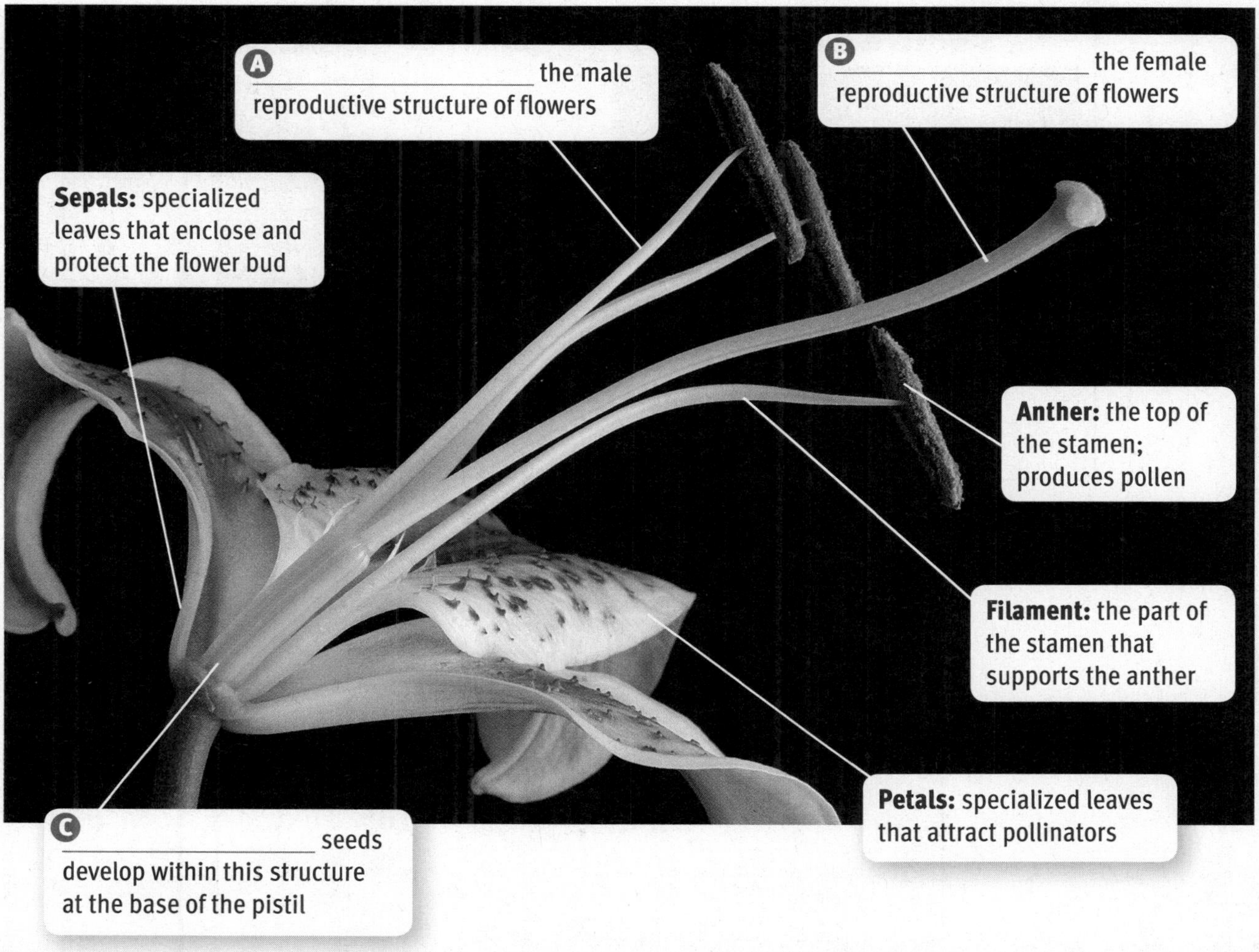

A ____________________ the male reproductive structure of flowers

B ____________________ the female reproductive structure of flowers

Sepals: specialized leaves that enclose and protect the flower bud

Anther: the top of the stamen; produces pollen

Filament: the part of the stamen that supports the anther

Petals: specialized leaves that attract pollinators

C ____________________ seeds develop within this structure at the base of the pistil

Visualize It!

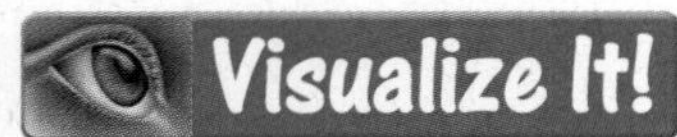

17 Compare Compare vascular and nonvascular plants, seedless and seed vascular plants, and nonflowering and flowering plants.

Nonvascular plants

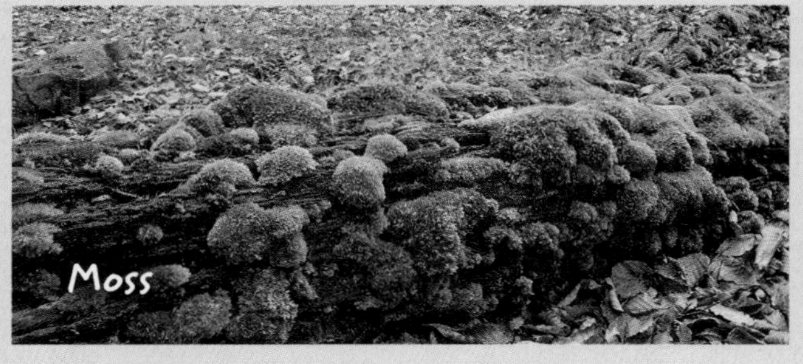

Moss

Vascular plants

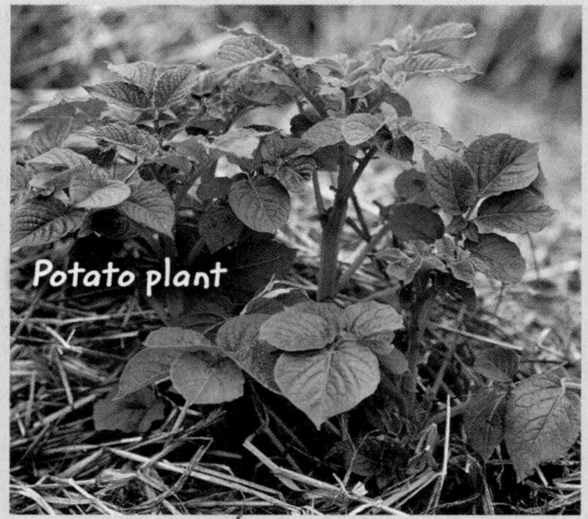

Potato plant

A Summarize the similarities and differences.

Seedless vascular plants

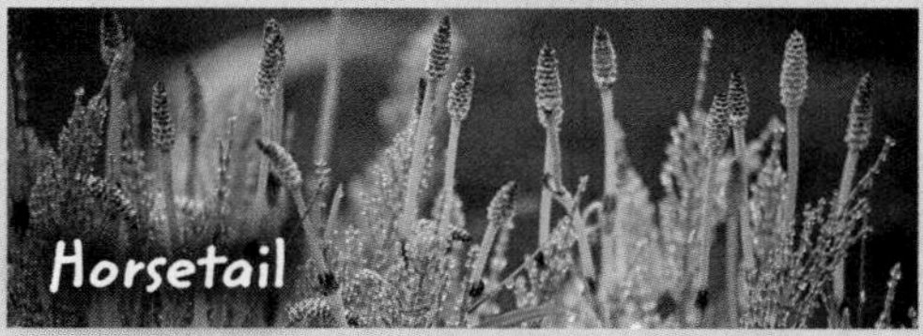

Horsetail

Seed vascular plants

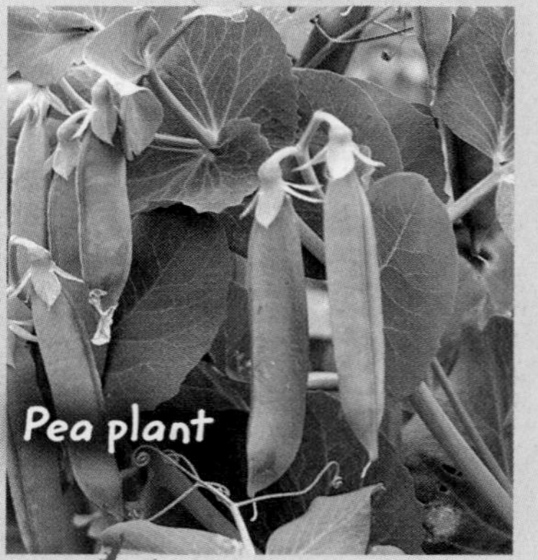

Pea plant

B Summarize the similarities and differences.

Gymnosperms (nonflowering plants)

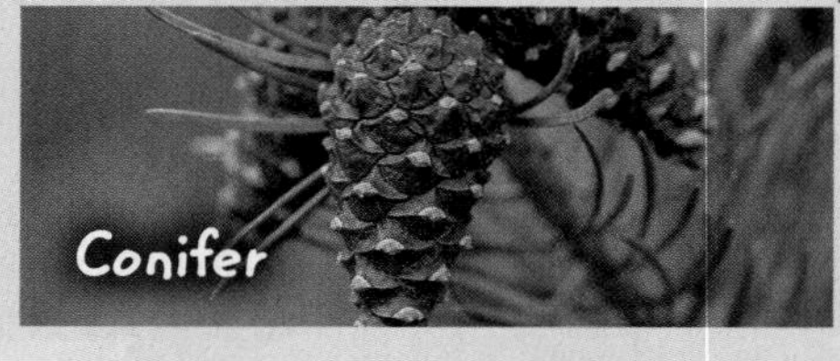

Conifer

Angiosperms (flowering plants)

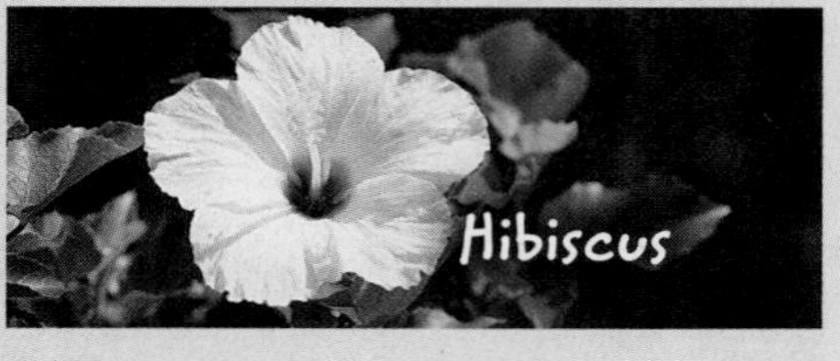

Hibiscus

C Summarize the similarities and differences.

Why It Matters

EYE ON THE ENVIRONMENT

Pharmaceuticals and Plants

Throughout history, plants have played an important role in medicine. Many modern medicines are derived from chemicals found in plants. Tropical rain forests are a source of many potential medicinal plants. For example, the cat's claw shown here is a woody vine found in the Amazon rain forest. It is used by local tribes to treat arthritis and some viral infections. Research is under way to find out if cat's claw might be useful for treating a variety of diseases. Scientists have discovered many useful compounds in rain-forest plants, and are likely to discover many more.

Cat's claw

White Willow Tree

The white willow tree is native to Europe and Asia. The medicinal value of white willow bark goes back to ancient Egyptians, who used white willow to treat inflammation. A compound in white willow, salicin, led to the development of aspirin.

Foxglove

Foxglove is a flowering plant commonly grown in gardens. This plant produces uncommon compounds that are used to make medicine for the heart.

Extend

Inquiry

18 Summarize How are the compounds derived from the foxglove plant and the white willow tree used in medicine?

19 Research Find out how another plant is used in modern medicine.

20 Propose How can we protect medicinal plants in rain forests?

Visual Summary

To complete this summary, write at least two facts on each card about the groups of plants. Then, use the key below to check your answers. You can use this page to review the main concepts of the lesson.

Introduction to Plants

Nonvascular plants do not have vessels to transport nutrients and water.

21 Summary points:

____

____

Seedless vascular plants have a vascular system, roots, and shoots, and reproduce using spores.

22 Summary points:

____

____

A gymnosperm is a vascular seed plant whose seeds are not enclosed by fruit.

23 Summary points:

____

____

An angiosperm is a flowering, vascular seed plant whose seeds are enclosed within a fruit.

24 Summary points:

____

____

Sample answers: 21 can grow in harsh environments, spores, rhizoids; 22 have vascular tissue, roots, rhizomes, and spores; 23 vascular plants, produce seeds without fruit, produce pollen, some produce cones; 24 produce seeds in fruit, produce flowers and pollen

25 Infer What characteristics of flowering plants have helped them to be successful?

Lesson Review

Vocabulary

Fill in the blank with the term that best completes the following sentence.

1 A(n) ______________________________ is a plant organ that consists of an embryo, tissues, and a protective coating.

2 Most plants are called ____________________ because they can make their own food using photosynthesis.

3 Vascular plants that have seeds surrounded by fruit are called __________________________

Key Concepts

4 Identify What characteristics do all plants share?

____

____

____

____

____

5 Summarize What is the importance of having a vascular system?

____

____

____

____

____

6 Identify List the function of each of the following parts of a flower: stamen, pistil, ovary, and sepal.

Critical Thinking

Use the image to answer the following questions.

7 Identify Which letter corresponds to the structure that absorbs water and minerals?

____

8 Label Which letter corresponds to the part of the plant that is primarily used for photosynthesis?

____

9 Infer Is this an example of a vascular plant? How do you know?

____

____

____

10 Conclude A scientist discovers a new plant that has vascular tissue and produces seeds. It has brightly colored, scented flowers. What type of plant did the scientist discover? How might this plant be pollinated, and what would lead you to draw that conclusion?

____

____

____

____

____

____

____

My Notes

S.T.E.M. Engineering & Technology

OHIO 6.LS.3, 6.SIA.4, 6.SIA.5, 6.SIA.8

Evaluating Technological Systems

Skills
✓ Identify inputs
✓ Identify outputs
✓ Identify system processes
✓ Identify system feedback
Examine system interactions
Apply system controls
✓ Communicate results

Objectives
• Identify inputs and outputs of a physical system.
• Differentiate between convective and radiative heat transfer.
• Graph temperature data versus time.
• Analyze and communicate results of an experiment.

Analyzing a Greenhouse

A greenhouse is an enclosed space that maintains a consistent environment and temperature to let people grow plants where the natural climate is not ideal. A greenhouse system needs to heat up and cool off in order to effectively grow plants. How the sun warms a greenhouse involves both radiation and convection. Objects on the ground absorb sunlight and become warm. At the same time, objects cool off primarily in two ways: (1) they get rid of heat by transferring energy as visible light or infrared (in•fruh•RED) light (radiation), or (2) they transfer energy in the form of heat to the air, which then carries it away (convection). A greenhouse retains energy in the form of heat primarily because its roof and walls prevent its warmed air from moving out into the atmosphere.

1 Infer Identify the processes shown at labels A and B as either convection or radiation.

A ______________________

B ______________________

Infer Why is convection the main process regulating the temperature in a greenhouse?

____

____

____

____

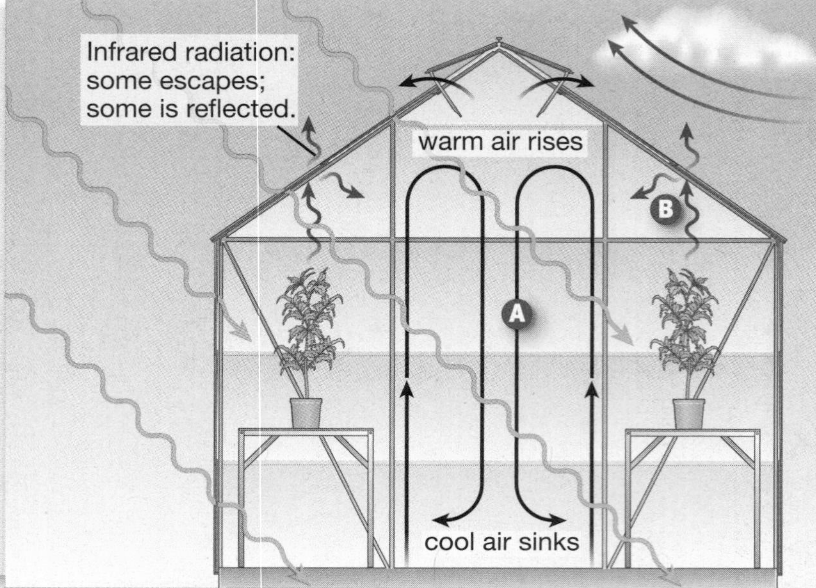

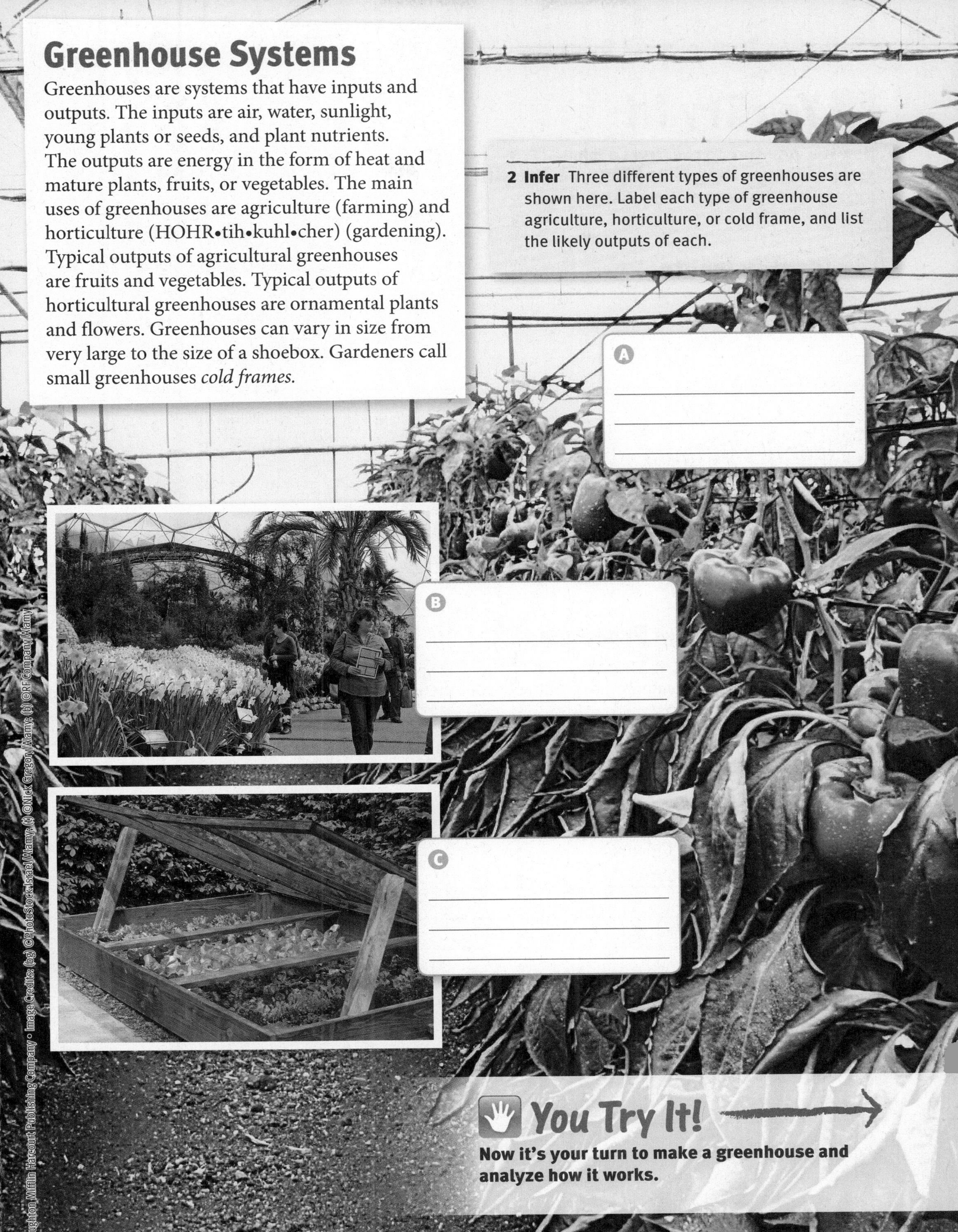

Greenhouse Systems

Greenhouses are systems that have inputs and outputs. The inputs are air, water, sunlight, young plants or seeds, and plant nutrients. The outputs are energy in the form of heat and mature plants, fruits, or vegetables. The main uses of greenhouses are agriculture (farming) and horticulture (HOHR•tih•kuhl•cher) (gardening). Typical outputs of agricultural greenhouses are fruits and vegetables. Typical outputs of horticultural greenhouses are ornamental plants and flowers. Greenhouses can vary in size from very large to the size of a shoebox. Gardeners call small greenhouses *cold frames*.

2 Infer Three different types of greenhouses are shown here. Label each type of greenhouse agriculture, horticulture, or cold frame, and list the likely outputs of each.

A ______________________

B ______________________

C ______________________

You Try It!

Now it's your turn to make a greenhouse and analyze how it works.

You Try It!

Now it's your turn to construct a mini-greenhouse and analyze its inputs, how it heats up, and how its temperature is regulated.

You Will Need

- ✔ small box, 8 in. (length) x 5 in. (width) x 3 in. (height)
- ✔ thermometer, digital if possible (1)
- ✔ marking pens, brown or black
- ✔ clear plastic wrap
- ✔ tape or rubber bands
- ✔ aluminum foil
- ✔ lamp

1 Identify Inputs

What are the inputs of your greenhouse?

____

____

2 Identify Outputs

What are the outputs of your greenhouse?

____

____

3 Identify System Processes

A First, record the room-temperature reading of your thermometer. ______________

B Then, begin to construct your greenhouse using the materials listed. With a marking pen, color the inside of your box to simulate the color of dirt.

C Place your thermometer in the box so that it does not touch any part of the box but so that you can still read it. Why should the thermometer not touch the box?

____

____

____

D Using the foil, make a tent-style barrier in the box to shade the thermometer so the lamp does not directly shine on it. Why is it important to shade the thermometer?

____

____

____

E Cover the box with clear plastic wrap, and seal it as best you can with tape or a rubber band to minimize air leaks. Place the lamp above the box to act as the sun.

F What physical processes are involved in your greenhouse system as it accumulates heat energy?

4 Identify System Feedbacks

Record the temperature of the air in the greenhouse every 5 minutes for at least 30 minutes. Add scale values on tick marks to both axes. Then, graph the temperature versus time in the space provided.

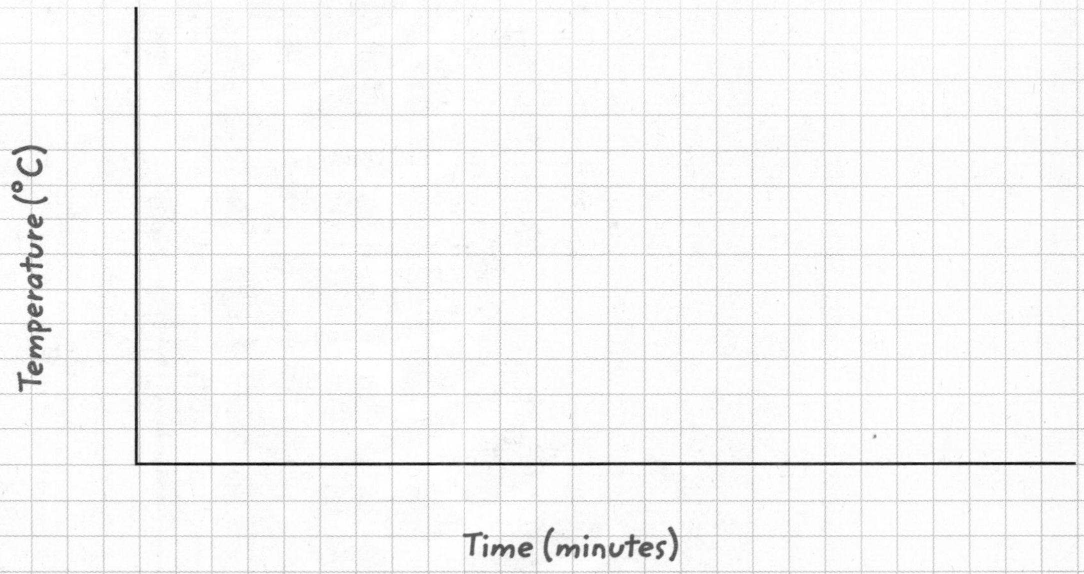

Temperature (°C)

Time (minutes)

5 Communicate Results

Describe what you learned from your greenhouse experiment.

Introduction to Animals

ESSENTIAL QUESTION

What are animals?

By the end of this lesson, you should be able to explain what characteristics define animals, and describe some different kinds of animals.

Animals come in many different sizes and shapes. Scientists have identified more than 1 million living species of animals.

OHIO 6.LS.1 Cells are the fundamental unit of life.

OHIO 6.LS.4 Living systems at all levels of organization demonstrate the complementary nature of structure and function.

Lesson Labs

Quick Labs
- Form and Motion
- Characteristics of Animals

Engage Your Brain

1 Predict Check T or F to show whether you think each statement is true or false.

T	F	
☐	☐	Animals are producers because they can make their own food.
☐	☐	An invertebrate is an animal that does not have a backbone.
☐	☐	Sponges are classified as animals.
☐	☐	Birds are more closely related to mammals than to reptiles.

2 Compare What do the two kinds of animals shown here have in common?

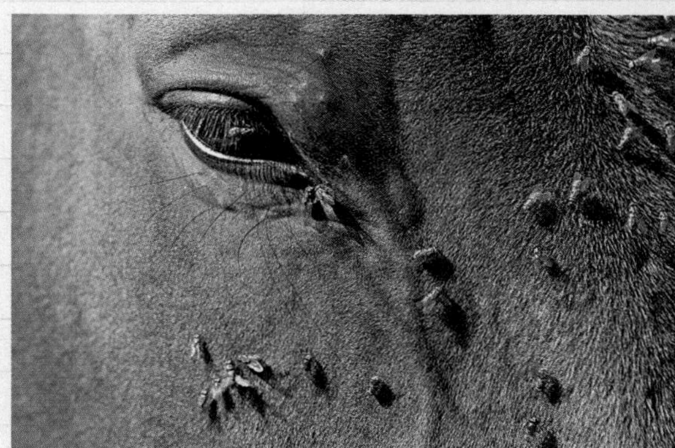

Active Reading

3 Synthesize You can often define an unknown word if you know the meaning of its word parts. Use the word parts and sentences below to make an educated guess about the meaning of the words *exoskeleton* and *endoskeleton*.

Word part	Meaning
exo-	outer, external
endo-	inner, internal
skeleton	framework

Example sentence:
An insect is covered by a hard exoskeleton.

exoskeleton

Example sentence:
The endoskeleton of a bird is made of bone.

endoskeleton

Vocabulary Terms

- **consumer**
- **invertebrate**
- **exoskeleton**
- **vertebrate**
- **endoskeleton**

4 Apply As you learn the definition of each vocabulary term in this lesson, create your own definition or sketch to help you remember the meaning of the term.

You Are an Animal!

What characteristics do animals share?

Animals come in many shapes and sizes. Pets, such as dogs and cats, are animals. Some sponges used in the shower are the remains of an animal. Some animals are too small to be seen without a microscope. Yet all animals share six characteristics.

Many Cells

Like other organisms, animals are made up of cells. All animals are *multicellular* organisms, which means that they are made up of many cells. Similar cells work together to perform the animal's life functions. Animal cells are eukaryotic, so they have a nucleus. In animals, all of the cells work together to perform the life functions of the animal.

Specialized Parts

The cells in a multicellular organism develop into different kinds of cells. This process is called differentiation. Some cells may become skin cells, and others may become gut cells. Each type of cell has a special function to play in an organism. For example, retinal cells of the eye function in vision.

Visualize It!

5 Infer These photos show different kinds of animal cells. Write down three other specialized cells that you think would be found in animal bodies.

____

____

____

Cell differentiation leads to different kinds of cells. Each type of cell performs a specific function in the animal.

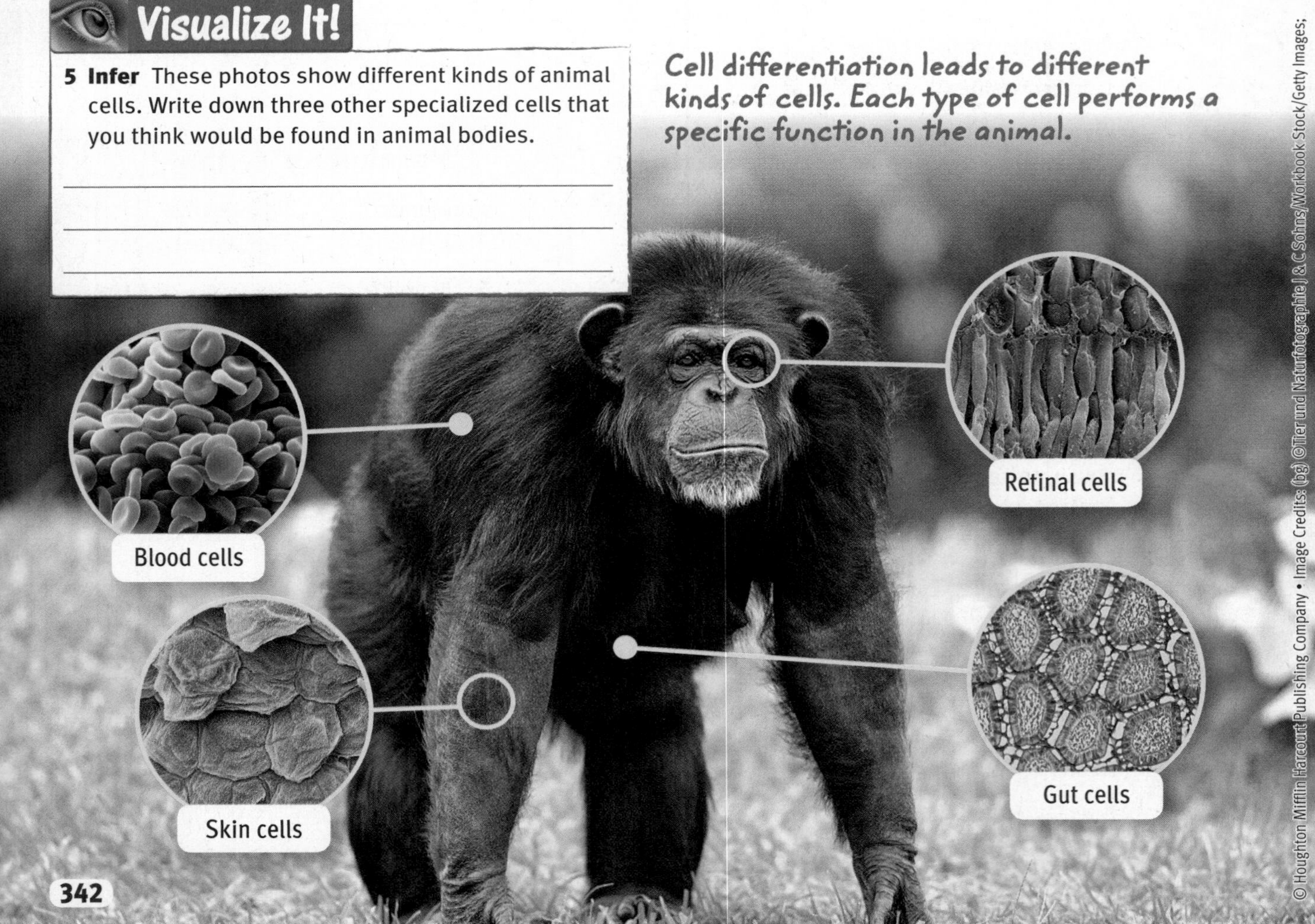

Movement

Animals move in various ways such as running, flying, and swimming. Some animals move to find food, shelter, and mates. Some animals move during only part of their life cycle. For example, the immature stage of a barnacle, the larva, swims around to find food. But adult barnacles are permanently attached to a hard surface, such as a rock, and catch food that passes by.

Some animals, like barnacles, can move from place to place only during the early larval stage of their life cycle.

Adult barnacles

Barnacle larva

Reproduction

Most animals use sexual reproduction. In sexual reproduction, a male sex cell, the sperm, fertilizes a female sex cell, the egg. Then the fertilized egg, or zygote, divides many times to form an embryo. Sexual reproduction leads to genetically diverse offspring. Some animals, such as hydras and sponges, can also reproduce asexually. Offspring of asexual reproduction are genetically identical to their parent.

Consume Food

Active Reading **6 Identify** As you read, underline the different kinds of food animals eat.

All organisms need energy to survive. Animals cannot produce their own food, so they are consumers. A **consumer** is an animal that eats other organisms, or parts of organisms, to get the energy it needs for life processes. Animals eat many kinds of food. Some animals eat plants, some eat animals or animal products, and some eat both plants and animals.

Some animals have specialized diets. South American vampire bats feed only on blood.

Maintain Body Temperature

To function well, all animals need to maintain their bodies within a specific range of temperatures. Birds and mammals maintain their own body temperatures by using some of the energy released by chemical reactions. Other animals rely on their environment to maintain their body temperature.

7 Infer How might an organism that relies on the environment to maintain body temperature do so?

Such Diversity!

What groups make up the diversity of animals?

Animals live in nearly every ecosystem on Earth. They are the most physically diverse kingdom of organisms. Some animals have four legs and some have none. Others, like rotifers, are smaller than the period ending this sentence. Blue whales are as big as two school buses! Besides shape and size, animals have body coverings that vary from feathers to hard shells to soft tissues.

One way to categorize animals is by symmetry or body plan. Some animals, such as sponges, are asymmetrical. You cannot draw a straight line to divide its body into equal parts. Animals like the sea anemone have a radial body plan, organized like the spokes of a wheel. Animals such as tortoises have bilateral symmetry with two mirror-image sides. Animals can also be categorized by internal traits, such as whether or not they have a backbone.

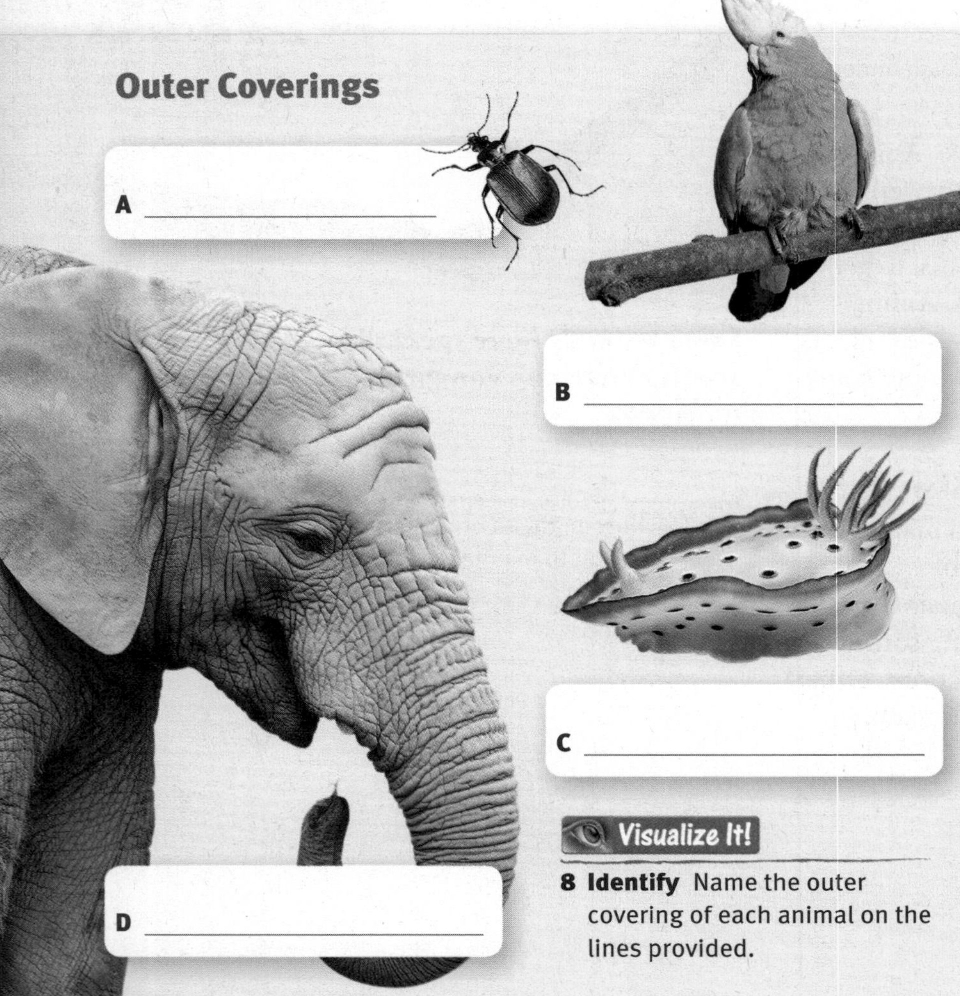

Visualize It!

8 Identify Name the outer covering of each animal on the lines provided.

Body Plans

Asymmetry In asymmetry, the animal is irregular in shape and, therefore, lacks symmetry.

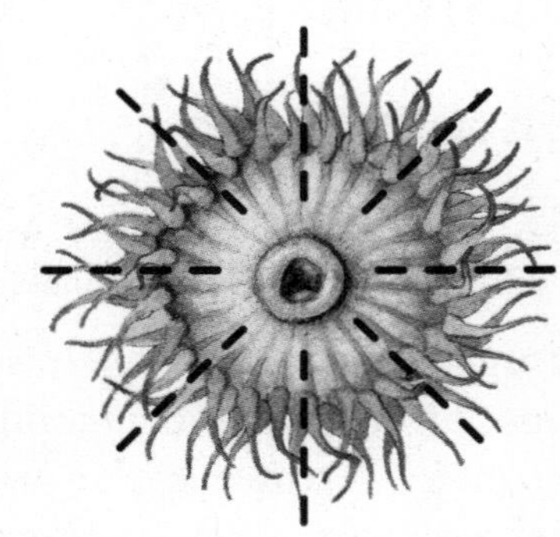

Radial symmetry The bodies of animals with radial symmetry are organized like spokes on a wheel.

Bilateral symmetry Animals with bilateral symmetry have two sides that mirror each other along one plane through the central axis.

Active Reading **9 Compare** As you read, underline the characteristics of invertebrates and vertebrates.

Invertebrates

An **invertebrate** is an animal without a backbone. In fact, invertebrates do not have any bones. Instead, many invertebrates have a hard, external covering, which supports the body, called an **exoskeleton**. Most animals on Earth—over 95% of all animal species—are invertebrates.

Asexual reproduction is more common in invertebrates than in other animals. For example, the phyla that include animals such as sponges, jellyfish, flatworms, and segmented worms use both sexual and asexual reproduction.

Two special kinds of invertebrates are tunicates and lancelets. Tunicates, such as sea squirts, are small, sac-shaped animals. Lancelets are small, fish-shaped animals as shown below. These invertebrate animals are unique because they share some characteristics with vertebrates.

Vertebrates

Tunicates and lancelets, along with vertebrates, are part of a group of animals called *chordates* (KOHR•dayts). Chordates have four traits at some point in their life: a notochord, a hollow nerve cord, pharyngeal (fuh•RIN•jee•uhl) slits, and a tail.

Animals that have a backbone are called **vertebrates**. The backbone is a part of an endoskeleton. An **endoskeleton** is an internal skeleton that supports an animal's body. The backbone is made up of bones called *vertebrae* (VER•tuh•bray) that protect part of the nervous system. Vertebrates also have a braincase, or skull, that protects their large brains. Almost all vertebrates reproduce sexually. In a few species, a female's egg can develop into an individual without being fertilized.

Visualize It!

10 Apply You may be unfamiliar with the lancelet shown here, but since lancelets are animals, what six things do you know must be true about them?

____

____

____

____

____

____

____

____

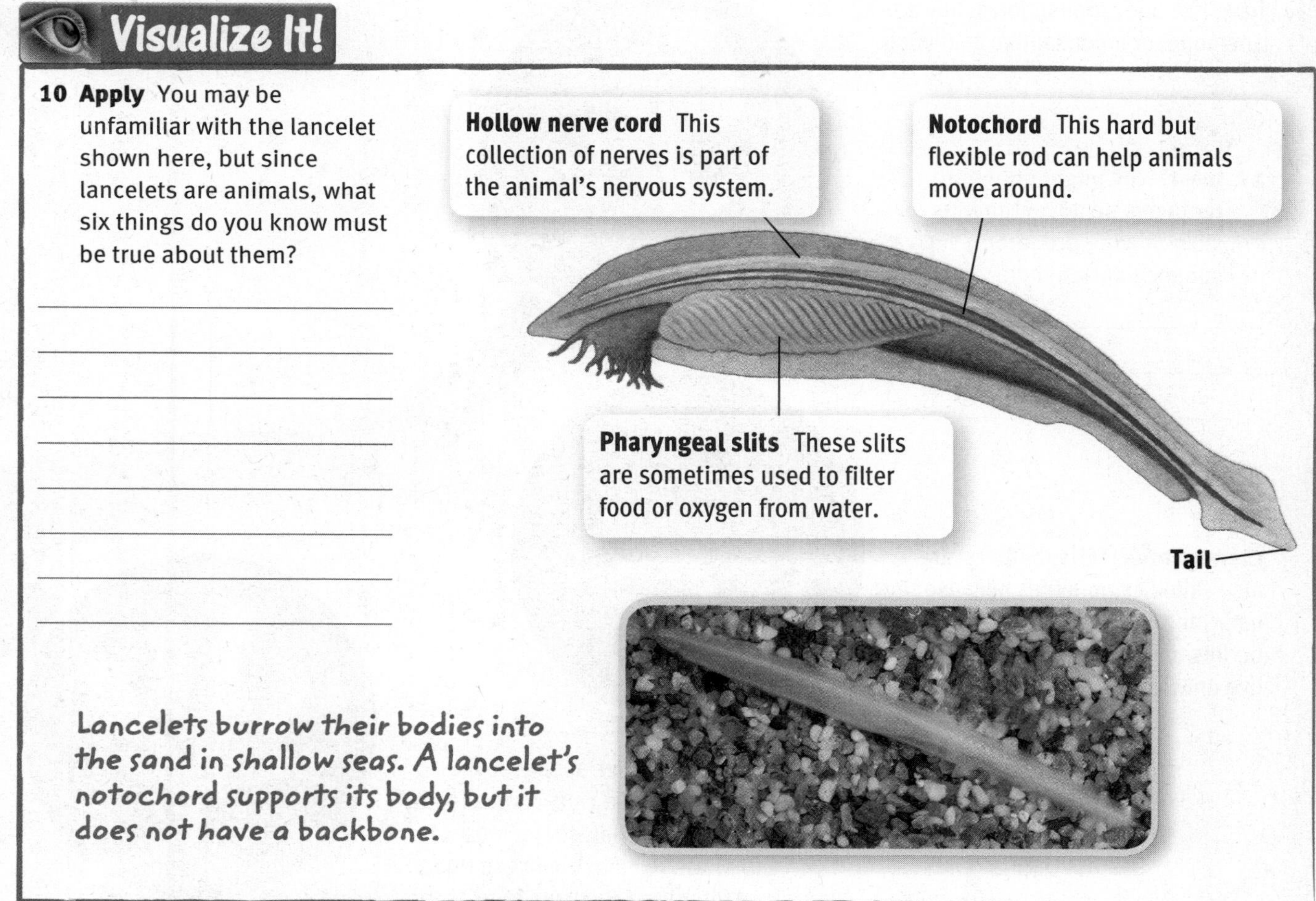

Hollow nerve cord This collection of nerves is part of the animal's nervous system.
Notochord This hard but flexible rod can help animals move around.
Pharyngeal slits These slits are sometimes used to filter food or oxygen from water.
Tail

Lancelets burrow their bodies into the sand in shallow seas. A lancelet's notochord supports its body, but it does not have a backbone.

Soft and Squishy?

What are some different kinds of invertebrates?

Most animal species are invertebrates. The figure shows some of the vast diversity of animals that make up this group. Scientists once used only structural characteristics to classify animals. Today, scientists also use DNA to place animals into groups related by their evolutionary history.

Active Reading **11 Identify** As you read the captions, underline the kind of environment where each group of invertebrates lives.

Invertebrate chordates

Echinoderms (ih•KY•nuh•dermz), such as sand dollars, live in oceans. Their endoskeleton has plates with spines, and a water vascular system helps them move. They have a complete digestive system.

Cnidarians (ny•DAIR•ee•uhnz) sting prey with their tentacles. They live in oceans and have two body forms: polyp, like a sea anemone, or medusa, like a jellyfish.

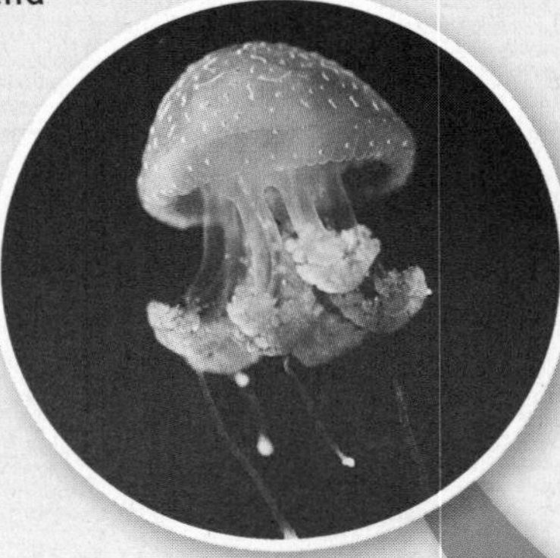

12 Infer Why might stinging tentacles be advantageous for slow-moving predators, such as some cnidarians?

____

____

____

____

Ctenophores (TEN•uh•fohrz) are also called comb jellies because they use comb-like rows of cilia on their bodies to move around. Comb jellies live only in marine environments.

Porifera includes sponges. They have specialized cells connected by jelly-like material, spend most of their lives fixed to the ocean floor, and filter food particles from water.

Arthropoda (ar•THRAHP•uh•duh) includes animals that live on land and in water. They have jointed appendages and an exoskeleton that protects them from predators and prevents drying out.

Annelida includes segmented worms that live on land and in the ocean. Earthworms break down dead organisms in the soil. Some marine annelids filter food from the water.

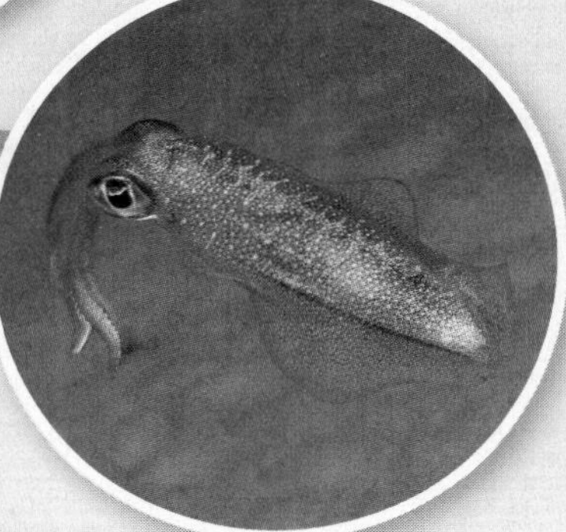

Mollusca live in water or on land, and have soft bodies. Many, such as snails and clams, have a protective outer shell and a muscular foot. Squids have complex eyes.

Nematoda are roundworms. They live in fresh water, soil, or other animals. Many of these animals, such as hookworms, are parasites that cause disease.

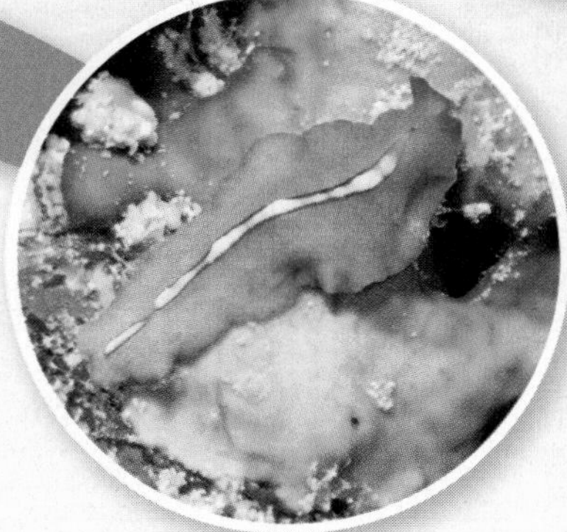

Platyhelminthes (plat•ih•hel•MIN•theez), such as planaria, flukes, and tapeworms, are the simplest worms. Parasitic flatworms have simple tissues and a head with eyespots.

Think Outside the Book

13 Apply On your way home from school, write a list of all the invertebrate animals you see. Then do research to try to classify each one.

Some Familiar Faces...

What are some different kinds of vertebrates?

Vertebrates are divided into five main groups: fish, amphibians, reptiles, birds, and mammals. Vertebrates live in water, on land, or in both places. Some eat only plants, only animals, or both plants and animals. Today, both DNA and body form and structure are used to classify vertebrates.

Active Reading **14 Identify** As you read the captions, underline how vertebrates reproduce.

Reptiles have bodies covered with scales or plates, and reproduce by laying eggs. Examples of reptiles include turtles, snakes, lizards, and crocodiles. Reptiles can live nearly anywhere on land because they can lay eggs out of the water. Their eggs are protected from drying out by membranes and shells.

Amphibians live both on land and in water. Most amphibians have four limbs. Most live near fresh water because their eggs and larvae need water to survive. Also, all amphibians have thin skins that must be kept moist. Frogs, toads, and salamanders are examples of amphibians.

15 Relate What is the difference between an invertebrate chordate and a vertebrate chordate?

____

____

____

____

____

Invertebrate chordates

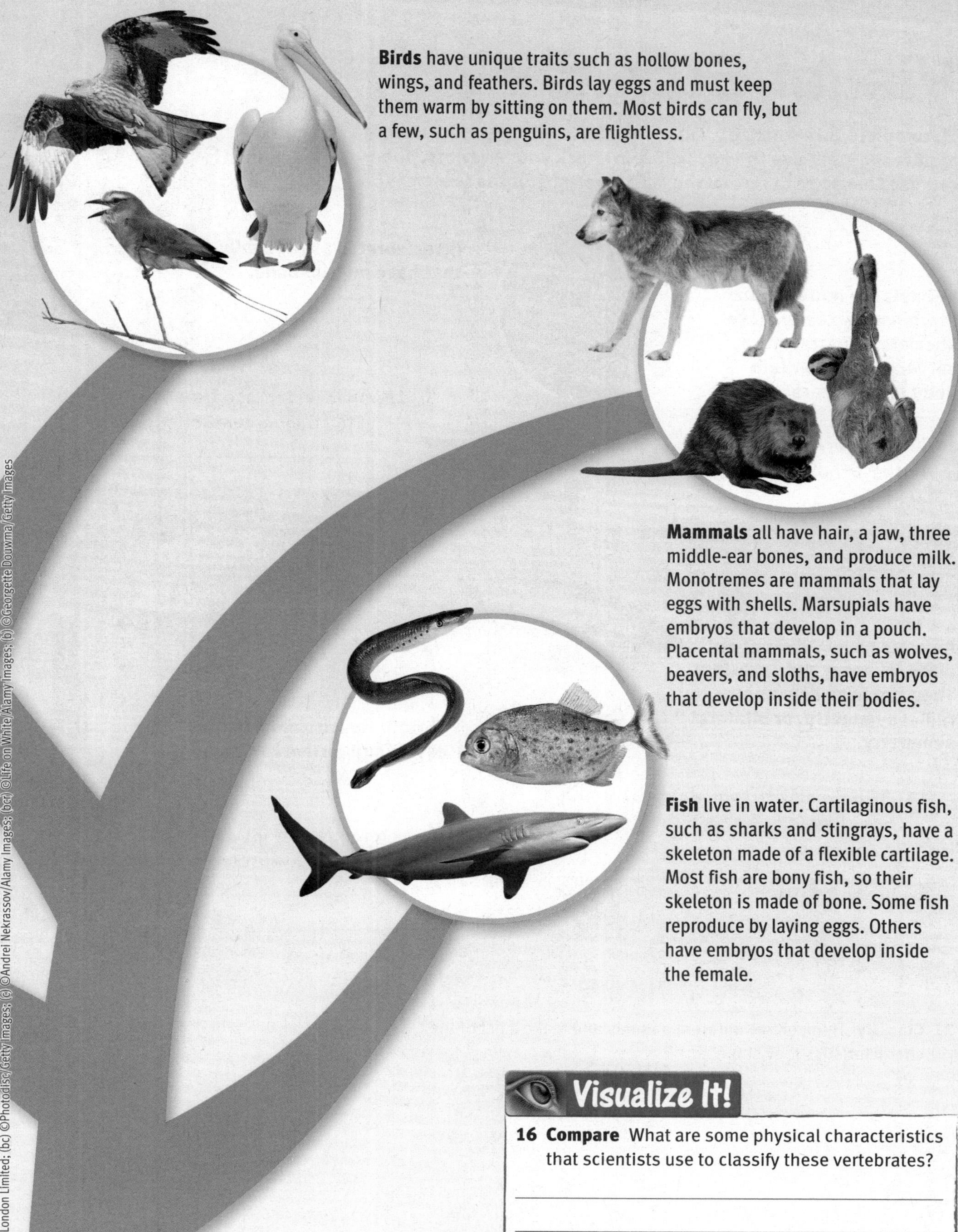

Birds have unique traits such as hollow bones, wings, and feathers. Birds lay eggs and must keep them warm by sitting on them. Most birds can fly, but a few, such as penguins, are flightless.

Mammals all have hair, a jaw, three middle-ear bones, and produce milk. Monotremes are mammals that lay eggs with shells. Marsupials have embryos that develop in a pouch. Placental mammals, such as wolves, beavers, and sloths, have embryos that develop inside their bodies.

Fish live in water. Cartilaginous fish, such as sharks and stingrays, have a skeleton made of a flexible cartilage. Most fish are bony fish, so their skeleton is made of bone. Some fish reproduce by laying eggs. Others have embryos that develop inside the female.

Visualize It!

16 Compare What are some physical characteristics that scientists use to classify these vertebrates?

____

____

____

____

Visual Summary

To complete this summary, fill in the blank with the correct word or phrase. Then, use the key below to check your answers. You can use this page to review the main concepts of the lesson.

Introduction to Animals

Animals are multicellular, reproduce sexually, have specialized parts, move, eat food, and maintain body temperature.

17 An organism that gets energy by eating other organisms is a(n) ____________________

Invertebrates are animals that have no backbone.

19 An invertebrate that hunts prey with stinging tentacles is a(n) ____________________

Animals have a diversity of sizes, shapes, and coverings. They can have asymmetry, radial symmetry, or bilateral symmetry.

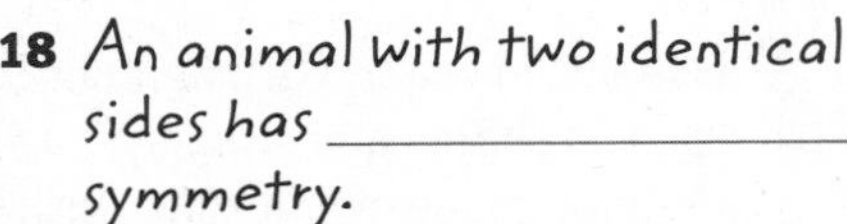

18 An animal with two identical sides has ____________________ symmetry.

Vertebrates are animals that have a supportive backbone.

20 A skeleton that is inside the body and attaches to muscles is called a(n) ____________________

Answers: 17 consumer; 18 bilateral; 19 cnidarian; 20 endoskeleton

21 Classify Think of five different animals and make a list of the characteristics they share.

Lesson Review

Vocabulary

Fill in the blank with the term that best completes the following sentence.

1 ______________________ are organisms with a backbone.

2 Tunicates and lancelets are classified as ______________________ chordates.

3 The hard external covering of some invertebrates is called an ______________________.

Key Concepts

4 Identify List the six characteristics that animals share.

5 Explain How do tunicates and lancelets differ from other chordates?

6 Compare What is the major difference between invertebrates and vertebrates?

7 Identify What are two unique characteristics shared by all birds?

Critical Thinking

Use the diagram to answer the following questions.

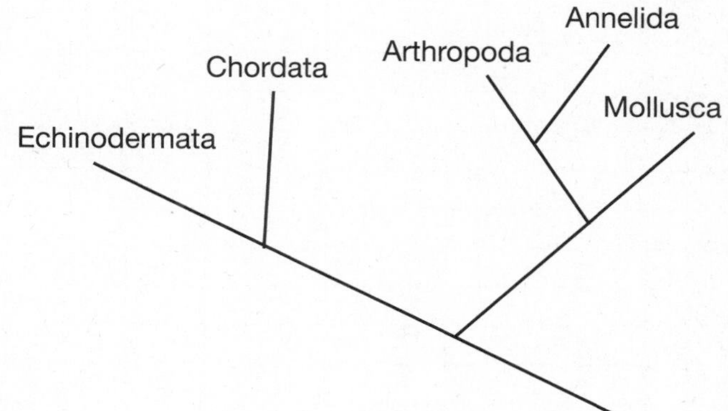

8 Analyze Which groups shown on the tree include invertebrates? Explain.

9 Infer Do any of the groups shown on this tree include vertebrates? Explain.

10 Conclude Assess what kinds of traits make invertebrates such a diverse group of animals.

My Notes

Unit 4 Big Idea

Living systems at all levels of organization demonstrate the complementary nature of structure and function.

Lesson 1
ESSENTIAL QUESTION
How are organisms classified?

Describe how people sort living things into groups based on shared characteristics.

Lesson 2
ESSENTIAL QUESTION
What are microorganisms?

Describe the characteristics of archaea, bacteria, and viruses, and explain how they reproduce or replicate.

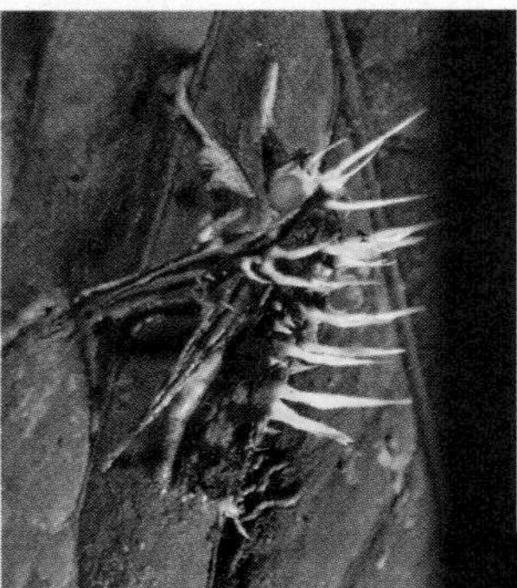

Lesson 3
ESSENTIAL QUESTION
What are protists and fungi?

Describe the characteristics of protists and fungi, and explain how they grow and reproduce.

Lesson 4
ESSENTIAL QUESTION
What are plants?

List the characteristics that all plants share, and explain how plants are classified into major plant divisions.

Lesson 5
ESSENTIAL QUESTION
What are animals?

Explain what characteristics define animals, and describe some different kinds of animals.

Connect ESSENTIAL QUESTIONS

Lessons 1, 2, 3, 4, and 5

1 Describe What characteristics do all living organisms share? In your answer, explain why viruses are not considered to be living things.

____

____

____

____

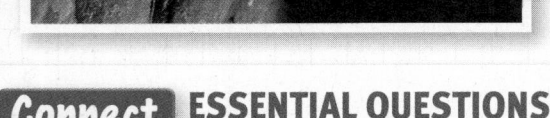

Think Outside the Book

2 Synthesize Choose one of these activities to help synthesize what you have learned in this unit.

☐ Using what you learned in lessons 1, 4, and 5, create a poster that compares the characteristics of plants and animals.

☐ Using what you learned in lessons 2, 3, 4, and 5, choose a living organism and create a brochure about its body structure, whether it is a consumer or producer, how it reproduces, and where it lives.

Unit 4 Review

Name ______________________________

Vocabulary

Check the box to show whether each statement is true or false.

T	F	
☐	☐	1 Binary fission is a form of sexual reproduction in single-celled organisms.
☐	☐	2 A lichen is a partnership between a fungus and a green algae or cyanobacterium.
☐	☐	3 A gymnosperm is a seed plant whose seeds are enclosed by a fruit.
☐	☐	4 A domain represents the largest difference among organisms.
☐	☐	5 In the most recent classification system, Animalia, Fungi, and Plantae are three of the major kingdoms of life.

Key Concepts

Choose the letter of the best answer.

6 The diagram below shows the relationships among some members of the phylum Chordata.

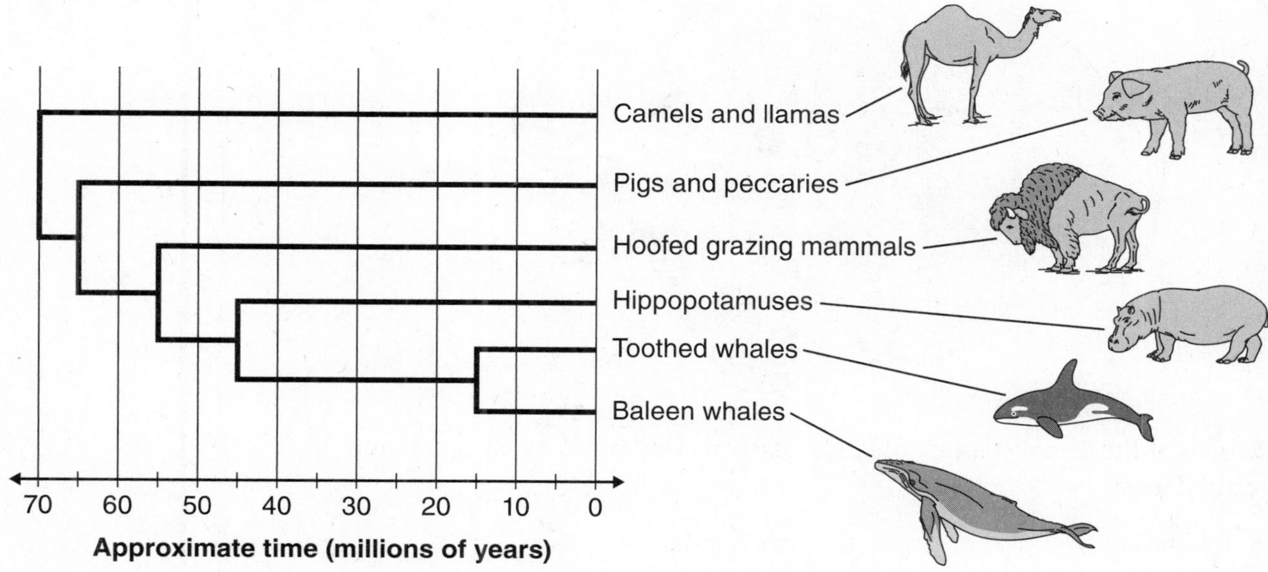

Which trait is shared by all members of the phylum Chordata?

A a notochord

B hollow bones

C gills

D radial symmetry

7 Where would you expect to see a plant that does not have a vascular system?

A in a botanical museum, because they are all extinct

B deeply rooted in a forest with a trunk that reaches 20 meters or more

C low and close to the ground

D climbing high while circling the branches of another plant

8 Which of the following is true of all animals?

A They are producers.

B They are multicellular.

C They reproduce asexually.

D They are unicellular.

9 The fossil below shows a well-preserved invertebrate with an exoskeleton and jointed appendages.

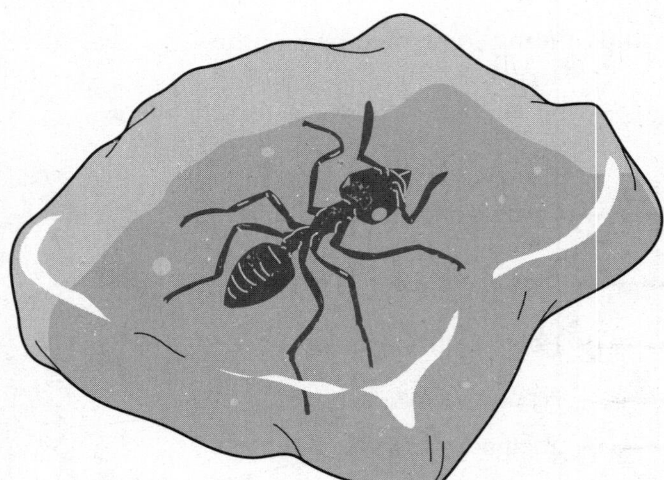

Which of these invertebrate phyla is characterized by an exoskeleton and jointed legs?

A Cnidaria

B Ctenophora

C Arthropoda

D Mollusca

Name ______________________________

10 The picture below shows a virus.

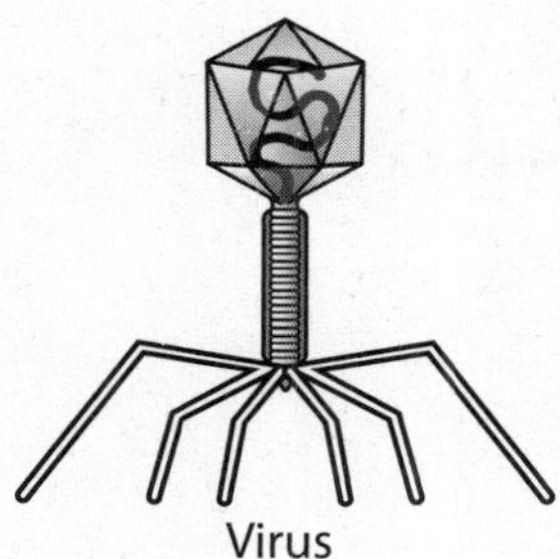

Which of the following is a task the host cell has during the replication of viruses?

A The host cell destroys the virus.

B The host cell replicates the virus's genetic material.

C The host cell is destroyed, and viral replication stops.

D The host cell's proteins block the replication of the viral proteins.

11 Which of the following is true of protists?

A Protists reproduce only by asexual reproduction.

B Some protists can photosynthesize.

C Protists cannot move on their own.

D Protists are prokaryotic.

12 As Carolus Linnaeus was growing up, he was interested in botany and in the names of plants. His ideas have influenced generations of biologists. How did Carolus Linnaeus contribute to modern classification systems?

A He identified the three domains of life.

B He developed two-part scientific names.

C He standardized common names of organisms.

D He used chemical characteristics to classify organisms.

Critical Thinking

Answer the following questions in the spaces provided.

13 How do flowering plants reproduce through sexual reproduction?

14 Name the two domains of prokaryotes and explain at least two key differences between the domains.

Connect ESSENTIAL QUESTIONS
Lessons 4 and 5

Answer the following question in the space provided.

15 Explain how the vascular systems of plants in the rainforests might have affected animal behavior and the diversity of life in the rainforests.

UNIT 5

Energy and Motion

Big Idea

Energy can be categorized as kinetic energy, which is related to the motion of an object, or potential energy, which is related to the position of an object.

A thermogram is a special type of image that shows the relative temperatures of objects.

Sealing windows keeps the warmth inside.

What do you think?

See all the red areas in this thermogram? These areas show where energy (in the form of heat) is escaping through gaps around windows and doors. Why is it important to reduce this loss of energy from a home?

Unit 5
Energy and Motion

CITIZEN SCIENCE

Saving Energy

Humans use many sources of energy in our everyday lives. For example, we need electricity to see at night, fuel to keep our cars running, and food to nourish our bodies. But we need to be careful in our use of energy resources. And you can help!

Ask A Question

How can individuals avoid wasting energy resources at home?

Make a list of all the sources of energy, such as electricity or natural gas, used in your home. Then, write down what those energy sources are used for, and estimate how much your family uses them each week. For example: "We use natural gas for cooking on our stove approximately three hours each week." Can your family reduce energy consumption in any areas? Work with your family to develop your ideas.

Using a programmable thermostat can help conserve energy.

2 Think About It

A What is one source of energy used in your home?

____

B Where is energy used most often in your school?

____

____

____

C Where is energy used most often in your home?

____

____

D What are some possible areas in the home and at school where energy usage can be easily reduced?

____

____

____

____

____

____

3 Apply Your Knowledge

A Choose some of the places you identified in your home. Develop strategies for reducing the amount of energy your family uses in those areas.

Area	Strategy

B Apply the strategies you listed above. Track how your energy usage changes as you conserve energy. Examine your utility bill if you have access to it.

____

____

____

____

Solar panels can convert energy from the sun into a form that can be used in a home.

Take It Home

As a class, create an energy conservation plan for your school. Implement it in your class and track how much energy you have saved. Share your results with your school.

Lesson 1

Introduction to Energy

ESSENTIAL QUESTION

What is energy?

By the end of this lesson, you should be able to describe how energy is conserved through transformation between different forms.

The chemical energy contained in fireworks is transformed into sound, light, and heat when the fireworks shells explode.

OHIO **6.PS.3** There are two categories of energy: kinetic and potential.

Lesson Labs

Quick Labs
- Setting Objects in Motion
- Conservation of Energy
- Bungee Jumping

S.T.E.M. Lab
- Designing a Simple Device

Engage Your Brain

1 Predict Check T or F to show whether you think each statement is true or false.

T	F	
☐	☐	Energy can change from one form to another.
☐	☐	An object can have only one type of energy at a time.
☐	☐	If an object has energy, it must be moving.
☐	☐	All energy travels in waves.

2 Describe Write a caption for this picture that includes the concept of sound energy.

____

____

____

Active Reading

3 Apply The phrase *conservation of energy* has an everyday meaning. We speak of trying to conserve, or save, energy for environmental reasons. It also refers to a law of nature. Use context clues to write your own definition for the meaning of the *law of conservation of energy*.

Example sentence

According to the law of conservation of energy, when a rolling ball slows, the energy of the ball does not disappear. Instead, it changes to energy as heat generated from moving across the ground.

law of conservation of energy:

____

____

____

____

Vocabulary Terms

- **energy**
- **kinetic energy**
- **potential energy**
- **mechanical energy**
- **energy transformation**
- **law of conservation of energy**

4 Apply As you learn the definition of each vocabulary term in this lesson, create your own definition or sketch to help you remember the meaning of the term.

Get Energized!

What are two types of energy?

Active Reading

5 Identify As you read this page and the next, underline the factors that affect an object's kinetic and potential energy.

In science, **energy** is the ability to cause change. Energy takes many different forms and has many different effects. There are two general types of energy: kinetic energy and potential energy.

Kinetic Energy

Kinetic energy (kih•NET•ik EN•er•jee) is the energy of an object that is due to motion. All moving objects have kinetic energy. The amount of kinetic energy an object has depends on its mass and its speed. Kinetic energy increases as mass increases. Imagine that a bowling ball and a soccer ball roll across the floor at the same speed. The bowling ball has more kinetic energy than the soccer ball has because the bowling ball has a greater mass.

Kinetic energy also increases as speed increases. If two bowling balls with the same mass roll across the floor at different speeds, the faster ball will have the greater kinetic energy.

D — As the skater moves up the ramp, he gains height but loses speed. Some of his kinetic energy is converted back to potential energy. The rest of it is transferred as heat due to friction.

C — At the bottom of the ramp, the skater's kinetic energy is at its peak because he is going the fastest. His potential energy is at its lowest because he is closer to the ground than at any other point on the ramp.

Potential Energy

Potential energy (puh•TEN•shuhl EN•er•jee) is the energy that an object has due to its position, condition, or chemical composition. A ball held above the ground has potential energy because the force of gravity can pull it to the ground. Potential energy that is the result of an object's position is called gravitational potential energy. Gravitational potential energy increases as the object's height or mass increases.

A change in condition can also affect potential energy. For example, stretching a rubber band increases its potential energy.

Chemical potential energy depends on chemical composition. As bonds break and new bonds form between atoms during a chemical change, energy can be released.

Think Outside the Book Inquiry

6 Diagram Think of another situation that shows kinetic and potential energy. Draw a sketch of and write a description explaining the situation in terms of potential and kinetic energy.

Can objects have potential and kinetic energy at the same time?

An object can have both kinetic and potential energy. For example, the skater in the picture below has kinetic energy as he moves down the ramp. He has potential energy due to his position on the ramp. A flying bird has kinetic energy because of its speed, mass, and potential energy due to its height from the ground.

A
At the top of the ramp, the skater has potential energy because gravity can pull him downward. He has no speed, so he has no kinetic energy.
B
As the skater moves closer to the ground, the decrease in potential energy is equal to the increase in his kinetic energy. As he rolls down the ramp, his potential energy decreases because his distance from the ground decreases. His kinetic energy increases because his speed increases.

7 Analyze Do you think that the skater has any gravitational potential energy at point C? Why?

In Perfect Form

What forms can energy take?

Kinetic energy and potential energy are two types of energy that can come in many different forms. Some common forms of energy include mechanical, sound, electromagnetic, electrical, chemical, thermal, and nuclear energy. Energy is expressed in joules (J) (JOOLZ).

Mechanical Energy

Mechanical energy is the sum of an object's kinetic energy and potential energy. Remember that kinetic energy is the energy of motion, and potential energy is the energy of position. So mechanical energy is the energy of position and motion. A moving car has mechanical energy. An object's mechanical energy can be all potential energy, all kinetic energy, or a combination of potential and kinetic energy.

Sound Energy

Sound energy is kinetic energy caused by the vibration of particles in a medium such as steel, water, or air. As the particles vibrate, they transfer the sound energy to other particles. The sound a guitar makes is caused by the vibrations of its strings transferring energy to the air around it. You hear the sound because special structures in your ears detect the vibrations of the particles in the air.

A ______________________________

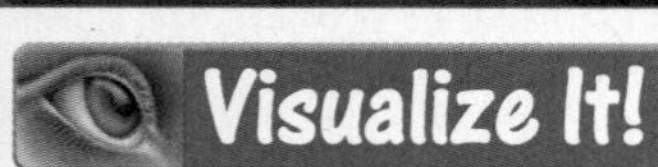

8 Identify Label the three forms of energy represented in this image.

B ______________________

C ______________________

Electromagnetic Energy

Electromagnetic energy is transmitted through space in the form of electromagnetic waves. These waves are caused by the vibration of electrically charged particles. Electromagnetic waves include visible light, x-rays, and microwaves. X-rays are high-energy waves used by doctors and dentists to look at your bones. Microwaves can be used to cook food or to transmit cellular telephone calls. The sun releases a large amount of electromagnetic energy, some of which reaches Earth as radiant energy.

Electrical Energy

Electrical energy is the energy that results from the position or motion of charged particles. The electrical energy that powers the lights overhead is associated with negatively charged particles moving in a wire. The wire also has positively charged particles that do not move. The negatively charged particles move within the wire and create an electric current.

9 Compare How does electrical energy differ from electromagnetic energy?

____

____

____

10 Infer Would you expect to detect electrical energy if you played the pinball game shown in the picture? Explain your answer.

____

____

____

____

____

11 Identify As you read, underline the source of energy in a chemical reaction.

Chemical Energy

Chemical energy is a form of potential energy. The amount of chemical energy in a molecule depends on the kinds of atoms and their arrangement. During a chemical change, bonds between these atoms break, and new bonds form. The foods you eat, batteries, and matches are sources of chemical energy.

Thermal Energy

The thermal energy of an object is the kinetic energy of its particles. Particles move faster at higher temperatures than at lower temperatures. The faster the molecules in an object move, the more thermal energy the object has. Also, the more particles an object has, the more thermal energy it has. Heat is the energy transferred from an object at a higher temperature to an object at a lower temperature.

Nuclear Energy

The nucleus of an atom is the source of nuclear energy. When an atom's nucleus breaks apart, or when the nuclei of two small atoms join together, energy is released. The energy given off by the sun comes from nuclear energy. In the sun, hydrogen nuclei join to make a helium nucleus. This reaction gives off a huge amount of energy. The sun's light and heat come from these reactions. Without nuclear energy from the sun, life would not exist on Earth.

12 Synthesize Why is the chemical energy of a battery potential energy and not kinetic energy?

____

____

____

____

____

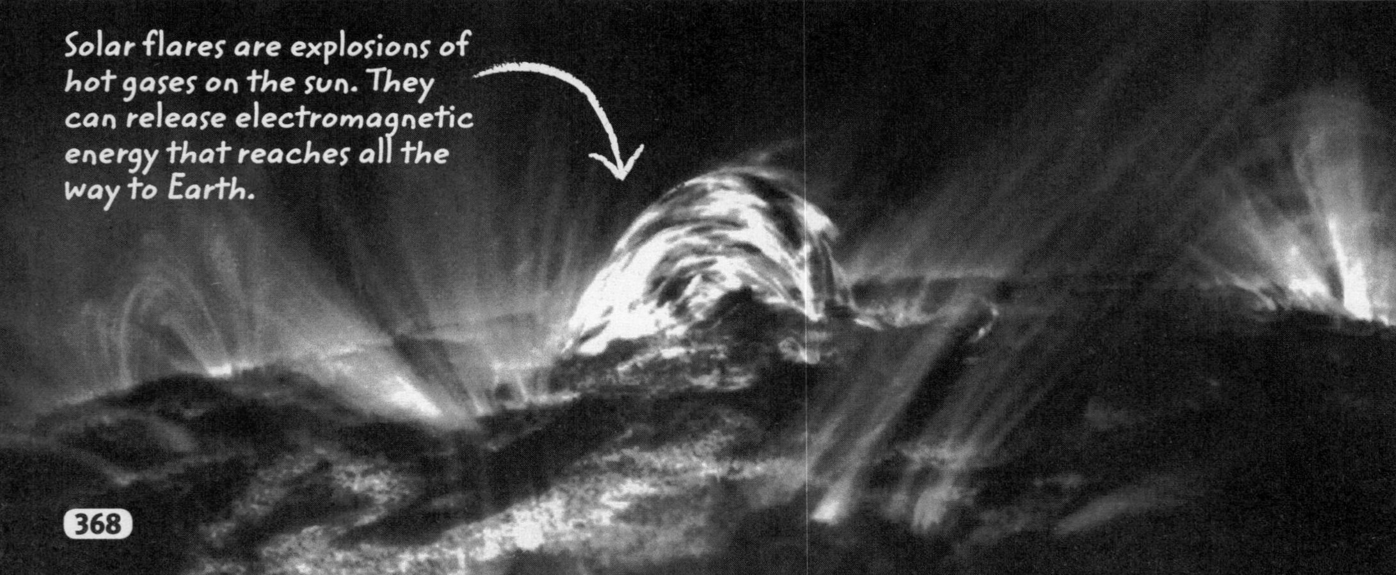

Solar flares are explosions of hot gases on the sun. They can release electromagnetic energy that reaches all the way to Earth.

Why It Matters

SOCIETY AND TECHNOLOGY

Space Weather and Technology

Every time you turn on a TV or use a cell phone, you may be affected by the "weather" in space. Space weather includes any activity happening in space that might affect Earth's environment, such as solar flares. A solar flare can release a million times more energy than the largest earthquake. It is an intense release of electromagnetic energy as a burst of radiation.

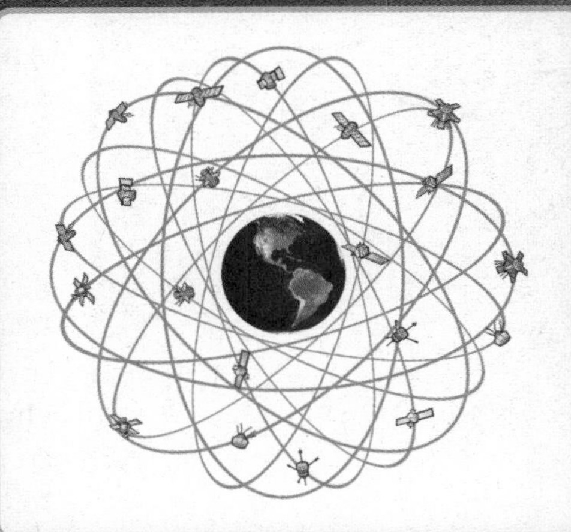

Space Weather Can Damage Satellites

Many of the satellites orbiting Earth provide telephone service. Damage from space weather can interrupt phone communications.

Space Weather Can Affect Navigation

Space weather can also cause navigation errors by interrupting satellite signals to Global Positioning System (GPS) receivers.

Space Weather Can Ground Planes

Auroras like the one shown here are caused by electrically charged particles of the solar winds hitting Earth's magnetic field. This activity can interrupt airplane communications, forcing the planes to land.

Extend

Inquiry

13 Identify What type of energy is monitored by scientists forecasting future space weather?

14 Infer Why is space weather a bigger concern now than it was in the past?

15 Research How do scientists forecast space weather? Why?

Transformers

What is an energy transformation?

An **energy transformation** (EN•er•jee trans•fohr•MAY•shuhn) takes place when energy changes from one form into another form. Any form of energy can change into any other form of energy. Often, one form of energy changes into more than one form. When you rub your hands together, you hear a sound, and your hands get warm. The mechanical energy of your moving hands was transformed into both sound energy and energy as heat.

Another example of an energy transformation is when chemical energy is converted in the body. Why is eating breakfast so important? Eating breakfast gives your body the energy needed to help you start your day. Chemical potential energy is stored in the food you eat. Your body breaks down the components of the food to access the energy stored in them. Some of this energy is then changed to the kinetic energy that allows you to move and play. Some of the chemical energy is converted into heat energy that keeps your body warm.

Some examples of energy transformation are illustrated in this flashlight. Follow the captions to learn how energy is transformed into the light energy that you rely on when you turn on a flashlight.

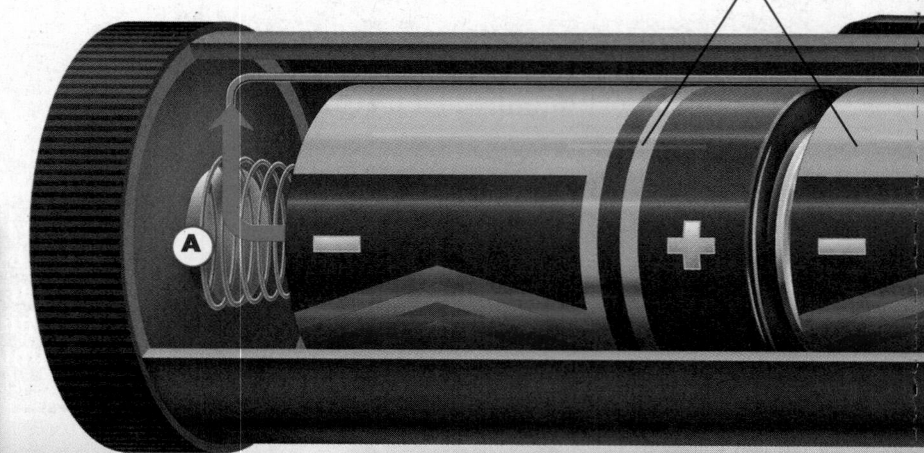

A *The chemical energy from the batteries is transformed into electrical energy.*

16 Describe Give two examples of other devices in which the chemical energy in a battery is transformed into electrical energy.

____

____

____

Is energy conserved?

A closed system is a group of objects that transfers energy only to one another. For example, a roller coaster can be considered a closed system if it includes everything involved, such as the track, the cars, and the air around them. Energy is conserved in all closed systems. The **law of conservation of energy** states that energy cannot be created or destroyed. It can only change forms. All of the different forms of energy in a closed system always add up to the same total amount of energy. It does not matter how many energy transformations take place.

For example, on a roller coaster some mechanical energy gets transformed into sound and heat energy as the roller coaster goes down a hill. The total of the coaster's mechanical energy at the bottom of the hill, the extra heat energy, and the sound energy is the same total amount of energy as the original amount of mechanical energy. In other words, total energy is conserved.

Active Reading **17 Relate** How are energy transformations related to the law of conservation of energy?

____

____

____

____

Think Outside the Book

18 Apply Have you ever thought about how an MP3 player works? What form of energy is used to power an MP3 player? What form of energy do you use from an MP3 player? Can you think of any other forms of energy that may be used inside of an MP3 player?

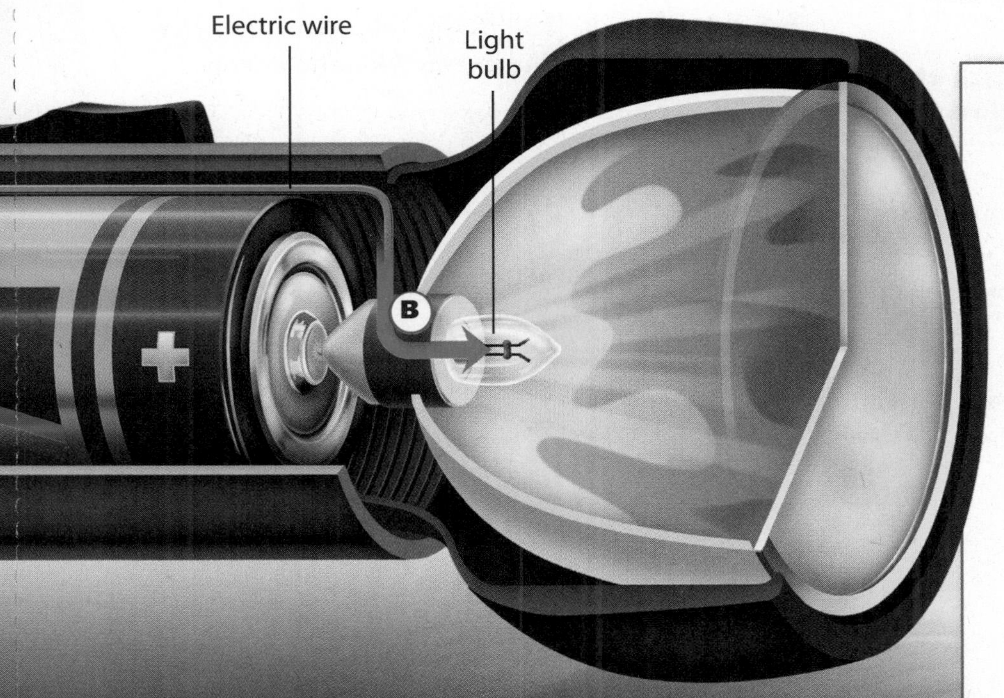

B The electrical energy in the wire is transformed into light in the light bulb. Some of the electrical energy is also transformed into energy as heat.

19 Describe Give another example of electrical energy being transformed into light.

____

____

____

____

____

Visual Summary

To complete this summary, circle the correct word. Then use the key below to check your answers. You can use this page to review the main concepts of the lesson.

Introduction to Energy

Energy is the ability to cause change; it cannot be created or destroyed.

20 The total energy in a closed system remains the same / changes as energy changes forms.

Potential energy results from an object's position, composition, or condition, and kinetic energy results from an object's motion.

21 A basketball that is balanced on the rim of a basketball hoop has potential energy / kinetic energy.

22 A basketball that is rolling across a floor has potential energy / kinetic energy.

Energy transformation takes place when energy changes from one form to another.

23 When a candle is burned, some chemical energy is transformed into nuclear / heat energy.

Answers: 20 remains the same; 21 potential energy; 22 kinetic energy; 23 heat

24 Apply Identify and give examples of at least three types of energy you see being used as you look around your classroom.

Lesson Review

Vocabulary

Draw a line to connect the following terms to their definitions.

1 kinetic energy	**A** energy of position
2 mechanical energy	**B** sum of energy of motion and energy of position
3 potential energy	**C** energy of motion

Key Concepts

4 Describe What happens to the kinetic energy of a snowball as it rolls across the lawn and gains mass?

5 Relate How is the sun related to nuclear, electromagnetic, and heat energy?

6 Apply When a person uses an iron to remove the wrinkles from a shirt, why does heat travel from the iron to the shirt?

7 Explain What determines the amount of chemical energy a substance has?

Critical Thinking

Use the picture below to answer the following questions.

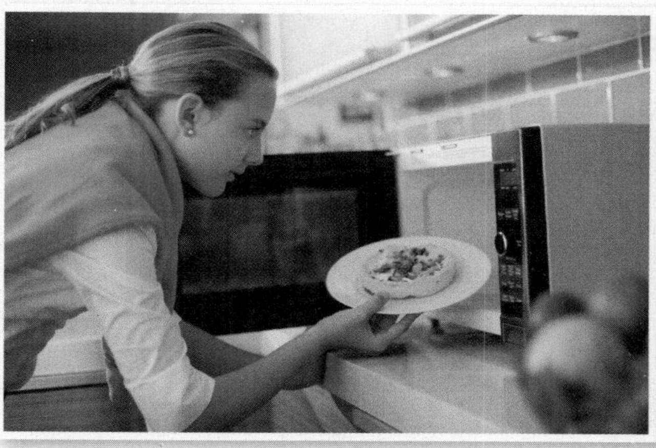

8 Identify Name at least three types of energy associated with the microwave.

9 Hypothesize How is electromagnetic energy from the microwave transformed into heat energy?

10 Infer Explain the law of conservation of energy.

My Notes

OHIO **6.SIA.2** Design and conduct a scientific investigation.

OHIO **6.SIA.6** Think critically and logically to connect evidence and explanations.

Planning an Investigation

Scientists ask many questions and develop hypotheses about the natural world. They conduct investigations to help answer these questions. A scientist must plan an investigation carefully. The investigation should gather information that might support or disprove the hypothesis.

Tutorial

Use the following steps to help plan an investigation.

1. **Write a hypothesis.**
   The hypothesis should offer an explanation for the question that you are asking. The hypothesis must also be testable. If it is not testable, rewrite the hypothesis.

2. **Identify and list the possible variables in your experiment.**
   Select the independent variable and the dependent variable. In your investigation, you will change the independent variable to see any effect it may have on the dependent variable.

3. **List the materials that you will need to perform the experiment.**
   This list should also include equipment that you need for safety.

4. **Determine the method you will use to test your hypothesis.**
   Clearly describe the steps you will follow. If you change any part of the procedure while you are conducting the investigation, record the change. Another scientist should be able to follow your procedure to repeat your investigation.

5. **Analyze the results.**
   Your data and observations from all of your experiments should be recorded carefully and clearly to maintain credibility. Record how you analyze your results so others can review your work and spot any problems or errors in your analysis.

6. **Draw conclusions.**
   Describe what the results of the investigation show. Tell whether the results support your hypothesis.

You Try It!

You are a member of a research team that is trying to design and test a roof system that can maintain a comfortable temperature inside a building during hot days. The system you design and test will be a scale model. To begin, you need to find an answer to the following question: What material will minimize the rate of heat transfer inside a building?

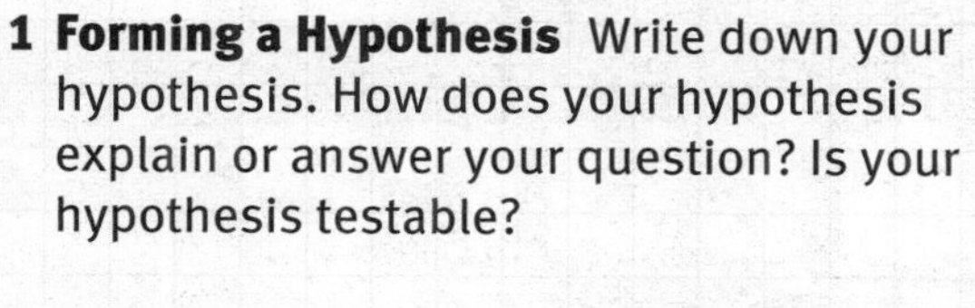

1 **Forming a Hypothesis** Write down your hypothesis. How does your hypothesis explain or answer your question? Is your hypothesis testable?

2 **Identifying Variables** List the possible variables in this experiment. Identify dependent variables and independent variables.

3 **Selecting Materials** What equipment and tools will you need to test this variable? What might happen if you select inappropriate tools?

4 **Testing Your Hypothesis** What will your system look like? Will it support your testing? You may sketch the system on a separate page.

5 **Maintaining Accurate Records** What steps will you need to follow in order to test your hypothesis? What kinds of measurements will you collect? What kind of graphic organizer will you use to record your information?

6 **Drawing Conclusions** What conclusions can you draw from your data? Was your hypothesis useful?

Take It Home

Look closely at objects and materials in your home. Write a list of things that help to prevent the transfer of energy as heat. Design an investigation using one or more of these items to learn more about the job they do. Record your observations. Evaluate your results to see if they might point to a further investigation or an improvement to a product. Present your results in a pamphlet.

Thermal Energy and Temperature

ESSENTIAL QUESTION

How are thermal energy and temperature related?

By the end of this lesson, you should be able to relate the temperature and thermal energy of a substance to the kinetic energy of its particles.

OHIO 6.PS.2 Changes of state are explained by a model of matter composed of atoms and/or molecules that are in motion.

OHIO 6.PS.3 There are two categories of energy: kinetic and potential.

What does it mean to be hot or cold? You can tell that this environment is cold because there is ice and because the person is in a hat and coat.

Lesson Labs

Quick Labs
- Exploring Temperature
- Understanding Temperature Scales

Engage Your Brain

1 Predict Check T or F to show whether you think each statement is true or false.

T	F	
☐	☐	Solids and liquids are made of particles, but gases are made of air, which is not made of particles.
☐	☐	Kinetic energy is the energy of motion.
☐	☐	Kinetic energy depends on mass and speed.
☐	☐	Thermal energy and temperature are the same thing.

2 Illustrate Think about a time when you were very cold. Then draw a picture of a time when you were very warm. Write a caption about the differences between the two situations.

Active Reading

3 Synthesize Many English words have their roots in other languages. Use the Greek words below to determine the meanings of the words *thermometer* and *thermal*. A context sentence is provided for *thermometer*. Then, write a sentence using the words correctly.

Greek word	Meaning
thermos	warm
metron	to measure

Example sentence
This thermometer indicates that it is 72 °F in this room.

thermometer:

____

____

thermal:

____

____

____

Vocabulary Terms

- **kinetic theory of matter**
- **temperature**
- **thermal energy**
- **degree**
- **thermometer**

4 Identify This list contains the key terms you'll learn in this lesson. As you read, circle the definition of each term.

Particle Party

What is the kinetic theory of matter?

All matter is made of atoms. These particles are always moving, even if it doesn't look like they are. The **kinetic theory of matter** states that all of the particles that make up matter are constantly in motion. Because the particles are in motion, they have kinetic energy. The faster the particles are moving, the more kinetic energy they have.

While the particles of matter are constantly moving, the particles move in different directions and at different speeds. This motion is random. Therefore, the individual particles of matter have different amounts of kinetic energy. The average kinetic energy of all these particles takes into account their different random movements. As seen in this picture, solids, liquids, and gases have different average kinetic energies.

This bridge is a solid, so its particles are close together and vibrate.

In this hot pool, the liquid particles are moving around.

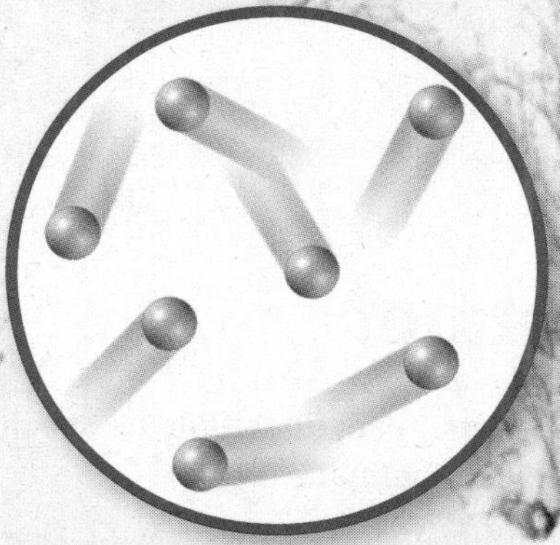

The particles in the gas in the air are far apart and moving quickly.

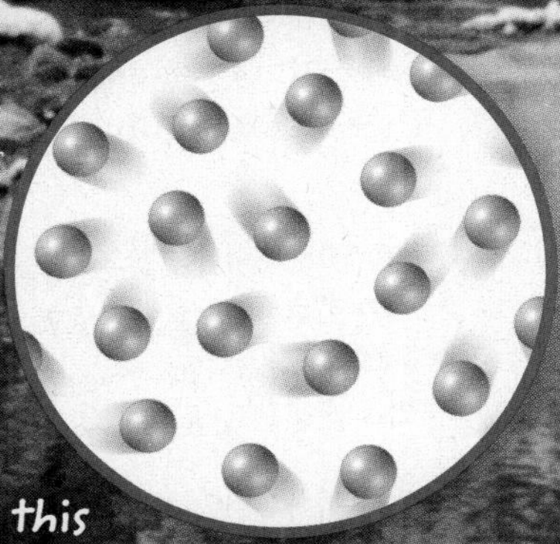

The particles in this cold river water are moving freely.

How do particles move in solids, liquids, and gases?

The kinetic theory of matter explains the motion of particles in solids, liquids, and gases.

- The particles in a solid, such as concrete, are not free to move around very much. They vibrate back and forth in the same position and are held tightly together by forces of attraction.
- The particles in a liquid, such as water in a pool, move much more freely than particles in a solid. They are constantly sliding around and tumbling over each other as they move.
- In a gas, such as the air around you, particles are far apart and move around at high speeds. Particles collide with one another, but otherwise they do not interact much.

Active Reading **5 Describe** In your own words, describe the difference between the movement of particles in liquids and the movement of particles in gases.

Visualize It!

6 Illustrate Locate another solid, liquid, or gas in this photo. Make a sketch of the particles that make up the solid, liquid, or gas. Also indicate how fast you think the particles might be moving based on the state of matter of the item you picked. Then, write a caption describing the particle movement.

Wear Your Thermals!

What is temperature?

Active Reading **7 Identify** As you read, underline the specific type of energy measured by temperature and thermal energy.

Each particle in an object has kinetic energy. The amount of energy these particles have can affect certain properties of the substance. As you saw on the previous page, the particles in solids such as concrete vibrate more slowly than the particles in liquids. This means that the water molecules in ice, which is a solid, have less average kinetic energy than the water molecules in liquid water. **Temperature** (TEM•per•uh•chur) is a measure of the average kinetic energy of all the particles in an object or substance. The higher the average kinetic energy of the particles in the object, the higher its temperature. The temperature of an object does not depend on the type or number of particles that make up the object.

The tea has a higher temperature than the lake, but the lake has more thermal energy than the tea because it contains more particles.

What is thermal energy?

Recall that each of the particles that makes up an object has kinetic energy. Every one of these moving particles adds to the total amount of kinetic energy within an object. The **thermal energy** of an object is the total amount of kinetic energy present in an object.

The thermal energy of an object depends on three things: the mass of the object (number of particles), the properties of the particles making up the object, and the average kinetic energy of the particles in the object. For example, a cup of hot tea has a higher temperature than a large, cold lake does. But the lake is made up of many more particles than the small volume of tea. So the total kinetic energy of the lake water is more than the total kinetic energy of the tea. Therefore, the lake has more thermal energy than the tea.

What is the difference between thermal energy and temperature?

Thermal energy and temperature are not the same thing. The temperature of an object is a measure of the *average* kinetic energy of all the particles in the object, while the thermal energy of an object is a measure of the *total* kinetic energy of all the particles in the object. The temperature of an object does not depend on the mass of the object, while the thermal energy the object has does depend on its mass.

For example, a 10 g sample and a 100 g sample of a substance such as mercury may have the same temperature, but the two masses would have different thermal energies. The 100 g sample contains more particles and therefore contains a greater amount of kinetic energy than the smaller sample. However, 10 g of boiling mercury likely has greater thermal energy than 100 g of room temperature mercury because of its higher temperature.

Although we use the terms *hot* and *cold* to describe the temperature of things in our environment, they are not very useful terms to scientists. Measuring the average kinetic energy of the particles that make up an object is more helpful. Temperature is a quantitative measurement.

The energy released as heat from the surface of objects is visualized by thermal-imaging cameras. The cooler a surface, the darker the color.

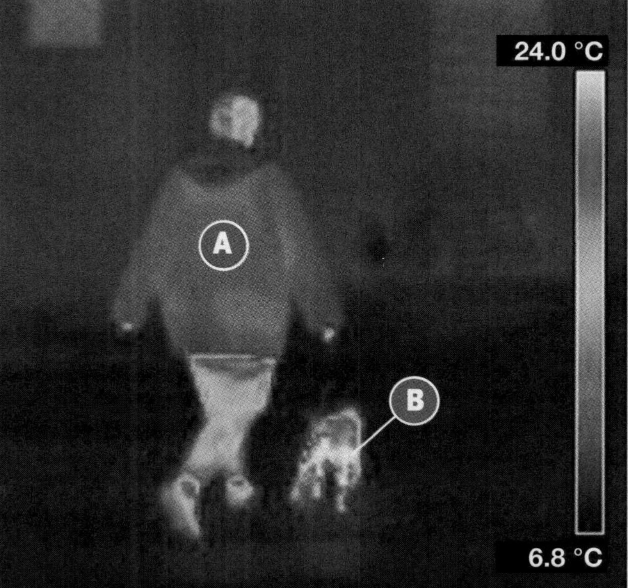

Visualize It!

8 Identify Which of these pumpkins has the most thermal energy? Explain your answer.

Visualize It!

9 Identify Which of the objects labeled has the higher surface temperature? Which one is cooler? Write your answers below.

A

B

Mercury Rising

How does temperature relate to kinetic energy?

Recall that temperature is a measure of the average kinetic energy of all the particles in an object. In the photo on the previous page, a person pours a cup of hot tea next to a large lake. The average movement of the particles that make up the lake is slower. In the warmer tea, the average movement of the particles is much faster. If an iron, which is a solid, has a high temperature the iron's particles are vibrating very fast and have a high average kinetic energy. If the iron has a low temperature, the iron's particles are vibrating more slowly and have a lower average kinetic energy.

Absolute zero is the temperature at which the motion of particles stops. It is not possible to actually reach absolute zero, though temperatures very close to absolute zero have been reached in laboratories.

How is temperature measured?

Suppose you hear on the radio that the temperature outside is 30 degrees. Do you need to wear a warm coat to spend the day outside? The answer depends on the temperature scale being used. There are three common temperature scales, all of which measure the average kinetic energy of particles. These scales are called Celsius, Fahrenheit, and Kelvin. However, 30 degrees on one scale is quite different from 30 degrees on the other scales.

To establish a temperature scale, two known values and the number of units between the values are needed. The freezing and boiling points of pure water are often used as the standard, known values. These points are always the same under the same conditions, and they are easy to reproduce. In the Celsius and Fahrenheit scales, temperature is measured in units called degrees. **Degrees** (°) are equally spaced units between two points. The space between degrees can vary from scale to scale. In the Kelvin scale, no degree sign is used. Instead, the unit is just called a kelvin. Temperature is measured using an instrument called a **thermometer**.

Active Reading **10 Explain** How does the temperature of a substance change when the average kinetic energy of its particles increases? When it decreases?

____

____

____

Think Outside the Book Inquiry

11 Produce Write a story about someone who travels from one place of extreme temperature to another. Identify how your character adjusts to the change in temperature. How are the character's daily activities and decisions affected?

Celsius Scale

The temperature scale most commonly used around the world, and often used by scientists, is the Celsius (SEL•see•uhs) scale (°C). This scale was developed in the 1740s by Anders Celsius. On the Celsius scale, pure water freezes at 0 °C and boils at 100 °C, so there are 100 degrees—100 equal units—between these two temperatures.

Fahrenheit Scale

The scale used most commonly in the United States for measuring temperature is the Fahrenheit scale (°F). It was developed in the early 1700s by Gabriel Fahrenheit. On the Fahrenheit scale, pure water freezes at 32 °F and boils at 212 °F. Thus, there are 180 degrees—180 equal units—between the freezing point and the boiling point of water.

Kelvin Scale

A temperature scale used commonly by physicists is the Kelvin scale. This scale was not developed until the 20th century. The equal units in the Kelvin scale are called kelvins, not degrees. On the Kelvin scale, pure water freezes at 273 K and boils at 373 K. There are 100 kelvins—100 equal units—between these two temperatures. The lowest temperature on the Kelvin scale is absolute zero, or 0 K.

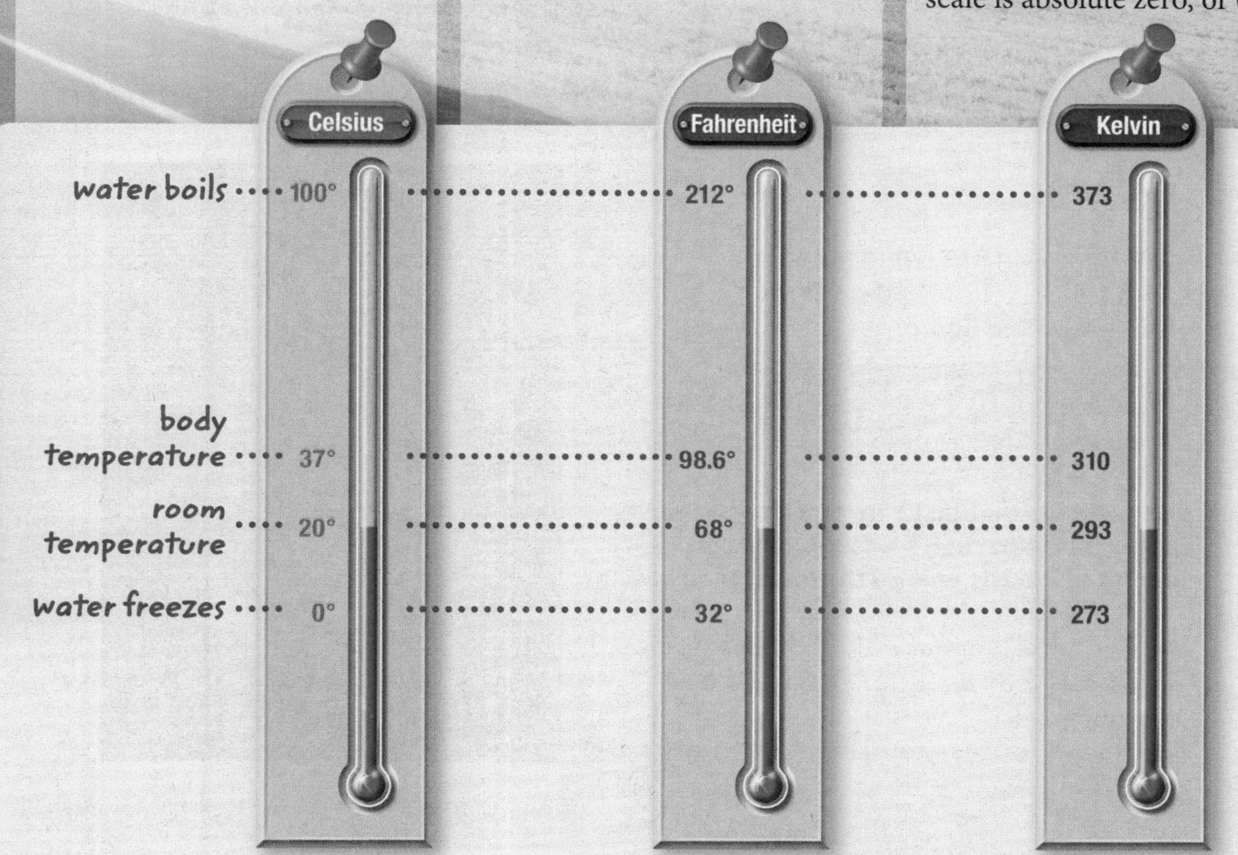

12 Identify What is body temperature in the Celsius scale? In the Fahrenheit scale? In the Kelvin scale?

____

____

13 Apply The water in swimming pools is typically about 80 °F. Mark this temperature on the Fahrenheit thermometer above. Estimate what temperature this is in the Celsius and Kelvin scales.

____

____

Visual Summary

To complete this summary, fill in the blanks with the correct word. Then use the key below to check your answers. You can use this page to review the main concepts of the lesson.

Thermal Energy and Temperature

All of the particles that make up matter are constantly in motion.

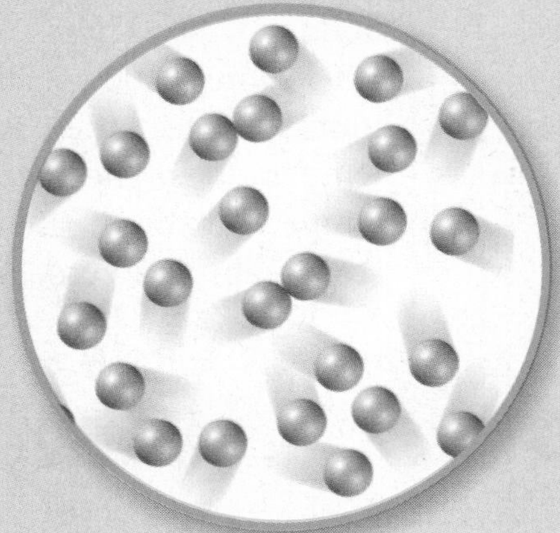

14 *The particles in a hot liquid move ________________ than the particles in a cold liquid.*

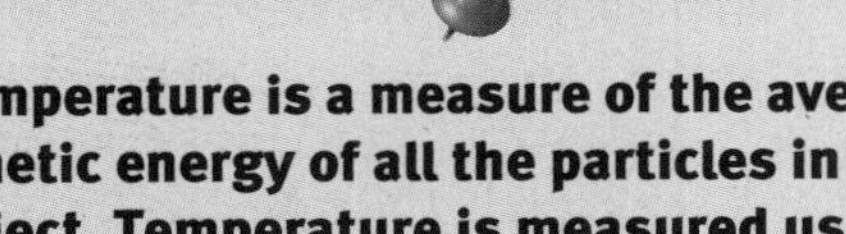

Temperature is a measure of the average kinetic energy of all the particles in an object. Temperature is measured using one of three scales: Celsius, Fahrenheit, or Kelvin.

15 *Temperature is measured using a tool called a ________________.*

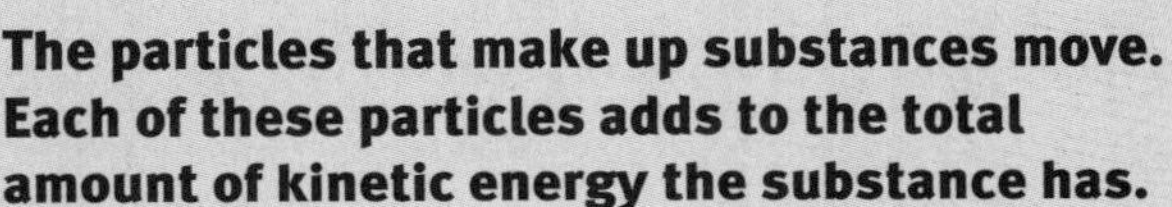

The particles that make up substances move. Each of these particles adds to the total amount of kinetic energy the substance has.

16 *The total amount of kinetic energy the particles of a substance have is the substance's ________________.*

Answers: 14 faster; 15 thermometer; 16 thermal energy

17 Infer If a puddle of water is frozen, do the particles in the ice have kinetic energy? Explain.

Lesson Review

Vocabulary

For each pair of terms, write a sentence using both terms that demonstrates the definition of each term.

1 *Kinetic theory of matter* and *thermal energy*

2 *Thermometer* and *degree*

Key Concepts

3 Relate Describe the relationship between temperature and kinetic energy.

4 Apply Particles in a substance that is 54 °C have a ____________ average kinetic energy than particles in a substance that is 95 °C.

5 Identify How does the thermal energy of an object differ from its temperature?

Critical Thinking

Use the art below to answer the following questions.

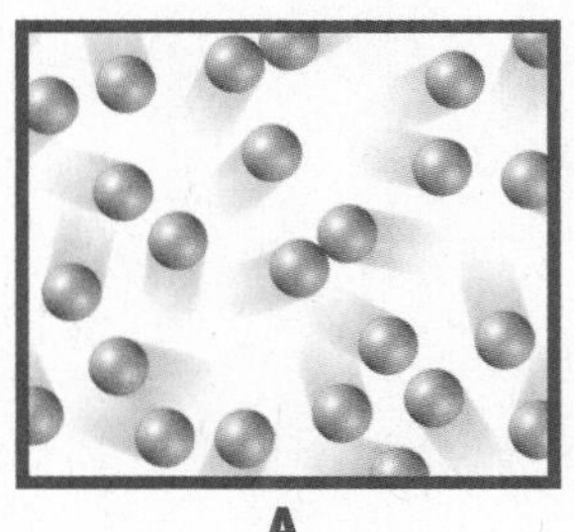
A

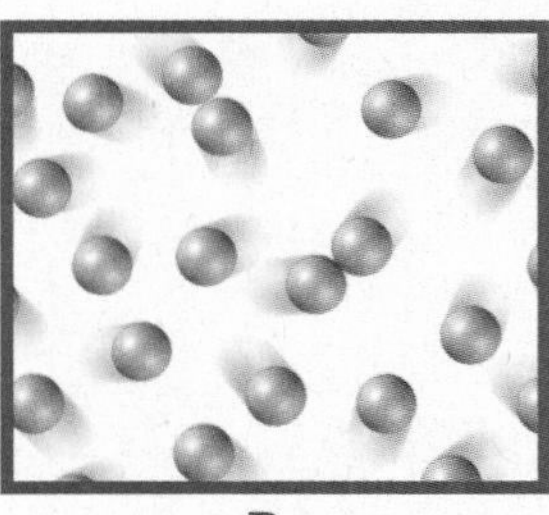
B

6 Observe Which illustration represents the substance at a higher temperature? Explain.

7 Predict What would happen to the particles in illustration A if the substance were chilled? What would happen if the particles in illustration B were warmed?

8 Apply Using your knowledge of the difference between the three different temperature scales, what do you think would happen if a human's body temperature were 98.6 °C? Why do doctors worry more about a fever of a couple of degrees Celsius than a fever of a couple of degrees Fahrenheit?

My Notes

Motion and Speed

ESSENTIAL QUESTION

How are distance, time, and speed related?

By the end of this lesson, you should be able to analyze how distance, time, and speed are related.

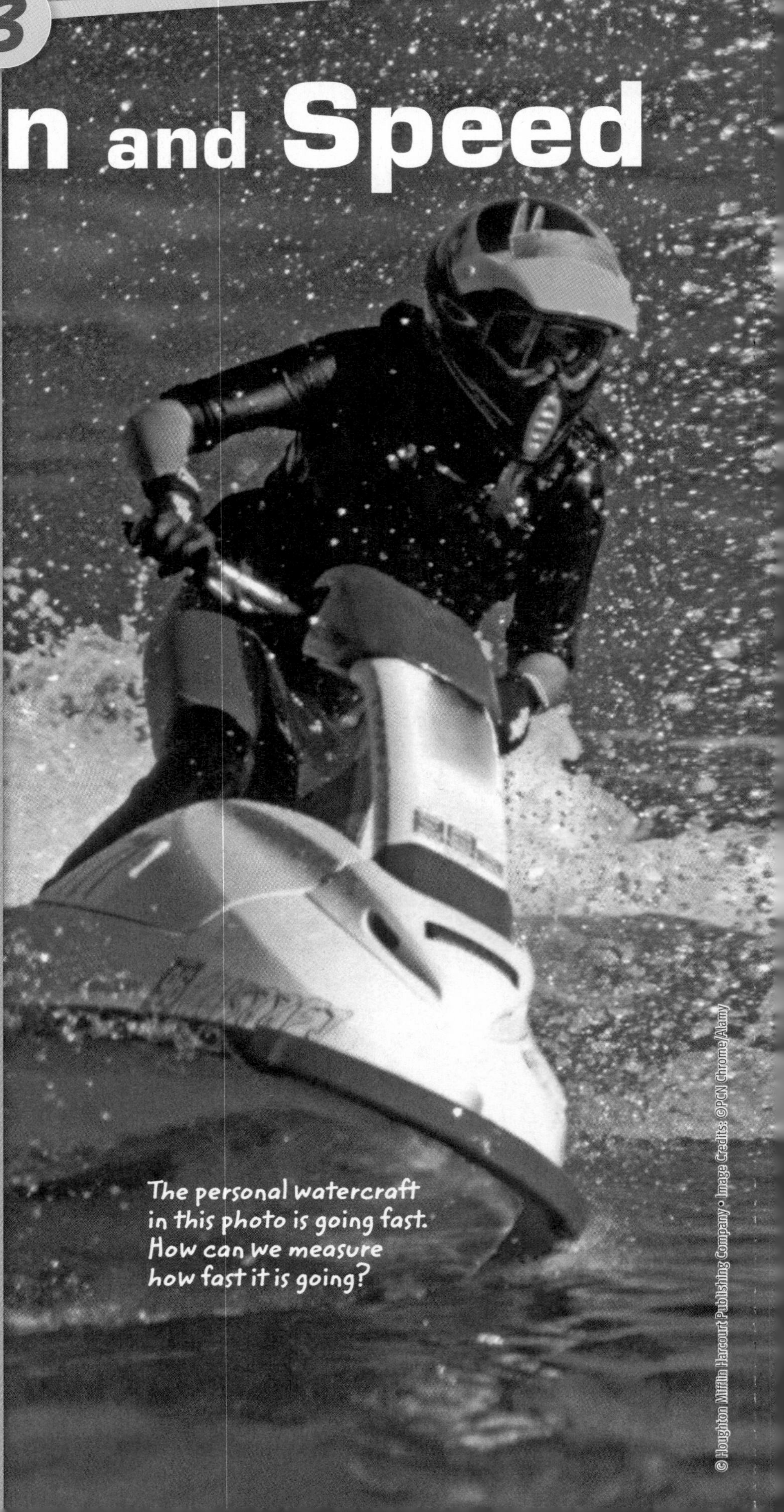

The personal watercraft in this photo is going fast. How can we measure how fast it is going?

OHIO 6.PS.4 An object's motion can be described by its speed and the direction in which it is moving.

OHIO 6.SIA.3 Use appropriate mathematics, tools and techniques to gather data and information.

OHIO 6.SIA.4 Analyze and interpret data.

Lesson Labs

Quick Labs
- Investigate Changing Positions
- Create a Distance-Time Graph

S.T.E.M. Lab
- Investigate Average Speed

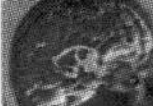

Engage Your Brain

1 Predict Circle the correct words in the paragraph below to make true statements.

A dog usually moves faster than a bug. That means that if I watch them move for one minute, then the dog would have traveled a *greater/smaller* distance than the bug. However, a car usually goes *faster/slower* than a dog. If the car and the dog both traveled to the end of the road, then the *car/dog* would get there first.

2 Explain Draw or sketch something that you might see move. Write a caption that answers the following questions: How would you describe its motion? Is it moving at a constant speed, or does it speed up and slow down?

Active Reading

3 Define Fill in the blank with the word that best completes the following sentences.

If an object changes its position, then it is

____

The speed of a car describes

____

____

Vocabulary Terms

- **position**
- **reference point**
- **motion**
- **speed**
- **vector**
- **velocity**

4 Apply As you learn the definition of each vocabulary term in this lesson, make your own definition or sketch to help you remember the meaning of the term.

Location, location,

How can you describe the location of an object?

Have you ever gotten lost while looking for a specific place? If so, you probably know that the description of the location can be very important. Imagine that you are trying to describe your location to a friend. How would you explain where you are? You need two pieces of information: a position and a reference point.

With a Position

Position describes the location of an object. Often, you describe where something is by comparing its position with where you currently are. For example, you might say that a classmate sitting next to you is two desks to your right, or that a mailbox is two blocks south of where you live. Each time you identify the position of an object, you are comparing the location of the object with the location of another object or place.

With a Reference Point

When you describe a position by comparing it to the location of another object or place, you are using a reference point. A **reference point** is a location to which you compare other locations. In the example above of a mailbox that is two blocks south of where you live, the reference point is "where you live."

Imagine that you are at a zoo with some friends. If you are using the map to the right, you could describe your destination using different reference points. Using yourself as the reference point, you might say that the red panda house is one block east and three blocks north of your current location. Or you might say the red panda house is one block north and one block east of the fountain. In this example, the fountain is your reference point.

Active Reading **5 Apply** How would you describe where this question is located on the page? Give two different answers using two different reference points.

____

____

____

____

location

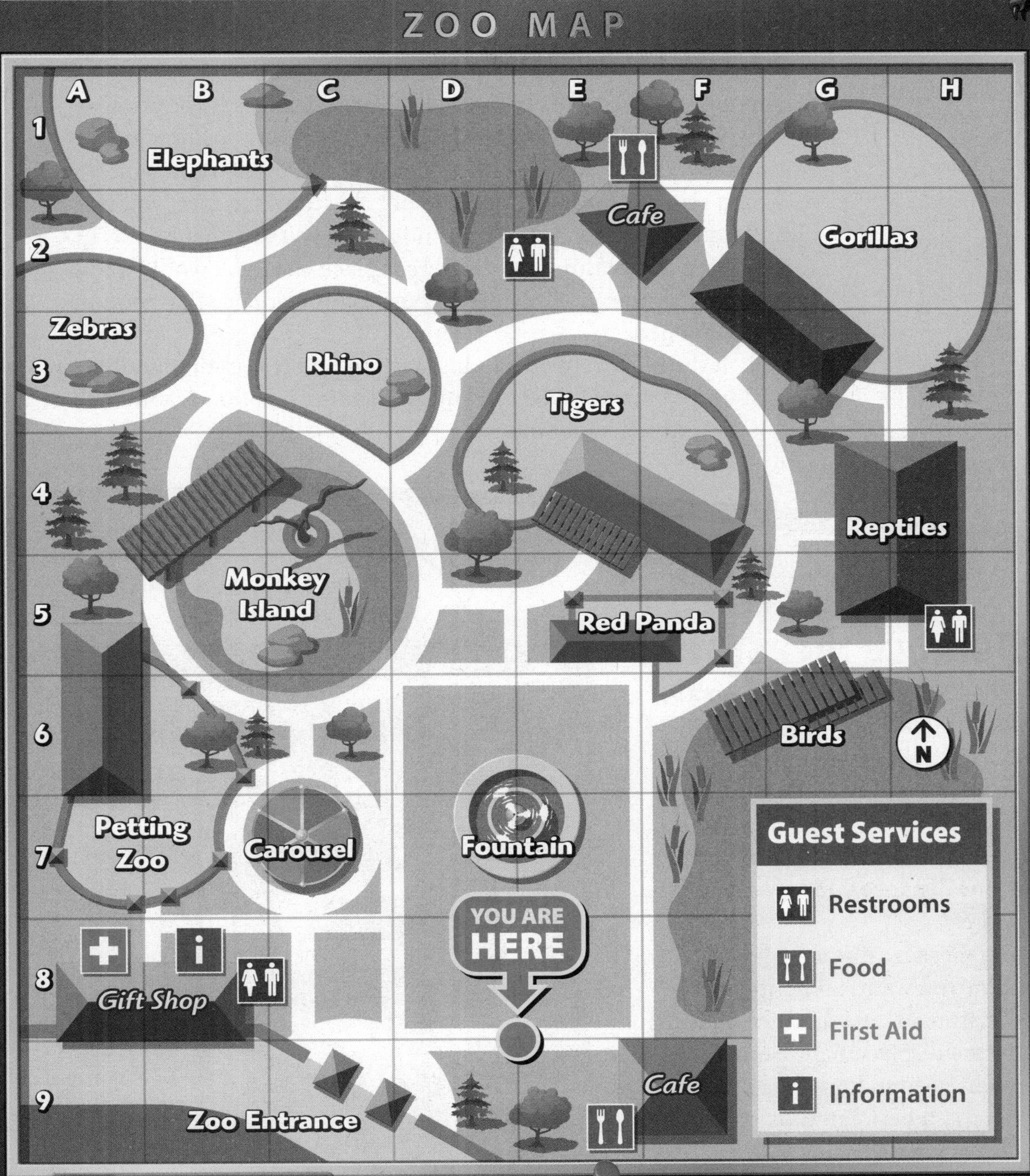

ZOO MAP

A B C D E F G H

1 2 3 4 5 6 7 8 9

Elephants

Zebras

Rhino

Cafe

Gorillas

Tigers

Monkey Island

Reptiles

Red Panda

Birds

N

Petting Zoo

Carousel

Fountain

YOU ARE HERE

Gift Shop

Zoo Entrance

Cafe

Guest Services

- Restrooms
- Food
- First Aid
- Information

Visualize It!

6 Apply One of your friends is at the southeast corner of Monkey Island. He would like to meet you. How would you describe your location to him?

____

____

____

7 Apply You need to go visit the first aid station. How would you describe how to get there?

____

____

____

____

MOVE It!

What is motion?

An object moves, or is in motion, when it changes its position relative to a reference point. **Motion** is a change in position over time. If you were to watch the biker pictured to the right, you would see him move. If you were not able to watch him, you might still know something about his motion. If you saw that he was in one place at one time and a different place later, you would know that he had moved. A change in position is evidence that motion has happened.

If the biker returned to his starting point, you might not know that he had moved. The starting and ending positions cannot tell you everything about motion.

How is distance measured?

Suppose you walk from one building to another building that is several blocks away. If you could walk in a straight line, you might end up 500 meters from where you started. The actual distance you travel, however, would depend on the exact path you take. If you take a route that has many turns, the distance you travel might be 900 meters or more.

The way you measure distance depends on the information you want. Sometimes you want to know the straight-line distance between two positions, or the displacement. Sometimes, however, you might need to know the total length of a certain path between those positions.

When measuring any distances, scientists use a standard unit of measurement. The standard unit of length is the meter (m), which is about 3.3 feet. Longer distances can be measured in kilometers (km), and shorter distances in centimeters (cm). In the United States, distance is often measured in miles (mi), feet (ft), or inches (in).

The distance from point A to point B depends on the path you take.

Visualize It!

8 Illustrate Draw a sample path on the maze that is a different distance than the one in red but still goes from the start point, "A," to the finish point, "B."

This biker is in motion.

What is speed?

A change in an object's position tells you that motion took place, but it does not tell you how quickly the object changed position. The **speed** of an object is a measure of how far something moves in a given amount of time. In other words, speed measures how quickly or slowly the object changes position. In the same amount of time, a faster object would move farther than a slower moving object would.

What is average speed?

The speed of an object is rarely constant. For example, the biker in the photo above may travel quickly when he begins a race but may slow down as he gets tired at the end of the race. *Average speed* is a way to calculate the speed of an object that may not always be moving at a constant speed. Instead of describing the speed of an object at an exact moment in time, average speed describes the speed over a stretch of time.

Active Reading **9 Compare** What is the difference between speed and average speed?

____

____

____

Think Outside the Book Inquiry

10 Analyze Research the top speeds of a cheetah, a race car, and a speed boat. How do they rank in order of speed? Make a poster showing which is fastest and which is slowest. How do the speeds of the fastest human runners compare to the speeds you found?

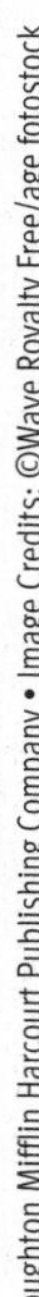

Speed It Up!

How is average speed calculated?

11 Identify As you read, underline sentences that relate distance and time.

Speed can be calculated by dividing the distance an object travels by the time it takes to cover the distance. Speed is shown in the formula as the letter *s*, distance as the letter *d*, and time as the letter *t*. The formula shows how distance, time, and speed are related. If two objects travel the same distance, the object that took a shorter amount of time will have the greater speed. An object with a greater speed will travel a longer distance in the same amount of time than an object with a lower speed will.

The following equation can be used to find average speed:

$$\text{average speed} = \frac{\text{distance}}{\text{time}}$$

$$s = \frac{d}{t}$$

The standard unit for speed is meters per second (m/s). Speed can also be given in kilometers per hour (km/h). In the United States, speeds are often given in miles per hour (mi/h or mph). One mile per hour is equal to 0.45 m/s.

Do the Math **Sample Problem**

A penguin swimming underwater goes 20 meters in 8 seconds. What is its average speed?

Identify

A. What do you know? $d = 20$ m, $t = 8$ s

B. What do you want to find out? average speed

Plan

C. Draw and label a sketch: 20 m / 8 sec

D. Write the formula: $s = d/t$

E. Substitute into the formula: $s = \frac{20 \text{ m}}{8 \text{ s}}$

Solve

F. Calculate and simplify: $s = \frac{20 \text{ m}}{8 \text{ s}} = 2.5 \text{ m/s}$

G. Check that your units agree: Unit is m/s. Unit of speed is distance/time. Units agree.

Answer: 2.5 m/s

Do the Math You Try It

12 Calculate This runner completed a 100-meter race with a time of 13.75 seconds. What was her average speed?

Identify

A. What do you know?

B. What do you want to find out?

Plan

C. Draw and label a sketch:

D. Write the formula:

E. Substitute into the formula:

Solve

F. Calculate and simplify:

G. Check that your units agree:

Answer:

Fast Graphs

How is constant speed graphed?

A convenient way to show the motion of an object is by using a graph that plots the distance the object has traveled against time. This type of graph is called a distance-time graph. You can use it to see how both distance and speed change with time.

How far away the object is from a reference point is plotted on the *y*-axis. So the *y*-axis expresses distance in units such as meters, centimeters, or kilometers. Time is plotted on the *x*-axis, and can display units such as seconds, minutes, or hours. If an object moves at a constant speed, the graph is a straight line.

You can use a distance-time graph to determine the average speed of an object. The slope, or steepness, of the line is equal to the average speed of the object. You calculate the average speed for a time interval by dividing the change in distance by the change in time for that time interval.

Suppose that an ostrich is running at a constant speed. The distance-time graph of its motion is shown below. To calculate the speed of the ostrich, choose two data points from the graph below and calculate the slope of the line. The calculation of the slope is shown below. Since we know that the slope of a line on a distance-time graph is its average speed, then we know that the ostrich's speed is 14 m/s.

How can you calculate slope?

$$\text{slope} = \frac{\text{change in } y}{\text{change in } x} = \frac{140\text{ m} - 70\text{ m}}{10\text{ s} - 5\text{ s}} = \frac{70\text{ m}}{5\text{ s}} = 14\text{ m/s}$$

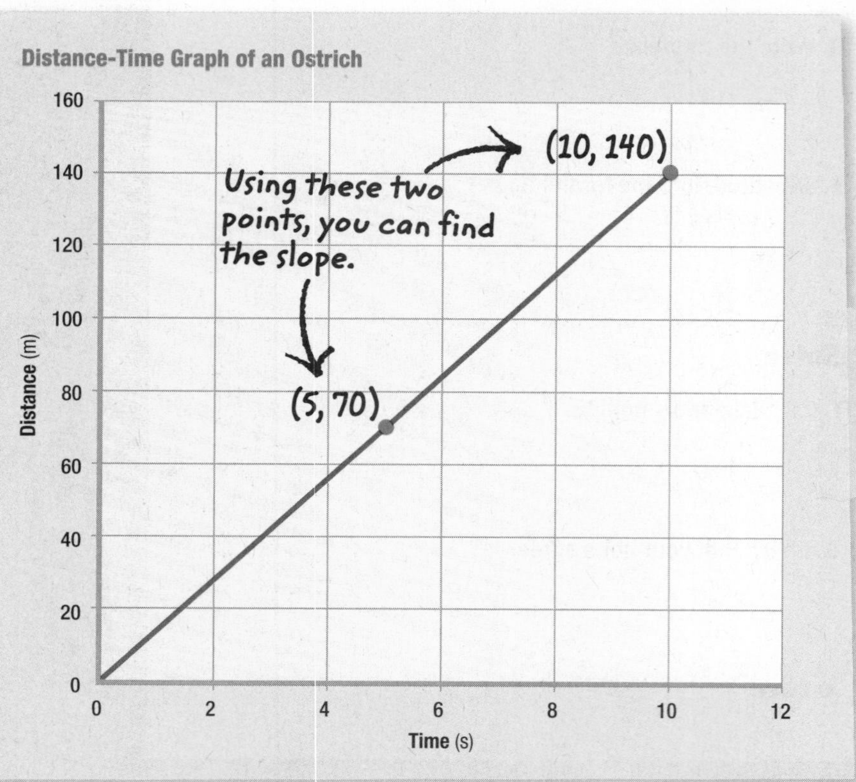

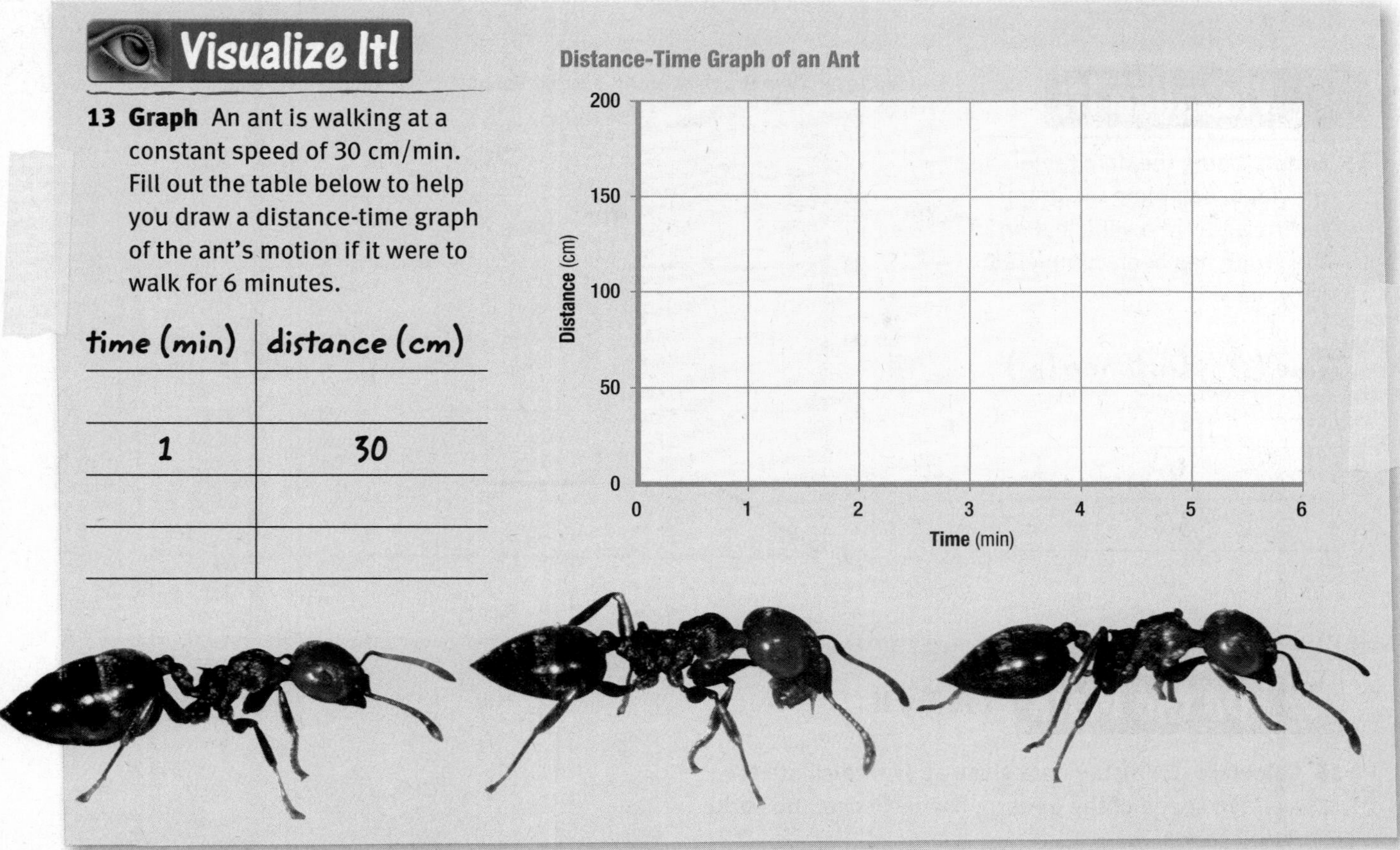

13 Graph An ant is walking at a constant speed of 30 cm/min. Fill out the table below to help you draw a distance-time graph of the ant's motion if it were to walk for 6 minutes.

time (min)	distance (cm)
1	30

How are changing speeds graphed?

Some distance-time graphs show the motion of an object with a changing speed. In these distance-time graphs, the change in the slope of a line indicates that the object has either sped up, slowed down, or stopped.

As an object moves, the distance it travels increases with time. The motion can be seen as a climbing line on the graph. The slope of the line indicates speed. Steeper lines show intervals where the speed is greater than intervals with less steep lines. If the line gets steeper, the object is speeding up. If the line gets less steep, the object is slowing. If the line becomes flat, or horizontal, the object is not moving. In this interval, the speed is zero meters per second.

For objects that change speed, you can calculate speed for a specific interval of time. You would choose two points close together on the graph. Or, you can calculate the average speed over a long interval of time. You would choose two points far apart on the graph to calculate an average over a long interval of time.

Active Reading **14 Analyze** If a line on a distance-time graph becomes steeper, what has happened to the speed of the object? What if it becomes a flat horizontal line?

Visualize It!

15 Graph Using the data table provided, complete the graph for the all-terrain vehicle. Part of the graph has been completed for you.

Time (s)	Distance (m)
1	10
3	10
4	30
5	50

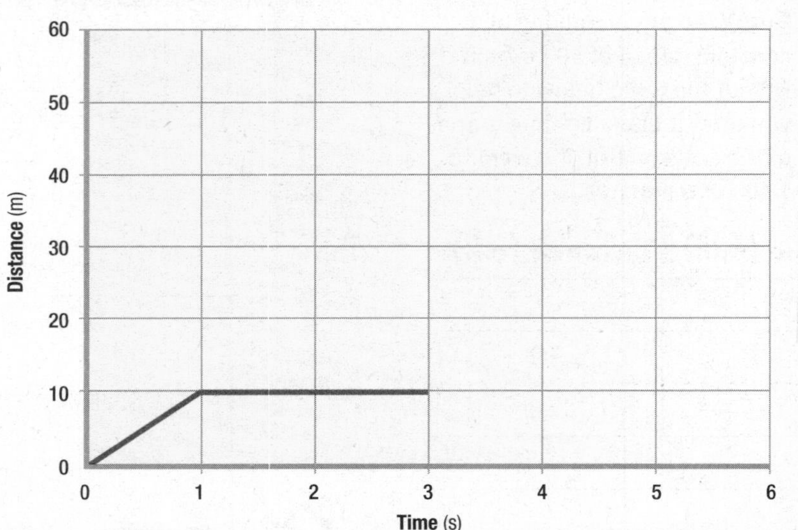

Do the Math You Try It

16 Calculate Using the data given above, calculate the average speed of the all-terrain vehicle over the entire five seconds.

Identify

A. What do you know?

B. What do you want to find out?

Plan

C. Draw and label a sketch:

D. Write the formula:

E. Substitute into the formula:

Solve

F. Calculate and simplify:

G. Check that your units agree:

Answer:

What would the distance-time graph of this ATV's motion look like?

Follow Directions

What is velocity?

Suppose that two birds start from the same place and fly at 10 km/h for 5 minutes. Why might they not end up at the same place? Because the birds were flying in different directions! There are times when the direction of motion must be included in a measurement. A **vector** is a quantity that has both size and direction.

In the example above, the birds' speeds were the same, but their velocities were different. **Velocity** [vuh•LAHS•ih•tee] is speed in a specific direction. If a police officer gives a speeding ticket for a car traveling 100 km/h, the ticket does not list a velocity. But it would list a velocity if it described the car traveling south at 100 km/h.

Because velocity includes direction, it is possible for two objects to have the same speed but different velocities. In the picture to the right, the chair lifts are going the same speed but in opposite directions: some people are going up the mountain while others are going down the mountain.

Average velocity is calculated in a different way than average speed. Average speed depends on the total distance traveled along a path. Average velocity depends on the straight-line distance from the starting point to the final point, or the displacement. A chair lift might carry you up the mountain at an average speed of 5 km/h, giving you an average velocity of 5 km/h north. After a round-trip ride, your average traveling speed would still be 5 km/h. Your average velocity, however, would be 0 km/h because you ended up exactly where you started.

These chair lifts have opposite velocities because they are going at the same speed but in opposite directions.

17 Compare Fill in the Venn diagram to compare and contrast speed and velocity.

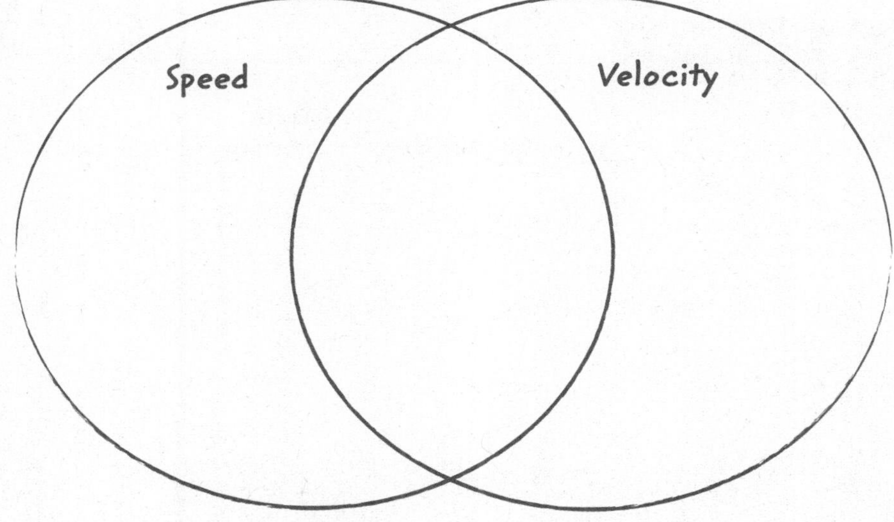

Visual Summary

To complete this summary, check the box that indicates true or false. Then use the key below to check your answers. You can use this page to review the main concepts of the lesson.

Motion is a change in position over time.

T F

18 ☐ ☐ A reference point is a location to which you compare other locations.

19 ☐ ☐ Distance traveled does not depend on the path you take.

Speed measures how far something moves in a given amount of time.

$$s = \frac{d}{t}$$

T F

20 ☐ ☐ To calculate speed, you first need to find the mass of an object.

21 ☐ ☐ Average speed is a way to describe the speed of an object that may not always be moving at a constant speed.

Motion and Speed

A distance-time graph plots the distance traveled by an object and the time it takes to travel that distance.

T F

22 ☐ ☐ In the graph at the right, the object is moving at a constant speed.

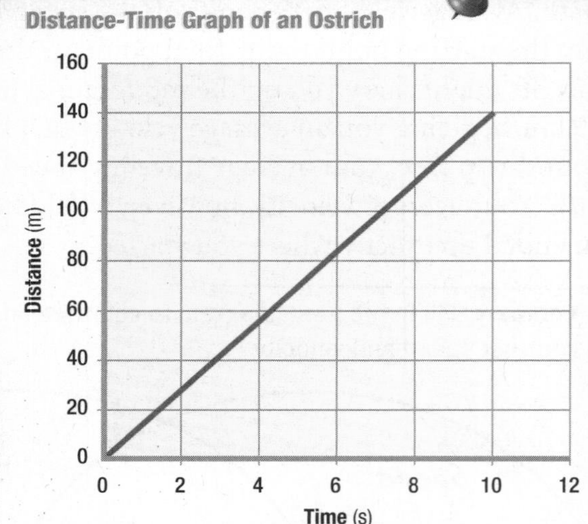

Answers: 18 T; 19 F; 20 F; 21 T; 22 T

23 Predict Amy and Ellie left school at the same time. Amy lives farther away than Ellie, but she and Ellie arrived at their homes at the same time. Compare the girls' speeds.

Lesson Review

Vocabulary

Draw a line to connect the following terms to their definitions.

1 velocity	**A** describes the location of an object
2 reference point	**B** speed in a specific direction
3 speed	**C** a location to which you compare other locations
4 position	**D** a measure of how far something moves in a given amount of time

Key Concepts

5 Describe What information do you need to describe an object's location?

6 Predict How would decreasing the time it takes you to run a certain distance affect your speed?

7 Calculate Juan lives 100 m away from Bill. What is Juan's average speed if he reaches Bill's home in 50 s?

8 Describe What do you need to know to describe the velocity of an object?

Use this graph to answer the following questions.

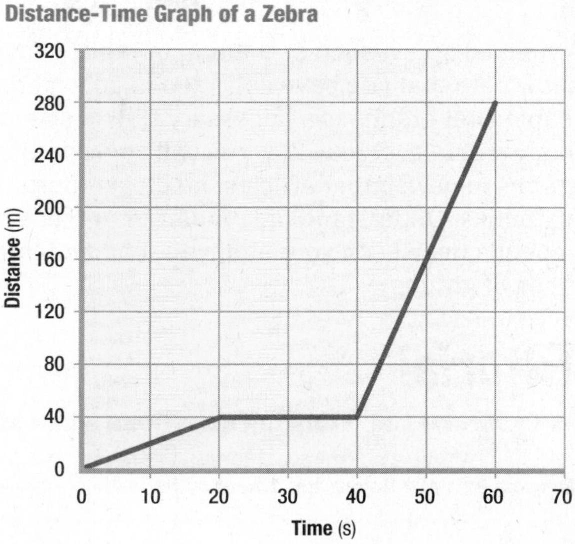

Distance-Time Graph of a Zebra

9 Analyze When is the zebra in motion? When is it not moving?

In motion: __________

Not moving: __________

10 Calculate What is the average speed of the zebra during the time between 0 s and 40 s?

Critical Thinking

11 Apply Look around you to find an object in motion. Describe the object's motion by discussing its position and direction of motion in relation to a reference point. Then explain how you could determine the object's speed.

OHIO 6.SIA.4 Analyze and interpret data.

OHIO 6.SIA.5 Develop descriptions, models, explanations and predictions.

OHIO 6.SIA.8 Communicate scientific procedures and explanations.

Interpreting Graphs

A visual display, such as a graph or table, is a useful way to show data that you have collected in an experiment. The ability to interpret graphs is a necessary skill in science, and it is also important in everyday life. You will come across various types of graphs in newspaper articles, medical reports, and, of course, textbooks. Understanding a report or article's message often depends heavily on your ability to read and interpret different types of graphs.

Tutorial

Ask yourself the following questions when studying a graph.

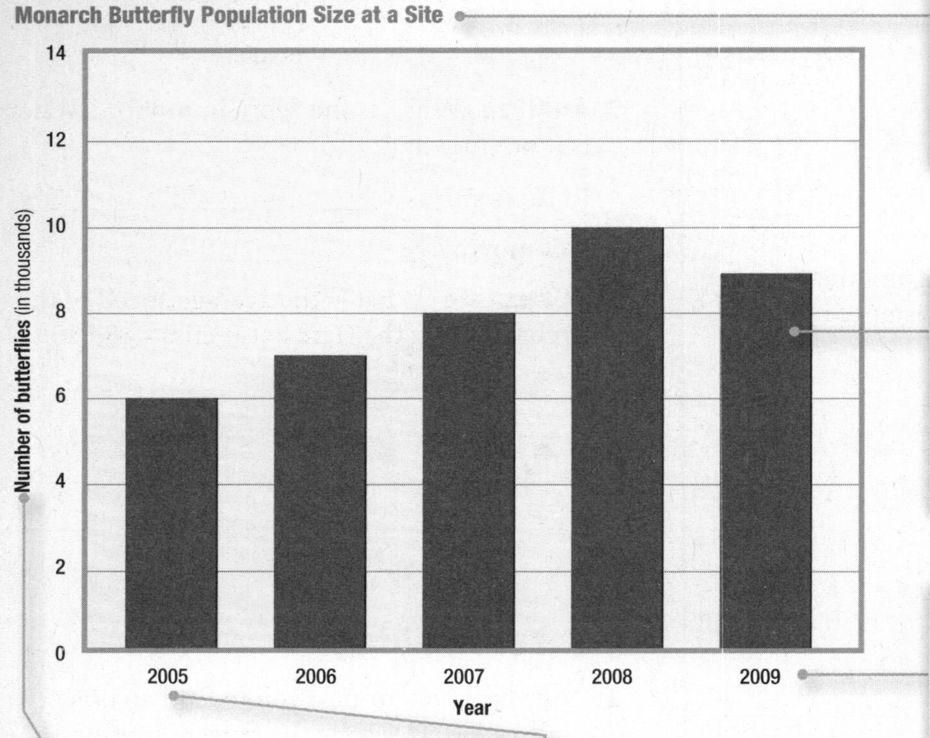

What is the title of the graph? Reading the title can tell you the subject or main idea of the graph. The subject here is monarch butterfly population size.

What type of graph is it? Bar graphs, like the one here, are useful for comparing categories or total values. The lengths of the bars are proportional to the value they represent.

Do you notice any trends in the graph? After you understand what the graph is about, look for patterns. For example, here the monarch butterfly population increased each year from 2005 to 2008. But in 2009, the monarch butterfly population decreased.

What are the labels and headings in the graph? What is on each axis of the graph? Here, the vertical axis shows the population in thousands. Each bar represents a different year from 2005 to 2009. So from 2005 to 2009, the monarch butterfly population ranged from 6,000 to 10,000.

Can you describe the data in the graph? Data can be numbers or text. Analyze the information you read at specific data points. For example, the graph here tells us that there were 6,000 monarch butterflies in 2005.

You Try It!

A member of your research group has made the graph shown below about an object in motion. Study the graph, then answer the questions that follow.

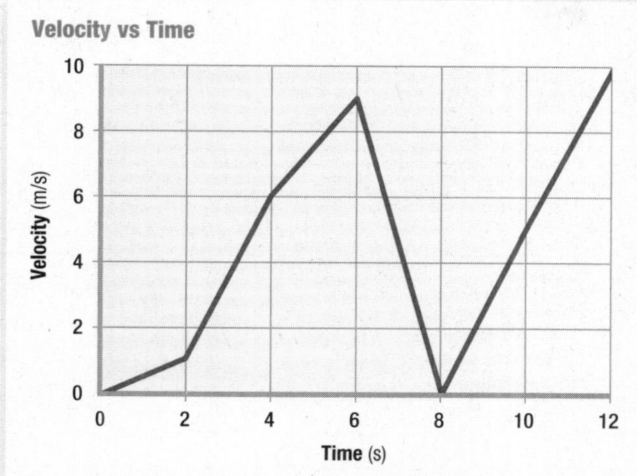

1 Interpreting Graphs Study the graph shown above. Identify the title of this graph, the *x*-axis, the *y*-axis, and the type of graph.

A title of graph ______________________

B *x*-axis ______________________

C *y*-axis ______________________

D type of graph ______________________

2 Identify Study the graph shown above and record the velocity at the indicated times.

Time (s)	Velocity (m/s)
2	
4	
6	
8	
10	

3 Using Graphs Use the graph to answer the following questions.

A What is the approximate velocity of the object at 5 seconds?

____

B During what time interval is the object slowing down? Explain how you can tell.

____

C At what time or times was the velocity of the object about 4 m/s?

____

4 Communicating Results In a short paragraph, describe the motion of the object.

____

Take It Home

Find a newspaper or magazine article that has a graph. What type of graph is it? Study the graph and determine its main message. Bring the graph to class and be prepared to discuss your interpretation of the graph.

My Notes

Unit 5 **Big Idea**

Energy can be categorized as kinetic energy, which is related to the motion of an object, or potential energy, which is related to the position of an object.

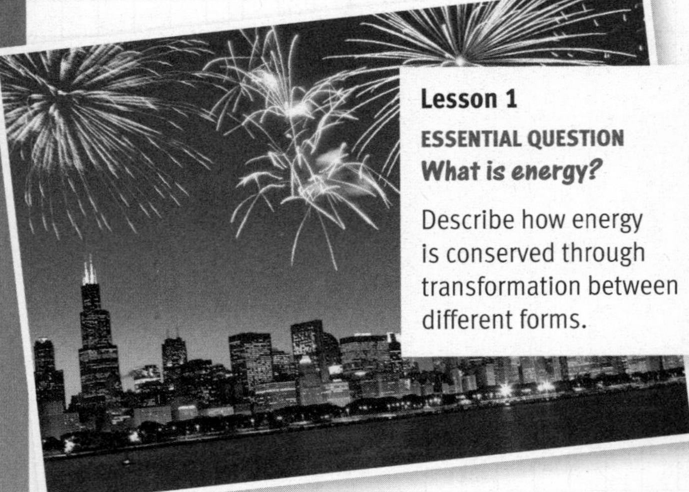

Lesson 1

ESSENTIAL QUESTION

What is energy?

Describe how energy is conserved through transformation between different forms.

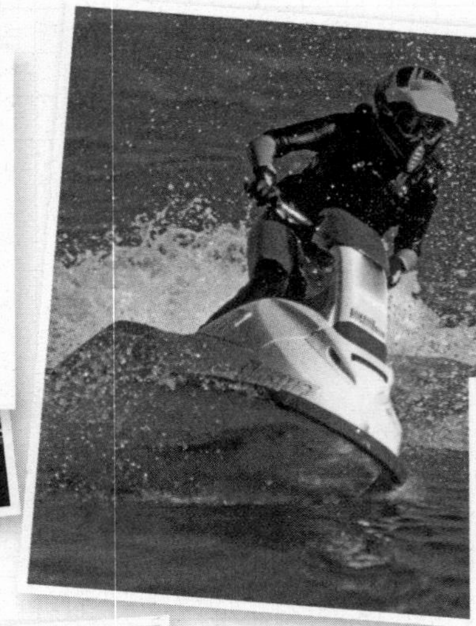

Lesson 3

ESSENTIAL QUESTION

How are distance, time, and speed related?

Analyze how distance, time, and speed are related.

Lesson 2

ESSENTIAL QUESTION

How are thermal energy and temperature related?

Relate the thermal energy and temperature of a substance to the kinetic energy of its particles.

Connect ESSENTIAL QUESTIONS

Lessons 1 and 2

1 Synthesize Give an example of an energy transformation that results in a temperature change.

____

____

____

____

____

____

Think Outside the Book

2 Synthesize Choose one of these activities to help synthesize what you have learned in this unit.

☐ Using what you learned in lessons 1 and 2, explain the movement of particles in a cold glass as energy is transferred to it from warm hands by making a poster presentation. Include captions and labels.

☐ Using what you learned in lessons 1, 2, and 3, create a presentation that describes how energy and motion relate to temperature.

Unit 5 Review

Name ______________________________

Vocabulary

Fill in the blank with the term that best completes the sentence.

1 The ____________________ of an object describes the speed and the direction in which it is going.

2 A vector is a quantity that has both size and ____________________.

3 The ____________________ theory of matter states that all of the particles that make up matter are constantly in motion.

4 ____________________ is the sum of an object's kinetic and potential energy.

5 ____________________ is the total amount of kinetic energy present in the particles of a substance.

Key Concepts

Choose the letter of the best answer.

6 Joanna's family drove 360 km on a trip. The graph below represents their motion.

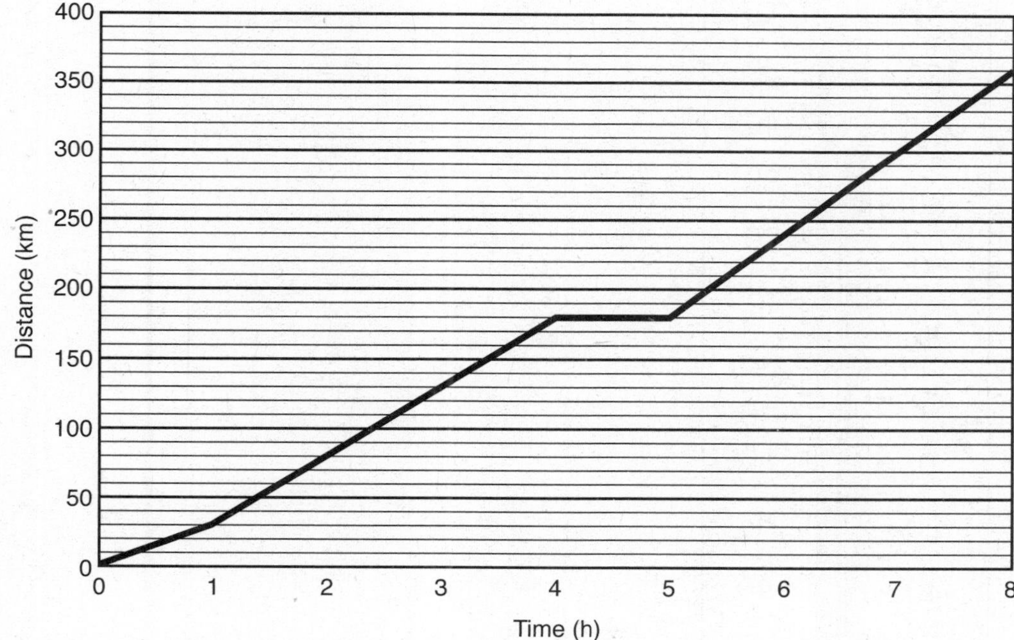

What was the average speed during the last 3 h of the trip?

A 45 km/h

B 60 km/h

C 120 km/h

D 180 km/h

7 An airplane leaves New York to fly to Los Angeles. It travels 3,850 km in 5.5 hours. What is the average speed of the airplane?

A 700 km

B 700 hours

C 700 km/hour

D 7,000 hours/km

8 A person flips a switch to turn on a lamp. Instantly, light is produced. What is one other form of energy that the person should expect to observe from the lamp?

A sound

B nuclear

C thermal

D chemical

9 The thermometer in the figure below shows the temperature on both the Fahrenheit scale and the Celsius scale.

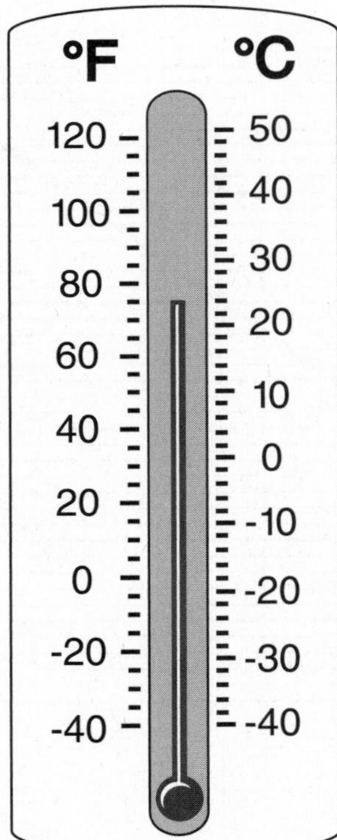

What temperature does the thermometer show on the Fahrenheit scale?

A 70 °F

B 75 °F

C 80 °F

D 85 °F

10 A student collects and records the following data throughout the day.

Time	Temperature (°C)
9 a.m.	12
11 a.m.	14
3 p.m.	16
5 p.m.	13

Which instrument did the student use to collect the temperature data?

A scale

B balance

C barometer

D thermometer

11 A mass hanging from a spring moves up and down. The mass stops moving temporarily each time the spring is extended to its fullest at Position 2 and each time it returns to its tight coil at Position 4.

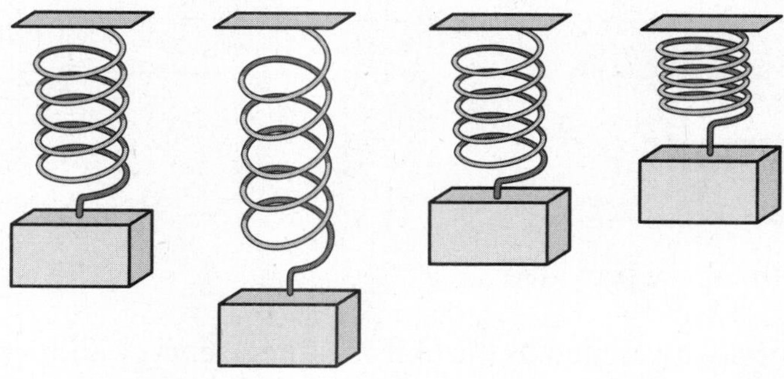

Which answer choice best describes the type of energy the spring has at Position 1?

A kinetic energy

B potential energy

C both potential energy and kinetic energy

D neither potential energy or kinetic energy

Critical Thinking

Answer the following questions in the spaces provided.

12 Substances freeze and boil at different temperatures. What are the freezing and boiling points of water on the Kelvin scale? The temperature of a substance is 75 K. How much higher or lower is this than the freezing point of water and from the boiling point of water?

13 Describe the law of conservation of energy. Give two examples of energy being transformed from one type to another.

Connect ESSENTIAL QUESTIONS

Lessons 1 and 3

Answer the following question in the space provided.

14 How are an object's speed and velocity related to the object's kinetic energy and total mechanical energy?

UNIT 6

Matter

Big Idea

Atoms are the basic building blocks of matter, and their motion determines the state of matter of the substance.

What do you think?

A large iceberg floats in water, but an anchor sinks. What is different about these two objects that causes them to behave differently in water?

Unit 6

Matter

CITIZEN SCIENCE

Deep Freeze

When outdoor temperatures reach 0 °C (32 °F), liquid water can freeze to form a solid. Snow, ice, sleet, and hail are examples of the solid form of water. Understanding the properties of water in its different states helps people to stay safe during icy weather.

1 Think About It

How is liquid water different from solid ice?

____

____

____

____

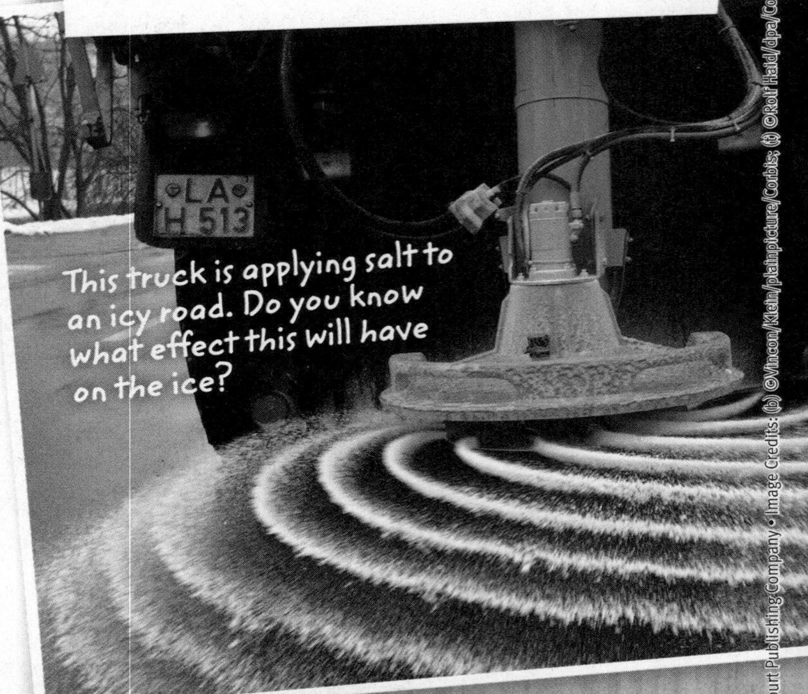

This truck is applying salt to an icy road. Do you know what effect this will have on the ice?

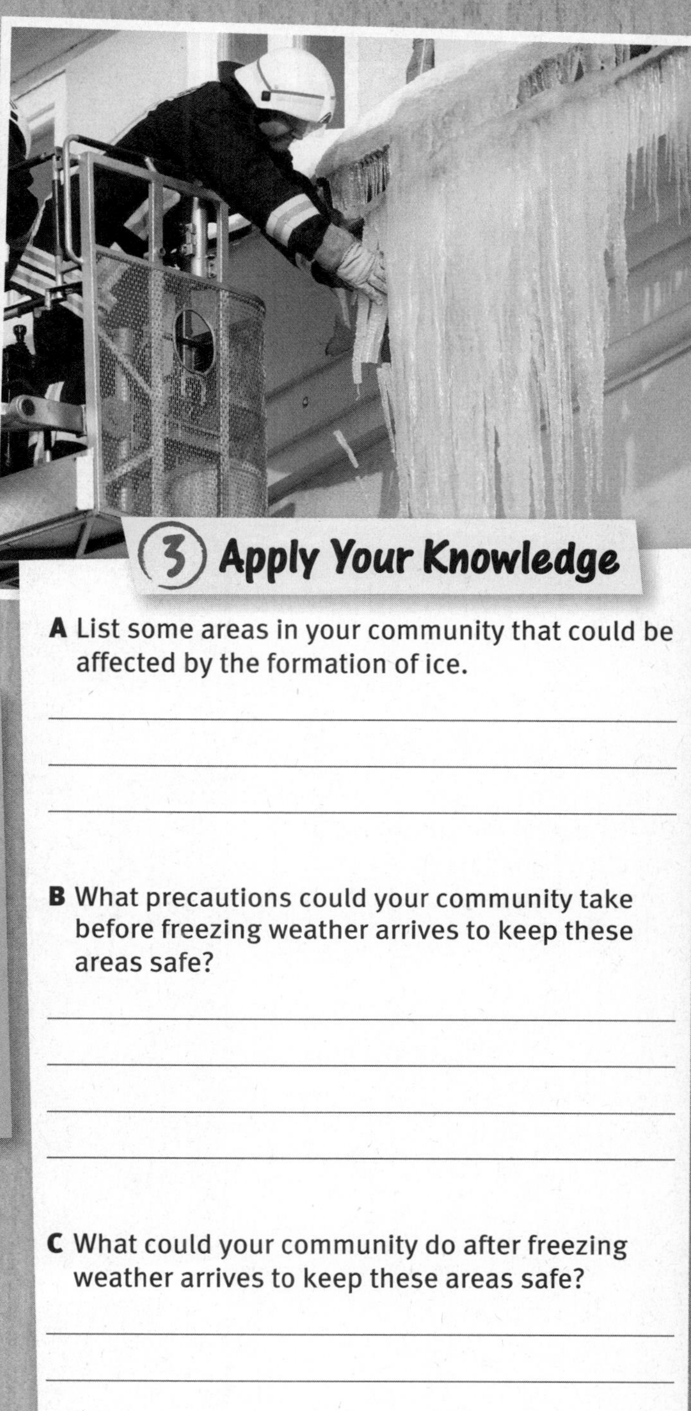

2 Ask A Question

What precautions should be taken during freezing weather?

Would you believe that the ice on these fruit trees is actually protecting them? The trees are being sprayed with water, which turns to ice in freezing weather. The formation of ice helps to keep the plants warmer. With a partner, research some of the ways in which people protect other areas and living things during icy weather.

Think about the impact that ice could have on

- ✓ plants
- ✓ people
- ✓ bodies of water
- ✓ pets and other animals

3 Apply Your Knowledge

A List some areas in your community that could be affected by the formation of ice.

____

____

____

B What precautions could your community take before freezing weather arrives to keep these areas safe?

____

____

____

____

C What could your community do after freezing weather arrives to keep these areas safe?

____

____

____

____

Take It Home

How do you prepare your home for icy weather? Draw a map of your home and the surrounding area. Identify areas on your map that could become hazardous in freezing conditions. Then, create a plan for protecting these areas.

Lesson 1

Introduction to Matter

ESSENTIAL QUESTION

What properties define matter?

By the end of this lesson, you should be able to relate mass, weight, volume, and density to one another.

Hot air takes balloons aloft because hot air is less dense than the cooler air around it.

OHIO 6.PS.1 All matter is made up of small particles called atoms.

OHIO 6.SIA.3 Use appropriate mathematics, tools and techniques to gather data and information.

OHIO 6.SIA.4 Analyze and interpret data.

Lesson Labs

Quick Labs
- Mass and Weight
- Finding Volume by Displacement
- How Much Mass?

Exploration Lab
- Comparing Buoyancy

Engage Your Brain

1 Describe Fill in the blank with the word or phrase that you think correctly completes the following sentences.

A(n) ____________________ can hold a greater volume of water than a mug.

A hamster weighs less than a(n) ____________________.

A bowling ball is harder to lift than a basketball because ____________________.

2 Explain List some similarities and differences between the golf ball on the left and the table-tennis ball on the right in the photo below.

Active Reading

3 Apply Many scientific words, such as *matter*, also have everyday meanings. Use context clues to write your own definition for each meaning of the word *matter*.

Example sentence
What is this gooey matter on the table?

Matter:

Example sentence
Please vote! Your opinions matter.

Matter:

Vocabulary Terms

- **matter**
- **mass**
- **weight**
- **volume**
- **density**

4 Identify This list contains the vocabulary terms you'll learn in this lesson. As you read, circle the definition of each term.

What's the MATTER?

What is matter?

Suppose your class takes a field trip to a museum. During the course of the day you see mammoth bones, sparkling crystals, hot-air balloons, and an astronaut's space suit. All of these things are matter.

As you will see, **matter** is anything that has mass and takes up space. Your body is matter. The air that you breathe and the water that you drink are also matter. Matter makes up the materials around you.

However, not everything is matter. Light and sound, for example, are not matter. Light does not take up space or have mass in the same way that a table does. Although air is matter, a sound traveling through air is not.

Active Reading **5 Explain** How can you tell if something is matter?

____

____

____

Visualize It!

6 Identify Name three examples of matter found in this photo.

____

____

____

What is mass?

You cannot always tell how much matter is in an object simply by observing the object's size. But you *can* measure the object's mass. **Mass** describes the amount of matter in an object.

Compare the two balloons at the right. The digital scales show that the balloon filled with compressed air has a greater mass than the other balloon. This is because the compressed air adds mass to the balloon. Air may seem to be made of nothing, but it has mass. The readings on the scale are in grams (g). A gram is the unit of mass you will use most often in science class.

Objects that are the same size can be made up of different amounts of matter. For example, a large sponge is about the same size as a brick. But the brick contains more matter. Therefore, the brick has a greater mass than the sponge.

The readings on these digital scales show that all matter, even air, has mass.

How does mass differ from weight?

The words *weight* and *mass* are often used as though they mean the same thing, but they do not. **Weight** is a measure of the gravitational force (grav•ih•TAY•shuhn•uhl FAWRS) on an object. Gravitational force keeps objects on Earth from floating into space. The gravitational force between an object and Earth depends partly on the object's mass. The greater that the mass of an object is, the greater the gravitational force on the object will be and the greater the object's weight will be.

An object's weight can change depending on the object's location. For example, you would weigh less on the moon than you do on Earth because the moon has less mass—and therefore exerts less gravitational force—than Earth does. However, you would have the same mass in both places. An object's mass does not change unless the amount of matter in an object changes.

Active Reading **7 Explain** Why do astronauts weigh less on the moon than they do on Earth?

____

____

The weight of this dachshund on the moon is about one-sixth of its weight on Earth.

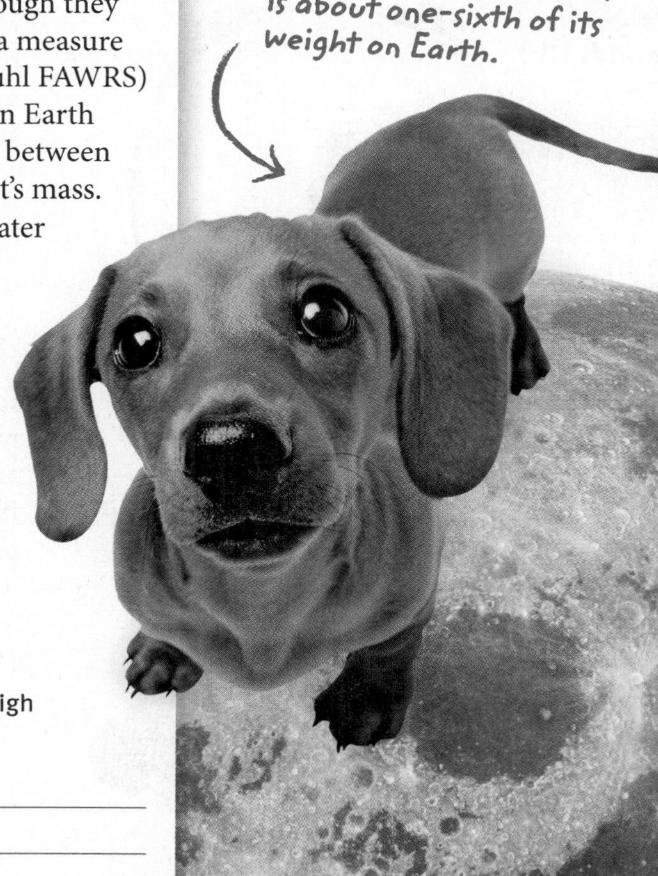

Visualize It!

The balance below works by moving the masses on the right along the beams until they "balance" the pan on the left. Moving the masses changes the amount of force the levers exert on the pan. The more massive the object on the pan, the more force will be needed on the levers to balance the two sides.

8 Infer Would this balance give the same value for mass if used on the moon? Explain.

____

____

____

____

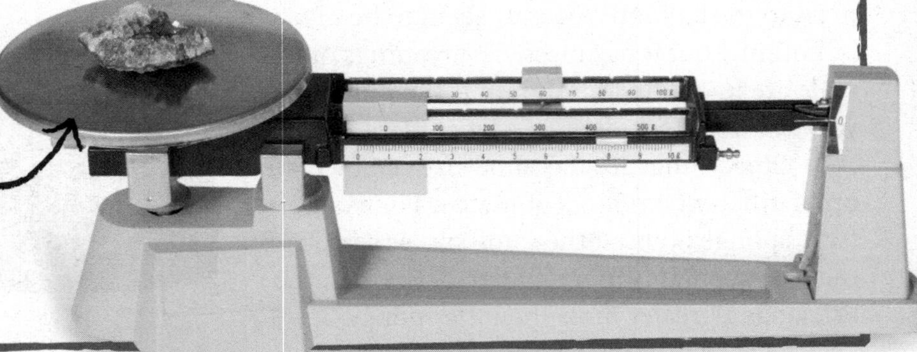

A triple-beam balance can be used to measure the mass of small objects such as this geode fragment.

The spring scale gives weight in pounds (lb).

How are mass and weight measured?

Mass is often measured by using a triple-beam balance such as the one shown above. The balance compares an object's mass to known standards of mass called *countermasses.* The countermasses slide across each of three beams. When the countermasses balance the mass of the object in the balance pan, the pointer will rest at 0. Then, the mass can be read from the position of the countermasses on the beams.

Weight is measured with devices such as the spring scale shown at the left. The spring measures the force between the mass in the pan and Earth. The more massive the object placed in the pan, the more forceful is the attraction between it and Earth, and the more the spring will stretch. Greater stretch means greater weight.

Because weight is a measure of gravitational force, it is given in units of force. You probably are most familiar with weight given in pounds (lb), like the units shown on the scale. The standard scientific unit for weight, however, is the newton (N). A 100-g mass weighs approximately 1 N on Earth. One newton is about one-fourth of a pound.

Measuring Space

How is the amount of space occupied by matter measured?

All matter takes up space. The amount of space that an object takes up, or occupies, is known as the object's **volume.**

Objects with the similar volumes do not always have the same mass. In the photos, the bowling ball and the balloon have about the same volume, but the bowling ball contains a lot more mass than the balloon. You know this because the bowling ball weighs much more than the balloon. The different masses take up about the same amount of space, so both objects have about the same volume.

Active Reading **9 Define** What does volume measure?

____

____

The bowling ball has a lot more mass than the balloon.

The balloon is similar in volume but has much less mass than the bowling ball.

Think Outside the Book Inquiry

10 Infer Big things can look very small when seen from far away. Describe how you know big things far away aren't really small.

How can volume be determined?

There are different ways to find the volume of an object. For objects that have well-defined shapes, you can take a few measurements and calculate the volume using a formula. For objects that are irregularly shaped, such as a rock, you can use water displacement to measure volume. For liquids, you can use a graduated cylinder.

Using a Formula

Some objects have well-defined shapes. For these objects, the easiest way to find their volume is to measure the dimensions of the object and use a formula. Different shapes use different volume formulas. For example, to find the volume of a rectangular box, you would use a different formula than if you were to find the volume of a spherical ball.

The volume of a solid is measured in units of length cubed. For example, if you measure the length, width, and height of a box in centimeters (cm), the volume of the box has units of centimeters multiplied by centimeters multiplied by centimeters, or cubic centimeters (cm^3). In order to calculate volume, make sure that all the measurements are in the same units.

To find the volume of a rectangular box, use the following formula:

Volume = (length)(width)(height)

$V = lwh$

Sample Problem

Find the volume of the lunch box.

Identify

A. What do you know?

length = 25 cm, width = 18 cm, height = 10 cm

B. What do you want to find? Volume

Plan

C. Draw and label a sketch:

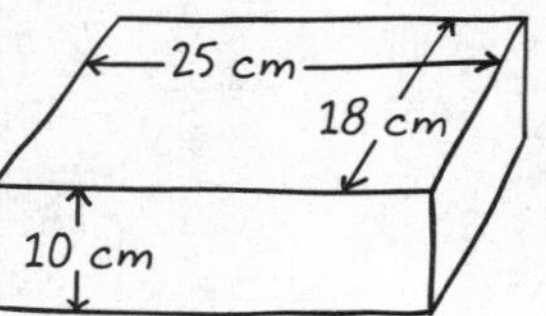

D. Write the formula: $V = lwh$

E. Substitute into the formula: $V = (25 \text{ cm})(18 \text{ cm})(10 \text{ cm})$

Solve

F. Multiply: $(25 \text{ cm})(18 \text{ cm})(10 \text{ cm}) = 4{,}500 \text{ cm}^3$

G. Check that your units agree: The given units are centimeters, and the measure found is volume. Therefore, the units should be cm^3. The units agree.

Answer: $4{,}500 \text{ cm}^3$

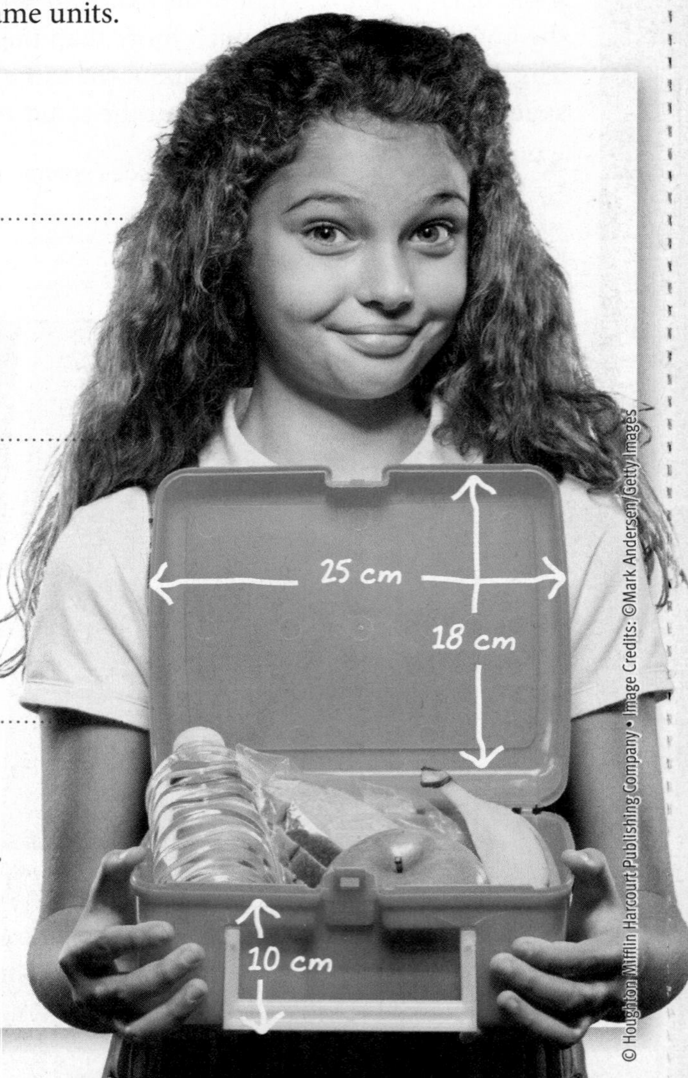

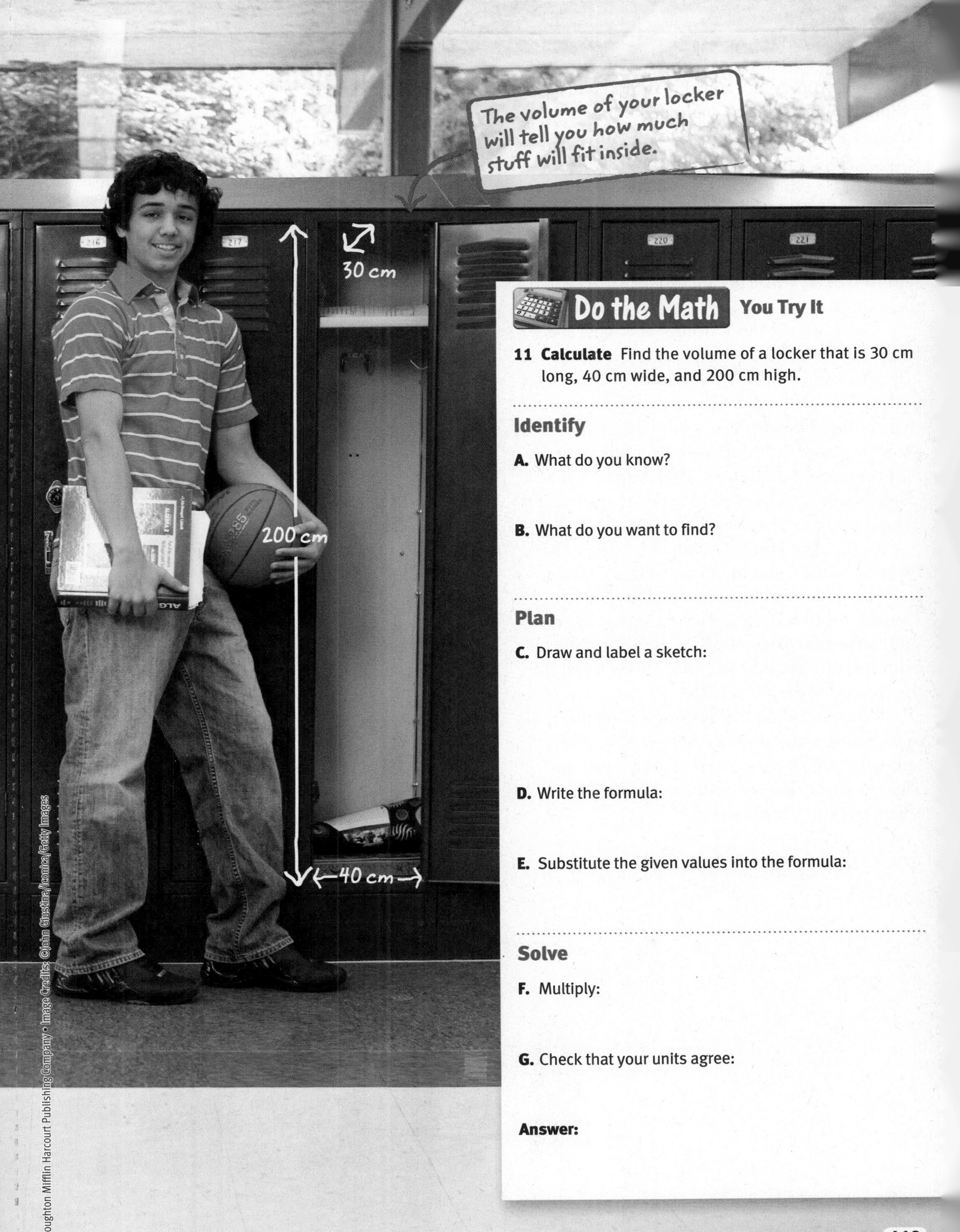
The volume of your locker will tell you how much stuff will fit inside.
30 cm
200 cm
40 cm

Do the Math You Try It

11 Calculate Find the volume of a locker that is 30 cm long, 40 cm wide, and 200 cm high.

Identify

A. What do you know?

B. What do you want to find?

Plan

C. Draw and label a sketch:

D. Write the formula:

E. Substitute the given values into the formula:

Solve

F. Multiply:

G. Check that your units agree:

Answer:

Using Water Displacement

In the lab, you can use a beaker or graduated cylinder to measure the volume of liquids. Graduated cylinders are used to measure liquid volume when accuracy is important. The volume of liquids is often expressed in liters (L) or milliliters (mL). Milliliters and cubic centimeters are equivalent; in other words, 1 mL = 1 cm^3. The volume of any amount of liquid, from one raindrop to an entire ocean, can be expressed in these units.

Two objects cannot occupy the same space at the same time. For example, as a builder stacks bricks to build a wall, she adds each brick on top of the other. No brick can occupy the same place that another brick occupies. Similarly, when an object is placed in water, the object pushes some of the water out of the way. This process, called *displacement*, can be used to measure the volume of an irregularly shaped solid object.

In the photos at the right, you can see that the level of the water in the graduated cylinder has risen after the chess piece is placed inside. The volume of water displaced is found by subtracting the original volume in the graduated cylinder from the new volume. This is equal to the volume of the chess piece.

When deciding the units of the volume found using water displacement, it is helpful to remember that 1 mL of water is equal to 1 cm^3. Therefore, you can report the volume of the object in cubic centimeters.

You Try It

12 Calculate The two images below show a graduated cylinder filled with water before and after a chess piece is placed inside. Use the images to calculate the volume of the chess piece.

Volume without chess piece = ___________

Volume with chess piece = ___________

Volume of chess piece = ___________

Don't forget to check the units of volume of the chess piece!

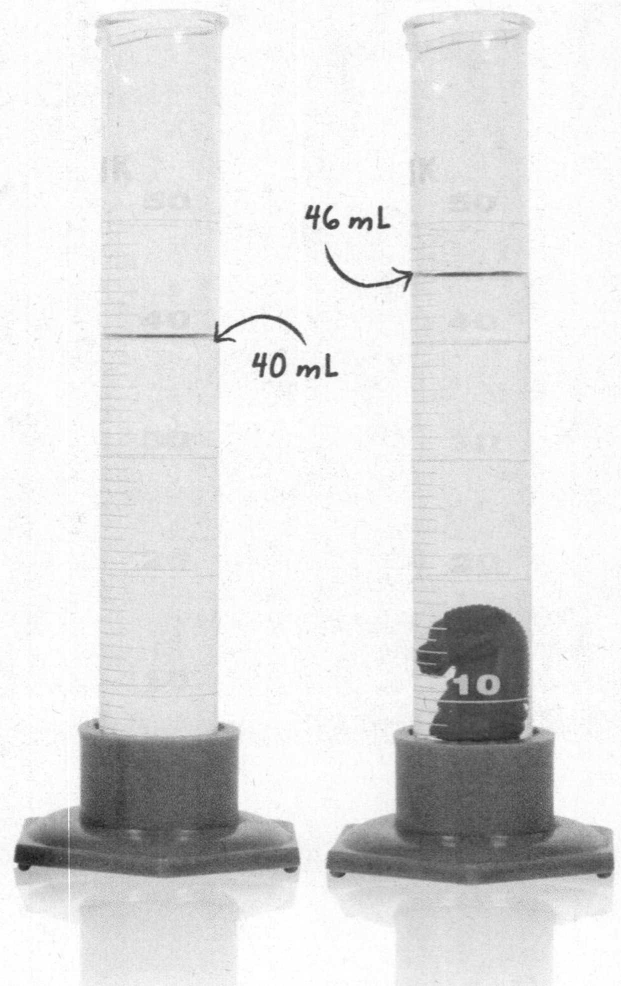

Packing It In!

What is density?

Mass and volume are properties of all substances. These two properties are related to another property called density (DEN•sih•tee). **Density** is a measure of the amount of mass in a given volume. Objects containing the same amount of mass can take up different amounts of space. For example, the pile of feathers above takes up more space than the tomato. But they have the same mass. This is because the tomato is more dense. The tomato has more mass in a smaller space.

The density of a given substance remains the same no matter how much of the substance you have. For example, if you divide a piece of clay in half, both halves will have the same density as the original piece.

The tomato and the pile of feathers have similar masses, but the tomato has less volume. This means that the tomato is more dense.

Active Reading

13 Explain What is density?

____

____

____

14 Predict Circle the item in each pair that is more dense.

Golf ball	Empty milk carton	Foam ball
Table-tennis ball	Milk carton full of milk	Baseball

How is density determined?

Units for density consist of a mass unit divided by a volume unit. Units that are often used for density are grams per cubic centimeter (g/cm^3) for solids, and grams per milliliter (g/mL) for liquids. In other words, density is the mass in grams divided by the volume in cubic centimeters or milliliters.

To find an object's density (*D*), find its mass (*m*) and its volume (*V*). Then, use the given formula to calculate the density of the object.

$$D = \frac{m}{V}$$

The density of water is 1 g/mL (g/cm^3). Any object with a density greater than 1 g/mL will sink in water and with a density less than 1 g/mL will float. Density, therefore, can be a useful thing to know. The sample problem below shows how to calculate the density of a volcanic rock called pumice.

Pumice and obsidian are two igneous volcanic rocks with very different densities.

Do the Math

Sample Problem

Pumice is an igneous volcanic rock, formed by the rapid cooling of lava. What is the density of a 49.8 g piece of pumice that has a volume of 83 cm^3?

Identify

A. What do you know?

mass = 49.8 g, volume = 83 cm^3

B. What do you want to find? Density

Plan

C. Write the formula: $D = \frac{m}{V}$

D. Substitute the given values into the formula:

$$D = \frac{49.8 \text{ g}}{83 \text{ cm}^3}$$

Solve

E. Divide: $\frac{49.8 \text{ g}}{83 \text{ cm}^3} = 0.6 \text{ g/cm}^3$

F. Check that your units agree: The given units are grams and cubic centimeters, and the measure found is density. Therefore, the units should be g/cm^3. The units agree.

Answer: 0.6 g/cm^3

You Try It

15 Calculate Obsidian is another type of igneous rock. What is the density of a piece of obsidian that has a mass of 239.2 g and a volume of 92 cm^3?

Identify

A. What do you know?

B. What do you want to find?

Plan

C. Write the formula:

D. Substitute the given values into the formula:

Solve

E. Divide:

F. Check that your units agree:

Answer:

Do the Math

Sample Problem

A basalt rock displaces 16 mL of water. The density of the rock is 3.0 g/cm^3. What is the mass of the rock?

Identify

A. What do you know?

volume = 16 mL, density = 3.0 g/cm^3

B. What do you want to find? Mass

Plan

C. Rearrange the formula $D = \frac{m}{V}$ to solve for mass. You can do this by multiplying each side by V.

$$D = \frac{m}{V}$$

$$m = D \cdot V$$

D. Substitute the given values into the formula. Recall that 1 mL = 1 cm^3, so 16 mL = 16 cm^3.

$$m = \frac{3.0\ \text{g}}{\text{cm}^3} \cdot 16\ \text{cm}^3$$

Solve

E. Multiply: $\frac{3.0\ \text{g}}{\text{cm}^3} \cdot 16\ \text{cm}^3 = 48\ \text{g}$

F. Check that your units agree: The given units are g/cm^3 and mL, and the measure found is mass. Therefore, the units should be g. The units agree.

Answer: 48 g

You Try It

16 Calculate A rhyolite rock has a volume of 9.5 mL. The density of the rock is 2.6 g/cm^3. What is the mass of the rock?

Identify

A. What do you know?

B. What do you want to find?

Plan

C. Write the formula:

D. Substitute the given values into the formula:

Solve

E. Multiply:

F. Check that your units agree:

Answer:

Kilauea is the youngest volcano on the Big Island of Hawaii. "Kilauea" means "spewing" or "much spreading," apparently in reference to the lava flows that it erupts.

Visual Summary

To complete this summary, check the box that indicates true or false. Then, use the key below to check your answers. You can use this page to review the main concepts of the lesson.

Relating Mass, Weight, Volume, and Density

Mass is the amount of matter in an object. Weight is a measure of the gravitational force on an object.

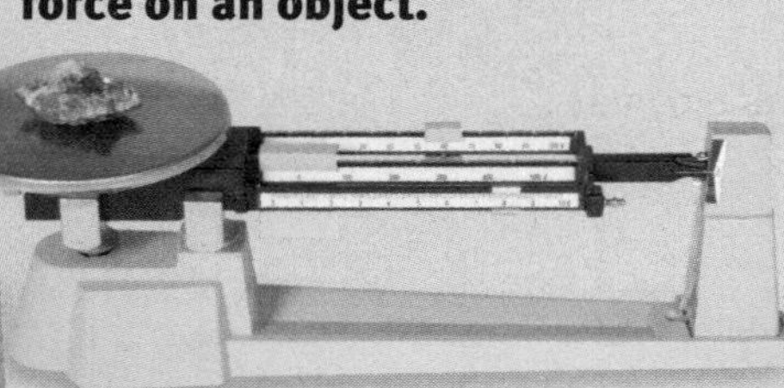

	T	F	
17	☐	☐	An object's weight is the amount of space it occupies.
18	☐	☐	The mass of an object is equal to its weight.

Volume is the amount of space that matter in an object occupies.
To find the volume of a rectangular box, use the formula:

$$V = lwh$$

	T	F	
19	☐	☐	The volume of a solid can be expressed in units of cm^3.

Density describes the mass of a substance in a given volume.
To find the density of a substance, use the formula:

$$D = \frac{m}{V}$$

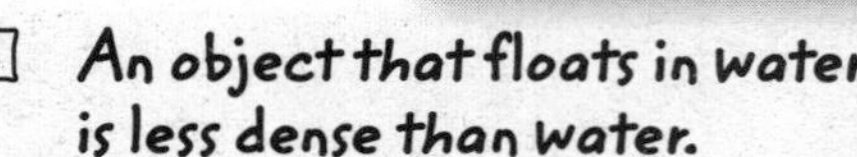

	T	F	
20	☐	☐	An object that floats in water is less dense than water.

Answers: 17 F; 18 F; 19 T; 20 T

21 Describe Write a set of instructions that describe how to find the density of an object. Write the instructions so that they work for a regularly shaped object and for an irregularly shaped object.

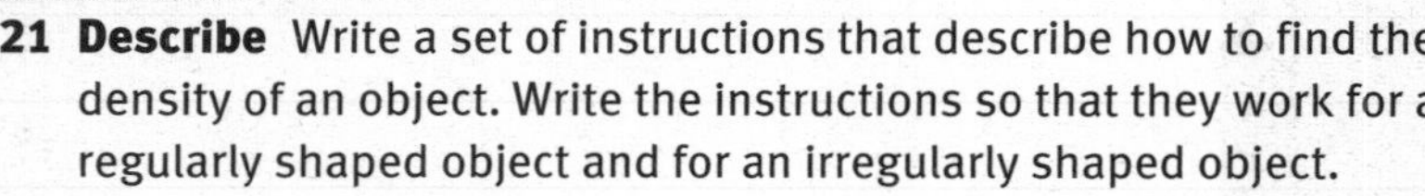

Lesson Review

Vocabulary

Fill in the blank with the term that best completes the following sentence.

1 ____________________ is the amount of space that matter in an object occupies.

2 ____________________ is anything that has mass and takes up space.

3 ____________________ is the amount of matter in an object.

4 ____________________ is a measure of the amount of matter in a given amount of space.

5 ____________________ is a measure of the gravitational force on an object.

Key Concepts

6 Classify Is air matter? How can you tell?

____

____

____

7 Describe Is it possible for an object's weight to change while its mass remains constant? Explain.

____

____

____

8 Compare Explain why a golf ball is heavier than a table-tennis ball, even though the balls are the same size.

____

____

____

9 Calculate A block of wood has a mass of 120 g and a volume of 200 cm^3. What is the density of the wood?

Critical Thinking

Use this table to answer the following questions.

Substance	Density (g/cm^3)
Zinc (solid)	7.13
Silver (solid)	10.50
Lead (solid)	11.35

10 Identify Suppose that 273 g of one of the substances listed above displaces 26 mL of water. What is the substance?

____

____

____

11 Evaluate How many mL of water would be displaced by 408 g of lead?

____

____

____

12 Predict How can you determine that a coin is not pure silver if you know the mass and volume of the coin?

____

____

____

____

____

13 Calculate A truck whose bed is 2.5 m long, 1.5 m wide, and 1.0 m high is delivering sand for a sand-sculpture competition. About how many trips must the truck make to deliver 7 m^3 of sand?

My Notes

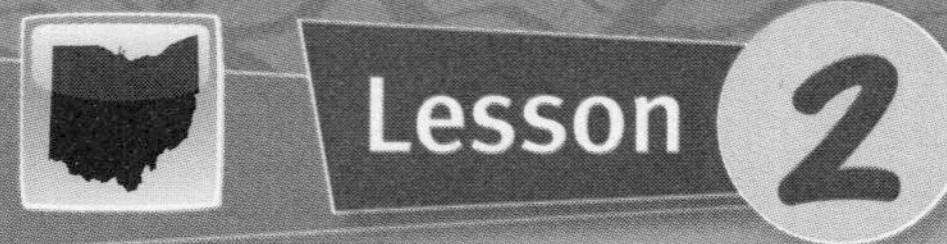

Properties of Matter

ESSENTIAL QUESTION

What are physical and chemical properties of matter?

By the end of this lesson, you should be able to classify and compare substances based on their physical and chemical properties.

To harvest cranberries, the dry beds are flooded with water. Next, water reels loosen the berries from the vines. Since cranberries are less dense than water, they float. Harvesters take advantage of this property to gather and easily float them toward collection sites.

OHIO **6.PS.1** All matter is made up of small particles called atoms.

OHIO **6.SIA.3** Use appropriate mathematics, tools and techniques to gather data and information.

OHIO **6.SIA.5** Develop descriptions, models, explanations and predictions.

Lesson Labs

Quick Labs
- Comparing Two Elements
- Observing Physical Properties

Exploration Lab
- Identifying an Unknown Substance

Engage Your Brain

1 Predict Check T or F to show whether you think each statement is true or false.

T	F	
☐	☐	Liquid water freezes at the same temperature at which ice melts: 0 °C.
☐	☐	A bowling ball weighs less than a Styrofoam ball of the same size.
☐	☐	An object with a density greater than the density of water will float in water.
☐	☐	Solubility is the ability of one substance to dissolve in another.

2 Describe If you were asked to describe an orange to someone who had never seen an orange, what would you tell the person?

Active Reading

3 Synthesize Many English words have their roots in other languages. The root of the word *solubility* is the Latin word *solvere,* which means "to loosen." Make an educated guess about the meaning of the word *solubility*.

Vocabulary Terms

- **physical property**
- **chemical property**

4 Apply As you learn the definition of each vocabulary term in this lesson, create your own definition or sketch to help you remember the meaning of the term.

Physical Education

What are physical properties of matter?

What words would you use to describe a table? A chair? A piece of cloth? You would probably say something about the shape, color, and size of each object. Next, you might consider whether the object is hard or soft, smooth or rough. Normally, when describing an object, you identify what it is about that object that you can observe without changing its identity.

They Are Used to Describe a Substance

A characteristic of a substance that can be observed and measured without changing the identity of the substance is called a **physical property**. Gold is one metal prized for its physical properties. Gold can be bent and shaped easily and has a lasting shine. Both properties make it an excellent metal for making coins and jewelry.

All of your senses can be used to detect physical properties. Color, shape, size, and texture are a few of the physical properties you encounter. Think of how you would describe an object to a friend. Most likely, your description would be a list of the object's physical properties.

Active Reading **5 Describe** Does observing a physical property of a substance change the identity of the substance? Explain.

____

____

____

____

____

Gold is a highly sought-after metal for making jewelry. Gold is dense, soft, and shiny, and it is resistant to tarnishing. Gold is often mixed with other metals to make it stronger.

In this factory, gold is being purified by the process of smelting. This process uses pressure, high heat, and chemicals to remove impurities from the gold.

They Can Be Observed without Changing the Identity of a Substance

The physical properties of an object can be observed with the senses. Some properties can be measured, too. For example, you can look at a table to observe its relative size. Or, you can measure its length, width, and height by using a tool like a measuring tape. When you observe a physical property, you do not change the substance's identity. The material that makes up the table keeps its identity.

Imagine that you conducted an experiment to measure the temperature at which water boils. This temperature, called the boiling point, is a physical property. You placed a beaker of water over a heating source and measured the increase in water temperature using a thermometer. Once the water reached its boiling point, some of the water had become a gas. In this experiment, the water had to change to a gas before you could record the boiling point of water. However, the water did not change in identity. It is water whether it is a solid, liquid, or gas.

Visualize It!

6 Observe Describe the physical properties of objects you see in this photo.

Think Outside the Book

7 Apply Describe a common object by naming its properties. Trade your mystery-object description with a classmate's and try to guess what object he or she has described.

Visualize It!

Common Physical Properties

On these two pages, you can read about some common physical properties. The physical properties of a substance often describe how the substance can be useful.

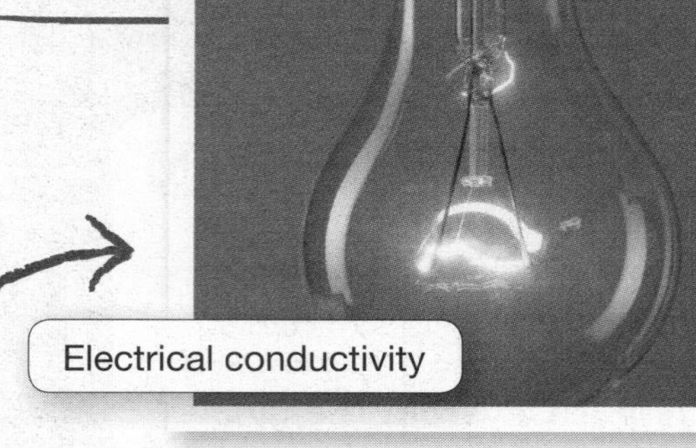

Electrical conductivity

Electrical conductivity is a measure of how well an electric current can move through a substance.

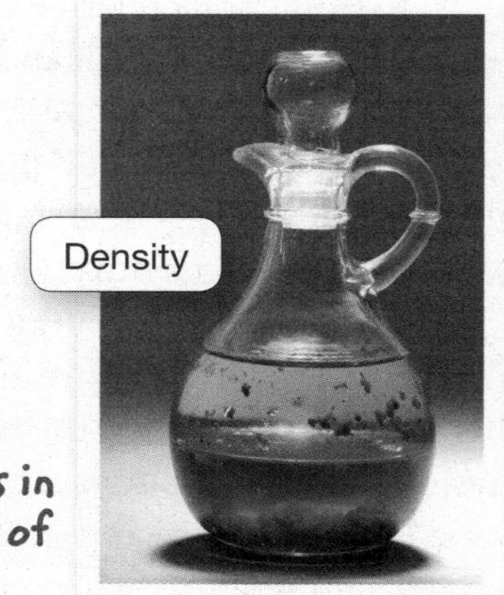

Density

Density is a measure of the amount of mass in a given amount of volume.

8 Explain The photo above shows oil and vinegar in a pitcher. The top layer is the oil. Describe the density of the vinegar compared to the density of the oil.

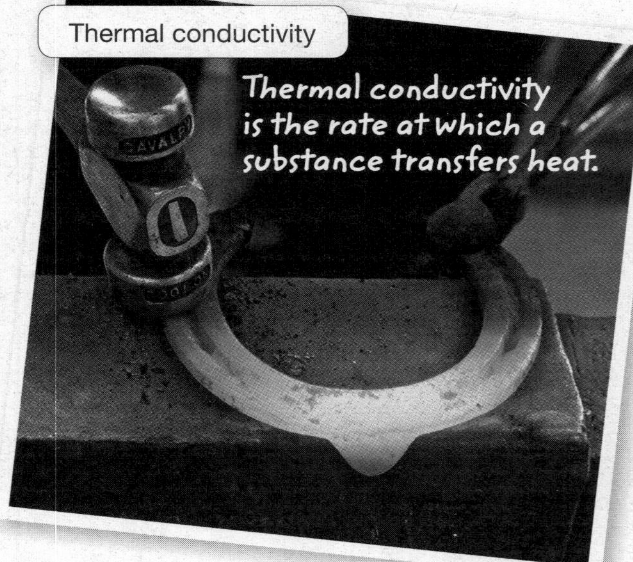

Thermal conductivity

Thermal conductivity is the rate at which a substance transfers heat.

Solubility

Solubility is the ability of a substance to dissolve in another substance. This powdered drink mix is dissolving in water. When fully dissolved, the particles of the drink mix will be spread throughout the water.

9 Predict If you let all of the liquid evaporate out of the pitcher, would you be able to see the solid particles of the drink mix? Explain.

Malleability (MAL•ee•uh•bil•i•tee) is the ability of a substance to be rolled or pounded into various shapes. Aluminum has the property of malleability.

10 Identify Name something made of aluminum and explain why malleability is a useful property.

Many metals often have a shine, or luster, that make them prized by decorators.

Some metals exert a magnetic attraction. Magnetic attraction can act at a distance.

Melting point

The melting point of a substance is the temperature at which it changes from a solid to a liquid.

Boiling water beneath the surface of Earth powers this geyser.

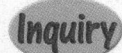

Inquiry

11 Infer Compare what happens when a geyser erupts to what happens when a tea kettle whistles.

Identity Theft

What are chemical properties of matter?

Active Reading **12 Identify** As you read, underline the definition of a chemical property.

Physical properties are not the only properties that describe matter. A **chemical property** describes a substance's ability to change into a new substance with different properties. Common chemical properties include flammability and reactivity with substances such as oxygen, water, and acids.

They Describe How a Substance Changes

Can you think of a chemical property for the metal iron? When left outdoors in wet weather, iron rusts. The ability to rust is a chemical property of iron. The metal silver does not rust, but eventually a darker substance, called tarnish, forms on its surface. You may have noticed a layer of tarnish on some silver spoons or jewelry. Rusting and tarnishing are chemical properties because the metal changes. After rusting or tarnishing, a portion of the metal is no longer the metal but a different substance.

13 Predict Why do automobiles rust more easily in wet climates than drier climates?

Iron can form rust, turning a once shiny car into a crumbling relic.

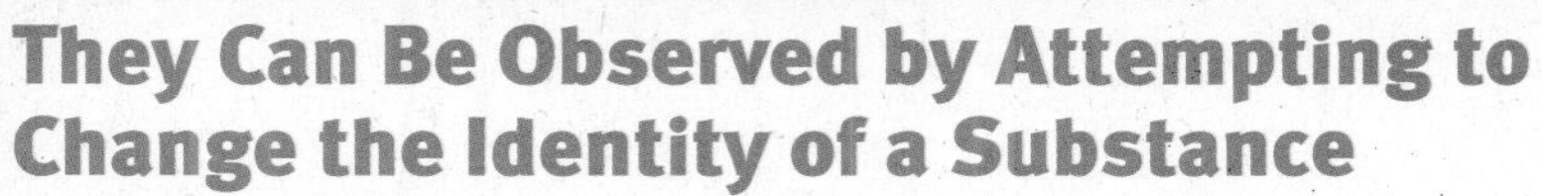

They Can Be Observed by Attempting to Change the Identity of a Substance

One way to identify a chemical property is to observe the changes that a substance undergoes. Wood for a campfire has the chemical property of flammability—the ability to burn. When wood burns, new substances are formed: water, carbon dioxide, and ash. These new substances have different properties than the wood had. Reactivity is another chemical property that can be identified by observing changes. Reactivity is the ability of a substance to interact with another substance and form one or more new substances.

You can also observe a chemical property of a substance by attempting to change the substance, even if no change occurs. For example, you can observe that gold is nonflammable by attempting to burn it. A chemical property of gold is that it is nonflammable.

Reactivity is a chemical property. Vinegar and baking soda react to make a salt, water, and carbon dioxide gas.

Flammability, or the ability of a substance to burn, is a chemical property. For example, the wood building in the photo is flammable, and the suits that help keep the firefighters safe are flame resistant.

Property Boundaries

What is the difference between physical and chemical properties?

A physical property can always be observed without changing the identity of a substance. The mass of a log can be observed without changing the log. A chemical property, however, is observed by attempting to change the identity of a substance. To witness a log's flammability, you must try to set the log on fire.

A substance always has physical and chemical properties. For example, a log is flammable even when it's not burning.

Active Reading **14 Compare** Describe the difference between a physical property and a chemical property.

___
___
___
___

Visualize It!

Bending an iron nail will change its shape but not its identity.

An iron nail can react with oxygen in the air to form iron oxide, or rust.

15 Distinguish What type of property is being shown by each nail?

___
___
___

16 Predict Check the correct box to show whether each property of an iron nail is a physical or a chemical property.

Property	
Malleable	☐ Physical ☐ Chemical
Reacts with oxygen	☐ Physical ☐ Chemical
Magnetic	☐ Physical ☐ Chemical
Nonflammable	☐ Physical ☐ Chemical

Why It Matters

At the Scene

The collection and study of physical evidence in a criminal investigation is known as *forensic science.* Forensic scientists are experts in observing the physical and chemical properties of evidence at crime scenes.

Arson Investigation

A forensic scientist can gently heat ashes from an arson scene to help determine what chemicals were used to start the fire. If detectives know how the fire began, then they might be able to determine who is responsible for the crime.

Studying Paint

Flecks of paint left on a tree where a car hit it can be examined with a special microscope. How the paint absorbs light can reveal what chemicals were used in the paint. This information could help authorities determine what kind of vehicle a criminal suspect drove.

Fiber Analysis

Magnified fibers, like those shown above, can provide clues, too. An acrylic fiber might be material from a boat cover or a rug. Or, polyester could have come from a suspect's shirt.

Extend

Inquiry

17 **Identify** List physical and chemical properties used to identify evidence at a crime scene.

18 **Predict** When examining evidence, why might investigators want to be more careful examining chemical properties than physical properties?

19 **Evaluate** By examining the physical and chemical properties of evidence at a crime scene, investigators can often be more certain about what a suspicious substance is not than about what it is. Why do you think this is the case?

Identify Yourself

How can physical and chemical properties identify a substance?

Properties unique to a substance are its *characteristic properties.* Characteristic properties can be physical properties, such as density, or chemical properties, such as flammability. Characteristic properties stay the same regardless of the amount of a sample. They can help identify a substance.

Iron pyrite is one of several minerals having a color similar to that of gold. Miners can find iron pyrite near deposits of gold, and sometimes mistake it for gold. Color and location, however, are about the only properties iron pyrite shares with gold. The two substances have quite different characteristic properties.

For example, gold flattens when hit with a hammer, but iron pyrite shatters. When rubbed on a ceramic plate, gold leaves a yellow streak, but iron pyrite leaves a greenish black one. Gold keeps its shine even if beneath the sea for years, but iron pyrite turns green if exposed to water.

An easy way for miners to tell iron pyrite and gold apart is by using the property of density. Miners collect gold by sifting through dirt in pans. Because of its high density, gold stays in the pan while dirt and most other substances wash over the side as the miner swirls the contents in the pan. Since gold has a density almost four times that of iron pyrite, distinguishing gold from iron pyrite should be an easy task for the experienced miner.

To find the density of a substance, use the following formula, where *D* is density, *m* is mass, and *V* is volume:

$$D = \frac{m}{V}$$

20 Infer Check the box to show which would tell you for sure if you had a sample of real gold.

	Yes	No
Color of your sample.	☐	☐
What happens when you strike your sample with a hammer.	☐	☐
The location where your sample was found.	☐	☐

In pan mining, as the contents in the pan are swirled, less dense substances are washed away.

Do the Math

Sample Problem

A sample of gold has a mass of 579 g. The volume of the sample is 30 cm³. What is the density of the gold sample?

Identify

A. What do you know?

mass = 579 g, volume = 30 cm³

B. What do you want to find? Density

Plan

C. Write the formula: $D = \frac{m}{V}$

D. Substitute the given values into the formula:

$$D = \frac{579\ \text{g}}{30\ \text{cm}^3}$$

Solve

E. Divide: $\frac{579\ \text{g}}{30\ \text{cm}^3} = 19.3\ \text{g/cm}^3$

F. Check that your units agree:

The given units are grams and cubic centimeters, and the measure found is density. Therefore, the units should be g/cm³. The units agree.

Answer: 19.3 g/cm³

You Try It

21 Calculate A student finds an object with a mass of 64.54 g and a volume of 14 cm³. Find the density of the object. Could the object be gold?

Identify

A. What do you know?

B. What do you want to find?

Plan

C. Write the formula:

D. Substitute the given values into the formula:

Solve

E. Divide:

F. Check that your units agree:

Answer:

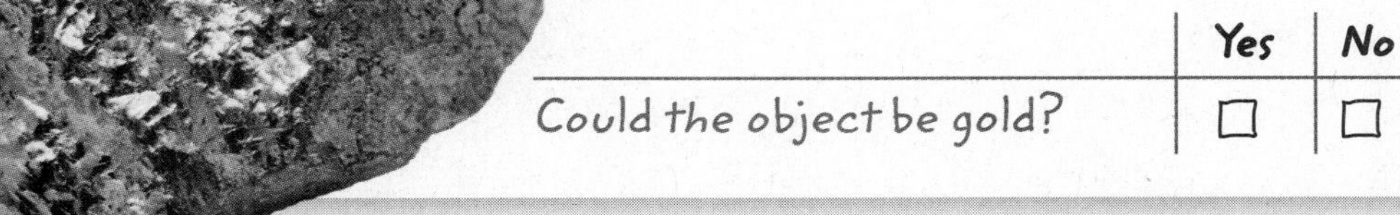

	Yes	No
Could the object be gold?	☐	☐

Visual Summary

To complete this summary, circle the correct word. Then use the key below to check your answers. You can use this page to review the main concepts of the lesson.

Physical and Chemical Properties

A physical property is a property that can be observed or measured without changing the identity of the substance.

22 Solubility / Flammability is a physical property.

23 The melting point of a substance is the temperature at which the substance changes from a solid to a gas / liquid.

A chemical property is a property that describes a substance's ability to form new substances.

24 Reactivity with water / Magnetism is a chemical property.

25 Flammability is the ability of a substance to transfer heat / burn.

The properties that are most useful in identifying a substance are its characteristic properties. Characteristic properties can be physical properties or chemical properties.

26 The characteristic properties of a substance do / do not depend on the size of the sample.

Answers: 22 Solubility; 23 liquid; 24 Reactivity with water; 25 burn; 26 do not

27 Synthesize You have two solid substances that look the same. What measurements would you take and which tests would you perform to determine whether they actually are the same?

Lesson Review

Vocabulary

Fill in the blanks with the term that best completes the following sentences.

1 Flammability is an example of a ________________ property.

2 Electrical conductivity is an example of a ________________ property.

Key Concepts

3 Identify What are three physical properties of aluminum foil?

4 Describe What effect does observing a substance's physical properties have on the substance?

5 Explain Describe how a physical property, such as mass or texture, can change without causing a change in the substance.

6 Justify Must new substances be formed when you observe a chemical property? Explain.

Critical Thinking

Use this table to answer the following question.

Element	Melting Point (°C)	Boiling Point (°C)
Bromine	−7.2	59
Chlorine	−100	−35
Iodine	110	180

7 Infer You are given samples of the substances shown in the table. The samples are labeled A, B, and C. At room temperature, sample A is a solid, sample B is a liquid, and sample C is a gas. What are the identities of samples A, B, and C? (Hint: Room temperature is about 20 °C.)

8 Conclude The density of gold is 19.3 g/cm^3. The density of iron pyrite is 5.0 g/cm^3. If a nugget of iron pyrite and a nugget of gold each have a mass of 50 g, what can you conclude about the volume of each nugget?

9 Predict Suppose you need to build a raft to cross a fast-moving river. Describe the physical and chemical properties of the raft that would be important to ensure your safety.

My Notes

People in Science

Wayne Rossi

METAL ARTISAN

Wayne Rossi works where art and science meet. Using a torch, he shapes pieces of steel into amazing works of art. The torch produces a flame that results from burning a combination of oxygen and acetylene. This action causes the steel to change from a solid to a liquid along the torch line. The change in matter results in the steel softening and separating into two pieces. Mr. Rossi uses the metal's change of state from solid to liquid to make his sculptures. In its liquid state, the steel can be easily cut or reshaped. Mr. Rossi brings art to his work as he imagines an interesting sculpture, envisions the cuts he needs, and guides the torch precisely to where he wants the cuts.

After he has cut out all of the pieces, Mr. Rossi uses more science to join the pieces together into the final sculpture. He joins them by welding, or melting metals together, and then letting them cool down and harden in place. When they harden, the metal pieces form one mass, and they are more strongly bonded to each other than if they were bolted together. Often, a third melted metal is added to help strengthen the bond. The end result is a nearly indestructible work of art!

Welding requires both precision and safety precautions.

The reddish color is from a chemical change that forms rust when rain and air react with the metal.

JOB BOARD

Sheet Metal Worker

What You'll Do: Set up and operate a shop that uses sheet metal. You may also manufacture, maintain, and repair metal products.

Where You Might Work: In a heating, air conditioning, and refrigeration shop. For a railroad cars and tracks manufacturer, sign manufacturer, or aircraft manufacturer. With an oil company, in construction, or various factories.

Education: High school diploma or equivalent

Other Job Requirements: You should be attentive to detail. You should also be able to read blueprints, take accurate measurements, and have knowledge of computerized saws, scissors, compressors, and lasers.

Geochemist

What You'll Do: Use physical and inorganic chemistry to study Earth's features related to rocks, minerals, fluids, and gases. Collect and analyze soil samples. Study the effects of Earth's movements. Write technical reports.

Where You Might Work: At a geochemical company, engineering firm, petroleum company, mining company, university, or environmental consulting firm.

Education: A master's or doctorate

Other Job Requirements: You need a strong background in math, science, English, and geography. You must be willing to work outdoors in all types of weather and to collaborate with a team.

PEOPLE IN SCIENCE NEWS

MIMI So

Rough gemstones are cut and polished into beautiful jewels.

The Science Behind Jewelry

When you look at an interesting necklace, do you think to yourself, "There's a scientist at work"? Perhaps you should! For jewelry designer Mimi So, every day at work includes a little science.

She uses her knowledge of stone size, hardness, color, grade, and cut to choose a gemstone for a piece of jewelry. Then she considers the hardness, melting point, color, and malleability of the metal she would like to use. For example, Mimi says that emeralds are soft and fragile. She explains that a platinum setting would be too hard and could damage the emerald. Therefore, emeralds are usually set in a softer metal, such as 18-karat gold.

Mimi So has a Bachelor's of Fine Arts and a Gemologist Certification. Another option for jewelry-making training is to go to gemology school to gain the needed technical knowledge.

Lesson 3

Atoms and Elements

ESSENTIAL QUESTION

How are atoms and elements related?

By the end of this lesson, you should be able to describe the properties of atoms and elements.

Earth is made of many elements. The fantastic formations in this cave contain atoms of calcium, carbon, and oxygen.

OHIO 6.PS.1 All matter is made up of small particles called atoms.

OHIO 6.SIA.3 Use appropriate mathematics, tools and techniques to gather data and information.

OHIO 6.SIA.4 Analyze and interpret data.

Lesson Labs

Quick Labs
- Model of an Atom
- Comparing Earth's Elements

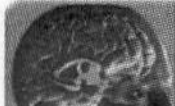

Engage Your Brain

1 Predict Check T or F to show whether you think each statement is true or false.

T	F	
☐	☐	Atoms are smaller than electrons.
☐	☐	Single atoms can be seen with a powerful light microscope.
☐	☐	There are more than 100 elements on the periodic table of elements.

2 Infer Why do the two elements silver and iron have different properties?

Active Reading

3 Synthesize Many English words have their roots in other languages. Use the Greek word below to make an educated guess about the meaning of the word *atom*.

Greek word	Meaning
atomos	indivisible

Example sentence
All matter is made up of particles called atoms.

atom:

Vocabulary Terms

- atom
- proton
- neutron
- electron
- element
- atomic number
- chemical symbol
- physical property

4 Identify As you read, create a reference card for each vocabulary term. On one side of the card, write the term and its meaning. On the other side, draw an image that illustrates or makes a connection to the term. These cards can be used as bookmarks in the text so that you can refer to them while studying.

A Small World

These dots of ink, like all matter, are made up of much smaller particles called atoms.

What are atoms?

When you magnify printed letters in a book, you can see that they are made up of small dots of ink. A fixed ratio of magenta and cyan ink dots make a light purple color. In the same way, all matter is made up of very small particles called atoms. **Atoms** are the basic building blocks of matter, because they are the smallest particles that can have the same properties as the stuff they make up. Different atoms can be combined in different ratios to form all of the substances we encounter every day. Unlike dots of ink, atoms are so small that they cannot be seen using a light microscope.

Think Outside the Book *Inquiry*

5 Model Create a model of an atom using materials of your choice. Include protons, neutrons, and the electron cloud in your model. Show your atom to the class, and explain how it models the structure or behavior of atoms.

What are the parts of an atom?

These tiny atoms contain even smaller particles called *subatomic* particles. **Protons** are subatomic particles that have a positive electric charge. Protons are found at the center, or *nucleus,* of the atom. The nucleus also contains another type of subatomic particle called **neutrons.** Neutrons have no charge. The protons and neutrons in the nucleus make up most of the mass of an atom.

A third type of subatomic particles are called **electrons.** Electrons are negatively charged and are much smaller than protons and neutrons. Electrons are found outside the nucleus in a region called the *electron cloud.* Atoms are electrically neutral overall because they have the same number of protons as electrons. The positive charges of the protons balance out the negative charges of the electrons.

6 Apply This model represents an atom and its parts. Label the parts of the atom.

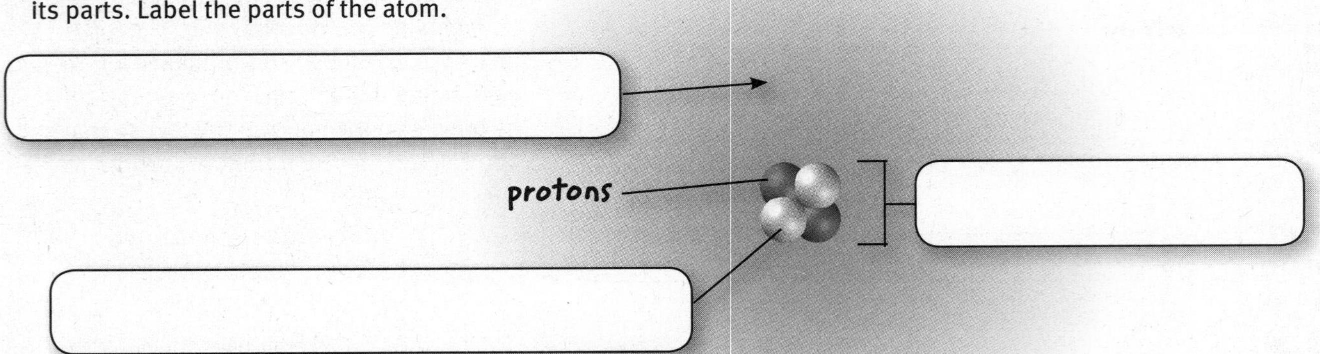

Why It Matters

Nanotechnology

Nanotechnology is the use of materials and processes designed on the atomic scale. Incredibly small electric circuits, machines, and medicine delivery systems are just a few nanotechnology applications that scientists are working to develop.

How It Works

In traditional manufacturing, materials are cut away or shaped to make a product. In nanotechnological manufacturing, materials are built by putting atoms together. The electric wires in this robotic "skin" are built from carbon atoms.

What Can You Make?

Scientists don't yet know all the possible uses of nanotechnology. Someday, tiny robots may be able to deliver medicine exactly where it is needed to treat disease. This drawing shows a model of a robot on a red blood cell.

Extend

Inquiry

7 Explain How does nanotechnology differ from other ways to make objects and materials?

8 Explain What could be the potential benefits of atomic-scale medicine delivery systems?

9 Research Use the library or the Internet to research a possible new device or material in the field of nanotechnology. Make a poster to present what you learn to your class.

The Element of Surprise

What is an element?

An **element** is a pure substance that is made up of only one type of atom. For example, the metal aluminum is an element made up of aluminum atoms. An atom is the smallest unit of an element that has the properties of that element.

How are elements described?

Each element has its own properties that differ from those of other elements. Elements can be identified by their atomic numbers and chemical symbols.

By Their Atomic Numbers

Atoms of one element differ from atoms of another element by the number of protons they have. The **atomic number** of an element is the number of protons in the nucleus of one of its atoms. Every atom of a given element has the same atomic number. For example, the atomic number of aluminum is 13. Each atom of aluminum contains 13 protons. While the number of protons in the nucleus is always the same for a given element, the number of neutrons can vary. All aluminum atoms found in nature have 14 neutrons.

The periodic table of elements is used to organize over 110 known elements. The periodic table is organized in rows by increasing atomic number. The atomic number of each element is listed at the top of that element's square in the periodic table.

These aluminum cans are made up of many aluminum atoms joined together.

Visualize It!

10 Apply In the space below, draw a model of an atom of the element aluminum. Use information from this lesson to determine how many protons, neutrons, and electrons to include in your model.

By Their Chemical Symbols

Active Reading **11 Identify** As you read, underline the chemical symbols of elements.

Elements can also be described by their chemical symbols. A **chemical symbol** is an abbreviation that represents an element. Most elements have a one- or two-letter chemical symbol. The first letter is always capitalized, and the other letters are always lowercase. These symbols are like nicknames that allow chemists to write chemical names in a shorter form. A few elements at the end of the periodic table have three-letter chemical symbols, such as Uut. These symbols are placeholders for elements that have not yet been discovered or that do not have official names. The discovery of a new element has to be approved by an international committee of scientists. Then the element is given a permanent name and a one- or two-letter chemical symbol.

A chemical symbol often contains letters from the element's name. For example, hydrogen is represented by H, and zinc is represented by Zn. Some chemical symbols come from the names of the elements in other languages. The chemical symbol of gold is Au, from the Latin word for gold—*aurum*. The symbol for tungsten, W, comes from its German name—*wolfram*.

13
Al
Aluminum
26.98

Different periodic tables may show different information about each element. The square above shows the atomic number, the chemical symbol, the full name, and the average atomic mass of aluminum. The table below shows less information about each element. Each square shows only the atomic number and the chemical symbol for each element.

Visualize It!

12 Describe Helium appears in the top-right corner of the periodic table. What are the atomic number and chemical symbol for helium?

____

____

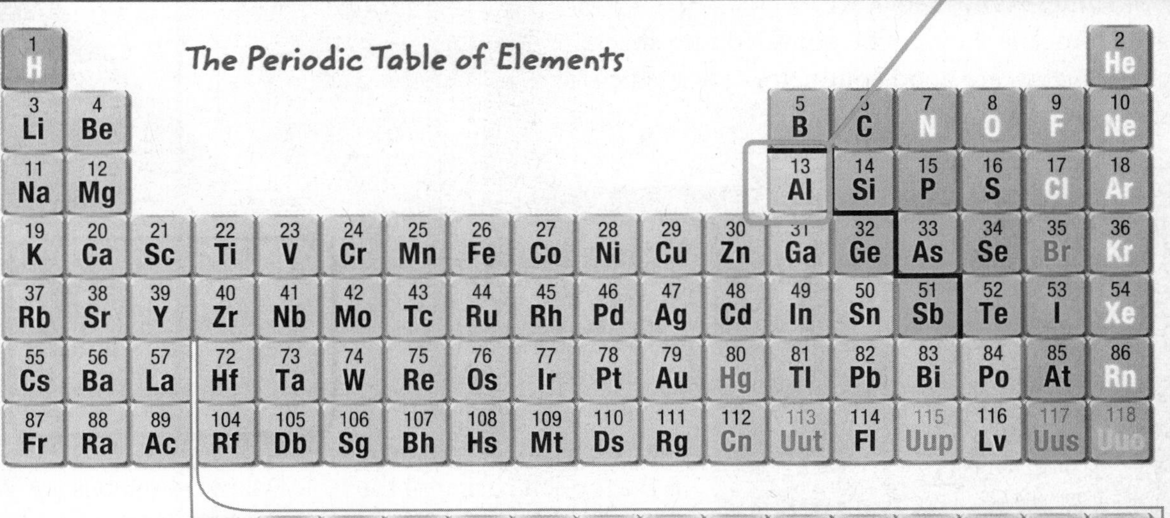

The Head of the Class

What are the three main classes of elements?

The periodic table is arranged into columns and rows. Elements in each column have similar properties. Also, the properties of the elements in each row change in a predictable way.

The periodic table contains three main classes of elements: metals, nonmetals, and metalloids. Each class of elements can be found in a specific area of the periodic table. A zigzag line on some periodic tables marks the locations of the metals, nonmetals, and metalloids. Each class of elements also has unique properties. A **physical property** is a characteristic of a substance that can be observed and measured without changing the identity of the substance. Color, density, and conductivity are all physical properties. Thermal conductivity is a measure of how well a substance transfers energy as heat. Conductivity also describes how well an electric current flows through a substance.

Metals

Most elements are classified as metals. Metals appear to the left of the zigzag line on the periodic table. Most metals are solid and can be recognized by their luster, or shine. Many metals are malleable, which means they can be pounded into sheets or other shapes. Metals are good conductors of electric current and of energy as heat.

This fence is made of wrought iron. Iron is a metal that is used in many building materials.

Nitrogen gas, N_2, is a nonmetal that makes up 78% of Earth's atmosphere.

Nonmetals

Nonmetals appear to the right of the zigzag line on the periodic table. The only exception is hydrogen, the first element in the top-left corner of the table. Many nonmetals are gases at room temperature. Nonmetals are typically dull; in other words, they lack luster. Solid nonmetals are brittle, or not malleable. Nonmetals are poor conductors of electric current and of energy as heat.

Metalloids

Metalloids appear between metals and nonmetals along the zigzag line on the periodic table. Metalloids are elements that have some properties of metals and some properties of nonmetals. Metalloids are typically solids and have a somewhat metallic luster. Metalloids are less malleable than metals but not as brittle as nonmetals. Metalloids are known as semiconductors. They conduct electric current better than nonmetals but not as well as metals.

Metalloids are used to make semiconductor chips found in computers and tablets.

Active Reading **13 Describe** Where are metalloids found on the periodic table?

____

Visualize It!

14 Compare Use the physical properties in the table to label each of these elements as a metal, nonmetal, or metalloid.

Substance	Appearance	Malleability	Thermal conductivity (mW/cm*K)
A	shiny solid	malleable	804
B	shiny solid	brittle	602
C	shiny solid	malleable	4,010
D	yellowish-green gas	not malleable	0.089

A _______________

B _______________

D _______________

C _______________

15 Extend What additional physical properties could help you compare these elements?

____

____

____

Elements in Our World

What elements make up Earth?

Nine elements account for almost all of the matter that makes up our planet. These elements are oxygen, silicon, aluminum, calcium, sodium, potassium, magnesium, nickel, and iron. Iron makes up about one-third of Earth's mass.

Earth has three layers: the crust, the mantle, and the core. Each layer has a different mix of elements. The continents and ocean floor are parts of the crust. The main elements in the crust are oxygen, silicon, and aluminum. Along with smaller amounts of other elements, they form the minerals found in rocks and soil. Earth's mantle is made of rock that is so hot that it flows slowly. Most of this rock is made of silicon, oxygen, iron, and magnesium. The main elements in Earth's core are the metals iron and nickel.

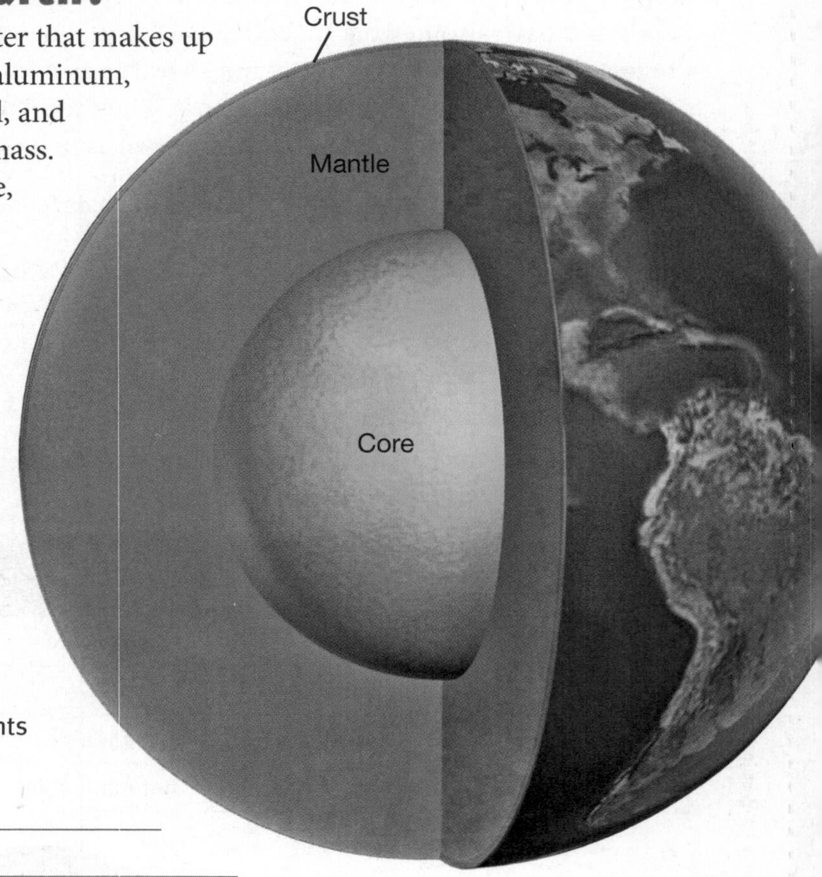

Active Reading **16 Identify** What are the main elements in Earth's core? Which class do these elements belong to?

____

____

17 Infer Despite the many different colors on the canyon walls, all the sandstone is mostly made of the same elements. What do you think the most common elements are? Check your answer with library or Internet resources.

____

____

____

____

____

____

What elements make up the atmosphere and ocean?

The atmosphere and ocean are above Earth's crust. The atmosphere is a layer of gases surrounding Earth. It is composed of about 78% nitrogen and 21% oxygen. The remaining 1% of the atmosphere is made up of gases such as argon, helium, neon, and carbon dioxide.

The ocean is mainly water. Water molecules are made of hydrogen and oxygen atoms joined together. These two elements are the most abundant in Earth's oceans. If you have ever tasted ocean water, you know that it is salty. Salt compounds make up a small percentage of the ocean. In all, ocean water contains about 30 elements. The salts in the ocean contain the elements sodium, chlorine, sulfur, magnesium, calcium, and potassium.

This sea lion, as well as the water and air that it needs to survive, is composed of just a few elements joined in different ways.

What elements make up living things?

All living things–and things that were once alive–contain the element carbon. This includes fossil fuels, such as coal and petroleum. These fuels come from the remains of organisms that lived millions of years ago. Other elements that are abundant in living things include hydrogen, oxygen, nitrogen, phosphorus, and calcium. Living things need a variety of other elements, such as iron, in small amounts. You can get some of these elements from the food you eat. Eating a variety of healthy foods will help you to get all the elements your body needs.

18 Compare In the table below, write the names and chemical symbols of elements found in Earth, the atmosphere, the oceans, and living things. Use the periodic table in the Look It Up! section to look up unfamiliar chemical symbols.

Earth	Earth's Atmosphere	Earth's Oceans	Living Things

Visual Summary

To complete this summary, fill in the blanks with the correct word or phrase. Then use the key below to check your answers. You can use this page to review the main concepts of the lesson.

Atoms and Elements

Atoms are the basic building blocks of matter.

19 Atoms are made up of protons, electrons, and ________________

An element is a pure substance that can be described by its atomic number and chemical symbol.

13
Al
Aluminum
26.98

20 The atomic number of an element is the number of ________________ in an atom's nucleus.

A small number of elements make up Earth, the atmosphere, the oceans, and living things.

21 The most common elements in the atmosphere are ________________ and ________________

22 The most common elements in the ocean are ________________ and ________________, which make up water.

Answers: 19 neutrons; 20 protons; 21 nitrogen, oxygen; 22 hydrogen, oxygen

23 Synthesize An unknown mineral sample contains the element calcium. What information could you learn about calcium and its properties from the periodic table?

Lesson Review

Vocabulary

Draw a line to connect the following terms to their definitions.

1 nucleus	**A** a pure substance made up of one type of atom
2 element	**B** letters that represent an element
3 chemical symbol	**C** the central region of an atom

Key Concepts

4 Relate Explain how the terms *atom* and *element* are related.

____

____

____

5 Summarize What are the three main classes of elements? Provide two physical properties for each class of elements.

____

____

____

____

____

____

____

6 Infer The atomic number of barium is 56. What do you know about the subatomic particles in an atom of this element?

____

____

____

7 Explain Atoms contain positively charged protons and negatively charged electrons. Why does an ordinary atom have no charge?

____

____

____

Critical Thinking

Use this diagram to answer the questions below.

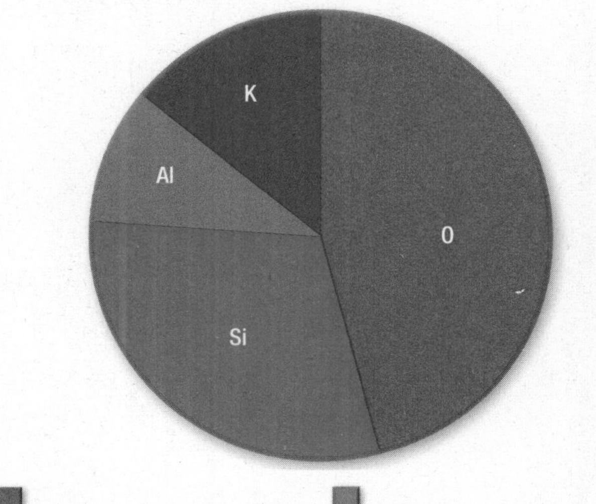

■ ______________ ■ ______________

■ ______________ ■ ______________

8 Classify Each color and chemical symbol on the chart represents an element. Write the name of each element next to the matching color box.

9 Analyze According to the chart, which element is most abundant in amazonite?

____

10 Infer Based on its chemical makeup, where do you think amazonite is found? Explain.

____

____

____

11 Synthesize Thermal energy is generated in Earth's core and mantle. Do you think this heat stays within those layers, or can it be transferred to Earth's surface? Explain.

____

____

____

____

My Notes

Pure Substances and Mixtures

ESSENTIAL QUESTION

How do pure substances and mixtures compare?

By the end of this lesson, you should be able to distinguish between pure substances and mixtures.

Seawater is a unique mixture that contains many dissolved substances. One such substance, called calcium carbonate, is used by these stony coral to build their hard skeletons.

OHIO 6.PS.1 All matter is made up of small particles called atoms.

Lesson Labs

Quick Labs
- Observing Mixtures
- Identifying Elements and Compounds

Exploration Lab
- Investigating Separating Mixtures

Engage Your Brain

1 Predict Check T or F to show whether you think each statement is true or false.

T	F	
☐	☐	Atoms combine in different ways to make up all of the substances you encounter every day.
☐	☐	Saltwater can be separated into salt and water.
☐	☐	A mixture of soil has the same chemical composition throughout.

2 Apply Think of a substance that does not dissolve in water. Draw a sketch below that shows what happens when this substance is added to water.

Active Reading

3 Synthesize Many English words have their roots in other languages. Use the Greek words below to make an educated guess about the meanings of the words *homogeneous* and *heterogeneous*.

Greek word	Meaning
genus	type
homos	same
heteros	different

Example sentence
Saltwater is homogeneous throughout.

homogeneous:

Example sentence
A heterogeneous mixture of rocks varies from handful to handful.

heterogeneous:

Vocabulary Terms

- **atom**
- **element**
- **molecule**
- **compound**
- **mixture**
- **pure substance**
- **heterogeneous**
- **homogeneous**

4 Identify This list contains the key terms you'll learn in this lesson. As you read, circle the definition of each term.

A Great Combination

How can matter be classified?

What kinds of food could you make with the ingredients shown below? You could eat slices of tomato as a snack. Or you could combine tomato slices with lettuce to make a salad. Combine more ingredients, such as bread and cheese, and you have a sandwich. Just as these meals are made up of simpler foods, matter is made up of basic "ingredients" known as *atoms*. **Atoms** are the smallest unit of an element that maintains the properties of that element. Atoms, like the foods shown here, can be combined in different ways to produce different substances.

The substances you encounter every day can be classified into one of the three major classes of matter: *elements, compounds,* and *mixtures*. Atoms are the basic building blocks for all three types of matter. Elements, compounds, and mixtures differ in the way that atoms are combined.

Active Reading **5 Compare** What do elements, compounds, and mixtures have in common?

____

____

Think Outside the Book **Inquiry**

6 Predict If you have ever baked a cake or bread, you know that the ingredients that combine to make it taste different from the baked food. Why do you think that is?

Just as these ingredients combine to make a tasty sandwich, atoms are the basic "ingredients" that make up matter.

Matter Can Be Classified into Elements, Compounds, and Mixtures

Atoms are the building blocks of matter. Like these toy blocks, atoms can be connected in different ways. The models below show how atoms make up elements, molecules, and compounds. Elements, molecules, and compounds make up mixtures.

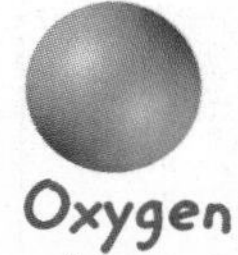

Oxygen atom

An **element** is a substance made up of one type of atom. Here, the element is oxygen.

Oxygen molecule

A **molecule** is a particle made up of two or more atoms that are joined together chemically. A molecule can be made up of atoms of one element, like this oxygen molecule.

An element can be more than one atom, and all atoms are the same type.

Water molecule

A **compound** is made up of different kinds of atoms chemically combined. Compounds have different properties from the elements that make them up.

A compound is always two or more elements, or different types of atoms.

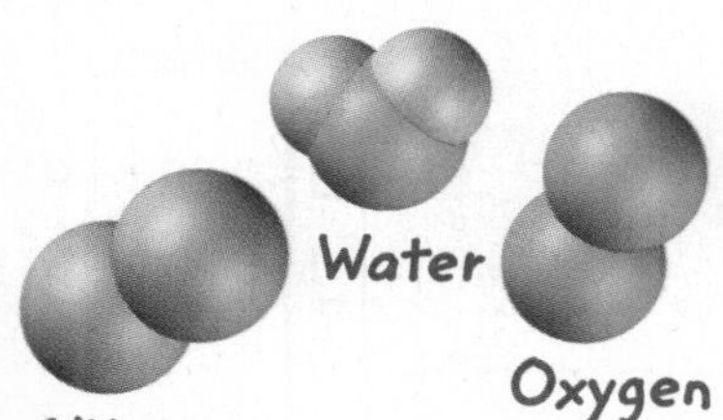

A **mixture** contains a variety of elements and compounds that are not chemically combined with each other.

Visualize It!

7 Analyze Why are the spheres representing nitrogen and oxygen different colors?

How do molecules and compounds differ?

If atoms combine to form molecules and compounds, what is the difference between a molecule and a compound? A molecule is a type of particle and the smallest combination of atoms that has the properties of the compound. A compound is a type of matter. For example, water is both a molecule and a compound. A water molecule is the combination of one oxygen atom and two hydrogen atoms. The compound water contains many molecules.

Key

Atoms of different elements

H Hydrogen

O Oxygen

C Carbon

Visualize It!

8 Identify A few of the different ways atoms can combine are shown below. Fill in the blanks with either *molecule* or *atom*. Draw the particle that goes in the box labeled "atom." To classify the type of matter that has been formed, check the box next to either element, compound, or mixture.

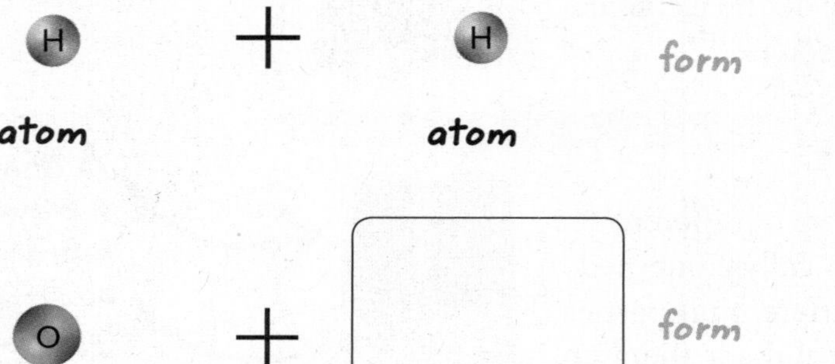

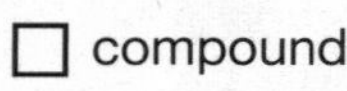

☐ element
☐ compound
☐ mixture

☐ element
☐ compound
☐ mixture

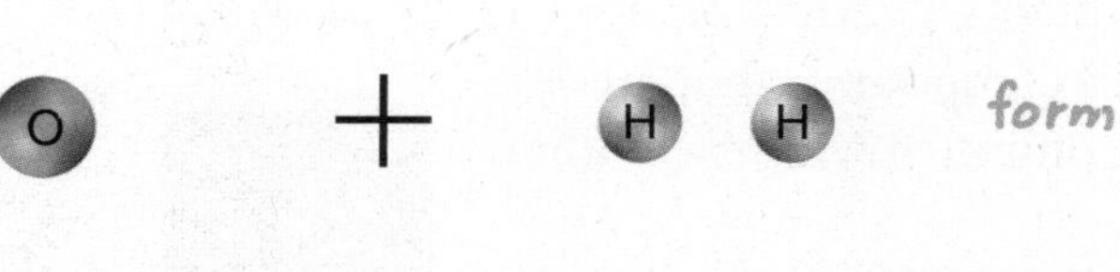

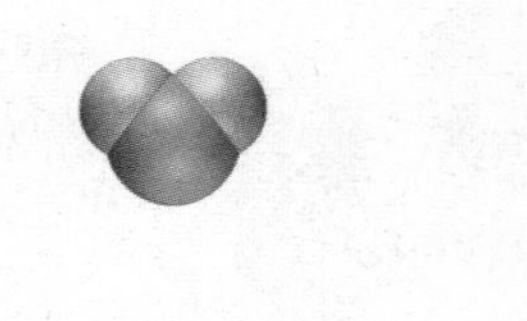

☐ element
☐ compound
☐ mixture

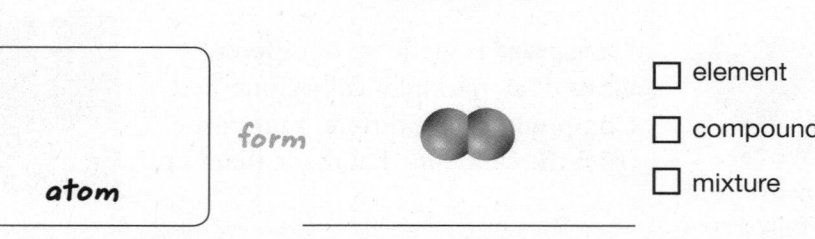

☐ element
☐ compound
☐ mixture

9 Analyze If sugar were dissolved in water, would the combination be a compound or a mixture? Explain your reasoning.

The Wonder of Water

Liquid water is essential for life. Every form of life spends some part of its life cycle dependent on water. For example, water is necessary for all cell processes. Water is called the *universal solvent* because it combines with so many other compounds. What makes water so special? The properties of cohesion and adhesion make water different from many other liquids.

Cohesion

Unlike many other molecules, water molecules are very attracted to each other. They stick together! Cohesion allows this spider to "walk" on top of the water.

Adhesion

Water molecules are also attracted to many other surfaces, such as this leaf. The attraction between the water and the leaf allows the water to bead up on the leaf or spread out without running off the edge.

Extend

Inquiry

10 Describe Explain how water molecules differ from many other molecules.

11 Research Investigate the causes of the unique properties of water. Write a summary of your findings.

12 Design Create a project that explains how water molecules are uniquely attracted to each other. Present your project as a poster or a model.

Pure Genius

What are pure substances?

Elements and compounds are pure substances. A **pure substance** is a substance that has definite physical and chemical properties such as appearance, melting point, and reactivity. No matter the amount of a pure substance you have, it will always have the same properties. This is because pure substances are made up of one type of particle.

Pure Substances Are Made Up of One Type of Particle

Copper, like all elements, is a pure substance. Take a look at the element copper, shown below. The atoms that make up copper are all the same. No matter where in the world you find pure copper, it will always have the same properties.

Molecules and compounds are also pure substances. Consider water, shown on the next page. Every water molecule is identical. Each molecule is made up of exactly two hydrogen atoms and one oxygen atom. Because water is a pure substance, it has properties that are always the same wherever water is found. For example, at standard pressure, water always freezes at 0 °C and boils at 100 °C.

Visualize It!

13 Identify Fill in the blanks to label the two particle models as either atoms or molecules.

A Copper ______________________

14 Explain Copper is an element. How do these images of copper illustrate this?

____

____

____

____

Pure Substances Cannot Be Formed or Broken Down by Physical Changes

Physical changes such as melting, freezing, cutting, or smashing do not change the identity of pure substances. For example, if you cut copper pipe into short pieces, the material is still copper. And if you freeze liquid water, the particles that make up the ice remain the same: two hydrogen atoms combined with one oxygen atom.

The chemical bonds that hold atoms together cannot be broken easily. To break or form chemical bonds, a chemical change is required. For example, when an electric current is passed through water, a chemical change takes place. The atoms that make up the compound break apart into two elements: hydrogen and oxygen. When a pure substance undergoes a chemical change, it is no longer that same substance. A chemical change changes the identity of the substance. Individual atoms cannot be broken down into smaller parts by normal physical or chemical changes.

Active Reading **15 Identify** What happens when a pure substance undergoes a chemical change?

____

____

____

____

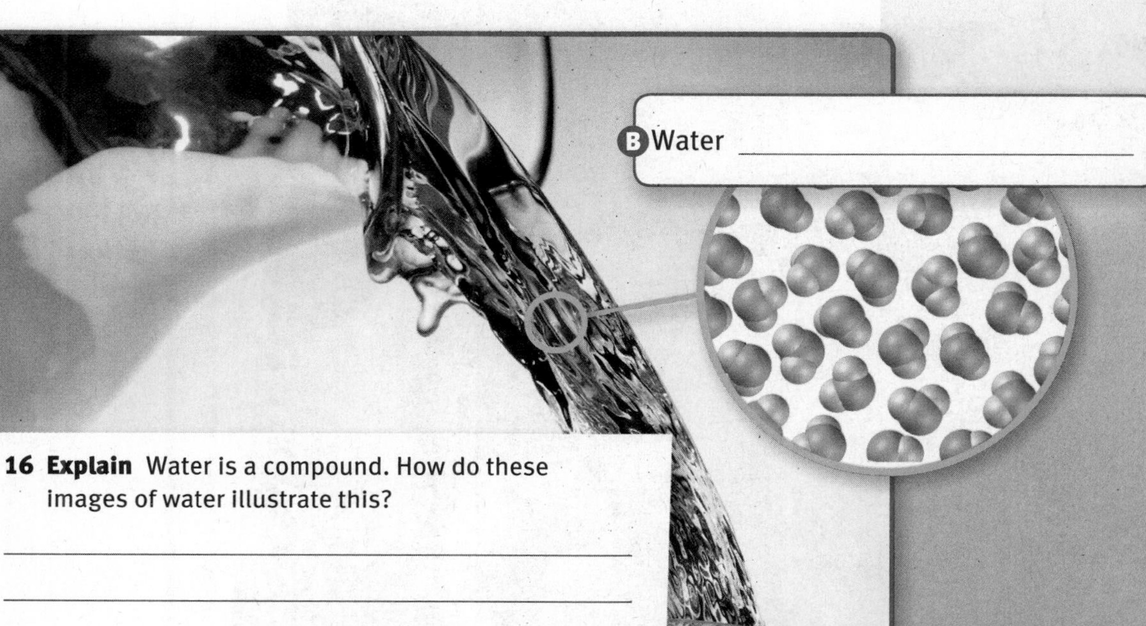

16 Explain Water is a compound. How do these images of water illustrate this?

____

____

____

____

Classified Information

How can elements be classified?

Active Reading

17 Identify As you read, underline the ways in which elements are organized on the periodic table.

Differences in physical and chemical properties allow us to classify elements. By knowing the category to which an element belongs, you can predict some of its properties. Elements are broadly classified as metals, nonmetals, or metalloids. Most metals are shiny, conduct heat and electricity well, and can be shaped into thin sheets and wires. Nonmetals are not shiny and do not conduct heat or electricity well. Metalloids have some properties of both metals and nonmetals.

There are over 100 elements known to exist. Each element has a place in an arrangement called *the periodic table of the elements.* The periodic table is a useful tool that can help you to identify elements that have similar properties. Metals, nonmetals, and metalloids occupy different regions in the periodic table. Metals start at the left and make up most of the elements in the periodic table. Nonmetals are at the right and are often shaded with a color different from that of the metals. Not surprisingly, the metalloids lie between the metals and nonmetals. In many instances, you can even predict which elements combine with others to form compounds based on their positions in the periodic table.

Aluminum, like many metals, can be formed into a thin foil.

Charcoal, made mostly of carbon atoms, is brittle and dull like many other nonmetals.

How can compounds be classified?

You are surrounded by compounds. Compounds make up the food you eat, the school supplies you use, and the clothes you wear—even you! There are so many compounds that it would be very difficult to list or describe them all. Fortunately, these compounds can be grouped into a few basic categories by their properties.

18 Classify Read about some of the ways in which compounds can be classified. Then fill in the blanks to complete the photo captions.

By Their pH

Compounds can be classified as acidic, basic, or neutral by measuring a special numerical value known as *pH.* Neutral compounds, such as pure water, have a pH value of 7. Acids have a pH value less than 7. Vinegar contains acetic acid, which gives a sharp, sour taste to salad dressings. Bases, on the other hand, have pH values greater than 7. Baking soda is an example of a basic compound. Bases have a slippery feel and a bitter taste. Water and salt are formed when an acid and a base react. A type of paper called *litmus paper* can be used to test whether a compound is an acid or a base. Blue litmus paper turns red in the presence of an acid. Red litmus paper turns blue in the presence of a base. Although some foods are acidic or basic, you should NEVER taste, smell, or touch a chemical to classify them. Many acids and bases can damage your body or clothing.

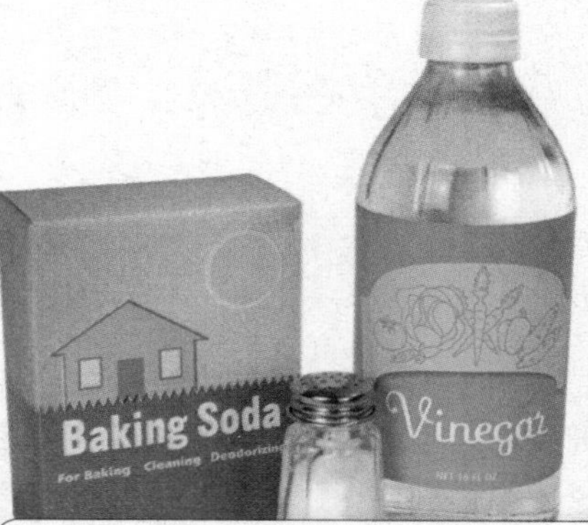

Baking soda is an example of a(n) ______________________.

The compounds that make up plastic are __________________ because they contain carbon.

As Organic or Inorganic

You may have heard of organically grown foods. But in chemistry, the word *organic* refers to compounds that contain carbon and hydrogen. Organic compounds are found in most foods. They can also be found in synthetic goods. For example, gasoline contains a number of organic compounds, such as octane and heptane.

By Their Role in the Body

Organic compounds that are made by living things are called *biochemicals.* Biochemicals are divided into four categories: carbohydrates, lipids, proteins, and nucleic acids. *Carbohydrates* are used as a source of energy and include sugars, starches, and fiber. *Lipids* are biochemicals that store excess energy in the body and make up cell membranes. Lipids include fats, oils, and waxes. *Proteins* are one of the most abundant types of compounds in your body. They regulate chemical activities of the body and build and repair body structures. *Nucleic acids* such as DNA and RNA contain genetic information and help the body build proteins.

Your body gets ______________________, such as sugars, starches, and fiber, from many of the foods you eat.

What are mixtures?

Imagine that you roll out some dough, add tomato sauce, and sprinkle some cheese on top. Then you add green peppers, mushrooms, and pepperoni. What have you just made? A pizza, of course! But that's not all. You have also created a mixture.

A mixture is a combination of two or more substances that are combined physically but not chemically. When two or more materials are put together, they form a mixture if they do not change chemically to form a new substance. For example, cheese and tomato sauce do not react when they are combined to make a pizza. They keep their original identities and properties. So, a pizza is a mixture.

Mixtures Are Made Up of More Than One Type of Particle

Unlike elements and compounds, mixtures are not pure substances. Mixtures contain more than one type of substance. Each substance in a mixture has the same chemical makeup it had before the mixture formed.

Unlike pure substances, mixtures do not have definite properties. Granite from different parts of the world could contain different minerals in different ratios. Pizzas made by different people could have different toppings. Mixtures do not have defined properties, because they do not have a defined chemical makeup.

Visualize It!

19 Describe This student is going to make and separate a mixture of sand and salt. Complete these captions to describe what is taking place in each photo.

A Sand and salt are poured into a single beaker. The result is a mixture because

______

______

______

______

Mixtures Can Be Separated by Physical Changes

You don't like mushrooms on your pizza? Just pick them off. This change is a physical change of the mixture because the identities of the substances do not change. But not all mixtures are as easy to separate as a pizza. You cannot just pick salt out of a saltwater mixture. One way to separate the salt from the water is to heat the mixture until the water evaporates. The salt is left behind. Other ways to separate mixtures are shown at the right and below.

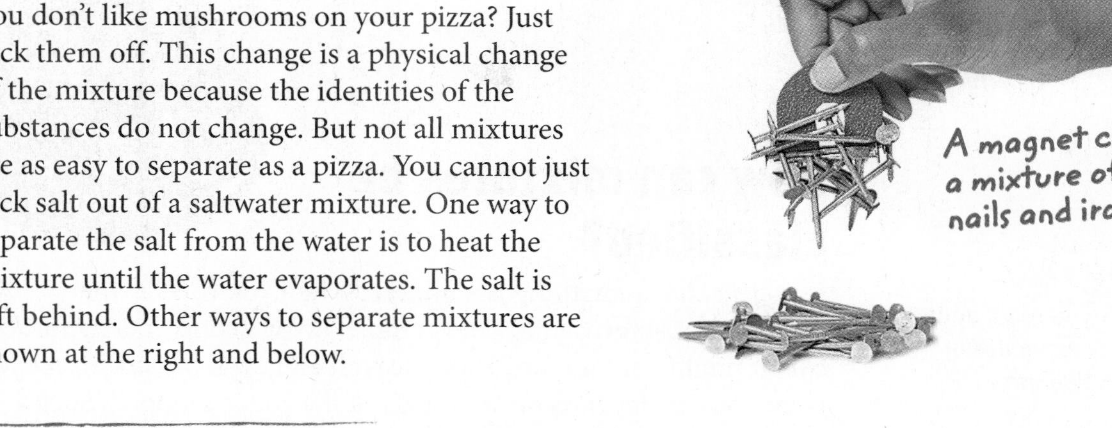

A magnet can separate a mixture of aluminum nails and iron nails.

20 Devise How could you separate a mixture of rocks and sand?

____
____
____
____

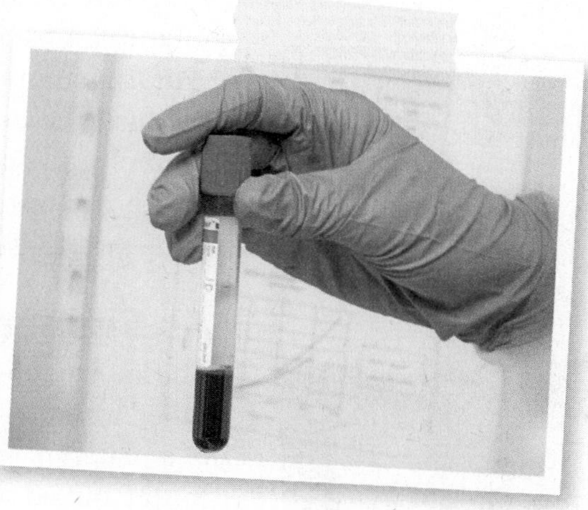

A machine called a centrifuge separates mixtures by the densities of the components. It can be used to separate the different parts of blood.

B When water is added to the sand-salt mixture,

____
____
____
____
____

C When the liquid is poured through a filter,

____
____
____
____
____

D The remaining saltwater is heated until

____
____
____
____
____

A Simple Solution

A snow globe contains a suspension.

How can mixtures be classified?

Active Reading

21 Identify As you read, underline the everyday examples of mixtures on this page.

It is clear that something is a mixture when you can see the different substances in it. For example, if you scoop up a handful of soil, it might contain dirt, rocks, leaves, and even insects. Exactly what you see depends on what part of the soil is scooped. Such a mixture is called a heterogeneous (het•uhr•uh•JEE•nee•uhs) mixture. A **heterogeneous** mixture is one that does not have a uniform composition. In a **homogenous** (hoh•muh•JEE•nee•uhs) mixture, the substances are evenly spread throughout. For example, if you add sugar to a cup of water, the sugar dissolves. When you taste it, each part of the sugar-water mixture has the same sweet taste.

As Suspensions

The snow globe (above) contains a type of heterogeneous mixture called a *suspension*. Suspensions are mixtures in which the particles of a material are spread throughout a liquid or gas but are too large to stay mixed without being stirred or shaken. If a suspension is allowed to sit, the particles will settle out.

Tea is a solution.

As Solutions

Tea is an example of a type of homogeneous mixture known as a *solution*. In a solution, one substance is dissolved in another substance. When you make tea, some of the compounds inside the tea leaves dissolve in the hot water. These compounds give your tea its unique color and taste. Many familiar solutions are liquids. However, solutions may also be gases or solids. Air is an example of a gaseous solution. Alloys, such as brass and steel, are solid solutions in which substances are dissolved in metals.

Gelatin is a colloid.

As Colloids

Colloids are a third type of mixture that falls somewhere between suspensions and solutions. As in a suspension, the particles in a colloid are spread throughout a liquid or gas. Unlike the particles in a suspension, colloid particles are small and do not settle out quickly. Milk and gelatin are colloids. Colloids look homogeneous, but we consider them to be heterogeneous.

22 Summarize Complete the graphic organizer below by filling in the blanks with terms from this lesson. Then, add definitions or sketches of each term inside the appropriate box.

Classifying Matter

Matter
Definition:
Matter is anything that has mass and takes up space. Matter is made up of building blocks called atoms.

Pure Substances
Definition:

Sketch:

Elements
Sketch:

Definition:

Sketch:

Homogeneous
Definition:

Suspensions
Sketch:

Colloids
Definition:

Definition:

Visual Summary

To complete this summary, circle the correct word or phrase. Then use the key below to check your answers. You can use this page to review the main concepts of the lesson.

Pure substances are made up of a single type of particle and cannot be formed or broken down by physical changes.

23 Water is a pure substance / mixture.

24 Water is a(n) element / compound.

Water molecules

Pure Substances and Mixtures

Mixtures are made up of more than one type of particle and can be separated into their component parts by physical changes.

25 Saltwater and sand can be separated with a magnet / filter.

26 Saltwater is a homogeneous / heterogeneous mixture.

Answers: 23 pure substance; 24 compound; 25 filter; 26 homogeneous

27 Predict Why do you think that the particles of a suspension settle out but the particles of a colloid do not?

Lesson Review

Vocabulary

Fill in the blanks with the term that best completes the following sentences.

1 The basic building blocks of matter are called

_______________________.

2 A(n) _______________ is a substance that is made up of a single kind of atom.

3 Elements and compounds are two types of

_______________________.

4 A(n) _______________ is a combination of substances that are combined physically but not chemically.

Key Concepts

5 Identify What kind of mixture is a solution? A suspension? A colloid?

6 Apply Fish give off the compound ammonia, which has a pH above 7. To which class of compounds does ammonia belong?

7 Compare Fill in the following table with properties of elements and compounds.

How are elements and compounds similar?	How are elements and compounds different?

Use this drawing to answer the following question.

8 Identify What type of mixture is this salad dressing?

Critical Thinking

9 Explain Could a mixture be made up of only elements and no compounds? Explain.

10 Synthesize Describe a procedure to separate a mixture of sugar, black pepper, and pebbles.

My Notes

States of Matter

ESSENTIAL QUESTION

How do particles in solids, liquids, and gases move?

By the end of this lesson, you should be able to model the motion of particles in solids, liquids, and gases.

At these hot springs in Japan, you can find water in the form of a solid, a liquid, and a gas.

The hot springs are a favorite winter getaway for these Japanese macaques, or "snow monkeys."

OHIO 6.PS.1 All matter is made up of small particles called atoms.

OHIO 6.PS.2 Changes of state are explained by a model of matter composed of atoms and/or molecules that are in motion.

Lesson Labs

Quick Labs
- Changing Volumes
- Can Crusher

Engage Your Brain

1 Describe Fill in the blank with a word or phrase that you think correctly completes the following sentences.

_________________ is an example of a solid.

_________________ is an example of a gas.

Unlike solids, gases can _________________

____

2 Identify Unscramble the letters below to find substances that are liquids. Write your words on the blank lines.

TWRAE _________________

EICJU _________________

RIVAENG _________________

LIKM _________________

PSAOMOH _________________

Active Reading

3 Apply Use context clues to write your own definitions for the words *definite* and *occupy*.

Example sentence
Solid is the state of matter that has a <u>definite</u> shape and volume.

definite:

____

____

Example sentence
A larger container will allow a gas to <u>occupy</u> more space.

occupy:

____

____

Vocabulary Terms

- **solid**
- **liquid**
- **gas**

4 Identify As you read, place a question mark next to any words that you don't understand. When you finish reading the lesson, go back and review the text that you marked. If the information is still confusing, consult a classmate or a teacher.

Particles in Motion

How do particles move in solids, liquids, and gases?

All matter is made of atoms or groups of atoms that are in constant motion. This idea is the basis for the *kinetic theory of matter.* How much the particles move and how often they bump into each other determine the state of matter of the substance. This view of a movie theater helps to illustrate the differences between the particle motion in each of the three common states of matter.

In Solids, Particles Vibrate in Place

A **solid** substance has a definite volume and shape. The particles in a solid are close together and do not move freely. The particles vibrate but are fixed in place. Often, the particles in a solid are packed together to form a regular pattern like the one shown at the right.

For most substances, the particles in a solid are closer together than the particles in a liquid. For example, the atoms in solid steel are closer together than the atoms in liquid steel. Water is an important exception to this rule. The molecules that make up ice actually have more space between them than the molecules in liquid water do.

Particles in a solid

5 Describe How are particles in a solid like people sitting in a movie theater?

____

____

____

____

____

____

In Liquids, Particles Slide Past One Another

A **liquid** substance has a definite volume but not a definite shape. Particles in a liquid, shown at the right, have more kinetic energy than particles in a solid do. The particles are attracted to one another and are close together. However, particles in a liquid are not fixed in place and can move from one place to another.

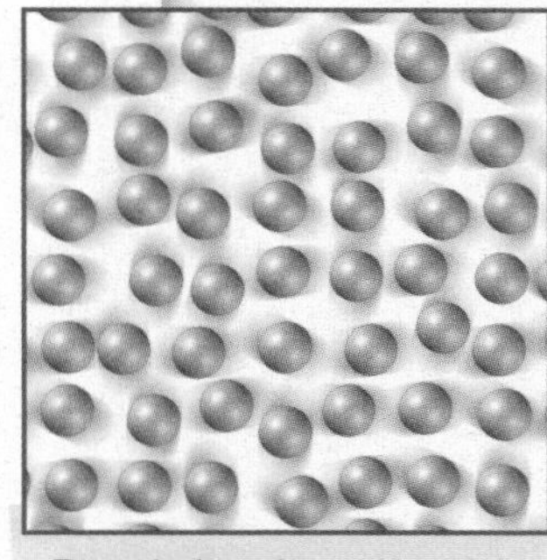
Particles in a liquid

6 Describe How are particles in a liquid like people in a movie theater lobby?

In Gases, Particles Move Freely

A **gas** does not have a definite volume or shape. A substance in the gaseous state has particles with the most kinetic energy of the three states. As you can see in the model at the right, gas particles are not as close to one another and can move easily in any direction. There is much more space between gas particles than there is between particles in a liquid or a solid. The space between gas particles can increase or decrease with changes in temperature or pressure.

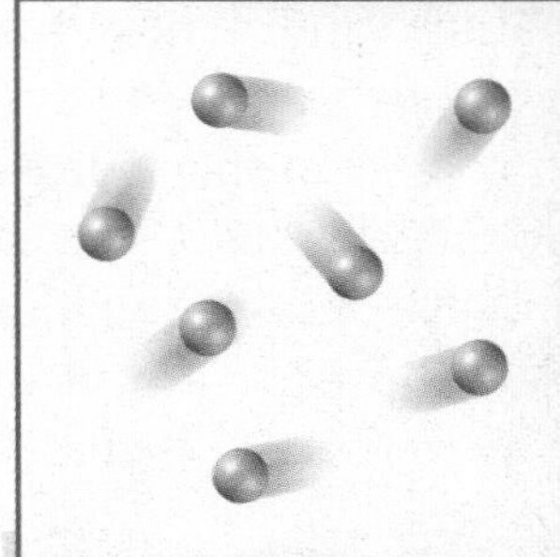
Particles in a gas

7 Describe How are particles in a gas like people outside of a movie theater?

Shape up!

How does particle motion affect the properties of solids, liquids, and gases?

Imagine what you would see if you put a few ice cubes into a pan on a hot stove. The hard blocks of ice would melt to form liquid water. If the pan is hot enough, the water would boil, giving off steam. Ice, liquid water, and the gaseous water in steam are all made up of the same water molecules. Yet ice looks and behaves differently than water or steam does. The kinetic theory of matter helps to explain the different properties of solids, liquids, and gases.

Active Reading **8 Identify** Underline words or phrases that describe the properties of solids, liquids, and gases.

Solids Have a Definite Volume and Shape

The fishbowl at the right contains a small toy castle. When the castle was added to the glass container, the castle kept its original size and shape. The castle, like all solid substances, has a definite shape and volume. The container does not change these properties of the toy. The particles in a solid are in fixed positions and are close together. Although the particles vibrate, they cannot move from one part of the solid to another part. As a result, a solid cannot easily change in shape or volume. If you force the particles apart, you can change the shape of a solid by breaking it into pieces. However, each of those pieces will still be a solid and have its own definite shape.

Think Outside the Book *Inquiry*

9 Model Think about the general shape and behavior of particles in solids, liquids, and gases within a container. What objects could be used as a model of particles? How could you model a container for your particles? Gather the materials and make your model. How does your model of solid, liquid, and gas particles compare to the real particles?

Liquids Have a Definite Volume but Can Change Shape

Unlike the solid toy castle, the water in this fishbowl does not have a definite shape. The water has taken the shape of the round fishbowl. If you poured this same water into a rectangular fish tank, the water would take the shape of that container. However, the water would have the same volume as it did before. It would still take up the same amount of space. Like water, all liquids have a definite volume but no definite shape. The particles in a liquid are close together, but they are not tightly attached to one another as the particles in a solid are. Instead, particles in liquids can slide past one another. As a result, liquids can flow. Instead of having a rigid form, the particles in a liquid move and fill the bottom of the container they are in.

Gases Can Change in Volume and Shape

The small bubbles in this fishbowl are filled with gas. Gases do not have a definite volume or shape. The particles in a gas are very far apart compared to the particles in a solid or a liquid. The amount of space between the particles in a gas can change more easily. If a rigid container has a certain amount of air inside and more air is pumped in, the volume of the gas does not change. The gas will still fill the entire container. Instead, the particles will become closer together. If the container is opened, the particles will spread out and mix with the air in the atmosphere.

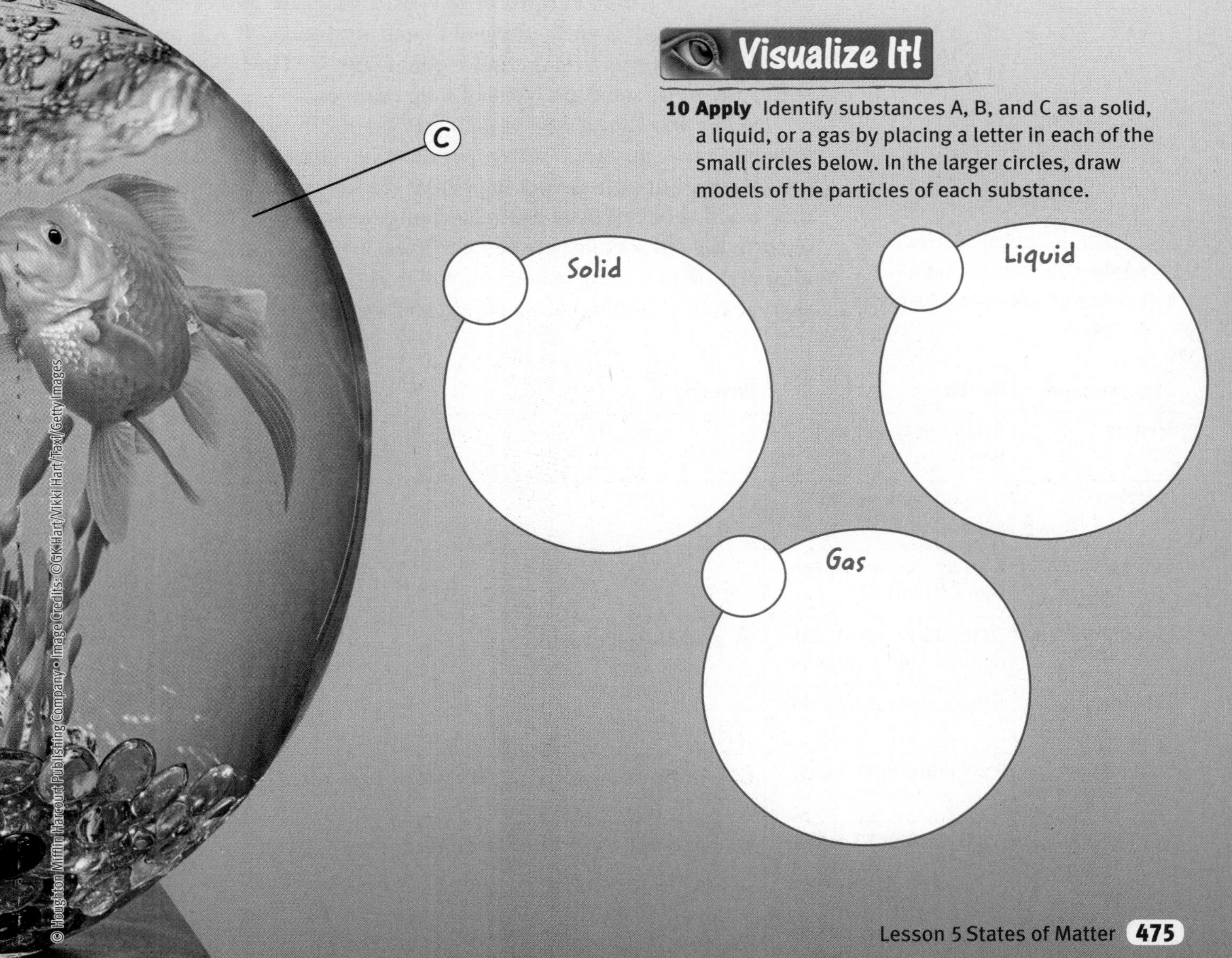

Visualize It!

10 Apply Identify substances A, B, and C as a solid, a liquid, or a gas by placing a letter in each of the small circles below. In the larger circles, draw models of the particles of each substance.

Icicles grow as water drips down them and then freezes, sticking to the ice that is already there. Freezing is an example of a change of state.

What happens when substances change state?

Ice, liquid water, and water vapor are different states of the same substance. As liquid water turns into ice or water vapor, the water molecules themselves do not change. What changes are the motion of the molecules and the amount of space between them.

The Motion of the Particles Changes

The particles of a substance, even a solid, are always in motion. As a solid is heated, its particles gain energy and vibrate faster. If the vibrations are fast enough, the particles break loose and slide past one another. The process in which a solid becomes a liquid is known as *melting.* As the temperature of a liquid is lowered, its particles lose energy. Eventually, the particles move slowly enough for the attractions between them to cause the liquid to become a solid. This process is called *freezing.* Because water freezes at 0 °C, you may associate freezing with cold temperatures. But some substances are frozen at room temperature or above. For example, an aluminum can is an example of frozen aluminum. It will not melt until it reaches a temperature above 660 °C! The table below shows the most common types of state changes.

When substances lose or gain energy, one of two things can happen to the substance: its temperature can change or its state can change. But both do not happen at the same time. The energy that is added or removed during a change of state is used to break or form the attractions between particles. If you measure the temperature of boiling water, you will find that the temperature stays at 100 °C until all of the liquid has become a gas.

11 Apply Complete the table below with examples of state changes.

State change	Result	Example
Melting	A solid becomes a liquid.	
Freezing	A liquid becomes a solid.	
Boiling	A liquid becomes a gas (throughout).	
Evaporation	A liquid becomes a gas (at the liquid's surface).	A puddle dries out.
Condensation	A gas becomes a liquid.	
Sublimation	A solid becomes a gas.	Dry ice becomes a gas at room temperature.
Deposition	A gas becomes a solid.	Frost forms on a cold windowpane.

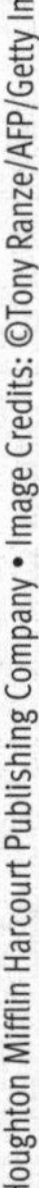

Why It Matters

Making Glass

WEIRD SCIENCE

You can see through it, drink water from it, and create objects of art with it. It's glass, a substance that has been crafted by humans for about 5,000 years! Read on to see how a few simple ingredients can become a beautiful work of art.

Glass Blowing

Glass blowing is the technique of shaping glass by blowing air into a blob of molten glass at the end of a tube. The *blowpipe* is the long, hollow tube that the glass blower uses to shape the molten glass. By blowing air through the blowpipe, a glass blower expands the open space inside the glass. This process is similar to inflating a balloon.

Glass from Sand?

Glass is made by heating a mixture of sand, soda ash, limestone, and other ingredients. Colored glass is made by adding small amounts of metal compounds. The mixture is melted in a roaring hot furnace at about 1,600 °C. Once the mixture melts, the molten glass can be shaped and allowed to cool into the solid state.

Extend

Inquiry

12 Describe In your own words, describe the glass-blowing process.

13 Investigate People once thought that old glass windows are thicker at the bottom because the solid glass had flowed to the bottom over time. Research this theory and report your findings.

14 Investigate Research the various methods of making glass objects. Present your findings by doing one of the following:

- make a poster
- write a short essay
- draw a graphic novel

Visual Summary

To complete this summary, check the box that indicates true or false. Then use the key below to check your answers. You can use this page to review the main concepts of the lesson.

The particles in solids vibrate in place.

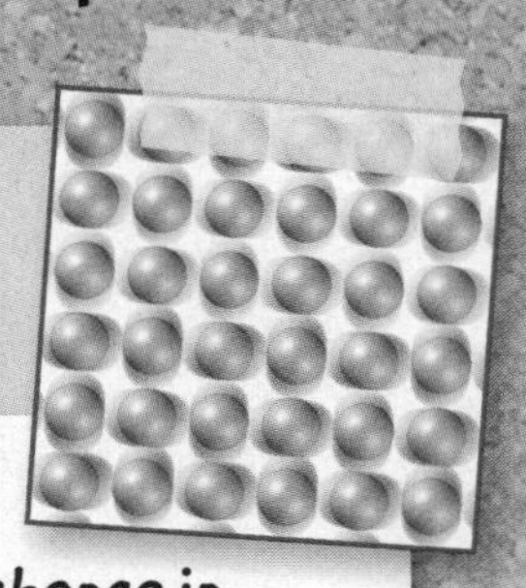

	T	F	
15	☐	☐	Solids can easily change in volume.

The particles in liquids slide past each other.

	T	F	
16	☐	☐	Liquids take the shape of their container.

The particles in gases move freely.

	T	F	
17	☐	☐	When the distance between gas particles increases, the volume of the gas increases.

Answers: 15 F; 16 T; 17 T

18 Describe What happens to the kinetic energy of the particles of a substance as the substance changes from a liquid to a gas?

Lesson Review

Vocabulary

Draw a line to connect the following terms to the description of their particle motion.

1 solid

2 liquid

3 gas

A particles are close together and locked in place

B particles are far apart and can move freely

C particles are close together and can slide past each other

Key Concepts

4 Define What is the kinetic theory of matter?

____

____

____

____

____

5 Analyze What happens to the temperature of a substance while it is changing state? Explain.

____

____

____

____

____

6 Analyze What could you do to change the volume of a gas?

____

____

____

Critical Thinking

7 Apply Can a tank of oxygen gas ever be half empty? Explain.

____

____

____

____

Use this drawing to answer the following questions.

8 Predict This jar contains helium gas. What would happen if the lid of this jar was removed?

____

____

____

____

____

9 Explain How are the helium atoms in this model different from real helium atoms?

____

____

____

____

____

10 Infer The particles that make up a rock are constantly in motion. However, a rock does not visibly vibrate. Why do you think this is?

____

____

____

____

____

____

____

____

____

My Notes

S.T.E.M. Engineering & Technology OHIO 6.SIA.5, 6.SIA.7, 6.SIA.8

Analysis—Risk/Benefit

Skills
✓ Identify risks
✓ Identify benefits
Evaluate cost of technology
✓ Evaluate environmental impact
✓ Propose improvements
✓ Propose risk reduction
✓ Compare technologies
✓ Communicate results

Objectives
• Research a desalination process.
• Conduct a risk/benefit analysis of a desalination process.
• Predict actions that may be taken to decrease the risks or improve the benefits of desalination.

Identifying Risks and Benefits of Desalination

Although our planet has a lot of water, vast areas of Earth are dry. Most of the water is too salty to use for drinking or to grow crops. Millions of people struggle to get enough drinking water. Many countries cannot grow enough food because of water shortages. If we could find an inexpensive and safe way to turn salt water into fresh water, people in drier parts of the world could benefit. Fresh water could be used to irrigate crops, and some dry areas could be turned into productive farmland. The removal of salt from salt water is called *desalination.* However, desalination technology is not appropriate for all areas of the world. There are a number of difficulties associated with this technology.

The Sahara Desert

1 Brainstorm What is a benefit of getting fresh water from the sea?

____

____

____

____

____

What Methods of Desalination Are Being Tried?

Thousands of desalination facilities exist worldwide. More than a dozen methods of desalination can be used effectively. However, most desalination occurs by the *multistage flash distillation* process. In this method, seawater is boiled so that the water turns to steam, leaving the salt behind. Then the steam is cooled and becomes liquid fresh water. This process must be repeated at different temperatures and pressures to remove as much salt as possible. It takes large amounts of energy to boil the water and run the pressure pumps.

Another desalination method is called *reverse osmosis*. Reverse osmosis uses high pressure to force water through a membrane. This membrane does not allow salt and other substances to pass through. So the liquid on the other side of the membrane is fresh water.

2 Apply What resources does multistage flash distillation require?

3 Brainstorm Research at least two other desalination methods. Which one would you like to do more research about?

Reverse osmosis module

Water storage tanks

Farmland made possible by irrigation

Desalination facility

Now it's your turn to research a method of desalination and perform a risk/benefit analysis.

You Try It!

Now it's your turn to more thoroughly research a method of desalination and perform a risk/benefit analysis. You will be comparing your analysis with the work of other class members.

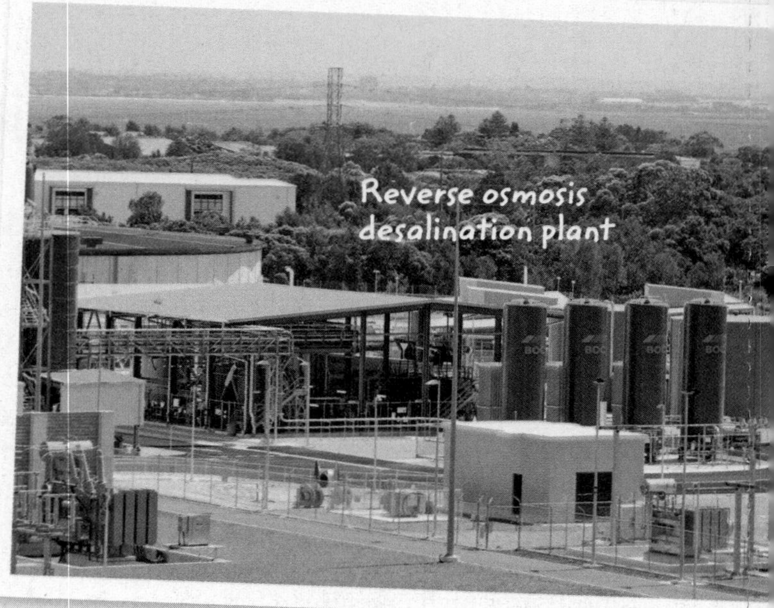

Reverse osmosis desalination plant

1 Identify Risks

Choose a desalination method to research. As you learn about your chosen desalination method, write down the risks or challenges this method has. They may be financial, social, or anything else that applies. Also, list the web sites you consulted.

2 Identify Benefits

What are the benefits to this method that would make it worth pursuing?

3 Evaluate Environmental Impact

How will this technology affect the land? How will it affect the atmosphere? If salt is returned to the sea, how could it affect marine life?

(4) Propose Improvements

What could be done to make this method even better? Can it be combined with another technology or process to enhance its benefits?

(5) Propose Risk Reduction

Is there anything that can be done to reduce the risks? Would combining it with another technology or process make it safer?

(6) Compare Technology

Discuss your analysis with classmates who chose different technologies. Record the ways in which the method you researched seems better or worse than the methods your classmates researched.

(7) Communicate Results

Overall, do you think the desalination method you researched should be used much more than it is? What is its best feature? What recommendations would you make about its use, including where it should be located?

Changes of State

ESSENTIAL QUESTION

What happens when matter changes state?

By the end of this lesson, you should be able to describe changes of state in terms of the attraction and motion of particles.

Two changes of state happen at the hot springs in Yellowstone National Park. Very hot liquid water changes to invisible water vapor, or gas, above the surface of the spring. Then the water vapor changes back into a liquid as it cools in the air. This liquid water can be seen as fog.

OHIO 6.PS.2 Changes of state are explained by a model of matter composed of atoms and/or molecules that are in motion.

OHIO 6.SIA.4 Analyze and interpret data.

OHIO 6.SIA.5 Develop descriptions, models, explanations and predictions.

Lesson Labs

Quick Labs
- Investigating Conservation of Mass
- Modeling Particle Motion
- Boiling Water Without Heating It

Exploration Lab
- Changes of State

Engage Your Brain

1 Identify Unscramble the letters of each word below to find objects in your classroom that are solids. Write the words on the blank lines.

PCLINE

____

SKED

____

OSBOK

____

ODRO

____

2 Describe Write your own caption for this photo.

____

Active Reading

3 Apply Use context clues to write your own definitions for the words *converted* and *constantly*.

Example sentence
When an ice cube melts, a solid is <u>converted</u> to a liquid.

converted:

____

Example sentence
The particles that make up matter are <u>constantly</u> in motion.

constantly:

____

Vocabulary Terms

- **freezing**
- **melting**
- **evaporation**
- **boiling**
- **condensation**
- **sublimation**
- **deposition**

4 Identify This list contains the vocabulary terms you'll learn in this lesson. As you read, circle the definition of each term.

The Fact of the Matter

Active Reading

5 **Identify** As you read, underline the three most familiar states of matter.

What happens when matter changes state?

Eating ice cream on a hot summer day can be messy business. Faster than you can lick it, the ice cream melts and drips down your hand. As ice cream melts, it goes through a change of state. The three most familiar states of matter are solid, liquid, and gas. A change of state is the change of a substance from one physical form of matter to another. When a substance undergoes a physical change, it does not change its identity, just its appearance.

Energy Is Gained and Lost

To change a substance from one state to another, energy must be added or removed. When a substance gains or loses energy, its temperature changes or its state changes. These two changes do not happen at the same time; the temperature remains constant until the change of state is complete. In the graph below, notice that the temperature of a solid remains the same until all of the solid has melted into a liquid. Also, the temperature of a substance remains the same until all of the liquid changes to a gas.

Solid wax becomes liquid when the warmth of the flame causes a change of state.

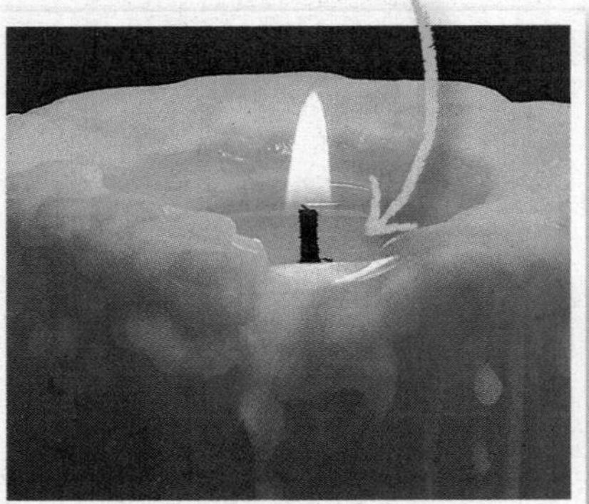

Visualize It!

6 **Apply** Use the graph to determine which point—A, B, or C—represents a candle melting. Circle the correct letter.

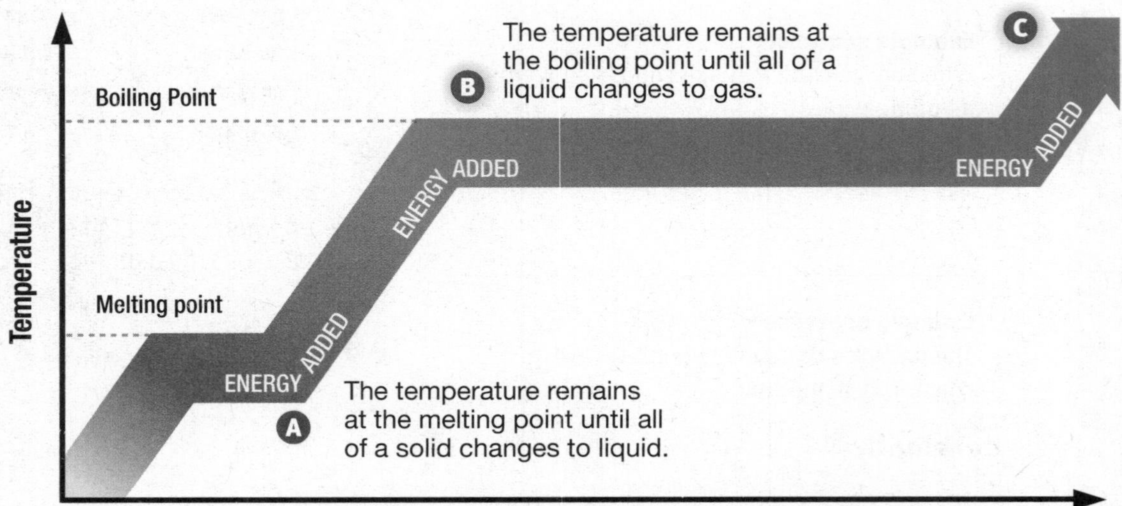
Boiling Point
Melting point
Temperature
Time
ENERGY ADDED
ENERGY ADDED
ENERGY ADDED
A
The temperature remains at the melting point until all of a solid changes to liquid.
B
The temperature remains at the boiling point until all of a liquid changes to gas.
C

Particle Motion Changes

All matter is made of tiny particles that are in constant motion. During a change of state, the motion of the particles changes. Particles can break away from each other and gain more freedom to move. This happens when a solid changes to a liquid, or a liquid changes to a gas. Particles can also attract each other more strongly, and have less freedom to move. This happens when gas changes to a liquid, or a liquid changes to a solid.

Energy Is Conserved

During a change of state, a substance must gain energy from the environment or lose energy to the environment, but the total amount of energy is conserved. Look at the diagram of the water cycle below. Water is converted from liquid water to water vapor, to solid snow, and back to liquid. Each change of state represents a transfer of energy either into or out of the water cycle from the surrounding environment, but energy is never created or destroyed.

7 Analyze Determine whether water particles will have more or less freedom to move at each stage, A, B, and C. Write *more freedom* or *less freedom* in each box.

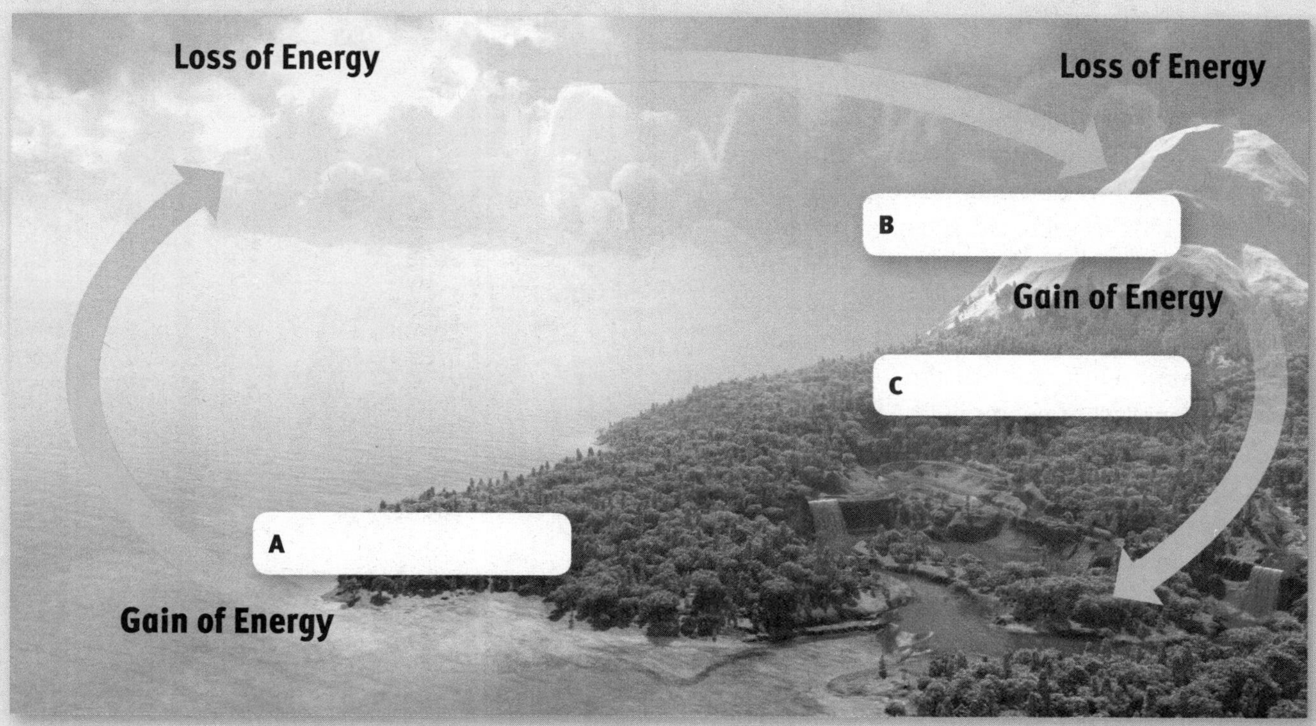

8 Categorize Identify whether each picture below shows a (1) gain of energy or a (2) loss of energy for the substance. Write the appropriate number in the box at the bottom of each picture.

Solid Facts

How do solids and liquids change states?

Particles in a liquid can slide past each other, but particles in a solid can only move enough to vibrate. Removing energy from a liquid can cause it to change to a solid as the particles stop sliding past each other. Adding energy to a solid can cause it to change to a liquid as particles begin sliding past each other.

By Freezing

The change in state in which a liquid becomes a solid is called **freezing**. When a liquid is cooled, its particles have less energy than they did before. The particles slow down, and the attractions between particles increase. Eventually, the particles lock into the fixed arrangement of a typical solid. The temperature at which a liquid substance changes into a solid is the liquid's *freezing point*. Different substances have different freezing points. For example, the freezing point of water is 0 °C. When energy is removed at 0 °C, water converts to its frozen state—ice. The freezing point of the element mercury is –38.8 °C. At 0 °C, mercury is still a liquid.

9 Predict In which sample of water do the water particles have more energy: 5 grams (g) of ice cubes at –10 °C, or 5 g of liquid water at 20 °C? How do you know?

____

____

____

____

____

Visualize It!

10 Identify In the box below each picture, write the state of the substance shown.

Solids can change to liquids.
Liquids can change to solids.

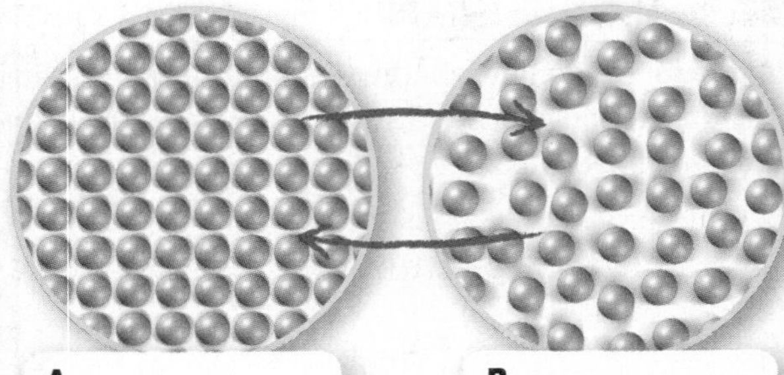

A ____________ B ____________

The freezing point of water is 0 °C (32 °F). Liquid water changes to solid ice at this temperature. You can see this change taking place in the waterfall.

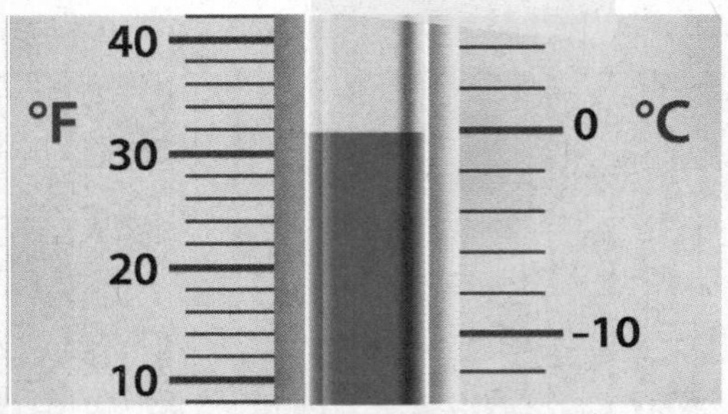

By Melting

Particles in a solid have an ordered arrangement. When a solid is warmed, its particles have more energy than they did before. The particles speed up, and the attraction between the particles decreases. Eventually the particles are able to slide past one another. This change of state from a solid to a liquid is called **melting**. The temperature at which the substance changes from a solid to a liquid is called the *melting point*. Melting is the reverse of freezing. Water freezes and melts at 0 °C. Mercury freezes and melts at −38.8 °C.

Think about a melting snowman. Energy from the sun is added to the solid snow. The particles in the snow begin to move faster. When the temperature of the snow reaches 0° C, the added energy of the particles will overcome some of the attractions that hold the particles in place. The snow starts to melt. As the sun continues to shine on the snowman, even more attractions are broken. Eventually, all the snow turns to liquid water.

Active Reading **11 Apply** Describe what happens to water particles when ice melts.

Inquiry

12 Infer Both the freezing temperature and the melting temperature of water are the same (0 °C). Explain why a substance like water freezes and melts at the same temperature.

Bubbling Over

How do liquids and gases change state?

Particles in a gas have a great deal of energy. Removing enough energy from a gas causes a gas to change into a liquid or a solid. Adding enough energy to a liquid or a solid causes it to change into a gas. The process by which a liquid or a solid changes to a gas is *vaporization*.

By Evaporation or Boiling

As a liquid is warmed, its particles gain energy. Some particles gain enough energy that they escape from the surface of the liquid and become a gas. This process is called **evaporation**. Evaporation occurs slowly at a range of temperatures, but it happens more quickly at higher temperatures.

A rapid change from a liquid to a gas, or vapor, is called **boiling**. This change takes place throughout a liquid, not just at the surface. As a liquid is warmed to a high enough temperature, bubbles form. The specific temperature at which this occurs in a liquid is called the *boiling point*. As air pressure changes at different elevations above sea level, so does the boiling point of liquids. The greater the air pressure, the higher the boiling point of a liquid.

13 Predict What would happen to the boiling point of water at 8,000 m above sea level, where air pressure is lower?

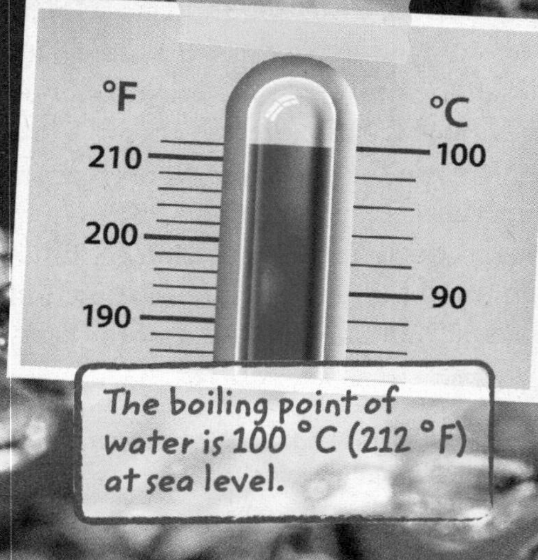

The boiling point of water is 100 °C (212 °F) at sea level.

Visualize It!

14 Identify In the box below each picture, write the state of the substance shown.

Liquids change to gases.
Gases change to liquids.

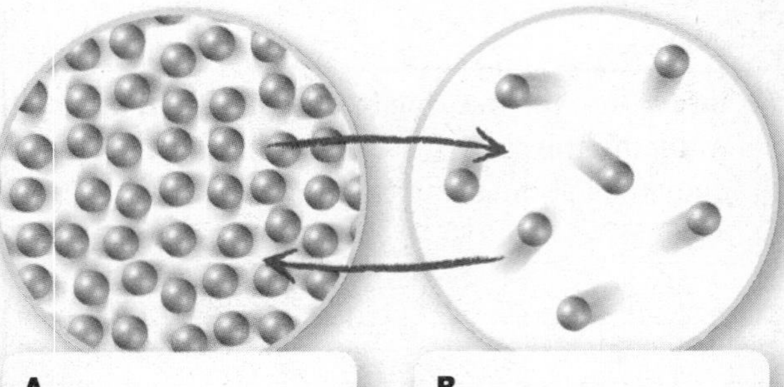

A

B

By Condensation

Particles in a gas have very little attraction to one another. As a gas is cooled its particles lose energy. The attraction between particles overcomes the speed of their motion, and a liquid forms. This change of state from a gas to a liquid is called **condensation**. Condensation is the reverse of evaporation.

Grass is often wet in early morning because gaseous water vapor in the air condenses on the cool grass. Water droplets form on the outside of a cold glass of lemonade when water vapor in the warm air condenses on the cool glass.

Look at the photo below of contrail lines left by jet planes. Water vapor and soot form when fuel burns in jet engines. The gaseous water vapor condenses as tiny liquid water droplets. The water droplets then freeze into ice crystals on the soot particles to form a contrail. The word *contrail* is short for condensation trail.

15 Apply Indicate whether the change of state in each process causes particles to (A) have more freedom or (B) have less freedom. Write the appropriate letter next to each process.

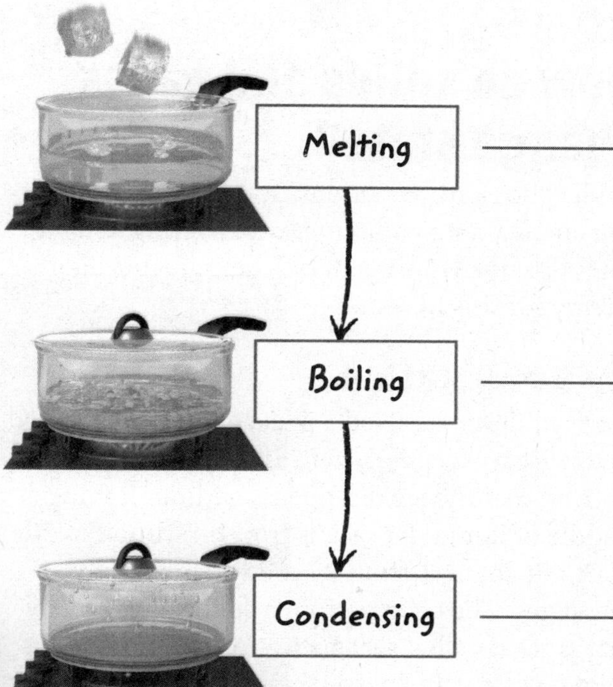

16 Compare How are the planes' contrail lines similar to clouds?

____

____

____

____

____

____

The dramatic effect of contrails is the result of condensation and freezing.

Into Thin Air

How do solids and gases change state?

Under the right conditions, some solids and gases can change state without ever becoming a liquid. The substance must gain or lose a great deal of energy for this to occur.

By Sublimation

Have you ever received a package of food shipped in dry ice to keep it frozen? If so, you may have noticed that the ice disappears without leaving a puddle of liquid. Dry ice is frozen carbon dioxide (CO_2). It changes from its solid state directly into a gas. The change from a solid state directly into a gas is called **sublimation**. As the particles of solid dry ice gain energy their motion completely overcomes the attraction between the particles, and the particles escape into the air as gas.

Dry ice is extremely cold, about –80 °C, and at room temperature, 25 °C, the air provides the energy for it to sublimate. A fog is observed as water vapor condenses when it comes in contact with cold CO_2 gas.

Snow and ice formed by water sublimate at below-freezing temperatures. To see sublimation in action, hang wet clothes outside on a day that temperatures are below freezing. First the water in the clothes freezes, and then the solid ice sublimates into the air.

No liquid is visible in the bowl as the solid CO_2 disappears. It sublimates from a solid directly to an invisible gas.

Think Outside the Book

17 Research With a partner, find another substance that can sublimate. Describe the conditions under which sublimation occurs.

By Deposition

In physical science, **deposition** is the change in state from a gas directly to a solid. Deposition is the process by which ice crystals form in clouds. The photo at the right shows deposition of invisible water vapor into ice crystals on a cold window.

When conditions are right, deposition occurs when the particles of a gas lose energy. Attraction between particles locks the particles into the rigid structure of a solid. No liquid is formed in the process.

Active Reading **18 Compare** Explain how sublimation and deposition are alike and how they are different.

____

____

____

____

Ice crystals form on a cold window when water vapor in the air is converted to ice by the process of deposition.

19 Relate Complete Column 1 and Column 2 to identify opposite processes. In the third column, indicate whether the process in Column 1 or Column 2 is the result of a gain of energy.

Column 1	Column 2	
The opposite of...	is	Gain in Energy
deposition		
	condensation	Column 1
melting		

Conserve

What happens to matter when a change of state occurs?

When matter changes from one state to another, it remains the same kind of matter. Its physical state changes, but its chemical identity does not. For example, an ice cube and the puddle it forms when it melts are both made up of water.

Active Reading

20 Identify As you read, underline the ways particles of matter are affected by a change of state.

Energy and Motion of Particles Changes

You might ask, "What *does* change as a result of a change of state?" The answer is that the energy of the particles, the movement of the particles, and the distance between them change. You can see these changes in the diagram below.

Visualize It!

21 Apply Label the state changes that are taking place in both directions of the arrows at stage A, B, and C. Draw the missing model for the gas state.

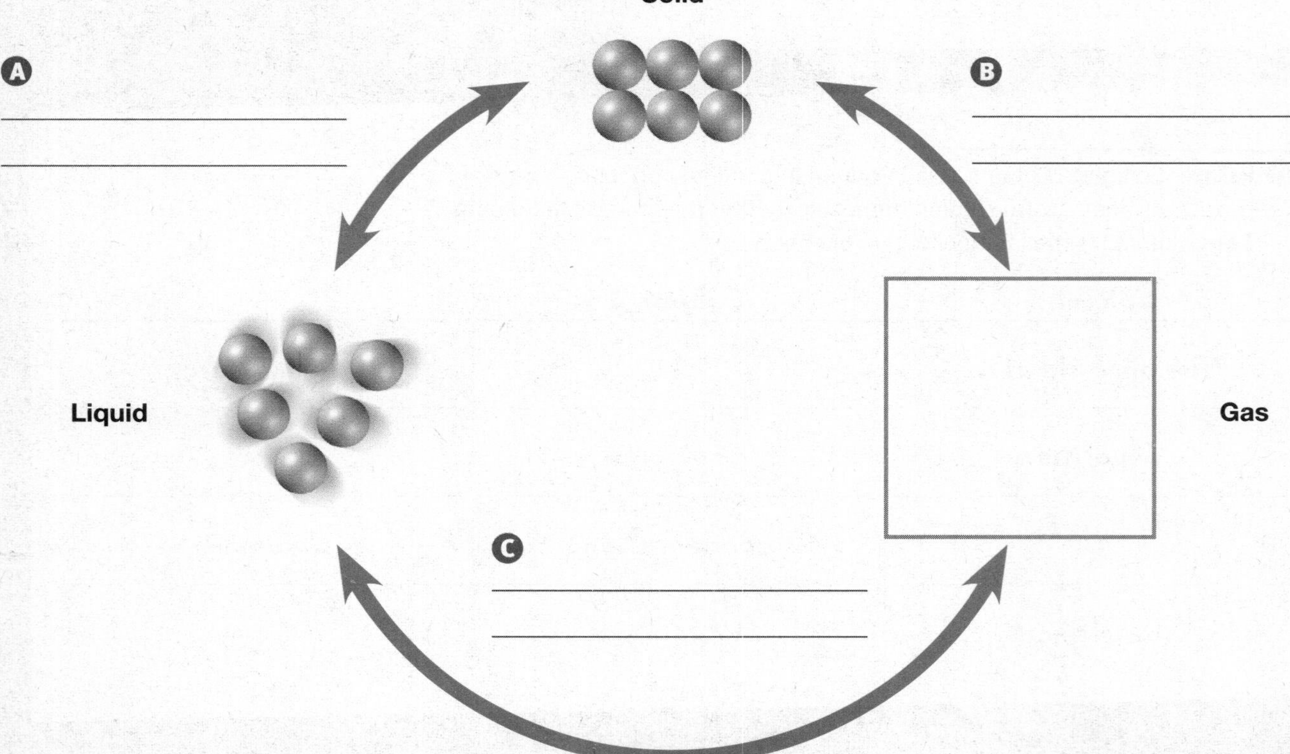

Mass Is Conserved

What happens to the *amount* of matter in a change of state? Suppose you do an experiment. You put ice cubes in a sealed container so that the container plus the ice has a total mass of 100 g. You warm the ice to the melting point. It becomes liquid water. Then you continue to warm the water to the boiling point so that it becomes a gas. After each step, you measure the mass of the water. You find no difference in the mass. The sealed container at each state has a mass of 100 g. You know that the mass of the container itself cannot change. So you can conclude that the gaseous water vapor has the same mass as the liquid water and the solid ice. The mass of a substance does not change when its state changes. Each state contains the same amount of matter.

Think about the particles of water in the closed container. They do not disappear. Even the particles that escape from the liquid state stay in the container as gas. Because the number of particles in the container stays the same, the amount of matter is conserved.

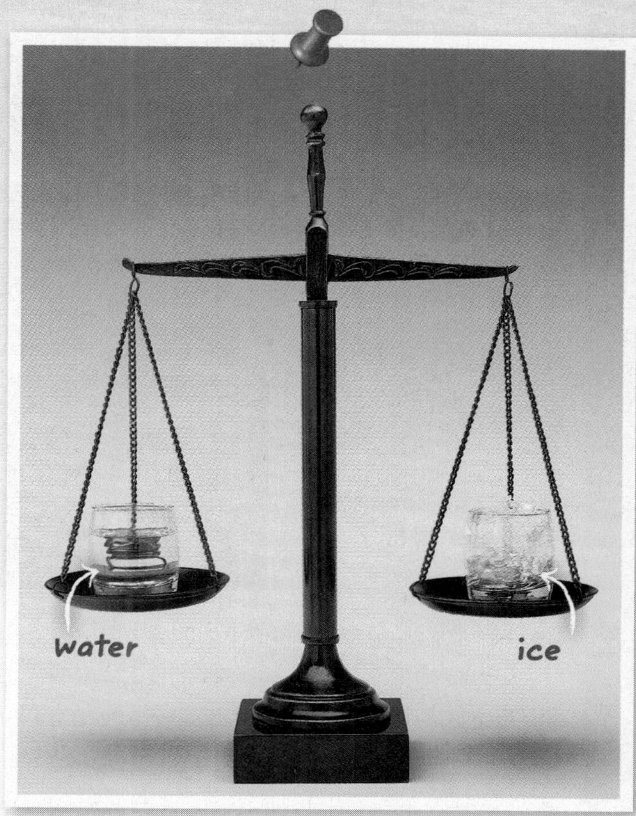

Mass is conserved when a change of state occurs.

Visualize It!

22 Apply A flask of water is sealed with a balloon and heated to various temperatures on a hot plate. Fill in the missing information below.

A $m =$ ________

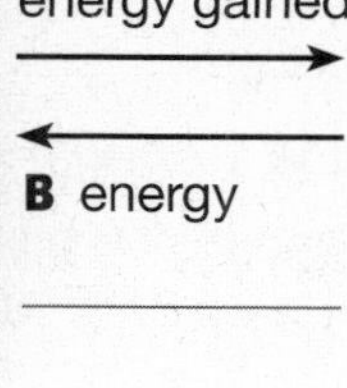

energy gained →

← **B** energy ________

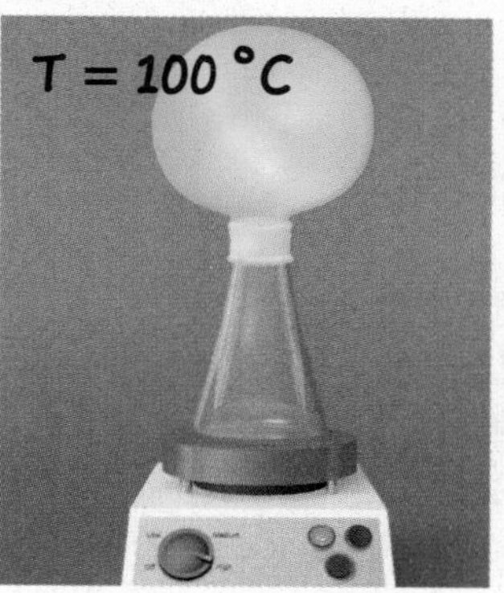

$m = 52$ g

C energy ________ ←

→ energy lost

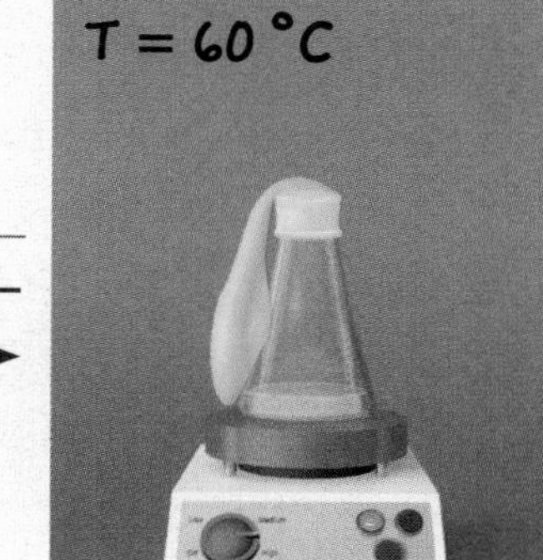

D $m =$ ________

23 Evaluate Explain how the system of the flask and the balloon illustrates the conservation of mass.

____

____

____

____

Visual Summary

To complete this summary, fill in the blanks with the correct word or phrase. Then use the key below to check your answers. You can use this page to review the main concepts of the lesson.

Changes of State

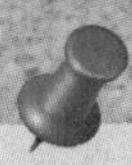

A solid can change to a liquid or gas.

24 The change from a solid to a liquid is called ____________________

25 The change of a solid directly to a gas is called ____________________

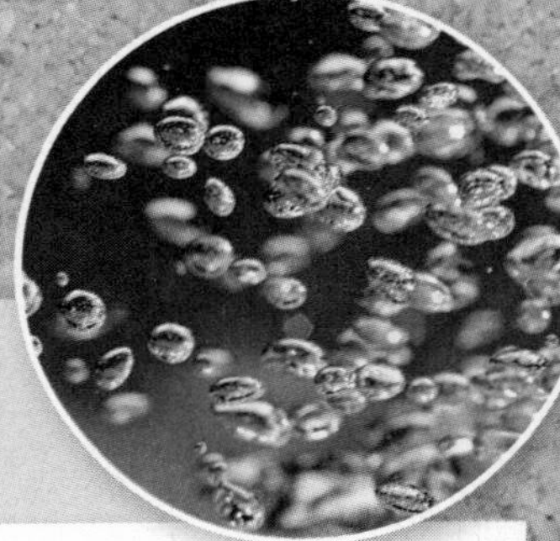

A liquid can change to a gas or a solid.

28 Ice is formed from liquid water during the process of ____________________

29 Two ways that liquid water can become a gas are by ____________________

Answers: 24 melting; 25 sublimation; 26 deposition; 27 Condensation; 28 freezing; 29 boiling and evaporation; 30 stays the same

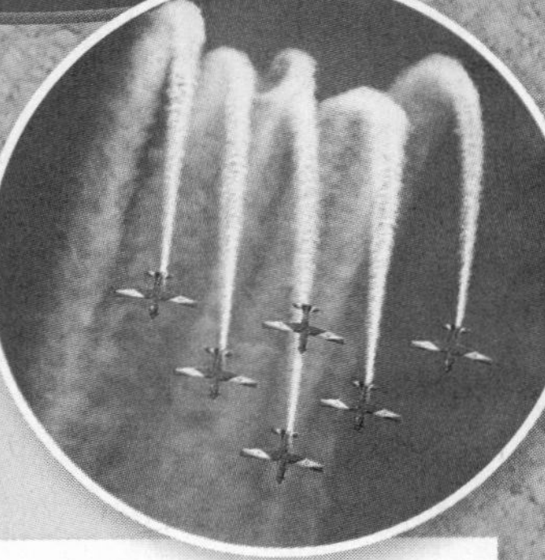

A gas can change to a solid or a liquid.

26 Water vapor changes directly to ice by ____________________

27 ____________________ is the process in which water vapor changes to a liquid.

Mass is conserved when a change of state occurs.

30 The amount of mass ____________________ ____________________ during a change of state.

31 Predict What would happen to the amount of matter on Earth if mass were not conserved during changes of state?

Lesson Review

Vocabulary

Draw a line to connect the following terms to their definitions.

1 freezing
2 evaporation
3 sublimation
4 melting

A change of state from solid to liquid
B change of state from liquid to gas
C change of state from solid to gas
D change of state from liquid to solid

Key Concepts

5 Describe What happens to particles when a substance gains energy and changes state?

6 Explain What happens to the energy that is lost when water freezes?

7 Compare How does the movement of particles in a stick of butter differ from the movement of particles in a dish of melted butter?

8 Identify As water is cooled, at what temperature do its particles become fixed in place?

Critical Thinking

Use this drawing to answer the following questions.

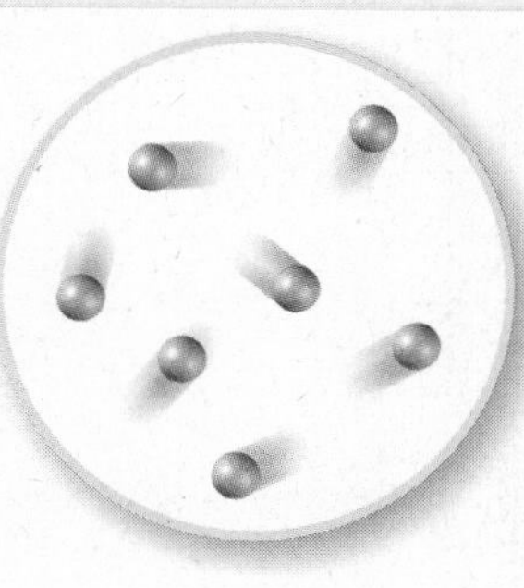

9 Relate The drawing represents the movement of particles in a substance. What changes of state can this substance undergo?

10 Describe What processes will the substance in the drawing undergo when those changes of state occur? Explain.

11 Compare How do evaporation and boiling differ?

12 Apply The boiling point of a substance in City A is found to be 145 °C. The boiling point of the same substance in City B is 141 °C. Which city, A or B, is at a higher elevation? How do you know?

My Notes

Unit 6 Big Idea

Atoms are the basic building blocks of matter, and their motion determines the state of matter of the substance.

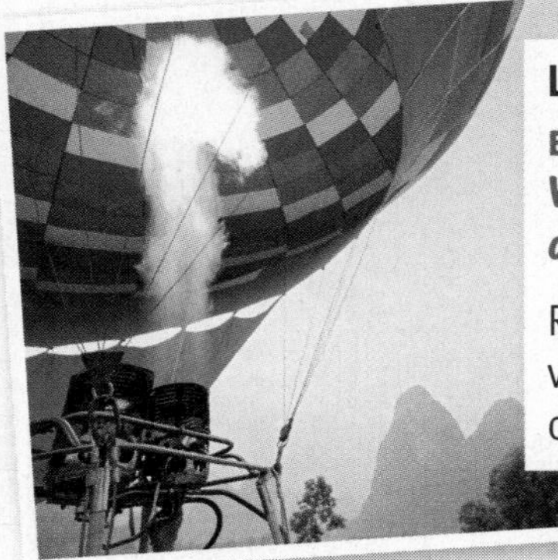

Lesson 1

ESSENTIAL QUESTION

What properties define matter?

Relate mass, weight, volume, and density to one another.

Lesson 2

ESSENTIAL QUESTION

What are physical and chemical properties of matter?

Classify and compare substances based on their physical and chemical properties.

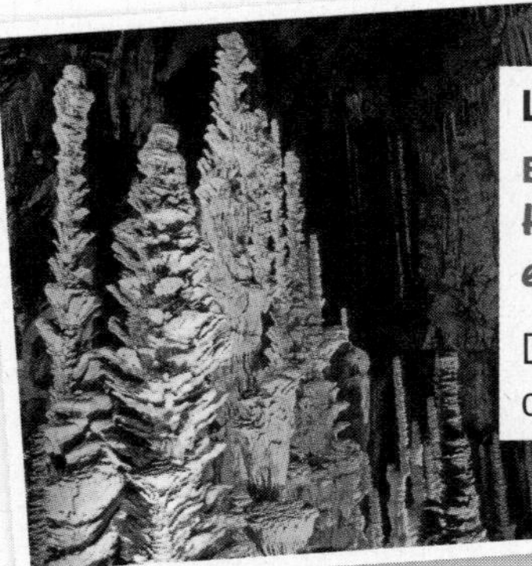

Lesson 3

ESSENTIAL QUESTION

How are atoms and elements related?

Describe the properties of atoms and elements.

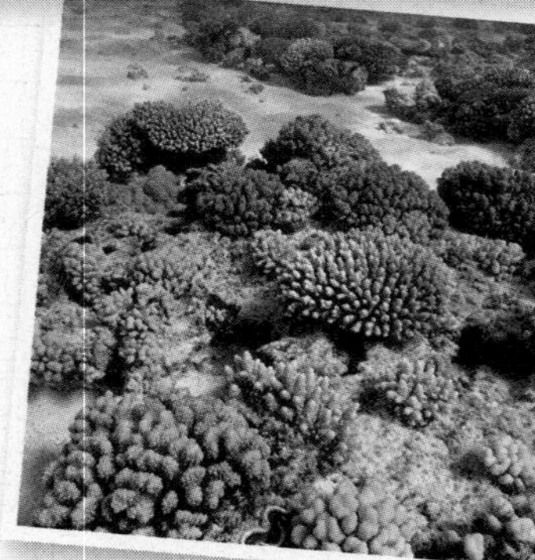

Lesson 4

ESSENTIAL QUESTION

How do pure substances and mixtures compare?

Distinguish between pure substances and mixtures.

Lesson 5

ESSENTIAL QUESTION

How do particles in solids, liquids, and gases move?

Model the motion of particles in solids, liquids, and gases.

Lesson 6

ESSENTIAL QUESTION

What happens when matter changes state?

Describe changes of state in terms of the attraction and motion of particles.

Connect ESSENTIAL QUESTIONS

Lessons 4 and 6

1 Synthesize How can understanding changes of state help you to separate a saltwater solution?

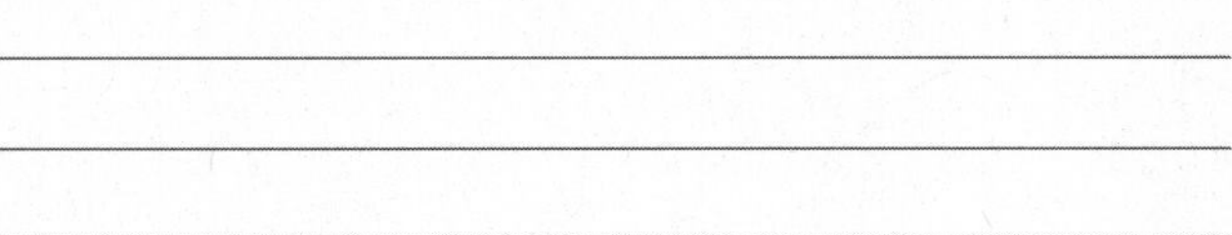

Think Outside the Book

2 Synthesize Choose one of these activities to help synthesize what you have learned in this unit.

☐ Using what you learned in lessons 1, 2, 3, and 4, explain how matter can be classified by its physical and chemical properties by creating an informative brochure. Include examples of both pure substances and mixtures.

☐ Using what you learned in lessons 5 and 6, create a presentation that describes the particle movement in a substance as it changes from a solid to a liquid to a gas and then back to a solid.

Unit 6 Review

Name ______________________________

Vocabulary

Check the box to show whether each statement is true or false.

T	F	
☐	☐	**1** Density is anything that has mass and takes up space.
☐	☐	**2** A physical property can be measured without changing the identity of the substance.
☐	☐	**3** Matter is anything that has mass and takes up space.
☐	☐	**4** A proton is a negatively charged subatomic particle.
☐	☐	**5** Each element is a pure substance that cannot be broken down into simpler materials by ordinary means and is represented by a unique chemical symbol.

Key Concepts

Choose the letter of the best answer.

6 Two balloons are blown up to an equal volume. Balloon 2 is placed in a freezer for 20 minutes.

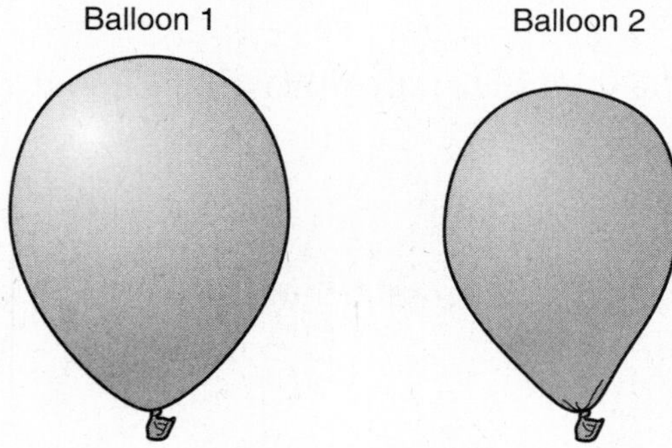

Why would freezing a balloon produce the results shown in Balloon 2?

A Increased kinetic energy decreases the attraction between particles of air in the balloon.

B Increased kinetic energy increases the attraction between particles of air in the balloon.

C Decreased kinetic energy decreases the attraction between particles of air in the balloon.

D Decreased kinetic energy increases the attraction between particles of air in the balloon.

7 The instrument below is used to measure an object.

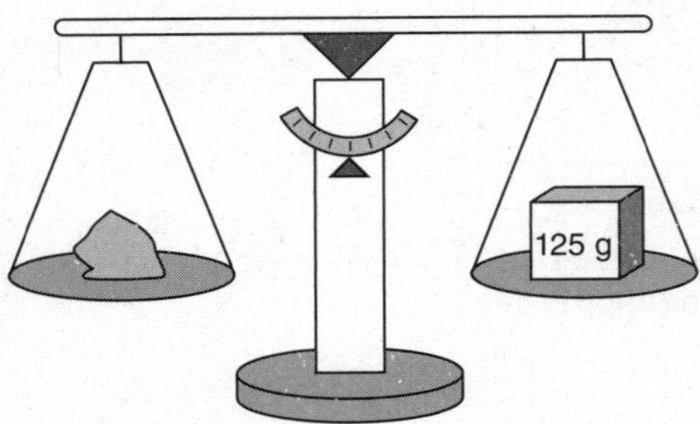

What is the instrument measuring?

A gravity

B weight

C density

D mass

8 Luster, conductivity, and malleability are physical properties of metals. What makes these properties different from chemical properties?

A Physical properties relate to elements rather than compounds.

B Physical properties appear only after a chemical change occurs.

C Physical properties can be observed without attempting to change the identity of the substance.

D Physical properties describe elements in the solid state rather than in the liquid or gas state.

9 Every atom has a nucleus and an electron cloud. The diagram below is a model of an atom.

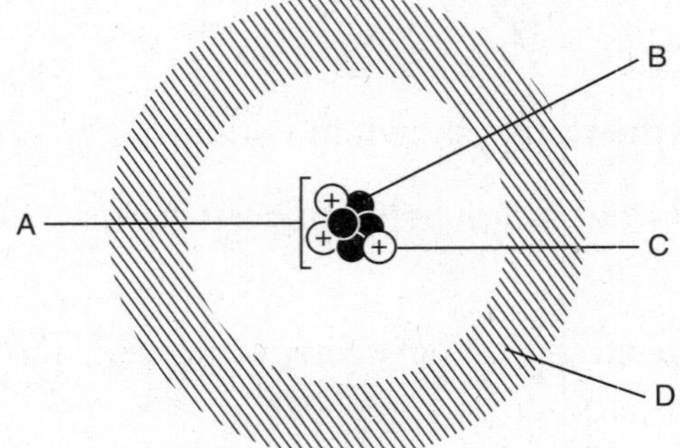

Which label points to a neutron?

A A

B B

C C

D D

10 Which of the following is a way in which elements and compounds are different?

A Elements are pure substances, but compounds are not.

B Compounds can be broken down by physical changes, but elements cannot.

C Elements are made of identical atoms, whereas compounds are made of identical molecules.

D A compound contains many different kinds of elements, whereas an element contains many different kinds of atoms.

11 A rock is dropped into a graduated cylinder filled with 35 mL of water.

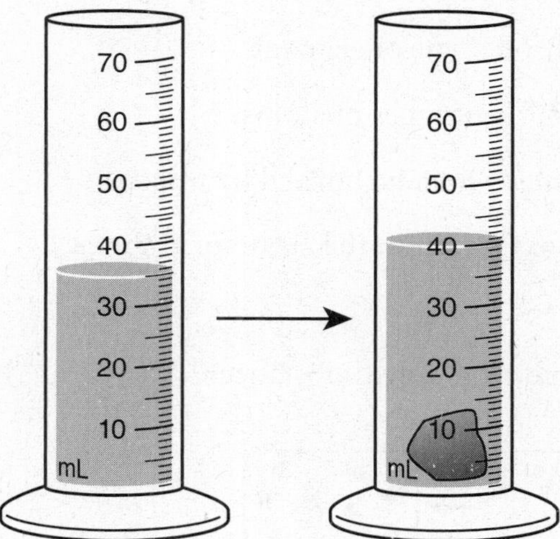

What is the volume of the rock?

A 40 cm^3

B 14 cm^3

C 5 cm^3

D 35 cm^3

12 What is the boiling point of water?

A 0 °C

B 32 °C

C 100 °C

D 212 °C

13 David found that water can be created in a lab by burning hydrogen gas in air. He concluded that water is not a compound because only hydrogen was used to form the water. What is wrong with David's conclusion?

A A compound does contain only one type of element.

B Hydrogen is made up of two different types of atoms.

C Water was not the product formed when he burned hydrogen.

D The hydrogen combined with oxygen from the air to form water.

14 Substance A and substance B combine to form substance C.

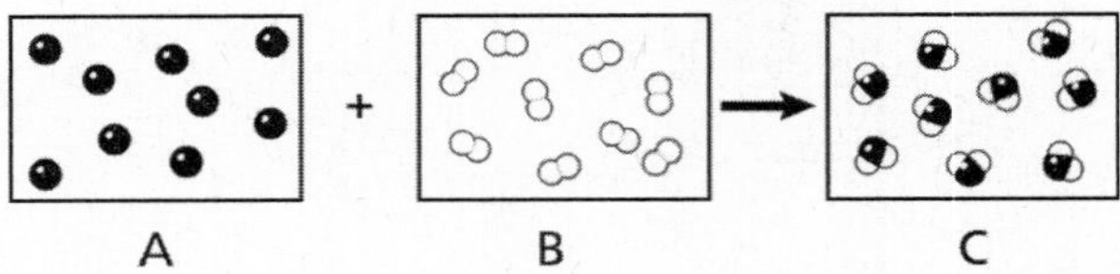

What is substance C?

A an atom

B a mixture

C an element

D a compound

Name ______________________________

Critical Thinking

Answer the following questions in the spaces provided.

15 An unknown substance has a volume of 2 cm^3 and a mass of 38.6 grams.

Material	Density (g/cm^3)
water	1.0
aluminum	2.7
iron	7.9
silver	10.5
gold	19.3

What is the density of the sample? Use the chart above to determine its identity.

____

____

List three other physical properties that could be used to identify this sample.

____

____

____

16 Sketch the particles in a solution, a suspension, and a colloid, and give an example of each.

Solution: ______________________

Suspension: ______________________

Colloid: ______________________

17 Although they both contain the same element, the metal copper (Cu) and the compound copper sulfate ($CuSO_4$) are very different substances. Why can substances that contain the same element have very different properties?

Connect ESSENTIAL QUESTIONS

Lessons 2, 3 and 5

Answer the following question in the space provided.

18 Living things are mostly made up of four elements: carbon, hydrogen, nitrogen, and oxygen. Explain why life on Earth depends on water. Describe how plants and animals get the water they need to survive.

Look It Up!

Mineral Properties

Here are five steps to take in mineral identification:

1 Determine the color of the mineral. Is it light-colored, dark-colored, or a specific color?

2 Determine the luster of the mineral. Is it metallic or nonmetallic?

3 Determine the color of any powder left by its streak.

4 Determine the hardness of your mineral. Is it soft, hard, or very hard? Using a glass plate, see if the mineral scratches it.

5 Determine whether your sample has cleavage or any special properties.

TERMS TO KNOW	DEFINITION
adamantine	a nonmetallic luster like that of a diamond
cleavage	how a mineral breaks when subject to stress on a particular plane
luster	the state or quality of shining by reflecting light
streak	the color of a mineral when it is powdered
submetallic	between metallic and nonmetallic in luster
vitreous	glass-like type of luster

Silicate Minerals					
Mineral	**Color**	**Luster**	**Streak**	**Hardness**	**Cleavage and Special Properties**
Beryl	deep green, pink, white, bluish green, or yellow	vitreous	white	7.5–8	1 cleavage direction; some varieties fluoresce in ultraviolet light
Chlorite	green	vitreous to pearly	pale green	2–2.5	1 cleavage direction
Garnet	green, red, brown, black	vitreous	white	6.5–7.5	no cleavage
Hornblende	dark green, brown, or black	vitreous	none	5–6	2 cleavage directions
Muscovite	colorless, silvery white, or brown	vitreous or pearly	white	2–2.5	1 cleavage direction
Olivine	olive green, yellow	vitreous	white or none	6.5–7	no cleavage
Orthoclase	colorless, white, pink, or other colors	vitreous	white or none	6	2 cleavage directions
Plagioclase	colorless, white, yellow, pink, green	vitreous	white	6	2 cleavage directions
Quartz	colorless or white; any color when not pure	vitreous or waxy	white or none	7	no cleavage

Nonsilicate Minerals					
Mineral	**Color**	**Luster**	**Streak**	**Hardness**	**Cleavage and Special Properties**
Native Elements					
Copper	copper-red	metallic	copper-red	2.5–3	no cleavage
Diamond	pale yellow or colorless	adamantine	none	10	4 cleavage directions
Graphite	black to gray	submetallic	black	1–2	1 cleavage direction
Carbonates					
Aragonite	colorless, white, or pale yellow	vitreous	white	3.5–4	2 cleavage directions; reacts with hydrochloric acid
Calcite	colorless or white to tan	vitreous	white	3	3 cleavage directions; reacts with weak acid; double refraction
Halides					
Fluorite	light green, yellow, purple, bluish green, or other colors	vitreous	none	4	4 cleavage directions; some varieties fluoresce
Halite	white	vitreous	white	2.0–2.5	3 cleavage directions
Oxides					
Hematite	reddish brown to black	metallic to earthy	dark red to red-brown	5.6–6.5	no cleavage; magnetic when heated
Magnetite	iron-black	metallic	black	5.5–6.5	no cleavage; magnetic
Sulfates					
Anhydrite	colorless, bluish, or violet	vitreous to pearly	white	3–3.5	3 cleavage directions
Gypsum	white, pink, gray, or colorless	vitreous, pearly, or silky	white	2.0	3 cleavage directions
Sulfides					
Galena	lead-gray	metallic	lead-gray to black	2.5–2.8	3 cleavage directions
Pyrite	brassy yellow	metallic	greenish, brownish, or black	6–6.5	no cleavage

Geologic Time Scale

Geologists developed the geologic time scale to represent the 4.6 billion years of Earth's history that have passed since Earth formed. This scale divides Earth's history into blocks of time. The boundaries between these time intervals (shown in millions of years ago, or mya, in the table below), represent major changes in Earth's history. Some boundaries are defined by mass extinctions, major changes in Earth's surface, and/or major changes in Earth's climate.

The four major divisions that encompass the history of life on Earth are Precambrian time, the Paleozoic era, the Mesozoic era, and the Cenozoic era. The largest divisions are eons. **Precambrian time** is made up of the first three eons, over 4 billion years of Earth's history.

The **Paleozoic era** lasted from 542 mya to 251 mya. All major plant groups, except flowering plants, appeared during this era. By the end of the era, reptiles, winged insects, and fishes had also appeared. The largest known mass extinction occurred at the end of this era.

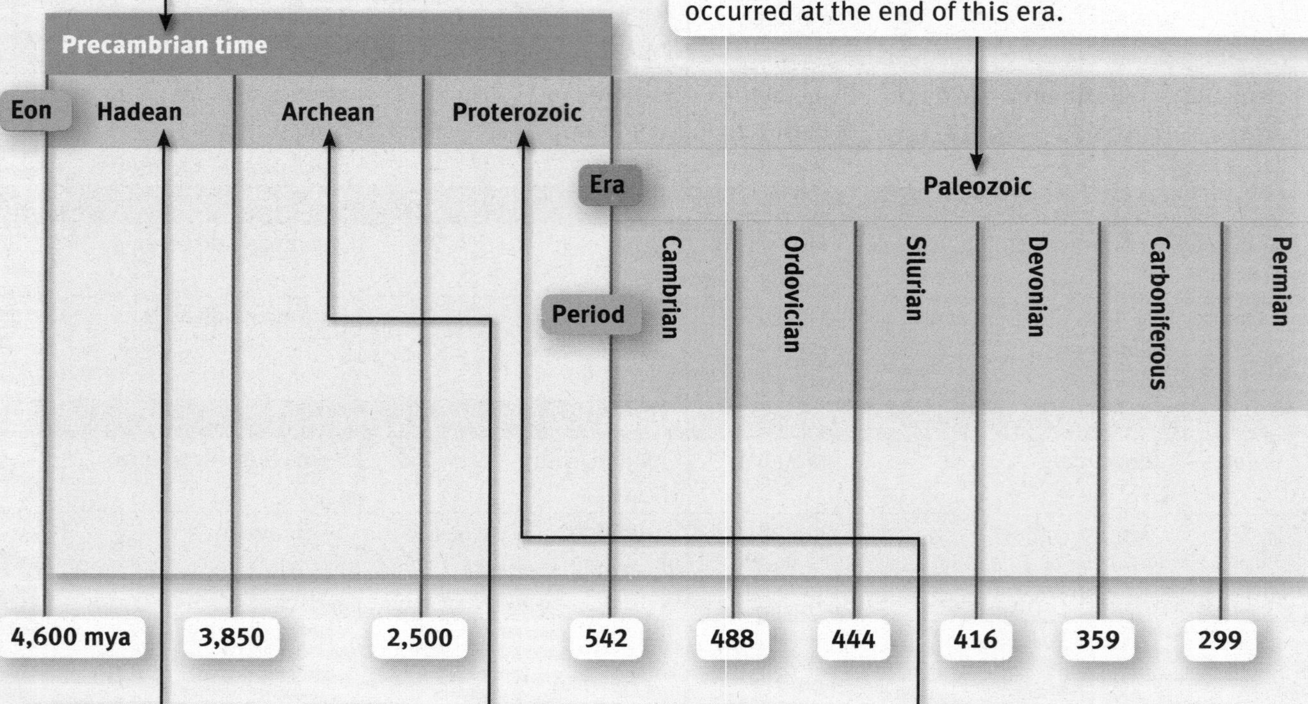

The **Hadean eon** lasted from about 4.6 billion years ago (bya) to 3.85 bya. It is described based on evidence from meteorites and rocks from the moon.

The **Archean eon** lasted from 3.85 bya to 2.5 bya. The earliest rocks from Earth that have been found and dated formed at the start of this eon.

The **Proterozoic eon** lasted from 2.5 bya to 542 mya. The first organisms, which were single-celled organisms, appeared during this eon. These organisms produced so much oxygen that they changed Earth's oceans and Earth's atmosphere.

Divisions of Time

The divisions of time shown here represent major changes in Earth's surface and when life developed and changed significantly on Earth. As new evidence is found, the boundaries of these divisions may shift. The Phanerozoic eon is divided into three eras. The beginning of each of these eras represents a change in the types of organisms that dominated Earth. And each era is commonly characterized by the types of organisms that dominated the era. These eras are divided into periods, and periods are divided into epochs.

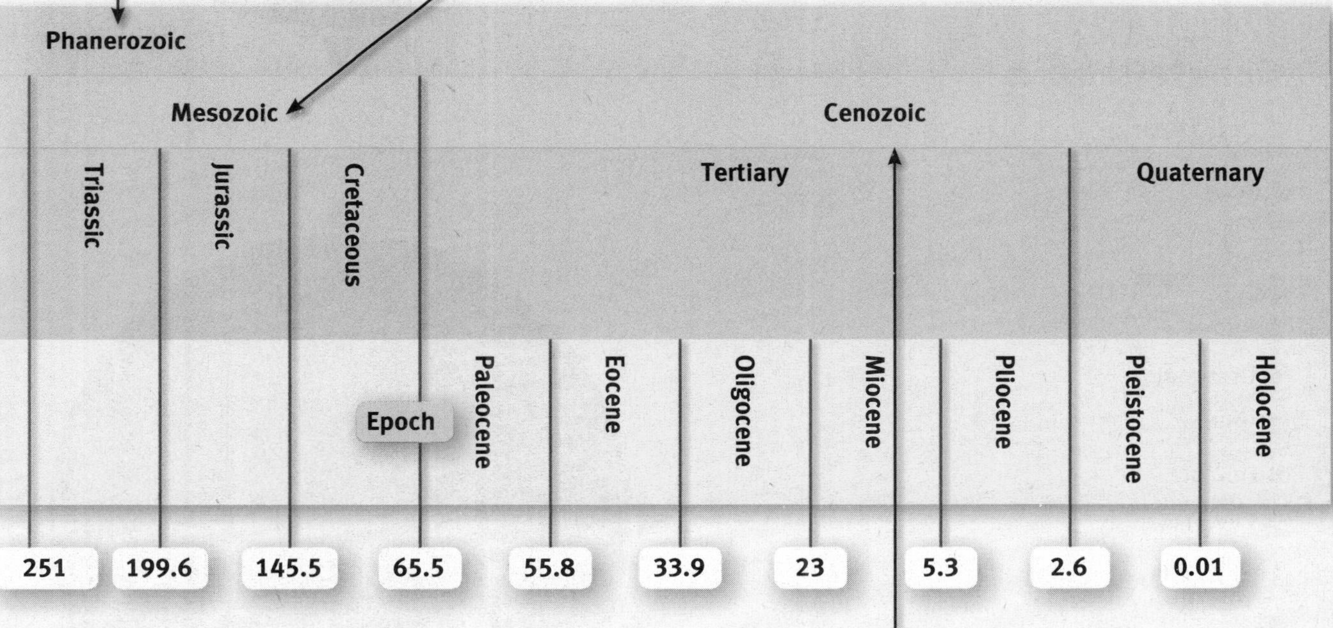

The **Mesozoic era** lasted from 251 mya to 65.5 mya. During this era, many kinds of dinosaurs dominated land, and giant lizards swam in the ocean. The first birds, mammals, and flowering plants also appeared during this time. About two-thirds of all land species went extinct at the end of this era.
The **Phanerozoic eon** began 542 mya. We live in this eon.
Phanerozoic
Mesozoic
Cenozoic
Triassic
Jurassic
Cretaceous
Tertiary
Quaternary
Epoch
Paleocene
Eocene
Oligocene
Miocene
Pliocene
Pleistocene
Holocene
251
199.6
145.5
65.5
55.8
33.9
23
5.3
2.6
0.01
The **Cenozoic era** began 65.5 mya and continues today. Mammals dominate this era. During the Mesozoic era, mammals were small in size but grew much larger during the Cenozoic era. Primates, including humans, appeared during this era.

References

Star Charts for the Northern Hemisphere

A star chart is a map of the stars in the night sky. It shows the names and positions of constellations and major stars. Star charts can be used to identify constellations and even to orient yourself using Polaris, the North Star.

Because Earth moves through space, different constellations are visible at different times of the year. The star charts on these pages show the constellations visible during each season in the Northern Hemisphere.

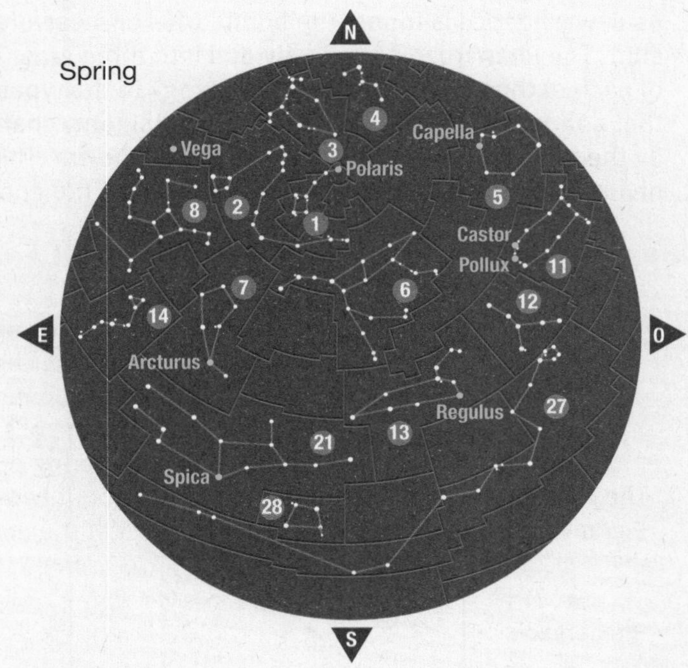

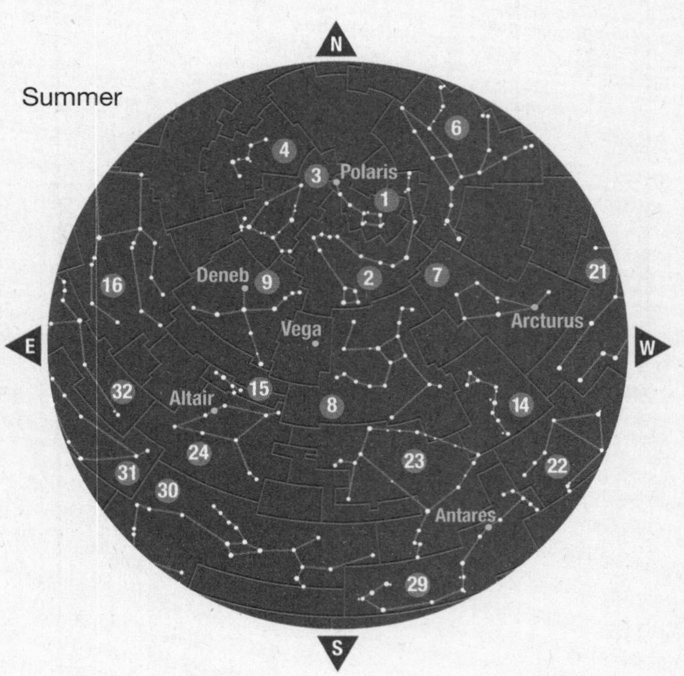

Constellations

1 Ursa Minor

2 Draco

3 Cepheus

4 Cassiopeia

5 Auriga

6 Ursa Major

7 Boötes

8 Hercules

9 Cygnus

10 Perseus

11 Gemini

12 Cancer

13 Leo

14 Serpens

15 Sagitta

16 Pegasus

17 Pisces

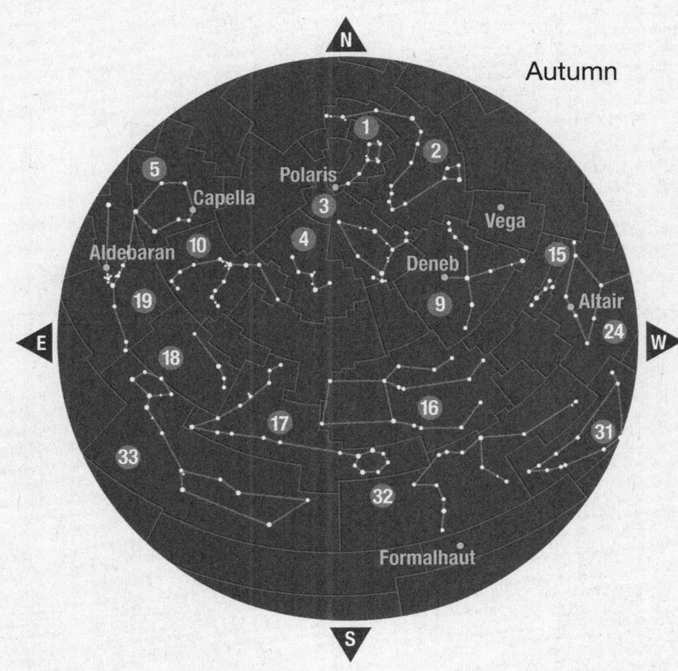

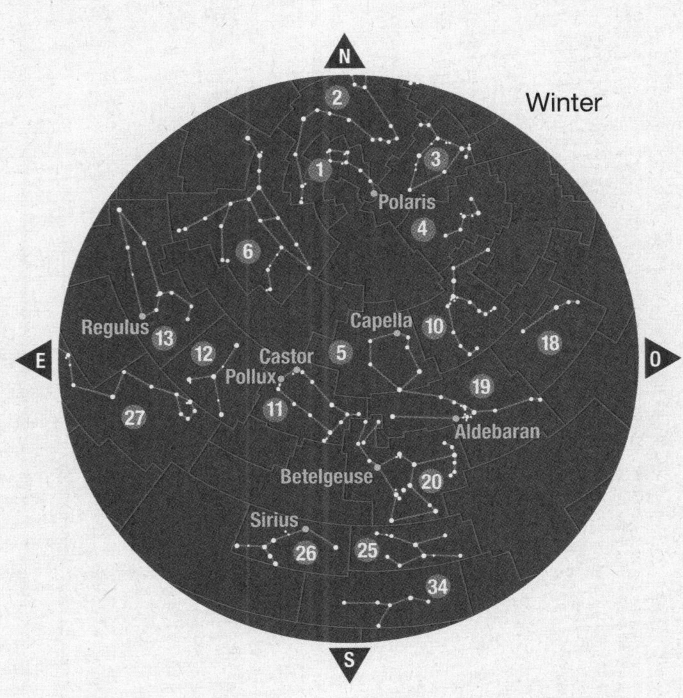

Constellations

18 Aries

19 Taurus

20 Orion

21 Virgo

22 Libra

23 Ophiuchus

24 Aquila

25 Lepus

26 Canis Major

27 Hydra

28 Corvus

29 Scorpius

30 Sagittarius

31 Capricornus

32 Aquarius

33 Cetus

34 Columba

World Map

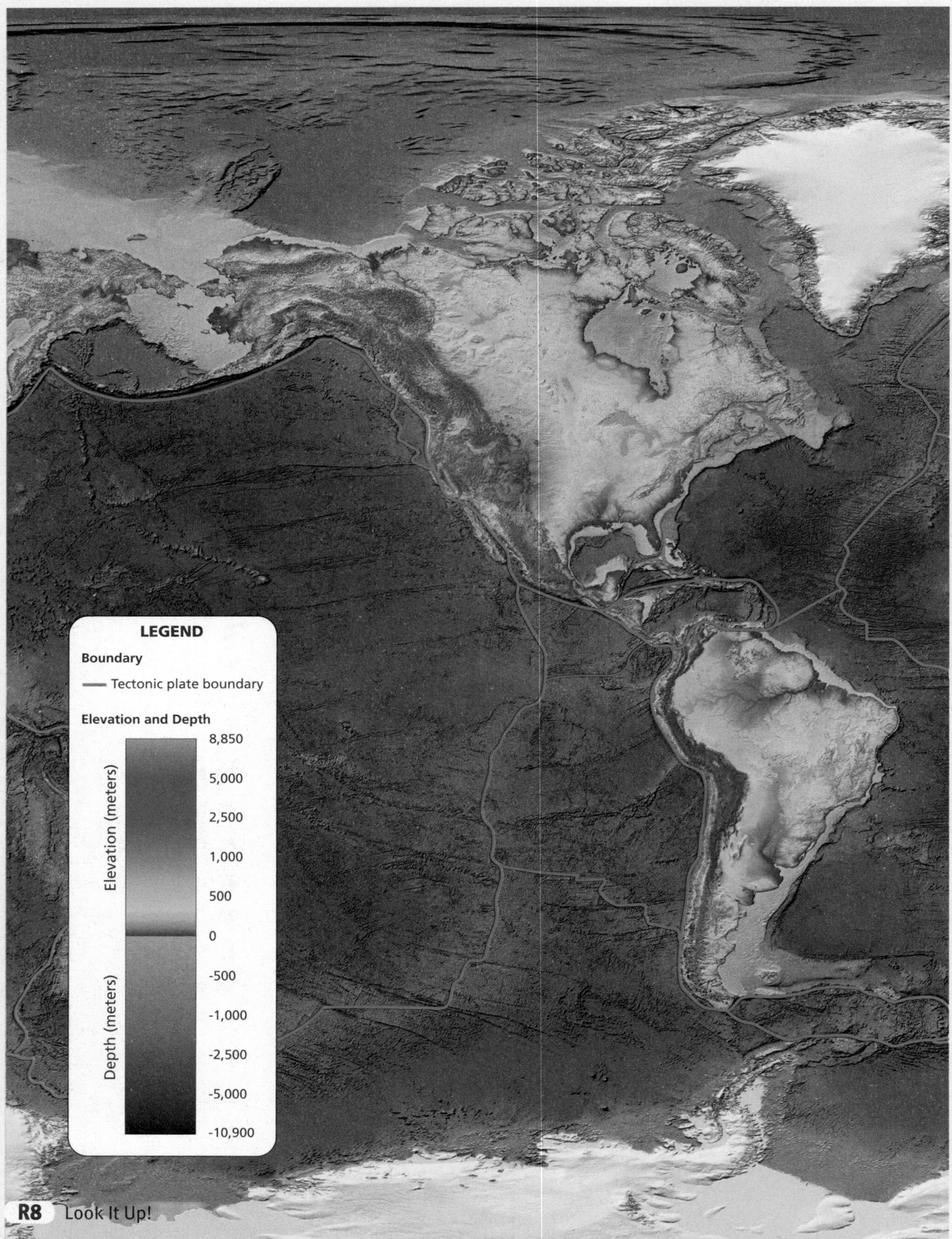
LEGEND
Boundary
Tectonic plate boundary
Elevation and Depth
Elevation (meters)
8,850
5,000
2,500
1,000
500
0
Depth (meters)
-500
-1,000
-2,500
-5,000
-10,900

References

Classification of Living Things

Domains and Kingdoms

All organisms belong to one of three domains: Domain Archaea, Domain Bacteria, or Domain Eukarya. Some of the groups within these domains are shown below. (Remember that genus names are italicized.)

Domain Archaea

The organisms in this domain are single-celled prokaryotes, many of which live in extreme environments.

Archaea		
Group	**Example**	**Characteristics**
Methanogens	*Methanococcus*	produce methane gas; can't live in oxygen
Thermophiles	*Sulfolobus*	require sulfur; can't live in oxygen
Halophiles	*Halococcus*	live in very salty environments; most can live in oxygen

Domain Bacteria

Organisms in this domain are single-celled prokaryotes and are found in almost every environment on Earth.

Bacteria		
Group	**Example**	**Characteristics**
Bacilli	*Escherichia*	rod shaped; some bacilli fix nitrogen; some cause disease
Cocci	*Streptococcus*	spherical shaped; some cause disease; can form spores
Spirilla	*Treponema*	spiral shaped; cause diseases such as syphilis and Lyme disease

Domain Eukarya

Organisms in this domain are single-celled or multicellular eukaryotes.

Kingdom Protista Many protists resemble fungi, plants, or animals but are smaller and simpler in structure. Most are single celled.

Protists		
Group	**Example**	**Characteristics**
Sarcodines	*Amoeba*	radiolarians; single-celled consumers
Ciliates	*Paramecium*	single-celled consumers
Flagellates	*Trypanosoma*	single-celled parasites
Sporozoans	*Plasmodium*	single-celled parasites
Euglenas	*Euglena*	single celled; photosynthesize
Diatoms	*Pinnularia*	most are single celled; photosynthesize
Dinoflagellates	*Gymnodinium*	single celled; some photosynthesize
Algae	*Volvox*	single celled or multicellular; photosynthesize
Slime molds	*Physarum*	single celled or multicellular; consumers or decomposers
Water molds	powdery mildew	single celled or multicellular; parasites or decomposers

Kingdom Fungi Most fungi are multicellular. Their cells have thick cell walls. Fungi absorb food from their environment.

Fungi		
Group	**Examples**	**Characteristics**
Zygote fungi	bread mold	spherical zygote produces spores; decomposers
Sac fungi	yeast; morels	saclike spore structure; parasites and decomposers
Club fungi	mushrooms; rusts; smuts	club-shaped spore structure; parasites and decomposers
Lichens	British soldier	a partnership between a fungus and an alga

Kingdom Plantae Plants are multicellular and have cell walls made of cellulose. Plants make their own food through photosynthesis. Plants are classified into divisions instead of phyla.

Plants		
Group	**Examples**	**Characteristics**
Bryophytes	mosses; liverworts	no vascular tissue; reproduce by spores
Club mosses	*Lycopodium;* ground pine	grow in wooded areas; reproduce by spores
Horsetails	rushes	grow in wetland areas; reproduce by spores
Ferns	spleenworts; sensitive fern	large leaves called fronds; reproduce by spores
Conifers	pines; spruces; firs	needlelike leaves; reproduce by seeds made in cones
Cycads	*Zamia*	slow growing; reproduce by seeds made in large cones
Gnetophytes	*Welwitschia*	only three living families; reproduce by seeds
Ginkgoes	*Ginkgo*	only one living species; reproduce by seeds
Angiosperms	all flowering plants	reproduce by seeds made in flowers; fruit

Kingdom Animalia Animals are multicellular. Their cells do not have cell walls. Most animals have specialized tissues and complex organ systems. Animals get food by eating other organisms.

Animals		
Group	**Examples**	**Characteristics**
Sponges	glass sponges	no symmetry or specialized tissues; aquatic
Cnidarians	jellyfish; coral	radial symmetry; aquatic
Flatworms	planaria; tapeworms; flukes	bilateral symmetry; organ systems
Roundworms	*Trichina;* hookworms	bilateral symmetry; organ systems
Annelids	earthworms; leeches	bilateral symmetry; organ systems
Mollusks	snails; octopuses	bilateral symmetry; organ systems
Echinoderms	sea stars; sand dollars	radial symmetry; organ systems
Arthropods	insects; spiders; lobsters	bilateral symmetry; organ systems
Chordates	fish; amphibians; reptiles; birds; mammals	bilateral symmetry; complex organ systems

Periodic Table of the Elements

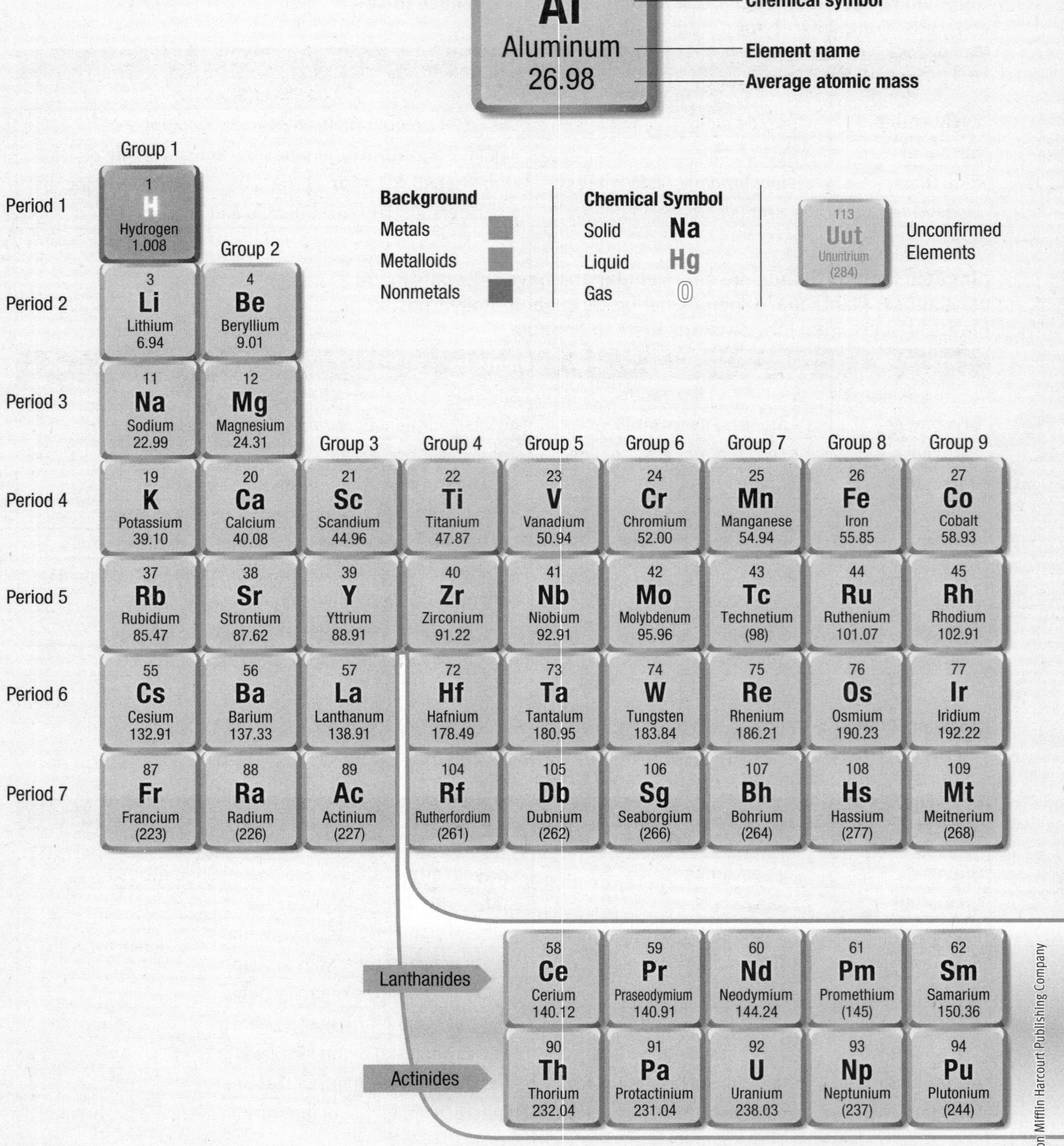

13 **Al** Aluminum 26.98	
13	Atomic number
Al	Chemical symbol
Aluminum	Element name
26.98	Average atomic mass

Background		Chemical Symbol		
Metals		Solid	Na	
Metalloids		Liquid	Hg	
Nonmetals		Gas	O	

113 **Uut** Ununtrium (284)	Unconfirmed Elements

	Group 1	Group 2	Group 3	Group 4	Group 5	Group 6	Group 7	Group 8	Group 9
Period 1	1 **H** Hydrogen 1.008								
Period 2	3 **Li** Lithium 6.94	4 **Be** Beryllium 9.01							
Period 3	11 **Na** Sodium 22.99	12 **Mg** Magnesium 24.31							
Period 4	19 **K** Potassium 39.10	20 **Ca** Calcium 40.08	21 **Sc** Scandium 44.96	22 **Ti** Titanium 47.87	23 **V** Vanadium 50.94	24 **Cr** Chromium 52.00	25 **Mn** Manganese 54.94	26 **Fe** Iron 55.85	27 **Co** Cobalt 58.93
Period 5	37 **Rb** Rubidium 85.47	38 **Sr** Strontium 87.62	39 **Y** Yttrium 88.91	40 **Zr** Zirconium 91.22	41 **Nb** Niobium 92.91	42 **Mo** Molybdenum 95.96	43 **Tc** Technetium (98)	44 **Ru** Ruthenium 101.07	45 **Rh** Rhodium 102.91
Period 6	55 **Cs** Cesium 132.91	56 **Ba** Barium 137.33	57 **La** Lanthanum 138.91	72 **Hf** Hafnium 178.49	73 **Ta** Tantalum 180.95	74 **W** Tungsten 183.84	75 **Re** Rhenium 186.21	76 **Os** Osmium 190.23	77 **Ir** Iridium 192.22
Period 7	87 **Fr** Francium (223)	88 **Ra** Radium (226)	89 **Ac** Actinium (227)	104 **Rf** Rutherfordium (261)	105 **Db** Dubnium (262)	106 **Sg** Seaborgium (266)	107 **Bh** Bohrium (264)	108 **Hs** Hassium (277)	109 **Mt** Meitnerium (268)

Lanthanides	58 **Ce** Cerium 140.12	59 **Pr** Praseodymium 140.91	60 **Nd** Neodymium 144.24	61 **Pm** Promethium (145)	62 **Sm** Samarium 150.36
Actinides	90 **Th** Thorium 232.04	91 **Pa** Protactinium 231.04	92 **U** Uranium 238.03	93 **Np** Neptunium (237)	94 **Pu** Plutonium (244)

The International Union of Pure and Applied Chemistry (IUPAC) has determined that, because of isotopic variance, the average atomic mass is best represented by a range of values for each of the following elements: hydrogen, lithium, boron, carbon, nitrogen, oxygen, silicon, sulfur, chlorine, and thallium. However, the values in this table are appropriate for everyday calculations.

Group 10	Group 11	Group 12	Group 13	Group 14	Group 15	Group 16	Group 17	Group 18
								2 He Helium 4.003
			5 B Boron 10.81	6 C Carbon 12.01	7 N Nitrogen 14.01	8 O Oxygen 16.00	9 F Fluorine 19.00	10 Ne Neon 20.18
			13 Al Aluminum 26.98	14 Si Silicon 28.09	15 P Phosphorus 30.97	16 S Sulfur 32.06	17 Cl Chlorine 35.45	18 Ar Argon 39.95
28 Ni Nickel 58.69	29 Cu Copper 63.55	30 Zn Zinc 65.38	31 Ga Gallium 69.72	32 Ge Germanium 72.63	33 As Arsenic 74.92	34 Se Selenium 78.96	35 Br Bromine 79.90	36 Kr Krypton 83.80
46 Pd Palladium 106.42	47 Ag Silver 107.87	48 Cd Cadmium 112.41	49 In Indium 114.82	50 Sn Tin 118.71	51 Sb Antimony 121.76	52 Te Tellurium 127.60	53 I Iodine 126.90	54 Xe Xenon 131.29
78 Pt Platinum 195.08	79 Au Gold 196.97	80 Hg Mercury 200.59	81 Tl Thallium 204.38	82 Pb Lead 207.2	83 Bi Bismuth 208.98	84 Po Polonium (209)	85 At Astatine (210)	86 Rn Radon (222)
110 Ds Darmstadtium (271)	111 Rg Roentgenium (272)	112 Cn Copernicium (285)	113 Uut Ununtrium (284)	114 Fl Flerovium (289)	115 Uup Ununpentium (288)	116 Lv Livermorium (293)	117 Uus Ununseptium (294)	118 Uuo Ununoctium (294)

63 Eu Europium 151.96	64 Gd Gadolinium 157.25	65 Tb Terbium 158.93	66 Dy Dysprosium 162.50	67 Ho Holmium 164.93	68 Er Erbium 167.26	69 Tm Thulium 168.93	70 Yb Ytterbium 173.05	71 Lu Lutetium 174.97
95 Am Americium (243)	96 Cm Curium (247)	97 Bk Berkelium (247)	98 Cf Californium (251)	99 Es Einsteinium (252)	100 Fm Fermium (257)	101 Md Mendelevium (258)	102 No Nobelium (259)	103 Lr Lawrencium (262)

Physical Science Refresher

Atoms and Elements

Every object in the universe is made of matter. **Matter** is anything that takes up space and has mass. All matter is made of atoms. An **atom** is the smallest particle into which an element can be divided and still be the same element. An **element**, in turn, is a substance that cannot be broken down into simpler substances by chemical means. Each element consists of only one kind of atom. An element may be made of many atoms, but they are all the same kind of atom.

Atomic Structure

Atoms are made of smaller particles called **electrons**, **protons**, and **neutrons**. Electrons have a negative electric charge, protons have a positive charge, and neutrons have no electric charge. Together, protons and neutrons form the **nucleus**, or small dense center, of an atom. Because protons are positively charged and neutrons are neutral, the nucleus has a positive charge. Electrons move within an area around the nucleus called the **electron cloud**. Electrons move so quickly that scientists cannot determine their exact speeds and positions at the same time.

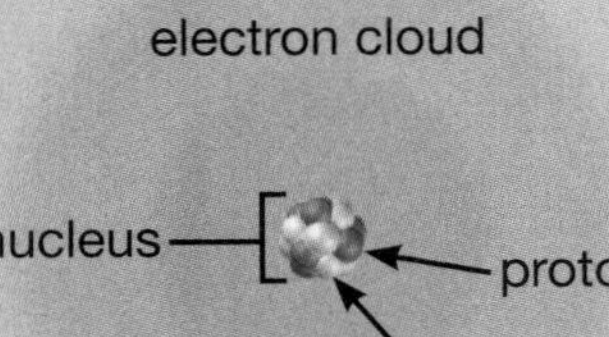

Atomic Number

To help distinguish one element from another, scientists use the atomic numbers of atoms. The **atomic number** is the number of protons in the nucleus of an atom. The atoms of a certain element always have the same number of protons.

When atoms have an equal number of protons and electrons, they are uncharged, or electrically neutral. The atomic number equals the number of electrons in an uncharged atom. The number of neutrons, however, can vary for a given element. Atoms of the same element that have different numbers of neutrons are called **isotopes**.

Periodic Table of the Elements

In the periodic table, each element in the table is in a separate box. And the elements are arranged from left to right in order of increasing atomic number. That is, an uncharged atom of each element has one more electron and one more proton than an uncharged atom of the element to its left. Each horizontal row of the table is called a **period**. Changes in chemical properties of elements across a period correspond to changes in the electron arrangements of their atoms.

Each vertical column of the table is known as a **group.** A group lists elements with similar physical and chemical properties. For this reason, a group is also sometimes called a family. The elements in a group have similar properties because their atoms have the same number of electrons in their outer energy level. For example, the elements helium, neon, argon, krypton, xenon, and radon all have similar properties and are known as the noble gases.

Molecules and Compounds

When two or more elements join chemically, they form a **compound.** A compound is a new substance with properties different from those of the elements that compose it. For example, water, H_2O, is a compound formed when hydrogen (H) and oxygen (O) combine. The smallest complete unit of a compound that has the properties of that compound is called a **molecule.** A chemical formula indicates the elements in a compound. It also indicates the relative number of atoms of each element in the compound. The chemical formula for water is H_2O. So each water molecule consists of two atoms of hydrogen and one atom of oxygen. The subscript number after the symbol for an element shows how many atoms of that element are in a single molecule of the compound.

Chemical Equations

A chemical reaction occurs when a chemical change takes place. A chemical equation describes a chemical reaction using chemical formulas. The equation indicates the substances that react and the substances that are produced. For example, when carbon and oxygen combine, they can form carbon dioxide, shown in the following equation: $C + O_2 \longrightarrow CO_2$

Acids, Bases, and pH

An **ion** is an atom or group of chemically bonded atoms that has an electric charge because it has lost or gained one or more electrons. When an acid, such as hydrochloric acid, HCl, is mixed with water, it separates into ions. An **acid** is a compound that produces hydrogen ions, H^+, in water. The hydrogen ions then combine with a water molecule to form a hydronium ion, H_3O^+. A **base**, on the other hand, is a substance that produces hydroxide ions, OH^-, in water.

To determine whether a solution is acidic or basic, scientists use pH. The **pH** of a solution is a measure of the hydronium ion concentration in a solution. The pH scale ranges from 0 to 14. Acids have a pH that is less than 7. The lower the number, the more acidic the solution. The middle point, pH = 7, is neutral, neither acidic nor basic. Bases have a pH that is greater than 7. The higher the number is, the more basic the solution.

The pH of Some Common Materials

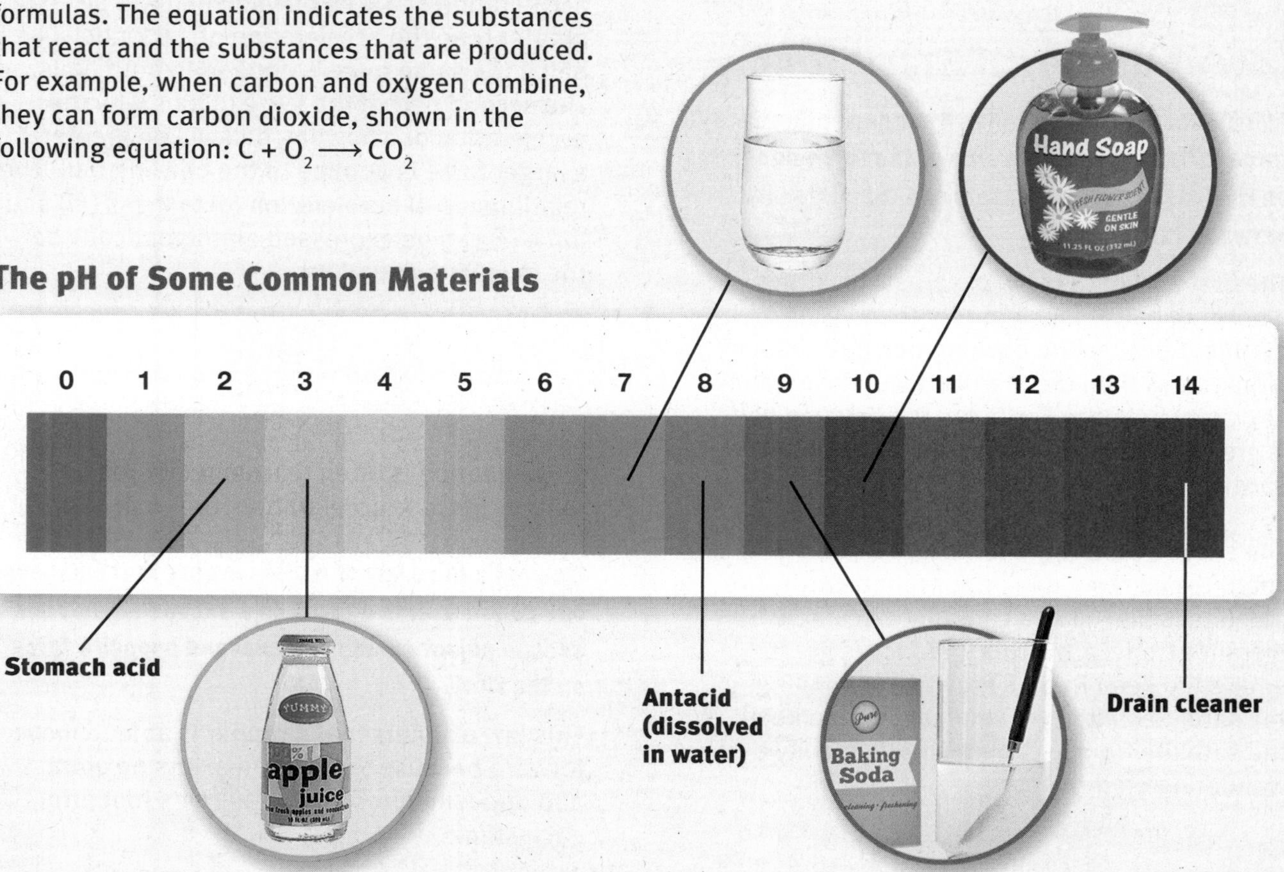

Physical Laws and Useful Equations

Law of Conservation of Mass

Mass cannot be created or destroyed during ordinary chemical or physical changes.

The total mass in a closed system is always the same no matter how many physical changes or chemical reactions occur.

Law of Conservation of Energy

Energy can be neither created nor destroyed.

The total amount of energy in a closed system is always the same. Energy can be changed from one form to another, but all of the different forms of energy in a system always add up to the same total amount of energy, no matter how many energy conversions occur.

Law of Universal Gravitation

All objects in the universe attract each other by a force called gravity. The size of the force depends on the masses of the objects and the distance between the objects.

The first part of the law explains why lifting a bowling ball is much harder than lifting a marble. Because the bowling ball has a much larger mass than the marble does, the amount of gravity between Earth and the bowling ball is greater than the amount of gravity between Earth and the marble.

The second part of the law explains why a satellite can remain in orbit around Earth. The satellite is placed at a carefully calculated distance from Earth. This distance is great enough to keep Earth's gravity from pulling the satellite down, yet small enough to keep the satellite from escaping Earth's gravity and wandering off into space.

Newton's Laws of Motion

Newton's first law of motion states that an object at rest remains at rest and that an object in motion remains in motion at constant speed and in a straight line unless acted on by an unbalanced force.

The first part of the law explains why a football will remain on a tee until it is kicked off or until a gust of wind blows it off. The second part of the law explains why a bike rider will continue moving forward after the bike comes to an abrupt stop. Gravity and the friction of the sidewalk will eventually stop the rider.

Newton's second law of motion states that the acceleration of an object depends on the mass of the object and the amount of force applied.

The first part of the law explains why the acceleration of a 4 kg bowling ball will be greater than the acceleration of a 6 kg bowling ball if the same force is applied to both balls. The second part of the law explains why the acceleration of a bowling ball will be greater if a larger force is applied to the bowling ball. The relationship of acceleration (*a*) to mass (*m*) and force (*F*) can be expressed mathematically by the following equation:

$$acceleration = \frac{force}{mass}, \text{ or } a = \frac{F}{m}$$

This equation is often rearranged to read $force = mass \times$ acceleration, or $F = m \times a$

Newton's third law of motion states that whenever one object exerts a force on a second object, the second object exerts an equal and opposite force on the first.

This law explains that a runner is able to move forward because the ground exerts an equal and opposite force on the runner's foot after each step.

Average Speed

$$\text{average speed} = \frac{\text{total distance}}{\text{total time}}$$

Example:
A bicycle messenger traveled a distance of 136 km in 8 h. What was the messenger's average speed?

$$\frac{136 \text{ km}}{8 \text{ h}} = 17 \text{ km/h}$$

The messenger's average speed was **17 km/h.**

Average Acceleration

$$\text{average acceleration} = \frac{\text{final velocity} - \text{starting velocity}}{\text{time it takes to change velocity}}$$

Example:
Calculate the average acceleration of an Olympic 100 m dash sprinter who reached a velocity of 20 m/s south at the finish line. The race was in a straight line and lasted 10 s.

$$\frac{20 \text{ m/s} - 0 \text{ m/s}}{10 \text{ s}} = 2 \text{ m/s/s}$$

The sprinter's average acceleration was **2 m/s/s south.**

Net Force

Forces in the Same Direction

When forces are in the same direction, add the forces together to determine the net force.

Example:
Calculate the net force on a stalled car that is being pushed by two people. One person is pushing with a force of 13 N northwest, and the other person is pushing with a force of 8 N in the same direction.

$$13 \text{ N} + 8 \text{ N} = 21 \text{ N}$$

The net force is **21 N northwest.**

Forces in Opposite Directions

When forces are in opposite directions, subtract the smaller force from the larger force to determine the net force. The net force will be in the direction of the larger force.

Example:
Calculate the net force on a rope that is being pulled on each end. One person is pulling on one end of the rope with a force of 12 N south. Another person is pulling on the opposite end of the rope with a force of 7 N north.

$$12 \text{ N} - 7 \text{ N} = 5 \text{ N}$$

The net force is **5 N south.**

Pressure

Pressure is the force exerted over a given area. The SI unit for pressure is the pascal. Its symbol is Pa.

$$\text{pressure} = \frac{\text{force}}{\text{area}}$$

Example:
Calculate the pressure of the air in a soccer ball if the air exerts a force of 10 N over an area of 0.5 m^2.

$$\text{pressure} = \frac{10 \text{ N}}{0.5 \text{ m}^2} = \frac{20 \text{ N}}{\text{m}^2} = 20 \text{ Pa}$$

The pressure of the air inside the soccer ball is **20 Pa.**

A How-To Manual for Active Reading

This book belongs to you, and you are invited to write in it. In fact, the book won't be complete until you do. Sometimes you'll answer a question or follow directions to mark up the text. Other times you'll write down your own thoughts. And when you're done reading and writing in the book, the book will be ready to help you review what you learned and prepare for tests.

Active Reading Annotations

Before you read, you'll often come upon an Active Reading prompt that asks you to underline certain words or number the steps in a process. Here's an example.

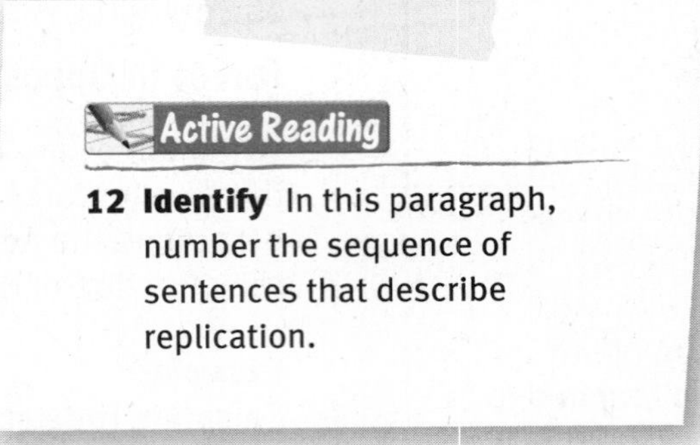

Active Reading
12 Identify In this paragraph, number the sequence of sentences that describe replication.

Marking the text this way is called **annotating,** and your marks are called **annotations.** Annotating the text can help you identify important concepts while you read.

There are other ways that you can annotate the text. You can draw an asterisk (*) by vocabulary terms, mark unfamiliar or confusing terms and information with a question mark (?), and mark main ideas with a double underline. And you can even invent your own marks to annotate the text!

Other Annotating Opportunities

Keep your pencil, pen, or highlighter nearby as you read so you can make a note or highlight an important point at any time. Here are a few ideas to get you started.

- Notice the headings in red and blue. The blue headings are questions that point to the main idea of what you're reading. The red headings are answers to the questions in the blue ones. Together these headings outline the content of the lesson. After reading a lesson, you could write your own answers to the questions.

- Notice the bold-faced words that are highlighted in yellow. They are highlighted so that you can easily find them again on the page where they are defined. As you read or as you review, challenge yourself to write your own sentence using the bold-faced term.
- Make a note in the margin at any time. You might
  - Ask a "What if" question
  - Comment on what you read
  - Make a connection to something you read elsewhere
  - Make a logical conclusion from the text

Use your own language and abbreviations. Invent a code, such as using circles and boxes around words to remind you of their importance or relation to each other. Your annotations will help you remember your questions for class discussions, and when you go back to the lesson later, you may be able to fill in what you didn't understand the first time you read it. Like a scientist in the field or in a lab, you will be recording your questions and observations for analysis later.

Active Reading Questions

After you read, you'll often come upon Active Reading questions that ask you to think about what you've just read. You'll write your answer underneath the question. Here's an example.

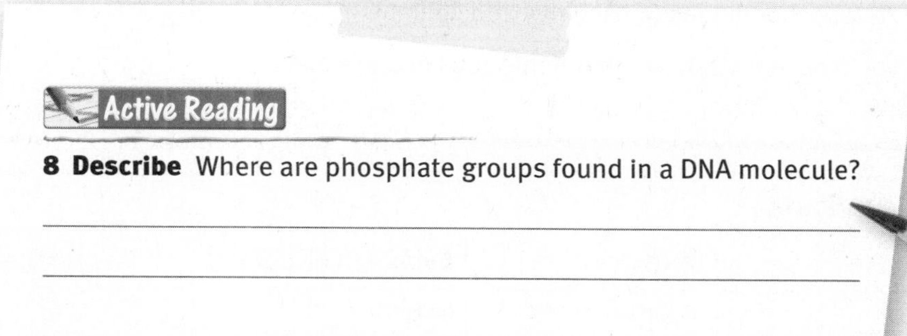

Active Reading
8 Describe Where are phosphate groups found in a DNA molecule?

This type of question helps you sum up what you've just read and pull out the most important ideas from the passage. In this case, the question asks you to **describe** the structure of a DNA molecule that you have just read about. Other times you may be asked to do such things as **apply** a concept, **compare** two concepts, **summarize** a process, or **identify a cause-and-effect** relationship. You'll be strengthening those critical thinking skills that you'll use often in learning about science.

Using Graphic Organizers to Take Notes

Graphic organizers help you remember information as you read it for the first time and as you study it later. There are dozens of graphic organizers to choose from, so the first trick is to choose the one that's best suited to your purpose. Following are some graphic organizers to use for different purposes.

To remember lots of information	To relate a central idea to subordinate details	To describe a process	To make a comparison
• Arrange data in a Content Frame • Use Combination Notes to describe a concept in words and pictures	• Show relationships with a Mind Map or a Main Idea Web • Sum up relationships among many things with a Concept Map	• Use a Process Diagram to explain a procedure • Show a chain of events and results in a Cause-and-Effect Chart	• Compare two or more closely related things in a Venn Diagram

Content Frame

1 Make a four-column chart.

2 Fill the first column with categories (e.g., snail, ant, earthworm) and the first row with descriptive information (e.g., group, characteristic, appearance).

3 Fill the chart with details that belong in each row and column.

4 When you finish, you'll have a study aid that helps you compare one category to another.

Invertebrates

NAME	GROUP	CHARACTERISTICS	DRAWING
snail	mollusks	mantle	
ant	arthropods	six legs, exoskeleton	
earthworm	segmented worms	segmented body, circulatory and digestive systems	
heartworm	roundworms	digestive system	
sea star	echinoderms	spiny skin, tube feet	
jellyfish	cnidarians	stinging cells	

Combination Notes

1 Make a two-column chart.

2 Write descriptive words and definitions in the first column.

3 Draw a simple sketch that helps you remember the meaning of the term in the second column.

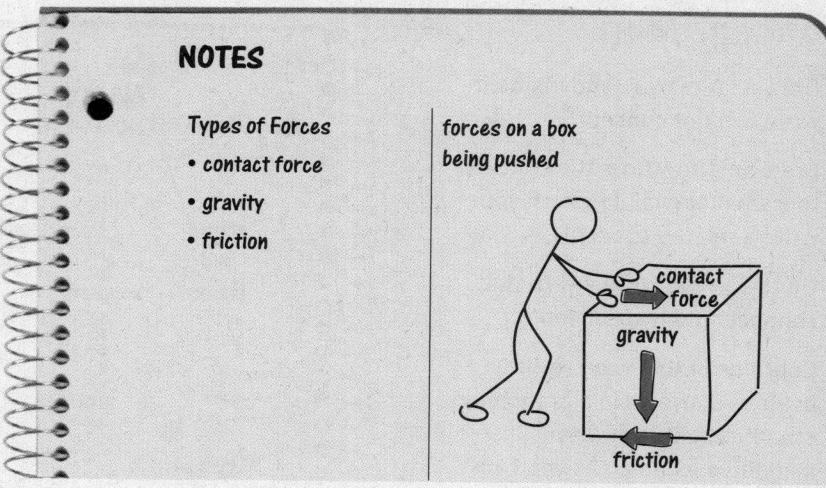

Mind Map

1 Draw an oval, and inside it write a topic to analyze.

2 Draw two or more arms extending from the oval. Each arm represents a main idea about the topic.

3 Draw lines from the arms on which to write details about each of the main ideas.

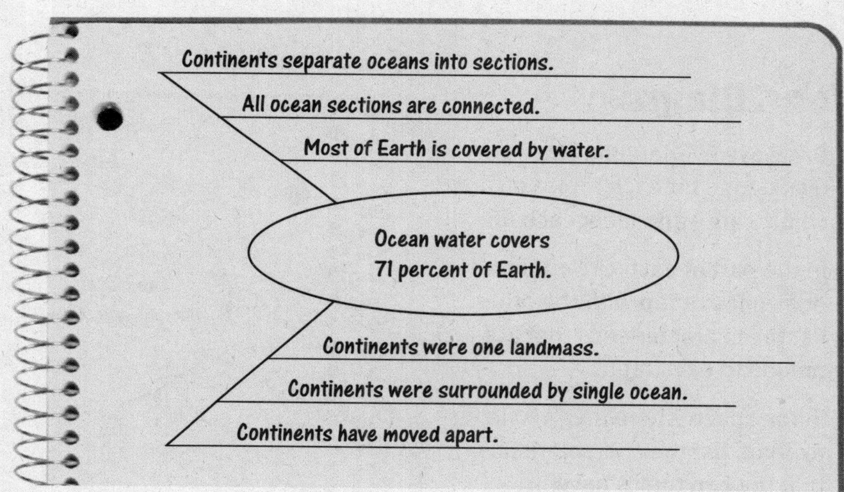

Main Idea Web

1 Make a box, and write a concept you want to remember inside it.

2 Draw boxes around the central box, and label each one with a category of information about the concept (e.g., definition, formula, descriptive details).

3 Fill in the boxes with relevant details as you read.

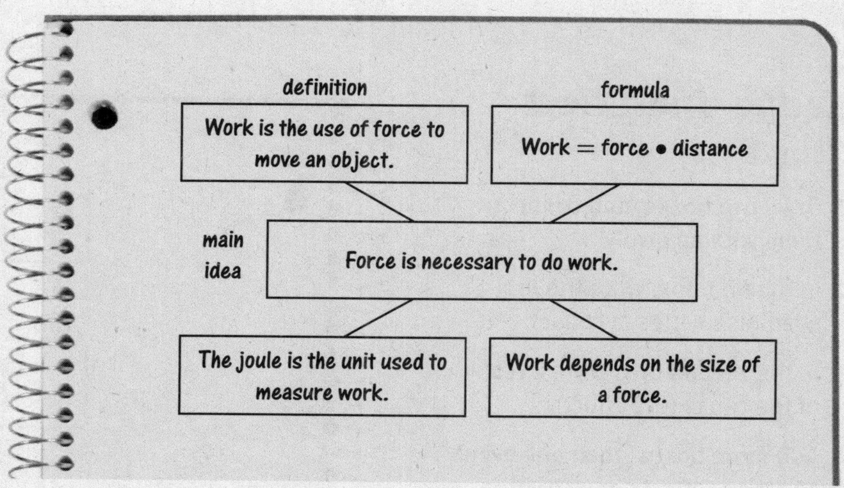

Reading and Study Skills

Concept Map

1 Draw a large oval, and inside it write a major concept.

2 Draw an arrow from the concept to a smaller oval, in which you write a related concept.

3 On the arrow, write a verb that connects the two concepts.

4 Continue in this way, adding ovals and arrows in a branching structure, until you have explained as much as you can about the main concept.

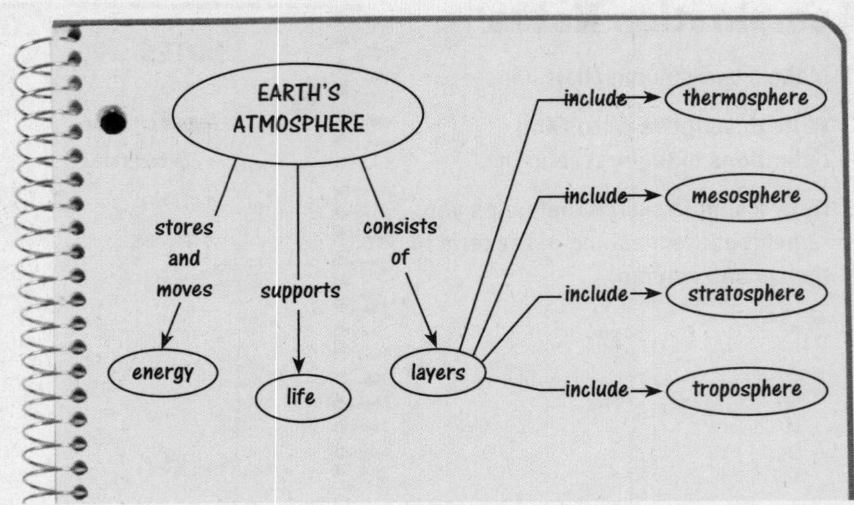

Venn Diagram

1 Draw two overlapping circles or ovals—one for each topic you are comparing—and label each one.

2 In the part of each circle that does not overlap with the other, list the characteristics that are unique to each topic.

3 In the space where the two circles overlap, list the characteristics that the two topics have in common.

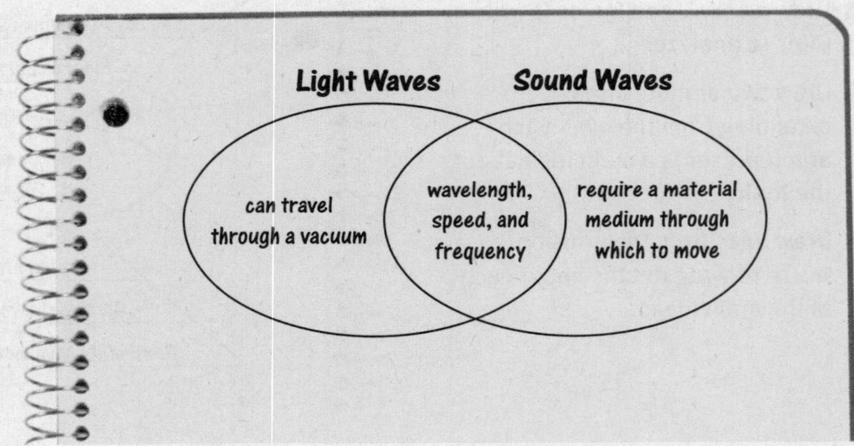

Cause-and-Effect Chart

1 Draw two boxes, and connect them with an arrow.

2 In the first box, write the first event in a series (a cause).

3 In the second box, write a result of the cause (the effect).

4 Add more boxes when one event has many effects or vice versa.

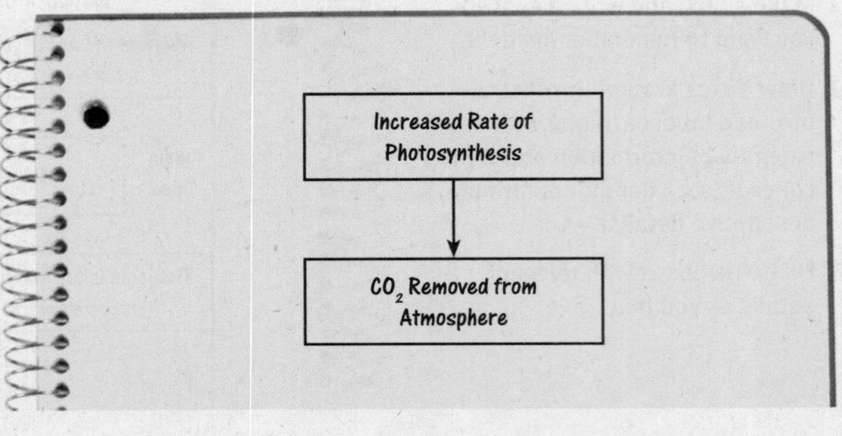

Process Diagram

A process can be a never-ending cycle. As you can see in this technology design process, engineers may backtrack and repeat steps, they may skip steps entirely, or they may repeat the entire process before a usable design is achieved.

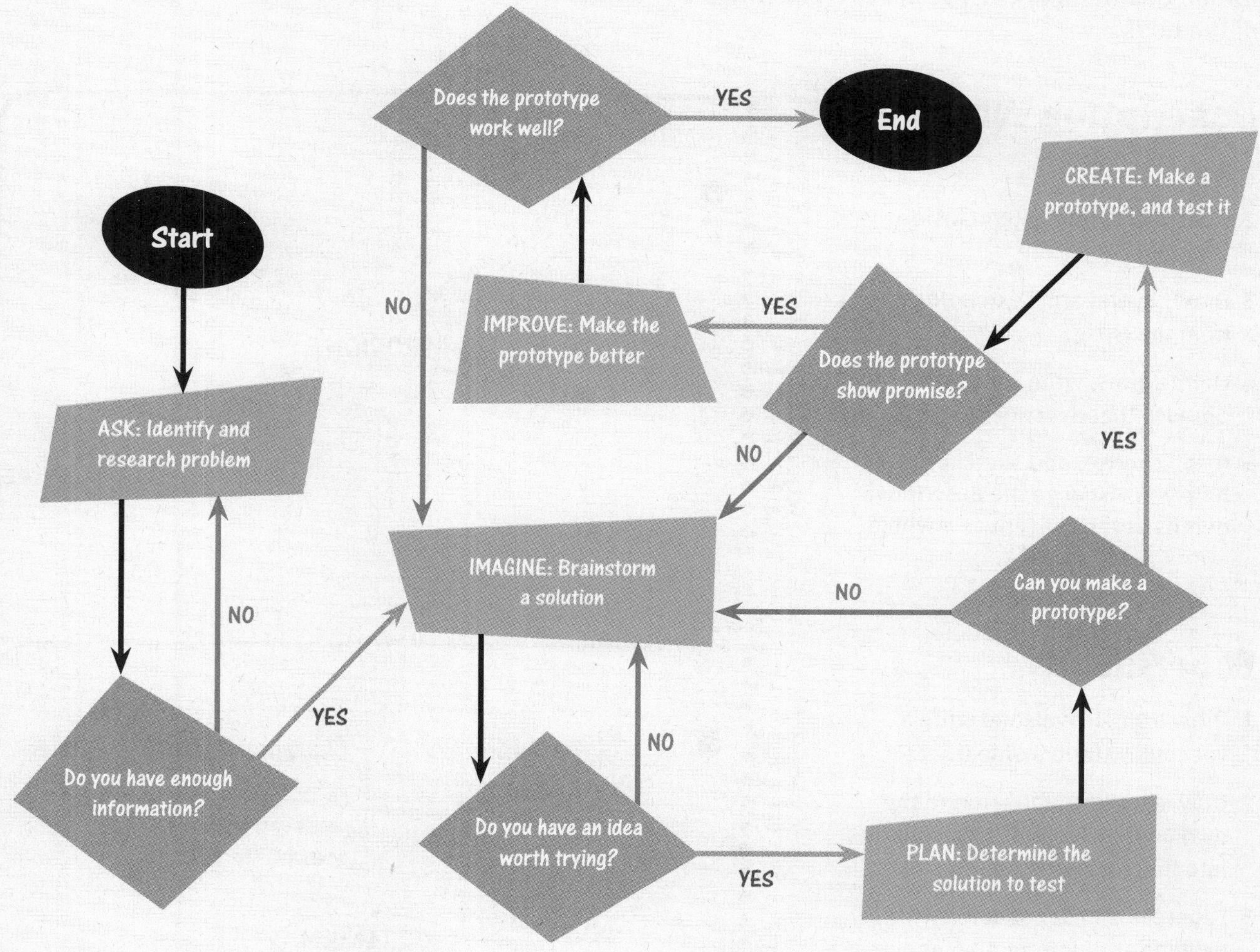

Using Vocabulary Strategies

Important science terms are highlighted where they are first defined in this book. One way to remember these terms is to take notes and make sketches when you come to them. Use the strategies on this page and the next for this purpose. You will also find a formal definition of each science term in the Glossary at the end of the book.

Description Wheel

1 Draw a small circle.

2 Write a vocabulary term inside the circle.

3 Draw several arms extending from the circle.

4 On the arms, write words and phrases that describe the term.

5 If you choose, add sketches that help you visualize the descriptive details or the concept as a whole.

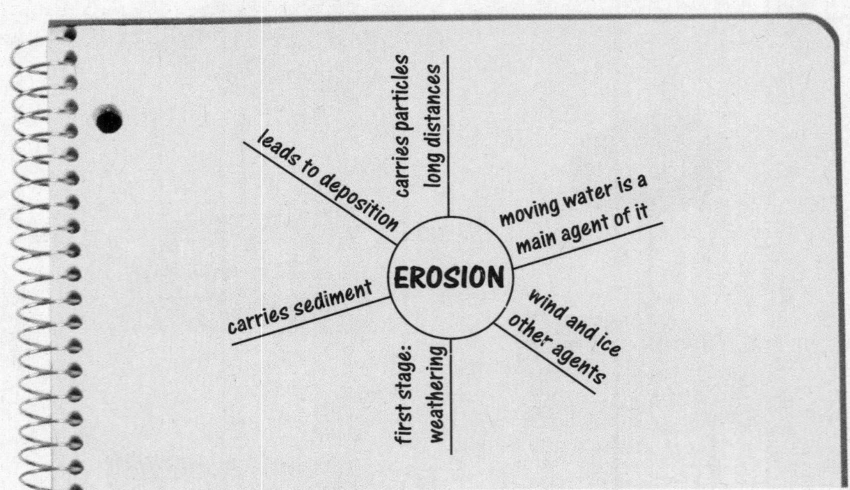

Four Square

1 Draw a small oval, and write a vocabulary term inside it.

2 Draw a large square around the oval, and divide the large square into four smaller squares.

3 Label the smaller squares with categories of information about the term, such as definition, characteristics, examples, non-examples, appearance, and root words.

4 Fill the squares with descriptive words and drawings that will help you remember the overall meaning of the term and its essential details.

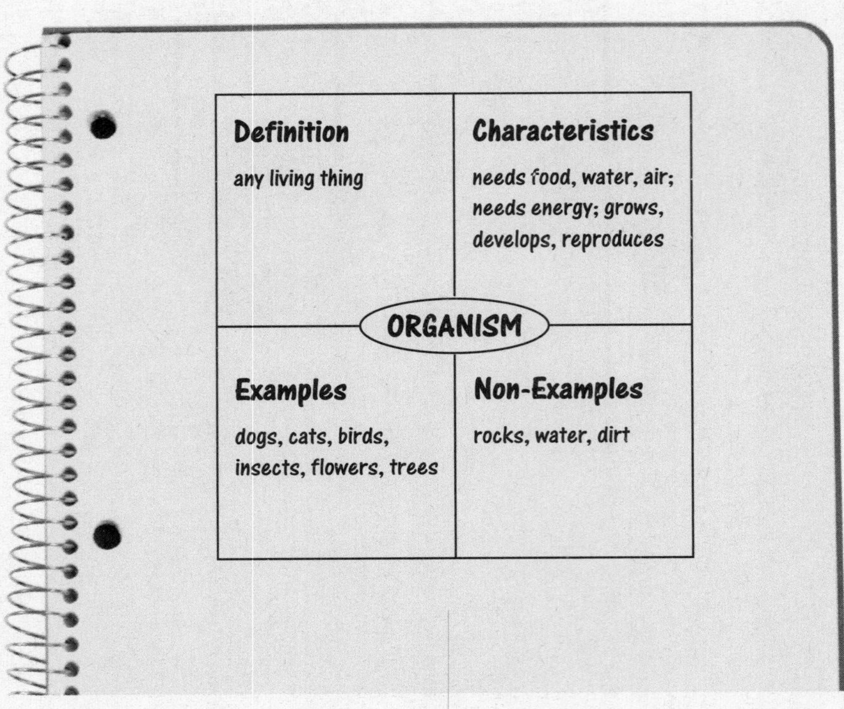

Frame Game

1 Draw a small rectangle, and write a vocabulary term inside it.

2 Draw a larger rectangle around the smaller one. Connect the corners of the larger rectangle to the corners of the smaller one, creating four spaces that frame the word.

3 In each of the four parts of the frame, draw or write details that help define the term. Consider including a definition, essential characteristics, an equation, examples, and a sentence using the term.

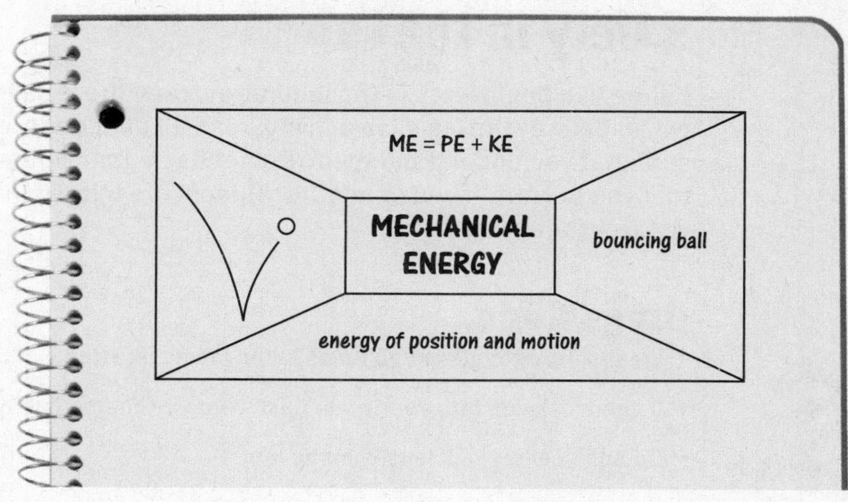

Magnet Word

1 Draw horseshoe magnet, and write a vocabulary term inside it.

2 Add lines that extend from the sides of the magnet.

3 Brainstorm words and phrases that come to mind when you think about the term.

4 On the lines, write the words and phrases that describe something essential about the term.

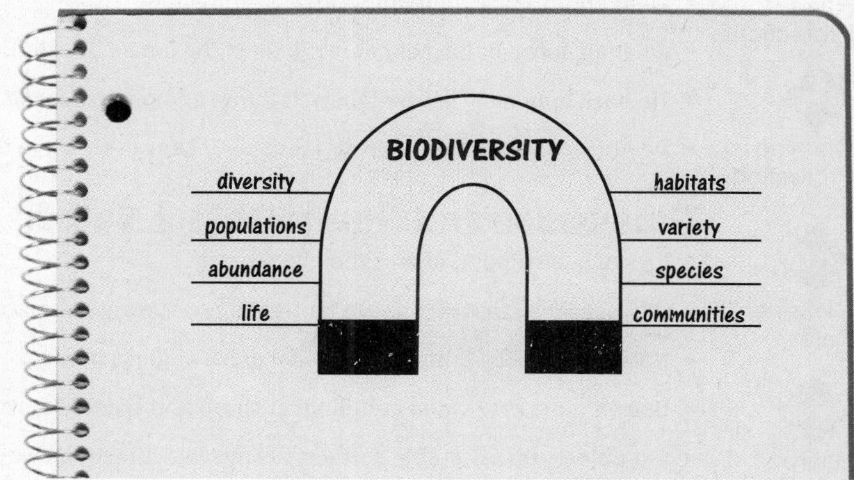

Word Triangle

1 Draw a triangle, and add lines to divide it into three parts.

2 Write a term and its definition in the bottom section of the triangle.

3 In the middle section, write a sentence in which the term is used correctly.

4 In the top section, draw a small picture to illustrate the term.

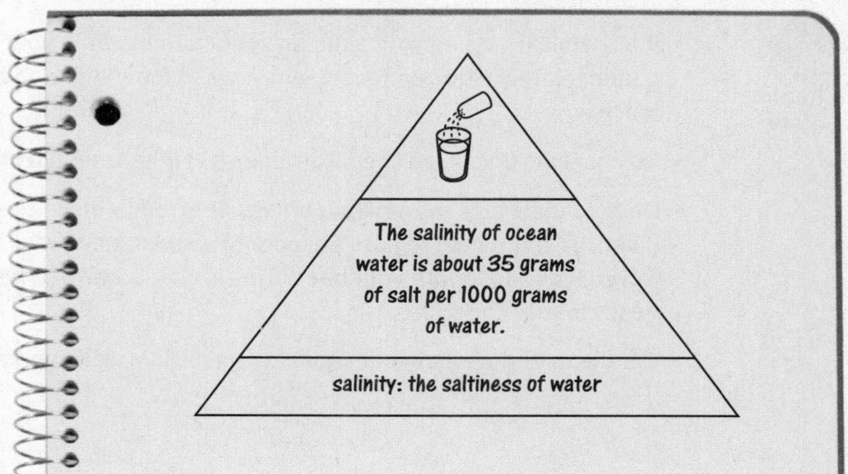

Safety in the Lab

Before you begin work in the laboratory, read these safety rules twice. Before starting a lab activity, read all directions, and make sure that you understand them. Do not begin until your teacher has told you to start. If you or another student are injured in any way, tell your teacher immediately.

Dress Code

Eye Protection

Hand Protection

Clothing Protection

- Wear safety goggles at all times in the lab as directed.
- If chemicals get into your eyes, flush your eyes immediately.
- Do not wear contact lenses in the lab.
- Do not look directly at the sun or any intense light source or laser.
- Do not cut an object while holding the object in your hand.
- Wear appropriate protective gloves as directed.
- Wear an apron or lab coat at all times in the lab as directed.
- Tie back long hair, secure loose clothing, and remove loose jewelry.
- Do not wear open-toed shoes, sandals, or canvas shoes in the lab.

Glassware and Sharp Object Safety

Glassware Safety

Sharp Objects Safety

- Do not use chipped or cracked glassware.
- Use heat-resistant glassware for heating or storing hot materials.
- Notify your teacher immediately if a piece of glass breaks.
- Use extreme care when handling all sharp and pointed instruments.
- Cut objects on a suitable surface, always in a direction away from your body.

Chemical Safety

Chemical Safety

- If a chemical gets on your skin, on your clothing, or in your eyes, rinse it immediately (shower, faucet, or eyewash fountain), and alert your teacher.
- Do not clean up spilled chemicals unless your teacher directs you to do so.
- Do not inhale any gas or vapor unless directed to do so by your teacher. If you are instructed to note the odor of a substance, wave the fumes toward your nose with your hand. This is called wafting. Never put your nose close to the source.
- Handle materials that emit vapors or gases in a well-ventilated area.

Electrical Safety

Electrical Safety

- Do not use equipment with frayed electrical cords or loose plugs.
- Do not use electrical equipment near water or when clothing or hands are wet.
- Hold the plug housing when you plug in or unplug equipment.

Heating and Fire Safety

Heating Safety

- Be aware of any source of flames, sparks, or heat (such as flames, heating coils, or hot plates) before working with any flammable substances.
- Know the location of lab fire extinguishers and fire-safety blankets.
- Know your school's fire-evacuation routes.
- If your clothing catches on fire, walk to the lab shower to put out the fire.
- Never leave a hot plate unattended while it is turned on or while it is cooling.
- Use tongs or appropriate insulated holders when handling heated objects.
- Allow all equipment to cool before storing it.

Wafting

Plant and Animal Safety

Plant Safety

Animal Safety

- Do not eat any part of a plant.
- Do not pick any wild plants unless your teacher instructs you to do so.
- Handle animals only as your teacher directs.
- Treat animals carefully and respectfully.
- Wash your hands thoroughly after handling any plant or animal.

Cleanup

Proper Waste Disposal

Hygienic Care

- Clean all work surfaces and protective equipment as directed by your teacher.
- Dispose of hazardous materials or sharp objects only as directed by your teacher.
- Keep your hands away from your face while you are working on any activity.
- Wash your hands thoroughly before you leave the lab or after any activity.

Designing, Conducting, and Reporting an Experiment

An experiment is an organized procedure to study something under specific conditions. Use the following steps of the scientific method when designing or conducting a controlled experiment.

1 Identify a Research Problem

Every day, you make observations by using your senses to gather information. Careful observations lead to good questions, and good questions can lead you to an experiment. Imagine, for example, that you pass a pond every day on your way to school, and you notice green scum beginning to form on top of it. You wonder what it is and why it seems to be growing. You list your questions, and then you do a little research to find out what is already known. A good place to start a research project is at the library. A library catalog lists all of the resources available to you at that library and often those found elsewhere. Begin your search by using:

- keywords or main topics.
- words similar to, or synonyms of, your keyword.

The types of resources that will be helpful to you will depend on the kind of information you are interested in. And some resources are more reliable for a given topic than others. Some different kinds of useful resources are:

- magazines and journals (or periodicals)—articles on a topic.
- encyclopedias—a good overview of a topic.
- books on specific subjects—details about a topic.
- newspapers—useful for current events.

The Internet can also be a great place to find information. Some of your library's reference materials may even be online. When using the Internet, however, it is especially important to make sure you are using appropriate and reliable sources. Websites of universities and government agencies are usually more accurate and reliable than websites created by individuals or businesses. Decide which sources are relevant and reliable for your topic. If in doubt, check with your teacher.

Take notes as you read through the information in these resources. You will probably come up with many questions and ideas for which you can do more research as needed. Once you feel you have enough information, think about the questions you have on the topic. Then write down the problem that you want to investigate. Your notes might look like those at the top of the next page.

Research Questions	Research Problem	Library and Internet Resources
• How do algae grow? • How do people measure algae? • What kind of fertilizer would affect the growth of algae? • Can fertilizer and algae be used safely in a lab? How?	How does fertilizer affect the algae in a pond?	Pond fertilization: initiating an algal bloom—from University of California Davis website. Blue-green algae in Wisconsin waters—from the Department of Natural Resources of Wisconsin website.

As you gather information from reliable sources, record details about each source, including author name(s), title, date of publication, and/or web address. Make sure to also note the specific information that you use from each source. Staying organized in this way will be important when you write your report and create a bibliography or works cited list. Recording this information and staying organized will help you credit the appropriate author(s) for the information that you have gathered.

Representing someone else's ideas or work as your own (without giving the original author credit) is known as plagiarism. Plagiarism can be intentional or unintentional. The best way to make sure that you do not commit plagiarism is to always do your own work and to always give credit to others when you use their words or ideas.

Current scientific research is built on scientific research and discoveries that have happened in the past. This means that scientists are constantly learning from each other and combining ideas to learn more about the natural world through investigation. But a good scientist always credits the ideas and research gathered from other people to those people. There are more details about crediting sources and creating a bibliography under step 9.

2 Make a Prediction

A prediction is a statement of what you expect will happen in your experiment. Before making a prediction, you need to decide in a general way what you will do in your procedure. You may state your prediction in an if-then format.

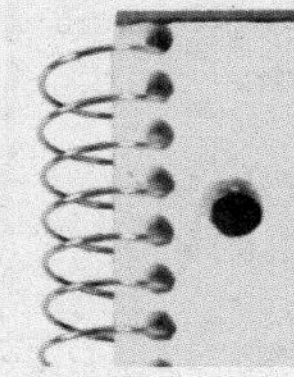

Prediction

If the amount of fertilizer in the pond water is increased, then the amount of algae will also increase.

3 Form a Hypothesis

Many experiments are designed to test a hypothesis. A hypothesis is a tentative explanation for an expected result. You have predicted that additional fertilizer will cause additional algae growth in pond water; your hypothesis should state the connection between fertilizer and algal growth.

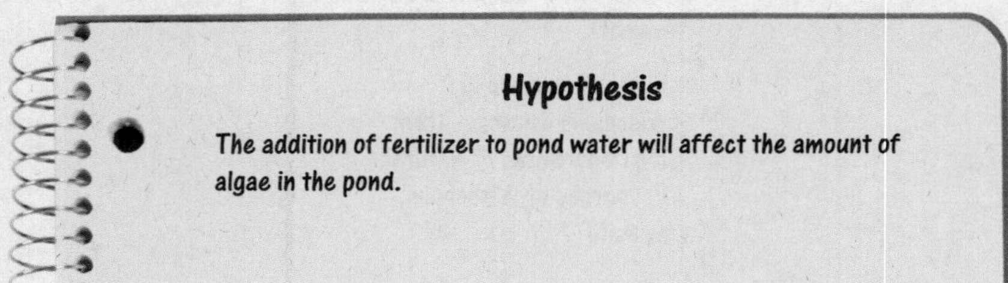

Hypothesis

The addition of fertilizer to pond water will affect the amount of algae in the pond.

4 Identify Variables to Test the Hypothesis

The next step is to design an experiment to test the hypothesis. The experimental results may or may not support the hypothesis. Either way, the information that results from the experiment may be useful for future investigations.

Experimental Group and Control Group

An experiment to determine how two factors are related has a control group and an experimental group. The two groups are the same, except that the investigator changes a single factor in the experimental group and does not change it in the control group.

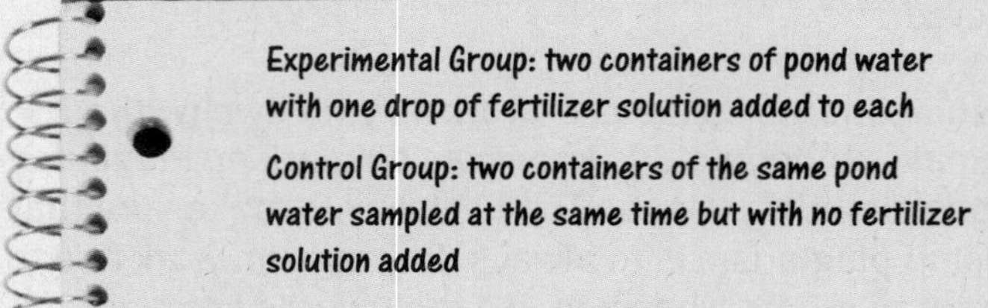

Experimental Group: two containers of pond water with one drop of fertilizer solution added to each

Control Group: two containers of the same pond water sampled at the same time but with no fertilizer solution added

Variables and Constants

In a controlled experiment, a variable is any factor that can change. Constants are all of the variables that are kept the same in both the experimental group and the control group.

The independent variable is the factor that is manipulated or changed in order to test the effect of the change on another variable. The dependent variable is the factor the investigator measures to gather data about the effect.

Independent Variable	Dependent Variable	Constants
Amount of fertilizer in pond water	Growth of algae in the pond water	• Where and when the pond water is obtained • The type of container used • Light and temperature conditions where the water is stored

5 Write a Procedure

Write each step of your procedure. Start each step with a verb, or action word, and keep the steps short. Your procedure should be clear enough for someone else to use as instructions for repeating your experiment.

Procedure

1. Use the masking tape and the marker to label the containers with your initials, the date, and the identifiers "Jar 1 with Fertilizer," "Jar 2 with Fertilizer," "Jar 1 without Fertilizer," and "Jar 2 without Fertilizer."
2. Put on your gloves. Use the large container to obtain a sample of pond water.
3. Divide the water sample equally among the four smaller containers.
4. Use the eyedropper to add one drop of fertilizer solution to the two containers labeled "Jar 1 with Fertilizer" and "Jar 2 with Fertilizer."
5. Cover the containers with clear plastic wrap. Use the scissors to punch ten holes in each of the covers.
6. Place all four containers on a window ledge. Make sure that they all receive the same amount of light.
7. Observe the containers every day for one week.
8. Place a ruler over the opening of the jar and measure the diameter of the largest clump of algae in each container. Record your measurements daily.

6 Experiment and Collect Data

Once you have all of your materials and your procedure has been approved, you can begin to experiment and collect data. Record both quantitative data (measurements) and qualitative data (observations), as shown below.

Algal Growth and Fertilizer

	Experimental Group		Control Group		
Date and Time	Jar 1 with Fertilizer (diameter of algal clump in mm)	Jar 2 with Fertilizer (diameter of algal clump in mm)	Jar 1 without Fertilizer (diameter of algal clump in mm)	Jar 2 without Fertilizer (diameter of algal clump in mm)	Observations
5/3 4:00 p.m.	0	0	0	0	condensation in all containers
5/4 4:00 p.m.	0	3	0	0	tiny green blobs in Jar 2 with fertilizer
5/5 4:15 p.m.	4	5	0	3	green blobs in Jars 1 and 2 with fertilizer and Jar 2 without fertilizer
5/6 4:00 p.m.	5	6	0	4	water light green in Jar 2 with fertilizer
5/7 4:00 p.m.	8	10	0	6	water light green in Jars 1 and 2 with fertilizer and Jar 2 without fertilizer
5/8 3:30 p.m.	10	18	0	6	cover off of Jar 2 with fertilizer
5/9 3:30 p.m.	14	23	0	8	drew sketches of each container

Drawings of Samples Viewed Under Microscope on 5/9 at 100x

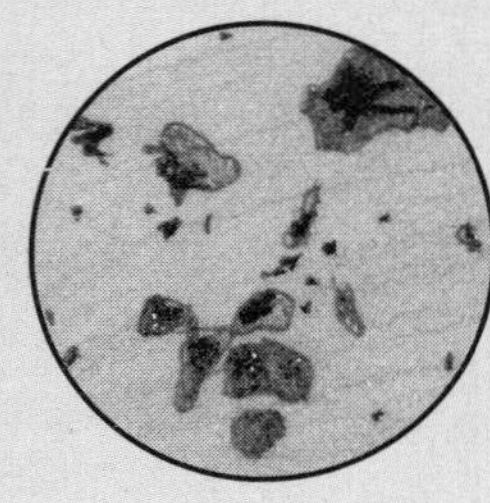
Jar 1 with Fertilizer

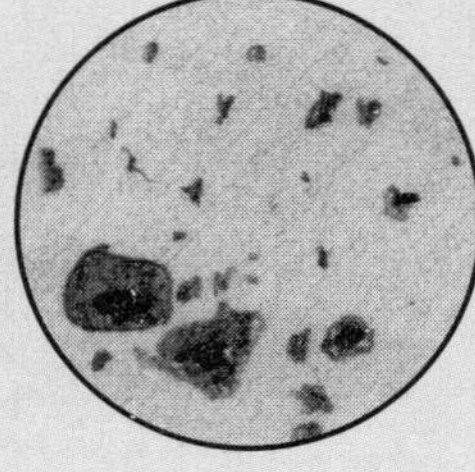
Jar 2 with Fertilizer

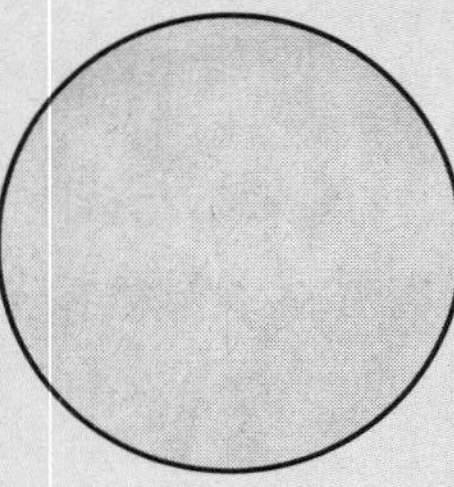
Jar 1 without Fertilizer

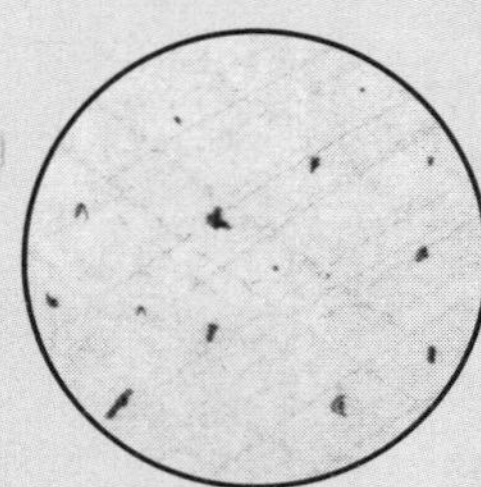
Jar 2 without Fertilizer

7 Analyze Data

After you complete your experiment, you must analyze all of the data you have gathered. Tables, statistics, and graphs are often used in this step to organize and analyze both the qualitative and quantitative data. Sometimes, your qualitative data are best used to help explain the relationships you see in your quantitative data.

Computer graphing software is useful for creating a graph from data you have collected. Most graphing software can make line graphs, pie charts, or bar graphs from data that have been organized in a spreadsheet. Graphs are useful for understanding relationships in the data and for communicating the results of your experiment.

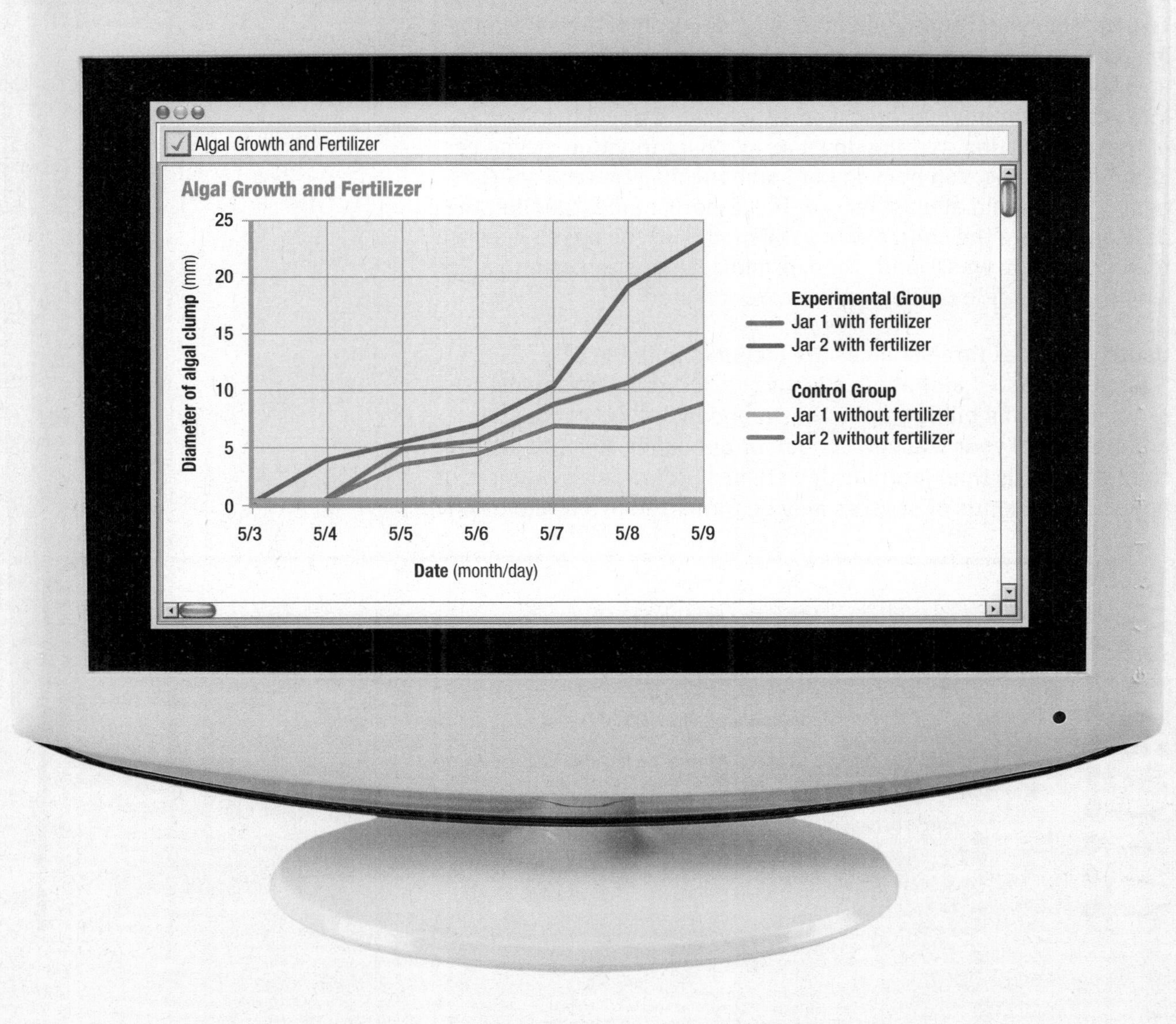

8 Make Conclusions

To draw conclusions from your experiment, first, write your results. Then, compare your results with your hypothesis. Do your results support your hypothesis? What have you learned?

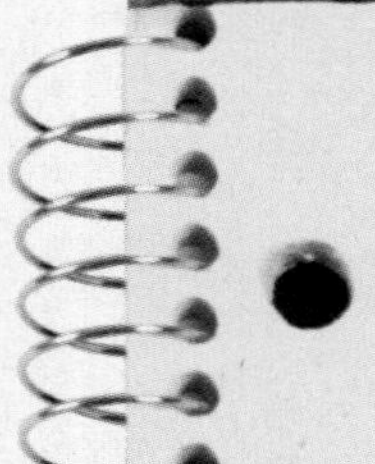

Conclusion

More algae grew in the pond water to which fertilizer had been added than in the pond water to which fertilizer had not been added. My hypothesis was supported. I conclude that it is possible that the growth of algae in ponds can be influenced by the input of fertilizer.

9 Create a Bibliography or Works Cited List

To complete your report, you must also show all of the newspapers, magazines, journals, books, and online sources that you used at every stage of your investigation. Whenever you find useful information about your topic, you should write down the source of that information. Writing down as much information as you can about the subject can help you or someone else find the source again. You should at least record the author's name, the title, the date and where the source was published, and the pages in which the information was found. Then, organize your sources into a list, which you can title Bibliography or Works Cited.

Usually, at least three sources are included in these lists. Sources are listed alphabetically, by the authors' last names. The exact format of a bibliography can vary, depending on the style preferences of your teacher, school, or publisher. Also, books are cited differently than journals or websites. Below is an example of how different kinds of sources may be formatted in a bibliography.

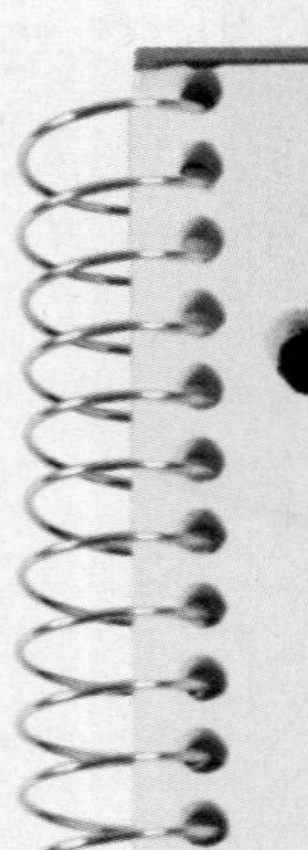

BOOK: Hauschultz, Sara. Freshwater Algae. Brainard, Minnesota: Northwoods Publishing, 2011.

ENCYCLOPEDIA: Lasure, Sedona. "Algae is not all just pond scum." Encyclopedia of Algae. 2009.

JOURNAL: Johnson, Keagan. "Algae as we know it." Sci Journal, vol 64. (September 2010): 201-211.

WEBSITE: Dout, Bill. "Keeping algae scum out of birdbaths." Help Keep Earth Clean. News. January 26, 2011. <www. SaveEarth.org>.

Using a Microscope

Scientists use microscopes to see very small objects that cannot easily be seen with the eye alone. A microscope magnifies the image of an object so that small details may be observed. A microscope that you may use can magnify an object 400 times—the object will appear 400 times larger than its actual size.

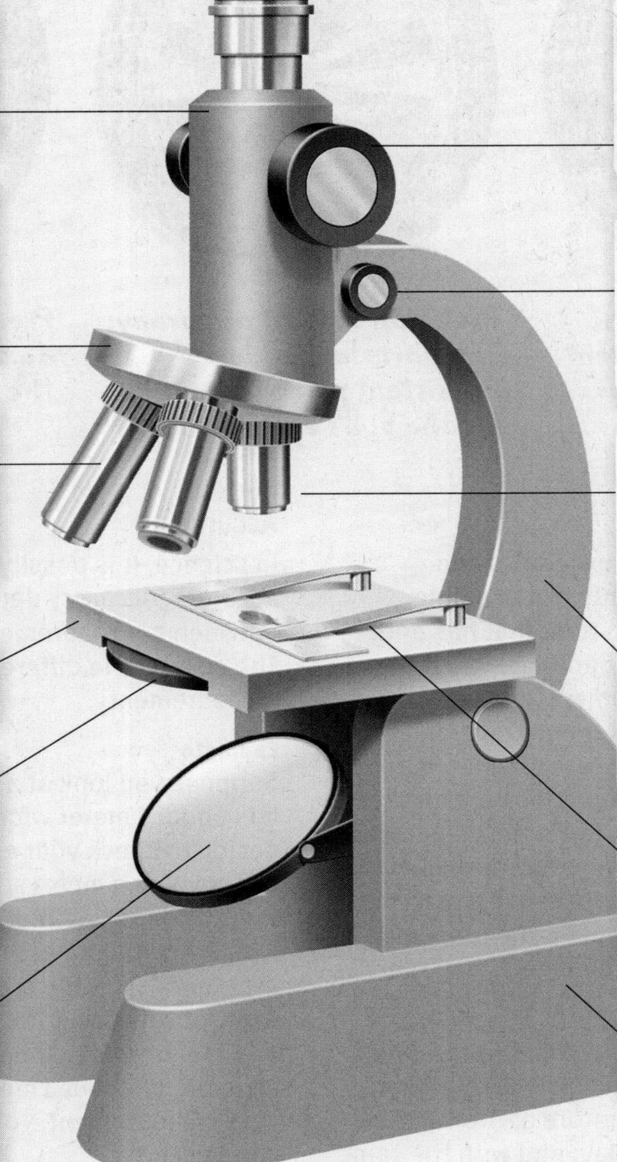

Eyepiece Objects are viewed through the eyepiece. The eyepiece contains a lens that commonly magnifies an image 10 times.

Body The body separates the lens in the eyepiece from the objective lenses below.

Coarse Adjustment This knob is used to focus the image of an object when it is viewed through the low-power lens.

Nosepiece The nosepiece holds the objective lenses above the stage and rotates so that all lenses may be used.

Fine Adjustment This knob is used to focus the image of an object when it is viewed through the high-power lens.

High-Power Objective Lens This is the largest lens on the nosepiece. It magnifies an image approximately 40 times.

Low-Power Objective Lens This is the smallest lens on the nosepiece. It magnifies images about 10 times.

Stage The stage supports the object being viewed.

Arm The arm supports the body above the stage. Always carry a microscope by the arm and base.

Diaphragm The diaphragm is used to adjust the amount of light passing through the slide and into an objective lens.

Stage Clip The stage clip holds a slide in place on the stage.

Mirror or Light Source Some microscopes use light that is reflected through the stage by a mirror. Other microscopes have their own light sources.

Base The base supports the microscope.

Measuring Accurately

Precision and Accuracy

When you do a scientific investigation, it is important that your methods, observations, and data be both precise and accurate.

Low precision: The darts did not land in a consistent place on the dartboard.

Precision but not accuracy: The darts landed in a consistent place but did not hit the bull's eye.

Precision and accuracy: The darts landed consistently on the bull's eye.

Precision

In science, *precision* is the exactness and consistency of measurements. For example, measurements made with a ruler that has both centimeter and millimeter markings would be more precise than measurements made with a ruler that has only centimeter markings. Another indicator of precision is the care taken to make sure that methods and observations are as exact and consistent as possible. Every time a particular experiment is done, the same procedure should be used. Precision is necessary because experiments are repeated several times and if the procedure changes, the results might change.

Example

Suppose you are measuring temperatures over a two-week period. Your precision will be greater if you measure each temperature at the same place, at the same time of day, and with the same thermometer than if you change any of these factors from one day to the next.

Accuracy

In science, it is possible to be precise but not accurate. *Accuracy* depends on the difference between a measurement and an actual value. The smaller the difference, the more accurate the measurement.

Example

Suppose you look at a stream and estimate that it is about 1 meter wide at a particular place. You decide to check your estimate by measuring the stream with a meter stick, and you determine that the stream is 1.32 meters wide. However, because it is difficult to measure the width of a stream with a meter stick, it turns out that your measurement was not very accurate. The stream is actually 1.14 meters wide. Therefore, even though your estimate of about 1 meter was less precise than your measurement, your estimate was actually more accurate.

Graduated Cylinders

How to Measure the Volume of a Liquid with a Graduated Cylinder

- Be sure that the graduated cylinder is on a flat surface so that your measurement will be accurate.
- When reading the scale on a graduated cylinder, be sure to have your eyes at the level of the surface of the liquid.
- The surface of the liquid will be curved in the graduated cylinder. Read the volume of the liquid at the bottom of the curve, or meniscus (muh•NIHS•kuhs).
- You can use a graduated cylinder to find the volume of a solid object by measuring the increase in a liquid's level after you add the object to the cylinder.

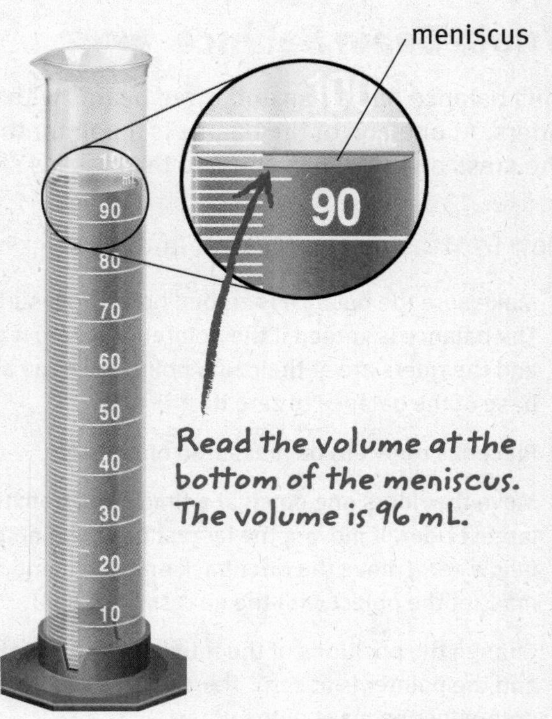

Metric Rulers

How to Measure the Length of a Leaf with a Metric Ruler

1. Lay a ruler flat on top of the leaf so that the 1-centimeter mark lines up with one end. Make sure the ruler and the leaf do not move between the time you line them up and the time you take the measurement.
2. Look straight down on the ruler so that you can see exactly how the marks line up with the other end of the leaf.
3. Estimate the length by which the leaf extends beyond a marking. For example, the leaf below extends about halfway between the 4.2-centimeter and 4.3-centimeter marks, so the apparent measurement is about 4.25 centimeters.
4. Remember to subtract 1 centimeter from your apparent measurement, since you started at the 1-centimeter mark on the ruler and not at the end. The leaf is about 3.25 centimeters long (4.25 cm − 1 cm = 3.25 cm).

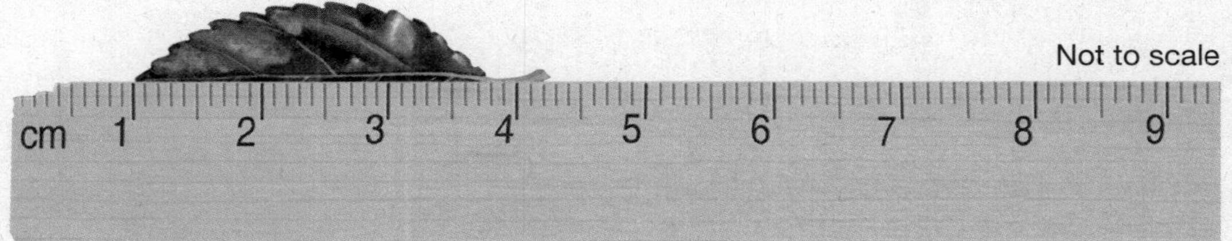

Triple Beam Balance

This balance has a pan and three beams with sliding masses, called riders. At one end of the beams is a pointer that indicates whether the mass on the pan is equal to the masses shown on the beams.

How to Measure the Mass of an Object

1 Make sure the balance is zeroed before measuring the mass of an object. The balance is zeroed if the pointer is at zero when nothing is on the pan and the riders are at their zero points. Use the adjustment knob at the base of the balance to zero it.

2 Place the object to be measured on the pan.

3 Move the riders one notch at a time away from the pan. Begin with the largest rider. If moving the largest rider one notch brings the pointer below zero, move the rider back one notch and begin measuring the mass of the object with the next smaller rider.

4 Change the positions of the riders until they balance the mass on the pan and the pointer is at zero. Then add the readings from the three beams to determine the mass of the object.

300 g	position of largest rider
90 g	position of middle rider
+ 3 g	position of smallest rider
393 g	mass of beaker and water

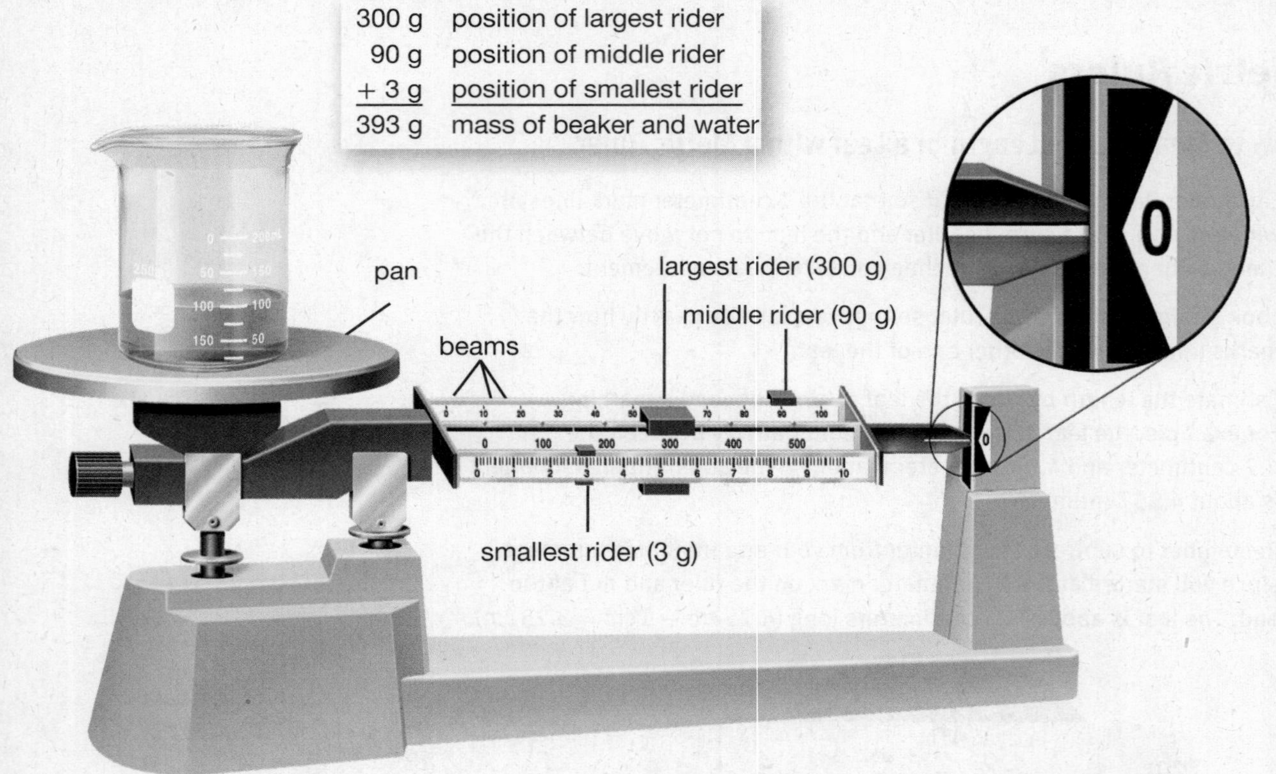

Electronic Balance

How to Measure the Mass of an Object

1 Be sure the balance is on a flat, stable surface.

2 Zero, or *tare*, the balance using the appropriate key. If you are measuring a specific quantity of a substance using a weigh boat or other container, place the weigh boat or container on the balance pan before zeroing the balance.

3 When the readout on the balance is steady and within a few thousandths of zero grams, place the object to be measured on the balance. If you are measuring out chemicals or other substances, wear gloves and use a clean spatula or similar tool to transfer the substance. Do not reach into containers or touch chemicals with your hands.

4 Record the mass of the object to the nearest milligram (1/1000 of one gram).

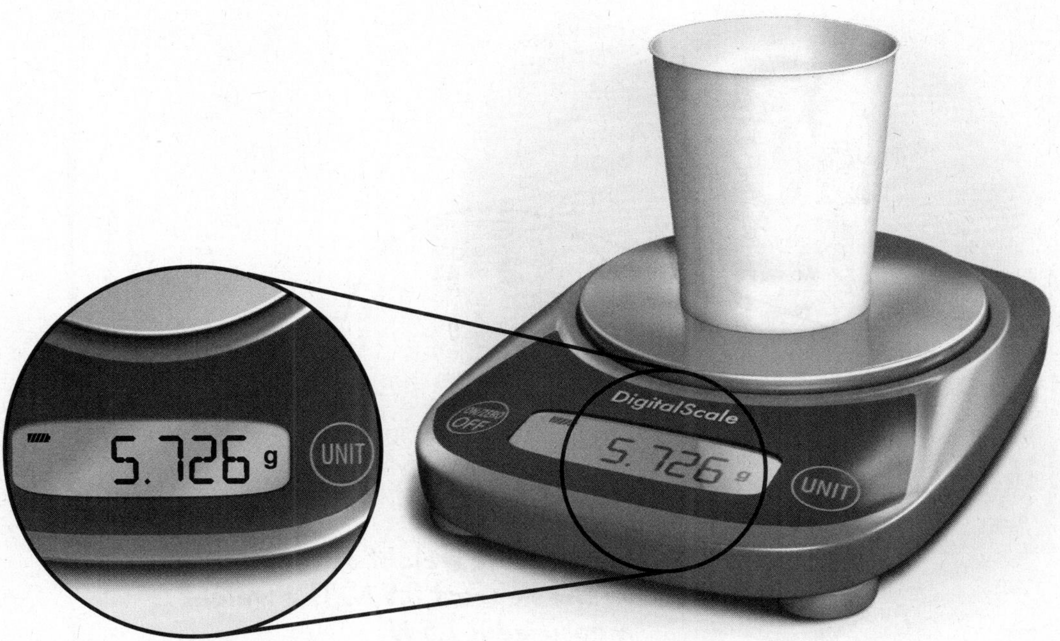

Record the mass of an object to the nearest milligram (mg). The mass measured is 5.726 grams.

Spring Scale

Spring scales are tools that measure forces, such as weight, or the gravitational force exerted on an object. A spring scale indicates an object's weight by measuring how far the spring stretches when an object is suspended from it. This type of scale is often used in grocery stores or to measure the weights of large loads of crops or industrial products. Spring scales are useful for measuring the weight of larger objects as well.

How to Measure the Weight of an Object

- Be sure the spring scale is securely suspended and is not touching the ground, wall, or desk. The pointer should be at zero.
- Hang the object to be weighed from the hook at the free end of the spring scale.
- When the object is still—not bouncing, swinging, or otherwise moving—read the object's weight to the nearest 0.5 N.

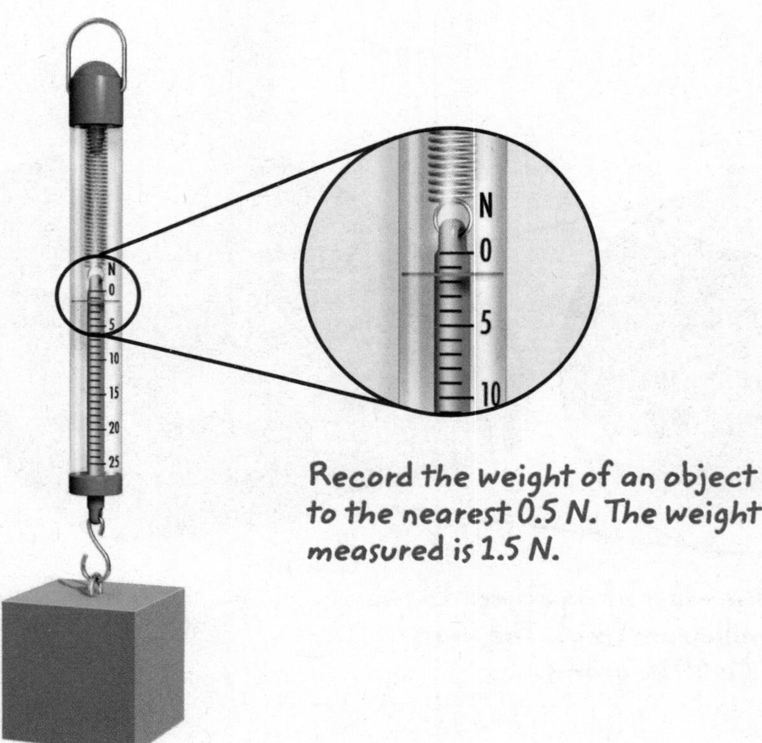

Record the weight of an object to the nearest 0.5 N. The weight measured is 1.5 N.

Thermometer

Many laboratory thermometers are the bulb type shown below. The sensing bulb of the thermometer is filled with a colored liquid (alcohol) that expands as it is heated. When the liquid expands, it moves up the stem of the thermometer through the capillary tube. Thermometers usually measure temperature in degrees Celsius (°C).

How to Measure the Temperature of a Substance

Caution: Do not hold the thermometer in your hand while measuring the temperature of a heated substance. Never use a thermometer to stir a solution. Always consult your teacher regarding proper laboratory techniques and safety rules when using a thermometer.

- Carefully lower the bulb of the thermometer into the substance. The stem of the thermometer may rest against the side of the container, but the bulb should never rest on the bottom. If the thermometer has an adjustable clip for the side of the container, use the clip to suspend the thermometer in the liquid.
- Watch the colored liquid as it rises in the thermometer's capillary tube. When the liquid stops rising, note the whole-degree increment nearest the top of the liquid column.
- If your thermometer is marked in whole degrees, report temperature to the nearest half degree.

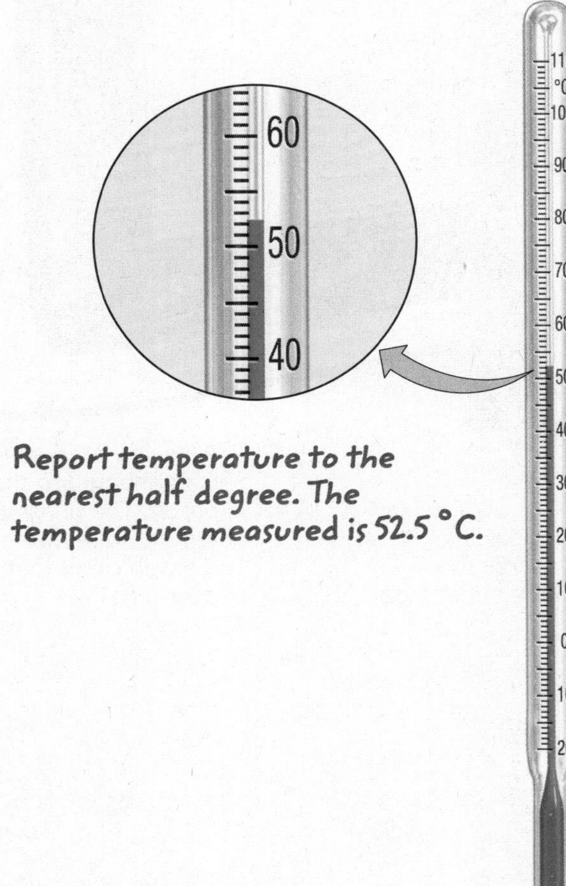

Introduction to Probeware

Probeware is a system of tools that offers a way to measure and analyze various physical properties, such as pressure, pH, temperature, or acceleration. Most probeware systems consist of a sensor, or probe, that is connected to a device such as a computer. As the sensor takes measurements, a computer program records the data. Users can then analyze data using tables, charts, or graphs. Some systems allow you to analyze more than one variable at a time.

Temperature Probe

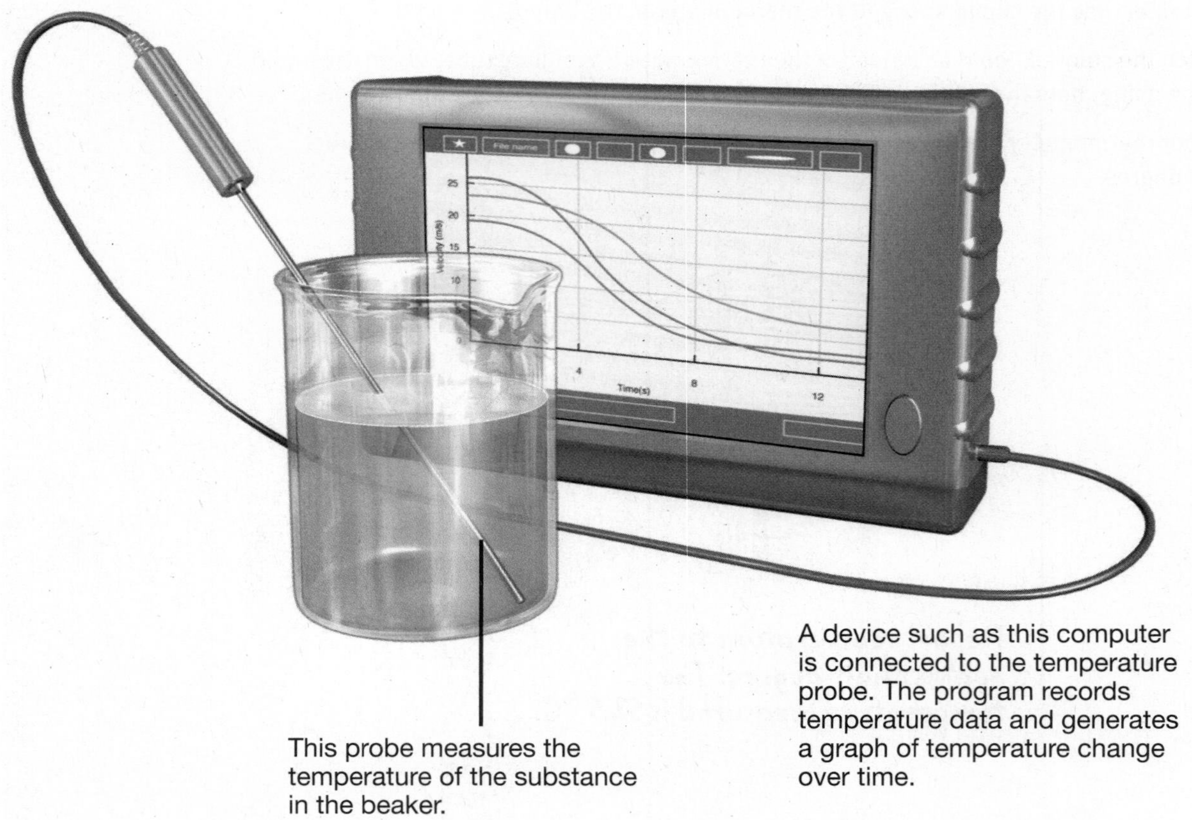

Time(s)
This probe measures the temperature of the substance in the beaker.
A device such as this computer is connected to the temperature probe. The program records temperature data and generates a graph of temperature change over time.

Motion Detector

Use a motion detector to gather information about an object's velocity, position, or acceleration.

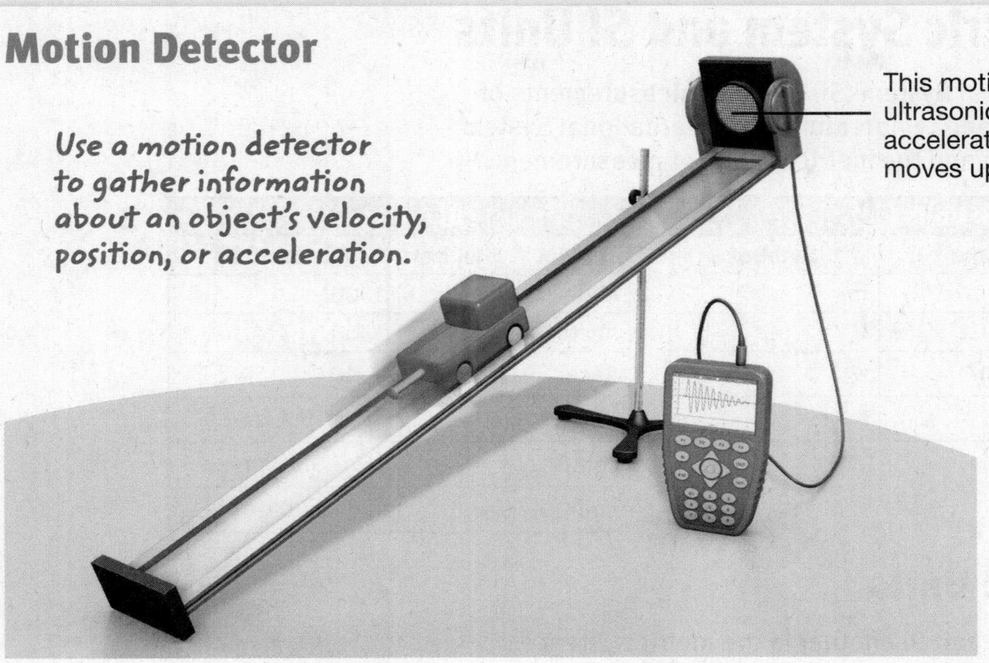

This motion detector uses ultrasonic waves to measure the acceleration of the toy car as it moves up and down the track.

pH Probe

Use a pH probe to determine whether a substance is acidic, neutral, or basic.

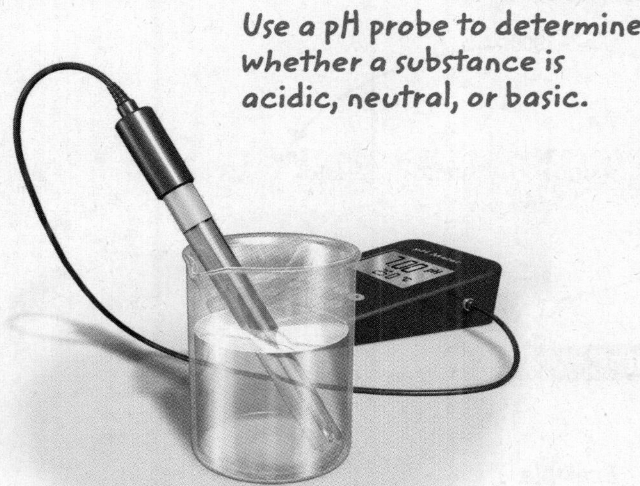

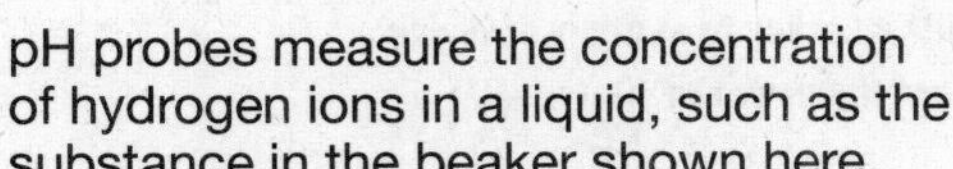

pH probes measure the concentration of hydrogen ions in a liquid, such as the substance in the beaker shown here.

The tip of a pH probe is a thin glass membrane that should not be allowed to dry out. Store pH probes in the appropriate container and solution when you are finished with your investigation.

Caution: Probeware equipment should always be handled carefully. Be sure to follow your teacher's instructions regarding the use and storage of all probeware equipment.

Using the Metric System and SI Units

Scientists use International System (SI) units for measurements of distance, volume, mass, and temperature. The International System is based on powers of ten and the metric system of measurement.

Basic SI Units		
Quantity	**Name**	**Symbol**
length	meter	m
volume	liter	L
mass	kilogram	kg
temperature	kelvin	K

SI Prefixes		
Prefix	**Symbol**	**Power of 10**
kilo-	k	1000
hecto-	h	100
deca-	da	10
deci-	d	0.1 or $\frac{1}{10}$
centi-	c	0.01 or $\frac{1}{100}$
milli-	m	0.001 or $\frac{1}{1000}$

Changing Metric Units

You can change from one unit to another in the metric system by multiplying or dividing by a power of 10

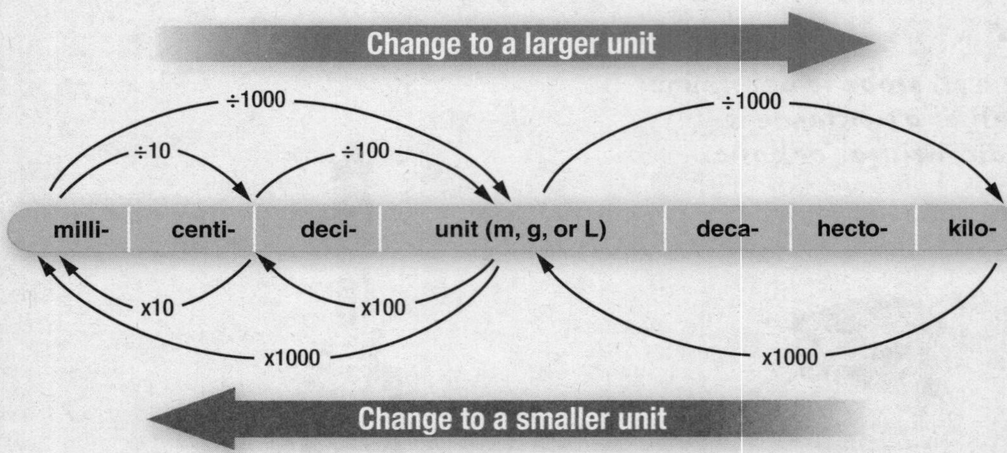

Example

Change 0.64 liters to milliliters.

1. *Decide whether to multiply or divide.*
2. *Select the power of 10.*

Change to a smaller unit by multiplying

mL ← x 1000 — L

0.64 x 1000 = 640.

ANSWER 0.64 L = 640 mL

Example

Change 23.6 grams to kilograms.

1. *Decide whether to multiply or divide.*
2. *Select the power of 10.*

Change to a larger unit by dividing

g — ÷ 1000 → kg

26.3 ÷ 1000 = 0.0263

ANSWER 23.6 g = 0.0236 kg

Converting Between SI and U.S. Customary Units

Use the chart below when you need to convert between SI units and U.S. customary units

SI Unit	From SI to U.S. Customary			From U.S. Customary to SI		
Length	**When you know**	**multiply by**	**to find**	**When you know**	**multiply by**	**to find**
kilometer (km) = 1000 m	kilometers	0.62	miles	miles	1.61	kilometers
meter (m) = 100 cm	meters	3.28	feet	feet	0.3048	meters
centimeter (cm) = 10 mm	centimeters	0.39	inches	inches	2.54	centimeters
millimeter (mm) = 0.1 cm	millimeters	0.04	inches	inches	25.4	millimeters
Area	**When you know**	**multiply by**	**to find**	**When you know**	**multiply by**	**to find**
square kilometer (km^2)	square kilometers	0.39	square miles	square miles	2.59	square kilometers
square meter (m^2)	square meters	1.2	square yards	square yards	0.84	square meters
square centimeter (cm^2)	square centimeters	0.155	square inches	square inches	6.45	square centimeters
Volume	**When you know**	**multiply by**	**to find**	**When you know**	**multiply by**	**to find**
liter (L) = 1000 mL	liters	1.06	quarts	quarts	0.95	liters
	liters	0.26	gallons	gallons	3.79	liters
	liters	4.23	cups	cups	0.24	liters
	liters	2.12	pints	pints	0.47	liters
milliliter (mL) = 0.001 L	milliliters	0.20	teaspoons	teaspoons	4.93	milliliters
	milliliters	0.07	tablespoons	tablespoons	14.79	milliliters
	milliliters	0.03	fluid ounces	fluid ounces	29.57	milliliters
Mass and Weight	**When you know**	**multiply by**	**to find**	**When you know**	**multiply by**	**to find**
kilogram (kg) = 1000 g	kilograms	2.2	pounds	pounds	0.45	kilograms
gram (g) = 1000 mg	grams	0.035	ounces	ounces	28.35	grams

Temperature Conversions

Even though the kelvin is the SI base unit of temperature, the degree Celsius will be the unit you use most often in your science studies. The formulas below show the relationships between temperatures in degrees Fahrenheit (°F), degrees Celsius (°C), and kelvins (K).

$°C = \frac{5}{9}(°F - 32)$ $\quad$ $°F = \frac{9}{5}°C + 32$ $\quad$ $K = °C + 273$

Examples of Temperature Conversions		
Condition	**Degrees Celsius**	**Degrees Fahrenheit**
Freezing point of water	0	32
Cool day	10	50
Mild day	20	68
Warm day	30	86
Normal body temperature	37	98.6
Very hot day	40	104
Boiling point of water	100	212

Math Refresher

Performing Calculations

Science requires an understanding of many math concepts. The following pages will help you review some important math skills.

Mean

The mean is the sum of all values in a data set divided by the total number of values in the data set. The mean is also called the *average*.

Example

Find the mean of the following set of numbers: 5, 4, 7, and 8.

Step 1 Find the sum.

$5 + 4 + 7 + 8 = 24$

Step 2 Divide the sum by the number of numbers in your set. Because there are four numbers in this example, divide the sum by 4.

$24 \div 4 = 6$

Answer The average, or mean, is 6.

Median

The median of a data set is the middle value when the values are written in numerical order. If a data set has an even number of values, the median is the mean of the two middle values.

Example

To find the median of a set of measurements, arrange the values in order from least to greatest. The median is the middle value.

13 mm 14 mm 16 mm 21 mm 23 mm

Answer The median is 16 mm.

Mode

The mode of a data set is the value that occurs most often.

Example

To find the mode of a set of measurements, arrange the values in order from least to greatest, and determine the value that occurs most often.

13 mm, 14 mm, 14 mm, 16 mm,
21 mm, 23 mm, 25 mm

Answer The mode is 14 mm.

A data set can have more than one mode or no mode. For example, the following data set has modes of 2 mm and 4 mm:

2 mm 2 mm 3 mm 4 mm 4 mm

The data set below has no mode because no value occurs more often than any other.

2 mm 3 mm 4 mm 5 mm

Ratios

A **ratio** is a comparison between numbers, and it is usually written as a fraction.

Example

Find the ratio of thermometers to students if you have 36 thermometers and 48 students in your class.

Step 1 Write the ratio.

$$\frac{36 \text{ thermometers}}{48 \text{ students}}$$

Step 2 Simplify the fraction to its simplest form.

$$\frac{36}{48} = \frac{36 \div 12}{48 \div 12} = \frac{3}{4}$$

The ratio of thermometers to students is 3 to 4 or 3:4. So there are 3 thermometers for every 4 students.

Proportions

A **proportion** is an equation that states that two ratios are equal.

$$\frac{3}{1} = \frac{12}{4}$$

To solve a proportion, you can use cross-multiplication. If you know three of the quantities in a proportion, you can use cross-multiplication to find the fourth.

Example

Imagine that you are making a scale model of the solar system for your science project. The diameter of Jupiter is 11.2 times the diameter of the Earth. If you are using a plastic-foam ball that has a diameter of 2 cm to represent the Earth, what must the diameter of the ball representing Jupiter be?

$$\frac{11.2}{1} = \frac{x}{2 \text{ cm}}$$

Step 1 Cross-multiply.

$$\frac{11.2}{1} = \frac{x}{2}$$

$$11.2 \times 2 = x \times 1$$

Step 2 Multiply.

$$22.4 = x \times 1$$

$$x = 22.4 \text{ cm}$$

You will need to use a ball that has a diameter of 22.4 cm to represent Jupiter.

Rates

A **rate** is a ratio of two values expressed in different units. A unit rate is a rate with a denominator of 1 unit.

Example

A plant grew 6 centimeters in 2 days. The plant's rate of growth was $\frac{6 \text{ cm}}{2 \text{ days}}$.

To describe the plant's growth in centimeters per day, write a unit rate.

Divide numerator and denominator by 2:

$$\frac{6 \text{ cm}}{2 \text{ days}} = \frac{6 \text{ cm} \div 2}{2 \text{ days} \div 2}$$

Simplify:

$$= \frac{3 \text{ cm}}{1 \text{ day}}$$

Answer The plant's rate of growth is 3 centimeters per day.

Math Refresher

Percent

A **percent** is a ratio of a given number to 100. For example, 85% = 85/100. You can use percent to find part of a whole.

Example
What is 85% of 40?

Step 1 Rewrite the percent as a decimal by moving the decimal point two places to the left.

$$0.85$$

Step 2 Multiply the decimal by the number that you are calculating the percentage of.

$$0.85 \times 40 = 34$$

85% of 40 is 34.

Decimals

To **add** or **subtract decimals**, line up the digits vertically so that the decimal points line up. Then add or subtract the columns from right to left. Carry or borrow numbers as necessary.

Example
Add the following numbers: 3.1415 and 2.96.

Step 1 Line up the digits vertically so that the decimal points line up.

$$\begin{array}{r} 3.1415 \\ +\ 2.96 \\ \hline \end{array}$$

Step 2 Add the columns from right to left, and carry when necessary.

$$\begin{array}{r} 3.1415 \\ +\ 2.96 \\ \hline 6.1015 \end{array}$$

The sum is 6.1015.

Fractions

A **fraction** is a ratio of two whole numbers. The top number is the numerator. The bottom number is the denominator. The denominator must not be zero.

Example
Your class has 24 plants. Your teacher instructs you to put 5 plants in a shady spot. What fraction of the plants in your class will you put in a shady spot?

Step 1 In the denominator, write the total number of parts in the whole.

$$\frac{?}{24}$$

Step 2 In the numerator, write the number of parts of the whole that are being considered.

$$\frac{5}{24}$$

So $\frac{5}{24}$ of the plants will be in the shade.

Simplifying Fractions

It is usually best to express a fraction in its simplest form. Expressing a fraction in its simplest form is called **simplifying a fraction.**

Example

Express the fraction $\frac{30}{45}$ in its simplest form.

Step 1 Find the largest whole number that will divide evenly into both the numerator and denominator. This number is called the greatest common factor (GCF).

Factors of the numerator 30:
1, 2, 3, 5, 6, 10, **15**, 30

Factors of the denominator 45:
1, 3, 5, 9, **15**, 45

Step 2 Divide both the numerator and the denominator by the GCF, which in this case is 15.

$$\frac{30}{45} = \frac{30 \div 15}{45 \div 15} = \frac{2}{3}$$

Thus, $\frac{30}{45}$ written in its simplest form is $\frac{2}{3}$.

Adding and Subtracting Fractions

To **add** or **subtract fractions** that have the same denominator, simply add or subtract the numerators.

Examples

$\frac{3}{5} + \frac{1}{5} = ?$ and $\frac{3}{4} - \frac{1}{4} = ?$

Step 1 Add or subtract the numerators.

$\frac{3}{5} + \frac{1}{5} = \frac{4}{\ }$ and $\frac{3}{4} - \frac{1}{4} = \frac{2}{\ }$

Step 2 Write in the common denominator, which remains the same.

$\frac{3}{5} + \frac{1}{5} = \frac{4}{5}$ and $\frac{3}{4} - \frac{1}{4} = \frac{2}{4}$

Step 3 If necessary, write the fraction in its simplest form.

$\frac{4}{5}$ cannot be simplified, and $\frac{2}{4} = \frac{1}{2}$.

To **add** or **subtract** fractions that have **different denominators,** first find the least common denominator (LCD).

Examples

$\frac{1}{2} + \frac{1}{6} = ?$ and $\frac{3}{4} - \frac{2}{3} = ?$

Step 1 Write the equivalent fractions that have a common denominator.

$\frac{3}{6} + \frac{1}{6} = ?$ and $\frac{9}{12} - \frac{8}{12} = ?$

Step 2 Add or subtract the fractions.

$\frac{3}{6} + \frac{1}{6} = \frac{4}{6}$ and $\frac{9}{12} - \frac{8}{12} = \frac{1}{12}$

Step 3 If necessary, write the fraction in its simplest form.

$\frac{4}{6} = \frac{2}{3}$, and $\frac{1}{12}$ cannot be simplified.

Multiplying Fractions

To **multiply fractions,** multiply the numerators and the denominators together, and then simplify the fraction if necessary.

Example

$\frac{5}{9} \times \frac{7}{10} = ?$

Step 1 Multiply the numerators and denominators.

$$\frac{5}{9} \times \frac{7}{10} = \frac{5 \times 7}{9 \times 10} = \frac{35}{90}$$

Step 2 Simplify the fraction.

$$\frac{35}{90} = \frac{35 \div 5}{90 \div 5} = \frac{7}{18}$$

Math Refresher

Dividing Fractions

To **divide fractions**, first rewrite the divisor (the number you divide by) upside down. This number is called the reciprocal of the divisor. Then multiply and simplify if necessary.

Example

$\frac{5}{8} \div \frac{3}{2} = ?$

Step 1 Rewrite the divisor as its reciprocal.

$\frac{3}{2} \rightarrow \frac{2}{3}$

Step 2 Multiply the fractions.

$\frac{5}{8} \times \frac{2}{3} = \frac{5 \times 2}{8 \times 3} = \frac{10}{24}$

Step 3 Simplify the fraction.

$\frac{10}{24} = \frac{10 \div 2}{24 \div 2} = \frac{5}{12}$

Using Significant Figures

The **significant figures** in a decimal are the digits that are warranted by the accuracy of a measuring device.

When you perform a calculation with measurements, the number of significant figures to include in the result depends in part on the number of significant figures in the measurements. When you multiply or divide measurements, your answer should have only as many significant figures as the measurement with the fewest significant figures.

Examples

Using a balance and a graduated cylinder filled with water, you determined that a marble has a mass of 8.0 grams and a volume of 3.5 cubic centimeters. To calculate the density of the marble, divide the mass by the volume.

Write the formula for density: Density $= \frac{\text{mass}}{\text{volume}}$

Substitute measurements: $= \frac{8.0\ g}{3.5\ cm^3}$

Use a calculator to divide: $\approx 2.285714286\ g/cm^3$

Answer Because the mass and the volume have two significant figures each, give the density to two significant figures. The marble has a density of 2.3 grams per cubic centimeter.

Using Scientific Notation

Scientific notation is a shorthand way to write very large or very small numbers. For example, 73,500,000,000,000,000,000,000 kg is the mass of the moon. In scientific notation, it is 7.35×10^{22} kg. A value written as a number between 1 and 10, times a power of 10, is in scientific notation.

Examples

You can convert from standard form to scientific notation.

Standard Form	Scientific Notation
720,000 5 decimal places left	7.2×10^5 Exponent is 5.
0.000291 4 decimal places right	2.91×10^{-4} Exponent is –4.

You can convert from scientific notation to standard form.

Scientific Notation	Standard Form
4.63×10^7 Exponent is 7.	46,300,000 7 decimal places right
1.08×10^{-6} Exponent is –6.	0.00000108 6 decimal places left

Making and Interpreting Graphs

Circle Graph

A circle graph, or pie chart, shows how each group of data relates to all of the data. Each part of the circle represents a category of the data. The entire circle represents all of the data. For example, a biologist studying a hardwood forest in Wisconsin found that there were five different types of trees. The data table at right summarizes the biologist's findings.

Wisconsin Hardwood Trees	
Type of tree	**Number found**
Oak	600
Maple	750
Beech	300
Birch	1,200
Hickory	150
Total	3,000

How to Make a Circle Graph

1 To make a circle graph of these data, first find the percentage of each type of tree. Divide the number of trees of each type by the total number of trees, and multiply by 100%.

$$\frac{600 \text{ oak}}{3{,}000 \text{ trees}} \times 100\% = 20\%$$

$$\frac{750 \text{ maple}}{3{,}000 \text{ trees}} \times 100\% = 25\%$$

$$\frac{300 \text{ beech}}{3{,}000 \text{ trees}} \times 100\% = 10\%$$

$$\frac{1{,}200 \text{ birch}}{3{,}000 \text{ trees}} \times 100\% = 40\%$$

$$\frac{150 \text{ hickory}}{3{,}000 \text{ trees}} \times 100\% = 5\%$$

A Community of Wisconsin Hardwood Trees

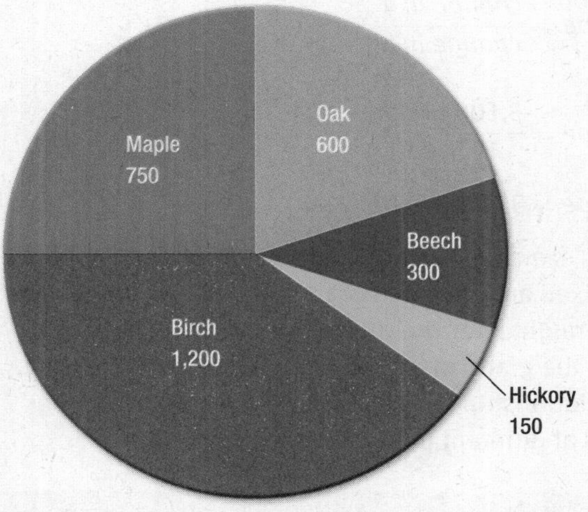

2 Now, determine the size of the wedges that make up the graph. Multiply each percentage by 360°. Remember that a circle contains 360°.

$20\% \times 360° = 72°$　　$25\% \times 360° = 90°$

$10\% \times 360° = 36°$　　$40\% \times 360° = 144°$

$5\% \times 360° = 18°$

3 Check that the sum of the percentages is 100 and the sum of the degrees is 360.

$$20\% + 25\% + 10\% + 40\% + 5\% = 100\%$$

$$72° + 90° + 36° + 144° + 18° = 360°$$

4 Use a compass to draw a circle, and mark the center of the circle.

5 Then, use a protractor to draw angles of 72°, 90°, 36°, 144°, and 18° in the circle.

6 Finally, label each part of the graph, and choose an appropriate title.

Math Refresher

Line Graphs

Line graphs are most often used to demonstrate continuous change. For example, Mr. Smith's students analyzed the population records for their hometown, Appleton, between 1910 and 2010. Examine the data at right.

Because the year and the population change, they are the variables. The population is determined by, or dependent on, the year. Therefore, the population is called the **dependent variable,** and the year is called the **independent variable**. Each year and its population make a **data pair**. To prepare a line graph, you must first organize data pairs into a table like the one at right.

Population of Appleton, 1910–2010	
Year	**Population**
1910	1,800
1930	2,500
1950	3,200
1970	3,900
1990	4,600
2010	5,300

How to Make a Line Graph

1 Place the independent variable along the horizontal (x) axis. Place the dependent variable along the vertical (y) axis.

2 Label the x-axis "Year" and the y-axis "Population." Look at your greatest and least values for the population. For the y-axis, determine a scale that will provide enough space to show these values. You must use the same scale for the entire length of the axis. Next, find an appropriate scale for the x-axis.

3 Choose reasonable starting points for each axis.

4 Plot the data pairs as accurately as possible.

5 Choose a title that accurately represents the data.

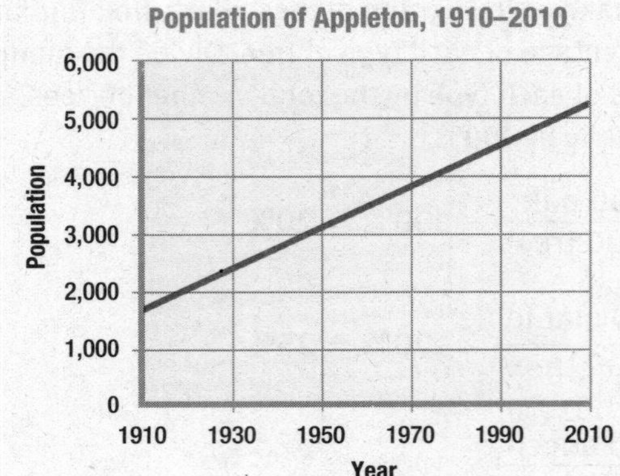

How to Determine Slope

Slope is the ratio of the change in the y-value to the change in the x-value, or "rise over run."

1 Choose two points on the line graph. For example, the population of Appleton in 2010 was 5,300 people. Therefore, you can define point A as (2010, 5,300). In 1910, the population was 1,800 people. You can define point B as (1910, 1,800).

2 Find the change in the y-value.
(y at point A) − (y at point B) =
5,300 people − 1,800 people =
3,500 people

3 Find the change in the x-value.
(x at point A) − (x at point B) =
2010 − 1910 = 100 years

4 Calculate the slope of the graph by dividing the change in y by the change in x.

$$slope = \frac{change\ in\ y}{change\ in\ x}$$

$$slope = \frac{3{,}500\ \text{people}}{100\ \text{years}}$$

$$slope = 35\ \text{people per year}$$

In this example, the population in Appleton increased by a fixed amount each year. The graph of these data is a straight line. Therefore, the relationship is **linear**. When the graph of a set of data is not a straight line, the relationship is **nonlinear**. As a result, the slope varies at different points on the graph.

Bar Graphs

Bar graphs can be used to demonstrate change that is not continuous. These graphs can be used to indicate trends when the data cover a long period of time. A meteorologist gathered the precipitation data shown here for Summerville for April 1–15 and used a bar graph to represent the data.

Precipitation in Summerville, April 1–15			
Date	**Precipitation (cm)**	**Date**	**Precipitation (cm)**
April 1	0.5	April 9	0.25
April 2	1.25	April 10	0.0
April 3	0.0	April 11	1.0
April 4	0.0	April 12	0.0
April 5	0.0	April 13	0.25
April 6	0.0	April 14	0.0
April 7	0.0	April 15	6.50
April 8	1.75		

How to Make a Bar Graph

1 Use an appropriate scale and a reasonable starting point for each axis.

2 Label the axes, and plot the data.

3 Choose a title that accurately represents the data.

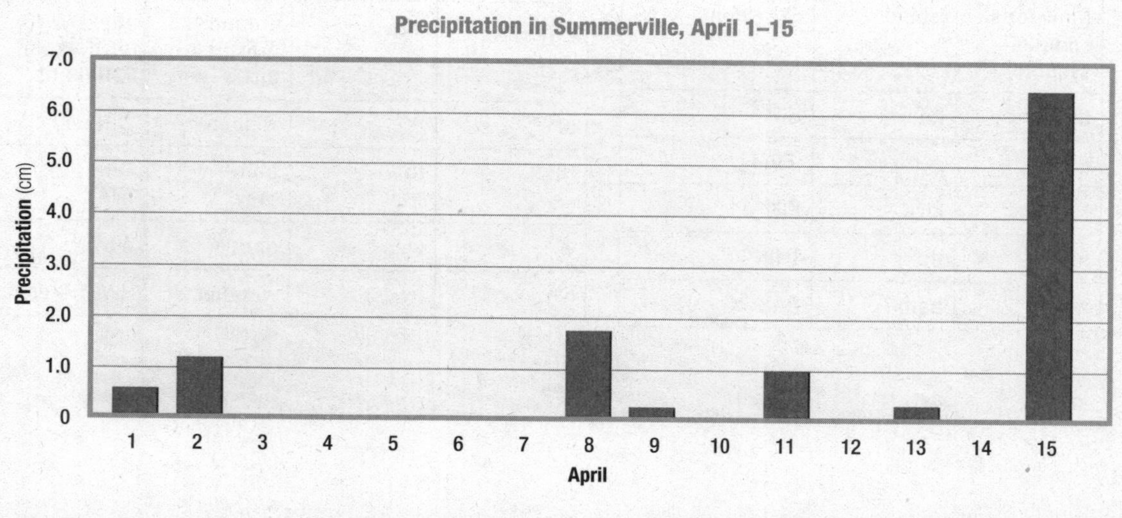

Glossary

Pronunciation Key							
Sound	Symbol	Example	Respelling	Sound	Symbol	Example	Respelling
ă	a	pat	PAT	ŏ	ah	bottle	BAHT•l
ā	ay	pay	PAY	ō	oh	toe	TOH
âr	air	care	KAIR	ô	aw	caught	KAWT
ä	ah	father	FAH•ther	ôr	ohr	roar	ROHR
är	ar	argue	AR•gyoo	oi	oy	noisy	NOYZ•ee
ch	ch	chase	CHAYS	o͝o	u	book	BUK
ĕ	e	pet	PET	o͞o	oo	boot	BOOT
ĕ (at end of a syllable)	eh	settee lessee	seh•TEE leh•SEE	ou	ow	pound	POWND
ĕr	ehr	merry	MEHR•ee	s	s	center	SEN•ter
ē	ee	beach	BEECH	sh	sh	cache	CASH
g	g	gas	GAS	ŭ	uh	flood	FLUHD
ĭ	i	pit	PIT	ûr	er	bird	BERD
ĭ (at end of a syllable)	ih	guitar	gih•TAR	z	z	xylophone	ZY•luh•fohn
ī	y eye (only for a complete syllable)	pie island	PY EYE•luhnd	z	z	bags	BAGZ
îr	ir	hear	HIR	zh	zh	decision	dih•SIZH•uhn
j	j	germ	JERM	ə	uh	around broken focus	uh•ROWND BROH•kuhn FOH•kuhs
k	k	kick	KIK	ər	er	winner	WIN•er
ng	ng	thing	THING	th	th	thin they	THIN THAY
ngk	ngk	bank	BANGK	w	w	one	WUHN
				wh	hw	whether	HWETH•er

accuracy (AK•yer•uh•see) a description of how close a measurement is to the true value of the quantity measured (50)
exactitud término que describe qué tanto se aproxima una medida al valor verdadero de la cantidad medida

active transport (AK•tiv TRANS•pohrt) the movement of substances across the cell membrane that requires the cell to use energy (261)
transporte activo el movimiento de sustancias a través de la membrana celular que requiere que la célula gaste energía

algae (AL•jee) eukaryotic organisms that convert the sun's energy into food through photosynthesis but that do not have roots, stems, or leaves (singular, *alga*) (315)
algas organismos eucarióticos que transforman la energía del Sol en alimento por medio de la fotosíntesis, pero que no tienen raíces, tallos ni hojas

angiosperm (AN•jee•uh•sperm) a flowering plant that produces seeds within a fruit (330)
angiosperma una planta que da flores y que produce semillas dentro de la fruta

Animalia (an•uh•MAYL•yuh) a kingdom made up of complex, multicellular organisms that lack cell walls, can usually move around, and quickly respond to their environment (285)
Animalia un reino formado por organismos pluricelulares complejos que no tienen pared celular, normalmente son capaces de moverse y reaccionan rápidamente a su ambiente

Archaea (ar•KEE•uh) a domain made up of prokaryotes most of which are known to live in extreme environments that are distinguished from other prokaryotes by differences in their genetics and in the makeup of their cell wall (282, 294)
Archaea un dominio compuesto por procariotes la mayoría de los cuales viven en ambientes extremos que se distinguen de otros procariotes por su genética y por la composición de su pared celular

atom (AT•uhm) the smallest unit of an element that maintains the properties of that element (112, 216, 444, 456)
átomo la unidad más pequeña de un elemento que conserva las propiedades de ese elemento

atomic number (uh•TAHM•ik NUM•ber) the number of protons in the nucleus of an atom; the atomic number is the same for all atoms of an element (446)
número atómico el número de protones en el núcleo de un átomo; el número atómico es el mismo para todos los átomos de un elemento

Bacteria (bak•TIR•ee•uh) a domain made up of prokaryotes that usually have a cell wall and that usually reproduce by cell division (282, 294)
Bacteria un dominio compuesto por procariotes que por lo general tienen pared celular y se reproducen por división celular

binary fission (BY•nuh•ree FISH•uhn) a form of asexual reproduction in single-celled organisms by which one cell divides into two cells of the same size (298)
fisión binaria una forma de reproducción asexual de los organismos unicelulares, por medio de la cual la célula se divide en dos células del mismo tamaño

biomass (BY•oh•mas) plant material, manure, or any other organic matter that is used as an energy source (188)
biomasa materia vegetal, estiércol o cualquier otra materia orgánica que se usa como fuente de energía

boiling (BOYL•ing) the change of state from a liquid to a gas that occurs at a specific temperature (490)
ebullición el cambio de estado de líquido a gaseoso que ocurre a una temperatura específica

carbohydrate (kar•boh•HY•drayt) a class of molecules that includes sugars, starches, and fiber; contains carbon, hydrogen, and oxygen (219)
carbohidrato una clase de moléculas entre las que se incluyen azúcares, almidones y fibra; contiene carbono, hidrógeno y oxígeno

cell (SEL) in biology, the smallest unit that can perform all life processes; cells are covered by a membrane and contain DNA and cytoplasm (206)
célula en biología, la unidad más pequeña que puede realizar todos los procesos vitales; las células están cubiertas por una membrana y tienen ADN y citoplasma

cell membrane (SEL MEM•brayn) a phospholipid layer that covers a cell's surface and acts as a barrier between the inside of a cell and the cell's environment (210)
membrana celular una capa de fosfolípidos que cubre la superficie de la célula y funciona como una barrera entre el interior de la célula y el ambiente de la célula

cellular respiration (SEL•yuh•luhr res•puh•RAY•shuhn) the process by which cells use oxygen to produce energy from food (258)
respiración celular el proceso por medio del cual las células utilizan oxígeno para producir energía a partir de los alimentos

cell wall (SEL WAWL) a rigid structure that surrounds the cell membrane and provides support to the cell (230)
pared celular una estructura rígida que rodea la membrana celular y le brinda soporte a la célula

chemical property (KEM•ih•kuhl PRAHP•uhr•tee) a property of matter that describes a substance's ability to participate in chemical reactions (432)
propiedad química una propiedad de la materia que describe la capacidad de una sustancia de participar en reacciones químicas

chemical symbol (KEM•ih•kuhl SIM•buhl) a one-, two-, or three-letter abbreviation of the name of an element (447)
símbolo químico una abreviatura de una, dos o tres letras del nombre de un elemento

chlorophyll (KLOHR•uh•fil) a green pigment that captures light energy for photosynthesis (325)
clorofila un pigmento verde que capta la energía luminosa para la fotosíntesis

chloroplast (KLOHR•uh•plast) an organelle found in plant and algae cells where photosynthesis occurs (231)
cloroplasto un organelo que se encuentra en las células vegetales y en las células de las algas, en el cual se lleva a cabo la fotosíntesis

cleavage (KLEE•vij) in geology, the tendency of a mineral to split along specific planes of weakness to form smooth, flat surfaces (119)
exfoliación en geología, la tendencia de un mineral a agrietarse a lo largo de planos débiles específicos y formar superficies lisas y planas

composition (kahm•puh•ZISH•uhn) the chemical makeup of a rock; describes either the minerals or other materials in the rock (142)
composición la constitución química de una roca; describe los minerales u otros materiales presentes en ella

compound (KAHM•pownd) a substance made up of atoms of two or more different elements joined by chemical bonds (112, 457)
compuesto una sustancia formada por átomos de dos o más elementos diferentes unidos por enlaces químicos

condensation (kahn•den•SAY•shuhn) the change of state from a gas to a liquid (491)
condensación el cambio de estado de gas a líquido

conservation (kahn•ser•VAY•shuhn) the wise use of and preservation of natural resources (106)
conservación el uso inteligente y la preservación de los recursos naturales

consumer (kuhn•SOO•mer) an organism that eats other organisms or organic matter (343)
consumidor un organismo que se alimenta de otros organismos o de materia orgánica

control (kuhn•TROHL) the part of an experiment for which the independent variable has not been changed; used as a way to determine the reliability and significance of the experimental results (34)
control parte de un experimento en la cual la variable independiente no cambia; se usa para determinar cuán confiables y significativos son los resultados del experimento

crystal (KRIS•tuhl) a solid whose atoms, ions, or molecules are arranged in a regular, repeating pattern (113)
cristal un sólido cuyos átomos, iones o moléculas están ordenados en un patrón regular y repetitivo

cytoplasm (SY•toh•plaz•uhm) the region of the cell within the membrane that includes the fluid, the cytoskeleton, and all of the organelles except the nucleus (210)
citoplasma la región de la célula dentro de la membrana, que incluye el líquido, el citoesqueleto y los organelos, pero no el núcleo

cytoskeleton (sy•toh•SKEL•ih•tn) the cytoplasmic network of protein filaments that plays an essential role in cell movement, shape, and division (227)
citoesqueleto la red citoplásmica de filamentos de proteínas que juega un papel esencial en el movimiento, forma y división de la célula

data (DAY•tuh) information gathered by observation or experimentation that can be used in calculating or reasoning (29)
datos la información recopilada por medio de la observación o experimentación que puede usarse para hacer cálculos o razonar

degree (dih•GREE) the units of a temperature scale (382)
grado la unidad de una escala de temperatura

density (DEN•sih•tee) the ratio of the mass of a substance to the volume of the substance (421)
densidad la relación entre la masa de una sustancia y su volumen

dependent variable (dih•PEN•duhnt VAIR•ee•uh•buhl) in a scientific investigation, the factor that changes as a result of manipulation of one or more independent variables (29, 56)
variable dependiente en una investigación científica, el factor que cambia como resultado de la manipulación de una o más variables independientes

deposition (dep•uh•ZISH•uhn) the process in which material is laid down (127, 493)
sublimación inversa el proceso por medio del cual un material se deposita

diffusion (dih•FYOO•zhuhn) the movement of particles from regions of higher density to regions of lower density (260)
difusión el movimiento de partículas de regiones de mayor densidad a regiones de menor densidad

domain (doh•MAYN) in a taxonomic system, one of the three broad groups that all living things fall into (282)
dominio en un sistema taxonómico, uno de los tres amplios grupos al que pertenecen todos los seres vivos

E

electron (ee•LEK•trahn) a subatomic particle that has a negative charge (444)
electrón una partícula subatómica que tiene carga negativa

element (EL•uh•muhnt) a substance that cannot be separated or broken down into simpler substances by chemical means (112, 446, 457)
elemento una sustancia que no se puede separar o descomponer en sustancias más simples por medio de métodos químicos

empirical evidence (em•PIR•ih•kuhl EV•ih•duhns) the observations, measurements, and other types of data that people gather and test to support and evaluate scientific explanations (7)
evidencia empírica las observaciones, mediciones y demás tipos de datos que se recopilan y examinan para apoyar y evaluar explicaciones científicas

endocytosis (en•doh•sy•TOH•sis) the process by which a cell membrane surrounds a particle and encloses the particle in a vesicle to bring the particle into the cell (262)
endocitosis el proceso por medio del cual la membrana celular rodea una partícula y la encierra en una vesícula para llevarla al interior de la célula

endoplasmic reticulum (en•doh•PLAZ•mik ri•TIK•yuh•luhm) a system of membranes that is found in a cell's cytoplasm and that assists in the production, processing, and transport of proteins and in the production of lipids (229)
retículo endoplásmico un sistema de membranas que se encuentra en el citoplasma de la célula y que tiene una función en la producción, procesamiento y transporte de proteínas y en la producción de lípidos

endoskeleton (en•doh•SKEL•ih•tn) an internal skeleton made of bone and cartilage (345)
endoesqueleto un esqueleto interno hecho de hueso y cartílago

energy (EN•er•jee) the ability to cause change (364)
energía la capacidad de producir un cambio

energy resource (EN•er•jee REE•sohrs) a natural resource that humans use to generate energy (101, 168, 182)
recurso energético un recurso natural que utilizan los humanos para generar energía

energy transformation (EN•er•jee trans•fohr•MAY•shuhn) the process of energy changing from one form into another (370)
transformación de energía el proceso de cambio de un tipo de energía a otro

engineering (en•juh•NIR•ing) the application of science and mathematics to solve real-life problems (75)
ingeniería la aplicación de las ciencias y las matemáticas para resolver problemas de la vida diaria

erosion (ee•ROH•zhuhn) the process by which wind, water, ice, or gravity transports soil and sediment from one location to another (127)
erosión el proceso por medio del cual el viento, el agua, el hielo o la gravedad transporta tierra y sedimentos de un lugar a otro

Eukarya (yoo•KAIR•ee•uh) in a modern taxonomic system, a domain made up of all eukaryotes; this domain aligns with the traditional kingdoms Protista, Fungi, Plantae, and Animalia (283)
Eukarya en un sistema taxonómico moderno, un dominio compuesto por todos los eucariotes; este dominio coincide con los reinos tradicionales Protista, Fungi, Plantae y Animalia

eukaryote (yoo•KAIR•ee•oht) an organism made up of cells that have a nucleus enclosed by a membrane; eukaryotes include protists, animals, plants, and fungi but not archaea or bacteria (211)
eucariote un organismo cuyas células tienen un núcleo contenido en una membrana; entre los eucariotes se encuentran protistas, animales, plantas y hongos, pero no arqueas ni bacterias

evaporation (ee•vap•uh•RAY•shuhn) the change of state from a liquid to a gas that usually occurs at the surface of a liquid over a wide range of temperatures (490)
evaporación el cambio de estado de líquido a gaseoso que ocurre generalmente en la superficie de un líquido en un amplio rango de temperaturas

exocytosis (ek•soh•sy•TOH•sis) the process in which a cell releases a particle by enclosing the particle in a vesicle that then moves to the cell surface and fuses with the cell membrane (262)
exocitosis el proceso por medio del cual una célula libera una partícula encerrándola en una vesícula que luego se traslada a la superficie de la célula y se fusiona con la membrana celular

exoskeleton (ek•soh•SKEL•ih•tn) a hard, external supporting structure (345)
exoesqueleto una estructura de soporte, dura y externa

experiment (ek•SPEHR•uh•muhnt) an organized procedure to study something under controlled conditions (28)
experimento un procedimiento organizado que se lleva a cabo bajo condiciones controladas para estudiar algo

fission (FISH•uhn) the process by which a nucleus splits into two or more fragments and releases neutrons and energy (173)
fisión el proceso por medio del cual un núcleo se divide en dos o más fragmentos y libera neutrones y energía

fossil fuel (FAHS•uhl FYOO•uhl) a nonrenewable energy resource formed from the remains of organisms that lived long ago; examples include oil, coal, and natural gas (99, 168)
combustible fósil un recurso energético no renovable formado a partir de los restos de organismos que vivieron hace mucho tiempo; algunos ejemplos incluyen el petróleo, el carbón y el gas natural

freezing (FREEZ•ing) the change of state from a liquid to a solid (485)
congelación el cambio de estado de líquido a sólido

function (FUNGK•shuhn) the special, normal, or proper activity of an organ or part (244)
función la actividad especial, normal o adecuada de un órgano o parte

Fungi (FUHN•jy) a kingdom made up of nongreen, eukaryotic organisms that have no means of movement, reproduce by using spores, and get food by breaking down substances in their surroundings and absorbing the nutrients (285, 316)
Fungi un reino formado por organismos eucarióticos no verdes que no tienen capacidad de movimiento, se reproducen por esporas y obtienen alimento al descomponer sustancias de su entorno y absorber los nutrientes

gamete (GAM•eet) a haploid reproductive cell that unites with another haploid reproductive cell to form a zygote (313)
gameto una célula reproductiva haploide que se une con otra célula reproductiva haploide para formar un cigoto

gas (GAS) a form of matter that does not have a definite volume or shape (473)
gas un estado de la materia que no tiene volumen ni forma definidos

genus (JEE•nuhs) the level of classification that comes after family and that contains similar species (280)
género el nivel de clasificación que viene después de la familia y que contiene especies similares

geothermal energy (jee•oh•THER•muhl EN•er•jee) the energy produced by heat within Earth (189)
energía geotérmica la energía producida por el calor del interior de la Tierra

Golgi complex (GOHL•jee KAHM•pleks) a cell organelle that helps make and package materials to be transported out of the cell (229)
aparato de Golgi un organelo celular que ayuda a hacer y a empacar los materiales que serán transportados al exterior de la célula

gymnosperm (JIM•nuh•sperm) a woody, vascular seed plant whose seeds are not enclosed by an ovary or fruit (330)
gimnosperma una planta leñosa vascular que produce semillas que no están contenidas en un ovario o fruto

H

heterogeneous (het•er•uh•JEE•nee•uhs) describes something that does not have a uniform structure or composition throughout (466)
heterogéneo término que describe algo que no tiene una estructura o composición totalmente uniforme

homeostasis (hoh•mee•oh•STAY•sis) the maintenance of a constant internal state in a changing environment (256)
homeostasis la capacidad de mantener un estado interno constante en un ambiente en cambio

homogeneous (hoh•muh•JEE•nee•uhs) describes something that has a uniform structure or composition throughout (466)
homogéneo término que describe a algo que tiene una estructura o composición global uniforme

host (HOHST) an organism from which a parasite takes food or shelter (302)
huésped el organismo del cual un parásito obtiene alimento y refugio

humus (HYOO•muhs) dark, organic material formed in soil from the decayed remains of plants and animals (157)
humus material orgánico obscuro que se forma en la tierra a partir de restos de plantas y animales en descomposición

hydroelectric energy (hy•droh•ee•LEK•trik EN•er•jee) electrical energy produced by the flow of water (185)
energía hidroeléctrica energía eléctrica producida por el flujo del agua

hypha (HY•fuh) a nonreproductive filament of a fungus (316)
hifa un filamento no-reproductor de un hongo

hypothesis (hy•PAHTH•ih•sis) a testable idea or explanation that leads to scientific investigation (28)
hipótesis una idea o explicación que conlleva a la investigación científica y que se puede probar

I-J

igneous rock (IG•nee•uhs RAHK) rock that forms when magma cools and solidifies (128)
roca ígnea una roca que se forma cuando el magma se enfría y se solidifica

independent variable (in•dih•PEN•duhnt VAIR•ee•uh•buhl) in a scientific investigation, the factor that is deliberately manipulated (29, 56)
variable independiente en una investigación científica, el factor que se manipula deliberadamente

invertebrate (in•VER•tuh•brit) an animal that does not have a backbone (345)
invertebrado un animal que no tiene columna vertebral

kinetic energy (kih•NET•ik EN•er•jee) the energy of an object that is due to the object's motion (364)
energía cinética la energía de un objeto debido al movimiento del objeto

kinetic theory of matter (kih•NET•ik THEE•uh•ree UHV MAT•er) a theory that states that all of the particles that make up matter are constantly in motion (378)
teoría cinética de la materia una teoría que establece que todas las partículas que forman la materia están en movimiento constante

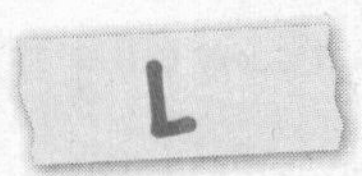

law of conservation of energy (LAW UHV kahn•suhr•VAY•shuhn UHV EN•er•jee) the law that states that energy cannot be created or destroyed but can be changed from one form to another (371)
ley de la conservación de la energía la ley que establece que la energía ni se crea ni se destruye, sólo se transforma de una forma a otra

lichen (LY•kuhn) a mass of fungal and algal cells that grow together in a symbiotic relationship and that are usually found on rocks or trees (319)
liquen una masa de células de hongos y de algas que crecen juntas en una relación simbiótica y que normalmente se encuentran en rocas o árboles

lipid (LIP•id) a fat molecule or a molecule that has similar properties; examples include oils, waxes, and steroids (218)
lípido una molécula de grasa o una molécula que tiene propiedades similares; algunos ejemplos son los aceites, las ceras y los esteroides

liquid (LIK•wid) the state of matter that has a definite volume but not a definite shape (473)
líquido el estado de la materia que tiene un volumen definido, pero no una forma definida

luster (LUHS•ter) the way in which a mineral reflects light (119)
brillo la forma en que un mineral refleja la luz

lysosome (LY•suh•sohm) a cell organelle that contains digestive enzymes (232)
lisosoma un organelo celular que contiene enzimas digestivas

mass (MAS) a measure of the amount of matter in an object (415)
masa una medida de la cantidad de materia que tiene un objeto

material resource (muh•TIR•ee•uhl REE•sohrs) a natural resource that humans use to make objects or to consume as food and drink (100)
recurso material un recurso natural que utilizan los seres humanos para fabricar objetos o para consumir como alimento o bebida

matter (MAT•er) anything that has mass and takes up space (112, 414)
materia cualquier cosa que tiene masa y ocupa un lugar en el espacio

measurement (MEZH•uhr•muhnt) a quantitative description of something that includes a number and a unit, such as 42 meters (44)
medida una descripción cuantitativa de algo, que incluye un número y una unidad, por ejemplo, 42 metros

mechanical energy (mih•KAN•ih•kuhl EN•er•jee) the sum of an object's kinetic energy and potential energy due to gravity or elastic deformation; does not include chemical energy or nuclear energy (366)
energía mecánica la suma de las energías cinética y potencial de un objeto debido a la gravedad o a la deformación elástica; no incluye la energía química ni nuclear

melting (MELT•ing) the change of state from a solid to a liquid (489)
fusión el cambio de estado de sólido a líquido

metamorphic rock (met•uh•MOHR•fik RAHK) a rock that forms from other rocks as a result of intense heat, pressure, or chemical processes (128)
roca metamórfica una roca que se forma a partir de otras rocas como resultado de calor intenso, presión o procesos químicos

mineral (MIN•er•uhl) a natural, usually inorganic solid that has a characteristic chemical composition and an orderly internal structure (112)
mineral un sólido natural, normalmente inorgánico, que tiene una composición química característica y una estructura interna ordenada

mitochondrion (my•toh•KAHN•dree•uhn) in eukaryotic cells, the organelle that is the site of cellular respiration, which releases energy for use by the cell (228)
mitocondria en las células eucarióticas, el organelo donde se lleva a cabo la respiración celular, la cual libera energía para que utilice la célula

mitosis (my•TOH•sis) in eukaryotic cells, a process of cell division that forms two new nuclei, each of which has the same number of chromosomes (259)
mitosis en las células eucarióticas, un proceso de división celular que forma dos núcleos nuevos, cada uno de los cuales posee el mismo número de cromosomas

mixture (MIKS•cher) a combination of two or more substances that are not chemically combined (457)
mezcla una combinación de dos o más sustancias que no están combinadas químicamente

molecule (MAHL•ih•kyool) a group of atoms that are held together by chemical forces; a molecule is the smallest unit of a compound that keeps all the properties of that compound (217, 457)
molécula un grupo de átomos unidos por fuerzas químicas; una molécula es la unidad más pequeña de un compuesto que conserva todas las propiedades de ese compuesto

motion (MOH•shuhn) an object's change in position relative to a reference point (390)
movimiento el cambio en la posición de un objeto respecto a un punto de referencia

mycorrhiza (my•kuh•RY•zuh) a symbiotic association between fungi and plant roots (319)
micorriza una asociación simbiótica entre los hongos y las raíces de las plantas

N

natural resource (NACH•uh•ruhl REE•sohrs) any natural material that is used by humans, such as water, petroleum, minerals, forests, and animals (98)
recurso natural cualquier material natural que es utilizado por los seres humanos, como agua, petróleo, minerales, bosques y animales

neutron (NOO•trahn) a subatomic particle that has no charge and that is located in the nucleus of an atom (444)
neutrón una partícula subatómica que no tiene carga y que está ubicada en el núcleo de un átomo

nonrenewable resource (nahn•rih•NOO•uh•buhl REE•sohrs) a resource that forms at a rate that is much slower than the rate at which the resource is consumed (99)
recurso no renovable un recurso que se forma a una tasa que es mucho más lenta que la tasa a la que se consume

nuclear energy (NOO•klee•er EN•er•jee) the energy released by a fission or fusion reaction; the binding energy of the atomic nucleus (168)
energía nuclear la energía liberada por una reacción de fisión o fusión; la energía de enlace del núcleo atómico

nucleic acid (noo•KLAY•ik AS•id) a molecule made up of subunits called *nucleotides* (219)
ácido nucleico una molécula formada por subunidades llamadas nucleótidos

nucleus (NOO•klee•uhs) in physical science, an atom's central region, which is made up of protons and neutrons (210)
núcleo en ciencias físicas, la región central de un átomo, la cual está constituida por protones y neutrones

O

observation (ahb•zer•VAY•shuhn) the process of obtaining information by using the senses (28)
observación el proceso de obtener información por medio de los sentidos

organ (OHR•guhn) a collection of tissues that carry out a specialized function of the body (242)
órgano un conjunto de tejidos que desempeñan una función especializada en el cuerpo

organelle (ohr•guhn•EL) one of the small bodies in a cell's cytoplasm that are specialized to perform a specific function (210)
organelo uno de los cuerpos pequeños del citoplasma de una célula que están especializados para llevar a cabo una función específica"

organism (OHR•guh•niz•uhm) a living thing; anything that can carry out life processes independently (206, 240)
organismo un ser vivo; cualquier cosa que pueda llevar a cabo procesos vitales independientemente

organ system (OHR•guhn SIS•tuhm) a group of organs that work together to perform body functions (243)
aparato (o sistema) de órganos un grupo de órganos que trabajan en conjunto para desempeñar funciones corporales

osmosis (ahz•MOH•sis) the diffusion of water through a semipermeable membrane (260)
ósmosis la difusión del agua a través de una membrana semipermeable

P

passive transport (PAS•iv TRANS•pohrt) the movement of substances across a cell membrane without the use of energy by the cell (260)
transporte pasivo el movimiento de sustancias a través de una membrana celular sin que la célula tenga que usar energía

phospholipid (fahs•foh•LIP•id) a lipid that contains phosphorus and that is a structural component in cell membranes (220)
fosfolípido un lípido que contiene fósforo y que es un componente estructural de la membrana celular

photosynthesis (foh•toh•SIN•thih•sis) the process by which plants, algae, and some bacteria use sunlight, carbon dioxide, and water to make food (258, 325)
fotosíntesis el proceso por medio del cual las plantas, las algas y algunas bacterias utilizan la luz solar, el dióxido de carbono y el agua para producir alimento

physical property (FIZ•ih•kuhl PRAHP•er•tee) a characteristic of a substance that does not involve a chemical change, such as density, color, or hardness (428, 448)
propiedad física una característica de una sustancia que no implica un cambio químico, tal como la densidad, el color o la dureza

Plantae (PLAN•tee) a kingdom made up of complex, multicellular organisms that are usually green, have cell walls made of cellulose, cannot move around, and use the sun's energy to make sugar by photosynthesis (284)
Plantae un reino formado por organismos pluricelulares complejos que normalmente son verdes, tienen una pared celular de celulosa, no tienen capacidad de movimiento y utilizan la energía del Sol para producir azúcar mediante la fotosíntesis

pollen (PAHL•uhn) the tiny granules that contain the male gametophyte of seed plants (330)
polen los gránulos diminutos que contienen el gametofito masculino en las plantas con semilla

position (puh•ZISH•uhn) the location of an object (368)
posición la ubicación de un objeto

potential energy (puh•TEN•shuhl EN•er•jee) the energy that an object has because of the position, condition, or chemical composition of the object (365)
energía potencial la energía que tiene un objeto debido a su posición, condición o composición química

precision (prih•SIZH•uhn) the exactness of a measurement (50)
precisión la exactitud de una medición

producer (pruh•DOO•ser) an organism that can make its own food by using energy from its surroundings (325)
productor un organismo que puede elaborar sus propios alimentos utilizando la energía de su entorno

prokaryote (proh•KAIR•ee•oht) a single-celled organism that does not have a nucleus or membrane-bound organelles; examples are archaea and bacteria (211)
procariote un organismo unicelular que no tiene núcleo ni organelos cubiertos por una membrana, por ejemplo, las arqueas y las bacterias

protein (PROH•teen) a molecule that is made up of amino acids and that is needed to build and repair body structures and to regulate processes in the body (218)
proteína una molécula formada por aminoácidos que es necesaria para construir y reparar estructuras corporales y para regular procesos del cuerpo

Protista (proh•TIS•tuh) a kingdom of mostly one-celled eukaryotic organisms that are different from plants, animals, archaea, bacteria, and fungi (284, 310)
Protista un reino compuesto principalmente por organismos eucarióticos unicelulares que son diferentes de las plantas, animales, arqueas, bacterias y hongos

proton (PROH•tahn) a subatomic particle that has a positive charge and that is located in the nucleus of an atom; the number of protons in the nucleus is the atomic number, which determines the identity of an element (444)
protón una partícula subatómica que tiene una carga positiva y que está ubicada en el núcleo de un átomo; el número de protones que hay en el núcleo es el número atómico, y éste determina la identidad del elemento

prototype (PROH•tuh•typ) a test model of a product (79)
prototipo prueba modelo de un producto

pseudoscience (SOO•doh•sy•uhns) a process of investigation that in one or more ways resembles science but deviates from the scientific methods (12)
pseudociencia un proceso de investigación que tiene semejanzas con la actividad científica, pero no cumple con los métodos científicos

pure substance (PYOOR SUHB•stuhns) a sample of matter, either a single element or a single compound, that has definite chemical and physical properties (460)
sustancia pura una muestra de materia, ya sea un solo elemento o un solo compuesto, que tiene propiedades químicas y físicas definidas

Q

qualitative (KWAHL•ih•tay•tiv) relating to information that concerns quality or kind (44)
cualitativo relativo a la información acerca de la cualidad o el tipo

quantitative (KWAHN•tih•tay•tiv) relating to information that is expressed by a number or quantity (44)
cuantitativo relativo a la información expresada por un número o una cantidad

reference point (REF•er•uhns POYNT) a location to which another location is compared (368)
punto de referencia una ubicación con la que se compara otra ubicación

renewable resource (rih•NOO•uh•buhl REE•sohrs) a natural resource that can be replaced at the same rate at which the resource is consumed (99)
recurso renovable un recurso natural que puede reemplazarse a la misma tasa a la que se consume

ribosome (RY•buh•sohm) a cell organelle composed of RNA and protein; the site of protein synthesis (228)
ribosoma un organelo celular compuesto de ARN y proteína; el sitio donde ocurre la síntesis de proteínas

rift zone (RIFT ZOHN) an area of deep cracks that forms between two tectonic plates that are pulling away from each other (132)
zona de rift un área de grietas profundas que se forma entre dos placas tectónicas que se están alejando una de la otra

rock (RAHK) a naturally occurring solid mixture of one or more minerals or organic matter (142)
roca una mezcla sólida de uno o más minerales o de materia orgánica que se produce de forma natural

rock cycle (RAHK SY•kuhl) the series of processes in which rock forms, changes from one type to another, is broken down or melted, and forms again by geologic processes (130)
ciclo de las rocas la serie de procesos por medio de los cuales una roca se forma, cambia de un tipo a otro, se destruye o funde y se forma nuevamente por procesos geológicos

science (SY•uhns) the knowledge obtained by observing natural events and conditions in order to discover facts and formulate laws or principles that can be verified or tested (6)
ciencia el conocimiento que se obtiene por medio de la observación natural de acontecimientos y condiciones con el fin de descubrir hechos y formular leyes o principios que puedan ser verificados o probados

scientific notation (sy•uhn•TIF•ik noh•TAY•shuhn) a method of expressing a quantity as a number multiplied by 10 to the appropriate power (46)
notación científica un método para expresar una cantidad en forma de un número multiplicado por 10 a la potencia adecuada

sedimentary rock (sed•uh•MEN•tuh•ree RAHK) a rock that forms from compressed or cemented layers of sediment (128)
roca sedimentaria una roca que se forma a partir de capas comprimidas o cementadas de sedimento

seed (SEED) a plant embryo that is enclosed in a protective coat (330)
semilla el embrión de una planta que está encerrado en una cubierta protectora

soil (SOYL) a loose mixture of rock fragments, organic material, water, and air that can support the growth of vegetation (156)
suelo una mezcla suelta de fragmentos de roca, material orgánico, agua y aire en la que puede crecer vegetación

soil horizon (SOYL huh•RY•zuhn) each layer of soil within a soil profile (159)
horizonte del suelo una de las capas en que se divide el perfil del suelo; tiene características bien definidas, es relativamente uniforme y se encuentra casi paralela a la superficie terrestre

soil profile (SOYL PROH•fyl) a vertical section of soil that shows the layers, or horizons (159)
perfil del suelo una sección vertical de suelo que muestra las capas u horizontes

solar energy (SOH•ler EN•er•jee) the energy received by Earth from the sun in the form of radiation (186)
energía solar la energía que la Tierra recibe del Sol en forma de radiación

solid (SAHL•id) the state of matter in which the volume and shape of a substance are fixed (472)
sólido el estado de la materia en el cual el volumen y la forma de una sustancia están fijos

species (SPEE•sheez) a group of organisms that are closely related and can mate to produce fertile offspring (280)
especie un grupo de organismos que tienen un parentesco cercano y que pueden aparearse para producir descendencia fértil

speed (SPEED) the distance traveled divided by the time interval during which the motion occurred (391)
rapidez la distancia que un objeto se desplaza dividida entre el intervalo de tiempo durante el cual ocurrió el movimiento

spore (SPOHR) a reproductive cell or multicellular structure that is resistant to stressful environmental conditions and that can develop into an adult without fusing with another cell (313)
espora una célula reproductora o estructura pluricelular que resiste las condiciones ambientales adversas y que se puede desarrollar hasta convertirse en un adulto sin necesidad de fusionarse con otra célula

stewardship (STOO•erd•ship) the careful and responsible management of a resource (107)
gestión ambiental responsable el manejo cuidadoso y responsable de un recurso

streak (STREEK) the color of a mineral in powdered form (118)
veta el color de un mineral en forma de polvo

structure (STRUHK•cher) the arrangement of parts in an organism (244)
estructura el orden y distribución de las partes de un organismo

sublimation (suhb•luh•MAY•shuhn) the change of state from a solid directly to a gas (492)
sublimación cambio de estado por el cual un sólido se convierte directamente en un gas

subsidence (suhb•SYD•ns) the sinking of regions of Earth's crust to lower elevations (132)
hundimiento del terreno el hundimiento de regiones de la corteza terrestre a elevaciones más bajas

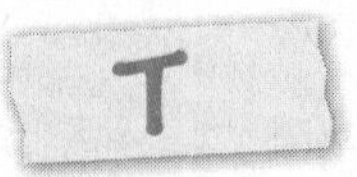

technology (tek•NAHL•uh•jee) the application of science for practical purposes; the use of tools, machines, materials, and processes to meet human needs (74)
tecnología la aplicación de la ciencia con fines prácticos; el uso de herramientas, máquinas, materiales y procesos para satisfacer las necesidades de los seres humanos

temperature (TEM•per•uh•chur) a measure of how hot (or cold) something is; specifically, a measure of the average kinetic energy of the particles in an object (381)
temperatura una medida de qué tan caliente (o frío) está algo; específicamente, una medida de la energía cinética promedio de las partículas de un objeto

texture (TEKS•cher) the quality of a rock that is based on the sizes, shapes, and positions of the rock's grains (127, 143)
textura la cualidad de una roca que se basa en el tamaño, la forma y la posición de los granos que la forman

thermal energy (THER•muhl EN•er•jee) the kinetic energy of a substance's atoms (380)
energía térmica la energía cinética de los átomos de una sustancia

thermometer (ther•MAHM•ih•ter) an instrument that measures and indicates temperature (382)
termómetro un instrumento que mide e indica la temperatura

tissue (TISH•oo) a group of similar cells that perform a common function (241)
tejido un grupo de células similares que llevan a cabo una función común

uplift (UHP•lift) the rising of regions of Earth's crust to higher elevations (132)
levantamiento la elevación de regiones de la corteza terrestre a elevaciones más altas

vacuole (VAK•yoo•ohl) a fluid-filled vesicle found in the cytoplasm of plant cells or protozoans (230)
vacuola una vesícula llena de líquido que se encuentra en el citoplasma de las células vegetales o de los protozoarios

variable (VAIR•ee•uh•buhl) a factor that changes in an experiment in order to test a hypothesis (29)
variable un factor que se modifica en un experimento con el fin de probar una hipótesis

vascular system (VAS•kyuh•ler SIS•tuhm) a conducting system of tissues that transport water and other materials in plants or in animals (326)
sistema vascular un sistema de transporte de los tejidos que lleva agua y otros materiales en las plantas o en los animales

vector (VEK•ter) a quantity that has both size and direction (397)
vector una cantidad que tiene tanto magnitud como dirección

velocity (vuh•LAHS•ih•tee) the speed of an object in a particular direction (397)
velocidad la rapidez de un objeto en una dirección dada

vertebrate (VER•tuh•brit) an animal that has a backbone (345)
vertebrado un animal que tiene columna vertebral

virus (VY•ruhs) a microscopic particle that gets inside a cell and often destroys the cell (300)
virus una partícula microscópica que se introduce en una célula y a menudo la destruye

volume (VAHL•yoom) the amount of space that an object takes up, or occupies (417)
volumen la cantidad de espacio que ocupa un objeto

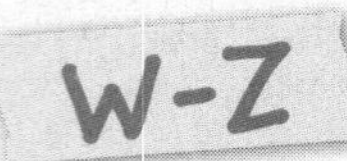

weathering (WETH•er•ing) the natural process by which atmospheric and environmental agents, such as wind, rain, and temperature changes, disintegrate and decompose rocks (127)
meteorización el proceso natural por medio del cual los agentes atmosféricos o ambientales, como el viento, la lluvia y los cambios de temperatura, desintegran y descomponen las rocas

weight (WAYT) a measure of the gravitational force exerted on an object; its value can change with the location of the object in the universe (415)
peso una medida de la fuerza gravitacional ejercida sobre un objeto; su valor puede cambiar en función de la ubicación del objeto en el universo

wind energy (WIND EN•er•jee) the use of the force of moving air to drive an electric generator (184)
energía eólica el uso de la fuerza del aire en movimiento para hacer funcionar un generador eléctrico

Index

Note: Italic page numbers represent illustrative material, such as figures, tables, margin elements, photographs, and illustrations. Boldface page numbers represent page numbers for definitions.

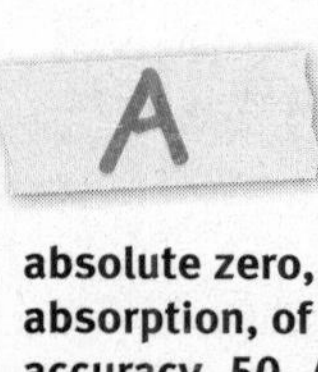

D

L

M

Q

R

S

T